REGULATORY LAW AND THE PUBLIC INTEREST

REGULATORY LAW AND THE PUBLIC INTEREST

Robert C. Fellmeth
and Marcus Friedman

Clarity Press, Inc.

ISBN: 978-1-949762-99-0
EBOOK ISBN: 978-1-949762-98-3

In-house editor: Diana G. Collier

Library of Congress Control Number: 2024909172

Clarity Press, Inc.
2625 Piedmont Rd. NE, Ste. 56
Atlanta, GA 30324, USA
https://www.claritypress.com

Table of Contents

About the Authors

Professor Robert C. Fellmeth is a graduate of Stanford University (AB 1967, Honors in Humanities), and Harvard University (JD 1970, Chair of the Civil Rights/Civil Liberties Committee). He was a part of the consumer movement in 1968–73, including scholarship and advocacy in the regulatory law area. He was co-author of the NADER REPORT ON THE FEDERAL TRADE COMMISSION (w/ Schulz and Cox, 1968, Baron Press) leading to the FTC Improvements Act of 1972. From 1969–72 he organized Ralph Nader's studies of federal regulatory agencies, including co-authoring and editing a study of the Interstate Commerce Commission (ICC): THE INTERSTATE COMMERCE OMISSION (Grossman, 1970). He studied the regulation of land use, editing THE POLITICS OF LAND (Grossman, 1972). He directed a study of the Congress involving 45 writers publishing profiles of 484 members of Congress, the book WHO RUNS CONGRESS, and five studies of Congressional Committees, contributing to the book THE COMMERCE COMMITTEES (edited by David Price, Grossman, 1976). He co-authored numerous treatises with Professor Ralph Folsom in the regulatory area, including CALIFORNIA REGULATORY LAW AND PRACTICE (Butterworths, 1983 with Supplements 1985, 1987, 1989).

Fellmeth became a White Collar Crime prosecutor in 1972, serving as a Deputy DA directing the San Diego office's antitrust unit, cross commissioned as an Assistant United States Attorney in 1979–81 to also bring white collar crime actions in federal court. He filed 22 major antitrust actions during his nine years serving in those positions. He has co-authored six editions of the treatise CALIFORNIA WHITE COLLAR CRIME AND BUSINESS LITIGATION (w/ Papageorge, Tower Publishing, 6th Edition, 2020).

Professor Fellmeth assumed the endowed Price Chair in Public Interest Law at the University of San Diego faculty in 1985 and has also served since that time as the executive director of its Centers for Public Interest Law (CPIL), including its Consumer Protection Policy Center. He has been involved in numerous regulatory law issues, including service as the State Bar Discipline Monitor (a position created by the Legislature) and proposing the current independent State Bar Court adjudicating attorney discipline. Other activities of the Centers have included its staff serving as the Medical Board Enforcement Monitor and as staff to the Contractors' State Licensing Board Enforcement Monitor. Professor Fellmeth has also served on a state regulatory agency, the Athletic Commission, chairing it for three years and proposing the current pension/disability system for professional boxers. CPIL has also published the CALIFORNIA REGULATORY LAW REPORTER for the past 35 years; available on Westlaw, the REPORTER describes the activities, rules, actions, and decisions of major California regulatory agencies, and is the only publication of its kind nationally. He has been involved in legislative revisions to state and federal regulatory law. Those revisions in California include approximately 100 enacted statutes and numerous agency-adopted rules. He has served as counsel in over 50 reported appellate cases, with holdings relevant to regulatory law standards and practice.

MARCUS FRIEDMAN is Administrative Director of the Consumer Protection Policy Center (CPPC) at the University of San Diego School of Law. He teaches California Regulatory Law and the Public Interest courses and clinics, writes and reviews legislation on behalf of CPPC, and participates in various regulatory agency proceedings. He is also editor and contributor to the CALIFORNIA REGULATORY LAW REPORTER. Further, he advocates for gun violence prevention and drafted multiple bills that have become law. Marcus previously worked as a Deputy City Attorney for the City of San Diego in the General Trial Unit and the Domestic Violence & Sex Crimes Unit. He is a graduate of Boston University (BA) and University of San Diego (JD).

Acknowledgments

Many have contributed to this text beyond the two authors, including Julianne D'Angelo Fellmeth. Professor Julianne Fellmeth co-taught Public Interest Law and Practice and edited the CALIFORNIA REGULATORY LAW REPORTER for over 30 years. She also served as the Medical Board Enforcement Monitor and as the staff for the Contractors' State Licensing Board Monitor. Bridget Gramme also co-taught the class for five years, edited the REPORTER during that period, and contributed much expertise to this subject matter. Tom Papageorge, head of the San Diego District Attorney's consumer protection section, contributed much material for this text. All three of these scholars have their publications included in various portions of the text, as appropriate.

In addition to these contributors, Elisa Weichel, Administrative Director of CPIL's Children's Advocacy Institute, contributed much to the information included herein. Katie Gonzalez, Associate Director of the Centers for Public Interest Law, similarly provided expert assistance and scholarship skills. The above have also helped to guide students covering major California agencies and have helped to write and to edit the CALIFORNIA REGULATORY LAW REPORTER, as noted above. Also contributing was Professor Margaret Dalton, former director of clinics and then part of the administrative leadership at USD School of Law and a recognized expert on disability issues. CPIL Executive Assistant, Ben Sims contributed important formatting and other editorial improvements. Finally, former student Andrew Kent skillfully provided research and related assistance.

Introduction and Basic Regulatory Terminology

INTRODUCTION

Many law schools teach basic Administrative Law, a course which includes the federal Administrative Procedure Act, sometimes the federal Freedom of Information Act, et al. But few focus on regulatory law at the state level. This omission is ironic since the vast majority of regulatory decisions occur in that forum. States manage education at all levels—both public and private. They directly regulate environmental issues far more extensively than does the federal jurisdiction, from land use to pollution to protection of natural resources. And they are central to the regulation of the economy, from utilities to insurance to virtually every trade and profession. The last commonly includes attorneys, physicians, nurses, dentists, veterinarians, accountants, real estate brokers, pharmacies, and contractors (from plumbers and electricians to drywall installers).

This text will include federal regulation for exemplary purposes, and includes a section on federal regulatory failure during the mortgage crisis of 2008—which concerned banking and mortgage finance with federal regulatory implications. But the focus will be on state level regulatory law and procedure. To be sure, states vary among themselves on some aspects of their respective regulatory systems. We include major constitutional and antitrust cases, among others, that have broad federal and state law impact. While this book primarily uses California as an example, the context within this book is applicable and useful to many other states.

REGULATORY FUNCTIONS AND TERMINOLOGY (CALIFORNIA EXAMPLE)[1]

Scope of Agency Functions

Enabling acts of administrative agencies commonly authorize them to engage in the following functions:

- Generally, rulemaking and rate making (for the Public Utilities Commission). Regulations adopted by an agency to carry out its statutory or constitutional duties are codified in the California Code of Regulations (CCR). Agencies may also adopt rules, policies, and guidelines governing internal agency matters, which can generally be obtained directly from the agency.

---

[1] This overview references information from Matthew Bender & Co., California Forms of Pleading and Practice, § 470.17 et seq.

- Licensing, registration, or certification of persons or business entities to engage in particular occupations or business activities.

- Adjudication (authorizing agencies to conduct disciplinary hearings), and enforcement of statutory standards and requirements under the agency's jurisdiction. Agencies may not act outside their constitutional or statutory scope of authority. An agency is not bound by any acts of its officers or employees that exceed the actor's scope of authority ("ultra vires" acts).

Most administrative agencies perform multiple functions. For example, administrative agencies involved in environmental law perform many functions, including the familiar division between rulemaking (quasi-legislative action) and administrative adjudication (quasi-judicial action). California's environmental agencies also engage in a wide variety of other more informal administrative actions, including investigations and information collection. Ministerial actions include the issuance of some permits and mandatory approvals, e.g., of subdivision tract maps.

Delegation of Duties by Agencies

An agency typically delegates to agency employees the various functions and duties imposed by its enabling act on the agency, its governing board, its employees, committees, or other persons. For example, many boards delegate the implementation of standards and disciplinary oversight to their respective executive officers, who are not a member of the applicable board. Many agencies delegate important authority to national testing entities relevant to their licensing examinations.

Unless an agency's enabling act specifically provides otherwise, the agency may not delegate its discretionary duties. A duty is "discretionary" if there is no clearly defined rule governing its exercise.

Types of Agencies: Five Categories

California administrative agencies can be divided into five major categories, depending on the major purpose of the agency:

- Regulatory agencies

- Rate-making agencies

- Licensing agencies

- Social welfare and entitlement agencies

- Permitting agencies.

Many agencies fit into only one category. For example, the Medical Board of California is primarily responsible for licensing physicians and surgeons. Its regulatory functions, as with most business regulations, include establishing criteria for licensure. Other agencies, however, fit into more than one category. For example, the Public Utilities Commission is both a regulatory and a rate-making agency.

a. Regulatory Agencies

A regulatory agency is responsible for regulating a specific business or industry for the protection of the public interest. California regulatory agencies supervise the operations and practices of diverse business ventures including: Real estate (Department of Real Estate); Horse racing (California Horse Racing Board); and State corporate securities transactions (Department of Financial Protection and Innovation).

b. Rate Making Agencies

A rate-making agency sets prices for goods or services provided by a business or industry that is a monopoly or common carrier. The Public Utilities Commission has the authority to establish rates to be charged by the following public utilities: intrastate water carriers, telephone companies, natural gas and electrical utilities, railroads and certain other transportation carriers. The CPUC will grant a rate change for a utility only on a showing that the utility's existing rates are insufficient, unlawful, unjust, unreasonable, discriminatory, or preferential.

c. Licensing Agencies

A licensing agency is responsible for setting and maintaining standards for entry into a business or occupation. In California, licensing standards have been established by administrative agencies for such diverse businesses and occupations as the furniture and bedding industry (Bureau of Household Goods and Services), structural pest control operators (Structural Pest Control Board), and various medical professionals (including physicians, nurses, and dentists).

Licensing agencies also engage in rulemaking functions (*e.g.*, authorizing divisions within Medical Board to adopt regulations concerning the licensing of medical professionals), but do not ordinarily engage in rate making.

d. Social Welfare and Entitlement Agencies

California has a Department of Social Services and other agencies that provide financial assistance and other help in a number of categories, including cash assistance for low-income families, food and nutrition programs, child protection services, foster care, adoption services, et al.

e. Permitting Agencies

Permitting agencies require practitioners within their practice definition to obtain a "permit" in order to conduct business. However, this does not generally involve an examination or any demonstration of competence. It involves, rather, simply the tracking of who is actively practicing the conduct requiring a permit.

Agency Structure Within the Executive Branch

a. Purpose and Function of Executive Branch Agencies

The placement of administrative agencies in the executive branch is significant for two reasons. First, it establishes law enforcement as a main function of the agencies. Second, it places the agencies under some direct influence from the Governor. The basic authority of the executive branch to execute duly enacted laws may not be usurped by the Legislature except through the alteration of a relevant enabling or other statute.

b. The Department of Consumer Affairs

The Department of Consumer Affairs (DCA) is a licensing and regulatory body that is responsible for regulating private businesses and various professions and occupations to protect the public health and safety. DCA consists of over 30 subagencies that establish licensing qualifications and competency standards, redress grievances against licensees, discipline licensees, and conduct investigations to ensure compliance with licensing standards. The DCA Director is the chief executive officer of the Department. They are appointed by the Governor and holds office at the Governor's pleasure (no specific assured term of office). This person is responsible for organizing the work of the Department; investigating the work of the subagencies within the Department; and protecting the interests of consumers and reporting to the Governor and the Legislature on the Department's functioning. The subagencies within DCA function autonomously in setting standards, holding meetings, preparing and conducting licensing examinations, investigating improper conduct by licensees, conducting disciplinary hearings, and imposing penalties following such hearings. However, the decisions of the subagencies are not generally subject to review by the Director.

The DCA Director must be provided the opportunity to review regulations proposed or promulgated by agencies within the Department before these regulations can take effect. The only exceptions to this requirement are regulations concerning examinations and qualifications for licensure. The agencies must notify the Director and give the Director the opportunity to specifically review agency-prepared notices of proposed action that are consistent with APA rulemaking procedure, including modifications, supplements, and the text of proposed new or changed regulations. The Director's review must be completed before that agency can file the regulation with the Office of Administrative Law.

c. The Governor's Role

As the head of the executive branch, the Governor has the responsibility to ensure that state laws are faithfully executed, including the following duties regarding state agencies:

- Supervising the agencies and their officers.
- Appointing heads of the five major executive branch and appointing a majority of the members of other agencies.
- Examining the organization of agencies and, as necessary for the public interest, preparing reorganization plans, which must be approved by the Senate and the Assembly.
- Preparing an annual state budget that, among other things, allocates funding to agencies.

The Governor exerts a great deal of control over the activities of administrative agencies through the appointment power. This power includes the ability to do the following:

- Remove without cause the secretary of any of the major executive branch agencies.
- Choose individuals to lead an agency, which can affect its policies, priorities, and efficacy.
- Provide or withhold funding through budget recommendations, which can increase or decrease the ability of an agency to carry out its duties.

d. Other Executive Officers

The Attorney General is the state's chief law enforcement officer, and it is his or her duty to see that state laws are uniformly and adequately enforced. The Attorney General heads the Department of Justice, which represents the state and most state agencies and other state entities in litigation matters. Indeed, most state agencies are assigned a Deputy Attorney General (DAG) to monitor their performance and assure compliance with applicable law.

The Lieutenant Governor's role in state government is similar to that of the vice president at the federal level. The Lieutenant Governor presides over the Senate, may vote in Senate matters in order to break a tie vote, and acts in the Governor's place if the Governor is incapacitated or out of the state.

The Secretary of State keeps the official records of the executive branch, the State Treasurer receives and deposits state funds, and the State Controller administers state expenditures and audits claims against the state, as well as payments made by state agencies.

Preliminary Diagnostic Quiz

1. Most of the agencies, boards, and commissions studied in this course are part of which branch of government?
   a. Legislative
   b. Executive
   c. Judicial

2. These agencies, boards, and commissions may be created by:
   a. A statute enacted by the state Legislature
   b. The state constitution (including amendments thereto)
   c. The voters, by initiative vote
   d. All of the above

3. The two houses of the California Legislature are called the ________ and the _________.

4. SB 118 (Johnson)
   In the above phrase, what does "SB" refer to? Why is there a name in parenthesis?

5. The agencies, boards, and commissions covered by this text have the power to adopt regulations that set forth the definitions, procedures, and details of the regulation of a trade or profession. The process by which agencies adopt regulations is called _______.

6. What is the difference between a statute and a regulation?

7. Most occupational licensing agencies are permitted to discipline their licensees (*e.g.*, revoke or suspend the license to practice for misconduct). This procedure is called:
   a. Legislation
   b. Rulemaking
   c. Adjudication

8. What is the difference between the State Board of Pharmacy and the California Pharmacists Association? Between a licensed real estate broker and a realtor?

9. What is the difference between a board or commission and a department or bureau?

10. Does the generic term "agency" include all of the entities in #9 above?

11. When a state agency "licenses" a trade or profession as a means of regulation it may (more than one may be correct):
    a. Set conditions to obtain a license without which one may not practice that trade.
    b. Set standards for acceptable performance of the trade through rulemaking.
    c. Discipline licensees who violate those standards.
    d. Fix fair prices or rates for the services provided by its licensees.

12. The attorneys who most often represent California's boards and commissions come from:
    a. The offices of the United States Attorney.
    b. The State Attorney General's Office.
    c. Local offices of the District Attorney.
    d. Private attorneys on contract.

13. What is the relationship between the appointed members of a regulatory board or commission and the board's "executive director" or "executive officer"?

14. In regulatory jargon, the term "sunset" means:
    a. The time all good government bureaucrats get to go home.
    b. The time to look for the "green flash" at Mission Beach.
    c. A regular, systematic review of the need for and effectiveness of a regulatory board or program; If the board or program is unnecessary or ineffective, it may be "sunsetted" (either the regulatory system or its current governing body may be terminated).

Chapter 1
The Basics of Regulation

A THEORY OF REGULATION

The following article by Robert C. Fellmeth was originally published in the California Regulatory Law Reporter, Vol. 5, No. 2, in 1985. That year was the initiation of Gorbachev's "Glasnost," liberalizing the Soviet Union in many ways. The discourse here also follows an example of California regulatory agencies that have changed in some respects. Agency names and the advent of new regulatory entities have occurred. However, most of the regulatory entities of that time remain in similar if not identical statutory frameworks. Its underlying thesis is to detail how a regulatory system can preserve or enhance the benefits of competition, while intervening to ameliorate its most troubling features. We acknowledge that the statistics and figures, and agency names may have changed over time, but the underlying theory of regulation remains the same.

We who grew up in the cold war remember well our ninth-grade civics picture of the Soviet state. We were told that you could not be what you wanted to be when you grew up. With special starkness, we could see a young Soviet boy driving a small pedal car up and down his sidewalk. A boy with eyes full of wonder about the big machines which hum down the cold streets. As he grows up he learns how the motors operate and he studies the various models year after year. He decides he wants to run a new automobile sales shop when he grows up. He wants to see and service the Ladka. He cannot raise capital and do it, the sales offices are government owned. He must apply for the position, or one which may lead to it.

In our cold war vision, before he applies, the Soviet youth faces a burly commissar, the quintessential bureaucrat. The boy walks into a sterile room of vaulted ceiling. He has waited for several hours for a 30-second interview. The commissar sheaves through a small stack of papers. Even before the boy reaches the lone chair in front of the desk, the official barks out his name and drones: "food factory canner, case receiver in tomato canning plan in Sochi next." He then dismisses the boy with a curt wave of the hand.

Most of us have since learned that the repressive Soviet central planning system works less intrusively. Our young boy would not be instructed to be a case receiver. He would not be told at an early age exactly what occupation he would have to take. But he would be told what he could not be. If he wanted to be a Ladka dealer he could apply. With the help of the party, a committee is likely to formulate the requirements. Based on their view of how many dealers there should be and what they should do to qualify, they would say "no" to all but those persons they select.

Although not totally manipulating, the Soviet system imposes a "prior restraint": people cannot be what they want to be unless they are first given permission. They are not permitted to try on their own calculation of risk and let a marketplace defeat them based only on their failure to perform.

The year is 1984. The place, Thousand Oaks, California. One Paul Rusnak wishes to start a BMW franchise. It has been his lifelong dream, he has learned the auto business with great care. He has saved his money. He has secured the permission of BMW. He knows of many possible customers. He is sure of his market and proud of the product he wants to offer.

He is well aware that government bodies circumscribe much of what he can do: he must be licensed by the Department of Motor Vehicles and by the Bureau of Automotive Repair. He must advertise honestly, obeying the standards of the Federal Trade Commission and the Unfair Competition Act of California. He must honor his warranties and comply with the Magnuson-Moss Act and its state counterpart, the Song-Beverly Act. He must offer financing only under the strict terms of the Rees-Levering Act. And his automobiles must meet the emission standards of the state Air Resources Board and the safety standards of the National Highway Traffic Safety Administration. His own business operations must meet the safety standards of Cal-OSHA and the labor restrictions of the Labor Code. And, of course, he must pay taxes, keeping appropriate records. For local government, he must meet all land use conditions, ranging from parking requirements to the size and candlepower of his sign.

He is prepared to do all of that.

But there is yet another Board, one of many which Californians know little about: the New Motor Vehicle Board. This Board, set up by a trade association of existing car dealers, created a Board of seven members, three of whom are dealers. If any person, including a competing dealer, complains about the plans of someone to open up a new dealership, he or she may protest to this Board, which can then impose a "prior restraint" and say "no" to Paul Rusnak. This Board said no.

Many of us are well aware that lawyers and physicians must be "licensed" by state regulatory boards. And we justify this prior restraint by citing what lawyers like to call "irreparable harm." We must make sure that certain trades and businesses do not operate unless they are competently conducted. This means both keeping out those who might cause severe public harm and excising those who are already in business whose performance falls below minimum standards. But it's not just lawyers and the medical profession who are involved with prior restraints. Our New Motor Vehicle Board is not an anomaly.

The fastest growing and most intrusive part of American government rests within the so- called fourth branch: regulatory agencies. Created by legislative bodies and given quasi- executive, legislative and judicial powers, these agencies increasingly predominate in the lives of our citizenry. Much is written about the so-called "alphabet soup" of federal regulatory bodies: the Federal Trade Commission (FTC), Civil Aeronautics Board (CAB), Federal Communications Commission (FCC), Securities and Exchange Commission (SEC), etc. Approximately 20 major regulatory bodies function in a relatively visible and open fashion in Washington, D.C., and through regional field offices. These agencies have been given enormous discretion by the Congress, which fashioned broadly framed mandates, and by the courts which have deferred to their expertise. They are subject to constitutional due process safeguards as to those they most directly affect. They are subject to an Administrative Procedure Act, a Freedom of Information Act, and other statutes. More importantly, their proceedings draw some interest from American journalism.

What is less known is that the greatest expansion in this fourth branch of government has occurred at the state and local levels, not at the federal level. Furthermore, the sometimes clear rationale for the development of regulatory bodies at the federal level has not guided state and local counterparts. State legislatures create new boards and commissions without considering economic rationale. They are viewed as "free" to the legislators authorizing them since they are "special funded" from the trade or industry subject to regulation. Legislators do not focus on marketplace flaws which might justify regulation, and the fashioning of specific means to compensate for or correct them.

Although new agencies are justified by consumer benefit, their initial proponents are often the trade group to be regulated. Where there is no one organized to oppose a new governmental body and it does not expend general fund monies, approval is not difficult. Legislators tend to count noses: who is for, who is against, and base decisions on the line-up. California now has over 60 regulatory agencies setting detailed policy in insurance, banking, utilities, transportation, and alcoholic beverage sales. Most of the trades are covered by regulatory agencies requiring licensure as a precondition to practice. In addition, agriculture has both state and federal (controlled regionally or locally) "marketing orders" government the promotion, distribution and/or supply of many agricultural commodities.

A typical citizen may be aware that local government regulates land use, that the Air Resources Board, Water Resources Control Board and California Occupational Safety and Health Administration affect the operations of many California businesses. Fewer are aware of the Milk Advisory Board, or the

Board of Landscape Architects or the California Beef Council or the Bureau of Home Furnishings.

Co-extensive with a plethora of agencies, boards and commissions for purposes which are not clearly understandable, is the expansion of existing agencies well beyond what might have been a defensible original justification. The numerous existing agencies are very rarely monitored, or ever seen by any outside entity.

On the other side of the same coin is the issue of lack of regulation where regulation is warranted. And related to the problem of underregulation is the artificial creation of a marketplace flaw, the conferral of antitrust immunity and the avoidance of any meaningful substitute for the absent marketplace.

It is time to posit a rational basis for regulation, to develop some kind of defensible theory on which to base a regulatory system and to fashion its limitations.

I. PRESUMPTIONS

Adherents of the Chicago "libertarian" school often define "regulation" simplistically as government interference in which would otherwise be a natural marketplace. It seems to be a libertarian thesis that the "state" is an inherently coercive and dangerous institution, possessing the power to tax, to draft and to imprison. These coercive powers make the limitation of the state vis-a-vis private power an essential concern of the citizenry. While there is more than a grain of truth to the libertarian presumption, the allegiance of its adherents to the symbols of the "marketplace," without reference to the mechanisms which make the marketplace work, marks the philosophy as more of a religion than a rational tool for weighing options. The libertarians will often simply define "good policy" as a removal of government to a "marketplace," without reference to what that might mean. It is accepted as an article of faith in the tradition of religious zealotry that the marketplace functions as a proper object of obeisance. Disciplines advocate the simple removal of those institutions which might prevent the "market" from achieving its "natural status."

The world is much more complicated than this. In fact, the condition of the market absent government is the product of custom, language, pre-existing economic power—a human creation. And in fact, private power can coerce and enslave almost as much as the "state" can. Any resident of a one-company town will testify to the power of private interest. Large institutions may interrelate in an extremely adhesive fashion with the common citizenry. A serious marketplace choice may not be actualized. Private parties, increasingly cartelized, and horizontally organized into trade associations, may preclude marketplace choice and otherwise bully the consumer, the taxpayer, the citizen.

It is difficult for any but the most obsequious worshiper of marketplace symbolism to doubt the limitations of the unfettered market as a guarantor of economic freedom, equity or even efficiency. We shall explore the more traditional flaws of the marketplace that preclude its status as a blind object of worship below. However, to the extent it does function to manifest consumer sovereignty and allocation of resources according to informed consumer choice from a wide variety of alternatives, it is a touchstone deserving of presumptive status. Hence, we shall assume that where the marketplace functions to allocate resources efficiently and fairly, where the prerequisites are present for the marketplace to so function, it should be initially relied upon to that end. This reliance is related to the viability of its prerequisites. These prerequisites include the following traditional elements:

1. Many entrepreneurs acting individually and independently in buying and selling.
2. No one buyer or seller is able to affect a significant market share.
3. Homogeneous products within types.
4. Perfect information about the characteristics of alternative products.
5. Rational decisionmaking by consumers.
6. No external costs which are unassessed by the marketplace.

Most regulations may be justified because of a breakdown of one or more of these factors. Although it is possible to exaggerate the impact of a marketplace deficiency, and to use it as an excuse to engage in unnecessary intervention, it is also true that where serious deficiencies exist in these prerequisites, the marketplace may not function to allocate resources fairly or efficiently. Where such an event occurs, it is inappropriate to rely on the mere absence of government as the solution. To the contrary, it is a primary function of government, as it provides checks and balances in our system, to intervene in order to restore or substitute for that absent prerequisite. The government should decline to do so only if the indirect and direct costs of that intervention exceed the benefits to be obtained from it. In determining what kind of intervention the government should choose, the benefits and costs of each must be measured. However, it is generally preferable to restore the marketplace, rather than to institutionally cripple it by providing for a substitute which may carry with it its own momentum and *raison d'etre*.

There are four major categories of breakdowns most often justifying some sort of governmental interference: (1) natural monopoly; (2) "scarcity;" (3) adhesive relationships, often accentuated with inadequate or misleading information; (4) external costs. The precise nature of a marketplace breakdown will dictate what is best suited to either restore the marketplace or to compensate for its absence.

II. WHAT IS REGULATION?

Regulation is not a simple yes-no proposition. There are degrees of regulation. As we are using the term, regulation can mean intervention by the state at any one of three different levels. The most extreme level is "licensing." Here, a regulatory body prohibits the practice of a trade, profession or enterprise until or unless a "license" has been obtained from a governmental body. The existence of this license gives the state a basis for barring entry into the trade or profession, and through its denial, or revocation, confers an ancillary power to promulgate rules. Violation of these rules may be enforced through the draconian denial of that right to practice one's trade or profession.

At a second level, the state can regulate through a system of "permits." Here, no one can practice a defined activity until or unless they have a permit. However, as we are defining the term, there are few barriers to entry to obtain a permit. A system of permits allows entry simply upon the registry of certain required information so the "regulator" knows who is practicing. It gives that regulator the power to suspend or revoke such a permit if certain adopted rules of behavior are transgressed. A system of permits, although little used in the regulatory process, theoretically gives the system an easy in—easy out format. The regulatory body does not bar entry, but once an abuse occurs by a practitioner, the state has the authority to remove the practitioner.

A third level of regulation is "certification." As with "licensing," there is a barrier to entry in order to achieve "certification." One must pass certain tests or otherwise prove special competence in a field. But contrary to a license or permit, one can practice in that field without obtaining "certification." One simply cannot use a defined label or "title" unless one has achieved entry and proven competence. This option involves the state in measuring the competence of various practitioners in order to provide information to consumers by associating the use of a certain "title" with the level of competence that must be obtained in order to use it. A private entity can theoretically "certify" a person, e.g., the use of the term "realtor" granted by a private trade association. But only the state can bar entry by directly prohibiting practice of a trade without prior approval.

Regulation may also take the form of specified maximum or minimum rates. This regulation usually occurs in the context of a "natural monopoly," and then only in conjunction with a "licensing scheme" as we have described.

In addition to the regulation of rates, entry and title use, government has numerous other options where there is a marketplace flaw. Unfortunately, traditionally few of these options are considered. Of course, prior to considering any regulatory alternative, the first priority should be to restore the marketplace by a "structural change" (discussed below) or by antitrust prosecution. Each of the remaining alternatives to traditional "regulation" has advantages and disadvantages, depending upon the marketplace flaw addressed. These alternatives include the following:

III. ALTERNATIVES TO TRADITIONAL REGULATION

A. Bond-Insurance Requirements

A bond or insurance requirement may involve a barrier to entry implicit from its acquisition, but may not involve any further regulation. It need require no government-set standards beyond the bond itself. It is most appropriate where there is the likelihood of incompetence damage and a likely inability by the consumer to collect on a readily obtainable civil judgment, due to insolvency or otherwise.

A bond or insurance requirement guarantees that should there be a small claims court or class action judgment, there will be some recovery. This alternative essentially allows the marketplace of bonding companies or insurance firms to regulate without government intervention. Where the courts sanction particular practices, the marketplace of bonds and insurance will reflect those decisions through higher rates or denial of coverage to those entities creating problems.

B. Disclosure

The second alternative is to require the disclosure of certain information by businesses. Disclosure requirements often address information failures or adhesive relationships, but only where there are alternatives in the marketplace. This alternative depends upon a meaningful enforcement system to guarantee the disclosures are made.

It can suffer from inequitable application in situations where failure to disclose carries with it no consumer wrong. The mechanical enforcement of a prophylactic requirement which may often prove unrelated to the wrong being addressed, can create injustice. Truth-in- lending may require disclosure of the total finance charge. A one-dollar error to the benefit of consumers can result in the mechanical application of a sanction which could gratuitously injure a small business.

C. Rule of Liability

Another alternative societal measure can be a change in a rule of liability by common law evolution or legislative act. Hence, strict product liability may make it easier for victims to recover damages where there has been an injury. The rule of *res ipsa loquitur* has a recovery-enhancing effect. A governmental alteration of the rules of the marketplace, which are themselves the product of custom and state intervention, facilitates the internalization of certain kinds of external costs. The change may utilize the currently existing court system.

Altering a rule of liability carries with it the disadvantage of depending upon the existing court system with all of its drawbacks and deficiencies. These include: enormous transaction costs due to inflated attorneys' fees, interminable delay, often incomprehensible rules of procedure, and in the federal courts, an aversion to the only meaningful way of internalizing many modern external costs through the court system: the class action. Of course, standards of licensing agencies are also rules of liability implicit in the licensing system and are discussed below. These standards are subject to confirmation in the courts and to their own procedural inefficiencies.

D. Straight Prohibition

Yet another alternative is deterrence by formulating broad marketplace rules grounded in fundamental fairness, and the punishment of those who transgress. Sanctions are based on the degree of transgression, the amount of unlawful gain and the extent of harm caused. The use of criminal prosecutions for consumer fraud is an example of such a deterrent- producing alternative. Generally, the deterrent-producing criminal prosecution alternative is under-utilized, even where the harm may be egregious, apparent and the result of *mens rea*.

E. Tax Incentives / Disincentives

Another form of societal intervention is through tax or fee incentives or disincentives. A tax incentive may be viewed as a public appropriation of funds to the extent it defers or excuses taxes by one person performing certain favored acts vis-a-vis others. Instead of not taxing citizen X $10,000 by allowing a deduction or credit for a favored private expenditure, we might instead simply take the same amount of tax money from all parties, and then turn around and hand citizen X a ten thousand dollar check. This mode of analyzing tax loopholes, terming them "tax expenditures," is now widely accepted. Tax incentives, although they produce a strong pull on private behavior, use a bureaucracy: the existing tax bureaucracy. Where this tax bureaucracy has excess capacity and economies of scale justifying further use as a cross-subsidy, it may make sense to use it. And it may also have the advantage of allowing allocation decisions to be made by many private actors in a kind of favor dispensing marketplace, rather than by a government agency.

However, there are several important deficiencies in using the tax system to accomplish cross-subsidies to stimulate or discourage behavior. Because of the progressive nature of the tax system, any tax incentive by way or deductions reduces the progressivity of the system. The tax deduction literally awards one person a greater benefit based on taxable income. Even a tax credit, which overcomes this difficulty, is limited since there are large numbers of people who do not pay taxes and cannot take advantage of the benefit.

Tax incentives or disincentives have a more serious deficiency. A tax incentive, once enacted, continues without further examination. It is often unclear how much it is costing. It does not automatically end until it is affirmatively removed. The benefits are received invisibly and without public scrutiny. If we had to appropriate the $10,000 for Citizen X, we would see who was getting it, why he was getting it and how much he was getting. If we had to give that money year after year, making that threshold decision to so appropriate it repeatedly, we might not make the same decisions we are making through the tax code. Of course, quite apart from the hidden nature of the subsidy, and its proclivity to continue unless specifically ended, we have its contribution to further complexity and inequity in a largely incomprehensible tax system. The current system undermines the legitimacy of all government, and indeed the allegiance of its citizens to the state.

F. Sale of Marketing Rights

Related to tax incentives/ disincentives are the possible sale of marketing rights. The state simply declares a given output allowed and then allocates excess demand to engage in that output by auction. The system is to create an artificial scarcity and allocate the permitted quantity by sale, either by letting those with current rights sell those rights in a marketplace, or by public auction.

G. Subsidy

The state can prevent an external cost or stimulate an external benefit by the obvious device of a direct subsidy. Or it can accomplish the same end with a more seemly appearing loan guarantee, supply limit, direct government purchase, government storage or marketing assistance, import protection, et al.

Despite the disadvantages of each of the seven alternatives we have listed, one or more may be superior to a system of comprehensive regulation. Indeed, the lesser forms of regulation described above may be superior to the more traditionally invoked "licensing" systems currently in vogue.

IV. COSTS OF REGULATION

The traditional comprehensive "licensing" mode of regulation has numerous costs. First is the cost of the regulation itself. Examination licensing fees, renewals and gate taxes, etc. are imposed industrywide by a board or commission under legislative authority. These direct costs of regulation are passed on to the consumer in the form of hidden taxes, although consumers may not identify them as such. Monies are not taken from the general fund for the purposes of financing most occupational licensing regulation, and hence these direct costs are not recognized by legislators either.

The second cost is an indirect cost, but is much more momentous than the direct cost of regulation. The barriers to entry which are created keep out of a trade or industry those who might compete. There is a cost in the denial of entry to those who would otherwise be practicing. There is the cost of overcoming the barrier by those who surmount it. There is the additional cost of the rules which are often promulgated. Because of some history of abuse by a practitioner, the legislature may categorically impose a barrier and exact a serious cost to the system as a whole.

Where there is an alternative more narrowly directed at a wrong, either by rulemaking or by some non-regulatory alternative, the cost may be unnecessary. There is a certain paternalism which pervades regulatory agencies over time and which has been the subject of much scholarly comment. When the optometrists of California were required to take CPR as a condition to obtaining an optometry license one begins to see the general trend.

The California Athletic Commission's concern about too many complimentary boxing match tickets to friends by certain promoters led it not merely to ban excessive gifts of tickets but to the licensing of ticket takers, ushers and even ticket printers! There is a large universe of examples of *in loco parentis*, often well intentioned, and often costly.

Perhaps the final cost is the cumulative effect of closing a large number of occupational and business opportunity doors before they can be tried. The notion of "prior restraint" imposed by the "state"—a kneeling servility to a bureaucratic official before one can start a commercial venture—is antithetical to the American character. Because someone somewhere has done someone wrong, you must be prevented from doing wrong—a wrong you have not done. So, you cede to the state the right to deprive you of the chance to offer your services or products unless it thinks you are not likely to do wrong. The American tradition has been to let me do what I want, and if I do wrong—then intervene, unless the wrong is so terrible and the state's accuracy in predicting who will do wrong justifies a contrary rule. No one categorically precludes prophylactic state intervention, but, rejecting the presumption of state paternalism, we better have a clear and damned good reason for it.

V. A FORMULA FOR JUDGING REGULATION

A. Presumption

Rather than using the current formula for evaluating the appropriateness of a new regulatory system by state legislatures (let's count noses, who is for it and who is against it), we might consider some form of rational analysis.

The appropriate societal response to market deficiency depends upon many variables. The first presumption is to employ the market to the extent it functions. This means the restoration of the market. If a market prerequisite is missing, perhaps it can be resurrected, or artificially supplied, to allow informed consumer sovereignty. One has a leak in the basement. One can hire workers to mop, and perhaps regulators to shut down the main water line when water is not needed for showers, drinking or watering. Of course, these moppers and regulators may become a regular part of a rather bloated household budget— unless we can work out a way to socialize their cost. Translated, this means getting others to pay for your lousy plumbing. One does not have to be a libertarian to propose calling in some plumbers, fixing the leak and then getting out of the house.

And our presumption has a corollary: pay for it yourself—unless we are prepared to subsidize a noble end, in which case the gift should be visible, debated and cease unless renewed annually.

B. Prioritization

Chart A presents a rough ranking of societal responses to the five types of market flaw traditionally justifying regulation.

1. Natural Monopoly

A natural monopoly exists, put in the simplest terms, when there is room for only one entrepreneur to operate efficiently, usually because of economies of scale. If it takes a billion dollars to acquire railroad or utility rights of way and there is room for only one such system, or only one is needed to carry all expected traffic, there may be a natural monopoly.

The priority societal response to a monopoly should be to try to restructure the enterprise to make competition meaningful. This could mean allowing new railroads to compete on the lines of another railroad in return for a fair rental charge for using their lines (called "wheeling"). Of course, government intervention would be required to set a fair rental charge.

It could mean public purchase and management of those aspects of the enterprise with high initial fixed costs (which create the economies of scale and the natural monopoly format). Hence, if the government owned railroad rights of way, track and switching facilities, the actual railroad carriage could be undertaken by competing lines. Technological change may also undermine natural monopoly by creating substitutes for the high fixed cost parts of previous monopolies (e.g., long distance telephone service by microwave/ satellite).

Where natural monopoly is inevitable, there is no competition, no natural selection of the most efficient entrepreneur, no competitive price. Once monopoly has been conceded, unless allowed for a limited period as a special socially beneficent reward (e.g., patent awards), there must be maximum rate regulation to preclude excess profits. Note that most natural monopolies are the result of government intervention to facilitate the enterprise (use of land grants, eminent domain powers, et al.).

Maximum rate regulation is not enough to preclude natural monopoly abuse. Lacking any competitor, the monopolist can give short shrift to consumer service, can become inefficient in operations, secure that most expenses will be compensated. The regulator is in a classic catch-22 quandary in attempting to provide an incentive to incompetent monopolists to improve. Although the regulator may inhibit monopoly power profits, it is obliged to provide the utility's private investors a "fair rate of return" on the investment. More important, the regulator knows well that the long run service depends upon the ability of the utility to attract capital for plant improvement. The denial of an attractive rate of return jeopardizes this utility asset. Yet most regulators believe that the only weapon they have with which to police or discipline utility imprudence is to deny requested rate increases. In so acting they are forced into the cliche to cut off their noses to spite their faces.

Natural monopoly regulation has suffered from a lack of imagination. In the private sector, a failure to perform results in an immediate impact — declining profits. This translates into lower dividends and the dismissal of management. There is a "natural selection" labor market in the competition for superior management. Unfortunately, there is little precedent for regulatory replication of this time-honored marketplace check, but it is easily accomplished.

Theoretically, a regulator could give an existing management group sufficient time to perform efficiently based on comparable market based standards. Repeated failure to achieve reasonable performance results in the conditioning of a future rate increase on the replacement of upper management with a new group. This is what the free market would do. The regulators do not specify who should be hired, just that there must be a change. The extremely well paid executives of a monopoly utility hold a position without tenure. They have a special duty to perform—since they function without immediate market challenge and often manage the provision of a necessity. As benign as the simple recognition that these positions are not lifetime sinecures may appear to be, there is a universal refusal to choose this regulatory option, even with the most egregious record of executive nonfeasance.

The third alternative, government ownership, is a last resort. The confluence of industry and the state removes a fundamental check in the American system: the independent state. With that precious independence, the citizenry can break through what might otherwise be a coordinated curtain of apologia or deceptive self-promotion obscuring failure.

2. Scarcity

The paradigm example of scarcity-based regulation is FCC licensing of radio and television over-the-air frequencies. There are a limited number of non-interfering stations and in many areas more entrepreneurs want to operate than can be supported. How do you decide who gets to broad or telecast? You do not need to limit maximum rates because there is presumably sufficient price competition. But there may be reasons why one does not want to simply allow those who got there first to have or keep these necessarily scarce resources.

The preferred method for allocating scarce resources is by auction. Leasing or selling these scarce resources to the highest bidder does two things: provides public revenues and allocates them to those willing to pay the most — willing to take the greatest risk or able to attract the most capital for the venture based, presumably, on their track record in anticipating consumer demand. To be sure, we may want to advance interests outside consumer demand, but if so, we should be willing to do so by direct and open subsidy.

The allocation of scarcity in the case of FCC regulation purportedly is based on "qualification." Licenses and renewals may be subject to competition along criteria designed to run consonant with the "public interest." In actual practice, with rare exception, the system is actually a "first come first served" system.

The least desirable method of scarcity allocation was illustrated in the gasoline shortages of the late 1970s. Artificial maximum prices prevented market allocation. Supplies were therefore allocated consistent with the Soviet practice: those willing to wait in lines the longest receive the service or product. Limiting demand by making those who wish to purchase something waste enormous quantities of productive time may be one way of seeing to it those who "want" it most (or who have no other demands on their time) get it, but is not the method of allocation favored by a rational society.

3. Adhesion / Imperfect Information

Much of consumer law is concerned with common adhesive relations between merchants and unorganized consumers. Take it or leave it boilerplate contracts imposed on consumers by merchants who spend their livelihood formulating them to their best advantage, has meant abuse. These abuses are often invoked to justify regulatory systems.

Certainly, where advertising is misleading, public civil and criminal remedies abound, at least in theory. The preferred remedy is competition: competitors challenge each other's advertising claims with counter advertising and provide product alternatives. And public education funded by the state may increase the consumer's ability to evaluate conflicting claims. Such an effort is especially warranted where purchasing decisions cannot be made easily by individual consumers. How does a consumer evaluate conflicting claims of tire longevity? The consequences of diet choices?

Notwithstanding vibrant competition and public education, imperfect information may warrant further intervention.

It is possible to identify certain kinds of transactions particularly subject to abuse. The most common of these has been in the area of consumer finance.

Hucksters advertise "8%" financing but fail to mention that 90% down is required for that rate; others advertise only "5%" down and fail to disclose high interest. A federal truth in lending statute was passed to require amount down, period of payment and interest rate if any one of these three is mentioned in an ad. Although an arguably helpful requirement, the statute then excluded any civil remedy for that requirement.

More typical are the direct "disclosure" requirements of Truth-in-Lending and many state counterparts at point of contract. In one reported case, a consumer bought two trucks with

$700 down on each as the disclosures represented on the contract. Because the consumer submitted a check for $1,000 and two others for $200 each, the statute was violated and the merchant severely sanctioned. Certainly requiring standard disclosures may help the marketplace and reduce the need for more intrusive forms of regulation, but the disclosures must be related to consumer need and the remedies must be measured against the wrong. It is better to have a general standard of fairness and hit egregious conduct with harsh sanctions in widely publicized cases than to impose debilitating sanctions on merchants for mechanical bona fide errors of no important concern. Every unnecessary merchant limitation and requirement imposed across an industry or trade is a cost imposed on all consumers.

Where disclosures will not suffice, certification is a possibility. Consumers cannot test many kinds of products individually. Marketplace information about the performance of an automobile in a collision cannot be obtained by buyers directly. The selection of a competent urologist may be a difficult task. In many cases, private groups ranging from Consumer Reports to Underwriter's Laboratory conduct testing to rate and certify performances. But many complex services or products may not be amenable to private testing and may justify public testing and promulgation of results (as with auto crash results) or publicly funded testing and certification for a "title use" to facilitate consumer marketplace information.

4. External Costs

External costs occur when the purchase or use of a product imposes costs on others which are not reflected in the price of the product. Typical examples include various forms of pollution, hazardous products imposing injury or death losses on others, and incompetent practitioners of essential professions or trades who injure those entrusted with their care. "External costs" justify most state and local regulation! Power plant A produces widgets and pollutes both the air and the water while doing so. Power plant B also produces identical widgets, but controls its pollution. Power plant A passes on certain costs to the environment, fishing interests or to the health and safety of future generations. These costs are not borne by the factory and hence are not internalized in the price of the product. The widgets produced in Factory B may cost a small amount more because of the controls preventing such pollution. Because this cost of control is included in the price of the widgets produced by Factory B, it is driven out of business. Factory A survives, even though the total cost of its production of widgets, including the cost imposed on others through the production or use of the product, is much greater than Factory B.

A possibly preferential way to deal with this flaw is rarely used: the compulsory tie-in. There is a harmful effect in the production or use of a product which is assessed outside the marketplace. Try to find a way to bring it into the marketplace by adjusting market rules, e.g., internalize the cost by direct tie-in. Take, for example, the non-fatal auto accident mission of the National Highway Traffic Safety Administration. We are talking about routine equipment standards, e.g., bumper strength for front end collisions. One can create an agency, hire experts and government civil servants, buy a series of office buildings, buy equipment, meet, hold hearings, establish standards for proper bumper production, inspect bumpers which are produced, test them against those standards and sanction those who fail to meet those standards.

On the other hand, one could simply declare that each automobile sold must include insurance according to very simple minimal standards of collision coverage. No bureaucracy. No standards. No enforcement. Those bumpers which result in the front end self-destruction of their accompanying vehicle at a bump under 5 mph (most current vehicles), would and do have horrendous insurance costs. But the manufacturer would have to pay them directly. At present, the external cost of gratuitous damage is cross-subsidized since imperfect information means that after-the-fact damage requires replacement parts whose production is dominated by the manufacturer. The high initial investment in the auto means a partially captive market leading manufacturers to set prices for extraordinary profit. The insurance tie-in requirement means that a manufacturer who designs a useful bumper will be able to offer insurance at a much lower cost than self-destructing bumpered autos. A vehicle with a better bumper is quite likely to cost less than one with a worse bumper, giving it a strong competitive advantage. If it does not obtain a competitive advantage, perhaps the cost of the better bumper is not justified.

The goal of the "tie-in" approach is to internalize external costs to let the self-regulating market determine the nature of the ameliorating action taken. There are other ways to accomplish the same end more efficiently than regulation with accompanying prior restraints.

Often, the tie-in cannot simply be legislated. Pollution is a paradigm case. We have listed in Chart A five kinds of measures to accomplish a tie-in or otherwise to ameliorate external damage: tax transfer, marketing rights sale, equipment standards, harm or output standards and a rule of liability enforced through the courts. We believe that the last alternative, often used, is among the least effective or equitable, but preference among the remaining measures is more difficult. We have expressed a certain ordering of priority, but qualify it by briefly explaining the advantages and disadvantages of each:

a. Tax Transfers

Where the harm increases in a relative straight line as the externality increases and where the harm can be measured, it may well be amenable to a tax or fee. Germany and France have used such a technique with some success in pollution control. Pollution emissions from a plant cause variable harm depending upon: the substance emitted, the atmospheric conditions in the locale, the kind of environment receiving the emission and, as many systems ignore, the synergistic effect of pollution mixes, including background pollution. Tax systems can adjust to at least some of these variables.

As with the three measures discussed immediately below, the remedy suffers from the conflict between an easily administered generalized tax by substance emitted and "individualizing" the tax. Theoretically, it could be varied according to: harm caused from a particular substance at a particular location at various levels of background pollution mixes. And it also suffers from the problem of monitoring and accurate assessment.

However, these difficulties are manageable. Perfect external assessment, as with the perfect due process, is a standard for measurement, not a minimum for action, and perhaps never completely achievable. Focusing on the imperfection of a system to correct a marketplace defect distorts the rational inquiry: what are its relative merits compared to the alternatives. The problems of a tax/fee system are formidable. If the rates are to vary by damage category in any detail, a regulatory body will likely have to set them, exercising expertise from specialized staff resources, engaging in public rulemaking hearings. To the extent the rates perfectly reflect individualized harm from emissions, they would vary literally by emitter and could be subject to the political process of advocacy from those larger entities able to afford it. One could even imagine the broadening of the tax-setting deliberation to include the tangential external costs of the tax itself — perhaps the closing of a plant which might entail some alleged externality.

In point of fact, if a polluter is using certain equipment and produces items by known processes, which is usually the case, it is possible to establish presumptive levels of emission. This is how the tax systems of Europe avoid the monitoring dilemma. It appears to be workable, although understandably imperfect. Likewise, the tax may well vary by pollutant and region without difficulty, and approximate the harm caused.

While most other forms of internalization have these same defects, they generally lack some critical advantages to taxes/fees. First, the tax/fee system is efficient. It does not depend upon detection, onerously expensive due process hearings for breach of standards, followed by assessment of unpredictable penalties. The sanction is relatively certain and calculable. Second, the system is continuous. As emissions increase, taxes increase and incentives to install controls may increase. Third, the system does not preclude new technology to control pollution — it stimulates it by providing an incentive-based demand. Fourth, the system misallocates resources less than alternatives by allowing certain emissions where the cost of reduction is extraordinarily high, while the marketplace first reduces emissions where they are gratuitous and more easily cut. Fifth, the system is capable of fine tuning. One can start the system at a politically acceptable low level and gradually increase until major reductions occur, or perhaps gradually decrease as overall air or water are clean enough so that their self-cleansing properties may allow for more emissions of certain types.

Finally, the system generates revenues which can be used to compensate the interests suffering damage from the emissions of those who choose to pay. The assess and pay dual aspect of a tax/fee system is especially attractive. In a sense it can accomplish what rules of liability attempt, except by automatic process without the need for detection, affirmative action by a sophisticated victim or public entity and without costly judicial proceedings.

It is important, however, to establish in advance where the taxes are going, or at least the criteria for tax adjustment. This information enables the private decisionmakers to make more rational decisions. One does not have the spectacle of auto emissions standards tightened so slowly and incrementally that the efficient stratified engine capable of meeting stringent standards is eschewed in favor of a clumsy technology of pollution control devices to meet what turn out to be interim standards.

b. Sale of Marketing Rights

The "public sale of marketing rights" shares many of the advantages of a tax/fee system. This remedy is appropriate where the harm done is closely related to some identifiable quantity of output and where at a certain level, the harm jumps in a curvilinear fashion. If we decide that if we have more than 1,000 taxi cabs serving the airport, the congestion creates an intolerable external cost due to lack of space for them, we can auction off the right to serve the airport to 999 cabs. If the emission of more than 500,000 pounds of sulfur dioxide per year in a given locale exceeds the self-cleansing properties of the atmosphere and creates intolerable harm, we can sell the right to emit sulfur dioxide up to the level, and compensate those possibly affected by more tolerable harm.

c. Standards

Equipment standards and performance standards may be needed where simple prohibition may not be effective by direct criminal or civil liability by statute.

These latter remedies may be sought where there is irreparable harm from the breach of definable standards and are discussed below. But it is also possible to set standards administratively through rulemaking to discourage an external cost. It is generally a power implicit in the general power to control entry through the granting of licenses (e.g., certificates of public convenience and necessity). The option of standards allows non-economic prescriptive rules of behavior. They are advantageous only where detailed control is needed, detection of violations is workable and the administrative sanction is efficiently applied or is deterrent-producing. Although there may be some basis for the use of standards to prevent forms of irreparable harm which come from their breach, as a means of internalizing external damage, it generally suffers from inflexibility and inefficiency.

The setting of the standards themselves has the problem of "generalizable rule versus individualized rule" in our tax/fee discussion, except the means of enforcing standard violations makes it more difficult. Should we limit sulfur dioxide total emissions in an area? By plant? By smokestack? Should we vary emissions if a given polluter is producing something which can be made nowhere else and the cost of lessening his emissions is enormous? Should we start granting exceptions? What often happens is the standard-setting system ends up describing through its standards what already exists, with little impact on the external damage. Additional emissions may be discouraged, but the same result would be achieved by freezing emissions at current levels and marketing the right to emit by public sale or from an entity currently emitting.

Where standards are set in too generalizable a manner they may misallocate resources and produce inequitable results. Enforcement is quasi-adjudicatory in nature and invokes the full panoply of due process rights. Due process may condition the sanction on years of discovery, hearings and appeals. Ironically, the chief weapon of the standard enforcer is the enormous cost of exercising these vaunted due process rights. It is precisely because they are too expensive to exercise that the standards have some efficacy. However, where the stakes are high for a private entrepreneur (i.e., under circumstances where the standards may have real import) the cost to the agency to establish the sanction is also high. As the disciplinary records of current state agencies make clear, very little enforcement of standards actually takes place. It is the likely disapproval of one's peers or the public from a prosecution, its cost (and in small measure the possibility of a draconian albeit rarely used license revocation) which gives standards what impact they have.

"Equipment" standards, rather than performance standards, limit many of these problems. However, requiring certain equipment or its equivalent can be accomplished without much regulatory presence beyond the approval of "equivalents." I.e., any equipment requirement should allow for substitute technology "equivalent" in performance to any existing equipment then specified. Review to warrant equivalence should be subsidized to encourage technological innovations. Such an equipment standard is appropriate where a certain kind of equipment precludes an unacceptable minimum external cost in a direct and equitable way, or where there are irreparable external costs without it, discussed below.

d. Rule of Liability: Judicial Assessment

One may create a rule of liability that allows those injured by Factory A to file a lawsuit and to use the existing bureaucracy of our legal system to internalize the cost of that damage into the price of the product by assessing damages against Factory A in court. A corollary way of accomplishing the same end is to simply ascertain the amount of damage being caused by Factory A and levy an assessment that would be internalized in the price of the product produced, as we have discussed above.

Whether the assessment is properly made by court adjudication, regulatory process or a more automatic tax levy will turn on a number of variables: the degree and diffusion of the external cost, its ease of calculation, et al. In general, the court system is a poor means to assess such costs where they are regular or widespread because of fundamental deficiencies in the American judicial system: lack of access by the poor or middle class, hostility to the class action mechanism theoretically able to accomplish internalization, unpredictability, the transfer of the dispute into a contest of resource exhaustion and delay, and overwhelming expense. Should a reasonable system of dispute resolution be created, it might be able to internalize costs more effectively. In some jurisdictions, easily detectable damage may be addressed where small claims reforms, alternative dispute resolution experiments or class actions occur meaningfully.

5. External Costs: Irreparable Harm

There are some external costs that cannot be "assessed" by any means of internalization satisfactorily. Attorneys have a concept: "irreparable harm." What do we do about harm which is unacceptable even if it can be paid for? Or harm which simply cannot be paid for? The law allows for preliminary injunctions in civil cases where such harm may befall one of the parties—where the "remedies at law," *e.g.*, money damages, are "not adequate" to provide relief, et al. There are obvious examples at the extremes. Nuclear safety is not a matter to leave for later damage assessment. The harm is irreparable, it must be prevented. Automobile collisions at high speed kill 40,000 Americans or more each year and disable many thousands for life. Preventive action would appear warranted. A consumer entrusts his life to a surgeon and preventive measures to assure a competent professional can be justified.

a. Mechanical Tie-In

The first checkpoint is the possibility of a "mechanical tie-in." Unlike the tie-in designed to internalize compensable damages, this tie-in seeks to prevent an incompensable cost. In the case of our automobile, a mechanical tie-in may consist of a simple requirement to equip vehicles with airbags. Assuming a benefit-cost ratio can justify a mechanical tie-in, which is rather obvious in the case of the airbag it can be imposed with a minimum of ancillary or misdirected restraint. As we have noted, it is important to qualify any such equipment requirement with an "or its equivalent" option, requiring regulatory review to certify equivalency; and there is a need for some enforcement means to assure compliance. But these tasks are focused, relatively easy and non-intrusive. They minimize the continuing generalized presence of government over an area of commerce and inhibit the kind of ultra vires extension and institutionalization of public bodies of control. And they are usually more effective in accomplishing their focused goals.

b. Standards: Civil or Criminal Prosecution

There is no set of equipment that will easily assure the safety of a nuclear power plant, disposal of hazardous wastes or the competence of a surgeon. For many practices which are simply unacceptably dangerous or harmful, a secondary approach might involve the issuance of a straight prohibition or mandatory instruction by statute, if easily articulated, and subject to preliminary relief and deterrent-producing civil or criminal sanctions as appropriate. The disposal of certain listed waste products must be made at specific sites where they are neutralized at a cost borne by those disposing of the products. Where (1) violations are prosecutable without the examination of the defendant, (2) the harm is attributable to individuals deciding to impose an irreparable harm on others, and (3) the danger is substantial, criminal remedies may be appropriate. Where one or more of these factors is absent, a public civil prosecution buttressed by the powers of preliminary injunction, restitution and civil penalties may be preferable. In some circumstances, a private cause of action may be used to assure adherence to a straight prohibitory rule with relaxed standing requirements and "private attorney general" attorney fee award provision.

Where the external harm requires complex and changing prohibitory conditions, e.g., the construction of a nuclear power plant, an agency may be needed to adjust and apply detailed rules of operation with expert staff guidance. Here, the agency applies the rules and the primary remedies for non-compliance, under general statutory authorization.

c. Standards: Licensing

The final alternative for external costs where there is irreparable harm is the licensing of a trade, profession or area of business. A board, commission, department or bureau prohibits business operations unless and until prior governmental permission is given. This prior restraint is justified so a public agency can filter out those who would cause irreparable harm. The same public purpose gives those public bodies the obligation to excise those who were admitted but who manifest the same danger. We have cited medicine as an example of a justifiable prior restraint, but there are non-health related candidates as well. An incompetent attorney can cause serious irreparable harm and a large number of such practitioners could threaten the efficient operation of a legal system which requires a high level of expertise. As with law, most non-health rationales for prior restraints involve: (1) the consumer lacking adequate information from which to evaluate competence in his or her own self-interest, (2) serious irreparable harm flowing from such incompetence, and (3) ability to exclude the incompetent.

VI. FUNDAMENTAL MIS-REGULATION

Using California as a case study reveals a symptomatic array of mis-regulation, not only by the theories set forth, but by any articulable theory.

A. Excessive Licensing to Ameliorate Incompetent Practice: Prior Restraints Gone Wild

The public knows little of the extent of regulation at the state level, nor of the indiscriminatory reliance on the last resort alternative of comprehensive licensing with prior restraints. For California does not just license doctors, dentists and lawyers. It licenses: landscape architects, accountants, boxing promoters, boxers, wrestling promoters, wrestlers, architects, barbers, counselors, psychologists, morticians, collection bureaus, contractors of all types, cosmetologists, polygraph examiners, personnel services, dry cleaners, geologists, geophysicists, nursing home administrators, optometrists, land surveyors, nuclear engineers, petroleum and other engineering title use, shorthand reporters, veterinarians, structural pest control operators, insurance agents, real estate brokers, auctioneers, chiropractors.

Further, within each of these licensing systems, enormous expansion has occurred over time. The Board of Fabric Care began by licensing dry cleaners; now it has separate approval for those who clean hats, those who clean furs. The dental regulators have expanded to license not only those who clean your teeth, but "dental auxiliaries" who put on your bib and show you where to spit. The regulation of boxing promoters resulted in the full scale licensing of everyone connected with the enterprise: matchmakers, timekeepers, even announcers...even the ushers! The Contractors State License Board is playing with separate licensing for each possible trade specialty: brickwork, drywall taping, solar device installation, etc.

More remarkable has been the continuing addition of new comprehensive licensing systems. There has been a great deal of publicity given to "deregulation," particularly by Republicans. Liberal Democrats have hailed the notion of "sunsetting," setting a date at which time an agency will automatically terminate unless it can affirmatively justify its existence. In fact, we have not been able to find a single licensing agency which has been deregulated significantly, nor one which has been effectively terminated within the past two decades. Even the source of the deregulation "sunset" movement, the state of Colorado, has failed. Although five agencies were terminated amidst much hoopla in the 1960s, we have traced the subsequent reappearance of all five. The trend has been in the opposite direction. And the efforts to expand this most intrusive form of regulation continue unabated. The last several years have seen serious bills to set up yet new boards to comprehensively license: "aestheticians" (people who advise on proper make-up), interior designers (people who advise on attractive interior decor), travel consultants, financial advisers. The most recent bill we reviewed proposed to license "recreational therapists." What is this? Those who: initiate, prescribe, direct, evaluate, educate or participate in any treatment involving "social, play, recreation, sports, game, or leisure oriented activity." Or it means anyone "using leisure education, leisure counseling, activity analysis, and leisure assessment." Or it means anyone else who performs: "any service requiring substantial specialized judgment and skills in the use of recreation activities for others based on the application of knowledge of principles of biological, physical, social, psychological sciences and recreation leader studies."

The list of currently licensed entities above is not meant to imply inappropriate government involvement in every case. For some, even a licensing system may be justified. But for most of them there is no justification for licensing under any theory, and for many of them, no need for any extraordinary government involvement. For many agencies with easily recognizable external costs, some irreparable, *e.g.*, the Occupational Safety and Health Administration (Cal-OSHA), water and air pollution control, we may wish to weigh the benefits and costs of the mode of regulation employed. But for many of the occupational and business licensing systems, they flunk a threshold test.

Chart B, below, includes an outlined listing of the regulatory abuses currently extant in California, allegedly a "model" state. The first columns indicate initial errors in regulatory format.

Threshold Test 1: Market Flaw

There is intrusive regulation, including prior restraint licensing, of dry cleaners, barbers, cosmetologists, shorthand reporters, et al. These trades are illustrative of not only low levels of irreparable harm, but of a generic need for repeat business. No dry cleaner or barber will remain in business long while incompetently disappointing successive populations of new customers and losing their repeat business. The performance of the tradesperson is readily evaluated by the consumer. The marketplace has no flaw justifying any intervention.

Threshold Test 2: Irreparable Harm

A second threshold test is the existence of sufficient irreparable harm to justify the extraordinary option of blocking entry. Does some incompetence by a landscape architect (persons who plan gardens for hire), a collection bureau, an appliance or electronic repairman, a retailer of bedding (or the dry cleaner, barber, or cosmetologist needing repeat business) create likely irreparable harm? Are not money damages sufficient? Note that these entrepreneurs are subject to Cal-OSHA regulations safety and are prohibited by criminal and civil statutes from deceptively advertising or defrauding consumers.

Threshold Test 3: Possible Assurance of Competence

A third test is the ability of the state to assure competence, at least in theory. Can the Board of Behavioral Science Examiners or the Psychology Examining Committee assure competent counselors or psychologists? By a written test? Is the state going to be able to set proper standards for make-up application for "aestheticians" or advisable interior decor of building for "interior designers?"

Threshold Test 4: Inability of Consumers to Judge Competence

There is a fourth group of trades improperly licensed. A number of these may involve encounters between consumers and trade persons where there is not a critical need for repeat business because of the one-time nature of each encounter. And there is sometimes the possibility of irreparable harm, perhaps even thought to warrant government intrusion of some sort. But are these situations where a final threshold test is met, an ability by the consumer to evaluate competence? Is assistance from the state needed because the consumer will be unable to make the evaluation himself? The Board of Landscape Architects has considered expansion to license "golf course architects." How many consumers need the assistance of the state to pick a good golf course architect? Are those who do this hiring in need of such assistance, even assuming irreparable harm from incompetence? What about collection bureaus? Geologists? Geophysicists? Petroleum engineers? Shorthand reporters? Auctioneers? Auto dealerships? Nuclear engineers? Who decides to hire or use these people? Is the role of the state here the assurance of competence or the reduction of competition from out-of-state practitioners?

A prime example of a board coalescing three of the above four deficiencies is the Board of Fabric Care licensing dry cleaners. There is a requirement for repeat business assuring competence, a lack of irreparable harm, and a system unrelated to competence. Safety problems are treated by Cal-OSHA. So what has the Board done? It has an interesting record. At its inception and for decades thereafter, it focused on price fixing attempts, eventually passing a rule requiring misdemeanor prosecution for anyone charging less than $1 to dry clean a suit (at a time when such a charge was profitable). Over the past decade, it has revoked the license of exactly one dry cleaner. But it administers a complex entry system. Cleaners are licensed by type, separately for three categories of clothing. The examination has little to do with competent cleaning or pressing and is not taken by those who do the cleaning and pressing, but by licensee "owners." But the Board manages to keep out of the trade the majority of those who seek entry.

B. Ineffective Regulation to Ameliorate Pollution and Hazard External Costs: Standard Setting Gone Wild

The California Administrative Code is a nightmare of detailed instructions. Boards, commissions and agencies have engaged in rulemaking with little restraint over the past two decades. Boxing promoters are required to file seating charts of the arenas where they hold their matches — repeating charts already on file. Rules concerning ladders at building sites consume over ten pages. Optometrists are now required to know CPR (a rule which interestingly was dropped for physicians by their Board). The consequences of extremely detailed standards are well documented: individualized standards and exceptions often related to the legal resources of the parties involved, gratuitous technology stultification, waste, misallocation, delay.

The agencies of California have not used or even considered seriously non-traditional means to internalize external costs. The Water Resources Control Board, Cal-OSHA covering worker safety, air pollution control agencies, et al., rely on detailed standards and traditional enforcement. The standards not only suffer from the defects we have discussed, but they are not effectively enforced. The tendency is for each of these systems to describe what is now through their standards.

Very few agencies, to the extent they use rulemaking, promulgate generally understood and broad standards related to their mandate and then aggressively follow up with deterrent-producing enforcement. Instead, a "negotiation" pattern is followed. A rule is proposed. A hearing is held. The industry raises problems. Exceptions are drawn to meet those problems. A violation occurs. On the rare occasions where it is detected, the violation is remedied with a warning and request to comply, which, if compliance is difficult, will yield a request to alter the rule accordingly.

The vast majority of standards are only distantly related to a real external harm. Those which are have very little impact on the industry allegedly affected. Of course there are a few exceptions where there has been some impact, but a careful review will reveal that these mostly concern what are actually equipment standards. These have their own disadvantages, but are enforceable enough to check what otherwise might be a degeneration of an external harm. Auto pollution control, minimum sewage treatment processes and electrostatic scrubbers are examples.

It is a vast oversimplification to conclude that standards by an expert regulatory body should never be used. There are criteria which can justify rulemaking, as we have discussed, especially in combination with other mechanisms where there is irreparable harm without them, as with the regulation of physicians, attorneys, et al. But the brunt of standard setting emanates from agencies which, as we note above, do not need to exist in the first place. Where they do need to exist because of a real and irreparable external cost (*e.g.*, Cal-OSHA, pollution control), the use of incentives which continuously and completely cover external cost production, provide relief for victims and do not misallocate resources, are not considered at the state level.

C. Regulatory Charade: Disguised Cartels

There are numerous areas of business suffering from serious market flaws. Some of these justify regulation at some level. But these justifications are often turned upside down by careless legislation and deferential courts. Two massive examples involve the regulation of agriculture and of alcoholic beverages, respectively.

In the case of agriculture, the external cost underlying initial government entry has largely turned on market volatility. Radical supply fluctuations create serious displacement costs as some farmers lacking a deep pocket to outlast an aberrational year are irretrievably driven out. Government intervenes to facilitate survival of small farmers to preserve vigorous competition and to smooth out violent market fluctuations.

At the federal and state levels, farmers were allowed to collude in the marketing of their products. These lawful cartels have functioned in federal so-called "marketing orders" to do far more than limit external costs. They have affirmatively engaged in price-enhancing traditional cartel practices: setting arbitrary "quality" standards and agreeing to limit the supply of their produce.

At the state level some of the same activity has occurred. Milk regulation historically, for example, has meant the division of milk into "classes" and limitations on the quantity and use of milk by collusive agreement of purported competitors. But most activity through state marketing orders has been to promote their product. There is nothing wrong with any entrepreneur promoting his product. But these entrepreneurs use the power of the state. They are able to coercively levy fees on all who produce a given product.

Those who pay the tax are quite willing to do so since it is imposed on all competitors and acts as a tax passed on to consumers.

In California, the most active promoters are the agricultural associations promoting beef, dairy products and avocados. The newest board is one created to promote wine ingestion financed by large scale assessment of California vintners. Where is the external cost being ameliorated? Where is the external benefit being conferred? The power of the state is used to collect monies and organize promotion of beef, milk, cheese, avocados and wine. Is there any indication that the diet of Californians suffers deficiencies in these food categories warranting public involvement in their promotion? One would have to guess that these would probably be about the last foods any competent nutritionist would list in need of promotion, given their current levels of ingestion.

Alcohol regulation is an example of more traditional "licensing" which is not based on a market flaw, but which itself creates an unintended defect. Concerned about the proliferation of bars in San Francisco during rather wild times, the state intervened to "cap" the number of liquor licenses at one per 2,500 population for on-site drinking and one per 2,000 for liquor stores. Limits were set county by county except for those who were licensed when the limits were passed. These people were grandfathered in.

The system is now justified on the same basis as was vertical price fixing in liquor: there is an external cost implicit in the drinking of alcohol. Although land use controls limit the location of the bars and stores, limiting the number of licensees makes liquor a bit more inaccessible and expensive, discouraging consumption. (The California Supreme Court has rejected a similar argument on behalf of the fixing of resale prices for liquor by the manufacturer.)

The result of this system is the same as with more artificial barriers, *e.g.*, the New Motor Vehicle Board approval system described above. It raises prices. But by creating extra profit it attracts investment to the enterprise, enhancing promotion. The value of a license increases over time, a cost which is borne by consumers but not collected by the state. It is collected by the person selling the license. If one wishes to discourage liquor consumption, a laudable goal conferring an indisputable external benefit, simply increase the tax. Use the proceeds to finance alcohol abuse programs, perhaps even alcohol education efforts to counter state-organized wine consumption promotion.

D. Fraudulent Regulation

Is there another side to the misregulation coin? Are there areas where regulation is warranted, even to the point of comprehensive prior restraint licensing? Of course. We have mentioned medicine and law as two areas where the alternatives at least appear to be unworkable. Where there is such an overwhelming need for competence that we are prepared to violate the basic right of our citizenry to offer their services in the marketplace, we should have a clear reason for doing so. Where we may have such a reason, does it guide our regulatory system? The answer is no.

The two primary examples where the licensing alternative may be justified illustrate the irony of prior restraints. Although we impose licensing on physicians, we confer a single all-purpose license to "practice medicine." Who "practices medicine?" One may go to an internist, a urologist, a dermatologist, or a neuro-surgeon. One must have a competent urologist if one needs kidney treatment.

There is a connection between a competent urologist and the general state license, but it is very indirect. Certainly, the licensure barrier keeps out those who are of particularly low general aptitude, although certifying medical schools appears to do that. But there is no significant testing of any physician even measuring to any relevant degree special competence in the area where he or she will be spending the rest of a professional life. As far as the state is concerned, a urologist can perform brain surgery. Perhaps malpractice fears (a rule of liability) or insurance requirements or private (e.g., hospital or private trade association) certification help limit such wandering, but these controls are unrelated to licensing.

Although the medical barriers to entry are severe in difficulty, and only distantly related to actual competence as a physician practices, there is little attention given to ensuring the competence of those who have made the club. Malpractice judgments are not even systematically reviewed.

Unsurprisingly, very few physicians of any description have their licenses revoked for anything short of felony drug or rape offenses.

Although the maintenance of competence in medical specialties requires constant re- education, there is no continuing education requirement. There is no re-testing at any point. (Note that nurses are, in contrast, required to submit to continuing education.)

Virtually an identical critique could be applied to the regulation of attorneys. No attorney practices immigration law, estate planning, criminal defense, patent law, tax law, divorce law and antitrust law. Attorneys may practice in more than one area competently, but no attorney can practice competently in a substantial number of the twenty-odd specialties which have evolved. As far as the state is concerned, they are perfectly free to do so. A patent attorney can defend a capital murder case.

The consumer expects that the onerous prior restraint of licensing assures counsel competent in the area where there is a problem needing services. The state does not do that. As with medicine, the Bar tests graduates on general principles unrelated to particular knowledge in most areas of actual practice.

It is true that persons with an ability to answer Bar questions will, in a very general sense, be somewhat more likely to gain competence in a given area of practice. What the state really tests is general aptitude, not relevant competence. A simple alternative to the massive regulatory systems in place: the required disclosure of schools, degrees and grades of physicians and attorneys (based on hundreds of examinations) provides a far better measure of such aptitude and some information about expertise.

As with medical regulation, the Bar does not require specialized competence of any kind, continuing education of any variety or re-testing. And its record of policing incompetence from within the existing profession is virtually non-existent. In California, for example, approximately 25 attorneys have their licenses revoked annually out of over 90,000 members of the Bar. Most of these have their licenses restored in short order. Once again, felony offenses against their own client is the basis of most of the revocation activity, such as it is–although one attorney was recently sanctioned for writing undignified remarks about a judge in an appellate brief.

If state determination of the right to do business is justified, given the extraordinary cost in the sacrifice of a basic freedom, it must occur only because of an extraordinary need for competence to avoid irreparable harm. Such a need means that the system must provide what its justification demands. This can be expected to mean not just a scorpion's club initiation ritual (scorpions are said to form a ring when attacked, like a besieged wagon train, each facing their sting-inducing tail outward toward the intruder). Justification demands proof of competence in the specific areas of practice where reliance occurs, continuing education, periodic testing and the assiduous removal of those who do not maintain their skills.

The message conveyed here can be summarized: use prior restraints only for good and unavoidable reason—but if the reason is there, fashion the system to it in a bona fide fashion. If competent practitioners are critical, then by God assure competent practitioners in the areas where they practice and are relied upon.

It is ironic that in the several areas where such prior restraints may be warranted, they are not applied in good faith.

VII. HOW TO REGULATE

Assuming a good faith basis for a regulatory system, particularly one appropriate for a licensing format, how should it be accomplished? How should it be monitored? What ancillary remedies (in addition to licensing powers) may be appropriate? Our watchword in analyzing structure, authority and standards is to preserve the basic check in the American system: the independence of the state. These systems exist because the marketplace is flawed. Its restoration or substitution must be entrusted to those who can represent the interests of the general citizenry in whose interests the intervention occurs.

A. Structure

1. Level of Regulation

State regulation may not be viable where it unduly burdens interstate commerce, or state systems imposed with variations between states affects a highly mobile regulated group. Only a national or international system can prevent jurisdictions from being played off against each other, to gravitate toward the lowest common denominator. *E.g.*, so long as Delaware offers minimal standards for incorporation, to what degree can individual states require more? Perhaps they should not require more, but the false competition for revenue between states is not conducive to a common rule which might ameliorate a market flaw. To impose such a curative rule it must be adopted at a level where it can be effective and cannot be avoided easily.

An Athletic Commission regulating boxing cannot reasonably function where it depends for revenues on gate tax receipts from high attraction matches and promoters can schedule events in any one of fifty different states. Promoters simply avoid the gate taxes, boxer pension systems, or safety-orientated regulations of any given state by seeking the state with the lowest regulatory standard.

Most regulation, however, does not unduly burden interstate commerce and does not involve a highly mobile licensee group. Regulation may involve legitimate differences between the cultures and peoples of the various states. Most regulation may be expected to occur at the state level.

Regulation at the local level may suffer from the same kind of destructive competition *vis- a-vis* the state that state regulation may suffer *vis-a-vis* the federal government. Except such destructive competition is much more likely given the relative mobility of practitioners in commerce within given states. Furthermore, although the nation has a tradition of direct local democracy, in fact, the reality of local government is quite different.

Local governments have been so fragmented by geography, function, and type, that direct democratic response is limited. Although there are equivalent problems at the state level with regard to gerrymandering, campaign contribution influence and other forms of abuse, at the local level these forms of abuse are supplemented by the relative invisibility of local officials. Los Angeles County, for example, includes 342 special districts. Each one of these districts performs a very fundamental and important governmental task. Special district governance at the local level accomplishes everything from mosquito abatement to parks, education, provision of water and other essential functions.

California has 5,000 special districts, 480 cities, and 58 counties. The special district, city and county lines do not follow rational boundaries. Drawing all of the governmental bodies within one urban county on paper would scarcely leave an unlined area. The shapes of the districts are not compact. Cities often run in corridors one hundred yards wide by ten miles long in order to capture a piece of tax-valuable property at the end. The governments of special districts are sometimes elected, and often appointed. The precise boundaries between cities and counties often go down the middle of the street, sometimes to one side, sometimes to the other.

Surveys of citizen awareness of fundamental local government functions have revealed responses concerning who provides basic water, trash, police and fire services approximating what one would expect with a roll of the dice: random guesses. Although local regulation may be advisable in a system where there is a multi-purpose government visibly governing a recognizable and compactly shaped area, that is not what we currently have. Local government, in the area of land use, "exclusive franchises," the letting out of preferential contracts, et al. manifests the most egregious abuse of any level of government.

Any system of local regulation depositing in the hands of local officials the authority to decide who should or should not practice a trade, who should or should not have a monopoly in a given enterprise, et al., should be accompanied by a state authorizing statute designed to systemically preclude abuses. The statute must specify the restraints of trade to be allowed, and provide for required checks to compensate for the absent marketplace. This minimal requirement is presumably the law of the land. The United States Supreme Court has declared the "state" to be the antitrust gatekeeper. Before a regulatory restraint of trade can contravene the federal antitrust statutes, the state must fulfill its obligations as sovereign. It must specifically authorize any restraint and provide for "independent state supervision," it cannot deliver a "blank check" to local government.

Examples of abuse proliferate. The starkest is in the area of trash hauling, where a trade association was able to obtain such a blank check for commercial trash hauling, normally subject to competition. The state law simply declared any arrangement approved by any of the 5,000 special districts, 480 cities, and 58 counties immune from antitrust exposure. The law issued such a blank check that monopolies without any possible competition or required rate regulation and lacking even competitive bidding were permitted. Local officials in the fragmented setting of local government could allow only one trash hauler into their jurisdiction to service businesses, apartments and construction sites, and make that monopoly grant worth millions of dollars. The largest firm dominating this industry is now successfully obtaining "exclusive franchises" (monopolies) throughout the state. Such an abdication by the state creates an atmosphere ripe for corruption as well as the violation of the most elementary principles of regulatory law.

B. Who Should Regulate

In most states, regulatory agencies consist of the trade, profession, or industry regulated. Such a system contravenes fundamental constitutional principles. We live in a system where the most fundamental civics concept commands that our government, the "state," represent the people. The state does not represent economic interests with a narrow profit stake in public policy, it represents the general public; the diffuse interests of all of us as citizens. It represents our concerns for the environment, the future and ourselves as a whole. We do not require governmental intervention if all it does is to replicate the functions of a private cartel.

Those persons making decisions on behalf of the public, precisely because the public has an interest separate and apart from the entities of profit stake interests, must have only the public at heart. It should be a fundamental axiom of American government that those regulatory bodies making decisions on behalf of all of us, and invoking the awesome power of the state, must not consist of those with a proprietary profit stake in the public policies being formulated. Yet in California and in almost every state to yet a greater degree, such is the case. By direct operation of law a majority of members of the Board of Medical Quality Assurance in California consists of physicians. The majority of the members of the Board of Accountancy consists of accountants. Even those boards which include "public" members count among them persons (for most agencies they constitute a voting majority of a quorum) with a direct profit stake in the public policies being formulated.

It is one thing for profit-stake interests to form trade associations to provide information, advice and opinion to government decision makers. It is quite another thing for them to be the government decision makers. Such a pattern transgresses fundamental notions of due process and cannot be tolerated in a constitutional democracy.

What is perhaps most interesting about current state regulation throughout the nation is the likely wholesale contravention of federal antitrust and Constitutional principles by these systems. The United States Supreme Court threw out the attempt by the Alabama Board of Optometrists to sanction an optometrist (*Gibson v. Berryhill*). The court held it violated fundamental notions of due process to have state officials with adjudicatory powers currently competing, however indirectly, with an object of Board enforcement. Most recently, California courts have tentatively voided part of the New Motor Vehicle Board Act because three of the Board's seven members are auto dealers and are therefore institutionally biased. An amendment was then passed precluding the vote by the dealers in any matter involving other dealers, but an appellate court has found that their very presence on the Board taints it. Meanwhile, federal courts are requiring state agencies which restrain trade to be immunized from federal antitrust exposure only if the state provides independent state supervision, i.e., supervision by state officials unconnected to those with a proprietary stake in the policies being formulated.

These precedents, if consistently and properly applied, void most of the current state regulatory systems in all fifty states—and they do so quite rightfully.

C. Funding

Almost all regulatory agencies are "special funded." That is, the industry or trade regulated is assessed charges which go into a separate fund financing the budget of the public agency regulating it. On the surface, an industry or trade producing an external cost should not only have that cost internalized if possible, but the cost of doing that internalization should also be internalized. However, the direct tie between fees and budget is improper. The legislature should first decide how an industry's or trade's market flaws should be addressed, determine the amount of money necessary to accomplish that end, and then and only then attempt to assess that industry or trade an amount not too different from that cost.

There are circumstances where such assessments may not be realistic. The Athletic Commission, for example, gains monies from gate tax receipts. Only "big" matches produce significant revenue, but promoters will take those matches out of California to avoid taxes. Where the external benefits of a regulatory system extend to society at large or where destructive interstate competition precludes collection, some contributions from the general fund may be warranted.

The other side of the same issue is the tendency of the legislature to see all special funding as free. A hidden tax without political resistance is considered no tax at all. Hence, any suggestion by a trade or commercial association to set up a licensing system funded by themselves is viewed as a proposal without political liability.

All monies collected from regulatory fees should go directly into the general fund. Budgets should be drawn from the general fund based on the public interest in the expenditures to be made. Then the legislature's finance committees should periodically adjust fees to approximate the money being spent where appropriate, which will usually be the case. The effect of this procedural change is to focus legislative attention on these budgets as public expenditures—which is what they are. They should compete for priority. And agencies should not be in the conflicting position of having to approve an unwise but revenue- producing boxing match or another remunerative examination entry barrier in order to add new equipment or more secretaries for their own shop. Nor should agencies be compelled to eschew removing the incompetent because of budget constraints. The revocation of a license is an expensive proposition. Currently, agencies pay for their own counsel, an administrative law judge and court reporter. For small agencies, the costs are formidable. And they are a very real bar to aggressive internal "clean ups" in the rare cases where the spirit is willing. Where budgets depend upon after-the-fact increased license renewal fees from those currently licensed, the prospects of major increases supported by a trade to finance internal policing are not sanguine.

The funding of such regulatory bodies is one of the few areas where Parkinson's Law that expenditures rise to meet income should be reversed, income should rise, after the fact, to meet expenditures. This is a very bad idea in public works and benefits budgeting, of course, but not in the financing of regulatory system mechanisms.

D. Bifurcation of Executive/Adjudicative

Regulatory agencies are very special legal creatures. They are given a very general mandate by the legislative branch to address a social purpose — often defined in a single clause. For example, the Federal Trade Commission is empowered to deal with undefined "deceptive advertising" and vaguely defined "unfair acts in competition." Agencies perform a major quasi-legislative role to fill in detailed meaning consonant with their authorizing statute's intent. Agencies "adopt rules." And they adopt thousands of them. State Administrative Codes now rival in extent and certainly surpass in detail the whole body of annually enacted statutes by state legislative bodies.

Rulemaking establishes standards of behavior which are often intended to give predictability and warning to agency action. Where there is a violation of a rule, the remedial powers of the agency may be invoked, powers which vary from the entry of an order to halt a given practice, to revocation of one's license to do business.

In enforcing its rules, the agency performs an executive function. It detects violations. It establishes enforcement priorities. It prosecutes the case. There is no conflict between the rulemaking and enforcement roles. But the regulatory body often fulfills yet a third role, a judicial one. For having decided to prosecute a violation of its statute or rules, it also establishes the procedures for "hearings" on the charges. And it even serves as judge. It may make findings of fact.

The dual prosecutorial/adjudicatory role is a troubling one in a common law adversarial system. Certainly, state Administrative Procedure Acts provide due process protection. And there is court review. But the fact remains that the entity who made the rule and who decided to prosecute is also sitting as judge. And court review is a very limited check given the deference paid to procedurally proper agency adjudications.

There are several ways to cure this imbalance. One is to use the Office of Attorney General or some other independent office as prosecutor. Staff simply turns over information concerning compliance to a separate entity with its own discretion to prosecute or not to prosecute. Another alternative for larger agencies is to restructure the agency as Commissioner Phil Elman has suggested for the FTC and as the California PUC has done: to bifurcate the agency staff. Those who perform as prosecutors or advocates are separated out into their own department with separate lines of authority from the "Commission" and its adjudicatory staff.

A more radical alternative would give a separate "Department of Consumer Affairs," which most states already have created, power to conduct investigations of violations and to prosecute them before the agency.

E. Representation of Diffuse Interests

Regardless of the reforms undertaken, regulatory agencies are bound to reflect "intensity of interest." That is, those with their own stake in agency policy will turn their attention to its influence. Even neutral board members will be subject to the regulatory environment described below. Trade association advocacy can be expected.

But since the agency exists to counter market flaws, it is critical that information and advocacy not be dominated by those whose interests often represent the very abuses the system was established to prevent or minimize. Several structural adjustments can facilitate a balanced consideration of the more diffuse interests which are otherwise underrepresented.

The first measure is the creation of an adequate and structurally independent staff. The "deferred bribe" of agency apprenticeship followed by trade employment must be precluded by terms of employment which prohibit employment with the trade regulated for at least several years after leaving the agency.

The second structural reform is the stimulation of those diffuse interests affected by an agency's actions to organize and represent themselves to counter the automatically organized profit stake interests. An agency, of course, should comply with the "sunshine" "standards of operation" discussed below. But beyond this, an agency can implement generous standing requirements to appear before it and argue, particularly in the rulemaking area. Proposals for de novo rulemaking should be entertained without standing impediments.

Some agencies can go much further to allow diffuse interests to have a role. The California PUC has allowed the Utility Consumers Action Network

(UCAN) to gain access to the bills of the local utility. The bills mailed out to ratepayers have always been financed as an expense item off the top by the ratepayers. The proponent for access proved there was "dead" or unused space in the envelopes requiring no additional postage. UCAN communicated with ratepayers, solicited funds, conducted elections. Over 75,000 ratepayers have joined the organization. The voting percentage of electors in the election of the Board of Directors was double that of the municipal elections. The organization is now funding professional and organized advocacy before the PUC. This organization has democratically institutionalized advocacy of an otherwise underrepresented group. It cost the taxpayers nothing. It cost the ratepayers nothing. The regulator simply used an available asset to facilitate more balanced advocacy before it. The requirements in the proposal for fair elections are of special import. They assure that the advocate is a legitimate representative of the interests it purports to represent, and they remove any taint that the regulator may be favoring any particular consumer group in allowing access.

Related to the UCAN reform is intervenor funding, allowing those who are able to represent diffuse interests and who benefit the regulatory process, to recover costs and fees. The California PUC has laudably adopted such a procedure.

Another structural feature which can address the profit stake vs. diffuse interest imbalance problem is a general Office of Consumer Advocacy, either within an agency or within the larger administration. Such an office can professionally represent diffuse interests where they are not capable of organization.

F. Proper Authority

Assuming a structure amenable to regulatory policy in the public interest, how should the authorizing statute be framed?

1. Statutory or constitutional

The first question is where should it exist, in the State Constitution or in statutory law? The answer is in statutory law. States nevertheless are persuaded by interest groups to put enabling provisions straight in the most fundamental document underlying our state. In California, our sacred guarantees or free speech and religion adjoin provisions creating a Board of Chiropractic Examiners, a Horse Racing Board, an Athletic Commission, a Board of Osteopathic Examiners, the State Bar and the Public Utilities Commission. One of the effects of such folly is the creation of regulatory arrogance. The State Bar contends that it is exempt from the open meetings and public records sunshine laws of the state. The Board of Osteopathic Examiners refused to seat two public members appointed by the Governor, contending that it did not have to obey a statute adding two public members to its Board since it was "created in the State Constitution." The Athletic

Commission notes that it does not have to comply with the Administrative Procedure Act.

If one were to create an exalted class of platonic regulators, this is not the crew one would assemble. There is no need to put any regulatory system designed to address a market flaw in so basic a document as a constitution.

2. Specificity

The second feature of the authorizing statute, apart from its creation of only public members to make decisions on behalf of the public, is specificity. The means assigned to compensate for a marketplace flaw must be set forth. If one allows a created board to "license" methadone clinics, does that mean it can specify how many staff must be on premises? How many medically qualified patients a clinic may treat? What prices may be charged?

The law must allow for a flexible response, but within some range of specified options.

3. Remedies

Confer remedies to effectively address the market flaw. The Federal Trade Commission is given the task of policing deceptive advertising, a task impossible without a deterrent punch. Its major remedy is the right to issue a complaint and establish a "cease and desist order." This order takes, on the average, 4.17 years to establish where it is contested. There is no prohibition on advertising and no sanction of any kind unless that cease and desist order is violated (or a similar one you have been served with). Since that will not happen for 4.17 years, what is the message conveyed? Is it, do not deceptively advertise or we shall sanction you more than you would gain? No. The message is: do whatever you want. We guarantee that we shall do nothing to you for four years or more. Only after we get our cease and desist order in place are penalties possible. So our remedy is actually a license to deceive—a grant of immunity.

By the same token, it is a mistake to confer only a single extreme remedy. Boards such as the California Contractors State License Board had only the draconian power to suspend or revoke licenses for many years. It could not fine. There was no gradient of sanctions consistent with the spectrum of wrongs it can be expected to address. Faced with depriving someone of his livelihood or doing nothing, it usually did nothing. Several years ago it was belatedly given the power to fine.

4. Who is regulated

The authorizing statute should define precisely what functions require licensure. The devolution of jurisdictional authority to the agency itself under a vague mandate leads toward excessive regulation. There is a marked tendency for boards and commissions to impose "prior restraint" licensing not only on the fundamental profession or trade capable of alleged irreparable harm, but directly to the ancillary services tangential to the enterprise. Hence, instead of licensing dentists and holding them responsible for their employees, the Board chose to directly license those employees, now under the appellation "dental auxiliaries." Real estate brokers are responsible for any transaction conducted under a broker's license and are fully responsible for the actions undertaken with apparent authority by salespersons working under the "license" of that broker. Nevertheless, the Real Estate Commissioner is licensing all salespersons, several hundred thousand of them. The Athletic Commission, as we have noted, is an extreme example. Although boxing promoters are fully responsible for their events, the Commission has licensed almost everyone they employ, from announcer to ushers, to even the ticket printers.

Some of these paternalistic expansions have occurred by the legislative direction, almost always at the behest of the trade involved. Others have been accomplished by the board or commission operating under an excessively vague statutory charter.

Often the motivation for such expansion is the creation of a "client" group of employees by the prime trade under regulation. Required apprenticeship as a part of licensure qualification can be a cheap source of labor while the apprenticeship is underway. Those who presently practice the ancillary function may support it because they will likely be grandfathered in and the licensing requirements serve as a barrier to entry increasing the long term value of their position. Well intentioned regulators can be persuaded to endorse expansion by a few egregious cases of abuse by these subordinates, and by a natural desire to territorially expand-often for the most beneficent of reasons.

Authorizing statutes should confine prior restraints as narrowly as possible. If there is one trade or profession whose members control an operation, those who are hired by that person, who have their work reviewed necessarily by him or her, need not be separately licensed except in the most extraordinary circumstances. The real estate broker, dentist, physician, etc. is well able to perform a far superior screening function than the mass testing process of standard licensing. Here is the person who reviews background and qualification carefully and individually because he or she is responsible and has both insurance and licensing on the line. The employee must work directly with the prime licensee day by day. A failure to review, an incompetent choice, and resulting harm to those protected by the regulatory system, can give rise to strong sanctions against the persons who are in the best position to hire, supervise the work, judge competency. Such a system avoids prior restraints while making responsible persons far more able to make these decisions than any single testing procedure. License dentists, doctors, brokers, boxing promoters, contractors, and hold them absolutely responsible for persons operating under their respective licenses as employees or subordinate contractors.

G. Standards of Operation

There are too many operational issues for comprehensive treatment in this forum. But two intra-agency issues belong in any discussion of reform.

1. Sunshine

Agencies have an obligation to operate publicly. The sunshine laws of most states which require open meetings and public records are sometimes avoided not only by those agencies with Constitutional identity, but by others subject to the law. To comply with the spirit as well as the letter of the law, members of small boards should not associate socially, the materials used by Board members at meetings should be available to the audience since meetings are incomprehensible without these materials, and document reproduction costs should be reasonable. It is remarkable how much mundane restrictions can bar public access.

2. Entry barriers

Entry barriers are the single most troublesome agency operation. Barriers should be imposed fairly and in a timely fashion. For example, a student attends a law school, an institution the Bar declares is acceptable to it, where a degree is a qualification to take the Bar examination. This institution takes \$6,000 to \$8,000 of hard-earned money. And it takes one year of his life. The student succeeds, passes basic courses and is promoted to a second year. The same thing occurs. Then into the third year. The student has expended three years of his life, over \$20,000 in tuition, and many more thousands in lost wages and opportunities elsewhere. But he or she is given a Juris Doctor degree. The university certifies the graduate as qualified not only to practice (which is presumably why people go to law school), but to hold a doctorate degree. Then the Bar flunks a large portion of those people. In California, the majority of those taking the exam are flunked. For some of the twice-yearly exams, the passage rate has been below 40%. For many of the law schools the passage rate is below 20%, and for some, consistently below 15%. Is something wrong here? To be sure, we inveigh against the state depriving anyone of an opportunity without good reason. But if we have a good reason to limit entry, is there any reason we lead so many down the primrose path for so long? If we're going to say no, why not say no a little earlier on? Why should the Bar preside over the gratuitous tragedy of so many? Why are schools certified which achieve less than 50% passage rates, much less 20%?

To be fair, entry barriers should relate to the kind of competence consumers will be relying upon. They should not be exercises in raising the drawbridge. Is it really necessary for an architect to know about the contents of an Egyptian tomb?

It is amusing to hear some laud the United States Marines who saved the medical students studying in Granada. We hailed as heroes the protectors of those important Americans. Did we do them a favor in allowing them to continue their studies? How many are going to achieve entry into the profession they were there to seek? They will be saved and brought home to White House gatherings, after which state medical regulators will attempt, with predictable success, to bar their entry into the profession.

The entry process itself should somehow measure the skills and information needed to perform. Few entry systems short of apprenticeships assure much more than a commitment to the enterprise and general aptitude.

Perhaps one of the more fascinating examples of entry irrelevance is the real estate sales and brokers exam. This is a multiple-choice question examination. The difficulty and ambiguity of a multiple-choice question is well known. And the questions are excellent. In fact, there are very few brokers who know the answers to them. The exam is honed by a process of reverse natural selection. Any question successfully answered by a majority of the examinees is dropped and a new one added. One can imagine the breed of those which remain, year after year. So how does one pass? A series of schools send in spies who memorize questions and answers and put together actual test questions and answers from exams going back three or four years. Most of these questions will be on the next exam. They are memorized. The critical barrier to entry is an ability to memorize and a willingness to pay one of the schools their substantial fee. The fee is a barrier to entry, which the state general fund could perhaps better use.

VIII. REGULATORY OVERSIGHT: THE ENVIRONMENT

Regulation exists in a political environment. These are public agencies. They must go to the Governor's Department of Finance for budget approval. They must submit to scrutiny by the legislature. They must deal with the general auditing and review agencies under the legislature and the Governor.

A. Horizontalization

The politics of regulation fully reflect what a sociologist might call the "horizontalization" of our society. We are less a nation of owner-operators than ever before. We are increasingly a nation of employees. We are organized around our peer groups. We identify with our peers. The prosecution of hospital kickback schemes by this author illustrated not only the well-documented vertical alienation between the hospital administrator and patient—but the concern of the administrator over what peer administrators in competing institutions are thinking and doing.

Politically, the horizontalization can be seen in burgeoning trade associations, thousands of them in Washington, D.C., and hundreds in most major state capitols. The massive, modern buildings housing the National Coal Institute,

American Petroleum Institute or the American Association of Railroads would not be mistaken for the site of a PTA meeting.

Although we have described the counter measures which can be taken to preserve some balanced advocacy before agencies, the campaign contribution and advocacy imbalance between profit stake interests and the general public interest is more serious in the surrounding legislative environment. On the positive side, the somewhat higher visibility of the legislature and possible contention between a greater mix of interest groups does create opportunities. One might build a coalition of interest groups who are not directly involved themselves in a given issue. If they can be persuaded to participate, they may represent a broader interest than the legislature would otherwise hear from, on issues apart from their primary concern.

However, there are structural and practical obstacles to an independent legislature. At a practical level most states lack even a critical mass of public interest private advocates to build a coalition. One study of land use policies in California surveyed lobbyists before the state legislature. There were 235 representing various profit stake interests. Two represented the general public, the taxpayer, the environment, the consumer, the future. And where an agent for coalition building appears, it is often difficult to persuade a narrower lobby to expend political capital on behalf of a cause outside the narrow mandate of the sponsoring association.

B. Campaign Finance

The direct corruption of campaign contribution influence is more lethal to the integrity of the state than is advocacy imbalance. The impact of more expensive campaigns and trade association contribution dependence has so undermined the independence of the state that the most basic check in the American system is in jeopardy. The solution may be politically difficult without major citizen upheaval. Only the public financing of campaigns, with fair rules for competitors, can remove what is now, at the risk of perceived hyperbole, nothing less than a dagger plunged into America's breast.

California has its quota of Lloyd Connellys, legislators who are willing to do the hard work to pierce into state government on behalf of broader interests. It is important that public financing occur to create more of them and to free those extant from the burden and shame of begging, however dignified it may appear. Contributions, even among the most ethical of legislators, buys at least access. Given time constraints on legislators, that is no small compromising commodity.

C. Oversight

What the regulatory environment needs is independent legislators with time and staff to oversee as well as to service. Rather than the benign nonfeasance of agency attention to keep it out of the general fund or to please a vocal constituent, there should be a schedule of oversight hearings. Each agency should have to expect a tough set of hearings at least once every three years on its performance in what will be a relatively more public forum than the agency's own environment creates. At present, it must account to very few indeed.

D. A Bold Reform: An Office of Administrative Law

One of the major oversight reforms attempted by the legislature created an Office of Administrative Law. This was a bona fide attempt by the legislature to clean up what it believed to be excessive and nonsensical rules by the state regulatory system. Recognizing its inability to oversee the kind of detail needed to have a real impact on the many agencies, it created an executive branch entity to complete the task. As an experiment in regulatory reform, it was imaginative and bold. And it has achieved some successes. After four years of operation, it is now possible to gauge more clearly what such a body can and cannot do responsibly.

The Office of Administrative Law was given the power to review existing rules and to approve new rules as they are adopted. OAL consists of a staff of some twenty young attorneys. They are empowered to use six criteria in reviewing a rule: reference, non- duplication, consistency, clarity, authority and necessity.

One can see the impact such a review may have on rulemaking. For example, conservative scholars have quite rightly critiqued many of these agencies for *ultra vires* rulemaking beyond any legislative mandate. Although there is a basis for legal challenge where an agency acts without authority, who is to sally forth with the challenge where the licensees enjoy a cartel benefit from the rule? In fact, well under 1% of all rules are challenged in court at all. This Office will now review each and every rule for proper authority. That is a momentous change.

Two problems exist which independently threaten this generally thoughtful idea—each will create a monster far worse than any abuse addressed by the new law. First, the sixth criteria, "necessity," is inappropriate for review by the Office. Whether a rule is "necessary" is a shorthand way of saying "sensible," "advisable," "a good idea." But the twenty attorneys who sit in the Office of Administrative Law have no knowledge of the substance of the regulation they are reviewing. They do not attend hearings. All they have before them is a file summarizing public comments and the agency's response.

It is possible that an Office of this kind can perform an academic "legal" review of rules. It can evaluate the statutory authority. It can address the clarity of the rule. It can survey for duplication and consistency. But to give it the authority to reject rules because of its perception that they are not "necessary" is a task which cannot be responsibly performed by them. This inability to second guess in ignorance is one of the reasons courts are not allowed to overturn normally the findings of the trier of fact. Courts, as outside parties do not present at the hearings, will examine proper authority and may critique in dicta lack of clarity. But they generally will not intrude into the expertise or fact finding of an agency. And they hesitate for good policy reasons.

Theoretically, the Office could argue that it merely examines the rulemaking file to make sure that there is some factual basis for a rule. But what does this mean? Does it mean there must be some words of justification placed after each clause in a rule? Does it matter what the words say? If it does not matter it is a futile exercise. If it does matter, who is judging whether the words provide justification such that the rule is "necessary" or "a good idea?" How is it making that judgment?

The eventual result of this process is two-fold. First will be the rejection of many rules which are quite necessary because of a technical failure to include a factual justification for a provision nobody contests. The second is the advent of gamesmanship. The agencies learn what words to use to justify what they want to do. Since the Office of Administrative Law lacks any expertise whatever in the area, since the process is not adversarial and the agency can provide whatever, it wishes and since factual justifications exist for everything from nuclear war (population control) to banning rock and roll music (damage to the inner ear), a great deal of impressive-looking paperwork will be produced.

Both consequences are now occurring with a vengeance, and the net result is, as the cynics would have predicted, far more red tape and regulatory delay than would now be the case without the reform.

The second flaw is the allowance of ex parte contacts between private parties and the Office of Administrative Law. The Office can and will become a conduit for improper reversal of rules by those who lost in the public forum but who now can meet secretly with officials from this Office and lodge complaints properly rejected or never made in the public forum. The Office in California has not only allowed such improper contacts, it has at least historically encouraged them.

The Office of Administrative Law idea is a reform of some promise if properly harnessed, and of great danger if not itself reformed.

IX. CONCLUSION

A first imperative is to articulate a defensible theory on which to base a regulatory system. The state must identify the flaw to be addressed and specify a means of amelioration precisely addressing it.

We have created some 60 regulatory agencies in California. They operate largely invisibly, with little legislative or public scrutiny. Many operate where there is no significant market flaw to address or consumer benefit resulting. We have expanded existing regulatory agencies into areas where they have no business. Where we have regulatory agencies with a legitimate purpose and a real market flaw to address, we have avoided that task in favor of cartel practices. And we have the system dominated by those with a narrow profit stake in the public policies they are adopting and imposing on all of us with the force of the law and in the name of the state.

While creating paternalistic rules and raising barriers to entry, few of the boards or commissions in the State of California, even those covering professions which create irreparable harm and whose regulation can be justified, have attempted to remove those currently practicing who are incompetent and who create that irreparable harm.

And the agencies continue to expand and new ones to proliferate. More and more trades and businesses are falling under the rule of "prior restraint." Alternatives are unexamined. We can be a psychologist when and if the state tells us we can, and what is worse, the Committee deciding consists largely of psychologists.

The Soviet system is comprehensive in its stultification. There, prior restraint does not require market flaw justification. It is presumed. And the system has the one failure which has long been anathema to the American experiment: a lack of checks and balances. In socialism there is no check between the state and the means of production. The state owns and operates the means of production. There is one system evolving here which is perhaps worse, and just as inimical to American principles; a system where that check is also obviated, except the means of production own and operate the state.

Chart A

Flaw	Societal Response
I. Natural Monopoly	1. Structural Change to Restore Market
	2. Maximum Rate Regulation/Management
	3. Government Ownership
II. Scarcity	1. Market sale
	2. Qualification
	3. First Come
	4. Line
III. Adhesion/Imperfect Information	1. Structural Change
	2. Consumer Education
	3. Disclosure Requirements with Nonmechanical Remedy
	4. Certification by the State
	5. Regulation by Permit with Rulemaking
IV. External Costs	1. Internalize through Required Tie-In
A. Damages	2. Internalize by Tax Transfer
	3. Internalize by Marketing Rights Sale
	4. Equipment Standards
	5. Harm or Output Standards
	6. Internalize by Judicial Assessment by:
	a. Rule of Liability
	b. Procedural Reform
B. Damages with Possible Inability to Assess/Collect	1. Bonding/Insurance Requirement
	2. Preliminary Relief
C. Damages with Health and Safety Irreparable Harm	1. Mechanical Tie-In by Statute
	2. Straight Civil Prohibition with Preliminary Relief
	3. Public Prosecution (Civil/Criminal)
	4. License Revocation

Chart B

California Flaws

1. Agency Wholly Unnecessary
2. Regulation Excessively Detailed
3. Regulation Cartel Oriented
4. Agency Dominated by Profit Stake Interests
5. Agency Includes Profit Stake Interests
6. Agency Purposes Addressable By Non Regulatory Measures
7. Agency Has Inadequate Practical Remedies to Accomplish Regulatory Purpose
8. Inadequately Staffed to Supervise Trade (Assuming Agency Justified)
9. Excessive or Irrational Barriers to Entry
10. Inadequate Quality Control of Existing Businesses/Tradesmen (Assuming Agency Justified)
11. Regulation at Wrong Level of Government
12. Wrongly in Constitution

List of Agencies	1	2	3	4	5	6	7	8	9	10	11	12
Board of Accountancy	?		✓	✓	✓	✓	✓	✓	?	✓		
Board of Architectural Examiners		✓	✓	✓	✓	✓	✓	✓	✓	✓		
Athletic Commission		✓			✓			✓	?		✓	✓
Bureau of Automotive Repair					✓	✓	✓	✓		✓		
Board of Barber Examiners	✓		✓	✓	✓	✓			✓			
Board of Behavioral Science Examiners	✓	✓	✓	✓	✓	✓	✓	✓	✓			
Cemetery Board				✓	✓	✓	?	?	?	✓		
Bureau of Collection and Investigative Services		?				✓	✓	?		✓		
Contractors State License Board		✓	?		✓	✓	?	✓	✓	✓		
Board of Cosmetology	✓	✓	✓	✓	✓	✓			✓			
Board of Dental Examiners		✓	✓	✓	✓		?	✓	✓	✓		
Bureau of Electronic and Appliance Repair	✓	?				✓	✓	?				
Board of Fabric Care	✓	✓	✓	✓	✓	✓	✓	✓	✓			
Board of Funeral Directors and Embalmers		✓	✓	✓	✓	✓			?	?		
Board of Registration for Geologists and Geophysicists	✓	✓	✓	✓	✓	✓	✓	✓	✓	✓		
Board of Guide Dogs for the Blind						✓		✓				
Bureau of Home Furnishings	✓	✓	✓			✓	✓	✓	✓			
Board of Landscape Architects	✓	✓	✓	✓	✓	✓	✓	✓		?		
Board of Medical Quality Assurance			✓	✓	✓			✓		✓		
Acupuncture Examining Committee			✓	✓	✓			✓		✓		
Hearing Aid Dispensers Examining Committee	✓		✓	✓	✓	✓		✓				
Physical Therapy Examining Committee		?	✓	✓	✓			✓	✓	?		
Physician's Assistants Examining Committee		✓	✓	?	✓	?	?	✓	?			
Podiatry Examining Committee		?	✓	✓	✓			✓	?			
Psychology Examining Committee	✓	✓	✓	✓	✓	✓	✓	✓	✓	✓		
Speech Pathology and Audiology Examining Committee		✓	✓	✓	✓	?			?			
Board of Examiners of Nursing Home Administrators		?	?	✓	✓	?	?	✓	?	✓		
Board of Optometry		?	✓	✓	✓	?			?			
Bureau of Personnel Services				?	✓	✓	?	✓				
Board of Pharmacy			✓	✓	✓			✓		✓		
Board of Registration for Professional Engineers and Land Surveyors	✓	✓	✓	✓	✓	✓	✓	✓	?	✓		
Board of Registered Nursing		?	?	✓	✓			✓	?	✓		
Board of Certified Shorthand Reporters	✓	?	✓	✓	✓	✓				?		
Structural Pest Control Board		✓	✓	✓	✓	?						
Tax Preparer Program			?	?	✓	✓	?	✓		✓		

Board of Examiners in Veterinary Medicine		✓	✓	✓	✓	?		✓	✓	✓		
Board of Vocational Nurse & Psychiatric Technician Examiners			?	✓	✓	✓		✓	✓	?		
Department of Alcoholic Beverage Control	✓	✓	✓			✓	?		✓	?		
Banking Department		✓	✓		✓			✓		✓	✓	
Department of Corporations		?			?		✓	✓		✓	✓	
Department of Insurance		✓	✓		✓			✓	?	✓	✓	
Department of Real Estate		✓	✓	✓	✓	?		✓	✓	✓		
Department of Savings and Loan		✓	✓		✓			?	?	✓	✓	
Cal-OSHA		✓				✓	✓	✓		✓	✓	
Department of Food and Agriculture		✓		✓	✓	✓		✓	✓			
Office of Statewide Health Planning and Development		✓			?	✓		✓	✓			
Air Resources Board		✓				✓	✓	✓		✓	✓	
California Waste Management Board						?	✓	✓		✓		
Coastal Commission		✓				?	✓	✓		?		
Department of Fish and Game					?		✓			✓		
Board of Forestry		✓	?			?	?	✓		✓	✓	
Water Resources Control Board		✓				✓	✓	✓		✓	✓	
Auctioneer Commission	✓	?	✓		✓	✓			✓			
Board of Chiropractic Examiners		?		✓	✓	✓			✓	✓		✓
Energy Commission		✓				✓	✓			?		
Horse Racing Board		✓	✓		✓	✓			?		?	✓
New Motor Vehicle Board	✓	✓	✓	✓	✓	✓			✓			
Board of Osteopathic Examiners		✓	✓	✓	✓		✓	✓	✓	✓		✓
Public Utilities Commission		?				?	✓	✓		✓		✓
State Bar of California			✓	✓	✓	?	✓	✓	✓	✓		

END OF ARTICLE

Hypotheticals

The Pharmacy Benefit Managers (PBMs) have been an unregulated group of persons who serve as agents for retail drug outlets and drug companies. They help to arrange products and prices and take a percentage of the proceeds as payment. They can serve as agents in making sales arrangements for competing drug companies and retailers. They are also involved in creating their own drug ordering systems. Some advocates contend that they are in a position to arrange product and price fixing in violation of antitrust law and have no transparency in their machinations.

In 2018, the California Governor signed a bill requiring the "registration" of PBMs in the state (Chapter 905, Statutes of 2018). Accordingly, they must notify the Department of Managed Health Care that they are operating in the state.

a) What are the likely effects of "registration"? Licensure permit requirements? What regulatory measures (checks and balances) should apply to this kind of enterprise? What type of adjudication regulations? Is licensing here justified?

b) What happens when AI-enhanced technology is operating in a field of endeavor that normally requires licensure? Should such technology use be regulated? What happens if the technology is wrong or its operations result in damages? Who is liable?

Sam Slippery is applying for a license from the Board of Pharmacy. He meets all qualifications and passes the licensure exam. However, he had a marijuana possession conviction within the last 7 years and served 90 days in custody.

a) Discuss whether the Board can deny him licensure based on that conviction. How would current law apply (assuming it was not after legalization and not so comporting).

Mike Tornado is applying for a boxing license. He meets all criteria, although he has a record of child abuse five years ago, involving the whipping of a preschooler with a cane leaving marks. No crime was charged, but the child was removed from his custody.

a) Discuss whether this kind of record can result in licensure denial. Discuss whether a criminal conviction for assault as the result of a fist fight can be a basis. What if Mike Tornado was the only injured party from the event?

Quiz

1. Which of these groups may be referred to as the "fourth branch" of government?

   a. Lobbyists
   b. Trade associations
   c. Regulatory agencies
   d. Licensed professionals

2. Which of these are the most frequent proponents of creating state regulatory boards?

   a. Trade associations
   b. Consumer groups
   c. Unions
   d. Federal agencies

3. Which is the most common "barrier to entry" created by occupational licensing boards?

   a. License revocation
   b. Continuing education requirements
   c. Disciplinary guidelines
   d. Licensing exams

4. California's "cap and trade" program is designed to remedy which market flaw?

   a. External costs
   b. Scarcity
   c. Natural monopoly
   d. Imperfect information

5. Requiring disclosure of licensee disciplinary history may address which market flaw?

   a. External costs
   b. Scarcity
   c. Natural monopoly
   d. Imperfect information

6. Which of these may be a negative by-product of occupational licensure increase?

   a. Price increases
   b. Limited employment opportunities
   c. Decreased mobility across state lines
   d. All of the above

Chapter 2
Regulation and Constitutional Law

CONSTITUTIONAL ANALYSIS FRAMEWORK

State agencies operate under both their state and the federal constitution. Their operations constitute "state action" by definition, and hence, any limitations on the state *vis-à-vis* individual rights may be prohibited or limited. Further, state constitutions may have more limitations on the state than may emanate from the federal counterpart. For example, California has an explicitly stated "right of individual privacy" (Art. I, Section 1) that is not explicitly provided federally.

Some individual rights may be analyzed under "strict scrutiny", requiring a "compelling state interest" and a lack of alternatives to approve state abridgement. A slightly more flexible second standard of "heightened scrutiny" may be applied where individual rights are at issue, but do not reach the level warranting "strict scrutiny." That more liberal standard is applied where there is a finding that the regulatory action is "substantially related to a legitimate state interest." Much state action falls under a third category, where the state must exercise a "rational relation" between a legitimate justification and the state action at issue.

Regulatory operations interfere with the underlying concept of (1) "freedom of contract" between private parties. This initial and seminal criterion for state intrusion was created by the leading and early case of *Munn v. Illinois* (*infra*), requiring that regulation must be "clothed with the public interest" to overcome the background premise of private freedom of contract. Other agency actions commonly subject to constitutional challenge and limitation include (2) due process taking—particularly as manifested in maximum rate regulation (also discussed in *Munn*) as well as in entry controls. Similar issues arise in minimum rate regulation and in entry controls (*e.g.*, licensing), and may arise agency operational standards (*e.g.*, rules). A wide variety of constitutional issues then arise in the context of agency actions—many of which require (3) procedural "due process" under constitutional standards. Next on the constitutional checklist is (4) interstate commerce—including the state requirement not to impede transportation or transactions between states. Finally, state agencies must comply with the standard civil liberty provisions of the federal constitution governing (5) 1st Amendment free speech, and (6) 4th Amendment right of privacy, particularly from unreasonable searches and seizure. Agencies must also comply with comparable provisions in their state constitutions—which can be more restrictive on their operations than the U.S.

Constitution. The provisions of the (7) federal 14th Amendment may apply to agency discrimination, rights of equal protection and right to travel.

FREEDOM OF CONTRACT

Seminal Regulatory Justification

Munn v. Illinois

94 U.S. 113 (1876)

Opinion

MR. CHIEF JUSTICE WAITE delivered the opinion of the court.

The question to be determined in this case is whether the general assembly of Illinois can, under the limitations upon the legislative power of the States imposed by the Constitution of the United States, fix by law the maximum of charges for the storage of grain in warehouses at Chicago and other places in the State having not less than one hundred thousand inhabitants, 'in which grain is stored in bulk, and in which the grain of different owners is mixed together, or in which grain is stored in such a manner that the identity of different lots or parcels cannot be accurately preserved.'

It is claimed that such a law is repugnant—

1. To that part of sect. 8, art. 1, of the Constitution of the United States which confers upon Congress the power 'to regulate commerce with foreign nations and among the several States;'

2. To that part of sect. 9 of the same article which provides that 'no preference shall be given by any regulation of commerce or revenue to the ports of one State over those of another;' and

3. To that part of amendment 14 which ordains that no State shall 'deprive any person of life, liberty, or property, without due process of law, nor deny to any person within its jurisdiction the equal protection of the laws.'

We will consider the last of these objections first.

Every statute is presumed to be constitutional. The courts ought not to declare one to be unconstitutional, unless it is clearly so. If there is doubt, the expressed will of the legislature should be sustained.

The Constitution contains no definition of the word 'deprive,' as used in the Fourteenth Amendment. To determine its signification, therefore, it is necessary to ascertain the effect which usage has given it, when employed in the same or a like connection.

While this provision of the amendment is new in the Constitution of the United States, as a limitation upon the powers of the States, it is old as a principle of civilized government. It is found in Magna Charta, and, in substance if not in form, in nearly or quite all the constitutions that have been from time to time adopted by the several States of the Union. By the Fifth Amendment, it was introduced into the Constitution of the United States as a limitation upon the powers of the national government, and by the Fourteenth, as a guaranty against any encroachment upon an acknowledged right of citizenship by the legislatures of the States.

When the people of the United Colonies separated from Great Britain, they changed the form, but not the substance, of their government. They retained for the purposes of government all the powers of the British Parliament, and through their State constitutions, or other forms of social compact, undertook to give practical effect to such as they deemed necessary for the common good and the security of life and property. All the powers which they retained they committed to their respective States, unless in express terms or by implication reserved to themselves. Subsequently, when it was found necessary to establish a national government for national purposes, a part of the powers of the States and of the people of the States was granted to the United States and the people of the United States.

When one becomes a member of society, he necessarily parts with some rights or privileges which, as an individual not affected by his relations to others, he might retain....

From this it is apparent that, down to the time of the adoption of the Fourteenth Amendment, it was not supposed that statutes regulating the use, or even the price of the use, of private property necessarily deprived an owner of his property without due process of law. Under some circumstances they may, but not under all. The amendment does not change the law in this particular: it simply prevents the States from doing that which will operate as such a deprivation.

This brings us to inquire as to the principles upon which this power of regulation rests, in order that we may determine what is within and what without its operative effect. Looking, then, to the common law, from whence came the right which the Constitution protects, we find that when private property is 'affected with a public interest, it ceases to be *juris privati* only.' This was said by Lord Chief Justice Hale more than two hundred years ago, in his treatise *De Portibus Maris*, 1 Harg. Law Tracts, 78, and has been accepted without objection as an essential element in the law of property ever since. Property does become clothed with a public interest when used in a manner to make it of public consequence, and affect the community at large. When, therefore, one devotes his property to a use in which the public has an interest, he, in effect, grants to the public an interest in that use, and must submit to be controlled by the public for the common good, to the extent of the interest he has thus created. He may withdraw his grant by discontinuing the use; but, so long as he maintains the use, he must submit to the control.

***

'There is no doubt that the general principle is favored, both in law and justice, that every man may fix what price he pleases upon his own property, or the use of it; but if for a particular purpose the public have a right to resort to his premises and make use of them, and he have a monopoly in them for that purpose, if he will take the benefit of that monopoly, he must, as an equivalent, perform the duty attached to it on reasonable terms....

And further on (p. 539):--

‘It is enough that there exists in the place and for the commodity in question a virtual monopoly of the warehousing for this purpose, on which the principle of law attaches, as laid down by Lord Hale in the passage referred to [that from *De Portibus Maris* already quoted], which includes the good sense as well as the law of the subject.’

***

In later times, the same principle came under consideration in the Supreme Court of Alabama. That court was called upon, in 1841, to decide whether the power granted to the city of Mobile to regulate the weight and price of bread was unconstitutional, and it was contended that ‘it would interfere with the right of the citizen to pursue his lawful trade or calling in the mode his judgment might dictate;’ but the court said, ‘there is no motive . . . for this interference on the part of the legislature with the lawful actions of individuals, or the mode in which private property shall be enjoyed, unless such calling affects the public interest, or private property is employed in a manner which directly affects the body of the people. Upon this principle, in this State, tavern-keepers are licensed; . . . and the County Court is required, at least once a year, to settle the rates of innkeepers. Upon the same principle is founded the control which the legislature has always exercised in the establishment and regulation of mills, ferries, bridges, turnpike roads, and other kindred subjects.’ *Mobile v. Yuille*, 3 Ala. N. S. 140.

***

Common carriers exercise a sort of public office, and have duties to perform in which the public is interested. *New Jersey Nav. Co. v. Merchants’ Bank*, 6 How. 382. Their business is, therefore, ‘affected with a public interest,’ within the meaning of the doctrine which Lord Hale has so forcibly stated.

But we need not go further. Enough has already been said to show that, when private property is devoted to a public use, it is subject to public regulation. It remains only to ascertain whether the warehouses of these plaintiffs in error, and the business which is carried on there, come within the operation of this principle.

For this purpose we accept as true the statements of fact contained in the elaborate brief of one of the counsel of the plaintiffs in error. From these it appears that 'the great producing region of the West and North-west sends its grain by water and rail to Chicago, where the greater part of it is shipped by vessel for transportation to the seaboard by the Great Lakes, and some of it is forwarded by railway to the Eastern ports---Vessels, to some extent, are loaded in the Chicago harbor, and sailed through the St. Lawrence directly to Europe.

. . . The quantity [of grain] received in Chicago has made it the greatest grain market in the world....It has been found impossible to preserve each owner's grain separate, and this has given rise to a system of inspection and grading, by which the grain of different owners is mixed, and receipts issued for the number of bushels which are negotiable, and redeemable in like kind, upon demand. This mode of conducting the business was inaugurated more than twenty years ago, and has grown to immense proportions. The railways have found it impracticable to own such elevators, and public policy forbids the transaction of such business by the carrier; the ownership has, therefore, been by private individuals, who have embarked their capital and devoted their industry to such business as a private pursuit.'

....Thus it is apparent that all the elevating facilities through which these vast productions 'of seven or eight great States of the West' must pass on the way 'to four or five of the States on the seashore' may be a 'virtual' monopoly.

Under such circumstances it is difficult to see why, if the common carrier, or the miller, or the ferryman, or the innkeeper, or the wharfinger, or the baker, or the cartman, or the hackney-coachman, pursues a public employment and exercises 'a sort of public office,' these plaintiffs in error do not. They stand, to use again the language of their counsel, in the very 'gateway of commerce,' and take toll from all who pass. Their business most certainly 'tends to a common charge, and is become a thing of public interest and use.' Every bushel of grain for its passage 'pays a toll, which is a common charge,' and, therefore, according to Lord Hale, every such warehouseman 'ought to be under public regulation, viz., that he . . . take but reasonable toll.' Certainly, if any business can be clothed 'with a public interest, and cease to be *juris privati* only,' this has been. It may not be made so by the operation of the Constitution of Illinois or this statute, but it is by the facts.

We also are not permitted to overlook the fact that, for some reason, the people of Illinois, when they revised their Constitution in 1870, saw fit to make it the duty of the general assembly to pass laws 'for the protection of producers, shippers, and receivers of grain and produce,' art. 13, sect. 7; and by sect. 5 of the same article, to require all railroad companies receiving and transporting grain in bulk or otherwise to deliver the same at any elevator to which it might be consigned, that could be reached by any track that was or could be used by such company, and that all railroad companies should permit connections to be made with their tracks, so that any public warehouse, &c., might be reached by the cars on their railroads. This indicates very clearly that during the twenty years in which this peculiar business had been assuming its present 'immense proportions,' something had occurred which led the whole body of the people to suppose that remedies such as are usually employed to prevent abuses by virtual monopolies might not be inappropriate here. For our purposes we must assume that, if a state of facts could exist that would justify such legislation, it actually did exist when the statute now under consideration was passed. For us the question is one of power, not of expediency. If no state of circumstances could exist to justify such a statute, then we may declare this one void, because is excess of the legislative power of the State. But if it could, we must presume it did. Of the propriety of legislative interference within the scope of legislative power, the legislature is the exclusive judge.

***

It matters not in this case that these plaintiffs in error had built their warehouses and established their business before the regulations complained of were adopted. What they did was from the beginning subject to the power of the body politic to require them to conform to such regulations as might be established by the proper authorities for the common good. They entered upon their business and provided themselves with the means to carry it on subject to this condition. If they did not wish to submit themselves to such interference, they should not have clothed the public with an interest in their concerns. The same principle applies to them that does to the proprietor of a hackney-carriage, and as to him it has never been supposed that he was exempt from regulating statutes or ordinances because he had purchased his horses and carriage and established his business before the statute or the ordinance was adopted.

It is insisted, however, that the owner of property is entitled to a reasonable compensation for its use, even though it be clothed with a public interest, and that what is reasonable is a judicial and not a legislative question.

As has already been shown, the practice has been otherwise. In countries where the common law prevails, it has been customary from time immemorial for the legislature to declare what shall be a reasonable compensation under such circumstances, or, perhaps more properly speaking, to fix a maximum beyond which any charge made would be unreasonable. Undoubtedly, in mere private contracts, relating to matters in which the public has no interest, what is reasonable must be ascertained judicially. But this is because the legislature has no control over such a contract. So, too, in matters which do affect the public interest, and as to which legislative control may be exercised, if there are no statutory regulations upon the subject, the courts must determine what is reasonable. The controlling fact is the power to regulate at all. If that exists, the right to establish the maximum of charge, as one of the means of regulation, is implied. In fact, the common-law rule, which requires the charge to be reasonable, is itself a regulation as to price. Without it the owner could make his rates at will, and compel the public to yield to his terms, or forego the use.

***

We know that this is a power which may be abused; but that is no argument against its existence. For protection against abuses by legislatures the people must resort to the polls, not to the courts.

***

We come now to consider the effect upon this statute of the power of Congress to regulate commerce.

It was very properly said in the case of the *State Tax on Railway Gross Receipts*, 15 Wall. 293, that 'it is not everything that affects commerce that amounts to a regulation of it, within the meaning of the Constitution.' The warehouses of these plaintiffs in error are situated and their business carried on exclusively within the limits of the State of Illinois. They are used as instruments by those engaged in State as well as those engaged in inter- state commerce, but they are no more necessarily a part of commerce itself than the dray or the cart by which, but for them, grain would be transferred from one railroad station to another. Incidentally they may become connected with inter-state commerce, but not necessarily so. Their regulation is a thing of domestic concern, and, certainly, until Congress acts in reference to their inter-state relations, the State may exercise all the powers of government over them, even though in so doing it may indirectly operate upon commerce outside its immediate jurisdiction. We do not say that a case may not arise in which it will be found that a State, under the form of regulating its own affairs, has encroached upon the exclusive domain of Congress in respect to inter-state commerce, but we do say that, upon the facts as they are represented to us in this record, that has not been done.

The remaining objection, to wit, that the statute in its present form is repugnant to sect. 9, art. 1, of the Constitution of the United States, because it gives preference to the ports of one State over those of another, may be disposed of by the single remark that this provision operates only as a limitation of the powers of Congress, and in no respect affects the States in the regulation of their domestic affairs.

We conclude, therefore, that the statute in question is not repugnant to the Constitution of the United States, and that there is no error in the judgment. In passing upon this case we have not been unmindful of the vast importance of the questions involved. This and cases of a kindred character were argued before us more than a year ago by most eminent counsel, and in a manner worthy of their well-earned reputations. We have kept the cases long under advisement, in order that their decision might be the result of our mature deliberations.

Judgment affirmed.

MR. JUSTICE FIELD and MR. JUSTICE STRONG dissented. MR. JUSTICE FIELD.

I am compelled to dissent from the decision of the court in this case, and from the reasons upon which that decision is founded. The principle upon which the opinion of the majority proceeds is, in my judgment, subversive of the rights of private property, heretofore believed to be protected by constitutional guaranties against legislative interference, and is in conflict with the authorities cited in its support.

The defendants had constructed their warehouse and elevator in 1862 with their own means, upon ground leased by them for that purpose, and from that time until the filing of the information against them had transacted the business of receiving and storing grain for hire. The rates of storage charged by them were annually established by arrangement with the owners of different elevators in Chicago, and were published in the month of January. In 1870 the State of Illinois adopted a new constitution, and by it 'all elevators or storehouses where grain or other property is stored for a compensation, whether the property stored be kept separate or not, are declared to be public warehouses.'

***

The question presented, therefore, is one of the greatest importance, -whether it is within the competency of a State to fix the compensation which an individual may receive for the use of his own property in his private business, and for his services in connection with it.

The declaration of the Constitution of 1870, that private buildings used for private purposes shall be deemed public institutions, does not make them so. The receipt and storage of grain in a building erected by private means for that purpose does not constitute the building a public warehouse. There is no magic in the language, though used by a constitutional convention, which can change a private business into a public one, or alter the character of the building in which the business is transacted. A tailor's or a shoemaker's shop would still retain its private character, even though the assembled wisdom of the State should declare, by organic act or legislative ordinance, that such a place was a public workshop, and that the workmen were public tailors or public shoemakers. One might as well attempt to change the nature of colors, by giving them a new designation. The defendants were no more public warehousemen, as justly observed by counsel, than the merchant who sells his merchandise to the public is a public merchant, or the blacksmith who shoes horses for the public is a public blacksmith; and it was a strange notion that by calling them so they would be brought under legislative control.

The Supreme Court of the State-divided, it is true, by three to two of its members-has held that this legislation was a legitimate exercise of State authority over private business; and the Supreme Court of the United States, two only of its members dissenting, has decided that there is nothing in the Constitution of the United States, or its recent amendments, which impugns its validity. It is, therefore, with diffidence I presume to question the soundness of the decision.

***

If this be sound law, if there be no protection, either in the principles upon which our republican government is founded, or in the prohibitions of the Constitution against such invasion of private rights, all property and all business in the State are held at the mercy of a majority of its legislature. The public has no greater interest in the use of buildings for the storage of grain than it has in the use of buildings for the residences of families, nor, indeed, anything like so great an interest; and, according to the doctrine announced. The legislature may fix the rent of all tenements used for residences, without reference to the cost of their erection. If the owner does not like the rates prescribed, he may cease renting his houses. He has granted to the public, says the court, an interest in the use of the buildings, and 'he may withdraw his grant by discontinuing the use; but, so long as he maintains the use, he must submit to the control.' The public is interested in the manufacture of cotton, woollen, and silken fabrics, in the construction of machinery, in the printing and publication of books and periodicals, and in the making of utensils of every variety, useful and ornamental; indeed, there is hardly an enterprise or business engaging the attention and labor of any considerable portion of the community, in which the public has not an interest in the sense in which that term is used by the court in its opinion; and the doctrine which allows the legislature to interfere with and regulate the charges which the owners of property thus employed shall make for its use, that is, the rates at which all these different kinds of business shall be carried on, has never before been asserted, so far as I am aware, by any judicial tribunal in the United States.

The doctrine of the State court, that no one is deprived of his property, within the meaning of the constitutional inhibition, so long as he retains its title and possession, and the doctrine of this court, that, whenever one's property is used in such a manner as to affect the community at large, it becomes by that fact clothed with a public interest, and ceases to be *juris privati* only, appear to me to destroy, for all useful purposes, the efficacy of the constitutional guaranty. All that is beneficial in property arises from its use, and the fruits of that use; and whatever deprives a person of them deprives him of all that is desirable or valuable in the title and possession. If the constitutional guaranty extends no further than to prevent a deprivation of title and possession, and allows a deprivation of use, and the fruits of that use, it does not merit the encomiums it has received. Unless I have misread the history of the provision now incorporated into all our State constitutions, and by the Fifth and Fourteenth Amendments into our Federal Constitution, and have misunderstood the interpretation it has received, it is not thus limited in its scope, and thus impotent for good. It has a much more extended operation that either court, State, or Federal has given to it. The provision, it is to be observed, places property under the same protection as life and liberty. Except by due process of law, no State can deprive any person of either. The provision has been supposed to secure to every individual the essential conditions for the pursuit of happiness; and for that reason has not been heretofore, and should never be, construed in any narrow or restricted sense.

No State 'shall deprive any person of life, liberty, or property without due process of law,' says the Fourteenth Amendment to the Constitution. By the term 'life,' as here used, something more is meant than mere animal existence. The inhibition against its deprivation extends to all those limbs and faculties by which life is enjoyed. The provision equally prohibits the mutilation of the body by the amputation of an arm or leg, or the putting out of an eye, or the destruction of any other organ of the body through which the soul communicates with the outer world. The deprivation not only of life, but of whatever God has given to every one with life, for its growth and enjoyment, is prohibited by the provision in question, if its efficacy be not frittered away by judicial decision.

By the term 'liberty,' as used in the provision, something more is meant than mere freedom from physical restraint or the bounds of a prison. It means freedom to go where one may choose, and to act in such manner, not inconsistent with the equal rights of others, as his judgment may dictate for the promotion of his happiness; that is, to pursue such callings and avocations as may be most suitable to develop his capacities, and give to them their highest enjoyment.

The same liberal construction which is required for the protection of life and liberty, in all particulars in which life and liberty are of any value, should be applied to the protection of private property. If the legislature of a State, under pretense of providing for the public good, or for any other reason, can determine, against the consent of the owner, the uses to which private property shall be devoted, or the prices which the owner shall receive for its uses, it can deprive him of the property as completely as by a special act for its confiscation or destruction. If, for instance, the owner is prohibited from using his building for the purposes for which it was designed, it is of little consequence that he is permitted to retain the title and possession; or, if he is compelled to take as compensation for its use less than the expenses to which he is subjected by its ownership, he is, for all practical purposes, deprived of the property, as effectually as if the legislature had ordered his forcible dispossession. If it be admitted that the legislature has any control over the compensation, the extent of that compensation becomes a mere matter of legislative discretion. The amount fixed will operate as a partial destruction of the value of the property, if it fall below the amount which the owner would obtain by contract, and, practically, as a complete destruction, if it be less than the cost of retaining its possession. There is, indeed, no protection of any value under the constitutional provision, which does not extend to the use and income of the property, as well as to its title and possession.

This court has heretofore held in many instances that a constitutional provision intended for the protection of rights of private property should be liberally construed. It has so held in the numerous cases where it has been called upon to give effect to the provision prohibiting the States from legislation impairing the obligation of contracts; the provision being construed to secure from direct attack not only the contract itself, but all the essential incidents which give it value and enable its owner to enforce it. Thus, in *Bronson v. Kinzie*, reported in the 1st of Howard, it was held that an act of the legislature of Illinois, giving to a mortgagor twelve months within which to redeem his mortgaged property from a judicial sale, and prohibiting its sale for less than two-thirds of its appraised value, was void as applied to mortgages executed prior to its passage. It was contended, in support of the act, that it affected only the remedy of the mortgagee, and did not impair the contract; but the court replied that there was no substantial difference between a retrospective law declaring a particular contract to be abrogated and void, and one which took away all remedy to enforce it, or incumbered the remedy with conditions that rendered it useless or impracticable to pursue it. And, referring to the constitutional provision, the court said, speaking through Mr. Chief Justice Taney, that 'it would be unjust to the memory of the distinguished men who framed it, to suppose that it was designed to protect a mere barren and abstract right, without any practical operation upon the business of life. It was undoubtedly adopted as a part of the Constitution for a great and useful purpose. It was to maintain the integrity of contracts, and to secure their faithful execution throughout this Union, by placing them under the protection of the Constitution of the United States. And it would but ill become this court, under any circumstances, to depart from the plain meaning of the words used, and to sanction a distinction between the right and the remedy, which would render this provision illusive and nugatory, mere words of form, affording no protection and producing no practical result.'

***

The power of the State over the property of the citizen under the constitutional guaranty is well defined. The State may take his property for public uses, upon just compensation being made therefor. It may take a portion of his property by way of taxation for the support of the government. It may control the use and possession of his property, so far as may be necessary for the protection of the rights of others, and to secure to them the equal use and enjoyment of their property. The doctrine that each one must so use his own as not to injure his neighbor-*sic utere tuo ut alienum non laedas*-is the rule by which every member or society must possess and enjoy his property; and all legislation essential to secure this common and equal enjoyment is a legitimate exercise of State authority. Except in cases where property may be destroyed to arrest a conflagration or the ravages of pestilence, or be taken under the pressure of an immediate and overwhelming necessity to prevent a public calamity, the power of the State over the property of the citizen does not extend beyond such limits.

***

'But though property be thus protected, it is still to be understood that the law-giver has the right to prescribe the mode and manner of using it, *so far as may be necessary to prevent the abuse of the right, to the injury or annoyance of others, or of the public.* The government may, by general regulations, interdict such uses of property as would create nuisances and become dangerous to the lives, or health, or peace, or comfort of the citizens. Unwholesome trades, slaughter-houses, operations offensive to the senses, the deposit of powder, the application of steam-power to propel cars, the building with combustible materials, and the burial of the dead, may all be interdicted by law, in the midst of dense masses of population, *on the general and rational principle that every person ought so to use his property as not to injure his neighbors, and that private interests must be made subservient to the general interests of the community.* 2 Kent, 340.

The Italics in these citations are mine. The citations show what I have already stated to be the case, that the regulations which the State, in the exercise of its police power, authorizes with respect to the use of property are entirely independent of any question of compensation for such use, or for the services of the owner in connection with it.

There is nothing in the character of the business of the defendants as warehousemen which called for the interference complained of in this case. Their buildings are not nuisances; their occupation of receiving and storing grain infringes upon no rights of others, disturbs no neighborhood, infects not the air, and in no respect prevents others from using and enjoying their property as to them may seem best. The legislation in question is nothing less than a bold assertion of absolute power by the State to control at its discretion the property and business of the citizen, and fix the compensation he shall receive. The will of the legislature is made the condition upon which the owner shall receive the fruits of his property and the just reward of his labor, industry, and enterprise. 'That government,' says Story, 'can scarcely be deemed to be free where the rights of property are left solely dependent upon the will of a legislative body without any restraint. The fundamental maxims of a free government seem to require that the rights of personal liberty and private property should be held sacred.' *Wilkeson v. Leland*, 2 Pet. 657. The decision of the court in this case gives unrestrained license to legislative will.

The several instances mentioned by counsel in the argument, and by the court in its opinion, in which legislation has fixed the compensation which parties may receive for the use of their property and services, do not militate against the views I have expressed of the power of the State over the property of the citizen. They were mostly cases of public ferries, bridges, and turnpikes, of wharfingers, hackmen, and draymen, and of interest on money. In all these cases, except that of interest on money, which I shall presently notice, there was some special privilege granted by the State or municipality; and no one, I suppose, has ever contended that the State had not a right to prescribe the conditions upon which such privilege should be enjoyed. The State in such cases exercises no greater right than an individual may exercise over the use of his own property when leased or loaned to others. The conditions upon which the privilege shall be enjoyed being stated or implied in the legislation authorizing its grant, no right is, of course, impaired by their enforcement. The recipient of the privilege, in effect, stipulates to comply with the conditions. It matters not how limited the privilege conferred, its acceptance implies an assent to the regulation of its use and the compensation for it. The privilege which the hackman and drayman have to the use of stands on the public streets, not allowed to the ordinary coachman or laborer with teams, constitutes a sufficient warrant for the regulation of their fares. In the case of the warehousemen of Chicago, no right or privilege is conferred by the government upon them; and hence no assent of theirs can be alleged to justify any interference with their charges for the use of their property.

***

I am of opinion that the judgment of the Supreme Court of Illinois should be reversed.

***

Discussion

Common carriage or other business of strong general social impact can justify state regulation, notwithstanding freedom of contract constitutional limitations. Prior to *Munn v. Illinois*, statutes setting maximum prices were successfully attacked as violating the due process clause of the Constitution. Such maximums were thought to be a taking of property without adequate compensation or due process because they limited earnings and reduced the market value of the property affected, or because they violated the freedom of private parties to contract.

In *Munn*, *supra*, the Court analogized the grain elevator business to common carriage and declared it to be "affected with a public interest" and therefore can be subject to state rate regulation. The Court above held that devoting "property to a use in which the public has an interest…in effect grants to the public an interest in that use...to be controlled by the public for the common good."

Although *Munn* upheld maximum prices on the nebulous rationale that the industry was "clothed with the public interest," the Court also noted that free and fair price competition was lacking in the grain elevator services at issue. The Court's recitation of simple industry import, rather than a market failure that a challenged regulatory system allegedly addresses, caused some future confusion. Industry import, not market flaw, became the focus of a series of conflicting cases either allowing or prohibiting state involvement, based on the relative import of retail gas sales, ice, milk, and numerous other products. The case of *Charles Wolff Packing Co. v. Court of Industrial Relations*, 262 U.S. 522 (1923), later striking a state wage court system as violative of freedom of contract principles, accepted the principle that any one of four bases for regulation could overcome a threshold due process challenge: (1) those who hold themselves out to the public, such as common carriers and public utilities; (2) business subject to monopoly control; (3) businesses historically regulated; and (4) businesses that have an exceptional impact on the public. As to the last alternative basis, there must be a "peculiarly close relation between the public and those engaged in [the business]." This uncertain test did not facilitate clear boundaries for constitutional state regulation. *See Williams v. Standard Oil Co.*, 278 U.S. 235, 239 (1929) (noting that "[n]othing is gained by reiterating the statement that the phrase [clothed with the public interest] is indefinite").

Cases have held a wide variety of industries in the modern economy to be sufficiently "clothed with the public interest" to warrant substantial state regulation. Although specific constitutional limitations apply to a particular manner or means of regulation and to possible rights to compensation, a threshold constitutional attack on regulation because it intrudes into a protected privacy interest in a commercial context in violation of due process or freedom of contract principles is not supported by recent case law. Rather, the major viable avenue of due process attack on the threshold constitutionality of government regulation is the contention that there is no rational basis for it as structured. The constitutional standard is not the generic right of the state to regulate, but its use of a gratuitously intrusive means of regulation unrelated to a legitimate state interest.

The traditional market flaws of natural monopoly, scarcity, imperfect information, external costs, and antitrust violations (ranging from collusive restraints of trade to monopolization and predation) may establish such a recognized legitimate state interest. When such market flaws are the justification for regulation, initial constitutional due process inquiry turns to the connection between those flaws and the regulatory system purportedly addressing them. As noted, this threshold qualification-that regulation be "rationally related" to such a state interest-does not exhaust due process inquiry. There are additional due process standards applicable to the execution of the regulatory system and requiring procedural due process, prohibiting arbitrary or discriminatory deprivations of property or liberty, and perhaps requiring just compensation for governmental takings.

Minimum Rate Regulation

State Board of Dry Cleaners v. Thrift-D-Lux Cleaners, Inc.

40 Cal. 2d 436 (1953)

Opinion by: SHENK

Plaintiff appeals from a judgment of dismissal after the defendants' general demurrer to the amended complaint was sustained without leave to amend. The demurrer is based on the ground that the minimum price provisions of the Dry Cleaners' Act of 1945 (Bus. & Prof. Code, ch. 18, art. 5, §§ 9560-9567), under which the plaintiff sought injunctive relief against the defendant's alleged violations of that act, are in violation of the due process clauses of the state and federal Constitutions. The ruling on the demurrer presents the sole question on appeal.

The act provides for the creation of a State Board of Dry Cleaners consisting of seven members: one from the general public; two owners of retail plants; two owners of wholesale plants; and two owners of shops. Article 5, in sections 9560 through 9567, provides for "Minimum Price Schedules." Section 9560 empowers the board to act; section 9561 permits the members of the board to have access to cleaning establishments; section 9562 provides for rules of procedure, notice and hearing. Section 9563 provides:

"The board may establish minimum price schedules for the various items of cleaning, dyeing and pressing services for any city or county or other area as may be determined by the board upon the filing of a petition with it, requesting a minimum price schedule for that. . . area signed by seventy-five per cent (75%) or more of the persons in that...area who are licensed under this chapter."

Section 9564 provides: "Upon receipt of a petition under this article the board shall investigate and ascertain those minimum prices which will enable cleaners, dyers, or pressers in that city or county or other area to furnish modern, proper, healthful and sanitary services, using such appliances and equipment as will minimize the danger to public health and safety incident to such services.

"In establishing minimum price schedules, the board shall consider all conditions affecting the business of cleaning, dyeing and pressing in that city, county, or other area and the relation of those conditions to the public health, welfare and safety."

Section 9565 provides that the board shall conduct a cost survey and states that "the board shall not fix a price for any service at a sum less than that which is shown to be the cost price of such service. "

Section 9566 provides for the readjustment of minimum price levels either on the initiative of the board or on complaint of 51 per cent or more of the persons licensed in the area, if the board determines that "the minimum price so established or any of them are insufficient properly to provide healthful and proper services to the public and to maintain a clean, healthful, safe and sanitary cleaning, dyeing or pressing establishment, or that any minimum price set creates an undue hardship on any licensee under this act." Section 9567 provides for injunctive relief upon complaint by the board against violators of the minimum price schedules established by the board.

In July 1947, 75 per cent of those licensed by the board in numerous cities in Los Angeles County petitioned the board to establish minimum prices in both wholesale and retail fields. Basing its action upon its own cost surveys, the board established and published its minimum Price Schedules. In September, 1949, the board filed a complaint charging the defendants with violations of the price schedule and with threats to continue to do so. The board had established a minimum price to be paid for cleaning and pressing a man's suit at $ 1.00. The defendant Thrift-D-Lux Cleaner was charging 69 cents for the same service.

If the statute can be sustained as constitutional it is because it is a reasonable exercise of the police power of the state....Under the law generally that power extends to legislation enacted to promote the public health, safety, morals and general welfare....It has rightly been said that "such [police] regulations may validly be imposed if they constitute a reasonable exertion of governmental authority for the public good. If there is a proper legislative purpose, a law enacted to carry out that purpose, if not arbitrary nor discriminatory, must be upheld by the courts." (*In re Fuller* (1940), 15 Cal.2d 425, 428 [102 P.2d 321].)...However, in the exercise of the police power the law places limits on the discretion of the Legislature. Whether there has been a reasonable exercise of this power is a court question.

It is first contended by the plaintiff that the price fixing features of the statute were designed to protect the public health and safety. The statutory law in California meets this contention head on for it has made detailed and adequate provisions elsewhere for the protection of the public's health and safety through the regulation of the dry cleaning industry. (Chapter 2 [Fire Protection -- Clothes Cleaning Establishments] and chapter 3 [Fire Protection -- Spotting, Sponging, and Pressing Establishments] of part 2, division 12 of the Health and Safety Code; subchapter 4 [Dry Cleaning Equipment Employing Volatile and Inflammable Solvents] and subchapter 5 [Spotting, Sponging and Pressing Establishments] of chapter 1 [State Fire Marshal], title 19 [Public Safety] of the California Administrative Code; article 6 [Laundry, Dry Cleaning, and Dyeing Industry], chapter 5 [Division of Industrial Welfare], title 8 [Industrial Relations] of the Administrative Code; chapter 2 [Safety Devices and Safeguards], part 1 [Workmen's Safety], division 5 [Safety in Employment] of the Labor Code.) It is not contended that the present statute is invalid merely because the Legislature could reach the purported objective through the enforcement of the provisions of the above cited statutes....The previous enactment of these statutes furnish support for the conclusion that they were designed to and do fully protect the public health and safety and that the price-fixing features of the present statute have no function to that end. On the contrary they constitute an unnecessary and unreasonable restriction on the pursuit of private and useful business activities. The asserted objective of those portions of the statute are not in fact their real objective. There is therefore nothing relating to the price charged for such services that has any real or substantial relationship to the public health or safety.

***

...It is claimed that the price-fixing portions of the statute were enacted to provide for the general welfare. But a legislative body may not, under the guise of providing for this component of the police power, impose unnecessary and unreasonable restrictions upon the pursuit of these useful activities....If a statute has no real or substantial relation to any legitimate police power objective, it is the duty of the court to so declare. (*McKay Jewelers, Inc. v. Bowron*, 19 Cal.2d 595, 600 [122 P.2d 543, 139 A.L.R. 1188].)...In this connection it is recognized that every intendment will be indulged in favor of the constitutionality of a legislative enactment (*Hart v. City of Beverly Hills*, 11 Cal.2d 343 [79 P.2d 1080]), but the presumption of constitutionality is not conclusive.

The question of the validity of a price fixing law as related to the general welfare was involved in the case of *In re Herrick* (1938), 25 Cal.App.2d 751 [77 P.2d 262]. There the court declared unconstitutional an ordinance which fixed a minimum price for the cleaning of a man's suit of clothes. The declared purpose of the ordinance was "the restoration and maintenance of the highest practical degree of public welfare." The court in that case relied on the decision in *In re Kazas* (1937), 22 Cal.App.2d 161 [70 P.2d 962], which had declared unconstitutional an ordinance for fixing minimum prices for a haircut and shave. In considering whether legislation aims to promote the public welfare as a component part of the police power, the court properly recognized that the concept of public welfare had undergone a process of development through the years. Traditionally the power to legislate for the public welfare was not much more comprehensive than the power to legislate for the public health, safety and morals. In *Munn v. Illinois* (1876), 94 U.S. 113 [24 L.Ed. 77] it was considered that only where a person had entered the field of public service in the use of his property did he consent to its regulation for the public welfare....In this state and elsewhere it is established that at least where a business is "affected with a public interest or clothed with a public use" it may be regulated under the general welfare concept. (*Nebbia v. New York*, 291 U.S. 502 [54 S.Ct. 505, 78 L.Ed. 940]; *Agricultural Prorate Com. v. Superior Court*, 5 Cal.2d 550, 582 [55 P.2d 495].) In the *Nebbia* case a New York statute establishing a minimum price for the milk industry of that state was upheld on the ground that the end sought was within the scope of the legislative power of the state to insure an adequate supply of wholesome milk for public consumption.

***

Regardless of the legal terminology used in defining the test employed, any legislation to be justified and supported by the concept of "general welfare" must aim to promote the welfare of a properly classified segment of the general public as contrasted with that of a small percentage or a special class of the body politic where no such classification can be justified. In the *Kazas* case the court held that the ordinance legislated for the benefit of barbers alone, who made up 2 per cent of the community, and that the "ordinance does not purport to consider the welfare of the other ninety-eight per cent of the population of the city nor the effect on them of fixing the minimum prices to be charged for cutting their hair or shaving their masculine faces." It was also held "that on the face of the ordinance it affirmatively appears that the legislation was not intended to promote the general welfare of the people...but only a small group composing a very small proportion of the population…" As further evidence that the ordinance did not consider the interests of the general public, the court noted that the ordinance "attempted to pour all barbers and barber shops into a common mold, turning them out exactly alike regardless of skill or efficiency of operation, excellence and completeness of equipment, desirability of location or expense of conducting business."

***

The statute before us is not dissimilar to that considered in the *Kazas* case. It seeks to establish but a single grade of work in the dry cleaning industry and to eliminate the economical cleaning job. It does not take into consideration the "skill or efficiency of operation, excellence and completeness of equipment, desirability of location or expense of conducting business." It does not consider that a substantial group of the public may choose to purchase a cheaper grade of cleaning for particular garments, knowing that they are not obtaining the quality of service offered by more expensive establishments. The statute does not purport to prevent the imposition of fraud upon the public, nor to eliminate destructive and unfair competition, which practices are adequately legislated against in the Unfair Practices Act (Bus. & Prof. Code, div. 7, pt. II, chap. IV). As in the *Kazas* case, this statute would seemingly have the effect of enhancing the economic status of the industry and enlarging the profits of each operator. The record shows that an advance in prices will benefit less than 1 per cent of those persons who comprise the dry cleaning operators in Los Angeles County. On principle the standards here involved are indistinguishable from the standards considered in that case. Indeed it is argued that the circumstances in that case presented an even greater reason for upholding the enactment; that it was decided upon a declared state of emergency in unemployment affecting the peace and welfare of the city, and affecting an industry more personal in nature and therefore more subject to regulation. But the court concluded that "the private advantage of a small group, not a class, composing a small percentage of the population...does not make a price fixing ordinance for that group alone legislation for the general welfare."

The plaintiff seeks a reversal on the ground that since the decision in the *Kazas* case in 1937 the judicial treatment of legislation dealing with an exercise of the police power has advanced to a point where the principles of that decision should not be controlling. It is particularly asserted that the "error in the *Kazas* case is the holding that in order to regulate the prices in an industry that industry must be 'clothed with a public use' in the old and traditional sense of that term." However the use of the phrase was in reference only to the fact that the barbering business is not so "clothed with a public interest" that the welfare of the industry itself is directly related to the welfare of the public. The use the court made of the phrase "affected with a public interest" in the *Kazas* case was in the same sense that the Olsen and the Nebbia cases (*Olsen v. Nebraska, supra,* 313 U.S. 236; *Nebbia v. New York, supra,* 291 U.S. 502) had used it, namely, as an aid to determine when a statute provides for the general welfare. This was indicated in the *Kazas* case by a citation of the following excerpt from *State v. Ives*, 123 Fla. 401 [167 So. 394]: "Such a regulation could be justified only upon the fact that the barber trade is a paramount industry of the state intimately connected with its welfare, so that the state may, through an agency such as the board of barber examiners, prescribe prices for the services to be rendered by each barber…."

"Reduced to its last analysis, the thought underlying the act seems to be not that the barber trade is a paramount industry affecting the general welfare, but that the prosperity of the barber class sufficient to maintain the average barber and his family 'properly' is a sufficient reason for the exercise by the state of the power of direction, control and management of the barber business."

***

Returning to the *Kazas* case it must be said that it correctly employed the "affected with a public interest" phrase in the same manner as that phrase was employed in the *Nebbia* case three years earlier. Because of the closeness of the milk industry to the public health the Supreme Court saw fit to classify it as "affected with a public interest," or subject to price regulation for the public good. But it does not follow that all other businesses in which the public is served should fall within the same classification. If they do there is no limit which the Legislature is bound to respect and all businesses are subject to its uncontrolled power to fix prices.

***

In *Wholesale Tobacco Dealers Bureau v. National Candy & Tobacco Co.* (1938), 11 Cal.2d 634 [82 P.2d 3, 118 A.L.R. 486], this court sustained the Unfair Practices Act. The court there held that the purpose of the act was the prevention of destructive competition and injury to competitors. That is a legitimate objective in the interest of the general welfare, and on this basis is distinguishable from the present statute.

***

It must be concluded that the price fixing provision of the statute here involved is invalid because it is not, by any recognized or recognizable standard, an enactment providing for the public health, safety, morals, or general welfare.

The defendant points to another ground upon which the invalidity of the statute may well be based. Section 9564 of the code requires that the "board shall investigate and ascertain those minimum prices which will enable cleaners, dyers, or pressers in that...area to furnish modern, proper, healthful and sanitary services, using such appliances and equipment as will minimize the danger to public health and safety incident to such services." The only other reference to an established standard is in section 9566 as follows: "At the conclusion of an investigation therefor, the board may establish a reasonable and just minimum price schedule conforming to the requirements of this article."…While the delegation of governmental authority to an administrative body is proper in some instances, the delegation of absolute legislative discretion is not. To avoid such a result it is necessary that a delegating statute establish an ascertainable standard to guide the administrative body…. Here the statute assumes to confer legislative authority upon those who are directly interested in the operation of the regulatory rule and its penal provisions with no guide for the exercise of the delegated authority. The board is made up of six active members of the industry, and one member of the public at large. The initiation of the proposed control is at the insistence of 75 per cent of the cleaners in the area. In declaring invalid the Bituminous Coal Conservation Act of 1935, the United States Supreme Court stated: "...one person may not be entrusted with the power to regulate the business of another, and especially of a competitor. And a statute which attempts to confer such power undertakes an intolerable and unconstitutional interference with personal liberty and private property. The delegation is so clearly arbitrary, and so clearly a denial of rights safeguarded by the due process clause of the Fifth Amendment, that it is unnecessary to do more than refer to decisions of this court which foreclose the question." (*Carter v. Carter Coal Co.*, 298 U.S. 238, 311 [56 S.Ct. 855, 80 L.Ed. 1160].)

In *Becker v. State*, *supra*, 7 Harr. 454, the Supreme Court of Delaware set aside the Delaware Dry Cleaning Law. It stated that "vast authority is centered in a governing board, a majority of which are directly interested in the industry, but who, nevertheless are empowered to act in a judicial capacity, and to sit in judgment over fellow members of the trade. Too great a strain is imposed upon human frailty. The practical tendency of the legislation is to create and foster monopoly, to prevent, not to encourage, competition, to maintain maximum, not minimum prices, all of which is against, not in aid of, the interests of a consuming public."

Where the Legislature attempts to delegate its powers to an administrative board made up of interested members of the industry, the majority of which can initiate regulatory action by the board in that industry, that delegation may well be brought into question.

From the foregoing it follows that the price fixing provisions of the statute under attack must fall on the constitutional grounds stated, and that the demurrer was properly sustained.

The judgment is affirmed.

EDMONDS, SCHAUER, and SPENCE, JJ., concur.

Dissent by: TRAYNOR

TRAYNOR, J. In my opinion the minimum price provisions of the Dry Cleaners' Act of 1945 do not violate the due process clause of either the United States Constitution or the California Constitution.

The Legislature has power to determine the rights of persons, subject only to the limitations of the United States Constitution and the California Constitution. (*Modern Barber Colleges, Inc. v. California Emp. Stab. Com.*, 31 Cal.2d 720, 726 [192 P.2d 916]; *Delaney v.

Lowery, 25 Cal.2d 561, 568 [154 P.2d 674]; *Collins v. Riley*, 24 Cal.2d 912, 916 [152 P.2d 169].) A statute regulating commercial transactions does not violate the due process clause of either Constitution unless it is proved so unreasonable as to dispel the presumption that it rests upon some rational basis within the knowledge and experience of the legislators. (*Olsen v. Nebraska*, 313 U.S. 236, 246 [61 S.Ct. 862, 85 L.Ed. 1305, 133 A.L.R. 1500]; *United States v. Carolene Products Co.*, 304 U.S. 144, 154 [58 S.Ct. 778, 82 L.Ed. 1234]; *Serve Yourself Gas. etc. Assn. v. Brock*, 39 Cal.2d 813, 817 [249 P.2d 545]; *In re Fuller*, 15 Cal.2d 425, 428 [102 P.2d 321]; *Jersey Maid Milk Products Co. v. Brock*, 13 Cal.2d 620, 636 [91 P.2d 577]; *Wholesale Tobacco Dealers Bureau v. National Candy & Tobacco Co.*, 11 Cal.2d 634, 643 [82 P.2d 3, 118 A.L.R. 486].) Judicial inquiry "where the legislative judgment is drawn into question, must be restricted to the issue whether any state of facts either known or which could reasonably be assumed affords support for it." (*United States v. Carolene Products Co., supra*, 304 U.S. 144, 154.) The statute in the present case, like any other regulation of private enterprise, must be considered in this light.

Although early decisions held that prices could not be regulated unless the industry was clothed with a public interest (see *Ribnik v. McBride*, 277 U.S. 350 [48 S.Ct. 454, 72 L.Ed. 913]), the United States Supreme Court discarded that test in *Nebbia v. New York*, 291 U.S. 502, 531-539 [54 S.Ct. 505, 78 L.Ed. 940]. (*See, also, West Coast Hotel Co. v. Parrish*, 300 U.S. 379 [57 S.Ct. 578, 81 L.Ed. 703, 108 A.L.R. 1330].) In *Olsen v. Nebraska*, 313 U.S. 236, 244 [61 S.Ct. 862, 85 L.Ed. 1305, 133 A.L.R. 1500], the court in a unanimous opinion overruled the *Ribnik* case and refused to inquire into the wisdom of the challenged legislation. The *Olsen* decision reversed the decision of the state court, 138 Neb. 574 [293 N.W. 393], holding the price-fixing statute in question unconstitutional. This court soon followed the lead of the United States Supreme Court. (*Wholesale Tobacco Dealers Bureau v. National Candy & Tobacco Co., supra*, 11 Cal.2d 634, 655.) The Legislature, therefore, is clearly empowered to prevent destructive price cutting, which has demoralizing effects on business itself and on its service to the public.

***

The dry cleaning business is highly vulnerable to price wars and their attendant evils. The industry represents millions of dollars in plants and equipment and requires the labor of thousands of skilled workers. It is subject to intense short-period fluctuations. The dry cleaner cannot hedge against these fluctuations by stock-piling inventory or by large-scale buying of raw materials. He cannot supply his market in advance, lay off help, and wait for demand to catch up with supply as a manufacturer ordinarily can. A dry cleaner is under constant pressure to cut his prices, increase his volume, and reduce his costs. Other cleaners follow suit and the price cuts inevitably result in downgrading of service. The cleaning industry is particularly susceptible to downgrading: its processes are highly specialized and it is difficult to police against slipshod performance or to detect it. Destructive price cutting quickly starts a vicious train of sabotage, violence, eventual bankruptcy for many cleaners, and disruption of a service industry essential to the public health.

The statute sets the minimum price schedule as low as is consistent with efficient and sanitary service. (Bus. & Prof. Code, § 9564.) Prices can be fixed only after a cost survey and due investigation by the board. (Bus. & Prof. Code, §§ 9564–9566.) If the board should abuse the discretion vested in it, its action is subject to judicial correction.... (Gov. Code, § 11440.) The statute thus limits the competitive struggle in the industry to the quality of service offered to the public.

The Legislature could reasonably conclude that the economic waste, the loss of property, the violation of law, the threat to health and public convenience, could be prevented by elimination of price warfare through establishment of minimum price schedules. It could reasonably conclude that a measure of economic security would encourage compliance with health and safety regulations and the maintenance of the industry's capacity to meet the fluctuating demand of the public at reasonable prices.

Disruption of business by destructive competition has long been recognized as an evil that may be controlled by the Legislature. Thus in *Max Factor & Co. v. Kunsman*, 5 Cal.2d 446 [55 P.2d 177], affirmed, 299 U.S. 198 [57 S.Ct. 147, 81 L.Ed. 122], this court held constitutional a statute requiring retailers to sell products at a price fixed by the wholesaler. The court said: "In the first place, this court has neither the power nor the duty to determine the wisdom of any economic policy; that function rests solely with the legislature. We recognize that economic and juridical thought is, and for many years has been, divided on the economic question as to the benefits to the consuming public of free and open competition, and its necessary corollary, price-cutting. The members of this court may or may not agree with the economic philosophy of the Fair Trade Act, but it is no part of the duty of this court to determine whether the policy embodied in the statute is wise or unwise." (5 Cal.2d at 454-455.) The majority opinion would distinguish the *Max Factor* case on the ground that the only question there decided was the right to enforce "implied" contracts between vendors and vendees who "should have known" that certain goods were fair trade items. The distinction is untenable. The retailer in the *Max Factor* case had not at any time agreed to sell at the fixed price and was being compelled by the court to abide by the price determined by the wholesaler. A statute requiring a nonsigning retailer to sell at a fixed price under penalty of an injunction is as much a price fixing statute as is the statute in the present case. The *Max Factor* case is clear authority for the proposition that the Legislature may enact price fixing legislation, if it determines that price cutting will adversely affect a particular industry to the detriment of the public.

***

The majority opinion holds that this case is governed by *In re Kazas* (1937), 22 Cal.App.2d 161 [70 P.2d 962], rather than by the cases discussed in the preceding paragraph. The *Kazas* case, however, turned on the question whether the barber trade was "affected with a public interest," a standard long since discarded by the United States Supreme Court and by this court. (*Olsen v. Nebraska, supra*; *Wholesale Tobacco Dealers v. National etc. Co., supra*.) Moreover, the *Kazas* case relied upon

State v. Ives, 123 Fla. 401 [167 So. 394], a case subsequently abandoned by the court that decided it. (*Miami Laundry Co. v. Florida Dry Cleaning & Laundry Board*, 134 Fla. 1, 54 [183 So. 759].) I would disapprove the *Kazas* case as clearly contrary to presently accepted principles of constitutional law.

It is contended that the Dry Cleaners' Act of 1945 could not have the objective of protecting the public health and safety because the Legislature could reach that objective by enforcement of provisions of the Health and Safety Code and of the Unfair Practices Act. This reasoning proceeds from a misconception of this court's function in passing upon the constitutionality of a legislative enactment. The only question before us is whether there is a rational basis for the statute. Questions regarding the wisdom of the legislation are irrelevant. (*Olsen v. Nebraska, supra*, 313 U.S. at p. 246.) It was for the Legislature to determine whether additional legislation was necessary to preclude conditions in the dry cleaning industry that would adversely affect the public welfare. An attack on a statute cannot be justified by an assumption that there are wiser methods of reaching the desired objective. (*Hunter v. Justice's Court*, 36 Cal.2d 315, 319 [223 P.2d 465].)

***

As an alternative ground of decision, the majority opinion states that the Dry Cleaners' Act "may well be" unconstitutional because it "assumes to confer legislative authority upon those who are directly interested in the operation of the regulatory rule and its penal provisions with no guide for the exercise of the delegated authority."

The members of the State Board of Dry Cleaners are appointed by the Governor and approved by the Senate. They are officials of the state, paid by the state for administering the law, and their acts are reviewed by the judiciary. The fact that six members of the board must be members of the cleaning industry has no constitutional significance. (*See Ex parte Gerino*, 143 Cal. 412, 414 [77 P. 166, 66 L.R.A. 249] [Board of Medical Examiners elected by members of regulated profession]; *Miami Laundry Co. v. Florida Dry Cleaning & Laundry Board*, 134 Fla. 1, 13 [183 So. 759, 764, 119 A.L.R. 956]; *see, also, Davis, Administrative Law*, pp. 380-381.) It may be debatable whether the manifest advantages of submitting highly technical problems to an informed tribunal are outweighed by the possible danger that an agency largely composed of members representing an interested economic group may be tempted to act for selfish ends. The Legislature is free to make its choice. (*See Opp Cotton Mills v. Administrator of Wage and Hour Div.*, 312 U.S. 126, 144 [61 S.Ct. 524, 85 L.Ed. 624].)

The fact that price regulation is initiated at the insistence of 75 per cent of the cleaners in the area does not present constitutional difficulties. Whatever their special interest in articulating the problem, it remains a general one, of the greatest concern to the public. Governmental processes are commonly set in motion by the petition, complaint, or other action by some individual or group. Thus, the Administrative Procedure Act provides that "Except where the right to petition for adoption of a regulation is restricted by statute to a designated group...any interested person may petition a state agency requesting the adoption or repeal of a regulation. [A] state agency shall within 30 days deny the petition in writing or schedule the matter for public hearing." (Gov. Code, §§ 11426–11427.) In *Agricultural Prorate Com. v. Superior Court*, 5 Cal.2d 550, 554, 586-587 [55 P.2d 495], this court upheld a statute providing that the details and area of a proration program be determined by the filing of a petition signed by two-thirds of the producers in the area. We rejected there a contention that apparently is accepted in the majority opinion: that the delegation of power to the industry to initiate action invalidated the statute. In *Jersey Maid Milk Products Co. v. Brock*, 13 Cal.2d 620, 645 [91 P.2d 577], we upheld a requirement that 65 per cent of the producers in the regulated industry decide that a stabilization plan should be formulated. (*See, also, Parker v. Brown*, 317 U.S. 341, 352 [63 S.Ct. 307, 87 L.Ed. 315] [upholding the statute involved in *Agricultural Prorate Com. v. Superior Court, supra*]; *Currin v. Wallace*, 306 U.S. 1, 15-16 [59 S.Ct. 379, 83 L.Ed. 441]; *Ray v. Parker*, 15 Cal.2d 275, 286-287 [101 P.2d 665]; Davis, Administrative Law, pp. 71-73.)

***

The provision in the present statute does no more than relieve the board from making an expensive survey at the instance of a few cleaners, and allows it to act only when the need for regulation is apparent to a substantial number of those who would be affected. Far from unlawfully delegating authority, the Legislature has merely restricted its regulations by withholding their operation from a given area until 75 per cent of the cleaners favor it. (*See Currin v. Wallace, supra*, 306 U.S. 1, 15-16.)

***

The real basis for the result reached by the majority opinion is an adherence to an economic view that minimum price legislation is not in the best interests of the general public. But as Mr. Justice Holmes long admonished, the economic and moral beliefs of the judiciary are not embedded in the Constitution. There is no reason to suppose that judges are better qualified than legislators to determine what social and economic programs should be adopted by the State of California.

I would reverse the judgment on the ground that plaintiff has stated a cause of action under a valid statute.

GIBSON, C. J. and CARTER, J. concur.

DUE PROCESS TAKING

Deprivation of Livelihood

Cornwell v. California Bd. of Barbering & Cosmetology

962 F. Supp. 1260 (1997)

Opinion by: Rudi M. Brewster

I. Introduction

***

Plaintiffs Dr. JoAnne Cornwell (Dr. Cornwell) and the American Hairbraiders and Natural Hair Care Association (AHNHCA) are suing two State of California agencies and various individuals alleging that California's licensing requirement for hairbraiders violates the due process, equal protection and privileges and immunities clauses of both the federal and California constitutions....

II. Background

A. The Parties

Plaintiff Dr. Cornwell is the owner of Sisterlocks, a sole proprietorship, which specializes in African hair styling. Plaintiff AHNHCA is a non-profit nationwide organization dedicated to protecting the rights of hairbraiders and natural hair stylists. Its members are individuals and salons engaged in the business of African hair styling and natural hair care....

***

Defendant Department of Consumer Affairs (DCA) is established as a State and Consumer Services Agency by Cal. Bus. & Prof. Code § 100 to regulate various occupations. The DCA is responsible for establishing minimum qualifications and standards of competency, issuing licenses, and ensuring compliance with regulations authorized under the California Business and Professions Code. The CBBC acts under the authority and supervision of the DCA....

Defendant Daniel E. Lungren is the Attorney General for the State of California. Pursuant to Cal. Bus. & Prof. Code § 321, the Attorney General has the authority to seek an injunction against any acts or practices in violation of any state law that the director of a regulatory agency finds may cause harm to consumers. Plaintiffs sue Lungren in his official capacity....

B. The Barbering and Cosmetology Act

Under the Barbering and Cosmetology Act, it is unlawful for a person to engage in barbering, cosmetology, or electrolysis for compensation without a valid license from the CBBC, to engage in barbering or cosmetology in an establishment that does not have a valid license, or to operate an establishment without a valid license. Cal. Bus. & Prof. Code

§ 7317. Cosmetology includes "arranging, dressing, curling, waving, machineless permanent waving, cleansing, cutting, shampooing, relaxing, singeing, bleaching, tinting, coloring, straightening, dyeing, brushing, applying hair tonics, beautifying, or otherwise treating by any means the hair of any person." Cal. Bus. & Prof. Code § 7316(b)(1).

On May 16, 1982, the Attorney General issued an opinion that the practice of African hair braiding falls within the definition of "cosmetology" and requires a cosmetology license. 65 Op. Atty. Gen. 284 (May 6, 1982). In order to obtain a license, a person must take a licensing examination. Cal. Bus. & Prof. Code § 7321. In order to be qualified to take the examination, a person must have at least a tenth grade education and must have completed a course in an approved cosmetology school, completed an apprenticeship program, or have practiced cosmetology outside of the state for a requisite period of time. Cal. Bus. & Prof. Code § 7321. In its regulations, the CBBC requires cosmetology schools to provide 1,600 hours of technical instruction and practical operations in cosmetology techniques. Cal. Code Reg. § 950.2. These courses must provide instruction in a broad range of cosmetology techniques as well as bacteriology, anatomy, physiology, disinfection and sanitation. Plaintiff alleges that completing such a course takes at least nine months of full- time study and costs between $5,000 and $7,000.

C. African Hair Styling

African hair styling is "a highly specialized artistic and cultural form of hair styling and hair care whose main techniques include hair braiding, locking, twisting, weaving, and cornrows."...These techniques originated centuries ago in Africa and were brought into this country by Africans where the methods have endured and been expanded....African hair styling is a form of natural hair care that does not use any chemicals....Plaintiff alleges that no CBBC-approved cosmetology schools teach African hair styling techniques as part of their required curriculum.....Further, the CBBC-mandated curriculum does not include any instruction in African hair styling, natural hair care, braiding, twisting, weaving, locking or cornrowing.

African hair styling is distinct from the type of styling taught in cosmetology schools in that it rejects the application of harsh chemicals to the hair of African-Americans. These chemicals can cause long-term damage to the hair. Instead, African hair styling uses the natural texture of the hair to style the hair....African hair styling involves physical manipulation of the hair and is labor intensive, often requiring between four and twelve hours to complete, including instruction in the proper maintenance of the hairstyle....

***

D. Facts Giving Rise to the Instant Action

Plaintiff Dr. Cornwell founded Sisterlocks, a San Diego based company, to meet the natural hair care needs of women with textured hair....Dr. Cornwell both styles the hair of African- American women, and trains others in African hair styling. She runs a two-day training seminar and has trained approximately 75 people....Dr. Cornwell seeks to open her own salon, but she cannot do so unless she obtains a license from the CBBC....Dr. Cornwell is not a CBBC-licensed cosmetologist, and believes that the instruction she would receive at a CBBC-approved cosmetology school would be irrelevant to the techniques of African hair styling that she employs....

***

Ali Rasheed and his salon, the Braderie, belong to AHNHCA. The Braderie is an African hairbraiding and weaving salon in San Diego. Rasheed owns the business with his wife and their business partner, Marguerite Sylva....Ms. Sylva is a Master Braider, certified by the National Braiders Guild, and a licensed cosmetologist....At the two Braderie salons, seven individuals, none of whom are licensed cosmetologists, perform braiding and weaving services for customers. Most of them, including Ms. Sylva, learned their craft in Africa....

On October 2, 1996, a CBBC inspector visited the Braderie in San Diego and issued a “Notice of Violation and Assessment of Fine” to the salon and to Ms. Sylva whose cosmetology license had expired. Ms. Sylva was cited for practicing cosmetology without a license and the Braderie was cited for “aiding and abetting unlicensed activity.” Both Ms. Sylva and the Braderie were fined $100.... The Braderie was also charged with operating an establishment without a license and for braiding activity by unlicensed people....Ms. Sylva and the Braderie have appealed their citations and fines. ...

Many of the braiders at the Braderie cannot afford to take a cosmetology course, and believe that such a course would not teach them anything relevant to African hair styling. Moreover, many of them emigrated from Africa and do not possess the tenth grade education required for eligibility to take the licensing examination....

The Braderie cannot continue to operate without a license, and cannot continue to employ African hair braiders who are not licensed cosmetologists....

E. Plaintiffs' Complaint

Plaintiffs' complaint asserts three main claims: (1) the Cosmetology and Barbering Act, as applied to African hair styling, violates plaintiffs' due process rights under the United States and California constitutions (claims 1 and 4); (2) the Barbering and Cosmetology Act, as applied to African hair styling, violates plaintiffs' equal protection rights under the U.S. and California constitutions (claims 2 and 5); and (3) the Barbering and Cosmetology Act, as applied to African hair styling, violates plaintiffs' rights under the privileges and immunities clauses of the U.S. and California constitutions (claims 3 and 6). Plaintiffs seek a declaratory judgment that the Barbering and Cosmetology Act is unconstitutional as applied to African hair styling, a permanent injunction against the enforcement of the statute and its attendant regulations, and attorney's fees and costs. Plaintiffs do not seek monetary damages.

***

III. Discussion

***

B. Whether Plaintiff's Claims Against the DCA are Barred by Eleventh Amendment Immunity

The Eleventh Amendment does not preclude suits against state officers for prospective injunctive relief, even when the remedy will enjoin the implementation of an official state policy. *Ex Parte Young*, 209 U.S. 123, 161-62, 52 L. Ed. 714; 28 S. Ct. 441 (1908); *Kentucky v. Graham*, 473

U.S. 159, 167 n. 14, 87 L. Ed. 2d 114, 105 S. Ct. 3099 (1985); *Chaloux v. Killeen*, 886 F.2d 247, 252 (9th Cir. 1989); *Hoohuli v. Ariyoshi*, 741 F.2d 1169, 1173-75 (9th Cir. 1984). Defendants are correct that neither state agencies nor state officials acting in their official capacities are "persons" for purposes of a § 1983 suit seeking monetary damages. *Will v. Michigan Department of State Police*, 491 U.S. 58, 70- 71, 105 L. Ed. 2d 45, 109 S. Ct. 2304 (1989). State officials acting in their official capacity, however, are "persons" for the purposes of § 1983 when sued only for prospective injunctive relief.

Of course a state official acting in his or her official capacity, when sued for injunctive relief, would be a person under § 1983 because "official-capacity actions for prospective relief are not treated as actions against the State." *Kentucky v. Graham*, 473 U.S. at 167 n. 14; *Ex Parte Young*, 209 U.S. 123, 159-60, 52 L. Ed. 714; 28 S. Ct. 441 (1908). The distinction is "commonplace in sovereign immunity doctrine." L. Tribe, American Constitutional Law § 3-27, p. 190, n. 3 (2d ed. 1988), and would not have been foreign to the 19th-century Congress that enacted § 1983[.]

***

Plaintiffs can only proceed against the individual CBBC board members and the Attorney General in their official capacities for their actions in administering and enforcing the allegedly unconstitutional provisions of the Barbering and Cosmetology Act and its attendant regulations.

All claims against the Department of Consumer Affairs and the California Board of Barbering and Cosmetology are DISMISSED without leave to amend.

***

D. Plaintiff Cornwell's Substantive Due Process Claims

1. Federal Due Process Claim

Plaintiff Cornwell contends that the BCA arbitrarily and unreasonably limits her right to practice her profession of choice — African hair styling. The Supreme Court has recognized that "the right to work for a living in the common occupations of the community is of the very essence of the personal freedom and opportunity" that the

Constitution was meant to protect. *Truax v. Raich*, 239 U.S. 33, 41, 60 L. Ed. 131, 36 S. Ct. 7 (1915). "The right to hold specific private employment and to follow a chosen profession free from unreasonable governmental interference comes within the 'liberty' and 'property' concepts of the Fifth Amendment." *Greene v. McElroy*, 360 U.S. 474, 492, 3 L. Ed. 2d 1377, 79 S. Ct. 1400 (1959); *see Hampton v. Mow Sun Wong*, 426 U.S. 88, 115-16, 48 L. Ed. 2d 495, 96 S. Ct. 1895 (1976) (holding statute barring aliens from Civil Service unconstitutional); *City of Mobile v. Bolden*, 446 U.S. 55, 64 L. Ed. 2d 47, 100 S. Ct. 1490 (1980) (Marshall, J. dissenting) (noting constitutional importance of opportunity for employment). The Ninth Circuit has consistently held that the due process clause provides people with a constitutional "right to pursue an occupation." *Benigni v. City of Hemet*, 879 F.2d 473, 478 (9th Cir. 1988); *Chalmers v. City of Los Angeles*, 762 F.2d 753, 757 (9th Cir. 1985).

Substantive due process challenges to economic regulations are subjected to rational basis review. *Exxon Corp. v. Governor of Maryland*, 437 U.S. 117, 124-25, 57 L. Ed. 2d 91, 98 S. Ct. 2207 (1978). The burden is on the party challenging the regulation "to establish that the legislature has acted in an arbitrary and irrational way." *Usery v. Turner Elkhorn Mining Co.*, 428 U.S. 1, 15, 49 L. Ed. 2d 752, 96 S. Ct. 2882 (1976). The regulation may only be struck down if there is no rational connection between the challenged statute and a legitimate government objective. *Williamson v. Lee Optical Inc.*, 348 U.S. 483, 488, 99 L. Ed. 563, 75 S. Ct. 461 (1955); *see Lange-Kessler v. Department of Education of the State of New York*, 109 F.3d 137, 1997 WL 134409 (2nd Cir. 1997) (finding a rational connection between education requirements for license to become a midwife and state's interest in protecting health and safety of mothers and children).

The issue before the Court is whether the CBBC regulations requiring 1600 hours of instruction in specific methods and techniques of cosmetology violate plaintiff's due process rights. The Court does not address the issues whether California can require licenses for hairbraiders or whether they can require schooling and a licensing examination prior to allowing African hair stylists to perform their craft. These two issues are so clearly within the legislature's prerogative that the Court will not entertain challenges to them.

On the issue of the legitimacy of the CBBC's required curriculum, plaintiff argues that since the required cosmetology courses contain no instruction on African hair styling, there is no rational reason why they should be required in order to perform African hair styling. Defendants respond that the required cosmetology curriculum contains instruction in health and safety, hazardous substances, bacteriology, anatomy, physiology, disinfection, and sanitation.... Requiring people who manipulate hair to have instruction in hygiene and sanitation, defendants contend, is rationally related to protecting the health, safety and welfare of California citizens. Plaintiff responds that African hair stylists do not shampoo, wet, or use any chemicals on clients' hair. Their method of hair styling simply involves physical manipulation of the hair. Since they use no chemicals, they argue that they have no need for instruction in disinfection and sanitation. Moreover, the instruction on disinfection and sanitation only comprises four percent of the required curriculum, so it would be unreasonable to require African hair stylists to attend cosmetology school for this one kernel of knowledge.

Defendants rely on *Ferguson v. Skrupa*, 372 U.S. 726, 10 L. Ed. 2d 93, 83 S. Ct. 1028 (1963), in which the Supreme Court upheld a Kansas statute which prohibited anyone from engaging "in the business of debt adjusting" except as incident to "the lawful practice of law." This effectively required all debt adjustors to be licensed attorneys. Debt adjustors who were not attorneys challenged the constitutionality of the law. The Supreme Court noted that courts should not "substitute their social and economic beliefs for the judgment of legislative bodies, who are elected to pass laws." *Id.* at 730. The court explained that states "have the power to legislate against what are found to be injurious practices in their internal commercial and business affairs, so long as their laws do not run afoul of some specific federal constitutional prohibition, or of some valid federal law." *Id.* 372 U.S. at 730–31. The majority did not mention rational basis review, but Justice Harlan concurred "in the judgment on the ground that this state measure bears a rational relation to a constitutionally permissible objective." *Id.* at 733.

Defendants do not argue that most of the CBBC curriculum requirements bear any rational relationship to a legitimate state objective....For instance, they do not contend that the required curriculum in manicures, pedicures, eyebrow arching and removal, facials, makeup, hair coloring, bleaching, permanent waving, chemical straightening, chemicals, press and curl, haircutting, scalp and hair treatments, cosmetology chemistry, thermal styling, theory of electricity in cosmetology, and wet hair styling are rationally related to legitimate state objectives. These topics comprise 935 hours of the 1600 hour required curriculum. Defendants argue that instruction in sanitation and hygiene-related topics is necessary to protect the health of its citizens. The CBBC-required curriculum contains 65 hours of instruction in health & safety, hazardous substances, bacteriology, anatomy, physiology, disinfection and sanitation...These 65 hours represent only four percent of the hours required for completion of cosmetology school.

Even if the Court were to assume that these 65 hours are rationally related to the state's interest in protecting the health and safety of its citizens, this education is one small part of a curriculum which plaintiff contends is 96% useless to her. To take an extreme example, the state could rationally believe that food preparers need instruction on hygiene, sanitation and disinfection prior to being allowed to prepare food in public schools. It would be irrational however, to require them to go to cosmetology school, even though they might benefit from the 65 hours related to health, hygiene and sanitation. Ninety-six percent of the curriculum would be irrelevant to the occupation for which they would be seeking licensure. Plaintiff in this suit contends that this is exactly what is happening to her. She does not provide manicures, pedicures, eyebrow waxing, dying, tinting, bleaching, wet styling, makeup or any of the other techniques which are taught in cosmetology school. Plaintiff argues that she is being lumped in with cosmetologists and barbers simply because she touches people's hair.

In March 1996, a Joint Legislative Sunset Review Committee (JLSRC) reviewed the CBBC and concluded that the number of hours and required curriculum erected an artificial barrier to individuals seeking to enter the barbering and cosmetology professions....The JLSRC further found "no evidence provided which justifies the need for lengthy training in these particular areas of specialty," and that there was "little evidence" to support the need for a licensing examination. Plaintiff contends that these findings demonstrate *a fortiori* that there is no rational relationship between the required curriculum and legitimate state objectives.

The Court finds that plaintiff has adequately alleged that there is no rational connection between the vast majority of the CBBC's required curriculum and a legitimate government objective, and that it acts as an barrier to the entry of African hair stylists into their chosen profession. For this reason, defendants' motion to dismiss plaintiff's claims for violation of the federal due process clause is DENIED.

2. California Due Process Claim

California courts interpret the due process clause of the California Constitution as co- extensive with the federal constitution on the issue of economic due process.

As we understand current doctrine, judicial examination of a statute under economic due process attack is completed when any fact or facts appear which the Legislature might rationally have accepted as the basis for a finding of public interest On this point federal and California doctrines appear to be parallel. *Doyle v. Board of Bar Examiners*, 219 Cal. App. 2d 504, 514, 33 Cal. Rptr. 349 (1963).

The constitutionality of the Cosmetology Act, the predecessor to the BCA, was challenged previously in *Whitcomb v. Emerson*, 46 Cal. App. 2d 263, 115 P.2d 892 (1941). Plaintiff engaged in "massaging, stimulating or beautifying the face, neck and upper part of the human body by means of the hands and use of oil lotions[.]" Id. at 265.... The Board of Cosmetology threatened to require her to obtain a license and to enforce its regulations on her. The California Court of Appeals stated that

> The right to labor or earn one's livelihood in any legitimate field of industry or business is a right of property, and any unlawful or unreasonable interference with, or abridgement of, such right is an invasion thereof and a restriction of the liberty of the citizen as guaranteed by the Constitution.

Id. at 273. The court noted that states may legitimately require certain qualifications for a profession, and that such regulations are unconstitutional only when "they have no relation to such calling or profession, or are unattainable by such reasonable study and application[.] *Id.* 46 Cal. App. 2d 263 at 273-74. The court continued:

> If, then, it is lawful for all to endeavor to preserve or to regain those treasured charms of yesteryear, it must also fall within the legal protection of the constitutional guarantees for those skilled in appropriate arts to serve the needs of those who seek the enhancement or preservation of personal beauty, subject only to the right of the state to impose such reasonable regulations as will protect the health, safety, morals and general welfare of the public.

Id. at 275. The court proceeded from a strong presumption of constitutionality of the statute. The court then noted that "in order to secure her right to labor as she chooses she must become a "hairdresser" in fact and to that end practice, have experience in, and pass an examination in shampooing, waving, coloring, dressing and care of the hair, or in the alternative starve or go to jail." *Id.* at 277. The court could "find nothing in the relation of facial massage with the arts of hair dressing which suggests that the public morals, safety, health or general welfare demands that the masseuse must be trained in those arts." *Id.* The court concluded that while the occupations specified in the Cosmetology Act could be subjected to legitimate regulation, there was no reasonable connection between regulating cosmetology and regulating facial massaging, and accordingly found the statute unconstitutional as applied to plaintiff. *Id.*

Whitcomb has never been overruled, but it was criticized in *Varanelli v. Structural Pest Control Board*, 1 Cal. App. 3d 217, 222, 81 Cal. Rptr. 492 (1969). In *Varanelli*, the Court of Appeals noted that Whitcomb was "decided in an era less receptive to economic legislation." Id. The court explained that the current doctrines of judicial review of the reasonableness of regulatory legislation is that judicial examination of a statute under economic due process attack is completed when any fact or facts appear, or may be hypothesized, which the Legislature might rationally have accepted as the basis for a finding of public interest.

Id. Most recently, the California Court of Appeals has stated that the "Legislature does not violate due process so long as an enactment is procedurally fair and reasonably related to a proper legislative goal." *In re Arthur W.*, 171 Cal. App. 3d 179, 185, 217 Cal. Rptr. 183 (1985).

The Court need not reach the specific issue of whether *Whitcomb* is still good law. Since the California and federal due process clauses are co-extensive, the Court DENIES defendants' motion to dismiss plaintiff's claims under the California due process clause for the same reasons.

E. Plaintiff Cornwell's Equal Protection Claims

1. Federal Equal Protection Claim

The equal protection clause requires that "all persons similarly situated should be treated alike." *City of Cleburne v. Cleburne Living Center*, 473 U.S. 432, 439, 87 L. Ed. 2d 313, 105 S. Ct. 3249 (1985). Defendants argue that the statutory scheme in the BCA treats all people alike by requiring everyone to qualify for and pass a licensing examination. "Plaintiffs are thus being treated exactly the same as all other persons who desire to engage in the practice of cosmetology." Def. Mem. P&A's, p. 20. As the Supreme Court has noted "sometimes the grossest discrimination can lie in treating things that are different as though they were exactly alike[.]" *Jenness v. Fortson*, 403 U.S. 431, 442, 29 L. Ed. 2d 554, 91 S. Ct. 1970 (1971); *see* Lawrence H. Tribe, American Constitutional Law 1438 (2nd ed. 1988) ("equality can be denied when government fails to classify, with the result that its rules or programs do not distinguish between persons who, for equal protection purposes, should be regarded as differently situated"). For instance, in *Williams v. Rhodes*, 393 U.S. 23, 21 L. Ed. 2d 24, 89 S. Ct. 5 (1968), the Supreme Court struck down an Ohio statute which regulated how political parties could get on the ballot. Although the statute was written in neutral terms, the burdens it imposed on new political parties, such as requiring petitions signed by 15% of the voters who voted in the last election, functioned to limit elections to the two dominant political parties. The regulations violated the equal protection clause even though they were facially neutral because they had a discriminatory effect.

Similarly, in Yick Wo v. Hopkins, 118 U.S. 356, 30 L. Ed. 220, 6 S. Ct. 1064 (1886), there was a neutral ordinance which required all laundries not housed in brick buildings to obtain permits, ostensibly out of a fear of fire. As applied, however, the statute effectively excluded Chinese laundry owners from operating their businesses.

Though the law itself be fair on its face, and impartial in appearance, yet, if it is applied and administered by public authority with an evil eye and an unequal hand, so as practically to make unjust and illegal discriminations between persons in similar circumstances, material to their rights, the denial of equal justice is still within the prohibition of the constitution. *Id.* 118 U.S. at 373–74.

In the instant case, it is not clear from the language of the BCA that it applies to African hair styling. The statute employs very broad language, defining cosmetology to include "arranging," "brushing," and "beautifying" the hair of any person. These broad terms can be interpreted to include the physical manipulation of the hair involved in African hair styling and hairbraiding. It is a discretionary decision on the part of the Attorney General and the CBBC to apply the BCA to hairbraiders and African hair stylists. Plaintiff's real challenge is to the way in which the CBBC and the Attorney General enforce and administer the statute. The CBBC has enacted all of the regulations setting forth the curriculum requirements at cosmetology schools. These requirements contain no instruction on African hair styling, but extensive instruction in "mainstream" hair styling. At the same time, the Attorney General has issued an opinion that the BCA applies to African hair styling and hairbraiding. 65 Op. Atty. Gen. 284 (May 6, 1982).... Plaintiff contends that the combination of these two requirements violates the equal protection clause. The Attorney General singled out a discrete group—African hair stylists—and subjected them to the requirements of the BCA. The CBBC's regulations allegedly bear no rational relationship to the performance of African hair styling. The effect of these regulations is to force African hair stylists out of business in favor of mainstream hair stylists and barbers.

Plaintiff and defendants agree that under an equal protection analysis, the BCA must be subjected to rational basis review. "If a law neither burdens a fundamental right nor targets a suspect class, we will uphold the legislative classification so long as it bears a rational relation to some legitimate end." *Romer v. Evans*, 134 L. Ed. 2d 855, 116 S. Ct. 1620, 1627 (1996)....

Even in the ordinary equal protection case calling for the most deferential of standards, we insist on knowing the relation between the classification adopted and the object to be obtained....In the ordinary case, a law will be sustained if it can be said to advance a legitimate government interest, even if the law seems unwise or works to the disadvantage of a particular group, or if the rationale seems tenuous. 116 S. Ct. at 1627. After citing several examples of cases in which the Supreme Court had upheld state statutes,...the Supreme Court continued:

By requiring that the classification bear a rational relationship to an independent and legitimate legislative end, we ensure that classifications are not drawn for the purpose of disadvantaging the group burdened by the law. *Id.* Although at trial, the burden would be on plaintiff to establish that there is no rational connection between the regulations and their asserted purpose, s*ee FCC v. Beach Communications, Inc.*, 508 U.S. 307, 314-15, 124 L. Ed. 2d 211, 113 S. Ct. 2096 (1993), in the context of a motion to dismiss, the Court must take all allegations in the complaint as true, must draw all inferences in favor plaintiffs, and must construe the complaint in the light most favorable to plaintiffs. *NL Industries*, 792 F.2d at 898.

In the instant case, the Court looks to see whether there is a rational basis for requiring African hair stylists to receive the 1600 hours of technical training required by the CBBC. 15 See Cal. Code Reg. § 950.2. The object to be obtained, according to the government, is a profession of hair care professionals who understand hygiene and sanitation. While 65 hours of the curriculum are geared towards this end, at least 935 hours are not. Almost one thousand hours of training are required in the techniques of "mainstream" hair styling and cosmetology. The object of this training is to produce better "mainstream" cosmetologists, not to promote hygiene and sanitation. The Court is left with the dilemma of whether a legitimate reason for four percent of the required curriculum makes the entire curriculum rationally related to a legitimate government interest. The Court cannot find as a matter of law that it does. This places an almost insurmountable barrier in front of anyone who seeks to practice African hair styling. They are required to spend nine months attending a cosmetology school, at a cost of $5,000–$7,000, learning skills, 96% of which, they will never use. Plaintiff has adequately alleged that there is no rational connection between the CBBC's required curriculum and the practice of African hair styling.

This case is similar to *Cleburne*, in which the city of Cleburne interpreted its zoning ordinance to require a special use permit for a group home for the mentally retarded. *Cleburne*, 473 U.S. at 436-37. The zoning ordinance provided that a special use permit was required for the construction of "hospitals for the insane or feeble-minded, or alcoholic [sic] or drug addicts, or penal or correctional institutions." *Id.* at 436. The city considered a group home for the mentally retarded a "hospital for the feeble-minded." The city then denied a permit to the group home. *Id.* at 437. The Supreme Court applied rational basis review to the city's interpretation of its zoning ordinance.

The general rule is that legislation is presumed to be valid and will be sustained if the classification drawn by the statute is rationally related to a legitimate state interest.

Id. at 440. The court noted that limitations on the functioning of mentally retarded individuals is a legitimate reason for state classification. For instance, the state could provide specialized educational programs for the mentally retarded. *Id.* 473 U.S. at 442–43. In the course of its rational basis review, the court noted that the city did not require special use permits for apartment houses, dormitories, hospitals (other than for the insane, feeble-minded, alcoholics or drug addicts), or nursing homes. *Id.* at 447. By insisting on a permit for the group home for the mentally retarded, the city was treating this group differently. The city provided no legitimate reason for this differential treatment, so the court invalidated the statute as applied to a group home for the mentally retarded. *Id.* at 448–50.

In the instant case, the CBBC and the Attorney General have interpreted the Barbering and Cosmetology Act to apply to African hair stylists and hairbraiders. It is this decision, as reflected in 65 Op. Atty. Gen. 284 and the CBBC's enforcement of the BCA against African hair stylists, that plaintiff challenges as unconstitutional. Just as there was no problem in *Cleburne* with applying the zoning ordinance to hospitals for the insane, there is no problem in this case with applying the BCA to barbers and "mainstream" hair stylists. It is the extension of the statute to a group for which the statute was not designed that plaintiffs in the instant case and in *Cleburne* challenge. Since the CBBC regulations require instruction that is unrelated to the practice of African hair styling, plaintiff argues that it is irrational to subject her to these requirements. Plaintiff suggests that just as the application of the zoning ordinance in *Cleburne* was a covert attempt to prevent a group home for the mentally retarded from being located within the community, the application of the BCA to African hair stylists is a covert attempt to prevent or minimize the practice of African hair styling in favor of "mainstream" hair styling.

The Court is unaware of what evidence there is to support this proposition, but if plaintiff comes forward with evidence of intentional discrimination, the enforcement of the statute could constitute a violation of the equal protection clause. See Yick Wo, 118 U.S. 356 at 377. The Court notes that the Joint Legislative Sunset Review

Committee concluded that the CBBC's required curriculum erected an artificial barrier to individuals seeking to enter these professions, and that there was no evidence that such lengthy and detailed training was justified.

For these reasons, the Court DENIES defendants' motion to dismiss plaintiff's federal equal protection claim. Plaintiff has stated a claim that there is no rational connection between 1535 hours of the 1600 hour required cosmetology curriculum and the practice of African hair styling.

2. California Equal Protection Claim

"The constitutional requirement that state regulation of a profession bear a rational relationship to a legitimate state interest imposes upon the courts the duty of fairly testing whether the state classification scheme is consistent with the asserted state interest." *Warden v. State Bar of California*, 53 Cal. App. 4th 510, 1997 Cal. App. LEXIS 190 (March 13, 1997). Defendants argue that the California equal protection claim must be dismissed for the same reasons as the federal equal protection claim. Similarly, plaintiff also conflates the federal and state equal protection analyses. For the same reasons, defendants' motion to dismiss the California equal protection claim is DENIED.

IV. Conclusion

Plaintiff Cornwell may maintain an action for prospective injunctive relief against the state officials responsible for administering and enforcing the Barbering and Cosmetology Act. Plaintiff cannot, however, maintain suit against the Department of Consumer Affairs or the Board of Barbering and Cosmetology. Accordingly, the DCA and the CBBC are DISMISSED without leave to amend.

The Court cannot abstain from adjudicating Dr. Cornwell's claims against the members of the CBBC on Younger grounds because she is not a party to an ongoing state proceeding. The Court must abstain, however, from adjudicating AHNHCA's claims against the members of the CBBC because the injunctive relief sought would interfere with the state proceedings in which one of

AHNHCA's members is involved. For this reason, plaintiff AHNHCA's claims are dismissed with 45 days leave to amend.

Defendants' motion to dismiss plaintiff's federal and California due process and equal protection claims is DENIED because the Court finds that plaintiff has adequately alleged that there is no rational relationship between the 1600 hours of training required by the CBBC and the practice of African hair styling.

IT IS SO ORDERED.

Procedural Taking

Bayside Timber Co. v. Board of Supervisors of San Mateo County

20 Cal.App.3d 1 (1971)

Opinion by: ELKINGTON, J.

This appeal is prosecuted by the San Mateo County Board of Supervisors and Planning Commission from a judgment against them in favor of Bayside Timber Company, Inc., directing the issuance of a peremptory writ of mandate.

By ordinance, San Mateo County purports to regulate logging operations within the county by "use permit."...The county also by ordinance, "to protect the natural beauty of the County and protect property owners from unnecessary loss from erosion and flooding from grading operations," regulates excavation and grading for road purposes.

Respondent Bayside Timber Company, Inc., was the owner of redwood timber land in San Mateo County. It had, under the State Forest Practice Act (Pub. Resources Code, §§ 4521–4618; sometimes herein called the Act), obtained a timber operations permit to log the land. The State Division of Highways had given the company an "encroachment permit" which authorized connection of logging roads with a state highway. Application was then made to the county by the company for a logging use permit and a grading permit for the logging roads which would become necessary to its operations. The applications were opposed by many residents, and organizations of residents, of San Mateo County. After generally favorable rulings by the county planning commission, on appeal to the board of supervisors each of the applications was denied. The latter decisions resulted in the company's mandamus petition to the superior court to compel issuance of the requested use and grading permits.

After a trial the superior court concluded that the state had preempted the field of regulation of timber operations by the enactment of the Forest Practice Act, that San Mateo County had "no power or authority to require, grant, or deny permits for timber operations," and that accordingly "issuance of a timber operations permit to plaintiff would be superfluous." The county's timber operations use permit ordinance was adjudged "invalid and unenforceable to the extent that [it purports] to require the issuance of a permit...prior to engaging in timber operations." A peremptory writ of mandate requiring the county to issue the requested road grading permit was ordered by the judgment.

It is this "Judgment Granting Peremptory Writ of Mandate" from which the San Mateo County officials have appealed.

The first issue presented by the appellants' briefs is the question of the constitutionality of the Forest Practice Act. The issue is raised for the first time on this appeal, counsel frankly confessing that "no one thought of the constitutional issue until preparation of appellants' opening brief."

Respondent, relying on *Jenner v. City Council*, 164 Cal.App.2d 490, 498 [331 P.2d 176], argues that such a constitutional issue may not now be considered since "'It is the general rule applicable in civil cases that a constitutional question must be raised at the earliest opportunity or it will be considered as waived.'..."

Jenner v. City Council, however, merely reiterates the general rule that appellate courts will not ordinarily consider matters raised for the first time on appeal. (See 3 Witkin, Cal. Procedure (1954) pp. 2261–2262, Appeal, § 94.) There are many situations where appellate courts will consider such matters. They will often be considered where the issue relates to questions of law only. (*Tyre v. Aetna Life Ins. Co.*, 54 Cal.2d 399, 405 [6 Cal.Rptr. 13, 353 P.2d 725]; *Jones v. Fireman's Fund Ins. Co.*, 270 Cal.App.2d 779, 783-784 [76 Cal.Rptr. 97].) Appellate courts are more inclined to consider such tardily raised legal issues where the public interest or public policy is involved. (*People v. Rodriguez*, 58 Cal.App.2d 415, 421 [136 P.2d 626].) And whether the rule shall be applied is largely a question of the appellate court's discretion. (*Isthmian Lines, Inc. v. Schirmer Stevedoring Co.*, 255 Cal.App.2d 607, 610 [63 Cal.Rptr. 458].)

The above quoted language of Jenner is taken verbatim from *Hershey v. Reclamation District No. 108*, 200 Cal. 550, 564 [254 P. 542], in which the court after stating the general rule, nevertheless did (apparently because the point was of public importance) proceed to pass upon the constitutionality of the subject statute. In *Higbie v. County of Los Angeles*, 47 Cal.App.2d 281, 289 [117 P.2d 933], where the appellate court was presented with a previously unraised constitutional question, it was said: "A sufficient answer to this argument should be that 'one who receives the benefit from an unconstitutional law is estopped from asserting its unconstitutionality.' (*Hershey v. Reclamation Dist. No. 108*, 200 Cal. 550 [254 Pac. 542], at 564.) As the questions are of considerable importance, we will not rest on this well-established rule, but will consider the several arguments of plaintiff on this phase of the case."

With considerable logic it has even been held that: "A fundamental public right,...which involves the interest of the citizens at large cannot be disregarded, and a constitutional question in respect thereof may be raised at any time, and even upon the court's own motion" (*Craig v. Board of Education of City of New York*, 173 Misc. 969 [19 N.Y.S.2d 293, 302]); and that it is contrary to the public interest to permit public officials to waive public constitutional rights by failure to raise them at the trial level. (*State v. Becker*, 194 Wis. 464 [215 N.W. 902, 904].)...

...Yet another consideration facing us at this point, however, is the long-established rule that an appellate court will not enter upon the resolution of constitutional questions unless absolutely necessary to a disposition of the appeal. (*Marin Municipal Water Dist. v. Dolge*, 172 Cal. 724, 726 [158 P. 187]; *Estate of Johnson*, 139 Cal. 532, 534 [73 P. 424]; *Estate of Crane*, 73 Cal.App.2d 93, 102 [165 P.2d 940].) In this respect we have concluded, as found by the trial court and here argued by respondent, that the Forest Practice Act does purport to preempt the field of logging and timber operations in California. To fully dispose of the appeal it would be necessary to pass upon the constitutional question raised by appellants.

Obviously the tendered constitutional issue concerns only a question of law. And we perceive no attendant prejudice to respondents were the matter to be considered by us at this time.

The remaining question is whether there is indeed a public interest in the Forest Practice Act, i.e., in the regulation of private logging and timber practices, and if so, whether our discretion should be exercised as requested by appellants.

We observe initially that the Forest Practice Act itself (§ 4541) declares "the existence of a public interest in the forest resources and timberlands of this state."

On the same subject we are invited to consider an abundance of published literature relating to private logging and timber operations in California and to the Forest Practice Act.

It seems to be widely recognized that few, if any, industries adversely affect the rights of others, and the public generally, as do timber and logging operations....

In much of California's forest areas soils are sedimentary, and ordinarily quite unstable. The erosion of such land is believed to be increased by a factor of 25 to 1 when the native vegetation is removed. The problem seems to be compounded by the practice of constructing and using logging and skid roads, and the operation of trucks and tractors up and down stream beds....

Normally such operations are said to send enormous quantities of silt and debris onto the land of lower riparian owners....Describing a recent flooding it was said,

"These lowlands were battered by tons of slash, cut logs, and whole trees washed down the rivers; worst of all was the three to six foot layer of silt left behind by the receding waters -- soil washed off the slopes of watersheds exposed to the torrents."...It is known that uprooted trees and unwanted logs by the thousands, left behind by loggers, have in time of flood backed up behind and then buckled and destroyed highway bridges.

Destructive erosion and siltation is blamed by some entirely on reckless logging;...others believe it to be but a major contributing cause. But there seems to be common agreement that the denuding of forest land intensifies flooding, and its effect upon the property of others....

***

Much criticism has been levelled at private logging and timber practices in California under the Forest Practice Act....Some illustrations: The use of "skyline cranes" instead of the more economical use of tractors in moving logs is said to reduce the necessary logging roads per 1,000 acres from 10 miles to 1 mile. The skyline operation would also reduce the exposed erosible area by from 60 to 75 percent. Nevertheless, the latter method appears to be seldom, if at all, used in California.... So-called "buffer strips" of untouched vegetation between eight and thirty feet wide have proven highly effective in preventing silt and slash from reaching streams, but they appear to be rarely used in our state....There is frequent complaint of "'gyppo' loggers who move quickly from job to job, leaving havoc in their wake, and starting a vicious cycle of erosion whose full implications may not appear for years to come."...This "fly by night logger still plays an important role in the industry."...And it has been said that a "close examination of the Act and of the local forest practice rules indicates that the self-regulation theory remains essentially fallacious."...

We do not arrive at any specific conclusions on the weight or credibility to be given the foregoing several comments -- they may well present an unfair and biased picture. But from any objective view, we believe all must agree that regardless of how they are actually conducted, private logging and timber operations of this state are a matter of fundamental public concern.

We have accordingly chosen to pass upon the constitutional issue presented.

We are concerned with the Public Resources Code and the Forest Practice Act (§§ 4521- 4618 of that code) as in effect prior to its 1970 amendments. Although for convenience the present tense will be used, statutory references, unless otherwise specified, will be to the Public Resources Code prior to its amendments of 1970.

Sections 630-631 create a State Board of Forestry consisting of seven members. One member shall "be appointed from the general public." In addition, "each of the following fields shall be represented by a member...: (1) The pine producing industry. (2) The redwood producing industry. (3) Forest land ownership. (4) The range livestock industry. (5) Agriculture. (6) The beneficial use of water."

The State Board of Forestry is charged with "the protection of the state's interests in forest resources on private lands, and [to] determine, establish, and maintain an adequate forest policy." (§ 639.)

Section 4541, as previously pointed out, declares "the existence of a public interest in the forest resources and timberlands of this state." It also expresses the purpose of the Forest Practice Act, among other things, to "(d) Authorize the creation of district forest practice committees which shall formulate and adopt forest practice rules, and approve forest management and alternate plans for final approval of the board."

Section 4551 provides that the "privately owned commercial forest areas of the state are divided into four regional groups known as forest districts..." One of these is known as the Redwood Forest District which generally comprises the northern California coastal counties including San Mateo County. (§ 4552.)

Section 4562 provides that a forest practice committee "consisting of five members shall be established for each district." Of these five members "two shall be private timber owner- operators..., one shall be a private timber owner [and nonoperator] owning 1,000 acres or more of commercial timber...and one shall be a farmer-timber owner owning not less than 160 acres nor more than 1,000 acres of commercial timber" (§ 4563.) The fifth member of the committee "shall be a member of the [State Board of Forestry or an employee designated by the board]" who "shall meet with and take part in all deliberations of the committee, but shall not have the power of a vote except in the case of a tie." (§ 4564.)

Each forest practice committee "shall formulate forest practice rules for the district to fulfill the purposes of the [Forest Practice Act]." (§ 4571.)

Section 4572 then provides that after formulation of its rules "the committee shall submit the rules to the private timber owners within the district for approval." If two-thirds of the "private timber ownership voting in the district" approve them, the rules shall then be submitted to the State Board of Forestry.

Sections 4574 and 4575 state that timber owners and timber operators of the district may themselves submit to the forest practice committee plans or alternate plans in lieu of the committee's formulated rules, which may be received and approved by the committee.

Section 4576 provides that if in the opinion of the State Board of Forestry the rules or plans of sections 4572, 4574 and 4575 are "within the purposes and intent" of the Act, they shall be approved by the board. If any rules or plans are disapproved by the board, they shall be returned to the committee with recommendations for amendments thereto. Thereafter "Resubmission of rules or plans in amended form may be made after repetition of the entire original procedure."

The Act (§ 4577) provides: "Forest practice rules, forest management plans, and alternate plans, approved by the [State Board of Forestry], have the force of law within the district in which the rules originated."

It seems proper at this point to summarize such portions of the Forest Practice Act as are directly relevant to the question before us.

The content of the rules under which private logging operations are conducted is decreed exclusively by persons pecuniarily interested in the timber industry, i.e., timber owners and operators. The ultimate basis of this exclusive control rests in the hands of the "private timber ownership," two-thirds of which must agree before any proposed rule may be adopted. Ordinarily such rules are formulated by the four timber owners or operators of the forest practice committee, but they may nevertheless be drafted by the district's private timber ownership. The rules are submitted to the State Board of Forestry which may approve or disapprove them. It is noteworthy that the board is powerless itself to promulgate any forest practice rule. It may only approve or disapprove those which are submitted.

It follows that without agreement of the "private timber ownership," no power in California has authority to impose rules to insure reasonable environmental and public protection from logging abuses.

Another noteworthy feature of the Forest Practice Act requires comment.

As pointed out, the Legislature has delegated to timber owners and operators the exclusive power to formulate forest practice rules which, when adopted, have the force and effect of law.

Yet in this delegation of legislative authority no guides or standards to prevent its abuse are laid down by the Act. The combination of forest practice committees and timber ownership, in their absolute discretion, are free to formulate, or not formulate, rules tending to prevent erosion, to lessen flooding, to protect wildlife, to preserve natural beauty, or otherwise to serve the public interest....As such rules are formulated, whether they be in the public interest or timber industry interest, or otherwise reasonable or effective, is likewise left to the uncontrolled discretion of the committee and the timber ownership.

It is contended by appellants that such an industry-oriented statutory scheme is an unreasonable exercise of the state's police power, that it abuses the due process rights of San Mateo County and its citizens, and that it amounts to an unconstitutional delegation of legislative power. The constitutional issues which we shall consider are accordingly framed.

It has repeatedly been held that (1) "truly fundamental issues" should be resolved by the Legislature, and (2) that any grant of legislative authority must be accompanied by "safeguards adequate to prevent its abuse." Lacking the required safeguards such a grant of authority is an unconstitutional delegation of legislative power. (*Wilke & Holzheiser, Inc. v. Dept. of Alcoholic Bev. Control,* 65 Cal.2d 349, 369 [55 Cal.Rptr. 23, 420 P.2d 735]; *Kugler v. Yocum*, 69 Cal.2d 371, 376 [71 Cal.Rptr. 687, 445 P.2d 303], and see authorities there cited.) And the Legislature cannot constitutionally avoid its responsibility as to such fundamental issues "by explicitly delegating that function to others or by failing to establish an effective mechanism to assure the proper implementation of its policy decisions." (*Kugler v. Yocum, supra*, pp. 376-377.)

It is most certainly a "truly fundamental issue" whether the state's environment and ecology, and the public generally, are to be protected by law from harmful practices of the logging and timber industry. It follows, since the Legislature has chosen to delegate such law-making power, that its failure to prescribe any standards or "safeguards to prevent its abuse" impresses upon the Act constitutional taint.

When legislative authority without standards for its guidance is delegated to an agency or group of individuals with a pecuniary interest in its subject matter, the constitutional fault is compounded.

In the case of *State Board v. Thrift-D-Lux Cleaners* (1953) 40 Cal.2d 436 [254 P.2d 29], a Dry Cleaners' Act of 1945 created a seven-member State Board of Dry Cleaners. The board's principle duty was the establishment and regulation of minimum price schedules for the industry. The act provided that the board's membership consist of "one from the general public; two owners of retail plants; two owners of wholesale plants; and two owners of shops." The court considered an argument (such as is made here) that the makeup of the board was unreasonable and a constitutionally invalid exercise of the state's police power.

It was said (p. 448): "Here the statute assumes to confer legislative authority upon those who are directly interested in the operation of the regulatory rule and its penal provisions with no guide for the exercise of the delegated authority. The board is made up of six active members of the industry, and one member of the public at large. " (Italics added.) The court likened the situation to that of *Carter v. Carter Coal Co.* (1935) 298 U.S. 238, 311 [80 L.Ed. 1160, 1189, 56 S.Ct. 855], where it was said: "'‘...one person may not be entrusted with the power to regulate the business of another, and especially of a competitor. And a statute which attempts to confer such power undertakes an intolerable and unconstitutional interference with personal liberty and private property. The delegation is so clearly arbitrary, and so clearly a denial of rights safeguarded by the due process clause of the Fifth Amendment, that it is unnecessary to do more than refer to decisions of this court which foreclose the question.'" The court (pp. 448-449) considered significant certain language of *Becker v. State*, 37 Del. 454 [185 A. 92] (where a similar public agency was found to be unconstitutionally composed), to the effect that "'‘vast authority is centered in a governing board, a majority of which are directly interested in the industry, but who, nevertheless are empowered to act in a judicial capacity, and to sit in judgment over fellow members of the trade. Too great a strain is imposed upon human frailty.'"

Stating (p. 449), "Where the Legislature attempts to delegate its powers to an administrative board made up of interested members of the industry, the majority of which can initiate regulatory action by the board in that industry, that delegation may well be brought into question," the California Supreme Court found the Dry Cleaner's Act of 1945 to be constitutionally invalid.

The rationale of *State Board v. Thrift-D-Lux Cleaners*, supra, was recently approved and followed in *Blumenthal v. Board of Medical Examiners* (1962) 57 Cal.2d 228, 235-236 [18 Cal.Rptr. 501, 368 P.2d 101].

A leading outside authority on the instant issue is found in *Johnson v. Michigan Milk Marketing Board* (1940) 295 Mich. 644 [295 N.W. 346]. In that case a constitutional attack was made on a legislatively created milk-marketing board. The court said (p. 351): "The chief difficulty with the present act is in the composition of the Board. Section 5 reads: 'There is hereby created a milk marketing board to consist of 5 members as follows: The commissioner of agriculture shall be a member and chairman of the board by virtue of his office and 4 other members to be appointed by the governor, by and with the advice and consent of the senate, as follows: 2 shall be milk producers not connected with the distribution of milk except by a bona fide producer cooperative marketing association, both of whom shall have as their principal occupation and earn their principal livelihood by the actual management of 1 or more dairy herds; 1 shall be a distributor, and 1 shall be a consumer not connected with the production or distribution of milk."

The *Johnson v. Michigan Milk Marketing Board* court was careful to point out that "No claim is made that any member of the present Board has acted unfairly or arbitrarily, but the facts remains that the act requires the appointment of a board, a majority of whose members have a direct pecuniary interest in the matters submitted to them...." It then continued, "In order that the administration of the milk industry may be conducted in a fair and impartial manner, it is essential that the Board be impartial in its composition. The act is fatally defective in its provision for the appointment of the personnel of the Board."

The court drew support from *Carter v. Carter Coal Co.*, *supra*, 298 U.S. 238, 311, from which it (on p. 352) quoted the following: "'This is legislative delegation in its most obnoxious form; for it is not even delegation to an official or an official body, presumptively disinterested, but to private persons whose interests may be and often are adverse to the interests of others in the same business'" The Michigan court then held (p. 353): "No one should act as a judge in his own cause. The Board, as constituted under the statute, is of such a nature that Johnson was not, and could not have been, accorded that impartial hearing which satisfies the requirements of due process" and that the statutory makeup of the Milk Marketing Board violated "both the spirit and letter of the Constitution."

We have been presented with no authority which in any way impugns the holdings of the cases we have cited, and we have been able to find none.

It is of course noted that the cited authority relates to presumed threats to individual private rights resulting from the creation of unfairly constituted public boards. In the case at bench the complaint is that public injury must inevitably result from placing exclusive control of the logging industry in the hands of persons who may be expected to profit most from the gathering of logs at the lowest cost and without environmental safeguards. But the rationale of the cited cases is equally, if not more strongly, applicable here, for we believe no one would contend that the law has lesser concern for the overall public welfare than for individual private rights.

It is an age-old principle of our law that no man should judge or otherwise officially preside over disputed matters in which he has a pecuniary interest. The rule is given expression in the law of trusts. "It is against public policy to permit any person occupying fiduciary relations to be placed in such a position that he may be tempted to betray his duty as a trustee." (*Sims v. Petaluma Gas Light Co.*, 131 Cal. 656, 659 [63 P. 1011].) California's Constitution, article IV, section 5, notices the same concept by providing that the Legislature shall enact laws to prohibit its members "from engaging in activities or having interests which conflict with the proper discharge of their duties and responsibilities,..." The same rule should reasonably apply to those persons empowered by law to promulgate the Forest Practice Act's rules which so vitally affect the public interest.

We are impelled to, and do, conclude that the Forest Practice Act, as in effect prior to its 1970 amendments, insofar as it provides for the promulgation of forest practice rules, is violative of the state and federal Constitutions; it unlawfully and without proper, or any, standards delegates legislative power, and otherwise denies due process of law to the interested and affected public. The judgment must be reversed and the cause remanded to the superior court for further and proper proceedings.

> We are required to "pass upon and determine all the questions of law involved in the case, presented upon [this] appeal, and necessary to the final determination of the case." (Code Civ. Proc. § 53.) Plaintiff will undoubtedly continue in its efforts to log its land; in such a case its application must again come before the county planning commission and, on review, perhaps before the board of supervisors and the superior court. A question which will undoubtedly require resolution in the future is the constitutionality of the Forest Practice Act as presently in effect, and including its 1970 amendments.
>
> ***
>
> The resolution of other points raised by the parties has become unnecessary to our disposition of the appeal.
>
> The judgment is reversed. The superior court will take further proceedings not inconsistent herewith.
>
> MOLINARI, P.J., and SIMS, J., concur.

Discussion

Section 1 of the 14th Amendment prohibits any state from depriving any person of "life, liberty, or property, without due process of law." An unconstitutional deprivation or "taking" may be accomplished by means other than low maximum rate regulation or prohibitions on exit. The state may require exit or may impose a multitude of conditions on operations that effectuate the taking of a business asset.

The 5th Amendment of the United States Constitution, applied to the states through the 14th Amendment, requires more than the procedural due process of notice, hearing, right to counsel, opportunity to present evidence, confront and cross-examine under oath, a neutral adjudicator, a record, and judicial review. Even with procedural fairness, a governmental taking may not be accomplished without fair compensation. A breach of the United States Constitution's 5th Amendment or its California counterpart (Cal. Const. Art 1, Section 7) requires the threshold elements of: (1) state action, (2) to take the property of another, (3) without procedural due process or without just compensation if compensation is compelled (substantive due process). Initially, there must be "state action." The federal and state constitutions do not prohibit private takings but limit only the power of the state.

The cases do not deal consistently with the involvement of the state as regulator or ministerial enforcer of prejudgment remedies. Although reconciling the case law is difficult, state action is most often found where the state itself acts to take or where the state creates a private right to take beyond rights extant at common law. Where private rights consistent with previous common law or accepted property rights are declared by statute, state action may be lacking–even where the industry is highly regulated and the state is relied on to accomplish the taking through both judicial and executive enforcement. Conversely, a statutory scheme that departs from common law or from previous commercial practice and standards may invoke state action notwithstanding minor state involvement in the taking. Hence, a bank setoff or a repossession may be accomplished with state operational assistance. However, if the setoff or repossession is consistent with prior common law remedies, it may not constitute state action.

In the regulatory context, state action is more easily found. Regulation derives from statutes departing from common law principles and extending state involvement into previously private areas. The most remarkable extension of state action in the regulatory context has been its application to hospitals engaging in peer review of physicians and other medical professionals. Here, the withdrawal of hospital privileges or similar private decertification has led some courts to apply due process procedural requirements of notice and hearing as if the state were directly disciplining the respondent. This case law is increasingly confused because of a misunderstanding by some courts of the distinction between "state action" required due process (not properly at issue in private hospital decertification cases) and the group boycott antitrust prohibition, which is potentially applicable to private parties.

A decision in restraint of trade by private competitors acting in concert (for example, by or through a hospital to effectively exclude a competitor from a marketplace) is lawfully accomplished only if allowed by federal statute or if the state is involved. There must be legitimate "state action" to immunize private hospitals from application of federal antitrust prohibitions. That state action requires both a state statute authorizing the anticompetitive acts and "independent state supervision" over them. "Independent state supervision" generally compels meaningful review by neutral regulators. Hence, antitrust law may compel review, which must be by the state and cannot be delegated to private parties. This state review, in turn, may well constitute state action, and if there is a "taking," will then trigger required procedural due process.

In the medical industry context, independent state review is not provided by mere opportunity for court review or the potential jurisdiction of a state department of health that oversees hospitals and the medical industry. Thus far, California has rejected any system of qualifying state hearings or state review, which would confer antitrust immunity on the private hospital privilege and disciplinary decisions of medical providers.

The Constitution's 5th Amendment protects against takings absent procedural due process and provides: "nor shall private property be taken for public use, without just compensation." A taking for purposes of this compensation is much more narrowly defined than takings invoking procedural due process. Rather, substantive due process requiring compensation is akin to a conversion of property for public use. However, a wide variety of restrictions on use are capable of accomplishing empirical conversions of property interests. The delineation of "taking" for these purposes suffers from inconsistent case law. A taking may not be found easily based only on additional commercial or personal costs imposed due to "police power" regulation. The "police power" of the state to regulate is broadly defined, and a generalized diminution in property value because of the police power's implementation will not create a compensable taking. Hence, the City of New Orleans may, for traffic control and other police power purposes, revoke the licenses of pushcart sales entrepreneurs without compensation, although it is a clear taking.

In the land use area in particular, California has been hesitant to apply the terse criterion of *Pennsylvania Coal Company v. Mahon*, 260 U.S. 393 (1922), that "while property may be regulated to a certain extent, if regulation goes too far, it will be recognized as a taking."

The appellate courts of California recognized in *Eldridge v. City of Palo Alto*, 77 Cal. App. 3d 329, 143 Cal. Rptr. 506 (1978), that a rezoning depriving an owner of all reasonable use was a taking requiring compensation. Although serving as a bright-line test, such a harsh application countenanced substantial public takings of private property.

However, beginning in 1982, a series of federal decisions based on the less protective federal takings clause seriously eroded the California refusal to recognize compensable takings by regulatory action. The most important first decision in this line is *Loretto v. Teleprompter Manhattan CATV Corp.*, 458 U.S. 419 (1982). In *Loretto*, a landlord was required by a New York statute to permit a cable television company to install cables on apartment buildings, with compensation to be set by a commission. The state commission set the appropriate fee at one dollar. The court held that the regulatory requirement of cable access through the landlord's property (to serve his property and others) was a regulatory taking, requiring compensation not provided by the fee. Although the incursion from the state was here a fixture attached to real property and involved an "occupation" of sorts (as the court characterized it). it was also minimal in degree, arguably enhanced rather than diminished property value, and involved the strong state interest of allowing tenants to have access to a major communications medium with educational and other public benefits.

The *Nollan v. California Coastal Commission*, 483 U.S. 825, 836 (1987), case cast further doubt on the previous wide latitude afforded regulatory property diminution without compensation. There, the coastal commission conditioned a permit to the *Nollans* to rebuild their house on an agreement to make an easement across their beachfront available to the public. The Court held that the appropriation of a public easement across a landowner's premises is the taking of a property interest and is not a "mere restriction on its use." This decision and related cases are especially significant because they limit uncompensated taking through land use controls. These powers lie at the heart of traditional court deference to state and local police powers affecting personal assets and have been used commonly to diminish the value of private property substantially without compensation, unless qualifying for eminent domain purchase. The *Nollan* case cites the rational relation test as part of the due process clause, holding that a taking must advance a "legitimate state interest." The Court found that test met in the public's right of access to beach resources but required compensation because the public easement deprived the plaintiff of "economically viable use of the land." Recent cases have narrowed *Nollan's* scope, including the stated limitation to "land use" restrictions. And more recent precedents otherwise reflect more deferential attitudes toward takings through regulatory decisions.

PROCEDURE FOR QUASI-JUDICIAL ENFORCEMENT

Gibson v. Berryhill

93 S.Ct. 1689 (1973)

MR. JUSTICE WHITE delivered the opinion of the Court.

Prior to 1965, the laws of Alabama relating to the practice of optometry permitted any person, including a business firm or corporation, to maintain a department in which "eyes are examined or glasses fitted," provided that such department was in the charge of a duly licensed optometrist. This permission was expressly conferred by § 210 of Title 46 of the Alabama Code of 1940, and also inferentially by § 211 of the Code which regulates the advertising practices of optometrists, and which, until 1965, appeared to contemplate the existence of commercial stores with optical departments....In 1965, § 210 was repealed in its entirety by the Alabama Legislature, and § 211 was amended so as to eliminate any direct reference to optical departments maintained by corporations or other business establishments under the direction of employee optometrists....

Soon after these statutory changes, the Alabama Optometric Association, a professional organization whose membership is limited to independent practitioners of optometry not employed by others, filed charges against various named optometrists, all of whom were duly licensed under Alabama law but were the salaried employees of Lee Optical Co. The charges were filed with the Alabama Board of Optometry, the statutory body with authority to issue, suspend, and revoke licenses for the practice of optometry. The gravamen of these charges was that the named optometrists, by accepting employment from Lee Optical, a corporation, had engaged in "unprofessional conduct" within the meaning of § 206 of the Alabama optometry statute, and hence were practicing their profession unlawfully....More particularly, the Association charged the named individuals with, among other things, aiding and abetting a corporation in the illegal practice of optometry; practicing optometry under a false name, that is, Lee Optical Co.; unlawfully soliciting the sale of glasses; lending their licenses to Lee Optical Co.; and splitting or dividing fees with Lee Optical....It was apparently the Association's position that, following the repeal of § 210 and the amendment of § 211, the practice of optometry by individuals as employees of business corporations was no longer permissible in Alabama, and that, by accepting such employment, the named optometrists had violated the ethics of their profession. It was prayed that the Board revoke the licenses of the individuals charged following due notice and a proper hearing.

Two days after these charges were filed by the Association in October 1965, the Board filed a suit of its own in state court against Lee Optical, seeking to enjoin the company from engaging in the "unlawful practice of optometry." The Board's complaint also named 13 optometrists employed by Lee Optical as parties defendant, charging them with aiding and abetting the company in its illegal activities, as well as with other improper conduct very similar to that charged by the Association in its complaint to the Board.

Proceedings on the Association's charges were held in abeyance by the Board while its own state court suit progressed. The individual defendants in that suit were dismissed on grounds that do not adequately appear in the record before us; and, eventually, on March 17, 1971, the state trial court rendered judgment for the Board, and enjoined Lee Optical both from practicing optometry without a license and from employing licensed optometrists....The company appealed this judgment.

Meanwhile, following its victory in the trial court, the Board reactivated the proceedings pending before it since 1965 against the individual optometrists employed by Lee, noticing them for hearings to be held on May 26 and 27, 1971....

A three-judge court was convened in August 1971, and shortly thereafter entered judgment for plaintiffs, enjoining members of the State Board and their successors "from conducting a hearing on the charges heretofore preferred against the Plaintiffs" and from revoking their licenses to practice optometry in the State of Alabama.

***

The court's ultimate conclusion was "that to require the Plaintiffs to resort to the protection offered by state law in these cases would effectively deprive them of their property, that is, their right to practice their professions, without due process of law and that irreparable injury would follow in the normal course of events."...331 F.Supp., at 126.

Appeal was taken to this Court and probable jurisdiction noted on June 26, 1972. 408 U.S. 920. Meanwhile, on March 30, 1972, the Supreme Court of Alabama reversed the judgment of the state trial court in the *Lee Optical Co.* case,...holding that nothing in the Alabama statutes pertaining to optometry evidenced "a legislative policy that an optometrist duly qualified and licensed under the laws of this state, may not be employed by another to examine eyes for the purpose of prescribing eyeglasses."...288 Ala. 338, 346, 261 So. 2d 17, 24.

***

I

We agree with the District Court that neither statute nor case law precluded it from adjudicating the issues before it and from issuing the injunction if its decision on the merits was correct.

Title 28 U. S. C. § 2283, the anti-injunction statute, prohibits federal courts from enjoining state court proceedings, but the statute excepts from its prohibition injunctions which are "expressly authorized" by another Act of Congress....Last Term, after the District Court's decision here, this Court determined that actions brought under the Civil Rights Act of 1871, 42 U. S. C. § 1983, were within the "expressly authorized" exception to the ban on federal injunctions.... *Mitchum v. Foster*, 407 U.S. 225 (1972).

Our decision in *Mitchum*, however, held only that a district court was not absolutely barred by statute from enjoining a state court proceeding when called upon to do so in a § 1983 suit. As we expressly stated in Mitchum, nothing in that decision purported to call into question the established principles of equity, comity, and federalism which must, under appropriate circumstances, restrain a federal court from issuing such injunctions. *Id.*, at 243. These principles have been emphasized by this Court many times in the past, albeit under a variety of different rubrics. First of all, there is the doctrine, usually applicable when an injunction is sought, that a party must exhaust his available administrative remedies before invoking the equitable jurisdiction of a court. *See, e.g., Prentis v. Atlantic Coast Line Co.*, 211 U.S. 210 (1908); *Illinois Commerce Comm'n v. Thomson*, 318 U.S. 675 (1943). Secondly, there is the basic principle of federalism, restated as recently as 1971 in *Younger v. Harris*, 401 U.S. 37, that a federal court may not enjoin a pending state criminal proceeding in the absence of special circumstances suggesting bad faith, harassment or irreparable injury that is both serious and immediate. And finally, there is the doctrine, developed in our cases at least since *Railroad Comm'n v. Pullman Co.*, 312 U.S. 496 (1941), that when confronted with issues of constitutional dimension which implicate or depend upon unsettled questions of state law, a federal court ought to abstain and stay its proceedings until those state law questions are definitively resolved.

In the instant case the matter of exhaustion of administrative remedies need not detain us long. Normally when a State has instituted administrative proceedings against an individual who then seeks an injunction in federal court, the exhaustion doctrine would require the court to delay action until the administrative phase of the state proceedings is terminated, at least where coverage or liability is contested and administrative expertise, discretion, or factfinding is involved....But this Court has expressly held in recent years that state administrative remedies need not be exhausted where the federal court plaintiff states an otherwise good cause of action under 42 U. S. C. § 1983. *McNeese v. Board of Education*, 373 U.S. 668 (1963); *Damico v. California*, 389 U.S. 416 (1967). Whether this is invariably the case even where, as here, a license revocation proceeding has been brought by the State and is pending before one of its own agencies and where the individual charged is to be deprived of nothing until the completion of that proceeding, is a question we need not now decide; for the clear purport of appellees' complaint was that the State Board of Optometry was unconstitutionally constituted and so did not provide them with an adequate administrative remedy requiring exhaustion. Thus, the question of the adequacy of the administrative remedy, an issue which under federal law the District Court was required to decide, was for all practical purposes identical with the merits of appellees' lawsuit....

II

This brings us to the question of whether *Younger v. Harris*, 401 U.S. 37 (1971); *Samuels v. Mackell*, 401 U.S. 66 (1971), or the principles of equity, comity, and federalism for which those cases stand, precluded the District Court from acting, in view of the fact that proceedings against appellees were pending before the Alabama Board of Optometry.

Those cases and principles would, under ordinary circumstances, forbid either a declaratory judgment or injunction with respect to the validity or enforcement of a state statute when a criminal proceeding under the statute has been commenced. Whether a like rule obtains where state civil proceedings are pending was left open in *Younger* and its companion cases.

Appellants now insist, not only that the issue is posed here by the pendency of proceedings before the state board, but also that the issue was actually decided following

Younger by our summary affirmance in the case of *Geiger v. Jenkins*, 401 U.S. 985 (1971). In that case, the State Medical Board of Georgia noticed hearings on charges filed against a medical practitioner who immediately brought suit in federal court under § 1983 seeking an injunction on the ground that the underlying statute the Medical Board sought to enforce was unconstitutional. The District Court dismissed the action without reaching the merits, holding that the state proceedings were "in the nature of criminal proceedings," sufficiently so in any event to trigger the 28 U. S. C. § 2283 bar to federal intervention. 316 F.Supp. 370, 372 (ND Ga. 1970). The decision was appealed to this Court and summarily affirmed without opinion but with citation to *Younger* and *Mackell*.

***

Unlike those situations where a federal court merely abstains from decision on federal questions until the resolution of underlying or related state law issues...—a subject we shall consider shortly in the context of the present case—*Younger v. Harris* contemplates the outright dismissal of the federal suit, and the presentation of all claims, both state and federal, to the state courts. Such a course naturally presupposes the opportunity to raise and have timely decided by a competent state tribunal the federal issues involved. Here the predicate for a *Younger v. Harris* dismissal was lacking, for the appellees alleged, and the District Court concluded, that the State Board of Optometry was incompetent by reason of bias to adjudicate the issues pending before it. If the District Court's conclusion was correct in this regard, it was also correct that it need not defer to the Board. Nor, in these circumstances, would a different result be required simply because judicial review, de novo or otherwise, would be forthcoming at the conclusion of the administrative proceedings. 16 Cf. *Ward v. Village of Monroeville*, 409 U.S. 57 (1972).

III

It is appropriate, therefore, that we consider the District Court's conclusions that the State Board of Optometry was so biased by prejudgment and pecuniary interest that it could not constitutionally conduct hearings looking toward the revocation of appellees' licenses to practice optometry. We affirm the District Court in this respect.

The District Court thought the Board to be impermissibly biased for two reasons. First, the Board had filed a complaint in state court alleging that appellees had aided and abetted Lee Optical Co. in the unlawful practice of optometry and also that they had engaged in other forms of "unprofessional conduct" which, if proved, would justify revocation of their licenses. These charges were substantially similar to those pending against appellees before the Board and concerning which the Board had noticed hearings following its successful prosecution of Lee Optical in the state trial court.

Secondly, the District Court determined that the aim of the Board was to revoke the licenses of all optometrists in the State who were employed by business corporations such as Lee Optical, and that these optometrists accounted for nearly half of all the optometrists practicing in Alabama. Because the Board of Optometry was composed solely of optometrists in private practice for their own account, the District Court concluded that success in the Board's efforts would possibly redound to the personal benefit of members of the Board, sufficiently so that in the opinion of the District Court the Board was constitutionally disqualified from hearing the charges filed against the appellees.

The District Court apparently considered either source of possible bias—prejudgment of the facts or personal interest—sufficient to disqualify the members of the Board. Arguably, the District Court was right on both scores, but we need reach, and we affirm, only on the latter ground of possible personal interest….

It is sufficiently clear from our cases that those with substantial pecuniary interest in legal proceedings should not adjudicate these disputes. *Tumey v. Ohio*, 273 U.S. 510 (1927). And *Ward v. Village of Monroeville*, 409 U.S. 57 (1972), indicates that the financial stake need not be as direct or positive as it appeared to be in *Tumey*. It has also come to be the prevailing view that "most of the law concerning disqualification because of interest applies with equal force to...administrative adjudicators." K. Davis, Administrative Law Text § 12.04, p. 250 (1972), and cases cited. The District Court proceeded on this basis and, applying the standards taken from our cases, concluded that the pecuniary interest of the members of the Board of Optometry had sufficient substance to disqualify them, given the context in which this case arose. As remote as we are from the local realities underlying this case and it being very likely that the District Court has a firmer grasp of the facts and of their significance to the issues presented, we have no good reason on this record to overturn its conclusion and we affirm it.

IV

Finally, we do not think that the doctrine of abstention, as developed in our cases from *Railroad Comm'n v. Pullman Co.*, 312 U.S. 496 (1941), to *Lake Carriers' Assn. v. MacMullan*, 406 U.S. 498 (1972), required the District Court to stay its proceedings until the appellees had presented unsettled questions of state law to the state courts. Those questions went to the reach and effect of the state optometry law and concerned the merits of the charges pending against the appellees, at the heart of which was the issue whether Alabama law permitted licensed optometrists to be employed by business corporations and others. That central question was pending in the Alabama Supreme Court in the *Lee Optical Co.* case at the time the District Court entered its order. As was noted earlier, however, appellees here had been dismissed from that case by the state trial court, and it was only after this dismissal, and after the Board had reactivated its charges against them, that appellees sought relief in federal court.

***

Nevertheless, the Alabama Supreme Court has since rendered its decision, not only in the *Lee Optical Co.* case, but also in a companion case, *House of $ 8.50 Eyeglasses v. State Board of Optometry*, 288 Ala. 349, 261 So. 2d 27 (1972). *See* n. 10, supra. Individual optometrists were parties to that latter case, and the Alabama Supreme Court entered judgment in their behalf, holding that nothing in the State's optometry law prohibited a licensed optometrist from accepting employment from a business corporation. Whether this judgment substantially

> devitalizes the position of the Board with respect to the appellees here, or in any way makes unnecessary or removes the "equity" from the injunction entered by the District Court, we are unable to determine. But we do think that considerations of equity, comity, and federalism warrant vacating the judgment of the District Court and remanding the case to that court for reconsideration in light of the Alabama Supreme Court's judgments in the *Lee Optical Co.* and *House of $ 8.50 Eyeglasses* cases. We in no way intimate whether or not the injunction should be reinstated by the District Court.
>
> It is so ordered.

***

Discussion

A property or liberty deprivation may only be accomplished by the state if procedural due process is afforded, regardless of whether compensation is compelled. The scope of state action considered "takings" for purposes of imposing procedural substantive due process requirements is substantially broader than for required compensation.

Regulatory takings often occur outside land use or property limitations. They may occur as state-established qualifications (barriers to entry) to practice in an industry, trade, or profession, or in revocation of permission to so practice. In general, courts have required the full panoply of due process guarantees prior to the taking of a "vested right." In the same settings, the bright-line point of licensure may be involved. Hence, a state disciplinary action directed at a licensee who is currently practicing requires detailed notice and hearing protections and calls for "independent judgment" court review.

However, a decision not to license an applicant may not involve the taking of a "vested right." Notice, hearing, and other due process rights may be reduced in required scope if the right is not vested. The extent of notice, hearing, and other due process rights may be somewhat diminished, the burden of proof to show qualification may be shifted to the applicant, and the decision to deny may be upheld if supported by substantial evidence, short of the "independent judgment" applied for revocation or limitation of an existing license.

The flexibility accorded to the degree and timing of due process is reflected in approved procedures for interim suspension or license restriction. License suspension while administrative proceedings are pending is analogous to standard superior court proceedings for temporary restraining orders and preliminary injunctions, but for Department of Consumer Affairs agencies. Here, courts may act (based on a balance of the irreparable harms involved) to suspend practice at the request of regulatory agencies responsible for licensing and concomitant discipline. Further, in more general superior court preliminary relief proceedings (such as those in which a civil complaint is contemporaneously filed), a defendant's suspension may trigger post-taking due process where exigencies preclude notice or hearing before the taking.

The California Supreme Court has upheld the authority of the State Bar to "interim suspend" attorney licenses. That interim suspension power clearly involves deprivation of a vested right. But the Bar's procedures require notice and an accelerated due process hearing prior to entry. Further, the adjudication of the underlying offense must be "expedited." However, there are no statutory or rule provisions specifying the conduct of these proceedings, and hearsay and affidavits are acceptable evidence.

Apart from licensure as a creator of a vested right, federal and California courts find vested property rights in most state entitlement programs, and they may not be terminated without providing notice and a reasonable pretermination opportunity to contest the determination. Hence, benefits must be maintained pending the hearing. Application of due process safeguards accrues where the state acts to deprive a person of contract rights or benefits in violation of reasonable expectations. Hence, the point of distinction is likely to be the difference between a contract cancellation (or a nonrenewal in which there has been substantial investment and reasonable expectation of continuation). This contrasts with a nonrenewal where the contract expires, and its renewal was conditional and discretionary. The California Supreme Court has found the requisite reasonable expectation and reliance in the case of applicants to the State Bar's client security fund. The fund was established to provide partial recompense to clients who had been the victims of their attorneys' theft while these attorneys were acting within the scope of legal authority.

IMPEDING INTERSTATE COMMERCE

Missouri ex rel. Koster v. Harris

847 F.3d 646 (2017)

GRABER, Circuit Judge:

***

In the 2008 general election, California voters adopted Proposition 2, which enacted new standards beginning on January 1, 2015, for housing farm animals within California including, as relevant here, egg-laying hens. Cal. Health & Safety Code §§ 25990-94. Under Proposition 2, hens may not be confined for the majority of any day "in a manner that prevents [them] from: (a) Lying down, standing up, and fully extending [their] limbs; and (b) Turning around freely." *Id.* § 25990. A violation of these standards is punishable by a $1,000 fine or imprisonment of 180 days in county jail, or both. *Id.* § 25993.

In 2010, California's legislature adopted Assembly Bill 1437 ("AB1437"), which mandated, also beginning on January 1, 2015, that "a shelled egg shall not be sold or contracted for sale for human consumption in California if the seller knows or should have known that the egg is the product of an egg-laying hen that was confined on a farm or place that is not in compliance with animal care standards set forth in [Proposition 2]." Cal. Health & Safety Code § 25996. Therefore, all eggs sold in California must comply with Proposition 2. In 2013, the California Department of Food and Agriculture promulgated egg-related regulations, including salmonella prevention measures and minimum cage sizes for egg-laying hens, all of which also carried an effective date of January 1, 2015. Cal. Code Regs. tit. 3, § 1350(d)(1).

On February 3, 2014, the State of Missouri filed a complaint in the Eastern District of California, asking the court to declare AB1437 and California Code § 1350(d)(1) (collectively the "Shell Egg Laws") invalid, as violating the Commerce Clause or as preempted by federal statute, and to enjoin California from enforcing the laws. Plaintiffs then filed their First Amended Complaint (the "complaint"), joining the States of Nebraska, Oklahoma, Alabama, and Kentucky and the Governor of Iowa as additional plaintiffs. The Humane Society of the United States and the Association of California Egg Farmers ("Intervenors") moved to intervene as defendants, which the court allowed. Defendants filed a motion to dismiss for lack of subject matter jurisdiction; Intervenors filed their own, similar motions. The district court granted the motions to dismiss, with prejudice. The court concluded that Plaintiffs lacked standing as *parens patriae*, held that their claim was not justiciable, and denied leave to amend as futile. Plaintiffs timely appeal.

A. *Parens Patriae* Standing

States asserting *parens patriae* standing must meet both the basic requirements of Article III standing and the unique requirements of that doctrine. *Table Bluff Reservation (Wiyot Tribe) v. Philip Morris, Inc.*, 256 F.3d 879, 885 (9th Cir. 2001). "To establish Article III standing, an injury must be concrete, particularized, and actual or imminent; fairly traceable to the challenged action; and redressable by a favorable ruling." *Clapper v. Amnesty Int'l USA*, 568 U.S. 398, 133 S. Ct. 1138, 1147, 185 L. Ed. 2d 264 (2013) (internal quotation marks omitted). In a *parens patriae* case, there are two additional requirements. First, "the State must articulate an interest apart from the interests of particular private parties, *i.e.*, the State must be more than a nominal party." *Alfred L. Snapp & Son, Inc. v. Puerto Rico ex rel. Barez ("Snapp")*, 458 U.S. 592, 607, 102 S. Ct. 3260, 73 L. Ed. 2d 995 (1982). Second, "[t]he State must express a quasi-sovereign interest." *Id.* On de novo review, *Habeas Corpus Res. Ctr. v. U.S. Dep't of Justice*, 816 F.3d 1241, 1247 (9th Cir. 2016), we conclude that Plaintiffs have not met the first requirement. We therefore need not, and do not, reach the second part of the test, nor do we reach the issue of ripeness.

There are no "definitive limits on the proportion of the population of the State that must be adversely affected." *Snapp*, 458 U.S. at 607. But "more must be alleged than injury to an identifiable group of individual residents." *Id.* "[T]he indirect effects of the injury must be considered as well in determining whether the State has alleged injury to a sufficiently substantial segment of its population." *Id.* …

Concerning the parties, the complaint alleges: "Missouri farmers produced nearly two billion eggs in 2012 and generated approximately $171 million in revenue for the state"; "Nebraska is one of the top ten largest egg producers in the United States"; "Alabama is one of the top fifteen largest egg producers in the United States"; "Kentucky farmers produced approximately 1.037 billion eggs in 2012 and generated approximately $116 million in revenue for the state"; "Oklahoma farmers produced more than 700 million eggs in 2012 and generated approximately $90 million in revenue for the state"; and "Iowa is the number one state in egg production[,] Iowa farmers produce over 14.4 billion eggs per year," and "[t]he cost to Iowa farmers to retrofit existing housing or build new housing that complies with AB1437 would be substantial."

The laws "forc[e] Plaintiffs' farmers either to forgo California's markets altogether or accept significantly increased production costs just to comply." That is, "Plaintiffs' egg farmers must choose either to bring their entire operations into compliance...or else simply leave the California marketplace." "[T]he necessary capital improvements [would] cost Plaintiffs' farmers hundreds of millions of dollars," and, without access to the California market, "supply would outpace demand by half a billion eggs, causing the price of eggs— as well as egg farmers' margins—to fall throughout the Midwest and potentially forc[e] some Missouri producers out of business. The same goes for egg producers in Nebraska, Alabama, Oklahoma, Kentucky, and Iowa."

***

Plaintiffs advance several theories to demonstrate "an interest apart from the interests of particular private parties" and an effect on "a sufficiently substantial segment of [the] population." *Id.* First, Plaintiffs allege harm to their egg farmers. Second, Plaintiffs argue that the Shell Egg Laws will cause harmful fluctuations in the price of eggs. Finally, Plaintiffs allege that they will suffer discrimination from the Shell Egg Laws. For the reasons that follow, none of these theories establishes standing.

1. Alleged Harm to Egg Farmers

Alleging harm to the egg farmers in Plaintiffs' States is insufficient to satisfy the first prong of *parens patriae* standing. Other courts have recognized that *parens patriae* standing is inappropriate where an aggrieved party could seek private relief. The Second Circuit, for example, held that "*[p]arens patriae* standing...requires a finding that individuals could not obtain complete relief through a private suit." *N.Y. ex rel. Abrams v. 11 Cornwell Co.*, 695 F.2d 34, 40 (2d Cir. 1982), *vacated in part on other grounds*, 718 F.2d 22 (2d Cir. 1983) (en banc); see also *Connecticut v. Physicians Health Servs. of Conn., Inc.*, 103 F. Supp. 2d 495, 504 (D. Conn. 2000) (noting that "the Second Circuit has interpreted Snapp to require a finding that the State act on behalf of individuals who could not obtain complete relief through a private suit"). Here, complete relief would be available to the egg farmers themselves, were they to file a complaint on their own behalf.

Supreme Court cases in which private relief was held to be unlikely or unrealistic illustrate why *parens patriae* standing does not lie here. In *Missouri v. Illinois*, 180 U.S. 208, 21 S. Ct. 331, 45 L. Ed. 497 (1901), though never explicitly calling it a *parens patriae* case, the Supreme Court heard a sewage dispute between two states. The Court observed that "the nature of the injury complained of is such that an adequate remedy can only be found in this court at the suit of the state of Missouri." *Id.* at 241. The Court emphasized that the "health and comfort of the large communities inhabiting those parts of the state situated on the Mississippi River are not alone concerned, but contagious and typhoidal diseases introduced in the river communities may spread themselves throughout the territory of the state." *Id.*; see also *Snapp*, 458 U.S. at 603 (describing "a line of cases ...in which States successfully sought to represent the interests of their citizens in enjoining public nuisances"). In other words, *Missouri* alleged that a public health hazard affected its entire population. By contrast, the Shell Egg Laws are not alleged to threaten the health of the entire population (or, indeed of anyone), and those directly affected—egg farmers—are capable of pursuing their own interests.

A rationale similar to that in *Missouri v. Illinois* supported *parens patriae* standing in *Maryland v. Louisiana*, 451 U.S. 725, 101 S. Ct. 2114, 68 L. Ed. 2d 576 (1981). There, Louisiana imposed a "First-Use Tax" on natural gas piped into the state from federal offshore drilling areas. A group of states, later joined by the federal government and several pipeline companies, filed an original jurisdiction suit in the Supreme Court challenging the tax under, among other sources, the Commerce Clause. The Court found jurisdiction on several theories, including the States' interest as *parens patriae*. *Id.* at 737. The Court observed that the incidence of the Tax [does not] fall on a small group of citizens who are likely to challenge the Tax directly. Rather, a great many citizens in each of the plaintiff States are themselves consumers of natural gas and are faced with increased costs aggregating millions of dollars per year. As the Special Master observed, individual consumers cannot be expected to litigate the validity of the First Use Tax given that the amounts paid by each consumer are likely to be relatively small.

Id. at 739. *Maryland v. Louisiana's* logic counsels the opposite result here: Whereas millions of consumers probably cannot challenge another state's tax on their commodities, large egg producers certainly could file an action like this one on their own.

2. Alleged Fluctuation in the Price of Eggs

Plaintiffs argue that fluctuations in the price of eggs will harm consumers, thereby affecting a substantial segment of their populations and establishing parens patriae standing. Plaintiffs filed their complaint before the Shell Egg Laws took effect. As a result, their allegations about the potential economic effects of those laws, after implementation, were necessarily speculative. Indeed, Plaintiffs' allegations are inconsistent; the complaint alleges that prices will go either up or down. On the one hand, Plaintiffs allege that farmers must bring all egg facilities into compliance with the Shell Egg Laws, regardless of the proportion of their product actually bound for California, because the demand across markets fluctuates. The cost of "compliant" eggs will thus increase across the board. On the other hand, Plaintiffs allege that, if farmers decline to comply and they exit the California market, "the price of eggs...[would] fall throughout the Midwest." Neither of these alleged results is sufficient to support *parens patriae* standing.

***

The result in *Maryland v. Louisiana* is not to the contrary. There, explaining that a state "may act as the representative of its citizens in original actions where the injury alleged affects the general population of a State in a substantial way," 451 U.S. at 737 (emphasis added), the Court found that the plaintiff states had alleged injury both to their proprietary interests as gas consumers and to their citizens "from substantial economic injury presented by imposition of the First-Use Tax," *id.* at 739 (emphasis added). Plaintiffs do not allege a similarly substantial injury here. Natural gas is a commodity so universally critical to state governments, businesses, and ordinary consumers that the Supreme Court has twice granted *parens patriae* standing to challenge state actions that directly threaten shortages or price increases. *Id.*; *Pennsylvania*, 262 U.S. at 592 (describing a cut-off in gas as "a matter of grave public concern"). An ordinary consumer commodity, such as eggs, lacks the central economic significance to a state of a utility's product, such as natural gas.

3. Alleged Discrimination

Finally, Plaintiffs' reliance on cases granting *parens patriae* standing to challenge discrimination against a state's citizens is misplaced. The Shell Egg Laws do not distinguish among eggs based on their state of origin. A statute that treats "both intrastate and interstate products" alike "is not discriminatory." *Ass'n des Eleveurs de Canards et d'Oies du Quebec v. Harris*, 729 F.3d 937, 948 (9th Cir. 2013).

...California egg farmers are subject to the same rules as egg farmers from all other states, including California itself.

...Plaintiffs allege no trade barriers erected against their broader economies and, again, the Shell Egg Laws are not discriminatory. Accordingly, Plaintiffs' allegations of discrimination do not establish *parens patriae* standing.

B. Leave to Amend

Plaintiffs urge us to reverse the district court's denial of leave to amend their complaint. They seek "[a]t the very least...to plead the additional information [that they have] gathered since the Shell Egg Laws went into effect."..."Denial of leave to amend is reviewed for an abuse of discretion." *Dougherty v. City of Covina*, 654 F.3d 892, 897 (9th Cir. 2011). "Dismissal without leave to amend is improper unless it is clear, upon de novo review, that the complaint could not be saved by any amendment." *Thinket Ink Info Res., Inc. v. Sun Microsystems, Inc.*, 368 F.3d 1053, 1061 (9th Cir. 2004).

But a "district court does not err in denying leave to amend where the amendment would be futile." Id. (internal quotation marks omitted). An amendment is futile when "no set of facts can be proved under the amendment to the pleadings that would constitute a valid and sufficient claim or defense." *Miller v. Rykoff-Sexton, Inc.*, 845 F.2d 209, 214 (9th Cir. 1988). We find no abuse of discretion.

First, Plaintiffs cannot satisfy the requirements of standing by adding events that have occurred after the Shell Egg Laws took effect. "[S]tanding is determined as of the commencement of litigation." *Yamada v. Snipes*, 786 F.3d 1182, 1203 (9th Cir.), cert. denied, 136 S. Ct. 569, 193 L. Ed. 2d 428 (2015) (internal quotation marks omitted); accord *D'Lil v. Best W. Encina Lodge & Suites*, 538 F.3d 1031, 1036 (9th Cir. 2008). Plaintiffs brought this action before the Shell Egg laws took effect. Accordingly, later developments cannot save the complaint.

Second, Plaintiffs argue that certain allegations were available when the complaint was filed and that they should be allowed to include them now. In particular, Plaintiffs wish to allege that eggs are an important, affordable source of protein with which the Shell Egg Laws threaten to interfere, and that the threat of increased egg prices affects not just egg farmers, but also "grocers, bakers, and restaurant owners." But Plaintiffs also allege that the price of eggs might drop. Again, as discussed above, the contingent and uncertain nature of the alternatives available to plead when this complaint was filed are inadequate to support Article III standing.

In short, Plaintiffs would be unable to assert *parens patriae* standing in an amended complaint. The district court did not err by denying leave to amend.

C. Dismissal With Prejudice

Finally, Plaintiffs argue that, because the district court dismissed the complaint for lack of subject matter jurisdiction, the dismissal should have been without prejudice. "We review for abuse of discretion a district court's decision to dismiss with prejudice." *Okwu v. McKim*, 682 F.3d 841, 844 (9th Cir. 2012).

> In general, dismissal for lack of subject matter jurisdiction is without prejudice. *See Kelly v. Fleetwood Enters., Inc.*, 377 F.3d 1034, 1036 (9th Cir. 2004)....As a result, the complaint should have been dismissed without prejudice. *See City of Oakland v. Hotels.com LP*, 572 F.3d 958, 962 (9th Cir. 2009) (affirming dismissal but remanding to dismiss without prejudice); *Kelly*, 377 F.3d at 1040 (affirming with instructions to enter order of dismissal without prejudice).
>
> The judgment of the district court is AFFIRMED and the case is REMANDED with instructions to dismiss this action without prejudice.

Discussion

A related case also came before the Ninth Circuit in 2021 and the petitioners (unsuccessfully) sought *certiorari* for reversal to the United States Supreme Court. *See National Pork Producers Council v. Ross*, 6 F.4th 1021 (2021). The case involved a challenge to Proposition 12, approved by the California electorate in 2018, and requiring all pork sold in the state must be born to pig mothers who are afforded at least 24 square feet of space (sufficient to allow them to lie down and turn around). The principles here are similar to the egg case above. And the result upheld the production condition notwithstanding additional costs incurred from production in other states where that restriction does not apply.

Note that other examples of regulatory policies that can potentially impede interstate commerce include: (a) a requirement from Arizona that "milk" must include additional Vitamin additives in order to be so labelled; (b) a requirement in Madison, Wisconsin that certain dairy products produced in other states where its own regulators cannot directly inspect production can be barred (see *Dean Milk Co. v. City of Madison*, 340 U.S. 349 (1951)); (c) a maximum rate for rail carriage of grain through one state (*e.g.*, Nebraska) is imposed that is lower than the normal charge in neighboring states where the trains must also traverse—resulting in a competitive price disadvantage for farmers producing in those other states (with higher rail costs thusly imposed); and (d) a requirement that no truck may carry more than one trailer on a highway in the state of Wisconsin. These examples do not enjoy the state deference of the egg or pork cases and tend to have either dubious bona fide justification or deal more directly with the actual transport between states—where a burden on interstate commerce from the actions of a single state are more likely to apply.

1ST AMENDMENT FREE SPEECH

Regulatory Use of Self-serving Labels

Moore v. California State Bd. of Accountancy

2 Cal. 4th 999 (1992)

Opinion by: BAXTER, J.

We granted review in this case to determine whether persons unlicensed by the State Board of Accountancy (Board), the public agency charged with administering the regulatory scheme governing the profession of public accountancy in California (Bus. & Prof. Code,

§ 5000 1 et seq., commonly known as the Accountancy Act), may hold themselves out to the public as "accountants," or as persons qualified and lawfully able to offer "accounting" services for compensation.

As will be shown, under California's regulatory scheme, accounting activities falling within the statutory definition of the "practice of public accountancy" are reserved to the Board's licensees. "Public accountancy" is broadly defined; a person is deemed to be practicing public accountancy, and is thus subject to the jurisdiction and licensing requirements of the Board, if the person does any of the following: "[h]olds himself or herself out to the public in any manner as one skilled in the knowledge, science and practice of accounting, and as qualified and ready to render professional service therein as a public accountant for compensation" (§ 5051, subd. (a), italics added); "[o]ffers to prospective clients to perform for compensation...professional services that involve or require an audit, examination, verification, investigation, certification, presentation, or review, of financial transactions and accounting records" (id., subd. (c)); or "[i]n general or as an incident to that work, renders professional services to clients for compensation in any or all matters relating to accounting procedure and to the recording, presentation, or certification of financial information or data" (id., subd. (e), italics added).

In contrast, unlicensed persons may offer to the public only a limited category of basic accounting services when performed "as a part of bookkeeping operations." (§ 5051, subd. (f), 5052.) Furthermore, they may not assume or use any title or designation "likely to be confused" with the two official titles reserved for licensed accountants: "certified public accountant" and "public accountant." (§ 5058.) Exercising the rulemaking authority granted to it in the Accountancy Act, the Board has adopted a regulation which prohibits the use of either the title "accountant" or the description of services offered as "accounting" by an unlicensed person. (Cal. Code Regs., tit. 16, § 2 [hereafter Regulation 2].) Appellants contend that in so doing the Board exceeded its authority, that the regulation is therefore invalid, and that even if the regulation is permissible under section 5058, the restriction denies them rights under the First Amendment to the United States Constitution.

***

The Board has determined that the terms "accountant" and "accounting" are misleading to members of the public, many of whom believe that a person who uses these terms must be licensed. For the reasons explained below, we conclude that the adoption and enforcement of Regulation 2 is a proper exercise of the Board's authority to administer the Accountancy Act, and, in particular, section 5058. We further conclude, however, that the regulatory scheme may constitutionally ban only those uses of the terms "accountant" and "accounting" that may potentially mislead the public regarding the user's licensee or nonlicensee status. Where the terms are used in conjunction with a modifier or modifiers that serve to dispel any possibility of confusion--for example, an express disclaimer stating that the "accounting" services being offered do not require a state license--their use in such a context may not be constitutionally enjoined.

I

FACTS AND PROCEDURAL BACKGROUND

In 1986, appellants Bonnie Moore, an unlicensed individual, Accounting Center, a California corporation of which Moore is president, and the California Association of Independent Accountants (CAIA), a nonprofit membership organization affiliated with the National Society of Public Accountants (NSPA), collectively filed suit against respondent Board for declaratory relief and a permanent injunction. (Code Civ. Proc., § 1060.) The complaint alleged that Moore had received a letter from the Board ordering her and Accounting Center to cease and desist from using the terms "accountant" and "accounting" in referring to herself, the business of Accounting Center, or the services she offered to the public. The complaint further alleged that resolution of the question of whether the Board may constitutionally prohibit use of generic terms such as "accountant" and "accounting" by unlicensed individuals will affect thousands of other unlicensed persons practicing throughout the state of California. At that time approximately 700 such individuals were members of CAIA, and the officers and directors of CAIA joined the lawsuit to challenge the Board's actions on behalf of CAIA's membership. The complaint sought a declaratory judgment that the Board may not constitutionally enjoin or prohibit appellants or members of CAIA from using the terms "accountant" and "accounting" in referring to unlicensed persons or the services rendered by them, and a permanent injunction ordering the Board to cease all enforcement actions against the use of those terms.

After its demurrer to the complaint was overruled, respondent Board filed an answer and a cross-complaint for injunctive relief against the named plaintiffs plus 2,000 Doe defendants. Does 1 through 1,000 were designated California members of CAIA, and Does 1,001 through 2,000 were designated as individuals who "have transacted and continue to transact business in the County of San Francisco and elsewhere in the State of California." The cross-complaint alleged that the cross-defendants were engaged in the practice of public accountancy and of tax preparation within California, yet were not licensed as public accountants or certified public accountants. The first amended cross-complaint prayed in part that cross- defendants be enjoined from using the words "accountant," "accounting," or "accounting services" in referring to themselves or their businesses, or representing themselves as "accountants" in any other manner which would tend to mislead or confuse the public.

During the ensuing court trial, evidence was introduced establishing that Moore possesses a college degree with a major in accounting. She has never taken the examination to become a certified public accountant (CPA), nor is she interested in doing so. Respondent Board concedes she meets the educational eligibility requirements for the CPA examination, but not the experience requirement for licensure. As a practical matter, in order to satisfy the latter requirement--two years of public accounting experience under the supervision of a licensed accountant (§ 5081.1, 5083)--she would have to secure employment with a CPA for at least two years.

Accounting Center primarily designs and installs basic accounting systems for small business clients. Once the system is set up, bookkeepers service the accounts, supervised by degreed accountants. The firm prepares monthly financial statements and long-range financial projections for its clients in furtherance of budgetary control and sound financial management practices. In a generic sense, the firm "audits" its client's books for internal purposes, although it does not produce formal signed audits. Moore conceded she is not qualified to perform the type of formal audits that a CPA does, nor is she qualified to perform services that require a certification of financial statements.

Moore uses the terms "accountant" and "accounting" to describe herself and her services in 90 percent of her advertising. She refers to her business on building directories, in the telephone directory, and in radio and television advertising as "Accounting Center."

***

In January 1987, after respondent Board had unsuccessfully demurred to appellants' complaint and filed its answer, the Board, through its counsel, the Office of the California Attorney General, contacted the Field Research Corporation, an independent opinion research firm that conducts the California Poll, an ongoing survey of Californians that attempts to measure public attitudes on various unrelated topics. All results from the polls are made public. The Attorney General sought to determine the public's perception of whether a person is licensed by the State of California when that person holds himself or herself out as an “accountant” ready and able to offer “accounting services.” To this end, the following two questions were included in the April 1987 California Poll: (1) “Do you think that persons who refer to themselves as accountants in advertising to the public are required to be licensed by the State of California?,” and (2) “Do you think persons who advertise accounting services to the public are required to be licensed by the State of California to offer such services?”

The results of the poll with respect to the first question indicated that 55 percent of those surveyed believed that a person who advertised as an “accountant” had to be licensed, 26 percent did not believe a license was required, and 19 percent did not know. The results of the second question indicated that 53 percent believed that a person who advertised “accounting services” to the public was required to be licensed by the state, 29 percent did not believe a license was required, and 18 percent did not know.

***

At the completion of trial, the court entered judgment denying relief to appellants, and granting respondent Board’s request for a permanent injunction enjoining appellants from “[u]sing the words ‘accountant,’ ‘accounting,’ or ‘accounting services’ in referring to themselves, their businesses or their services in the context of holding themselves out to the public in the offering or rendering of professional services, or representing themselves as ‘accountants’ in any other manner which would tend to mislead or confuse the public.”

This appeal followed. The Court of Appeal, relying in part on the only California case to have considered whether use of the terms at issue here may be banned--*People v. Hill* (1977) 66 Cal.App.3d 320 [136 Cal.Rptr. 30] (*Hill*)--concluded that statutory scheme prohibited an unlicensed person from holding himself or herself out to the public as an “accountant,” or as a person otherwise qualified to provide “accounting services” for compensation. Crediting the California Poll survey evidence introduced by respondent Board, the Court of Appeal found that “the terms ‘accountant’ and ‘accounting,’ standing alone, are misleading to the public and may not be utilized by unlicensed persons."

***

II

At the threshold, it is undisputed that the Legislature, in the public interest and in furtherance of the general welfare, is empowered to regulate the profession of public accountancy. (See, e.g., 1 Am.Jur.2d, Accountants (1962) § 2.) California's first entry into the regulation of the profession came in 1901, when the Legislature established a five- member State Board of Accountancy, and vested in it the power to examine applicants, and grant certificates of qualification to practice public accountancy. (Stats. 1901, ch. 213, p. 645.) The regulatory scheme underwent a major revision in 1945, and the Board was expanded to seven members. (Stats. 1945, ch. 1353, § 2, pp. 2529-2545.) Presently, the Board consists of 12 members, 8 of them state-licensed accountants, and 4 public members. (§ 5000.) It is empowered, among other things, to adopt regulations as may be reasonably necessary to administer the Accountancy Act (§ 5010), and to adopt rules of professional conduct governing its licensees. (§ 5018.) The Board is also authorized to seek injunctions against persons who have engaged or are about to engage in conduct or practices which violate the Accountancy Act. (§ 5122.)

Under the present California licensing scheme, certified public accountants must satisfy rigorous educational, experience, and examination requirements prior to obtaining licensure. Applicants must take and pass a written examination in accounting theory and practice, auditing, commercial law as affecting accountancy, and other related subjects. (§ 5082.) They may be denied a license (or a licensee's license may be suspended or revoked, or renewal of a license refused) if they have committed certain crimes, committed an act of fraud or dishonesty, or done other specified acts which would be cause for discipline by the Board. (§ 480, 5081, 5100.) The Board's licensees must adhere to professional standards and continuing education requirements in order to maintain licensure; noncompliance with such professional standards or other licensure requirements can lead to suspension or revocation of, or refusal to renew, a license. (§ 5100.)

In contrast, the Board's enforcement activities against unlicensed persons engaged in the practice of public accountancy are limited to responding to those consumer complaints over which it has jurisdiction. It has jurisdiction over complaints involving unlicensed persons holding themselves out to the public as licensed accountants. It has no jurisdiction over complaints involving the quality of "accounting" work or services performed by nonlicensees. Section 5050 provides that "No person shall engage in the practice of public accountancy in this State unless such person is the holder of a valid permit to practice public accountancy issued by the board[.]" According to the testimony of the executive officer of the Board, violators of section 5050 may be referred to the Division of Investigation, a state agency, for investigation and possible referral to the local district attorney's office for civil or criminal prosecution, but the Board itself is not empowered to "prosecute" unlicensed persons for the unlawful practice of public accountancy.

Accordingly, for purposes of our analysis herein, the term "unlicensed person" includes any person who does not hold a valid permit issued by the Board to practice public accountancy. It includes persons, like appellant Bonnie Moore, who, the Board concedes, can meet the educational eligibility requirements for the CPA examination but not the experience requirement for licensure. It would also include persons without any formal educational background or experience in the accounting profession whatsoever, who nonetheless attempt to seek compensation from members of the public for the rendering of "accounting" services. And it would include a former Board licensee who, due to a breach of professional ethics or the commission of a crime or act of fraud or dishonesty, has had his or her license revoked by the Board. All such persons, although unlicensed, may nonetheless seek to offer to the public for compensation a limited category of basic accounting services "*as a part of bookkeeping operations.*" (§ 5051, subd. (f), italics added; § 5052.)...

With this background in mind, we turn to the principal statute at issue in this case, section 5058. Section 5058 provides, in pertinent part: "No person or partnership shall assume or use the title or designation 'chartered accountant,' 'certified accountant,' 'enrolled accountant, 'registered accountant' or 'licensed accountant,' or any other title or designation likely to be confused with 'certified public accountant' or 'public accountant,' or any of the abbreviations 'C.A.,' 'E.A.,' 'R.A.,' or 'L.A.,' or similar abbreviations likely to be confused with 'C.P.A.' or 'P.A.'" ....

Appellants urge us to invoke the principle of statutory construction known by the Latin names ejusdem generis and noscitur a sociis, that when a statute contains a list or catalogue of items, a court should determine the meaning of each by reference to the others, giving preference to an interpretation that uniformly treats items similar in nature and scope. (See *People v. Rogers* (1971) 5 Cal.3d 129, 142 [95 Cal.Rptr. 601, 486 P.2d 129] [conc. & dis. opn. of Mosk, J.]; *Armenta v. Churchill* (1954) 42 Cal.2d 448, 454 [267 P.2d 303]; *People v. Thomas* (1945) 25 Cal.2d 880, 899-900 [156 P.2d 7]; *Treasure I.C. Co. v. St. Bd. Of Equal.* (1941) 19 Cal.2d 181, 188 [120 P.2d 1]; see generally, 2A Sutherland, Statutory Construction (4th ed. 1984) § 47.16-47.22, pp. 161-193.) In accordance with this principle of construction, a court will adopt a restrictive meaning of a listed item if acceptance of a more expansive meaning would make other items in the list unnecessary or redundant, or would otherwise make the item markedly dissimilar to the other items in the list. (See *Harris v. Capital Growth Investors XIV* (1991) 52 Cal.3d 1142, 1159-1160 [278 Cal.Rptr. 614, 805 P.2d 873]; *Peralta Community College Dist. v. Fair Employment & Housing Com.* (1990) 52 Cal.3d 40, 50 [276 Cal.Rptr. 114, 801 P.2d 357]; [*Dyna-Med, Inc. v. Fair Employment & Housing Com.* (1987) 43 Cal.3d 1379, 1390-1391 [241 Cal.Rptr. 67, 743 P.2d 1323].)

Appellants point to the fact that section 5058 contains a list of titles that, the Legislature has determined, are designations "likely to be confused" with the two titles reserved to Board-licensed accountants: "certified public accountant" and "public accountant." Each of the five expressly prohibited titles is comprised of the generic term "accountant" coupled with a modifier. Appellants urge that if the Legislature deemed the unadorned generic term "accountant" a title "likely to be confused" by the public with the two official designations denoting licensure, its unmodified use would have been expressly prohibited in section 5058.

Respondent urges us to instead focus on section 5058's catchall language prohibiting an unlicensed person's use of "any other title or designation likely to be confused with [the two official terms denoting licensure]…." The generic terms "accountant" and "accounting" services are two such confusing designations, argues respondent, and thus the statute should be construed to include the use of the unadorned generic terms within the statutory ban.

In construing a statute a court's objective is to ascertain and effectuate the underlying legislative intent. (*People v. Woodhead* (1987) 43 Cal.3d 1002, 1007 [239 Cal.Rptr. 656, 741 P.2d 154].) This fundamental rule overrides the ejusdem generis doctrine, just as it would any maxim of jurisprudence, if application of the doctrine or maxim would frustrate the intent underlying the statute. (Civ. Code, § 3509; *Larcher v. Wanless* (1976) 18 Cal.3d 646, 658 [135 Cal.Rptr. 75, 557 P.2d 507]; *Irwin v. City of Manhattan Beach* (1966) 65 Cal.2d 13, 21 [51 Cal.Rptr. 881, 415 P.2d 769]; *Matter of Societe Francaise etc.* (1899) 123 Cal. 525, 530-531 [56 P. 458, 56 P. 787]; *Worthington v. Unemployment Ins. Appeals Bd.* (1976) 64 Cal.App.3d 384, 388 [134 Cal.Rptr. 507]; *Coleman v. City of Oakland* (1930) 110 Cal.App. 715 [295 P. 59].)

We are not persuaded that the approach of either party is consistent with the legislative intent reflected in section 5058. Application of the doctrine of *ejusdem generis* would be inappropriate in this context. The Legislature used all-encompassing language in banning not only the expressly identified designations but also "any other title or designation that is likely to be confused with 'certified public accountant or 'public accountant.'" (§ 5058, italics added.) Appellants' construction of section 5058 would require us to assume that notwithstanding that broad prohibition of potentially confusing titles, use of the unmodified terms "accountant" and "accounting" was permissible regardless of whether that use was then or proved at some later date to be "likely confused with" licensed status, i.e., that use of those terms was to be permitted no matter how misleading they were. That construction cannot be reconciled with the clear purpose of the statute--ensuring that members of the public who seek the services of a licensed accountant are not misled regarding the status of the person who provides accounting services.

We agree with appellants, however, that section 5058 does not itself expressly prohibit the use of the unmodified terms "accountant" and "accounting." To read the section in that manner would render the identification of the specific terms which were banned surplusage, since the ban on "any…title or designation likely to be confused with 'certified public accountant' or 'public accountant' "encompasses those terms. The Legislature therefore had some other purpose for both identifying specific terms that are not to be used and banning other potentially misleading designations that it did not identify. Since that purpose could not have been to permit the use of misleading terms, it is reasonable to conclude that when the statute was amended in 1945 the Legislature was aware that the titles or designations it specifically identified were or had been in use and were misleading. Recognizing that other terms it had not then identified as misleading could be so, or might become misleading in the future, however, the Legislature made provision for that possibility by prohibiting the use of "any" misleading term.

Inasmuch as enforcement of the provisions of the Accountancy Act, including section 5058, is entrusted to the Board, it seems apparent that the Legislature delegated to the Board the authority to determine whether a title or designation not identified in the statute is likely to confuse or mislead the public. Since the Board was also authorized to seek an injunction against the use of such terms, its authority to "adopt, repeal, or amend such regulations as may be reasonably necessary and expedient for the…administration of [the Accountancy Act]" (§ 5010) includes the power to identify by regulation those terms which it finds are "likely to be confused with 'certified public accountant' or 'public accountant,' " the use of which may be enjoined under the broad prohibition of section 5058. To conclude otherwise would contravene the intent and purpose behind the statute.

In 1948, the Board exercised its authority to identify other potentially misleading designations that were subject to the catchall prohibition of what was then section 5065 (the predecessor statute to § 5058, identical in all respects relevant here) by the adoption of Regulation 2, which provides:

> "§ 2 Confusing Titles
>
> "The following are titles or designations likely to be confused with the titles Certified Public Accountant and Public Accountant within the meaning of Section 5058 of the Business and Professions Code:
>
> "(a) 'Accountant,' 'auditor,' 'accounting,' or 'auditing,' when used either singly or collectively or in conjunction with other titles.
>
> "(b) Any other titles or designations which imply that the individual is engaged in the practice of public accountancy."

In considering whether Regulation 2 is a valid exercise of the Board's power to adopt regulations necessary for the administration of the Accountancy Act, and in particular section 5058,..."our task is to inquire into the legality of the...regulation, not its wisdom. (*Morris v. Williams* (1967) 67 Cal.2d 733, 737 [63 Cal.Rptr. 689, 433 P.2d 697].)...[I]n reviewing the legality of a regulation adopted pursuant to a delegation of legislative power, the judicial function is limited to determining whether the regulation (1) is 'within the scope of the authority conferred' (Gov. Code, [former] § 11373 [see current Gov. Code § 11342.1]) and (2) is 'reasonably necessary to effectuate the purpose of the statute' (Gov. Code, [former] § 11374 [see current Gov. Code § 11342.2]). [Fn. omitted.] Moreover, 'these issues do not present a matter for the independent judgment of an appellate tribunal; rather, both come to this court freighted with the strong presumption of regularity accorded administrative rules and regulations.' (*Ralphs Grocery Co. v. Reimel* (1968) 69 Cal.2d 172, 175 [70 Cal.Rptr. 407, 444 P.2d 79].) And in considering whether the regulation is 'reasonably necessary' under the foregoing standards, the court will defer to the agency's expertise and will not 'superimpose its own policy judgment upon the agency in the absence of an arbitrary and capricious decision.' (*Pitts v. Perluss* (1962) 58 Cal.2d 824, 832 [27 Cal.Rptr. 19, 377 P.2d 83].)" (*Agricultural Labor Relations Bd. v. Superior Court* (1976) 16 Cal.3d 392, 411 [128 Cal.Rptr. 183, 546 P.2d 687].)

The promulgation of Regulation 2, which implements the catchall language of section 5058, appears well within the authority conferred on the Board by the Legislature to "adopt...such regulations as may be reasonably necessary and expedient for the...administration of [the Accountancy Act]." (§ 5010.) Furthermore, Regulation 2's declaration--that the generic terms "accountant" and "accounting" are themselves titles or designations likely to be confused with "certified public accountant" and "public accountant"--appears reasonably necessary to effectuate the purpose and intent behind section 5058: the protection of the public from the unlicensed practice of public accountancy through the elimination of any likelihood of confusion from the use of potentially misleading or confusing titles. The results of the California Poll survey evidence introduced in this case tend to bear this out.

***

In a somewhat analogous context--attorney advertising--it has been observed that special considerations apply to advertising by professionals: "[I]t has been noted that special considerations apply to advertising by lawyers because they 'do not dispense standardized products; they render professional services of almost infinite variety and nature, with the consequent enhanced possibility for confusion and deception if they were to undertake certain kinds of advertising.' (*Va. Pharmacy Board. v. Va. Consumer Council* (1976) 425 U.S. 748, 773, fn. 25 [48 L.Ed.2d 346, 365, 96 S.Ct. 1817].) This court analyzed the above quoted language in *Jacoby v. State Bar* (1977) 19 Cal.3d 359 [138 Cal.Rptr. 77, 562 P.2d 1326, 4 A.L.R.4th 273]. Writing for the court, Justice Mosk explained that the footnote 'stands for the proposition that while the First Amendment values in commercial advertising remain constant regardless of the profession involved, the governmental regulatory interest may vary from profession to profession.' (*Id.*, at p. 377.)" (*Leoni v. State Bar* (1985) 39 Cal.3d 609, 625 [217 Cal.Rptr. 423, 704 P.2d 183].)

As the court in *Texas State Board of Public Accountancy v. Fulcher* (Tex.Civ.App. 1974) 515 S.W.2d 950 observed nearly two decades ago: "[T]he need to protect the public against fraud, deception [and] the consequences of ignorance or incompetence in the practice of most professions makes regulation necessary. The state may exact the requisite degree of skill and learning in professions which affect the public, or at least a substantial portion of the public, such as the practice of law, medicine, engineering, dentistry, and many others. The [accountancy] Act before us recognizes public accountancy as one of such professions. Public accountancy now embraces many intricate and technical matters dealing with many kinds of tax laws, unfair trade practices, rate regulations, stock exchange regulations, reports required by many governmental agencies, financial statements and the like." (*Id.*, at pp. 954-955.)

These observations apply with even more force to the practice of the profession of public accountancy in the 1990's. We conclude that the Board's determination, embodied in Regulation 2, that the terms "accountant" and "accounting" are titles or designations likely to be confused with the official titles denoting licensure, is consistent with the intent and purpose behind section 5058 and the provisions of the related statutes, and is "reasonably necessary" to effectuate the purpose and intent underlying the legislation. (*Pitts v. Perluss* (1962) 58 Cal.2d 824, 832 [27 Cal.Rptr. 19, 377 P.2d 83].)

As further evidence that Regulation 2 is consistent with the legislative intent behind section 5058, it is significant that in the nearly half a century since the Board adopted the regulation, shortly after enactment of the statutory provision, the Legislature has not sought to amend section 5058 to defeat the Board's interpretation of the scope of its authority under section 5058. Although the Legislature twice amended section 5058, first in 1959 (Stats. 1959, ch. 310, § 42, p. 2228) and again in 1979 (Stats. 1979, ch. 25, § 1, p. 70), the substantive provisions with which we are here concerned have remained unchanged in the 44 years since the Board adopted Regulation 2.

In this regard, a presumption that the Legislature is aware of an administrative construction of a statute should be applied if the agency's interpretation of the statutory provisions is of such longstanding duration that the Legislature may be presumed to know of it. (*Robinson v. Fair Employment & Housing Com.* (1992) 2 Cal.4th 226, 235, fn. 7 [5 Cal.Rptr. 782, 825 P.2d 767]; *El Dorado Oil Works v. McColgan* (1950) 34 Cal.2d 731, 739 [215 P.2d 4].)

Such a presumption should also be applied on a showing that the construction or practice of the agency has been made known to the Legislature. (*Robinson v. Fair Employment & Housing Com., supra,* 2 Cal.4th at p. 235, fn. 7; *Pacific Greyhound Lines v. Johnson* (1942) 54 Cal.App.2d 297, 303 [129 P.2d 32].) To this end we note that in 1965, an assemblyman from the Third Assembly District requested an opinion from the California Attorney General as to whether a member of the public, who is not licensed as a certified public accountant or public accountant to practice accounting in California, is in violation of the Accountancy Act when he or she uses the word "accounting" on a building directory or on an office door. The Attorney General's conclusion was that: "The use of the word 'accounting' on a building directory and an office door by an unlicensed individual is a representation to the public that such individual is skilled in accounting and that the user is qualified and ready to perform professional services. Such a representation by an unlicensed individual is in violation of the Accountancy Act …." (46 Ops.Cal.Atty.Gen. 140, 141 (1965).)

Finally, the Legislature may also be presumed to have been aware of the decision filed in 1977 in *Hill, supra,* 66 Cal.App.3d 320, the only published California case to have addressed the right of an unlicensed person to use the terms in issue here. The *Hill* court concluded that use of a business name. "A-Accounting--Jack M. Hill & Co." violated section 5050, and affirmed an order granting a preliminary injunction against use of the words "accountant" and "accounting" by the defendant in conjunction with his business title.

Section 5050 prohibits the practice of public accountancy by an unlicensed person. The *Hill* court reasoned that by use of the name in issue the defendant was holding himself out to the public as being engaged in the provision of professional accounting services. That conduct constituted the practice of public accountancy as defined in section 5051. "[T]he use of the title 'A-Accounting' like the use of the word 'accounting' on the building directory and office door can only be interpreted to mean that he is representing to the public that he is skilled in the practice of accounting and is qualified and ready to provide accounting services to the public, a representation that an unlicensed person is prohibited from doing." (*Hill, supra*, 66 Cal.App.3d at 329.)

The *Hill* court recognized that an unlicensed person is permitted by law to offer certain basic accounting services to the public for compensation when offered in connection with bookkeeping operations (see § 5051, subd. (f), 5052), but concluded nonetheless that because the public may be misled concerning whether such a person is licensed when he or she uses the title "accountant" or the term "accounting services," use of those terms could be enjoined under the Accountancy Act. (66 Cal.App.3d at pp. 328–330.)...While the *Hill* court relied on sections 5050 and 5051, rather than section 5058 and Regulation 2 in upholding the injunction against use of the title "accountant" and term "accounting" by an unlicensed person in describing services offered to the public, the Legislature is presumed to be aware of that decision and to have acquiesced in the result, one identical to the result under Regulation 2 and the trial court ruling in this case.

In sum, we conclude that by inclusion of the catchall language in section 5058, the Legislature plainly intended that the enumerated list of five prohibited titles not be deemed an exclusive one. The Board's determination, embodied in Regulation 2, that the generic terms "accountant" and "accounting" fall within the legislatively defined class of titles or designations "likely to confuse the public," appears reasonably necessary to effectuate the purpose and intent underlying section 5058. Pursuant to section 5010, Regulation 2 is well within the scope of the rulemaking authority conferred upon the

Board to "adopt…such regulations as may be reasonably necessary…for the…administration of [the Accountancy Act]." Moreover, for the reasons discussed, the Legislature may also be presumed to have acquiesced in the Board's long-standing interpretation of section 5058. The regulatory scheme thus validly prohibits unlicensed persons from using the generic terms "accountant" or "accounting" standing alone, or in combination with other words that comprise a title or designation "likely to be confused" with the official titles reserved to the Board's licensees….

III

The Court of Appeal in this case reached substantially the same conclusion in construing the scope of section 5058,…and went on to hold: "The rulings by the *United States Supreme Court in Virginia Pharmacy* [*Va. Pharmacy Board. v. Va. Consumer Council* (1975) 425 U.S. 748 (48 L.Ed.2d 346, 365, 96 S.Ct. 1817)] and *Bates [v. State Bar of Arizona* (1977) 433 U.S. 350 (53 L.Ed.2d 810, 97 S.Ct. 2691)] make it clear that to satisfy the First Amendment, we must permit the use of [the generic terms 'accountant' and 'accounting'] if they are qualified by a warning or disclaimer that avoids their misleading impact."

Respondent urges that section 5058, as interpreted by the Board in Regulation 2, prohibits any and all use of the generic terms "accountant" and "accounting" by unlicensed persons. As stated in respondent's brief on the merits, "[The Court of Appeal] decision did not go far enough by failing to unqualifiedly affirm the state's prohibition of the misleading terms in question rather than permitting unlicensed persons to use disclaimer language qualifying such terms." We disagree.

The First Amendment cases do not question the authority of the state to regulate misleading advertising….

***

The high court's most recent commercial speech decisions have consistently applied the holding of I*n re R. M. J., supra. Thus, in Peel v. Attorney Disciplinary Comm'n of Ill.* (1990) 496 U.S. 91 [110 L.Ed.2d 83, 110 S.Ct. 2281], it was held that an attorney holding a

"Certificate in Civil Trial Advocacy" from the "National Board of Trial Advocacy" could not be enjoined by the State of Illinois, which had no similar officially sanctioned certification program of its own, from advertising on his letterhead the truthful fact of his "certification" by that organization. Following its decisions in *Bates v. State Bar of Arizona, supra*, 433 U.S. 350, and *In re R. M. J., supra*, 455 U.S. 191, the court concluded that Attorney Peel's letterhead was entitled to First Amendment protection since the facts stated thereon were "true and verifiable." (496 U.S. at p. 100 [110 L.Ed.2d at p. 94, 110 S.Ct. at p. 2288].)

The high court in Peel explained further: "Even if we assume that petitioner's letterhead may be potentially misleading to some consumers, that potential does not satisfy the State's heavy burden of justifying a categorical prohibition against the dissemination of accurate factual information to the public. *In re R. M. J.*, [*supra*,] 455 U.S., at 203." (*Peel v. Attorney Disciplinary Comm'n of Ill., supra*, 496 U.S. at p. 109 [110 L.Ed.2d at p. 100, 110 S.Ct. at p. 2292].) The court went on to conclude:

> "To the extent that potentially misleading statements of private certification or specialization could confuse consumers, a State might consider screening certifying organizations or requiring a disclaimer about the certifying organization or the standards of a specialty. *In re R. M. J.*, [*supra*,] 455 U.S., at 201-203. A State may not, however, completely ban statements that are not actually or inherently misleading…." (*Peel v. Attorney Disciplinary Comm'n of Ill., supra*, 496 U.S. at p. 110, fn. omitted [110 L.Ed.2d at pp. 100-101, 110 S.Ct. at pp. 2292- 2293]; accord *Bates v. State Bar of Arizona, supra*, 433 U.S. at p. 384 [53 L.Ed.2d at p. 836]; *Va. Pharmacy Board. v. Va. Consumer Council, supra*, 425 U.S. 748, 771-772 [48 L.Ed.2d 346, 363-365].),,,

We believe the Maryland Court of Appeals in *Comprehensive, etc. v. Maryland State Bd.* (1979) 284 Md. 474 [397 A.2d 1019, 4 A.L.R.4th 1188], correctly applied the commercial speech principles first announced by the high court in *Va. Pharmacy Board. v. Va. Consumer Council, supra*, 425 U.S. 748, and *Bates v.*

State Bar of Arizona, supra, 433 U.S. 350, to the arena of state regulation of the profession of accountancy. In that case, the Comprehensive Accountancy Service Company, which did not hold an enrollment certificate to practice public accounting in Maryland, challenged a Maryland statute that provided no person, partnership or corporation not holding an enrollment certificate "'shall practice or hold himself or itself out to the public as "accountant" or "auditor" in connection with his own or any other name, nor describe or designate the services offered or performed by him or it as "accounting" or "auditing," with or without any other designation or description ....'" (397 A.2d at p. 1020.) Comprehensive Accounting Service Company argued that Maryland's express statutory ban unconstitutionally abridged its right of free speech because the statute prevented uncertified persons, who were otherwise permitted to perform ordinary accounting work under that state's so-called "bookkeeping exception," from advertising the true nature of their services.

Invoking the rationale of the United States Supreme Court's decisions in *Va. Pharmacy Board. v. Va. Consumer Council, supra,* 425 U.S. 748, and *Bates v. State Bar of Arizona, supra,* 433 U.S. 350, the Comprehensive court concluded that the State of Maryland could not, consistent with the First Amendment, completely suppress the dissemination of truthful information about an entirely lawful business activity. (*Comprehensive, etc. v. Maryland State Bd., supra,* 397 A.2d at pp. 1023–1027.) But the Comprehensive court also acknowledged the high court's recognition in *Va. Pharmacy Board. v. Va. Consumer Council, supra,* and *Bates v. State Bar of Arizona, supra,* that, "in some cases it may be 'appropriate to require that a commercial message appear in such a form, or include such additional information, warning, and disclaimers as are necessary to prevent its being deceptive.'" (397 A.2d, at p. 1025, quoting *Va. Pharmacy Bd. v. Va. Consumer Council, supra,* 425 U.S. at pp. 771-772, fn. 24.)

As the rulings by the United States Supreme Court in *Va. Pharmacy Board. v. Va. Consumer Council,* Bates v. *State Bar of Arizona, In re R. M. J.,* and *Peel v. Attorney Disciplinary Comm'n of Ill.,* all *supra,* make clear, in order to satisfy the First Amendment, appellants must be permitted to use the terms "accountant," "accounting," or "accounting services," if the use of those terms is further qualified by an explanation, disclaimer or warning stating that the advertiser is not licensed by the state, or that the services being offered do not require a state license, thereby eliminating any potential or likelihood of confusion regarding those terms.

In sum, section 5058 may constitutionally ban only those uses of the generic terms "accountant" and "accounting" that stand to potentially mislead the public regarding the user's licensee or nonlicensee status. The evidence in this case supports the long-standing interpretation of section 5058 as including within its ban the unqualified use of those terms as misleading, to the public's detriment. In contrast, where the generic terms are used in conjunction with a modifier or modifiers that serve to dispel any possibility of confusion--for example, an express disclaimer stating that the "accounting" services being offered do not require a state license--their use in such a context may not be constitutionally enjoined.

IV

The trial court's judgment and injunction provided, in pertinent part: "Plaintiffs and Cross- Defendants...who are not licensed as certified public accountants or public accountants are hereby permanently enjoined directly or indirectly from engaging in any of the following acts or practices:...[P] b. Engaging in the practice of public accountancy without prior compliance with the requirements of sections 5000 et seq. of the Business and Professions Code relating to the licensing of accountants; provided, however, nothing herein is intended to enjoin unlicensed persons from preparing compilation reports, review reports, or audit reports, *although such activities are declared to be unlawful.*" (Italics added.)

Appellants contended on appeal that the trial court exceeded its authority in holding the preparation of compilation reports, review reports and audit reports by unlicensed persons to be illegal. The Court of Appeal agreed, explaining that the Board had never alleged *in its cross-complaint* that appellants were engaged in such illegal activities, and presented no evidence at trial to establish that such activities are illegal; hence, the trial court erred in rendering judgment outside the issues raised by the pleadings or at trial. (7 Witkin, Cal. Procedure (3d ed. 1985) Judgment, § 30, p. 472.) In its answer to the petition for review, respondent Board has asked this court to further consider whether the Court of Appeal erred in this regard.

We agree with the conclusions of the Court of Appeal respecting the procedural bar. In any event, the trial court's injunction, as worded, is erroneous; unlicensed persons are permitted to make "audits" and prepare "reports," when such is performed "as a part of bookkeeping operations." (§ 5052; ante, at p. 1011, fn. 3.)

V

The judgment of the Court of Appeal is affirmed.

Lucas, C. J., Panelli, J., and Arabian, J., concurred.

Dissent by: MOSK, J. GEORGE, J.

I dissent. The majority opinion not only violates the intent of the Accountancy Act (Bus. & Prof. Code, § 5000 et seq.), as Justice George's dissent points out, but it also violates the First Amendment of the United States Constitution and article I, section 2(a) of the California Constitution.

On the first of these issues, the State Board of Accountancy (Board) in issuing regulations to effectuate the Accountancy Act (Cal. Code Regs., tit. 16, § 2, hereinafter Regulation 2) prohibits what the statute permits. That is, section 5052 allows nonlicensed persons to offer basic accounting services "in connection with bookkeeping operations." Thus, such persons are authorized by law to perform accounting; it is axiomatic that those who perform accounting are accountants. Even *People v. Hill* (1977) 66 Cal.App.3d 320, 325 [136 Cal.Rptr. 30], a case on which the majority rely, acknowledges that unlicensed persons perform accounting services.

In the face of specific statutory authorization, the Board has in Regulation 2 prohibited unlicensed persons to hold themselves out as accountants or as performing accounting services. The majority uphold this anomalous result by which a truthful representation specifically sanctioned by statute is labelled as misleading to the public.

Indeed, the holding of the majority would render improper a representation by an unlicensed person couched in the specific words of section 5052. The majority hold that an unlicensed person must include an "express disclaimer stating that the 'accounting' services being offered do not require a state license." Thus, such a person who advertises that he or she offers accounting services "in connection with bookkeeping operations," the very language used in section 5052, would run afoul of Regulation 2, according to the majority. An incomprehensible result indeed.

Nor do I agree with the majority's analysis of the purpose of section 5058. They attempt to circumvent application of the doctrine of ejusdem generis by holding that the purpose of the catchall phrase ("any other title or designation that is likely to be confused with 'certified public accountant' or 'public accountant' ") in that provision was to prevent the use of "other terms" the Legislature "had not then identified as misleading…or might become misleading in the future." The Legislature could not have had "accountant" in mind as a misleading term not then identified, since that designation was in common use then, as it is now. If the Legislature had wanted to prohibit use of the term by unlicensed persons, it would have done so.

The majority fail to mention that every jurisdiction but one that has considered the issue before us has held, on either statutory or constitutional grounds, that use of the term "accountant" or "accounting" by unlicensed persons is proper. (*People v. Freedman* (1960) 144 Colo. 438 [356 P.2d 899]; *Florida Accountants Association v. Dandelake* (Fla. 1957) 98 So.2d 323 [70 A.L.R.2d 425]; *Comprehensive, etc. v. Maryland State Bd.* (1979) 284 Md. 474 [397 A.2d 1019]; *State v. Riedell* (1924) 109 Okla. 35 [233 P. 684, 42 A.L.R. 765]; *Burton v. Accountant's Society of Virginia, Inc.* (1973) 213 Va. 642 [194 S.E.2d 684]; *Tom Welch Accounting Service v. Walby* (1965) 29 Wis.2d 123 [138 N.W.2d 139].) Only a single intermediate appellate court in Texas has held to the contrary. (*Fulcher v. Texas State Bd. of Public Acc.* (Tex.Civ.App. 1978) 571 S.W.2d 366; *Texas State Board of Public Accountancy v. Fulcher* (Tex.Civ.App. 1974) 515 S.W.2d 950.)

I have serious doubts also whether the majority's conclusion complies with the First Amendment of the federal Constitution or with the California Constitution. While *Peel v. Attorney Disciplinary Comm'n of Ill.* (1990) 496 U.S. 91, 109–110 [110 L.Ed.2d 83, 100, 110 S.Ct. 2281, 2292–2293], does hold that some form of disclaimer may be required if commercial speech would be misleading without it, it also warns that the state has a "heavy burden of justifying a categorical prohibition against the dissemination of accurate factual information to the public." (*Ibid*; see also *Anderson v. Department of Real Estate* (1979) 93 Cal.App.3d 696 [155 Cal.Rptr. 307].) As we point out above, the unadorned designations "accountant" and "accounting" are accurate as applied to unlicensed persons. The state's interest in preventing misrepresentation can be met by prohibiting persons who are not certified public accountants or public accountants to advertise themselves as such, or to use terms that indicate they have been licensed by the state, rather than insisting upon an express disclaimer, as the majority gratuitously require.

Furthermore, Regulation 2 is itself of questionable validity. In 1948, at the time it was adopted, the Board consisted entirely of licensed accountants. (Stats. 1945, ch. 1353, § 2, p. 2530.) The membership of the Board was broadened in 1961 to include public members (Stats. 1961, ch. 1821, § 39, p. 3877); presently, it consists of 12 persons, 8 of them accounting professionals licensed by the state, and 4 public members. (Bus. & Prof. Code, § 5000, 5001.) None of the members of the Board, according to amicus curiae, the Center for Public Interest Law, is an unlicensed person performing accounting work. Amicus curiae states that a large percentage of the accounting work available is of the type that is performed by both licensed and unlicensed accountants. The Board majority has an obvious pecuniary interest in preventing those without a license from advertising to the public that they are performing accounting services. Regulation 2 furthers that interest. The law has long looked with disfavor on rules adopted by a regulatory body the majority of which consists of members of a profession with a pecuniary stake in restricting the rights of competitors. (*State Board v. Thrift-D-Lux Cleaners* (1953) 40 Cal.2d 436, 449 [254 P.2d 29]; *Allen v. California Board of Barber Examiners* (1972) 25 Cal.App.3d 1014, 1017 [102 Cal.Rptr. 368, 54 A.L.R.3d 910]; *Bayside Timber Co. v. Board of Supervisors* (1971) 20 Cal.App.3d 1, 12-14 [97 Cal.Rptr. 431].)

One additional point needs to be made. Court opinions should not rely on public opinion polls to support their conclusions. Judicial integrity suffers when judges hold a finger up to see which way the wind is blowing. Indeed, I doubt that poll results--which are notoriously inaccurate--should be admitted in evidence. (There may be one exception, however: in change of venue motions in criminal cases, surveys are often used merely to reveal if the crime, the victim and the alleged perpetrator are generally known in the community in which the case is to be tried.)

I would reverse the judgment of the Court of Appeal.

GEORGE, Justice, dissenting.

I respectfully dissent.

The majority affirms a judgment granting a permanent injunction enjoining appellants from referring to themselves as “accountants” or describing the services they offer as “accounting.” Appellants include Bonnie Moore, who possesses a college degree with a major in accounting, and officers and members of the California Association of Independent Accountants, a non- profit membership organization affiliated with the National Society of Public Accountants. I would reverse the judgment.

As explained more fully below, the Legislature has not required that all accountants be licensed. Instead, it has defined a special class of accountants comprised of certified public accountants and public accountants who exclusively are authorized to perform certain types of accountancy and thus must be licensed. Other accountants are prohibited by Business and Professions Code section

5058 and related statutes from using these titles, or similar titles that might be confused with these titles.

The majority acknowledges that unlicensed accountants may perform basic accounting services, but holds that such persons may not call themselves "accountants" or describe the services they offer as "accounting." This holding is not based upon the language of section 5058, which does not expressly prohibit use of the terms "accountant" and "accounting" by unlicensed accountants, but upon a regulation promulgated by the Board of Accountancy (the Board) which prohibits such use of these terms. I disagree with the majority.

I would hold that the Legislature has authorized unlicensed accountants to perform a wide range of accounting services and did not intend to prohibit such persons from accurately referring to themselves as accountants or describing the services they provide as accounting. Because an administrative regulation may not expand the scope of the statute it purports to enforce, the Board lacked the authority to alter this statutory scheme by prohibiting unlicensed accountants from using the terms "accountant" and "accounting." Accordingly, I find it unnecessary to consider the impact of the First Amendment on this issue. (*Ashwander v. Valley Authority* (1936) 297 U.S. 288, 347 [80 L.Ed. 688, 711, 56 S.Ct. 466].)

***

The "general words" in section 5058 form the catchall phrase, upon which the majority relies, prohibiting unlicensed persons from using "any *other* title or designation likely to be confused with 'certified public accountant' or 'public accountant'...." (Italics added.) Considered apart from the context of the statute and the overall scheme of which the statute is a part, this phrase could be construed to prohibit unlicensed accountants from using the term "accountant." But under this construction, which the majority adopts, the enumeration of examples which precede the general words becomes mere surplusage, in violation of the principle of ejusdem generis.

This is so because each of the enumerated examples of titles likely to be confused with the titles C.P.A. and P.A.

is comprised of the term "accountant" coupled with a modifier, as are the titles C.P.A. and P.A. themselves. The principle of *ejusdem generis* leads me to conclude, therefore, that the catchall phrase in section 5058 does not prohibit the use of the title "accountant" standing alone.

***

Had the Legislature meant to prohibit use of the unmodified term "accountant," it simply would have said so. Just as sections 5055 and 5056 expressly prohibit unlicensed accountants from using the titles "certified public accountant" and "public accountant," the Legislature could have added a similar provision expressly prohibiting unlicensed accountants from using the term "accountant" as well. Presumably the Legislature would have done so, had it intended to prohibit such accountants from calling themselves "accountants." "'Where the [Legislature] has demonstrated the ability to make [its] intent clear, it is not the province of this court to imply an intent left unexpressed.' [Citation.]" (*Peralta Community College Dist. v. Fair Employment & Housing Com.* (1990) 52 Cal.3d 40, 50 [276 Cal.Rptr. 114, 801 P.2d 357].)

***

The majority concludes that by including the catchall phrase in section 5058, the Legislature vested the Board with discretion to prohibit unlicensed accountants from using the title "accountant" if the Board determined the public otherwise might be misled. I disagree for two reasons.

First, the Legislature would not have prefaced the catchall phrase in section 5058 with a list of examples, all of which consist of the term "accountant" coupled with a modifier, had it intended to prohibit, or to authorize the Board to prohibit, the use of the term "accountant" standing alone. Had the Legislature intended to vest the Board with unfettered discretion to prohibit the use of any title the Board found to be misleading, including the unadorned term "accountant," it would have used only the catchall phrase employed in section 5058.

By including the examples found in section 5058, the Legislature described the types of titles which might be confused with the titles C.P.A. and P.A. and which the Legislature intended to prohibit unlicensed accountants from using. The title "accountant," standing alone, does not fit this description. To ignore these examples, as does the majority, violates the doctrine of ejusdem generis, a doctrine which merely reflects our common experience with the manner in which language is used.

Second, the Board's decision to prohibit use of the term "accountant," because it may be confused with the terms C.P.A. and P.A., constitutes a significant alteration of the statutory scheme. The Accountancy Act creates a rather subtle distinction between "public accountancy," which only C.P.A.'s and P.A.'s may perform, and other types of accountancy, which unlicensed accountants may perform. If the public finds this distinction confusing and erroneously believes that all accountants must be licensed, it must be left to the Legislature to alleviate this confusion by amending the statutes. Neither the Board nor this court possesses the authority to alter the statutory scheme established by the Accountancy Act, however beneficial such alterations might appear to be.

The majority finds persuasive the results of a public opinion poll, commissioned by the state, which posed the following questions: (1) "Do you think that persons who refer to themselves as accountants in advertising to the public are required to be licensed by the State of California," and (2) "Do you think persons who advertise accounting services to the public are required to be licensed by the State of California to offer such services?" More than half the number of persons queried believed that a license was required in both situations.

***

Section 5058 prohibits unlicensed accountants from using any title that might be confused with the titles C.P.A. and P.A. Contrary to the conclusion reached by the majority, the statute was not intended to prohibit, or to authorize the Board to prohibit, an accountant's use of any term that the public might construe as implying licensure by the state. (Maj. opn., ante, p. 1004.) The importance of this distinction is demonstrated by the following example. The majority concedes that unlicensed accountants may use the term "accountant" if "used in conjunction with a modifier or modifiers that serve to dispel any possibility of confusion...." (Maj. opn., *ante*, pp. 1005, 1024.) Consider an unlicensed accountant who uses the title "accountant" but adds an express disclaimer that he or she is not a C.P.A. or P.A. Such a designation certainly would dispel any possibility that the term "accountant" might be confused with the titles C.P.A. or P.A. and, accordingly, would satisfy even the most stringent interpretation of section 5058. It would not, however, dispel possible confusion concerning whether the accountant was licensed by the state because, according to the poll upon which the majority relies, the public mistakenly believes that all accountants are required to be licensed. It can be seen, therefore, that the public's belief as to whether accountants must be licensed is irrelevant to the determination of the proper scope of section 5058.

Neither the Accountancy Act in general, nor section 5058 in particular, prohibits an unlicensed accountant from using the title "accountant." As the majority recognizes, it is lawful for unlicensed accountants to perform certain types of accounting services. Nothing in the statutory scheme prohibits unlicensed accountants who lawfully provide accounting services from referring to themselves as accountants, nor does anything in the act authorize the Board to prohibit by regulation what the Legislature has permitted by statute.

Accordingly, I would reverse the judgment of the Court of Appeal. I reach this conclusion on the basis of the plain meaning of the words of the statute as interpreted with the aid of settled principles of statutory construction, and in the absence of any clear expression of legislative intent to the contrary, without regard, of course, to whether it would be good public policy for the Legislature to prohibit unlicensed accountants, whatever their level of education and experience, from calling themselves "accountants."

Mosk, J., and Kennard, J., concurred.

Pickup v. Brown

740 F.3d 1208 (2014)

Opinion by: GRABER

The California legislature enacted Senate Bill 1172 to ban state-licensed mental health providers from engaging in "sexual orientation change efforts" ("SOCE") with patients under 18 years of age. Two groups of plaintiffs sought to enjoin enforcement of the law, arguing that SB 1172 violates the First Amendment and infringes on several other constitutional rights.

In *Welch v. Brown*, No. 13-15023, the district court ruled that Plaintiffs were likely to succeed on the merits of their First Amendment claim and that the balance of the other preliminary-injunction factors tipped in their favor; thus, the court granted a preliminary injunction. In *Pickup v. Brown*, No. 12-17681, the district court ruled that Plaintiffs were unlikely to succeed on the merits of any of their claims and denied preliminary relief. The losing parties timely appealed. We address both appeals in this opinion.

***

FACTUAL AND PROCEDURAL BACKGROUND

A. *Sexual Orientation Change Efforts ("SOCE")*

SOCE, sometimes called reparative or conversion therapy, began at a time when the medical and psychological community considered homosexuality an illness. SOCE encompasses a variety of methods, including both aversive and non-aversive treatments, that share the goal of changing an individual's sexual orientation from homosexual to heterosexual....

In 1973, homosexuality was removed from the Diagnostic and Statistical Manual of Mental Disorders. Shortly thereafter the American Psychological Association declared that homosexuality is not an illness. Other major mental health associations followed suit. Subsequently, many mental health providers began questioning and rejecting the efficacy and appropriateness of SOCE therapy. Currently, mainstream mental health professional associations support affirmative therapeutic approaches to sexual orientation that focus on coping with the effects of stress and stigma. But a small number of mental health providers continue to practice, and advocate for, SOCE therapy.

B. *Senate Bill 1172*

Senate Bill 1172 defines SOCE as "any practices by mental health providers…that seek to change an individual's sexual orientation[,]...includ[ing] efforts to change behaviors or gender expressions, or to eliminate or reduce sexual or romantic attractions or feelings toward individuals of the same sex." Cal. Bus. & Prof. Code § 865(b)(1). SOCE, however,

> does not include psychotherapies that: (A) provide acceptance, support, and understanding of clients or the facilitation of clients' coping, social support, and identity exploration and development, including sexual orientation-neutral interventions to prevent or address unlawful conduct or unsafe sexual practices; and (B) do not seek to change sexual orientation. *Id.* § 865(b)(2). A licensed mental health provider's use of SOCE on a patient under 18 years of age is "considered unprofessional conduct," which will subject that provider to "discipline by the licensing entity for that mental health provider." *Id.* § 865.2.

Importantly, SB 1172 does not do any of the following:

- Prevent mental health providers from communicating with the public about SOCE
- Prevent mental health providers from expressing their views to patients, whether children or adults, about SOCE, homosexuality, or any other topic
- Prevent mental health providers from recommending SOCE to patients, whether children or adults
- Prevent mental health providers from administering SOCE to any person who is 18 years of age or older

- Prevent mental health providers from referring minors to unlicensed counselors, such as religious leaders
- Prevent unlicensed providers, such as religious leaders, from administering SOCE to children or adults
- Prevent minors from seeking SOCE from mental health providers in other states

Instead, SB 1172 does just one thing: it requires licensed mental health providers in California who wish to engage in "practices...that seek to change a [minor's] sexual orientation" either to wait until the minor turns 18 or be subject to professional discipline. Thus, SB 1172 regulates the provision of mental treatment, but leaves mental health providers free to discuss or recommend treatment and to express their views on any topic.

The legislature's stated purpose in enacting SB 1172 was to "protect[] the physical and psychological well-being of minors, including lesbian, gay, bisexual, and transgender youth, and [to] protect[] its minors against exposure to serious harms caused by sexual orientation change efforts." 2012 Cal. Legis. Serv. ch. 835, § l(n). The legislature relied on the well-documented, prevailing opinion of the medical and psychological community that SOCE has not been shown to be effective and that it creates a potential risk of serious harm to those who experience it....

In particular, the legislature relied on a report created by a Task Force of the American Psychological Association. That report resulted from a systematic review of the scientific literature on SOCE. Methodological problems with some of the reviewed studies limited the conclusions that the Task Force could draw. Nevertheless, the report concluded that SOCE practitioners have not demonstrated the efficacy of SOCE and that anecdotal reports of harm raise serious concerns about the safety of SOCE.

***

DISCUSSION

A. *Free Speech Rights*

At the outset, we must decide whether the First Amendment requires heightened scrutiny of SB 1172. As explained below, we hold that it does not.

The first step in our analysis is to determine whether SB 1172 is a regulation of conduct or speech. "[W]ords can in some circumstances violate laws directed not against speech but against conduct." *R.A.V. v. City of St. Paul*, 505 U.S. 377, 389, 112 S. Ct. 2538, 120 L.Ed. 2d 305 (1992). "Congress, for example, can prohibit employers from discriminating in hiring on the basis of race. The fact that this will require an employer to take down a sign reading 'White Applicants Only' hardly means that the law should be analyzed as one regulating the employer's speech rather than conduct." *Rumsfeld v. Forum for Academic & Institutional Rights, Inc.* ("*FAIR II*"), 547 U.S. 47,62, 126 S. Ct. 1297, 164 L. Ed. 2d 156 (2006). The Supreme Court has made clear that First Amendment protection does not apply to conduct that is not "inherently expressive." *Id.* at 66. In identifying whether SB 1172 regulates conduct or speech, two of our cases guide our decision: *National Association for the Advancement of Psychoanalysis v. California Board of Psychology ("NAAP")*, 228 F.3d 1043 (9th Cir. 2000), and *Conant v. Walters*, 309 F.3d 629 (9th Cir. 2002).

***

We distill the following relevant principles from NAAP and Conant: (1) doctor-patient communications about medical treatment receive substantial First Amendment protection, but the government has more leeway to regulate the conduct necessary to administering treatment itself; (2) psychotherapists are not entitled to special First Amendment protection merely because the mechanism used to deliver mental health treatment is the spoken word; and (3) nevertheless, communication that occurs during psychotherapy does receive *some* constitutional protection, but it is not immune from regulation.

Because those principles, standing alone, do not tell us whether or how the First Amendment applies to the regulation of specific mental health treatments, we must go on to consider more generally the First Amendment rights of professionals, such as doctors and mental health providers. In determining whether SB 1172 is a regulation of speech or conduct, we find it helpful to view this issue along a continuum.

At one end of the continuum, where a professional is engaged in a public dialogue, First Amendment protection is at its greatest. Thus, for example, a doctor who publicly advocates a treatment that the medical establishment considers outside the mainstream, or even dangerous, is entitled to robust protection under the First Amendment—just as any person is—even though the state has the power to regulate medicine. See *Lowe v. SEC*, 472 U.S. 181, 232, 105 S. Ct. 2557, 86 L. Ed. 2d 130 (1985) (White, J., concurring) ("Where the personal nexus between professional and client does not exist, and a speaker does not purport to be exercising judgment on behalf of any particular individual with whose circumstances he is directly acquainted, government regulation ceases to function as legitimate regulation of professional practice with only incidental impact on speech; it becomes regulation of speaking or publishing as such, subject to the First Amendment's command that 'Congress shall make no law...abridging the freedom of speech, or of the press.'"); Robert Post, *Informed Consent to Abortion: A First Amendment Analysis of Compelled Physician Speech*, 2007 U. 111. L. Rev. 939, 949 (2007) ("When a physician speaks to the public, his opinions cannot be censored and suppressed, even if they are at odds with preponderant opinion within the medical establishment."); cf. *Bailey v. Huggins Diagnostic & Rehab. Ctr., Inc.*, 952 P.2d 768, 773 (Colo. Ct. App. 1997) (holding that the First Amendment does not permit a court to hold a dentist liable for statements published in a book or made during a news program, even when those statements are contrary to the opinion of the medical establishment). That principle makes sense because communicating to the *public* on matters of *public concern* lies at the core of First Amendment values. See, e.g., *Snyder v. Phelps*, 562 U.S. 443, 131 S. Ct. 1207, 1215, 179 L. Ed. 2d 172 (2011) ("Speech on matters of public concern is at the heart of the First Amendment's protection." (internal quotation markets, brackets, and ellipsis omitted)). Thus, outside the doctor- patient relationship, doctors are constitutionally equivalent to soapbox orators and pamphleteers, and their speech receives robust protection under the First Amendment.

At the midpoint of the continuum, within the confines of a professional relationship, First Amendment protection of a professional's speech is somewhat diminished. For example, in *Planned Parenthood of Southeastern Pennsylvania v. Casey*, 505 U.S. 833, 884, 112 S. Ct. 2791, 120 L. Ed. 2d 674 (1992), the plurality upheld a requirement that doctors disclose truthful, nonmisleading information to patients about certain risks of abortion:

> All that is left of petitioners' argument is an asserted First Amendment right of a physician not to provide information about the risks of abortion, and childbirth, in a manner mandated by the State. To be sure, the physician's First Amendment rights not to speak are implicated, but only as part of the practice of medicine, *subject to reasonable licensing and regulation by the State*. We see no constitutional infirmity in the requirement that the physician provide the information mandated by the State here....

(Citations omitted; emphasis added.) Outside the professional relationship, such a requirement would almost certainly be considered impermissible compelled speech. Cf. *Wooley v. Maynard*, 430 U.S. 705, 97 S. Ct. 1428, 51 L. Ed. 2d 752 (1977) (holding that a state could not require a person to display the state motto on his or her license plate).

Moreover, doctors are routinely held liable for giving negligent medical advice to their patients, without serious suggestion that the First Amendment protects their right to give advice that is not consistent with the accepted standard of care. A doctor "may not counsel a patient to rely on quack medicine. The First Amendment would not prohibit the doctor's loss of license for doing so." *Conant v. McCaffrey*, No. C 97-00139 WHA, 2000 U.S. Dist. LEXIS 13024, 2000 WL 1281174, at *13 (N.D. Cal. Sept. 7, 2000) (order) (unpublished)....

At the other end of the continuum, and where we conclude that SB 1172 lands, is the regulation of professional conduct, where the state's power is great, even though such regulation may have an incidental effect on speech. See *id.* ("Just as offer and acceptance are communications incidental to the regulable transaction called a contract, the professional's speech is incidental to the conduct of the profession."). Most, if not all, medical and mental health treatments require speech, but that fact does not give rise to a First Amendment claim when the state bans a particular treatment. When a drug is banned, for example, a doctor who treats patients with that drug does not have a First Amendment right to speak the words necessary to provide or administer the banned drug. Cf. *Conant*, 309 F.3d at 634-35 (noting the government's authority to ban prescription of marijuana). Were it otherwise, then any prohibition of a particular medical treatment would raise First Amendment concerns because of its incidental effect on speech. Such an application of the First Amendment would restrict unduly the states' power to regulate licensed professions and would be inconsistent with the principle that "it has never been deemed an abridgement of freedom of speech or press to make a course of conduct illegal merely because the conduct was in part initiated, evidenced, or carried out by means of language, either spoken, written, or printed." *Giboney*, 336 U.S. at 502.

Senate Bill 1172 regulates conduct. It bans a form of treatment for minors; it does nothing to prevent licensed therapists from discussing the pros and cons of SOCE with their patients. Senate Bill 1172 merely prohibits licensed mental health providers from engaging in SOCE with minors. It is the limited reach of SB 1172 that distinguishes the present cases from *Conant*, in which the government's policy prohibited speech wholly apart from the actual provision of treatment. Pursuant to its police power, California has authority to regulate licensed mental health providers' administration of therapies that the legislature has deemed harmful. Under *Giboney*, 336 U.S. at 502, the fact that speech may be used to carry out those therapies does not turn the regulation of conduct into a regulation of speech. In fact, the *Welch* Plaintiffs concede that the state has the power to ban aversive types of SOCE. And we reject the position of the *Pickup* Plaintiffs—asserted during oral argument—that even a ban on aversive types of SOCE requires heightened scrutiny because of the incidental effect on speech....Here, unlike in *Conant*, 309 F.3d at 639, the law *allows* discussions about treatment, recommendations to obtain treatment, and expressions of opinions about SOCE and homosexuality.

***

As we have explained, SB 1172 regulates only (1) therapeutic treatment, not expressive speech, by (2) licensed mental health professionals acting within the confines of the counselor-client relationship. The statute does not restrain Plaintiffs from imparting information or disseminating opinions; the regulated activities are therapeutic, not symbolic. And an act that "symbolizes nothing," even if employing language, is not "an act of communication" that transforms conduct into First Amendment speech. *Nev. Comm'n on Ethics v. Carrigan*, 564 U.S. 117, 131 S. Ct. 2343, 2350, 180 L. Ed. 2d 150 (2011). Indeed, it is well recognized that a state enjoys considerable latitude to regulate the conduct of its licensed health care professionals in administering treatment. See, e.g., *Gonzales v. Carhart*, 550 U.S. 124, 157, 127 S. Ct. 1610, 167 L. Ed. 2d 480 (2007) ("Under our precedents it is clear the State has a significant role to play in regulating the medical profession.").

***

We further conclude that the First Amendment does not prevent a state from regulating treatment even when that *treatment* is performed through speech alone. As we have already held in NAAP, talk therapy does not receive special First Amendment protection merely because it is administered through speech. 228 F.3d at 1054. That holding rested on the understanding of talk therapy as "the treatment of emotional suffering and depression, not speech." *Id.* (internal quotation marks omitted) (first emphasis added). Thus, under NAAP, to the extent that talk therapy implicates speech, it stands on the same First Amendment footing as other forms of medical or mental health treatment. Senate Bill 1172 is subject to deferential review just as are other regulations of the practice of medicine.

Our conclusion is consistent with *NAAP's* statement that "communication that occurs during psychoanalysis is entitled to constitutional protection, but it is not immune from regulation." *Id.* Certainly, under *Conant*, content- or viewpoint-based regulation of communication about treatment must be closely scrutinized. But a regulation of only treatment itself—whether physical medicine or mental health treatment—implicates free speech interests only incidentally, if at all. To read *NAAP* otherwise would contradict its holding that talk therapy is not entitled to "special First Amendment protection," and it would, in fact, make talk therapy virtually "immune from regulation." *Id.*

Nor does *NAAP's* discussion of content and viewpoint discrimination change our conclusion. There, we used both a belt and suspenders. In addition to holding that the licensing scheme at issue was a permissible regulation of conduct, we reasoned that even if California's licensing requirements implicated First Amendment interests, the requirements did not discriminate on the basis of content or viewpoint. *Id.* at 1053, 1055–56. But here, SB 1172 regulates only treatment, and nothing in *NAAP* requires us to analyze a regulation of treatment in terms of content and viewpoint discrimination....

Because SB 1172 regulates only treatment, while leaving mental health providers free to discuss and recommend, or recommend against, SOCE, we conclude that any effect it may have on free speech interests is merely incidental. Therefore, we hold that SB 1172 is subject to only rational basis review and must be upheld if it bears a rational relationship to a legitimate state interest. See *Casey*, 505 U.S. at 884, 967-68 (a plurality of three justices, plus four additional justices concurring in part and dissenting in part, applied a reasonableness standard to the regulation of medicine where speech maybe implicated incidentally).

According to the statute, SB 1172 advances California's interest in "protecting the physical and psychological well-being of minors, including lesbian, gay, bisexual and transgender youth, and in protecting its minors against exposure to serious harms caused by sexual orientation change efforts." 2012 Cal. Legis. Serv. ch. 835, § 1(n).

Without a doubt, protecting the well-being of minors is a legitimate state interest. And we need not decide whether SOCE actually causes "serious harms"; it is enough that it could "reasonably be conceived to be true by the governmental decisionmaker." *NAAP*, 228 F.3d at 1050 (internal quotation marks omitted).

The record demonstrates that the legislature acted rationally when it decided to protect the well-being of minors by prohibiting mental health providers from using SOCE on persons under 18.8 The legislature relied on the report of the Task Force of the American Psychological Association, which concluded that SOCE has not been demonstrated to be effective and that there have been anecdotal reports of harm, including depression, suicidal thoughts or actions, and substance abuse....

Plaintiffs argue that the legislature acted irrationally when it banned SOCE for minors because there is a lack of scientifically credible proof of harm. But, under rational basis review, "[w]e ask only whether there are plausible reasons for [the legislature's] action, and if there are, our inquiry is at an end." *Romero-Ochoa v. Holder*, 712 F.3d 1328, 1331 (9th Cir. 2013) (internal quotation marks omitted).

Therefore, we hold that SB 1172 is rationally related to the legitimate government interest of protecting the well-being of minors....

B. *Expressive Association*

We also reject the Pickup Plaintiffs' argument that SB 1172 implicates their right to freedom of association because the First Amendment protects their "choices to enter into and maintain the intimate human relationships between counselors and clients."...

First, SB 1172 does not prevent mental health providers and clients from entering into and maintaining therapeutic relationships. It prohibits only "practices . . . that seek to change [a minor] individual's sexual orientation." Cal. Bus. & Prof. Code § 865(b)(1). Therapists are free, but not obligated, to provide therapeutic services, as long as they do not "seek to change [the] sexual orientation" of minor clients.

Moreover, the therapist-client relationship is not the type of relationship that the freedom of association has been held to protect. The Supreme Court's decisions "have referred to constitutionally protected 'freedom of association' in two distinct senses." *Roberts v. U.S. Jaycees*, 468 U.S. 609, 617, 104 S. Ct. 3244, 82 L. Ed. 2d 462 (1984). The first type of protected association concerns "intimate human relationships," which are implicated in personal decisions about marriage, childbirth, raising children, cohabiting with relatives, and the like. *Id.* at 617–19. That type of freedom of association "receives protection as a fundamental element of personal liberty." *Id.* at 618. The second type protects association "for the purpose of engaging in those activities protected by the First Amendment—speech, assembly, petition for the redress of grievances, and the exercise of religion." *Id.* at 618. Plaintiffs in *Pickup* claim an infringement of only the first type of freedom of association.

Although we have not specifically addressed the therapist-client relationship in terms of freedom of association, we have explained why the therapist-client relationship is not protected by the Due Process Clause of the Fourteenth Amendment: "The relationship between a client and psychoanalyst lasts only as long as the client is willing to pay the fee. Even if analysts and clients meet regularly and clients reveal secrets and emotional thoughts to their analysts, these relationships simply do not rise to the level of a fundamental right." *NAAP*, 228 F.3d at 1050 (internal quotation marks and citation omitted). Because the type of associational protection that the *Pickup* Plaintiffs claim is rooted in "personal liberty," *U.S. Jaycees*, 468 U.S. at 618, and because we have already determined that the therapist-client relationship does not "implicate the fundamental rights associated with... close-knit relationships," *NAAP*, 228 F.3d at 1050, we conclude that the freedom of association also does not encompass the therapist-client relationship.

C. *Vagueness*

We next hold that SB 1172 is not void for vagueness.

"It is a basic principle of due process that an enactment is void for vagueness if its prohibitions are not clearly defined." *Grayned v. City of Rockford*, 408 U.S. 104, 108,

92 S. Ct. 2294, 33 L. Ed. 2d 222 (1972). Nevertheless, "perfect clarity and precise guidance have never been required even of regulations that restrict expressive activity." *Ward v. Rock Against Racism*, 491 U.S. 781, 794, 109 S. Ct. 2746, 105 L. Ed. 2d 661 (1989).

"[U]ncertainty at a statute's margins will not warrant facial invalidation if it is clear what the statute proscribes 'in the vast majority of its intended applications.'" *Cal. Teachers Ass'n v. State Bd. of Educ.*, 271 F.3d 1141, 1151 (9th Cir. 2001) (quoting *Hill v. Colorado*, 530 U.S. 703, 733, 120 S. Ct. 2480, 147 L. Ed. 2d 597 (2000)). "A defendant is deemed to have fair notice of an offense if a reasonable person of ordinary intelligence would understand that his or her conduct is prohibited by the law in question." *United States v. Weitzenhoff*, 35 F.3d 1275, 1289 (9th Cir. 1994) (internal quotation marks omitted). But, "if the statutory prohibition involves conduct of a select group of persons having specialized knowledge, and the challenged phraseology is indigenous to the idiom of that class, the standard is lowered and a court may uphold a statute which uses words or phrases having a technical or other special meaning, well enough known to enable those within its reach to correctly apply them." *Id.* (internal quotation marks omitted).

Although the *Pickup* Plaintiffs argue that they cannot ascertain where the line is between what is prohibited and what is permitted—for example, they wonder whether the mere dissemination of information about SOCE would subject them to discipline—the text of SB 1172 is clear to a reasonable person. Discipline attaches only to "practices" that "seek to change" a minor "patient['s]" sexual orientation. Cal. Bus. & Prof. Code §§ 865-865.1. A reasonable person would understand the statute to regulate only mental health treatment, including psychotherapy, that aims to alter a minor patient's sexual orientation. Although Plaintiffs present various hypothetical situations to support their vagueness challenge, the Supreme Court has held that "speculation about possible vagueness in hypothetical situations not before the Court will not support a facial attack on a statute when it is surely valid in the vast majority of its intended applications." *Hill*, 530 U.S. at 733 (internal quotation marks omitted).

Moreover, considering that SB 1172 regulates licensed mental health providers, who constitute "a select group of persons having specialized knowledge," the standard for clarity is lower. *Weitzenhoff*, 35 F.3d at 1289. Indeed, it is hard to understand how therapists who identify themselves as SOCE practitioners can credibly argue that they do not understand what practices qualify as SOCE.

Neither is the term "sexual orientation" vague. Its meaning is clear enough to a reasonable person and should be even more apparent to mental health providers. In fact, several provisions in the California Code—though not SB 1172 itself—provide a simple definition: "heterosexuality, homosexuality, or bisexuality." Cal. Educ. Code §§ 212.6, 66262.7; Cal. Gov't Code § 12926(s); Cal. Penal Code §§ 422.56(h), 11410(b)(7). Moreover, courts have repeatedly rejected vagueness challenges that rest on the term "sexual orientation." E.g., *United States v. Jenkins*, 909 F. Supp. 2d 758, 778–79 (E.D. Ky. 2012); *Hyman v. City of Louisville*, 132 F. Supp. 2d 528, 546 (W.D. Ky. 2001), vacated on other grounds, 53 F. App'x 740 (6th Cir. 2002) (unpublished).

D. *Overbreadth*

We further hold that SB 1172 is not overbroad....

Overbreadth doctrine permits the facial invalidation of laws that prohibit "a substantial amount of constitutionally protected speech." *City of Houston v. Hill*, 482 U.S. 451, 466, 107 S. Ct. 2502, 96 L. Ed. 2d 398 (1987). "[T]he mere fact that one can conceive of some impermissible applications of a statute is not sufficient to render it susceptible to an overbreadth challenge." *Members of City Council v. Taxpayers for Vincent*, 466 U.S. 789, 800, 104 S. Ct. 2118, 80 L. Ed. 2d 772 (1984). Rather, "particularly where conduct and not merely speech is involved, ... the overbreadth of a statute must not only be real, but substantial as well, judged in relation to the statute's plainly legitimate sweep." *Broadrick v. Oklahoma*, 413 U.S. 601, 615, 93 S. Ct. 2908, 37 L. Ed. 2d 830 (1973).

Senate Bill 1172's plainly legitimate sweep includes SOCE techniques such as inducing vomiting or paralysis, administering electric shocks, and performing castrations.

> And, as explained above, it also includes SOCE techniques carried out solely through words. As with any regulation of a particular medical or mental health treatment, there may be an incidental effect on speech. Any incidental effect, however, is small in comparison with the "plainly legitimate sweep" of the law. *Broadrick*, 413 U.S. at 615.
>
> Thus, SB 1172 is not overbroad.
>
> ***
>
> CONCLUSION
>
> Senate Bill 1172 survives the constitutional challenges presented here. Accordingly, the order granting preliminary relief in *Welch*, No. 13-15023, is REVERSED, and the order denying preliminary relief in *Pickup*, No. 12-17681, is AFFIRMED. We remand both cases for further proceedings consistent with this opinion.

4TH AMENDMENT PRIVACY AND REGULATORY SEARCHES

The U.S. Constitution's 4th Amendment covers "search and seizure" by the state (at any level, federal to local). Some states have provisions that may limit the state to a greater degree. For example, as noted in this chapter's introduction, the California Constitution provides for a stated "right of privacy" not as directly stated at the federal level. (*See* Art. I, Section 1: "All people are by nature free and independent and have inalienable rights. Among these are enjoying and defending life and liberty, acquiring, possessing, and protecting property, and pursuing and obtaining safety, happiness, and privacy.")

In terms of regulatory law, this issue is affected by the crucial criteria for privacy protection, the "reasonable expectation of privacy" that may be infringed by governmental searches. For those who are regulated, that expectation is materially reduced. The fact of licensure by the state, with its implicit element of state supervision and monitoring apparently connected to the public need for state involvement, means that state intrusions for *bona fide* regulatory purposes have a measure of latitude not otherwise extant. However, complications occur where information is sought of the clients, patients or customers of licensees. This is particularly so with legal and medical professionals, where such communications have general confidential status due to the nature of the relationship with a licensee. In particular, the clients of a licensed attorney or the patients of a medical professional are granted a high measure of privacy *vis-à-vis* state searches than are the licensees themselves. That distinction is based on the sensitive subject area of the professional relationship and the explicit privilege of confidentiality in established law.

California's example of this duality for physicians is reflected in Business and Professions Code Section 2225(a), which provides that "...a communication between a physician and surgeon or a doctor of podiatric medicine and his or her patients [is] a privileged communication, [but] those provisions shall not apply to investigations or proceedings conducted under this chapter. Members of the [Medical or Podiatric Board and the Attorney General] shall keep in confidence during the course of investigations, the names of any patients whose records are reviewed and shall not disclose or reveal those names, except as is necessary during the course of an investigation, unless and until proceedings are instituted...."

Business and Profession Code Section 2225(b) provides in part that relevant state officials "may inquire into any alleged violation of the Medical Practice Act or any other federal or state law, regulation, or rule relevant to the practice of medicine...and may inspect documents relevant to those investigations in accordance with the following procedures:

> (1) Any document relevant to an investigation may be inspected, and copies may be obtained, where patient consent is given.
>
> (2) Any document relevant to the business operations of a licensee, and not involving medical records attributable to identifiable patients, may be inspected and copied if relevant to an investigation of a licensee."

Where a patient has died, the Board may inspect and copy all relevant medical records. A court order may be required for such inspection only where the beneficiary or personal representative of the deceased patient has been located and refused to consent to the inspection and copying of the patient's medical records (Bus. & Prof. Code Section 2225(c)(1)).

In general, a licensee has 15 business days to produce requested records, and a failure to do so may constitute unprofessional conduct subject to discipline (Bus. & Prof. Code Section 2225(e)).

These provisions are consistent with the general federal statute protecting medical patient privacy (the federal Health Insurance Portability and Accountability Act (HIPAA) (Bus. & Prof. Code Section 2225(c)(2)).

The other area of major 4th Amendment search and seizure complexity involves the records of a licensed attorney concerning clients. As with medical communications, an attorney has a confidentiality privilege vis-à-vis his or her clients. That shield complicates what would normally be the reduced expectation of privacy allowing the state licensor (or law enforcement) to review occupational records. As with medical records, states allow such searches, but they add checks not otherwise present. Hence, the relevant investigations must generally be confidential and commonly require subpoena justification. Some states require such client files to be "reviewed in the first instance by a neutral party (or "special master"), appointed by and answerable to the court. This third-party check may ensure that the prosecutors, regulators and investigators obtain the evidence that is relevant and is legally authorized (see, e.g., *Doyle v. State Bar*, 32 Cal.3d (1982)).

Medical Bd. of California v. Chiarottino

225 Cal. App. 4th 623 (2014)

Opinion by: Dondero, J.

Defendant Michael Chiarottino, a physician licensed to practice in California, appeals from the trial court's order to comply with investigative subpoenas issued by plaintiff Medical Board of California (Board). The Board issued the subpoenas in connection with an investigation into defendant's prescribing activities as they pertain to controlled substances. On appeal, defendant contends the court erred in rejecting his argument that the Board violated his patients' right to privacy by accessing a computerized database of controlled substance prescription records prior to issuing the subpoenas. We affirm.

FACTUAL BACKGROUND AND PROCEDURAL HISTORY

In August 2011, the Board obtained information that defendant was possibly prescribing excessive medications to patients in violation of the Medical Practice Act. (Bus. & Prof. Code, § 2000 et seq.) A Board investigator obtained a Controlled Substance Utilization Review and Evaluation System (CURES)...report of defendant's prescribing history between August 22, 2009, and February 22, 2012. The investigator also obtained CURES reports of the prescription histories for five of defendant's patients over a 12-month period between 2011 and 2012 and the corresponding pharmacy records for these same patients.

The Board's medical expert, Rick Chavez, M.D., conducted an independent review of the CURES reports and the patients' pharmacy records. He identified significant concerns and irregularities in defendant's prescribing of controlled substances to these patients, including prescribing large quantities of highly addictive and dangerous narcotics, prescribing highly unusual combinations of drugs, prescribing buprenorphine (a drug used to resolve opiate addiction) to patients who were concurrently receiving opioids from several other physicians, prescribing at irregular time intervals, and prescribing highly addictive drugs for lengthy periods of time. Chavez concluded defendant's conduct was alarming and difficult to justify.

On February 7, 2012, the Board's investigator sent letters to the five patients requesting authorization for the release of their medical records with respect to the treatment they received from defendant. Defendant was subsequently served with subpoenas directing him to produce the patients' medical records. After the patients were notified of the subpoenas, they informed the investigator that they objected. Defendant's counsel indicated to the investigator that defendant would not produce the requested information because the patients had objected to the release of their medical records.

On December 26, 2012, the Board filed a petition for an order compelling compliance with the investigative subpoenas. (Gov. Code, § 11180 et seq.)...In its supporting papers, it argued that the five patients' medical records were needed to properly assess whether the narcotics and controlled substances defendant had prescribed were or were not warranted, and whether he was in compliance with standards of care and practice. The Board asserted these records were necessary to allow it to "fulfill its monitoring responsibilities of public protection as mandated by California law." It claimed the subpoenas were "reasonably tailored to seek only the records that are necessary and material to the Board's investigation."

On January 2, 2013, the trial court issued an order to show cause regarding the Board's petition.

On January 31, 2013, defendant filed his opposition to the Board's petition. He claimed his refusal was based on protecting the privacy rights of his patients, as well as their rights not to be subjected to unwarranted search and seizure.

On April 18, 2013, the trial court granted the Board's petition to compel defendant's compliance with the subpoenas. The court found the Board had set forth sufficient facts to support a finding of good cause. The court limited the disclosure to records that "are relevant and material to the pending investigation," by setting forth certain substantive and time-based limitations. This appeal followed.

DISCUSSION

I. *Standard of Review*

The standard of review generally applicable to review of a trial court's order involving discovery matters or other matters where the trial court has discretionary power is abuse of discretion. (See *Britts v. Superior Court* (2006) 145 Cal.App.4th 1112, 1123 [52 Cal. Rptr. 3d 185].) An abuse of discretion is found where a court exceeds the bounds of reason in light of the circumstances under consideration. (*Loomis v. Loomis* (1960) 181 Cal.App.2d 345, 348 [5 Cal. Rptr. 550].) Unless there has been a clear miscarriage of justice, a reviewing court will not substitute its opinion for that of the trial court so as to avoid divesting the trial court of its discretionary power. (*Id.* at p. 349.)

Issues of law are reviewed de novo. (*Szold v. Medical Bd. of California* (2005) 127 Cal.App.4th 591, 596 [25 Cal. Rptr. 3d 665].) Construction of a statute is a question of law and, as such, is subject to de novo review. (*Ibid.*)

II. *Contentions on Appeal*

As noted above, the trial court found the Board had established good cause to support the issuance of the subpoenas. Defendant's sole basis for challenging the trial court's good cause finding is his claim that the CURES reports themselves were obtained in violation of his patients' rights to privacy under article I, section 1, of the California Constitution. More specifically, he contends their rights were violated when the Board was given "unfettered and extensive access to two-and-a-half years' worth of all of his patients' CURES prescription information." As will be demonstrated, the Board's actions were entirely authorized under Health and Safety Code section 11165 (the CURES statute). Thus, defendant is implicitly attacking the constitutionality of the statute itself. The weight of authority supports the Board's position that the statute, and its actions taken pursuant thereto, pass constitutional muster.

III. *The CURES Statute*

(1) The prescribing and dispensing of controlled substances in California are strictly regulated and are monitored by the Department of Justice (DOJ). (See Health & Saf. Code, § 11150 et seq.) The CURES statute provides for the reporting of prescription records to the DOJ, and specifically authorizes the DOJ to disclose such records to state enforcement and regulatory agencies. (Health & Saf. Code, § 11165, subd. (c).) The DOJ maintains a database for the electronic monitoring of, and Internet access to, information regarding the prescribing and dispensing of schedule II, schedule III, and schedule IV controlled substances by all practitioners authorized to prescribe or dispense these controlled substances. The primary purpose of the CURES statute is to "assist…law enforcement and regulatory agencies in their efforts to control the diversion and resultant abuse of…controlled substances." (Health & Saf. Code, § 11165, subd. (a).) It is undisputed that the Board qualifies for authorization under the CURES statute to access and review prescription records for controlled substances that pharmacists and other dispensing providers are required to report.

The CURES statute does not require the Board to obtain either patient consent or judicial approval prior to accessing CURES data. The statute does, however, contain its own confidentiality requirements. Specifically, it provides that the database system "shall operate under existing provisions of law to safeguard the privacy and confidentiality of patients." (Health & Saf. Code, § 11165, subd. (c).) The statute further prohibits the disclosure, sale, or transfer of patient data to any third party. (*Ibid.*)

IV. *The Medical Board of California*

In *Arnett v. Dal Cielo* (1996) 14 Cal.4th 4 [56 Cal. Rptr. 2d 706, 923 P.2d 1] (*Arnett*), our Supreme Court provided a useful overview of the Board's role in protecting the health and safety of the public. As the court observed, California has long regulated the practice of medicine as an exercise of the state's police power. (*Id.* at p. 7.) "A key instrument of that regulation has been the statewide agency authorized to license and discipline medical practitioners...," now known as the Medical Board of California. (*Ibid.*; see Bus. & Prof. Code, § 101, subd. (b).) "A primary power exercised by the Board in carrying out its enforcement responsibilities is the power to *investigate*: the statute broadly vests the Board with the power of 'Investigating complaints from the public, from other licensees, from health care facilities, or from a division of the board that a physician and surgeon may be guilty of unprofessional conduct.' [Citation.]" (*Arnett*, supra, at pp. 7–8.)

"The Board's investigators have the status of peace officers [citation], and possess a wide range of investigative powers. In addition to interviewing and taking statements from witnesses, the Board's investigators are authorized to exercise delegated powers [citation] to 'Inspect books and records' and to 'Issue subpoenas for the attendance of witnesses and the production of papers, books, accounts, documents and testimony in any inquiry [or] investigation...in any part of the state.' [Citation.]" (*Arnett*, *supra*, 14 Cal.4th at p. 8.)

Further, because the Board is authorized "to issue a subpoena 'in any inquiry [or] investigation' [citation], the Board may do so for purely investigative purposes; it is not necessary that a formal accusation be on file or a formal adjudicative hearing be pending. [Citation.]" (*Ibid.*) The Court in *Arnett* further observed "'the power to make administrative inquiry is not derived from a judicial function but is more analogous to the power of a grand jury, which does not depend on a case or controversy to get evidence but can investigate "merely on suspicion that the law is being violated, or even just because it wants assurance that it is not."' [Citation.]" (*Ibid.*)

The Board is specifically charged with enforcement of the Medical Practice Act, and many of the act's provisions focus particularly on the use and misuse of prescription drugs, as illustrated by the following statutes: Business and Professions Code sections 2238 (violation of state or federal statute regulating dangerous drugs and controlled substances), 2241 and 2241.5 (furnishing prescription drugs to an addict), and 2242 (furnishing prescription drugs without an appropriate prior examination and medical indication).

In the present case, defendant does not challenge the Board's investigative powers directly. Instead, he repeatedly asserts the Board violated his patients' privacy rights when it obtained "unfettered access" to the CURES data, data the Board subsequently relied on to justify the issuance of the five subpoenas....

V. *The Board's Actions Taken Pursuant to the CURES Statute Did Not Violate Patients' Privacy Rights*

A. *The State Constitutional Right to Privacy*

"In 1972, Californians, by initiative, added an explicit right to privacy in the state's Constitution: 'All people are by nature free and independent and have inalienable rights. Among these are enjoying and defending life and liberty, acquiring, possessing, and protecting property, and pursuing and obtaining safety, happiness, and privacy.' (Cal. Const., art. I, § 1, italics added.)" (*County of Los Angeles v. Los Angeles County Employee Relations Com.* (2013) 56 Cal.4th 905, 926 [157 Cal. Rptr. 3d 481, 301 P.3d 1102] (*County of Los Angeles*).)

In *Hill v. National Collegiate Athletic Assn.* (1994) 7 Cal.4th 1 [26 Cal. Rptr. 2d 834, 865 P.2d 633] (*Hill*), our Supreme Court "established a framework for analyzing constitutional invasion of privacy claims. An actionable claim requires three essential elements: (1) the claimant must possess a legally protected privacy interest [citation]; (2) the claimant's expectation of privacy must be objectively reasonable...[citation]; and (3) the invasion of privacy complained of must be serious in both its nature and scope [citation]. If the claimant establishes all three required elements, the strength of that privacy interest is balanced against countervailing interests. [Citation.] In general, the court should not proceed to balancing unless a satisfactory threshold showing is made. A defendant is entitled to prevail if it negates any of the three required elements. [Citations.] A defendant can also prevail at the balancing stage. An otherwise actionable invasion of privacy may be legally justified if it substantively furthers one or more legitimate competing interests. [Citation.] Conversely, the invasion may be unjustified if the claimant can point to 'feasible and effective alternatives' with 'a lesser impact on privacy interests.' [Citation.]" (*County of Los Angeles*, *supra*, 56 Cal.4th at p. 926.)

It is established that patients do have a right to privacy in their medical information under our state Constitution....(See, e.g., *Gross v. Recabaren* (1988) 206 Cal.App.3d 771, 782–783 [253 Cal. Rptr. 820] [substantial privacy concerns are raised whenever there is an intrusion into a patient's confidential relationship with a physician]; *Ruiz v. Podolsky* (2010) 50 Cal.4th 838, 851 [114 Cal. Rptr. 3d 263, 237 P.3d 584] [the same with respect to disclosure of confidential medical information regarding the condition a patient seeks to treat].) This right would appear to extend to prescription records....However, it is also well settled that an individual's constitutional right to privacy is not absolute. (*Hill*, *supra*, 7 Cal.4th at p. 37.)

Even assuming defendant has satisfied the three-prong prima facie elements under *Hill*, we conclude any invasion of his patients' privacy rights with respect to the Board's review of information obtained from the CURES database is justified by a compelling competing interest: "Invasion of a privacy interest is not a violation of the state constitutional right to privacy if the invasion is justified by a competing interest. Legitimate interests derive from the legally authorized and socially beneficial activities of government and private entities. Their relative importance is determined by their proximity to the central functions of a particular public or private enterprise. Conduct alleged to be an invasion of privacy is to be evaluated based on the extent to which it furthers legitimate and important competing interests." (*Hill*, *supra*, 7 Cal.4th at p. 38.) Here, the balance favors disclosure.

B. *Defendant Does Not Challenge the CURES Statute on Its Face*

As the Board correctly notes, to the extent defendant is contending on appeal that the CURES statute is facially unconstitutional, he did not raise this argument in the proceeding below; thus, this argument may be deemed waived. (*Ochoa v. Pacific Gas & Electric Co.* (1998) 61 Cal.App.4th 1480, 1488, fn. 3 [72 Cal. Rptr. 2d 232] ["arguments not asserted below are waived and will not be considered for the first time on appeal"].) We also observe he has not cited to any legal authority to support an argument that the CURES statute is facially unconstitutional. Accordingly, we deem the argument waived and abandoned....(*Ibid.*)

C. *The Board Did Not Violate Defendant's Patients' Right to Privacy*

Defendant concedes that the CURES statute "appears to authorize the [Board] to obtain CURES data in its investigation of doctors for potential disciplinary purposes, as in the instant case." Our research has not disclosed a California case directly addressing an invasion of privacy claim with respect to activities undertaken pursuant to the CURES statute. However, a recent case lends support for the proposition that the Board's conduct can be justified by a compelling governmental interest. In *420 Caregivers, LLC v. City of Los Angeles* (2012) 219 Cal.App.4th 1316 [163 Cal. Rptr. 3d 17] (*420 Caregivers*), the Court of Appeal reversed an order granting a preliminary injunction against the enforcement of an ordinance regulating the number and geographic distribution of medical marijuana collectives and requiring their registration. Among its conclusions, the appellate court found the collectives did not have a reasonable expectation of privacy in the limited information sought by the ordinance. (*Id.* at p. 1350.) Alternatively, it found any invasion of a reasonable expectation of privacy to be justified by a legitimate and competing state interest. (*Id.* at p. 1349.) Because the collectives did not demonstrate a likelihood of prevailing on the merits at trial, the appellate panel concluded the trial court had erred in granting the request for a preliminary injunction. (*Id.* at p. 1350.)

In arriving at its holding, the appellate court observed "statutes already allow the disclosure of patient contact information by traditional health care providers upon demand.…Insofar as schedules II, III, and IV controlled substances (drugs which may be legally prescribed) are concerned, pharmacies are already required weekly to provide the state Department of Justice with the names, addresses, and phone numbers of prescribed users. [Citation.] This information, in turn, may be given to state, local, or federal agencies for purposes of criminal *or disciplinary investigations.* [Citation.]" (*420 Caregivers, supra*, 219 Cal.App.4th at p. 1350, italics added & omitted.) The reviewing court concluded: "In short, even where the privacy rights of individual collective members are concerned, the information sought is extremely limited and nonintimate in nature and the information— plus more—is typically *already subject to disclosure in the context of more traditional health care treatments and providers*.…[W]e see no reason to give medical marijuana users greater privacy rights than patients utilizing more traditional health care providers and more traditional prescription drugs. Indeed, given the continued illegal nature of marijuana under most circumstances, even more substantial invasions of privacy would likely be justified under the current state of the law. Whether analyzed as an unreasonable expectation of privacy or a reasonably justified invasion of a reasonable expectation of privacy, we find no violation of the Collectives' members' individual privacy rights." (*Ibid.*, italics added.)

In rejecting defendant's unreasonable search and seizure claim, the trial court in the present case specifically rejected his right-to-privacy arguments, concluding that, under the circumstances of this case, neither defendant nor his patients have a reasonable expectation of privacy in the records maintained in the CURES database. Several other jurisdictions have addressed this issue more directly and have found that a state law enforcement official's access to controlled substance prescription records does not violate the patient's right of privacy under federal law or under applicable local privacy statutes. We find those opinions to be persuasive.

Significantly, in *Whalen v. Roe* (1977) 429 U.S. 589 [51 L. Ed. 2d 64, 97 S. Ct. 869] (*Whalen*), the United States Supreme Court addressed a statute similar to the CURES statute. In *Whalen*, a group of patients and physicians, among others, challenged the constitutionality of a New York statutory scheme requiring physicians to forward records of prescriptions for schedule II drugs, which contained detailed patient information, to a centralized database maintained by that state's department of health. (*Id.* at pp. 593–595.) Although, like the CURES statute at issue here, public disclosure of the identity of the patient was prohibited under New York law, certain state regulatory employees and personnel responsible for investigating violations of that state's controlled substance statutes were afforded access to that information. (*Id.* at pp. 594–595.) After finding that the statute furthered the state's "vital interest in controlling the distribution of dangerous drugs," the court concluded that the challenged statutory scheme, by mandating the disclosure of the prescription information to representatives of the state having responsibility for the health and welfare of the community, did not create an impermissible invasion of privacy. (*Id.* at pp. 603–604.) As more-recent cases demonstrate, other jurisdictions are in accord.

In *State of Nebraska v. Wiedeman* (2013) 286 Neb. 193 [835 N.W.2d 698], a criminal defendant argued that state law enforcement officers violated her due process privacy rights through their warrantless investigatory access to her prescription records. As in the present case, she did not challenge the statute that authorized the access. (*Id.*, 835 N.W.2d at p. 707.) The state's high court found Whalen to be dispositive of her privacy arguments under the federal Constitution. (835 N.W.2d at pp. 707–708.) The Nebraska court observed "there is a long history of governmental scrutiny in the area of narcotics and other controlled substances. All states highly regulate prescription narcotics, and many state statutes specifically allow for law enforcement investigatory access to those records without a warrant. This well-known and long-established regulatory history significantly diminishes any societal expectation of privacy against governmental investigation of narcotics prescriptions." (*Id.* at p. 711, fn. omitted.) The court concluded the defendant had no legitimate expectation that governmental inquiries would not occur with respect to a pharmacy's prescription records. (*Id.* at p. 712.)

In *State of Connecticut v. Russo*, *supra*, 790 A.2d 1132 (*Russo*), the Supreme Court of Connecticut held a patient's privacy rights were not violated under a state statute that allowed government officials with the duty to enforce state and federal controlled substance statutes to inspect prescription records. (*Id.* at p. 1146.) The local police department was investigating a defendant accused of multiple counts of forgery and obtaining controlled substances by forging a prescription. Pursuant to the challenged statute, an authorized law enforcement agent had obtained, with the pharmacists' consent, records of the defendant's prescriptions for controlled substances. The court, largely relying on Whalen, found the defendant's privacy rights had not been violated. (*Id.* at p. 1155.)

The court in *Russo* noted that the Connecticut statutory scheme was indistinguishable from the statutes at issue in *Whalen*. (*Russo*, *supra*, 790 A.2d at pp. 1150-1151.) Specifically, both schemes safeguarded the privacy interest of the affected patients by restricting access to those records to a limited class of persons, and by prohibiting the dissemination of such information to the general public. (*Ibid.*) The court further observed that nothing in the court records in either case suggested that the law enforcement officials involved had failed to abide by the nondisclosure provisions, or that they would likely flout those provisions in the future. (*Id.* at p. 1151.)

In *State of Vermont v. Welch* (1992) 160 Vt. 70 [624 A.2d 1105], the Supreme Court of Vermont held that a criminal defendant had a privacy interest in her pharmaceutical records, based on a reasonable expectation that those records would not be arbitrarily disclosed. (*Id.*, 624 A.2d at p. 1109.) The court concluded, however, that the "'pervasively regulated industry'" exception to the warrant requirement allowed for the warrantless inspection of her records in furtherance of the enforcement of statutes pertaining to closely regulated businesses such as pharmacies. (*Id.* at pp. 1110–1111.) The court specifically noted the state interest in the regulation of dangerous drugs (*id.* at p. 1111), and concluded the warrantless inspection of pharmacy records undertaken in compliance with statutory procedures was reasonable (*id.* at p. 1112).

Finally, in *Stone v. City of Stow* (1992) 64 Ohio St.3d 156 [593 N.E.2d 294], a contingent of doctors, patients, and a pharmacist sued several municipalities contending that Ohio statutes providing for the inspection of pharmacy prescription records without a warrant violated the right of privacy and the prohibition against unreasonable searches and seizures found in the United States and Ohio Constitutions. (593 N.E.2d at p. 297.) The court found *Whalen* dispositive of the privacy issue, declining to apply a balancing test that would weigh the need for access to prescription records against the deprivation of privacy caused by the regulatory provisions. The court noted that, on the state of the record before it, there was no basis for speculating that any unauthorized disclosure of the prescription records would occur. (593 N.E.2d at p. 299.)

In the present case, defendant argues that the Board violated the privacy rights of *all* of his patients by, essentially, conducting a fishing expedition into records of his prescribing activities as reflected in the CURES database. However, there is no evidence that the Board acted outside the scope of its investigative mandate. For example, defendant does not contend the Board used its authority to investigate the records of individuals who were not his patients, or that the Board improperly disclosed any CURES information to third parties. Nor does he contend that the Board had any improper motive in deciding to investigate his own prescribing activities. Thus, it is undisputed that the Board acted within the scope of its authority and in compliance with all relevant statutory law.

Further, the cases defendant relies on are inapposite in that they concern subpoena requests for medical records made by the Board in the absence of good cause. For example, in *Bearman v. Superior Court* (2004) 117

Cal.App.4th 463 [11 Cal. Rptr. 3d 644], the appellate court held that the Board "must demonstrate through competent evidence that the particular records it seeks are relevant and material to its inquiry sufficient for a trial court to independently make a finding of good cause to order the materials disclosed." (*Id.* at p. 469.) The appellate court concluded the Board had failed to set forth facts suggesting that the prescribing physician had engaged in any unethical conduct with respect to his prescribing medical marijuana to a patient. Further, the court found the request was overbroad. (*Id.* at pp. 471–472.) Here, defendant does not challenge the adequacy of the Board's good cause showing to the trial court. Instead, he challenges the legitimacy of the Board's conduct in compiling the factual justification that enabled the court to make an independent assessment of good cause.

For purposes of our decision here, we assume patients have a reasonable expectation that their prescription records will not be disclosed to persons who are not actively involved in their care. Balancing society's substantial interest in reducing the illegitimate use of dangerously addictive prescription drugs against the relatively minor intrusion upon a patient's reasonable expectations of privacy when he or she is given a prescription by a treating physician, we conclude that, as applied to such patients, the Board's actions here in accessing and compiling data from the CURES database did not violate article I, section 1 of the state Constitution. This is particularly so in light of the fact that the Board is prohibited by law from disclosing this data to third parties. Further, even a reasonable expectation of privacy is somewhat diminished as it is widely known that such investigative actions are possible with respect to controlled substances. In this setting, we conclude that the limited incremental intrusion upon a patient's privacy is justified by the state's countervailing interest in preventing the abuse of controlled substances. Accordingly, we hold the trial court correctly found there was good cause to enforce the subpoenas of the five patients' medical records.

DISPOSITION

The order is affirmed.

14TH AMENDMENT DUE PROCESS AND EQUAL PROTECTION

The 14th Amendment to the U.S. Constitution pertains to "equal protection," "due process," and the "right to travel." Regulatory practice can violate each of them. The general "equal protection" assurance involves a "strict scrutiny" standard where based on a "suspect" classification, such as religion or race,[2] or where it impedes a "fundamental liberty interest" (FLI). Other distinctions not within a "suspect" category may trigger a "heightened scrutiny" examination, e.g., based on age or disability. If neither of these two tests apply, the discrimination may then be based on a more deferential "rational relation" test. Apart from equal protection, the 14th Amendment also commands both procedural due process and "substantive" due process.

Jackson v. Metropolitan Edison Co.

419 U.S. 345 (1974)

MR. JUSTICE REHNQUIST delivered the opinion of the Court.

Respondent Metropolitan Edison Co. is a privately owned and operated Pennsylvania corporation which holds a certificate of public convenience issued by the Pennsylvania Public Utility Commission empowering it to deliver electricity to a service area which includes the city of York, Pa. As a condition of holding its certificate, it is subject to extensive regulation by the Commission. Under a provision of its general tariff filed with the Commission, it has the right to discontinue service to any customer on reasonable notice of nonpayment of bills....

Petitioner Catherine Jackson is a resident of York, who has received electricity in the past from respondent. Until September 1970, petitioner received electric service to her home in York under an account with respondent in her own name. When her account was terminated because of asserted delinquency in payments due for service, a new

---

[2] Note that the *Cornwell* case *supra*, could have been decided based on a strict scrutiny racial analysis. Those who are braiding African American hair have apparent association with African-American practitioners. But rather than engage in a strict scrutiny examination, the district court found that licensure of this profession lacked "rational relation" justification since the requirements and barriers to entry for practitioners bore little relationship to the skill or other regulatory justification for licensure.

account with respondent was opened in the name of one James Dodson, another occupant of the residence, and service to the residence was resumed. There is a dispute as to whether payments due under the Dodson account for services provided during this period were ever made. In August 1971, Dodson left the residence. Service continued thereafter but concededly no payments were made. Petitioner states that no bills were received during this period.

On October 6, 1971, employees of Metropolitan came to the residence and inquired as to Dodson's present address. Petitioner stated that it was unknown to her. On the following day, another employee visited the residence and informed petitioner that the meter had been tampered with so as not to register amounts used. She disclaimed knowledge of this and requested that the service account for her home be shifted from Dodson's name to that of one Robert Jackson, later identified as her 12-year-old son. Four days later on October 11, 1971, without further notice to petitioner, Metropolitan employees disconnected her service.

Petitioner then filed suit against Metropolitan in the United States District Court for the Middle District of Pennsylvania under the Civil Rights Act of 1871, 42 U. S. C. § 1983, seeking damages for the termination and an injunction requiring Metropolitan to continue providing power to her residence until she had been afforded notice, a hearing, and an opportunity to pay any amounts found due. She urged that under state law she had an entitlement to reasonably continuous electrical service to her home...and that Metropolitan's termination of her service for alleged nonpayment, action allowed by a provision of its general tariff filed with the Commission, constituted "state action" depriving her of property in violation of the Fourteenth Amendment's guarantee of due process of law....

The District Court granted Metropolitan's motion to dismiss petitioner's complaint on the ground that the termination did not constitute state action and hence was not subject to judicial scrutiny under the Fourteenth Amendment....On appeal, the United States Court of Appeals for the Third Circuit affirmed, also finding an absence of state action.…We granted certiorari to review this judgment.…

The Due Process Clause of the Fourteenth Amendment provides: "[Nor] shall any State deprive any person of life, liberty, or property, without due process of law." In 1883, this Court in the *Civil Rights Cases*, 109 U.S. 3, affirmed the essential dichotomy set forth in that Amendment between deprivation by the State, subject to scrutiny under its provisions, and private conduct, "however discriminatory or wrongful," against which the Fourteenth Amendment offers no shield. *Shelley v. Kraemer*, 334 U.S. 1 (1948).

We have reiterated that distinction on more than one occasion since then. See, e. g., *Evans v. Abney*, 396 U.S. 435, 445 (1970); M*oose Lodge No. 107 v. Irvis*, 407 U.S. 163, 171-179 (1972). While the principle that private action is immune from the restrictions of the Fourteenth Amendment is well established and easily stated, the question whether particular conduct is "private," on the one hand, or "state action," on the other, frequently admits of no easy answer. *Burton v. Wilmington Parking Authority*, 365 U.S. 715, 723 (1961); *Moose Lodge No. 107 v. Irvis*, *supra*, at 172.

Here the action complained of was taken by a utility company which is privately owned and operated, but which in many particulars of its business is subject to extensive state regulation. The mere fact that a business is subject to state regulation does not by itself convert its action into that of the State for purposes of the Fourteenth Amendment.… 407 U.S., at 176-177. Nor does the fact that the regulation is extensive and detailed, as in the case of most public utilities, do so. *Public Utilities Comm'n v. Pollak*, 343 U.S. 451, 462 (1952). It may well be that acts of a heavily regulated utility with at least something of a governmentally protected monopoly will more readily be found to be "state" acts than will the acts of an entity lacking these characteristics. But the inquiry must be whether there is a sufficiently close nexus between the State and the challenged action of the regulated entity so that the action of the latter may be fairly treated as that of the State itself. *Moose Lodge No. 107*, *supra*, at 176. The true nature of the State's involvement may not be immediately obvious, and detailed inquiry may be required in order to determine whether the test is met. *Burton v. Wilmington Parking Authority, supra.*

Petitioner advances a series of contentions which, in her view, lead to the conclusion that this case should fall on the *Burton* side of the line drawn in the *Civil Rights Cases, supra*, rather than on the *Moose Lodge* side of that line. We find none of them persuasive.

Petitioner first argues that "state action" is present because of the monopoly status allegedly conferred upon Metropolitan by the State of Pennsylvania. As a factual matter, it may well be doubted that the State ever granted or guaranteed Metropolitan a monopoly....But assuming that it had, this fact is not determinative in considering whether Metropolitan's termination of service to petitioner was "state action" for purposes of the Fourteenth Amendment. In *Pollak, supra*, where the Court dealt with the activities of the District of Columbia Transit Co., a congressionally established monopoly, we expressly disclaimed reliance on the monopoly status of the transit authority. 343 U.S., at 462. Similarly, although certain monopoly aspects were presented in *Moose Lodge No. 107, supra*, we found that the Lodge's action was not subject to the provisions of the Fourteenth Amendment. In each of those cases, there was insufficient relationship between the challenged actions of the entities involved and their monopoly status. There is no indication of any greater connection here.

Petitioner next urges that state action is present because respondent provides an essential public service required to be supplied on a reasonably continuous basis by Pa. Stat. Ann., Tit. 66, § 1171 (1959), and hence performs a "public function." We have, of course, found state action present in the exercise by a private entity of powers traditionally exclusively reserved to the State. See, e. g., *Nixon v. Condon*, 286 U.S. 73 (1932) (election); *Terry v. Adams*, 345 U.S. 461 (1953) (election); *Marsh v. Alabama*, 326 U.S. 501 (1946) (company town); *Evans v. Newton*, 382 U.S. 296 (1966) (municipal park). If we were dealing with the exercise by Metropolitan of some power delegated to it by the State which is traditionally associated with sovereignty, such as eminent domain, our case would be quite a different one. But while the Pennsylvania statute imposes an obligation to furnish service on regulated utilities, it imposes no such obligation on the State. The Pennsylvania courts have rejected the contention that the furnishing of utility services is either a state function or a municipal duty. *Girard Life Insurance Co. v. City of Philadelphia*, 88 Pa. 393 (1879); *Baily v. Philadelphia*, 184 Pa. 594, 39 A. 494 (1898).

Perhaps in recognition of the fact that the supplying of utility service is not traditionally the exclusive prerogative of the State, petitioner invites the expansion of the doctrine of this limited line of cases into a broad principle that all businesses "affected with the public interest" are state actors in all their actions.

We decline the invitation for reasons stated long ago in *Nebbia v. New York*, 291 U.S. 502 (1934), in the course of rejecting a substantive due process attack on state legislation:

> "It is clear that there is no closed class or category of businesses affected with a public interest. The phrase 'affected with a public interest' can, in the nature of things, mean no more than that an industry, for adequate reason, is subject to control for the public good. In several of the decisions of this court wherein the expressions 'affected with a public interest,' and 'clothed with a public use,' have been brought forward as the criteria...it has been admitted that they are not susceptible of definition and form an unsatisfactory test...." Id., at 536.

See, e. g., *Tyson & Brother v. Banton*, 273 U.S. 418, 451 (1927) (Stone, J., dissenting).

Doctors, optometrists, lawyers, Metropolitan, and Nebbia's upstate New York grocery selling a quart of milk are all in regulated businesses, providing arguably essential goods and services, "affected with a public interest." We do not believe that such a status converts their every action, absent more, into that of the State....

We also reject the notion that Metropolitan's termination is state action because the State "has specifically authorized and approved" the termination practice. In the instant case, Metropolitan filed with the Public Utility Commission a general tariff -- a provision of which states Metropolitan's right to terminate service for nonpayment....This provision has appeared in Metropolitan's previously filed tariffs for many years and has never been the subject of a hearing or other scrutiny by the Commission....Although the Commission did hold hearings on portions of Metropolitan's general tariff relating to a general rate increase, it never even considered the reinsertion of this provision in the newly filed general tariff....The provision became effective 60 days after filing when not disapproved by the Commission....As a threshold matter, it is less than clear under state law that Metropolitan was even required to file this provision as part of its tariff or that the Commission would have had the power to disapprove it....The District Court observed that the sole connection of the Commission with this regulation was Metropolitan's simple notice filing with the Commission and the lack of any Commission action to prohibit it....

The case most heavily relied on by petitioner is *Public Utilities Comm'n v. Pollak, supra*. There the Court dealt with the contention that Capital Transit's installation of a piped music system on its buses violated the First Amendment rights of the bus riders. It is not entirely clear whether the Court alternatively held that Capital Transit's action was action of the "State" for First Amendment purposes, or whether it merely assumed, *arguendo*, that it was and went on to resolve the First Amendment question adversely to the bus riders....In either event, the nature of the state involvement there was quite different than it is here. The District of Columbia Public Utilities Commission, on its own motion, commenced an investigation of the effects of the piped music, and after a full hearing concluded not only that Capital Transit's practices were "not inconsistent with public convenience, comfort, and safety," 81 P. U. R. (N. S.) 122, 126 (1950), but also that the practice "in fact, through the creation of better will among passengers,...tends to improve the conditions under which the public ride." *Ibid*. Here, on the other hand, there was no such imprimatur placed on the practice of Metropolitan about which petitioner complains. The nature of governmental regulation of private utilities is such that a utility may frequently be required by the state regulatory scheme to obtain approval for practices a business regulated in less detail would be free to institute without any approval from a regulatory body. Approval by a state utility commission of such a request from a regulated utility, where the commission has not put its own weight on the side of the proposed practice by ordering it, does not transmute a practice initiated by the utility and approved by the commission into "state action." At most, the Commission's failure to overturn this practice amounted to no more than a determination that a Pennsylvania utility was authorized to employ such a practice if it so desired. Respondent's exercise of the choice allowed by state law where the initiative comes from it and not from the State, does not make its action in doing so "state action" for purposes of the Fourteenth Amendment.

We also find absent in the instant case the symbiotic relationship presented in *Burton v. Wilmington Parking Authority*, 365 U.S. 715 (1961). There where a private lessee, who practiced racial discrimination, leased space for a restaurant from a state parking authority in a publicly owned building, the Court held that the State had so far insinuated itself into a position of interdependence with the restaurant that it was a joint participant in the enterprise. *Id.*, at 725. We cautioned, however, that while "a multitude of relationships might appear to some to fall within the Amendment's embrace," differences in circumstances beget differences in law, limiting the actual holding to lessees of public property. *Id.*, at 726.

Metropolitan is a privately owned corporation, and it does not lease its facilities from the State of Pennsylvania. It alone is responsible for the provision of power to its customers. In common with all corporations of the State it pays taxes to the State, and it is subject to a form of extensive regulation by the State in a way that most other business enterprises are not. But this was likewise true of the appellant club in *Moose Lodge No. 107 v. Irvis*, *supra*, where we said:

> "However detailed this type of regulation may be in some particulars, it cannot be said to in any way foster or encourage racial discrimination. Nor can it be said

to make the State in any realistic sense a partner or even a joint venturer in the club's enterprise." 407 U.S., at 176–177.

All of petitioner's arguments taken together show no more than that Metropolitan was a heavily regulated, privately owned utility, enjoying at least a partial monopoly in the providing of electrical service within its territory, and that it elected to terminate service to petitioner in a manner which the Pennsylvania Public Utility Commission found permissible under state law. Under our decision this is not sufficient to connect the State of Pennsylvania with respondent's action so as to make the latter's conduct attributable to the State for purposes of the Fourteenth Amendment.

We conclude that the State of Pennsylvania is not sufficiently connected with respondent's action in terminating petitioner's service so as to make respondent's conduct in so doing attributable to the State for purposes of the Fourteenth Amendment. We therefore have no occasion to decide whether petitioner's claim to continued service was "property" for purposes of that Amendment, or whether "due process of law" would require a State taking similar action to accord petitioner the procedural rights for which she contends. The judgment of the Court of Appeals for the Third Circuit is therefore

Affirmed.

MR. JUSTICE DOUGLAS, dissenting.

I reach the opposite conclusion from that reached by the majority on the state-action issue.

The injury alleged took place when respondent discontinued its service to this householder without notice or opportunity to remedy or contest her alleged default, even though its tariff provided that respondent might "discontinue its service on reasonable notice." May a State allow a utility -- which in this case has no competitor -- to exploit its monopoly in violation of its own tariff? May a utility have complete immunity under federal law when the State allows its regulatory agency to become the prisoner of the utility or, by a listless attitude of no concern, to permit the utility to use its monopoly power in a lawless way?

In *Burton v. Wilmington Parking Authority*, 365 U.S. 715 (1961), we said: "Only by sifting facts and weighing circumstances can the nonobvious involvement of the State in private conduct be attributed its true significance." *Id.*, at 722. A particularized inquiry into the circumstances of each case is necessary in order to determine whether a given factual situation falls within "the variety of individual-state relationships which the [Fourteenth] Amendment was designed to embrace." Ibid. As our subsequent discussion in Burton made clear, the dispositive question in any state-action case is not whether any single fact or relationship presents a sufficient degree of state involvement, but rather whether the aggregate of all relevant factors compels a finding of state responsibility....*Id.*, at 722–726. See generally *Moose Lodge No. 107 v. Irvis*, 407 U.S. 163 (1972).

It is not enough to examine seriatim each of the factors upon which a claimant relies and to dismiss each individually as being insufficient to support a finding of state action. It is the aggregate that is controlling.

It is said that the mere fact of respondent's monopoly status, assuming arguendo that that status is state conferred or state protected, "is not determinative in considering whether Metropolitan's termination of service to petitioner was 'state action' for purposes of the Fourteenth Amendment." *Ante*, at 351-352. Even so, a state-protected monopoly status is highly relevant in assessing the aggregate weight of a private entity's ties to the State....

It is said that the fact that respondent's services are "affected with a public interest" is not determinative. I agree that doctors, lawyers, and grocers are not transformed into state actors simply because they provide arguably essential goods and services and are regulated by the State. In the present case, however, respondent is not just one person among many; it is the only public utility furnishing electric power to the city. When power is denied a householder, the home, under modern conditions, is likely to become unlivable.

Respondent's procedures for termination of service may never have been subjected to the same degree of state scrutiny and approval, whether explicit or implicit, that was present in *Public Utilities Comm'n v. Pollak*, 343 U.S. 451 (1952). Yet in the present case the State is heavily involved in respondent's termination procedures, getting into the approved tariff a requirement of "reasonable notice." Pennsylvania has undertaken to regulate numerous aspects of respondent's operations in some detail,...and a "hands-off" attitude of permissiveness or neutrality toward the operations in this case is at war with the state agency's functions of supervision over respondent's conduct in the area of servicing householders, particularly where (as here) the State would presumably lend its weight and authority to facilitate the enforcement of respondent's published procedures. Cf. *Adickes v. S. H. Kress & Co.*, 398 U.S. 144 (1970); *Reitman v. Mulkey*, 387 U.S. 369 (1967); *Railway Employes' Dept. v. Hanson*, 351 U.S. 225 (1956); *Shelley v. Kraemer*, 334 U.S. 1 (1948).

In the aggregate, these factors depict a monopolist providing essential public services as a licensee of the State and within a framework of extensive state supervision and control. The particular regulations at issue, promulgated by the monopolist, were authorized by state law and were made enforceable by the weight and authority of the State. Moreover, the State retains the power of oversight to review and amend the regulations if the public interest so requires. Respondent's actions are sufficiently intertwined with those of the State, and its termination-of-service provisions are sufficiently buttressed by state law to warrant a holding that respondent's actions in terminating this householder's service were "state action" for the purpose of giving federal jurisdiction over respondent under 42 U. S. C. § 1983. Though the Court pays lip service to the need for assessing the totality of the State's involvement in this enterprise, *ante*, at 358, its underlying analysis is fundamentally sequential rather than cumulative. In that perspective, what the Court does today is to make a significant departure from our previous treatment of state-action issues.

Mr. Justice Brandeis in *Liggett Co. v. Lee*, 288 U.S. 517 (1933), in speaking of the competition among the States to ease the opportunities and methods of incorporation, said: "The race was one not of diligence but of laxity." *Id.*, at 559 (dissenting opinion). One has only to peruse the 84-part Utility Corporations Report by the Federal Trade Commission (under the direction of its able counsel the late Robert E. Healy) to realize that state regulation of utilities has largely made state commissions prisoners of the utilities. See especially S. Doc. No. 92, 70th Cong., 1st Sess., pt. 73-A (1936); and see id., pt. 72-A, p. 880. In this connection it should be noted that successful attempts by public utilities to exclude themselves from the antitrust laws have been based on the assertion that their monopoly activity constitutes "state action." See *Washington Gas Light Co. v. Virginia Electric & Power Co.*, 438 F.2d 248, 250-252 (CA4 1971); *Gas Light Co. of Columbus v. Georgia Power Co.*, 440 F.2d 1135, 1138–1140 (CA5 1971).

By like token the tariff prescribing termination-of-service procedures was possible only because of "state action." And it would be compatible only with administrative abdication of authority to equate "administrative silence with abandonment of administrative duty." *Washington Gas Light Co. v. Virginia Electric & Power Co., supra*, at 252.

Section 1983 was designed to give citizens a federal forum...for civil rights complaints wherever, by direct or indirect actions, a State, acting "in cahoots" with a private group or through neglect or listless oversight, allows a private group to perpetrate an injury. The theory is that in those cozy situations, local politics and the pressure of economic overlords on subservient state agencies make recovery in state courts unlikely. I realize we are in an area where we witness a great retreat from the exercise of federal jurisdiction which the Congress has conferred on federal courts. The sentiment here is that state courts are as hospitable as federal courts to federal claims. That may well be true, in some instances. But it is for the Senate and the House to make that decision. We should not tolerate an erosion of the policy Congress expressed in drafting § 1983.

Section 1983 addresses itself to grievances inflicted "under color of any statute, ordinance, [or] regulation...of any State...." The regulatory regime imposed by Pennsylvania on respondent utility seems to fit this statute like a glove. Electrical service, being a necessity of life under the circumstances of this case, is an entitlement which under our decisions may not be taken without the requirements of procedural due process. *Fuentes v. Shevin*, 407 U.S. 67, 80 (1972); *Goldberg v. Kelly*, 397 U.S. 254 (1970); *Palmer v. Columbia Gas of Ohio, Inc.*, 479 F.2d 153 (CA6 1973).

***

MR. JUSTICE MARSHALL, dissenting.

***

I

The Metropolitan Edison Co. provides an essential public service to the people of York, Pa. It is the only entity, public or private, that is authorized to supply electric service to most of the community. As a part of its charter to the company, the State imposes extensive regulations, and it cooperates with the company in myriad ways. Additionally, the State has granted its approval to the company's mode of service termination -- the very conduct that is challenged here. Taking these factors together, I have no difficulty finding state action in this case. As the Court concluded in *Burton v. Wilmington Parking Authority,* 365 U.S. 715, 725 (1961), the State has sufficiently "insinuated itself into a position of interdependence with [the company] that it must be recognized as a joint participant in the challenged activity."

Our state-action cases have repeatedly relied on several factors clearly presented by this case: a state-sanctioned monopoly; an extensive pattern of cooperation between the "private" entity and the State; and a service uniquely public in nature. Today the Court takes a major step in repudiating this line of authority and adopts a stance that is bound to lead to mischief when applied to problems beyond the narrow sphere of due process objections to utility terminations.

A

When the State confers a monopoly on a group or organization, this Court has held that the organization assumes many of the obligations of the State. *Railway Employees' Dept. v. Hanson*, 351 U.S. 225 (1956). Even when the Court has not found state action based solely on the State's conferral of a monopoly, it has suggested that the monopoly factor weighs heavily in determining whether constitutional obligations can be imposed on formally private entities. See *Steele v. Louisville & Nashville R. Co.*, 323 U.S. 192 (1944). Indeed, in *Moose Lodge No. 107 v. Irvis*, 407 U.S. 163, 177 (1972), the Court was careful to point out that the Pennsylvania liquor-licensing scheme "falls far short of conferring upon club licensees a monopoly in the dispensing of liquor in any given municipality or in the State as a whole."

The majority distinguishes this line of cases with a cryptic assertion that public utility companies are "natural monopolies." *Ante*, at 351-352, n. 8. The theory behind the distinction appears to be that since the State's purpose in regulating a natural monopoly is not to aid the company but to prevent its charging monopoly prices, the State's involvement is somehow less significant for state-action purposes. I cannot agree that so much should turn on so narrow a distinction. Initially, it is far from obvious that an electric company would not be subject to competition if the market were unimpeded by governmental restrictions. Certainly the "start-up" costs of initiating electric service are substantial, but the rewards available in a relatively inelastic market might well be sufficient under the right circumstances to attract competitive investment. Instead, the State has chosen to forbid the high profit margins that might invite private competition or increase pressure for state ownership and operation of electric power facilities.

The difficulty inherent in this kind of economic analysis counsels against excusing natural monopolies from the reach of state-action principles. To invite inquiry into whether a particular state-sanctioned monopoly might have survived without the State's express approval grounds the analysis in hopeless speculation. Worse, this approach ignores important implications of the State's policy of utilizing private monopolies to provide electric service. Encompassed within this policy is the State's determination not to permit governmental competition with the selected private company, but to cooperate with and regulate the company in a multitude of ways to ensure that the company's service will be the functional equivalent of service provided by the State....

B

The pattern of cooperation between Metropolitan Edison and the State has led to significant state involvement in virtually every phase of the company's business. The majority, however, accepts the relevance of the State's regulatory scheme only to the extent that it demonstrates state support for the challenged termination procedure. Moreover, after concluding that the State in this case had not approved the company's termination procedures, the majority suggests that even state authorization and approval would not be sufficient: the State would apparently have to order the termination practice in question to satisfy the majority's state-action test, see *ante*, at 357.

I disagree with the majority's position on three separate grounds. First, the suggestion that the State would have to "put its own weight on the side of the proposed practice by ordering it" seems to me to mark a sharp departure from our previous state-action cases. From the *Civil Rights Cases*, 109 U.S. 3 (1883), to *Moose Lodge*, *supra*, we have consistently indicated that state authorization and approval of "private" conduct would support a finding of state action....

Second, I question the wisdom of giving such short shrift to the extensive interaction between the company and the State, and focusing solely on the extent of state support for the particular activity under challenge. In cases where the State's only significant involvement is through financial support or limited regulation of the private entity, it may be well to inquire whether the State's involvement suggests state approval of the objectionable conduct. See *Powe v. Miles*, 407 F.2d 73, 81 (CA2 1968); *Grossner v. Trustees of Columbia University*, 287 F.Supp. 535, 547-548 (SDNY 1968). But where the State has so thoroughly insinuated itself into the operations of the enterprise, it should not be fatal if the State has not affirmatively sanctioned the particular practice in question.

Finally, it seems to me in any event that the State *has* given its approval to Metropolitan Edison's termination procedures. The State Utility Commission approved a tariff provision under which the company reserved the right to discontinue its service on reasonable notice for nonpayment of bills.

The majority attempts to make something of the fact that the tariff provision was not challenged in the most recent Utility Commission hearings, and that it had apparently not been challenged before. But the provision had been included in a tariff required to be filed and approved by the State pursuant to statute. That it was not seriously questioned before approval does not mean that it was not approved. It suggests, instead, that the Commission was satisfied to permit the company to proceed in the termination area as it had done in the past. The majority's test puts potential plaintiffs in a difficult position: if the Commission approves the tariff without argument or a hearing, the State has not sufficiently demonstrated its approval and support for the company's practices. If, on the other hand, the State challenges the tariff provision on the ground, for example, that the "reasonable notice" does not meet the standards of fairness that it expects of the utility, then the State has not put its weight behind the termination procedure employed by the company, and again there is no state action. Apparently, authorization and approval would require the kind of hearing that was held in Pollak, where the Public Utilities Commission expressly stated that the bus company's installation of radios in buses and streetcars was not inconsistent with the public convenience, safety, and necessity. I am afraid that the majority has in effect restricted Pollak to its facts if it has not discarded it altogether....

C

The fact that the Metropolitan Edison Co. supplies an essential public service that is in many communities supplied by the government weighs more heavily for me than for the majority. The Court concedes that state action might be present if the activity in question were "traditionally associated with sovereignty," but it then undercuts that point by suggesting that a particular service is not a public function if the State in question has not required that it be governmentally operated. This reads the "public function" argument too narrowly. The whole point of the "public function" cases is to look behind the State's decision to provide public services through private parties. See *Evans v. Newton*, 382 U.S. 296 (1966); *Terry v. Adams*, 345 U.S. 461 (1953); *Marsh v. Alabama*, 326 U.S. 501 (1946).

In my view, utility service is traditionally identified with the State through universal public regulation or ownership to a degree sufficient to render it a "public function."

I agree with the majority that it requires more than a finding that a particular business is "affected with the public interest" before constitutional burdens can be imposed on that business. But when the activity in question is of such public importance that the State invariably either provides the service itself or permits private companies to act as state surrogates in providing it, much more is involved than just a matter of public interest. In those cases, the State has determined that if private companies wish to enter the field, they will have to surrender many of the prerogatives normally associated with private enterprise and behave in many ways like a governmental body. And when the State's regulatory scheme has gone that far, it seems entirely consistent to impose on the public utility the constitutional burdens normally reserved for the State.

Private parties performing functions affecting the public interest can often make a persuasive claim to be free of the constitutional requirements applicable to governmental institutions because of the value of preserving a private sector in which the opportunity for individual choice is maximized. See *Evans v. Newton*, *supra*, at 298; H. Friendly, The Dartmouth College Case and the Public-Private Penumbra (1969). Maintaining the private status of parochial schools, cited by the majority, advances just this value. In the due process area, a similar value of diversity may often be furthered by allowing various private institutions the flexibility to select procedures that fit their particular needs. See *Wahba v. New York University*, 492 F.2d 96, 102 (CA2), cert. denied, *post*, p. 874. But it is hard to imagine any such interests that are furthered by protecting privately owned public utility companies from meeting the constitutional standards that would apply if the companies were state owned. The values of pluralism and diversity are simply not relevant when the private company is the only electric company in town.

II

The majority's conclusion that there is no state action in this case is likely guided in part by its reluctance to impose on a utility company burdens that might ultimately hurt consumers more than they would help them. Elaborate hearings prior to termination might be quite expensive, and for a responsible company there might be relatively few cases in which such hearings would do any good. The solution to this problem, however, is to require only abbreviated pretermination procedures for all utility companies, not to free the "private" companies to behave however they see fit. At least on occasion, utility companies have failed to demonstrate much sensitivity to the extreme importance of the service they render, and in some cities, the percentage of error in service termination is disturbingly high. See *Palmer v. Columbia Gas Co. of Ohio, Inc.*, 342 F.Supp. 241, 243 (ND Ohio 1972), aff'd, 479 F.2d 153 (CA6 1973); *Bronson v. Consolidated Edison Co.*, 350 F.Supp. 443, 448 (SDNY 1972) Accordingly, I think that at the minimum, due process would require advance notice of a proposed termination with a clear indication that a responsible company official can readily be contacted to consider any claim of error.

III

What is perhaps most troubling about the Court's opinion is that it would appear to apply to a broad range of claimed constitutional violations by the company. The Court has not adopted the notion, accepted elsewhere, that different standards should apply to state-action analysis when different constitutional claims are presented. See *Adickes v. S. H. Kress & Co.*, 398 U.S. 144, 190–191 (1970) (BRENNAN, J., concurring and dissenting); *Grafton v.*

Brooklyn Law School, 478 F.2d 1137, 1142 (CA2 1973). Thus, the majority's analysis would seemingly apply as well to a company that refused to extend service to Negroes, welfare recipients, or any other group that the company preferred, for its own reasons, not to serve. I cannot believe that this Court would hold that the State's involvement with the utility company was not sufficient to impose upon the company an obligation to meet the constitutional mandate of nondiscrimination. Yet nothing in the analysis of the majority opinion suggests otherwise.

I dissent.

***

Quiz

1) Which of the following are the factors the state must show in order to validate a proposed regulation that may impact interstate commerce? (Choose two)

   a. The state regulation is substantially related to accomplishing an important state objective.

   b. The state regulation is rationally related to a legitimate state interest.

   c. The state's interest in enforcing the regulation outweighs the burden the regulation imposes on interstate commerce.

   d. The federal government occupies the field that is the subject matter of the proposed regulation.

2) Assuming it does not involve a discriminatory purpose, which of these is an effective means for the federal government to impose its desired outcome of state regulation even where it does not occupy the field of the subject matter of the regulations?

   a. Conditioning availability of federal funding on the state's adoption of the desired policy

   b. Imposition of the supremacy clause

   c. Imposition of the privileges and immunities clause

   d. None of the above.

3) In *Missouri v Harris*, the Ninth Circuit upheld the District Court's dismissal of the case on the grounds that the plaintiff states lacked standing to challenge California's law requiring chickens to be given minimal space. If the case would have been permitted to proceed on the merits and the court would have considered the states' arguments that California's law is unconstitutional because it places a burden on interstate commerce, which of the following would be California's most persuasive argument that the court should uphold its statute?

   a. If producers in any of the six suing states want to sell products in another state, they should have to comply with the laws of the state with jurisdiction over the purchasing consumers.

   b. California consumers find it reprehensible to engage in animal cruelty to lower costs. Here, there is no inherent difficulty or discriminatory effect in complying with the statute. It confers no unfair advantage on California producers and all producers are able to comply.

c. This law isn't discriminatory because California egg producers have to comply with the same restrictions too.

d. The Federal government does not occupy the field of regulation involving egg production and therefore the commerce clause does not apply.

4) Which of the following best describes the holding in *Welch v. Brown* with respect to California's statute banning Sexual Orientation Change Efforts (SOCE), AKA "Gay Conversion Therapy" for minors?

a. The law does not infringe upon religious rights because homosexuality is not so connected to religious belief that strict scrutiny would properly apply.

b. The First Amendment Rights of regulated professionals are subject to some state control along a spectrum. If a doctor is making a political comment about a medicine or treatment it is entitled to strong protection, but where it is part of a "treatment" itself subject to regulation, that speech right may be limited.

c. There is much latitude in the "how" of licensed practice, but the "what" that is to be proffered as therapy may be imposed by the state.

d. All of the above

5) Under which constitutional principle would an individual have the strongest argument if challenging a Board's decision to revoke his license to practice accounting where the Board is comprised of a majority of accountants?

a. Freedom of Contract

b. First Amendment Freedom of Speech

c. Interstate Commerce Clause

d. Due process procedure

Chapter 3
Antitrust Law

Discussion

Antitrust law reflects Aristotle's "golden mean" concept. There is a spectrum from collusion between competitors to bullying by one over others. Antitrust law attempts to block both extremes to allow consumers at the bottom of the market to have choices and to decide in their own respective best interests. The idea is to have "bottom up" control of the market by consumers, not top down through horizontal arrangements or single firm tyranny.

Federal antitrust law begins with Sherman Act section one prohibiting "unreasonable combinations in restraint of trade." Sherman Act section two prohibits "monopolization." Note that monopoly itself may not be an offense, but achieving or maintaining monopoly by unfair means transforms a practice into unlawful "monopolization." In addition, federal antitrust law also includes the Robinson-Patman Act and the Clayton Act, applying to price discrimination and anticompetitive mergers, respectively. The above statutes are enforced through public prosecutions by U.S. Attorneys and the Department of Justice, and many have private civil remedies for treble damages and attorney fees for successful plaintiff counsel. Violations may also be criminal felony offenses. Finally, federal law also has the Federal Trade Commission Act which confers civil authority to the FTC to enforce the above statutes, as well as unfair competition more generally, using cease and desist powers and civil penalties. The FTC is also empowered to review mergers, and to adopt "trade regulation rules" to assure lawful and competitive commercial practices.

The jurisdiction of these federal statutes is broad and covers a transaction that "affects" interstate commerce. Such an "affect" is broadly defined.

State antitrust law generally parallels the above federal statutes. Taking California as an example, the "Cartwright Act" (California Business and Professions Code Section 16700 et seq.) covers "trusts"—which are collusive arrangements that violate the law, similar to Sherman Act Section 1, above. And as with the federal statute, violations may be felony offenses, as well as yielding civil treble damage remedies. In addition to the state Cartwright Act, Section 17200 is the "Unfair Competition Law (UCL)" which covers the broad range of the federal FTC jurisdiction above. It may be enforced with injunctive relief and civil penalties by the state Attorney General, any county district attorney, and the city attorneys of the largest cities in the state. And it can also be enforced civilly by private parties—including equitable remedies such as injunctions, disgorgement, and restitution, as well as attorneys' fees. However, no civil penalties will accrue for private action, and such general private prosecutions must qualify the allegedly damaged consumers as a qualifying "class" under applicable criteria. This broad statute covers any "unfair, unlawful, or fraudulent" act in competition. And is sometimes referred to as "the Little FTC Act," with counterparts in most of the 50 states. Also, related to these prohibitions in California is Section 17500 of the Business and Professions Code—which broadly prohibits deceptive advertising and with similar public prosecution and private civil remedies.

The first step in applying antitrust law is to define the "market" at issue. *I.e.*, it is necessary to begin analysis by spelling out that is the "relevant market" to gauge impact. This may have two dimensions: (a) the product or service market, and (b) the geographic market. In the modern market, geography has become less significant given the growing large space for competitive choice as communications and delivery advances create larger geographically defined markets.

As to both federal and state laws in this field, only "unreasonable" combinations are prohibited, since competitors may have legitimate reasons to agree among themselves on certain practices. To this end, such agreements are generally examined under what is termed the "rule of reason." But some types of offenses are considered "*per se*" unreasonable.

One aspect of the market to be examined is whether the competition at issue is "horizontal" or "vertical." Horizontal restraints involve agreements or practices between direct competitors, *e.g.*, gas stations or retail stores. Vertical restraints pertain to arrangements between a manufacturer and wholesaler and/or retailer up or down the chain of distribution. Courts tend to more easily find per se offenses that involve horizontally competing entities.

Certain types of restraints are considered "per se" unreasonable and the plaintiff in such cases need not prove it to be substantively so. The categories so qualifying include price fixing—applicable where an agreement artificially affects prices. Note that in the regulatory sphere, any supply restriction agreement has such an artificial impact—including that of licensure. But as discussed below, restraints, including those qualifying as per se unreasonable may be lawful if covered by the "state action" exception. If state law provides for or authorizes such agreements, they may be lawful notwithstanding anticompetitive impact.

Other commonly condemned restraints include what are termed "group boycotts" (or an arrangement to exclude a competitor from a market). Also considered to be a per se offense is a "tying arrangement" where the purchase of one product or service where there is substantial market power is used to require purchase of other (or tied) purchases.

An example of an antitrust violation in an allegedly regulated area of commerce is an antitrust case brought by Professor Fellmeth while a public prosecutor. *People v. National Association of Realtors*, 120 Cal.App.3d 465

(1981), was brought against the San Diego Board of Realtors, as well as their state and national associations. Importantly, "realtors" is the name of those who belong to a private trade association. They may also be state-licensed brokers authorized to sell real property, but the realtor organization is not a state entity but is a private association of allegedly competing practitioners. The case involved two major allegations. First, the association entirely controlled what is termed a "multiple listing service," which contained information about properties offered for sale. Every real estate broker or agent has to have access to that service in order to market their client's real property, both to buy and sell. But in order to get access to that necessary market document, each broker or agent also had to join the "realtor" trade association and pay fees for its operations, including lobbying, et al. This was alleged as a per se "tie-in," requiring the purchase of a separate tied product ("realtor" membership and political activities) as a condition to access to the "tying" product—the multiple listing service market information.

Second, the thousands of allegedly competing members of the realtor associations all charged the same fee, 6% of the selling price of a piece of real property. This fee was unrelated to costs and increased dramatically as real property values increased. By linking it to a percentage of that number, they assured themselves dramatically increasing revenue and profit. In the case brought, a small competitor (Twin Palms Realty) was the only broker offering a commission charge unrelated to sale price, but instead offered to charge $1,600 for brokerage services. The San Diego Board of Realtors responded by sanctioning the lower priced competitor in a variety of ways, including the denial of any commission as to properties where it provided a buyer more than the amount it was charging.

Both of these offenses were *per se* horizontal violations and judgment was returned for the People. Importantly, these offenders were all licensed by the State of California and allegedly regulated by a Department of Real Estate state agency. That agency did nothing to detect, prevent, or in any way review these long-standing felony practices.

Every day, agencies:

- Combine to preclude prospective competitors from the marketplace (licensing)
- Engage in a group boycott to preclude competitors from the marketplace (licensing)
- Combine to adopt regulations affecting price or supply of services (rulemaking)
- Collude to exclude competitors from the marketplace (discipline).

How can they do what they do? The answer is known as "state action."

STATE ACTION

The Sherman Act contains no purpose to nullify state powers. Actions of the state itself are not subject to federal antitrust laws. And in terms of state antitrust law, state statutes authorizing a restraint of trade trumps the more general competition protecting laws under standard "conflict of law" doctrine.

Cal. Retail Liquor Dealers Ass'n v. Midcal Aluminum

445 U.S. 97 (1980)

A California statute requires all wine producers and wholesalers to file fair trade contracts or price schedules with the State. If a producer has not set prices through a fair trade contract, wholesalers must post a resale price schedule and are prohibited from selling wine to a retailer at other than the price set in a price schedule or fair trade contract. A wholesaler selling below the established prices faces fines or license suspension or revocation. After being charged with selling wine for less than the prices set by price schedules and also for selling wines for which no fair trade contract or schedule had been filed, respondent wholesaler filed suit in the California Court of Appeal asking for an injunction against the State's wine pricing scheme. The Court of Appeal ruled that the scheme restrains trade in violation of the Sherman Act, and granted injunctive relief, rejecting claims that the scheme was immune from liability under that Act under the "state action" doctrine of *Parker v. Brown*, 317 U.S. 341, and was also protected by § 2 of the Twenty-first Amendment, which prohibits the transportation or importation of intoxicating liquors into any State for delivery or use therein in violation of the State's laws.

Held:

1. California's wine pricing system constitutes resale price maintenance in violation of the Sherman Act, since the wine producer holds the power to prevent price competition by dictating the prices charged by wholesalers. And the State's involvement in the system is insufficient to establish antitrust immunity under *Parker v. Brown, supra*. While the system satisfies the first requirement for such immunity that the challenged restraint be "one clearly articulated and affirmatively expressed as state policy," it does not meet the other

requirement that the policy be "actively supervised" by the State itself. Under the system the State simply authorizes price setting and enforces the prices established by private parties, and it does not establish prices, review the reasonableness of price schedules, regulate the terms of fair trade contracts, monitor market conditions, or engage in any "pointed reexamination" of the program. The national policy in favor of competition cannot be thwarted by casting such a gauzy cloak of state involvement over what is essentially a private price-fixing arrangement....

2. The Twenty-first Amendment does not bar application of the Sherman Act to California's wine pricing system....

(a) Although under that Amendment States retain substantial discretion to establish liquor regulations over and above those governing the importation or sale of liquor and the structure of the liquor distribution system, those controls may be subject to the federal commerce power in appropriate situations....

(b) There is no basis for disagreeing with the view of the California courts that the asserted state interests behind the resale price maintenance system of promoting temperance and protecting small retailers are less substantial than the national policy in favor of competition. Such view is reasonable and is supported by the evidence, there being nothing to indicate that the wine pricing system helps sustain small retailers or inhibits the consumption of alcohol by Californians....

***

Discussion

The gist of the full *Midcal* decision is the following proposition: To qualify for state action immunity, a challenged state action must meet a two-pronged test: (1) the challenged action must be a "clearly articulated and affirmatively expressed" state policy (*e.g.*, contained in a state statute or constitutional provision), **and** (2) the action must be "actively supervised" in a meaningful way by the state.

Goldfarb v. Va. State Bar

421 U.S. 773 (1975)

MR. CHIEF JUSTICE BURGER delivered the opinion of the Court.

We granted certiorari to decide whether a minimum fee schedule for lawyers published by the Fairfax County Bar Association and enforced by the Virginia State Bar violates § 1 of the Sherman Act, 26 Stat. 209, as amended, 15 U.S.C. § 1. The Court of Appeals held that, although the fee schedule and enforcement mechanism substantially restrained competition among lawyers, publication of the schedule by the County Bar was outside the scope of the Act because the practice of law is not "trade or commerce," and enforcement of the schedule by the State Bar was exempt from the Sherman Act as state action as defined in *Parker v. Brown*, 317 U.S. 341 (1943).

I

In 1971 petitioners, husband and wife, contracted to buy a home in Fairfax County, Va. The financing agency required them to secure title insurance; this required a title examination, and only a member of the Virginia State Bar could legally perform that service....Petitioners therefore contacted a lawyer who quoted them the precise fee suggested in a minimum-fee schedule published by respondent Fairfax County Bar Association; the lawyer told them that it was his policy to keep his charges in line with the minimum-fee schedule which provided for a fee of 1% of the value of the property involved. Petitioners then tried to find a lawyer who would examine the title for less than the fee fixed by the schedule. They sent letters to 36 other Fairfax County lawyers requesting their fees. Nineteen replied, and none indicated that he would charge less than the rate fixed by the schedule; several stated that they knew of no attorney who would do so.

The fee schedule the lawyers referred to is a list of recommended minimum prices for common legal services. Respondent Fairfax County Bar Association published the fee schedule although, as a purely voluntary association of attorneys, the County Bar has no formal power to enforce it. Enforcement has been provided by respondent Virginia State Bar which is the administrative agency...through which the Virginia Supreme Court regulates the practice of law in that State; membership in the State Bar is required in order to practice in Virginia....Although the State Bar has never taken formal disciplinary action to compel adherence to any fee schedule, it has published reports...condoning fee schedules, and has issued two ethical opinions...indicating that fee schedules cannot be ignored. The most recent opinion states that "evidence that an attorney habitually charges less than the suggested minimum fee schedule adopted by his local bar Association, raises a presumption that such lawyer is guilty of misconduct...."

***

We granted certiorari, 419 U.S. 963 (1974), and are thus confronted for the first time with the question of whether the Sherman Act applies to services performed by attorneys in examining titles in connection with financing the purchase of real estate.

II

Our inquiry can be divided into four steps: did respondents engage in price fixing? If so, are their activities in interstate commerce or do they affect interstate commerce? If so, are the activities exempt from the Sherman Act because they involve a "learned profession?" If not, are the activities "state action" within the meaning of *Parker v. Brown*, 317 U.S. 341 (1943), and therefore exempt from the Sherman Act?

A

The County Bar argues that because the fee schedule is merely advisory, the schedule and its enforcement mechanism do not constitute price fixing. Its purpose, the argument continues, is only to provide legitimate information to aid member lawyers in complying with Virginia professional regulations. Moreover, the County Bar contends that in practice the schedule has not had the effect of producing fixed fees. The facts found by the trier belie these contentions, and nothing in the record suggests these findings lack support.

A purely advisory fee schedule issued to provide guidelines, or an exchange of price information without a showing of an actual restraint on trade, would present us with a different question, e.g., *American Column Co. v. United States*, 257 U.S. 377 (1921); *Maple Flooring Assn. v. United States*, 268 U.S. 563, 580 (1925). But see *United States v. National Assn. of Real Estate Boards*, 339 U.S. 485, 488-489, 495 (1950). The record here, however, reveals a situation quite different from what would occur under a purely advisory fee schedule. Here a fixed, rigid price floor arose from respondents' activities: every lawyer who responded to petitioners' inquiries adhered to the fee schedule, and no lawyer asked for additional information in order to set an individualized fee. The price information disseminated did not concern past standards, cf. *Cement Mfrs. Protective Assn. v. United States*, 268 U.S. 588 (1925), but rather minimum fees to be charged in future transactions, and those minimum rates were increased over time. The fee schedule was enforced through the prospect of professional discipline from the State Bar, and the desire of attorneys to comply with announced professional norms, see generally *American Column Co., supra*, at 411; the motivation to conform was reinforced by the assurance that other lawyers would not compete by underbidding. This is not merely a case of an agreement that may be inferred from an exchange of price information, *United States v. Container Corp.*, 393 U.S. 333, 337 (1969), for here a naked agreement was clearly shown, and the effect on prices is plain.... *Id.*, at 339 (Fortas, J., concurring).

Moreover, in terms of restraining competition and harming consumers like petitioners the price-fixing activities found here are unusually damaging. A title examination is indispensable in the process of financing a real estate purchase, and since only an attorney licensed to practice in Virginia may legally examine a title, see n. 1, supra, consumers could not turn to alternative sources for the necessary service. All attorneys, of course, were practicing under the constraint of the fee schedule. See generally *United States v. Container Corp., supra*, at 337. The County Bar makes much of the fact that it is a voluntary organization; however, the ethical opinions issued by the State Bar provide that any lawyer, whether or not a member of his county bar association, may be disciplined for "habitually [charging] less than the suggested minimum fee schedule adopted by his local bar Association…." See *supra*, at 777-778, and n. 4. These factors coalesced to create a pricing system that consumers could not realistically escape. On this record respondents' activities constitute a classic illustration of price fixing.

B

The County Bar argues, as the Court of Appeals held, that any effect on interstate commerce caused by the fee schedule's restraint on legal services was incidental and remote. In its view the legal services, which are performed wholly intrastate, are essentially local in nature and therefore a restraint with respect to them can never substantially affect interstate commerce. Further, the County Bar maintains, there was no showing here that the fee schedule and its enforcement mechanism increased fees, and that even if they did there was no showing that such an increase deterred any prospective homeowner from buying in Fairfax County.

These arguments misconceive the nature of the transactions at issue and the place legal services play in those transactions. As the District Court found,… "a significant portion of funds furnished for the purchasing of homes in Fairfax County comes from without the State of Virginia," and "significant amounts of loans on Fairfax County real estate are guaranteed by the United States Veterans Administration and Department of Housing and Urban Development, both headquartered in the District of Columbia." Thus in this class action the transactions which create the need for the particular legal services in question frequently are interstate transactions. The necessary connection between the interstate transactions and the restraint of trade provided by the minimum-fee schedule is present because, in a practical sense,… title examinations are necessary in real estate transactions to assure a lien on a valid title of the borrower. In financing realty purchases lenders require, "as a condition of making the loan, that the title to the property involved be examined…."…Thus a title examination is an integral part of an interstate transaction…and this Court has long held that "there is an obvious distinction to be drawn between a course of conduct wholly within a state and conduct which is an inseparable element of a larger program dependent for its success upon activity which affects commerce between the states." *United States v. Frankfort Distilleries*, 324 U.S. 293, 297 (1945). See *United States v. Yellow Cab Co.*, 332 U.S. 218, 228-229 (1947).

***

Where, as a matter of law or practical necessity, legal services are an integral part of an interstate transaction, a restraint on those services may substantially affect commerce for Sherman Act purposes. Of course, there may be legal services that involve interstate commerce in other fashions, just as there may be legal services that have no nexus with interstate commerce and thus are beyond the reach of the Sherman Act.

C

The County Bar argues that Congress never intended to include the learned professions within the terms "trade or commerce" in § 1 of the Sherman Act,...and therefore the sale of professional services is exempt from the Act. No explicit exemption or legislative history is provided to support this contention; rather, the existence of state regulation seems to be its primary basis. Also, the County Bar maintains that competition is inconsistent with the practice of a profession because enhancing profit is not the goal of professional activities; the goal is to provide services necessary to the community....That, indeed, is the classic basis traditionally advanced to distinguish professions from trades, businesses, and other occupations, but it loses some of its force when used to support the fee control activities involved here.

In arguing that learned professions are not "trade or commerce" the County Bar seeks a total exclusion from antitrust regulation. Whether state regulation is active or dormant, real or theoretical, lawyers would be able to adopt anticompetitive practices with impunity. We cannot find support for the proposition that Congress intended any such sweeping exclusion. The nature of an occupation, standing alone, does not provide sanctuary from the Sherman Act, *Associated Press v. United States*, 326 U.S. 1, 7 (1945), nor is the public-service aspect of professional practice controlling in determining whether § 1 includes professions. *United States v. National Assn. of Real Estate Boards*, 339 U.S., at 489. Congress intended to strike as broadly as it could in § 1 of the Sherman Act, and to read into it so wide an exemption as that urged on us would be at odds with that purpose.

The language of § 1 of the Sherman Act, of course, contains no exception. "Language more comprehensive is difficult to conceive." *United States v. South-Eastern Underwriters Assn.*, 322 U.S. 533, 553 (1944). And our cases have repeatedly established that there is a heavy presumption against implicit exemptions, *United States v. Philadelphia National Bank*, 374 U.S. 321, 350-351 (1963); *California v. FPC*, 369 U.S. 482, 485 (1962). Indeed, our cases have specifically included the sale of services within § 1. E.g., *American Medical Assn. v. United States*, 317 U.S. 519 (1943); *Radovich v. National Football League*, 352 U.S. 445 (1957). Whatever else it may be, the examination of a land title is a service; the exchange of such a service for money is "commerce" in the most common usage of that word. It is no disparagement of the practice of law as a profession to acknowledge that it has this business aspect,...and § 1 of the Sherman Act "[o]n its face... shows a carefully studied attempt to bring within the Act every person engaged in business whose activities might restrain or monopolize commercial intercourse among the states." *United States v. South-Eastern Underwriters Assn.*, *supra*, at 553.

In the modern world it cannot be denied that the activities of lawyers play an important part in commercial intercourse, and that anticompetitive activities by lawyers may exert a restraint on commerce.

D

In *Parker v. Brown*, 317 U.S. 341 (1943), the Court held that an anticompetitive marketing program which "derived its authority and its efficacy from the legislative command of the state" was not a violation of the Sherman Act because the Act was intended to regulate private practices and not to prohibit a State from imposing a restraint as an act of government. *Id.*, at 350-352; *Olsen v. Smith*, 195 U.S. 332, 344-345 (1904). Respondent State Bar and respondent County Bar both seek to avail themselves of this so-called state- action exemption.

Through its legislature Virginia has authorized its highest court to regulate the practice of law....That court has adopted ethical codes which deal in part with fees, and far from exercising state power to authorize binding price fixing, explicitly directed lawyers not "to be controlled" by fee schedules....The State Bar, a state agency by law,...argues that in issuing fee schedule reports and ethical opinions dealing with fee schedules it was merely implementing the fee provisions of the ethical codes. The County Bar, although it is a voluntary association and not a state agency, claims that the ethical codes and the activities of the State Bar "prompted" it to issue fee schedules and thus its actions, too, are state action for Sherman Act purposes.

The threshold inquiry in determining if an anticompetitive activity is state action of the type the Sherman Act was not meant to proscribe is whether the activity is required by the State acting as sovereign. *Parker v. Brown*, 317 U.S., at 350-352; *Continental Co. v. Union Carbide*, 370 U.S. 690, 706-707 (1962). Here we need not inquire further into the state- action question because it cannot fairly be said that the State of Virginia through its Supreme Court Rules required the anticompetitive activities of either respondent. Respondents have pointed to no Virginia statute requiring their activities; state law simply does not refer to fees, leaving regulation of the profession to the Virginia Supreme Court; although the Supreme Court's ethical codes mention advisory fee schedules they do not direct either respondent to supply them, or require the type of price floor which arose from respondents' activities. Although the State Bar apparently has been granted the power to issue ethical opinions, there is no indication in this record that the Virginia Supreme Court approves the opinions. Respondents' arguments, at most, constitute the contention that their activities complemented the objective of the ethical codes. In our view that is not state action for Sherman Act purposes. It is not enough that, as the County Bar puts it, anticompetitive conduct is "prompted" by state action;

rather, anticompetitive activities must be compelled by direction of the State acting as a sovereign.

The fact that the State Bar is a state agency for some limited purposes does not create an antitrust shield that allows it to foster anticompetitive practices for the benefit of its members....Cf. *Gibson v. Berryhill*, 411 U.S. 564, 578-579 (1973). The State Bar, by providing that deviation from County Bar minimum fees may lead to disciplinary action, has voluntarily joined in what is essentially a private anticompetitive activity, and in that posture cannot claim it is beyond the reach of the Sherman Act....*Parker v. Brown*, *supra*, at 351-352. Its activities resulted in a rigid price floor from which petitioners, as consumers, could not escape if they wished to borrow money to buy a home.

III

We recognize that the States have a compelling interest in the practice of professions within their boundaries, and that as part of their power to protect the public health, safety, and other valid interests they have broad power to establish standards for licensing practitioners and regulating the practice of professions. We also recognize that in some instances the State may decide that "forms of competition usual in the business world may be demoralizing to the ethical standards of a profession." *United States v. Oregon State Medical Society*, 343 U.S. 326, 336 (1952). See also *Semler v. Oregon State Board of Dental Examiners*, 294 U.S. 608, 611-613 (1935). The interest of the States in regulating lawyers is especially great since lawyers are essential to the primary governmental function of administering justice, and have historically been "officers of the courts." See *Sperry v. Florida ex rel. Florida Bar*, 373 U.S. 379, 383 (1963); *Cohen v. Hurley*, 366 U.S. 117, 123-124 (1961); *Law Students Research Council v. Wadmond*, 401 U.S. 154, 157 (1971). In holding that certain anticompetitive conduct by lawyers is within the reach of the Sherman Act we intend no diminution of the authority of the State to regulate its professions.

The judgment of the Court of Appeals is reversed and the case is remanded to that court with orders to remand to the District Court for further proceedings consistent with this opinion.

Reversed and remanded.

Patrick v. Burget

486 U.S. 94 (1988)

Justice MARSHALL delivered the opinion of the Court.

The question presented in this case is whether the state-action doctrine of *Parker v. Brown*, 317 U.S. 341, 87 L. Ed. 315, 63 S. Ct. 307 (1943), protects physicians in the State of Oregon from federal antitrust liability for their activities on hospital peer-review committees.

I

Astoria, Oregon, where the events giving rise to this lawsuit took place, is a city of approximately 10,000 people located in the northwest corner of the State. The only hospital in Astoria is the Columbia Memorial Hospital (CMH). Astoria also is the home of a private group-medical practice called the Astoria Clinic. At all times relevant to this case, a majority of the staff members at the CMH were employees or partners of the Astoria Clinic.

Petitioner Timothy Patrick is a general and vascular surgeon. He became an employee of the Astoria Clinic and a member of the CMH's medical staff in 1972. One year later, the partners of the Clinic, who are the respondents in this case,…invited petitioner to become a partner of the Clinic. Petitioner declined this offer and instead began an independent practice in competition with the surgical practice of the Clinic. Petitioner continued to serve on the medical staff of the CMH.

After petitioner established his independent practice, the physicians associated with the Astoria Clinic consistently refused to have professional dealings with him. Petitioner received virtually no referrals from physicians at the Clinic, even though the Clinic at times did not have a general surgeon on its staff. Rather than refer surgery patients to petitioner, Clinic doctors referred them to surgeons located as far as 50 miles from Astoria. In addition, Clinic physicians showed reluctance to assist petitioner with his own patients.

Clinic doctors often declined to give consultations, and Clinic surgeons refused to provide backup coverage for patients under petitioner's care. At the same time, Clinic physicians repeatedly criticized petitioner for failing to obtain outside consultations and adequate backup coverage.

In 1979, respondent Gary Boelling, a partner at the Clinic, complained to the executive committee of the CMH's medical staff about an incident in which petitioner had left a patient in the care of a recently hired associate, who then left the patient unattended. The executive committee decided to refer this complaint, along with information about other cases handled by petitioner, to the State Board of Medical Examiners (BOME). Respondent Franklin Russell, another partner at the Clinic, chaired the committee of the BOME that investigated these matters. The members of the BOME committee criticized petitioner's medical practices to the full BOME, which then issued a letter of reprimand that had been drafted by Russell. The BOME retracted this letter in its entirety after petitioner sought judicial review of the BOME proceedings.

Two years later, at the request of respondent Richard Harris, a Clinic surgeon, the executive committee of the CMH's medical staff initiated a review of petitioner's hospital privileges. The committee voted to recommend the termination of petitioner's privileges on the ground that petitioner's care of his patients was below the standards of the hospital. Petitioner demanded a hearing, as provided by hospital bylaws, and a five-member ad hoc committee, chaired by respondent Boelling, heard the charges and defense. Petitioner requested that the members of the committee testify as to their personal bias against him, but they refused to accommodate this request. Before the committee rendered its decision, petitioner resigned from the hospital staff rather than risk termination....

During the course of the hospital peer-review proceedings, petitioner filed this lawsuit in the United States District Court for the District of Oregon. Petitioner alleged that the partners of the Astoria Clinic had violated §§ 1 and 2 of the Sherman Act, ch. 647, 26 Stat. 209, 15 U.S. C. §§ 1, 2. Specifically, petitioner contended that the Clinic partners had initiated and participated in the hospital peer-review proceedings to reduce competition from petitioner rather than to improve patient care. Respondents denied this assertion, and the District Court submitted the dispute to the jury with instructions that it could rule in favor of petitioner only if it found that respondents' conduct was the result of a specific intent to injure or destroy competition.

The jury returned a verdict against respondents Russell, Boelling, and Harris on the § 1 claim and against all of the respondents on the § 2 claim. It awarded damages of $650,000 on the two antitrust claims taken together. The District Court, as required by law, see 15 U.S. C. § 15(a), 38 Stat. 731, trebled the antitrust damages.

The Court of Appeals for the Ninth Circuit reversed. 800 F.2d 1498 (1986). It found that there was substantial evidence that respondents had acted in bad faith in the peer-review process....The court held, however, that even if respondents had used the peer-review process to disadvantage a competitor rather than to improve patient care, their conduct in the peer-review proceedings was immune from antitrust scrutiny. The court reasoned that the peer-review activities of physicians in Oregon fall within the state-action exemption from antitrust liability because Oregon has articulated a policy in favor of peer review and actively supervises the peer-review process....The court therefore reversed the judgment of the District Court as to petitioner's antitrust claims.

We granted certiorari, 484 U.S. 814 (1987), to decide whether the state-action doctrine protects respondents' hospital peer-review activities from antitrust challenge.... We now reverse.

II

In *Parker v. Brown*, 317 U.S. 341, 87 L. Ed. 315, 63 S. Ct. 307 (1943), this Court considered whether the Sherman Act prohibits anticompetitive actions of a State. Petitioner in that case was a raisin producer who brought suit against the California Director of Agriculture to enjoin the enforcement of a marketing plan adopted under the State's Agricultural Prorate Act. That statute restricted competition among food producers in the State in order to stabilize prices and prevent economic waste. Relying on principles of federalism and state sovereignty, this Court refused to find in the Sherman Act "an unexpressed purpose to nullify a state's control over its officers and agents." *Id.*, at 351. The Sherman Act, the Court held, was not intended "to restrain state action or official action directed by a state." *Ibid.*

Although Parker involved a suit against a state official, the Court subsequently recognized that Parker's federalism rationale demanded that the state-action exemption also apply in certain suits against private parties. See, *e.g.*, *Southern Motor Carriers Rate Conference, Inc. v. United States*, 471 U.S. 48, 85 L. Ed. 2d 36, 105 S. Ct. 1721 (1985). If the Federal Government or a private litigant always could enforce the Sherman Act against private parties, then a State could not effectively implement a program restraining competition among them. The Court, however, also sought to ensure that private parties could claim state-action immunity from Sherman Act liability only when their anticompetitive acts were truly the product of state regulation. We accordingly established a rigorous two- pronged test to determine whether anticompetitive conduct engaged in by private parties should be deemed state action and thus shielded from the antitrust laws. See *California Retail Liquor Dealers Assn. v. Midcal Aluminum, Inc.*, 445 U.S. 97, 63 L. Ed. 2d 233, 100 S. Ct. 937 (1980). First, "the challenged restraint must be 'one clearly articulated and affirmatively expressed as state policy.'" *Id.*, at 105, quoting *Lafayette v. Louisiana Power & Light Co.*, 435 U.S. 389, 410, 55 L. Ed. 2d 364, 98 S. Ct. 1123 (1978) (opinion of BRENNAN, J.). Second, the anticompetitive conduct "must be 'actively supervised' by the State itself." *California Retail Liquor Dealers Assn. v. Midcal Aluminum, Inc.*, *supra*, at 105, quoting *Lafayette v. Louisiana Power & Light Co.*, *supra*, at 410 (opinion of BRENNAN, J.). Only if an anticompetitive act of a private party meets both of these requirements is it fairly attributable to the State.

In this case, we need not consider the "clear articulation" prong of the *Midcal* test, because the "active supervision" requirement is not satisfied. The active supervision requirement stems from the recognition that "where a private party is engaging in the anticompetitive activity, there is a real danger that he is acting to further his own interests, rather than the governmental interests of the State." *Hallie v. Eau Claire*, 471 U.S. 34, 47, 85 L. Ed. 2d 24, 105 S. Ct. 1713 (1985); see *id.*, at 45 ("A private party . . . may be presumed to be acting primarily on his or its own behalf"). The requirement is designed to ensure that the state-action doctrine will shelter only the particular anticompetitive acts of private parties that, in the judgment of the State, actually further state regulatory policies. *Id.*, at 46-47. To accomplish this purpose, the active supervision requirement mandates that the State exercise ultimate control over the challenged anticompetitive conduct. Cf. *Southern Motor Carriers Rate Conference, Inc. v. United States*, *supra*, at 51 (noting that state public service commissions "have and exercise ultimate authority and control over all intrastate rates"); *Parker v. Brown*, *supra*, at 352 (stressing that a marketing plan proposed by raisin growers could not take effect unless approved by a state board). The mere presence of some state involvement or monitoring does not suffice. See *324 Liquor Corp. v. Duffy*, 479 U.S. 335, 345, n. 7, 93 L. Ed. 2d 667, 107 S. Ct. 720 (1987) (holding that certain forms of state scrutiny of a restraint established by a private party did not constitute active supervision because they did not "exer[t] any significant control over" the terms of the restraint). The active supervision prong of the *Midcal* test requires that state officials have and exercise power to review particular anticompetitive acts of private parties and disapprove those that fail to accord with state policy. Absent such a program of supervision, there is no realistic assurance that a private party's anticompetitive conduct promotes state policy, rather than merely the party's individual interests.

Respondents in this case contend that the State of Oregon actively supervises the peer- review process through the State Health Division, the BOME, and the state judicial system. The Court of Appeals, in finding the active supervision requirement satisfied, also relied primarily on the powers and responsibilities of these state actors. Neither the Court of Appeals nor respondents, however, have succeeded in showing that any of these actors reviews—or even could review—private decisions regarding hospital privileges to determine whether such decisions comport with state regulatory policy and to correct abuses.

Oregon's Health Division has general supervisory powers over "matters relating to the preservation of life and health," Ore. Rev. Stat. § 431.110(1) (1987), including the licensing of hospitals, see § 441.025, and the enforcement of health laws, see §§ 431.120(1), 431.150, 431.155(1). Hospitals in Oregon are under a statutory obligation to establish peer- review procedures and to review those procedures on a regular basis. See §§ 441.055(3)(c), (d). The State Health Division, exercising its enforcement powers, may initiate judicial proceedings against any hospital violating this law. See §§ 431.150, 431.155. In addition, the Health Division may deny, suspend, or revoke a hospital's license for failure to comply with the statutory requirement. See § 441.030(2). Oregon law specifies no other ways in which the Health Division may supervise the peer-review process.

This statutory scheme does not establish a state program of active supervision over peer- review decisions. The Health Division's statutory authority over peer review relates only to a hospital's procedures;...that authority does not encompass the actual decisions made by hospital peer-review committees. The restraint challenged in this case (and in most cases of its kind) consists not in the procedures used to terminate hospital privileges, but in the termination of privileges itself. The State does not actively supervise this restraint unless a state official has and exercises ultimate authority over private privilege determinations. Oregon law does not give the Health Division this authority: under the statutory scheme, the Health Division has no power to review private peer-review decisions and overturn a decision that fails to accord with state policy. Thus, the activities of the Health Division under Oregon law cannot satisfy the active supervision requirement of the state-action doctrine.

Similarly, the BOME does not engage in active supervision over private peer-review decisions. The principal function of the BOME is to regulate the licensing of physicians in the State. As respondents note, Oregon hospitals are required by statute to notify the BOME promptly of a decision to terminate or restrict privileges. See Ore. Rev. Stat. § 441.820(1) (1987). Neither this statutory provision nor any other, however, indicates that the BOME has the power to disapprove private privilege decisions. The apparent purpose of the reporting requirement is to give the BOME an opportunity to determine whether additional action on its part, such as revocation of a physician's license, is warranted.... Certainly, respondents have not shown that the BOME in practice reviews privilege decisions or that it ever has asserted the authority to reverse them.

The only remaining alleged supervisory authority in this case is the state judiciary. Respondents claim, and the Court of Appeals agreed, that Oregon's courts directly review privilege-termination decisions and that this judicial review constitutes active state supervision. This Court has not previously considered whether state courts, acting in their judicial capacity, can adequately supervise private conduct for purposes of the state-action doctrine. All of our prior cases concerning state supervision over private parties have involved administrative agencies, see, *e.g.*, *Southern Motor Carriers Rate Conference, Inc. v. United States*, 471 U.S. 48, 85 L. Ed. 2d 36, 105 S. Ct. 1721 (1985), or State Supreme Courts with agency-like responsibilities over the organized bar, see *Bates v. State Bar of Arizona*, 433 U.S. 350, 53 L. Ed. 2d 810, 97 S. Ct. 2691 (1977). This case, however, does not require us to decide the broad question whether judicial review of private conduct ever can constitute active supervision, because judicial review of privilege-termination decisions in Oregon, if such review exists at all, falls far short of satisfying the active supervision requirement.

As an initial matter, it is not clear that Oregon law affords any direct judicial review of private peer-review decisions. Oregon has no statute expressly providing for judicial review of privilege terminations. Moreover, we are aware of no case in which an Oregon court has held that judicial review of peer-review decisions is available.

The two cases that respondents have cited certainly do not hold that a physician whose privileges have been terminated by a private hospital is entitled to judicial review. In each of these cases, the Oregon Supreme Court assumed, but expressly did not decide, that a complaining physician was entitled to the kind of review he requested. See *Straube v. Emanuel Lutheran Charity Board*, 287 Ore. 375, 383, 600 P.2d 381, 386 (1979) ("We have assumed (but not decided) for the purpose of this case that plaintiff is entitled to 'fair procedure' as a common law right"); *Huffaker v. Bailey*, 273 Ore. 273, 275, 540 P.2d 1398, 1399 (1975) ("In view of our conclusion that petitioner cannot prevail even assuming the case is properly before us, we find it unnecessary to decide these interesting questions [of reviewability]. Therefore, we assume, but do not decide, that the hospital's decisions are subject to review by mandamus . . .").

Moreover, the Oregon courts have indicated that even if they were to provide judicial review of hospital peer-review proceedings, the review would be of a very limited nature. The Oregon Supreme Court, in its most recent decision addressing this matter, stated that a court "should [not] decide the merits of plaintiff's dismissal" and that "it would be unwise for a court to do more than to make sure that some sort of reasonable procedure was afforded and that there was evidence from which it could be found that plaintiff's conduct posed a threat to patient care." *Straube v. Emanuel Lutheran Charity Board*, *supra*, at 384, 600 P.2d at 386. This kind of review would fail to satisfy the state-action doctrine's requirement of active supervision. Under the standard suggested by the Oregon Supreme Court, a state court would not review the merits of a privilege termination decision to determine whether it accorded with state regulatory policy. Such constricted review does not convert the action of a private party in terminating a physician's privileges into the action of the State for purposes of the state-action doctrine.

Because we conclude that no state actor in Oregon actively supervises hospital peer-review decisions, we hold that the state-action doctrine does not protect the peer-review activities challenged in this case from application of the federal antitrust laws. In so holding, we are not unmindful of the policy argument that respondents and their *amici* have advanced for reaching the opposite conclusion. They contend that effective peer review is essential to the provision of quality medical care and that any threat of antitrust liability will prevent physicians from participating openly and actively in peer-review proceedings. This argument, however, essentially challenges the wisdom of applying the antitrust laws to the sphere of medical care, and as such is properly directed to the legislative branch. To the extent that Congress has declined to exempt medical peer review from the reach of the antitrust laws,...peer review is immune from antitrust scrutiny only if the State effectively has made this conduct its own. The State of Oregon has not done so. Accordingly, we reverse the judgment of the Court of Appeals.

It is so ordered.

Justice BLACKMUN took no part in the consideration or decision of this case.

INVALID STATE ACTION

N.C. State Bd. of Dental Exam'rs v. FTC

574 U.S. 494 (2015)

Justice KENNEDY delivered the opinion of the Court.

This case arises from an antitrust challenge to the actions of a state regulatory board. A majority of the board's members are engaged in the active practice of the profession it regulates. The question is whether the board's actions are protected from Sherman Act regulation under the doctrine of state-action antitrust immunity, as defined and applied in this Court's decisions beginning with *Parker v. Brown*, 317 U. S. 341, 63 S. Ct. 307, 87 L. Ed. 315 (1943).

I

A

In its Dental Practice Act (Act), North Carolina has declared the practice of dentistry to be a matter of public concern requiring regulation. N. C. Gen. Stat. Ann. §90-

22(a) (2013). Under the Act, the North Carolina State Board of Dental Examiners (Board) is "the agency of the State for the regulation of the practice of dentistry." §90-22(b).

The Board's principal duty is to create, administer, and enforce a licensing system for dentists. See §§90-29 to 90-41. To perform that function it has broad authority over licensees. See §90-41. The Board's authority with respect to unlicensed persons, however, is more restricted: Like "any resident citizen," the Board may file suit to "perpetually enjoin any person from . . . unlawfully practicing dentistry." §90-40.1.

The Act provides that six of the Board's eight members must be licensed dentists engaged in the active practice of dentistry. §90-22. They are elected by other licensed dentists in North Carolina, who cast their ballots in elections conducted by the Board. *Ibid.* The seventh member must be a licensed and practicing dental hygienist, and he or she is elected by other licensed hygienists. *Ibid.* The final member is referred to by the Act as a "consumer" and is appointed by the Governor. Ibid. All members serve 3-year terms, and no person may serve more than two consecutive terms. *Ibid.* The Act does not create any mechanism for the removal of an elected member of the Board by a public official. See *ibid.*

Board members swear an oath of office, §138A-22(a), and the Board must comply with the State's Administrative Procedure Act, §150B-1 *et seq.*, Public Records Act, §132-1 *et seq.*, and open-meetings law, §143-318.9 *et seq.* The Board may promulgate rules and regulations governing the practice of dentistry within the State, provided those mandates are not inconsistent with the Act and are approved by the North Carolina Rules Review Commission, whose members are appointed by the state legislature. See §§90-48, 143B- 30.1, 150B-21.9(a).

B

In the 1990's, dentists in North Carolina started whitening teeth. Many of those who did so, including 8 of the Board's 10 members during the period at issue in this case, earned substantial fees for that service. By 2003, nondentists arrived on the scene. They charged lower prices for their services than the dentists did. Dentists soon began to complain to the Board about their new competitors. Few complaints warned of possible harm to consumers. Most expressed a principal concern with the low prices charged by nondentists.

Responding to these filings, the Board opened an investigation into nondentist teeth whitening. A dentist member was placed in charge of the inquiry. Neither the Board's hygienist member nor its consumer member participated in this undertaking. The Board's chief operations officer remarked that the Board was "going forth to do battle" with nondentists. App. to Pet. for Cert. 103a. The Board's concern did not result in a formal rule or regulation reviewable by the independent Rules Review Commission, even though the Act does not, by its terms, specify that teeth whitening is "the practice of dentistry."

Starting in 2006, the Board issued at least 47 cease-and-desist letters on its official letterhead to nondentist teeth whitening service providers and product manufacturers. Many of those letters directed the recipient to cease "all activity constituting the practice of dentistry"; warned that the unlicensed practice of dentistry is a crime; and strongly implied (or expressly stated) that teeth whitening constitutes "the practice of dentistry." App. 13, 15. In early 2007, the Board persuaded the North Carolina Board of Cosmetic Art Examiners to warn cosmetologists against providing teeth whitening services. Later that year, the Board sent letters to mall operators, stating that kiosk teeth whiteners were violating the Act and advising that the malls consider expelling violators from their premises.

These actions had the intended result. Nondentists ceased offering teeth whitening services in North Carolina.

C

In 2010, the Federal Trade Commission (FTC) filed an administrative complaint charging the Board with violating §5 of the Federal Trade Commission Act, 38 Stat. 719, as amended, 15 U. S. C. §45. The FTC alleged that the Board's concerted action to exclude nondentists from the market for teeth whitening services in North

Carolina constituted an anticompetitive and unfair method of competition. The Board moved to dismiss, alleging state-action immunity. An Administrative Law Judge (ALJ) denied the motion. On appeal, the FTC sustained the ALJ's ruling. It reasoned that, even assuming the Board had acted pursuant to a clearly articulated state policy to displace competition, the Board is a "public/private hybrid" that must be actively supervised by the State to claim immunity. App. to Pet. for Cert. 49a. The FTC further concluded the Board could not make that showing.

Following other proceedings not relevant here, the ALJ conducted a hearing on the merits and determined the Board had unreasonably restrained trade in violation of antitrust law. On appeal, the FTC again sustained the ALJ. The FTC rejected the Board's public safety justification, noting, *inter alia*, "a wealth of evidence...suggesting that non-dentist provided teeth whitening is a safe cosmetic procedure." *Id.*, at 123a.

The FTC ordered the Board to stop sending the cease-and-desist letters or other communications that stated nondentists may not offer teeth whitening services and products. It further ordered the Board to issue notices to all earlier recipients of the Board's cease-and-desist orders advising them of the Board's proper sphere of authority and saying, among other options, that the notice recipients had a right to seek declaratory rulings in state court.

On petition for review, the Court of Appeals for the Fourth Circuit affirmed the FTC in all respects. 717 F. 3d 359, 370 (2013). This Court granted certiorari. 571 U. S. 1236, 134 S. Ct. 1491, 188 L. Ed. 2d 375 (2014).

II

Federal antitrust law is a central safeguard for the Nation's free market structures. In this regard it is "as important to the preservation of economic freedom and our free-enterprise system as the Bill of Rights is to the protection of our fundamental personal freedoms." *United States v. Topco Associates, Inc.*, 405 U. S. 596, 610, 92 S. Ct. 1126, 31 L. Ed. 2d 515 (1972). The antitrust laws declare a considered and decisive prohibition by the

Federal Government of cartels, price fixing, and other combinations or practices that undermine the free market.

The Sherman Act, 26 Stat. 209, as amended, 15 U. S. C. §1 *et seq.*, serves to promote robust competition, which in turn empowers the States and provides their citizens with opportunities to pursue their own and the public's welfare. See *FTC v. Ticor Title Ins. Co.*, 504 U. S. 621, 632, 112 S. Ct. 2169, 119 L. Ed. 2d 410 (1992). The States, however, when acting in their respective realm, need not adhere in all contexts to a model of unfettered competition. While "the States regulate their economies in many ways not inconsistent with the antitrust laws," *id.*, at 635-636, 112 S. Ct. 2169, 119 L. Ed. 2d 410, in some spheres they impose restrictions on occupations, confer exclusive or shared rights to dominate a market, or otherwise limit competition to achieve public objectives. If every duly enacted state law or policy were required to conform to the mandates of the Sherman Act, thus promoting competition at the expense of other values a State may deem fundamental, federal antitrust law would impose an impermissible burden on the States' power to regulate. See *Exxon Corp. v. Governor of Maryland*, 437 U. S. 117, 133, 98 S. Ct. 2207, 57 L. Ed. 2d 91 (1978); see also Easterbrook, Antitrust and the Economics of Federalism, 26 J. Law & Econ. 23, 24 (1983).

For these reasons, the Court in *Parker v. Brown* interpreted the antitrust laws to confer immunity on anticompetitive conduct by the States when acting in their sovereign capacity. See 317 U. S., at 350-351, 63 S. Ct. 307, 87 L. Ed. 315. That ruling recognized Congress' purpose to respect the federal balance and to "embody in the Sherman Act the federalism principle that the States possess a significant measure of sovereignty under our Constitution." *Community Communications Co. v. Boulder*, 455 U. S. 40, 53, 102 S. Ct. 835, 70 L. Ed. 2d 810 (1982). Since 1943, the Court has reaffirmed the importance of *Parker's* central holding. See, *e.g.*, *Ticor*, *supra*, at 632-637, 112 S. Ct. 2169, 119 L. Ed. 2d 410; *Hoover v. Ronwin*, 466 U. S. 558, 568, 104 S. Ct. 1989, 80 L. Ed. 2d 590 (1984); *Lafayette v. Louisiana Power & Light Co.*, 435 U. S. 389, 394-400, 98 S. Ct. 1123, 55 L.Ed. 2d 364 (1978).

III

In this case the Board argues its members were invested by North Carolina with the power of the State and that, as a result, the Board's actions are cloaked with *Parker* immunity. This argument fails, however. A nonsovereign actor controlled by active market participants—such as the Board—enjoys *Parker* immunity only if it satisfies two requirements: "first that 'the challenged restraint...be one clearly articulated and affirmatively expressed as state policy,' and second that 'the policy...be actively supervised by the State.'" *FTC v. Phoebe Putney Health System, Inc.*, 568 U. S. 216, 225, 568 U.S. 216, 133 S. Ct. 1003, 1010, 185 L. Ed. 2d 43, 53 (2013) (quoting *California Retail Liquor Dealers Assn. v. Midcal Aluminum, Inc.*, 445 U. S. 97, 105, 100 S. Ct. 937, 63 L.Ed. 2d 233 (1980)). The parties have assumed that the clear articulation requirement is satisfied, and we do the same. While North Carolina prohibits the unauthorized practice of dentistry, however, its Act is silent on whether that broad prohibition covers teeth whitening. Here, the Board did not receive active supervision by the State when it interpreted the Act as addressing teeth whitening and when it enforced that policy by issuing cease-and-desist letters to nondentist teeth whiteners.

A

Although state-action immunity exists to avoid conflicts between state sovereignty and the Nation's commitment to a policy of robust competition, *Parker* immunity is not unbounded. "[G]iven the fundamental national values of free enterprise and economic competition that are embodied in the federal antitrust laws, 'state-action immunity is disfavored, much as are repeals by implication.'" *Phoebe Putney, supra*, at 225, 133 S. Ct. 1003, 1010, 185 L. Ed. 2d 43, 53) (quoting *Ticor, supra*, at 636, 112 S. Ct. 2169, 119 L.Ed. 2d 410).

An entity may not invoke *Parker* immunity unless the actions in question are an exercise of the State's sovereign power. See *Columbia v. Omni Outdoor Advertising, Inc.*, 499 U.S. 365, 374, 111 S. Ct. 1344, 113 L. Ed. 2d 382 (1991). State legislation and "decision[s] of a state supreme court, acting legislatively rather than judicially," will satisfy this standard, and "ipso facto are exempt from the operation of the antitrust laws" because they are an undoubted exercise of state sovereign authority. *Hoover, supra*, at 567-568, 104 S. Ct. 1989, 80 L. Ed. 2d 590.

But while the Sherman Act confers immunity on the States' own anticompetitive policies out of respect for federalism, it does not always confer immunity where, as here, a State delegates control over a market to a nonsovereign actor. See *Parker, supra*, at 351, 63 S. Ct. 307, 87 L.Ed. 315 ("[A] state does not give immunity to those who violate the Sherman Act by authorizing them to violate it, or by declaring that their action is lawful"). For purposes of *Parker*, a nonsovereign actor is one whose conduct does not automatically qualify as that of the sovereign State itself. See *Hoover, supra*, at 567-568, 104 S. Ct. 1989, 80 L. Ed. 2d 590. State agencies are not simply by their governmental character sovereign actors for purposes of state-action immunity. See *Goldfarb v. Virginia State Bar*, 421 U.S. 773, 791, 95 S. Ct. 2004, 44 L.Ed. 2d 572 (1975) ("The fact that the State Bar is a state agency for some limited purposes does not create an antitrust shield that allows it to foster anticompetitive practices for the benefit of its members"). Immunity for state agencies, therefore, requires more than a mere facade of state involvement, for it is necessary in light of *Parker's* rationale to ensure the States accept political accountability for anticompetitive conduct they permit and control. See *Ticor, supra*, at 636, 112 S. Ct. 2169, 119 L. Ed. 2d 410.

Limits on state-action immunity are most essential when the State seeks to delegate its regulatory power to active market participants, for established ethical standards may blend with private anticompetitive motives in a way difficult even for market participants to discern. Dual allegiances are not always apparent to an actor. In consequence, active market participants cannot be allowed to regulate their own markets free from antitrust accountability. See *Midcal, supra*, at 106, 100 S. Ct. 937, 63 L. Ed. 2d 233 ("The national policy in favor of competition cannot be thwarted by casting...gauzy cloak of state involvement over what is essentially a private price-fixing arrangement"). Indeed, prohibitions against anticompetitive self-regulation by active market participants are an axiom of federal antitrust policy. See, *e.g.*, *Allied Tube & Conduit Corp. v. Indian Head, Inc.*, 486 U. S. 492, 501, 108 S. Ct. 1931, 100 L. Ed. 2d 497 (1988); *Hoover*, *supra*, at 584, 104 S. Ct. 1989, 80 L. Ed. 2d 590 (Stevens, J., dissenting) ("The risk that private regulation of market entry, prices, or output may be designed to confer monopoly profits on members of an industry at the expense of the consuming public has been the central concern of...our antitrust jurisprudence"); see also Elhauge, The Scope of Antitrust Process, 104 Harv. L. Rev. 667, 672 (1991). So it follows that, under *Parker* and the Supremacy Clause, the States' greater power to attain an end does not include the lesser power to negate the congressional judgment embodied in the Sherman Act through unsupervised delegations to active market participants. See Garland, Antitrust and State Action: Economic Efficiency and the Political Process, 96 Yale L. J. 486, 500 (1986).

Parker immunity requires that the anticompetitive conduct of nonsovereign actors, especially those authorized by the State to regulate their own profession, result from procedures that suffice to make it the State's own. See *Goldfarb*, *supra*, at 790, 95 S. Ct. 2004, 44 L. Ed. 2d 572; see also 1A P. Areeda & H. Hovenkamp, Antitrust Law ¶226, p. 180 (4th ed. 2013) (Areeda & Hovenkamp). The question is not whether the challenged conduct is efficient, well functioning, or wise. See *Ticor*, 504 U. S., at 634-635, 112 S.Ct. 2169, 119 L.Ed. 2d 410. Rather, it is "whether anticompetitive conduct engaged in by [nonsovereign actors] should be deemed state action and thus shielded from the antitrust laws." *Patrick v. Burget*, 486 U. S. 94, 100, 108 S. Ct. 1658, 100 L. Ed. 2d 83 (1988).

To answer this question, the Court applies the two-part test set forth in *California Retail Liquor Dealers Assn. v. Midcal Aluminum, Inc.*, 445 U.S. 97, 100 S.Ct. 937, 63 L.Ed. 2d 233, a case arising from California's delegation of price-fixing authority to wine merchants. Under *Midcal*, "[a] state law or regulatory scheme cannot be the basis for antitrust immunity unless, first, the State has articulated a clear...policy to allow the anticompetitive conduct, and second, the State provides active supervision of [the] anticompetitive conduct." *Ticor*, *supra*, at 631,

112 S. Ct. 2169, 119 L. Ed. 2d 410 (citing *Midcal, supra*, at 105, 100 S. Ct. 937, 63 L. Ed. 2d 233.

Midcal's clear articulation requirement is satisfied "where the displacement of competition [is] the inherent, logical, or ordinary result of the exercise of authority delegated by the state legislature. In that scenario, the State must have foreseen and implicitly endorsed the anticompetitive effects as consistent with its policy goals." *Phoebe Putney*, 568 U.S., at 229, 133 S.Ct. 1003, 185 L.Ed. 2d 43, 56). The active supervision requirement demands, *inter alia*, "that state officials have and exercise power to review particular anticompetitive acts of private parties and disapprove those that fail to accord with state policy." *Patrick, supra*, at 101, 108 S. Ct. 1658, 100 L. Ed. 2d 83.

The two requirements set forth in *Midcal* provide a proper analytical framework to resolve the ultimate question whether an anticompetitive policy is indeed the policy of a State. The first requirement—clear articulation— rarely will achieve that goal by itself, for a policy may satisfy this test yet still be defined at so high a level of generality as to leave open critical questions about how and to what extent the market should be regulated. See *Ticor*, *supra*, at 636-637, 112 S.Ct. 2169, 119 L.Ed. 2d 410. Entities purporting to act under state authority might diverge from the State's considered definition of the public good. The resulting asymmetry between a state policy and its implementation can invite private self-dealing. The second *Midcal* requirement—active supervision—seeks to avoid this harm by requiring the State to review and approve interstitial policies made by the entity claiming immunity.

Midcal's supervision rule "stems from the recognition that '[w]here a private party is engaging in anticompetitive activity, there is a real danger that he is acting to further his own interests, rather than the governmental interests of the State.'" *Patrick, supra*, at 100, 108 S. Ct. 1658, 100 L. Ed. 2d 83. Concern about the private incentives of active market participants animates *Midcal's* supervision mandate, which demands "realistic assurance that a private party's anticompetitive conduct promotes state policy, rather than merely the party's individual interests." *Patrick, supra*, at 101, 108 S.Ct. 1658, 100 L.Ed. 2d 83.

B

In determining whether anticompetitive policies and conduct are indeed the action of a State in its sovereign capacity, there are instances in which an actor can be excused from *Midcal's* active supervision requirement. In *Hallie v. Eau Claire*, 471 U. S. 34, 45, 105 S.Ct. 1713, 85 L.Ed. 2d 24 (1985), the Court held municipalities are subject exclusively to *Midcal's* "'clear articulation'" requirement. That rule, the Court observed, is consistent with the objective of ensuring that the policy at issue be one enacted by the State itself. *Hallie* explained that "[w]here the actor is a municipality, there is little or no danger that it is involved in a private price-fixing arrangement. The only real danger is that it will seek to further purely parochial public interests at the expense of more overriding state goals." 471 U. S., at 47, 105 S.Ct. 1713, 85 L.Ed. 2d 24 (emphasis deleted). *Hallie* further observed that municipalities are electorally accountable and lack the kind of private incentives characteristic of active participants in the market. See *id.*, at 45, n. 9, 105 S. Ct. 1713, 85 L. Ed. 2d 24. Critically, the municipality in *Hallie* exercised a wide range of governmental powers across different economic spheres, substantially reducing the risk that it would pursue private interests while regulating any single field. See *ibid.* That *Hallie* excused municipalities from *Midcal's* supervision rule for these reasons all but confirms the rule's applicability to actors controlled by active market participants, who ordinarily have none of the features justifying the narrow exception *Hallie* identified. See 471 U. S., at 45, 105 S.Ct. 1713, 85 L.Ed. 2d 24.

Following Goldfarb, *Midcal*, and *Hallie*, which clarified the conditions under which *Parker* immunity attaches to the conduct of a nonsovereign actor, the Court in *Columbia v. Omni Outdoor Advertising, Inc.*, 499 U.S. 365, 111 S.Ct. 1344, 113 L.Ed. 2d 382, addressed whether an otherwise immune entity could lose immunity for conspiring with private parties. In *Omni*, an aspiring billboard merchant argued that the city of Columbia, South Carolina, had violated the Sherman Act—and forfeited its *Parker* immunity—by anticompetitively conspiring with an established local company in passing an ordinance restricting new billboard construction. 499 U.S., at 367-368, 111 S.Ct. 1344, 113 L.Ed. 2d 382. The Court disagreed, holding there is no "conspiracy exception" to *Parker*. *Omni*, *supra*, at 374, 111 S.Ct. 1344, 113 L.Ed. 2d 382.

Omni, like the cases before it, recognized the importance of drawing a line "relevant to the purposes of the Sherman Act and of *Parker*: prohibiting the restriction of competition for private gain but permitting the restriction of competition in the public interest." 499 U. S., at 378, 111 S.Ct. 1344, 113 L.Ed. 2d 382. In the context of a municipal actor which, as in *Hallie*, exercised substantial governmental powers, *Omni* rejected a conspiracy exception for "corruption" as vague and unworkable, since "virtually all regulation benefits some segments of the society and harms others" and may in that sense be seen as "'corrupt.'" 499 U.S., at 377, 111 S.Ct. 1344, 113 L.Ed. 2d 382. *Omni* also rejected subjective tests for corruption that would force a "deconstruction of the governmental process and probing of the official 'intent' that we have consistently sought to avoid." *Ibid.* Thus, whereas the cases preceding it addressed the preconditions of *Parker* immunity and engaged in an objective, *ex ante* inquiry into nonsovereign actors' structure and incentives, *Omni* made clear that recipients of immunity will not lose it on the basis of ad hoc and *ex post* questioning of their motives for making particular decisions.

Omni's holding makes it all the more necessary to ensure the conditions for granting immunity are met in the first place. The Court's two state-action immunity cases decided after *Omni* reinforce this point. In *Ticor*, the Court affirmed that *Midcal's* limits on delegation must ensure that "[a]ctual state involvement, not deference to private price-fixing arrangements under the general auspices of state law, is the precondition for immunity from federal law." 504 U.S., at 633, 112 S.Ct. 2169, 119 L.Ed. 2d 410. And in *Phoebe Putney*, the Court observed that *Midcal's* active supervision requirement, in particular, is an essential condition of state-action immunity when a nonsovereign actor has "an incentive to pursue [its] own self-interest under the guise of implementing state policies." 568 U.S., at 226, 133 S.Ct. 1003, 1011, 185 L.Ed. 2d 43, 54) (quoting *Hallie*, *supra*, at 46-47, 105 S. Ct. 1713, 85 L. Ed. 2d 24). The lesson is clear: *Midcal's* active supervision test is an essential prerequisite of *Parker* immunity for any nonsovereign entity—public or private—controlled by active market participants.

C

The Board argues entities designated by the States as agencies are exempt from *Midcal's* second requirement. That premise, however, cannot be reconciled with the Court's repeated conclusion that the need for supervision turns not on the formal designation given by States to regulators but on the risk that active market participants will pursue private interests in restraining trade.

State agencies controlled by active market participants, who possess singularly strong private interests, pose the very risk of self-dealing *Midcal's* supervision requirement was created to address. See Areeda & Hovenkamp ¶227, at 226. This conclusion does not question the good faith of state officers but rather is an assessment of the structural risk of market participants' confusing their own interests with the State's policy goals. See *Patrick*, 486 U.S., at 100-101, 108 S.Ct. 1658, 100 L.Ed. 2d 83.

The Court applied this reasoning to a state agency in *Goldfarb*. There the Court denied immunity to a state agency (the Virginia State Bar) controlled by market participants (lawyers) because the agency had "joined in what is essentially a private anticompetitive activity" for "the benefit of its members." 421 U.S., at 791, 792, 95 S.Ct. 2004, 44 L.Ed. 2d 572. This emphasis on the Bar's private interests explains why *Goldfarb*, though it predates *Midcal*, considered the lack of supervision by the Virginia Supreme Court to be a principal reason for denying immunity. See 421 U.S., at 791, 95 S.Ct. 2004, 44 L.Ed. 2d 572; see also *Hoover*, 466 U. S., at 569, 104 S.Ct. 1989, 80 L.Ed. 2d 590 (emphasizing lack of active supervision in *Goldfarb*); *Bates v. State Bar of Ariz.*, 433 U.S. 350, 361-362, 97 S.Ct. 2691, 53 L.Ed. 2d 810 (1977) (granting the Arizona Bar state-action immunity partly because its "rules are subject to pointed re-examination by the policymaker").

While *Hallie* stated "it is likely that active state supervision would also not be required" for agencies, 471 U.S., at 46, n. 10, 105 S.Ct. 1713, 85 L.Ed. 2d 24, the entity there, as was later the case in *Omni*, was an electorally accountable municipality with general regulatory powers and no private price-fixing agenda. In that and other respects the municipality was more like prototypical state agencies, not specialized boards dominated by active market participants. In important regards, agencies controlled by market participants are more similar to private trade associations vested by States with regulatory authority than to the agencies *Hallie* considered. And as the Court observed three years after *Hallie*, "[t]here is no doubt that the members of such associations often have economic incentives to restrain competition and that the product standards set by such associations have a serious potential for anticompetitive harm." *Allied Tube*, 486 U.S., at 500, 108 S.Ct. 1931, 100 L.Ed. 2d 497. For that reason, those associations must satisfy *Midcal's* active supervision standard. See *Midcal*, 445 U.S., at 105-106, 100 S.Ct. 937, 63 L.Ed. 2d 233.

The similarities between agencies controlled by active market participants and private trade associations are not eliminated simply because the former are given a formal designation by the State, vested with a measure of government power, and required to follow some procedural rules. See *Hallie*, *supra*, at 39, 105 S.Ct. 1713, 85 L.Ed. 2d 24 (rejecting "purely formalistic" analysis). *Parker* immunity does not derive from nomenclature alone. When a State empowers a group of active market participants to decide who can participate in its market, and on what terms, the need for supervision is manifest. See Areeda & Hovenkamp ¶227, at 226. The Court holds today that a state board on which a controlling number of decisionmakers are active market participants in the occupation the board regulates must satisfy *Midcal's* active supervision requirement in order to invoke state-action antitrust immunity.

D

The State argues that allowing this FTC order to stand will discourage dedicated citizens from serving on state agencies that regulate their own occupation. If this were so—and, for reasons to be noted, it need not be so— there would be some cause for concern. The States have a sovereign interest in structuring their governments, see *Gregory v. Ashcroft*, 501 U. S. 452, 460, 111 S. Ct. 2395, 115 L. Ed. 2d 410 (1991), and may conclude there are substantial benefits to staffing their agencies with experts in complex and technical subjects, see *Southern Motor Carriers Rate Conference, Inc. v. United States*, 471 U.S. 48, 64, 105 S.Ct. 1721, 85 L.Ed. 2d 36 (1985). There is, moreover, a long tradition of citizens esteemed by their professional colleagues devoting time, energy, and talent to enhancing the dignity of their calling.

Adherence to the idea that those who pursue a calling must embrace ethical standards that derive from a duty separate from the dictates of the State reaches back at least to the Hippocratic Oath. See generally S. Miles, The Hippocratic Oath and the Ethics of Medicine (2004). In the United States, there is a strong tradition of professional self-regulation, particularly with respect to the development of ethical rules. See generally R. Rotunda & J. Dzienkowski, Legal Ethics: The Lawyer's Deskbook on Professional Responsibility (2014); R. Baker, Before Bioethics: A History of American Medical Ethics From the Colonial Period to the Bioethics Revolution (2013). Dentists are no exception. The American Dental Association, for example, in an exercise of "the privilege and obligation of self-government," has "call[ed] upon dentists to follow high ethical standards," including "honesty, compassion, kindness, integrity, fairness and charity." American Dental Association, Principles of Ethics and Code of Professional Conduct 3-4 (2012). State laws and institutions are sustained by this tradition when they draw upon the expertise and commitment of professionals.

Today's holding is not inconsistent with that idea. The Board argues, however, that the potential for money damages will discourage members of regulated occupations from participating in state government. Cf.

Filarsky v. Delia, 566 U.S. 377, 390, 132 S.Ct. 1657, 1666, 182 L.Ed. 2d 662, 672 (2012)) (warning in the context of civil rights suits that "the most talented candidates will decline public engagements if they do not receive the same immunity enjoyed by their public employee counterparts"). But this case, which does not present a claim for money damages, does not offer occasion to address the question whether agency officials, including board members, may, under some circumstances, enjoy immunity from damages liability. See *Goldfarb*, 421 U.S., at 792, n. 22, 95 S.Ct. 2004, 44 L.Ed. 2d 572; see also Brief for Respondent 56. And, of course, the States may provide for the defense and indemnification of agency members in the event of litigation.

States, furthermore, can ensure *Parker* immunity is available to agencies by adopting clear policies to displace competition; and, if agencies controlled by active market participants interpret or enforce those policies, the States may provide active supervision. Precedent confirms this principle. The Court has rejected the argument that it would be unwise to apply the antitrust laws to professional regulation absent compliance with the prerequisites for invoking Parker immunity:

> "[Respondents] contend that effective peer review is essential to the provision of quality medical care and that any threat of antitrust liability will prevent physicians from participating openly and actively in peer-review proceedings. This argument, however, essentially challenges the wisdom of applying the antitrust laws to the sphere of medical care, and as such is properly directed to the legislative branch. To the extent that Congress has declined to exempt medical peer review from the reach of the antitrust laws, peer review is immune from antitrust scrutiny only if the State effectively has made this conduct its own." *Patrick*, 486 U.S., at 105-106, 108 S.Ct. 1658, 100 L.Ed. 2d 83 (footnote omitted).

The reasoning of *Patrick v. Burget* applies to this case with full force, particularly in light of the risks licensing boards dominated by market participants may pose to the free market. See generally Edlin & Haw, Cartels by

Another Name: Should Licensed Occupations Face Antitrust Scrutiny? 162 U. Pa. L. Rev. 1093 (2014).

E

The Board does not contend in this Court that its anticompetitive conduct was actively supervised by the State or that it should receive *Parker* immunity on that basis.

By statute, North Carolina delegates control over the practice of dentistry to the Board. The Act, however, says nothing about teeth whitening, a practice that did not exist when it was passed. After receiving complaints from other dentists about the nondentists' cheaper services, the Board's dentist members—some of whom offered whitening services—acted to expel the dentists' competitors from the market. In so doing the Board relied upon cease-and-desist letters threatening criminal liability, rather than any of the powers at its disposal that would invoke oversight by a politically accountable official. With no active supervision by the State, North Carolina officials may well have been unaware that the Board had decided teeth whitening constitutes "the practice of dentistry" and sought to prohibit those who competed against dentists from participating in the teeth whitening market. Whether or not the Board exceeded its powers under North Carolina law, cf. *Omni*, 499 U.S., at 371-372, 111 S.Ct. 1344, 113 L.Ed. 2d 382, there is no evidence here of any decision by the State to initiate or concur with the Board's actions against the nondentists.

IV

The Board does not claim that the State exercised active, or indeed any, supervision over its conduct regarding nondentist teeth whiteners; and, as a result, no specific supervisory systems can be reviewed here. It suffices to note that the inquiry regarding active supervision is flexible and context dependent. Active supervision need not entail day-to- day involvement in an agency's operations or micromanagement of its every decision. Rather, the question is whether the State's review mechanisms provide "realistic assurance" that a nonsovereign actor's anticompetitive conduct "promotes state policy, rather than merely the party's individual interests." *Patrick, supra,* at 100-101, 108 S.Ct. 1658, 100 L.Ed. 2d 83; see also *Ticor,* 504 U.S., at 639-640, 112 S.Ct. 2169, 119 L.Ed. 2d 410.

The Court has identified only a few constant requirements of active supervision: The supervisor must review the substance of the anticompetitive decision, not merely the procedures followed to produce it, see *Patrick,* 486 U.S., at 102-103, 108 S.Ct. 1658, 100 L.Ed. 2d 83; the supervisor must have the power to veto or modify particular decisions to ensure they accord with state policy, see *ibid.*; and the "mere potential for state supervision is not an adequate substitute for a decision by the State," *Ticor, supra,* at 638, 112 S.Ct. 2169, 119 L.Ed. 2d 410. Further, the state supervisor may not itself be an active market participant. In general, however, the adequacy of supervision otherwise will depend on all the circumstances of a case.

* * *

The Sherman Act protects competition while also respecting federalism. It does not authorize the States to abandon markets to the unsupervised control of active market participants, whether trade associations or hybrid agencies. If a State wants to rely on active market participants as regulators, it must provide active supervision if state-action immunity under *Parker* is to be invoked.

The judgment of the Court of Appeals for the Fourth Circuit is affirmed.

It is so ordered.

Justice ALITO, with whom Justice SCALIA and Justice THOMAS join, dissenting.

The Court's decision in this case is based on a serious misunderstanding of the doctrine of state-action antitrust immunity that this Court recognized more than 60 years ago in *Parker v. Brown,* 317 U.S. 341, 63 S.Ct. 307, 87 L.Ed. 315 (1943). In *Parker,* the Court held that the Sherman Act does not prevent the States from continuing their age-old practice of enacting measures, such as licensing requirements, that are designed to protect the public health and welfare. *Id.,* at 352, 63 S.Ct. 307, 87

L.Ed. 315. The case now before us involves precisely this type of state regulation—North Carolina's laws governing the practice of dentistry, which are administered by the North Carolina State Board of Dental Examiners (Board).

Today, however, the Court takes the unprecedented step of holding that *Parker* does not apply to the North Carolina Board because the Board is not structured in a way that merits a good-government seal of approval; that is, it is made up of practicing dentists who have a financial incentive to use the licensing laws to further the financial interests of the State's dentists. There is nothing new about the structure of the North Carolina Board. When the States first created medical and dental boards, well before the Sherman Act was enacted, they began to staff them in this way....Nor is there anything new about the suspicion that the North Carolina Board—in attempting to prevent persons other than dentists from performing teeth whitening procedures—was serving the interests of dentists and not the public. Professional and occupational licensing requirements have often been used in such a way....But that is not what *Parker* immunity is about. Indeed, the very state program involved in that case was unquestionably designed to benefit the regulated entities, California raisin growers.

The question before us is not whether such programs serve the public interest. The question, instead, is whether this case is controlled by *Parker*, and the answer to that question is clear. Under *Parker*, the Sherman Act (and the Federal Trade Commission Act, see F*TC v. Ticor Title Ins. Co.*, 504 U.S. 621, 635, 112 S.Ct. 2169, 119 L.Ed. 2d 410 (1992)) do not apply to state agencies; the Board is a state agency; and that is the end of the matter. By straying from this simple path, the Court has not only distorted *Parker*; it has headed into a morass. Determining whether a state agency is structured in a way that militates against regulatory capture is no easy task, and there is reason to fear that today's decision will spawn confusion. The Court has veered off course, and therefore I cannot go along.

I

In order to understand the nature of *Parker* state-action immunity, it is helpful to recall the constitutional landscape in 1890 when the Sherman Act was enacted. At that time, this Court and Congress had an understanding of the scope of federal and state power that is very different from our understanding today. The States were understood to possess the exclusive authority to regulate "their purely internal affairs." *Leisy v. Hardin*, 135 U.S. 100, 122, 10 S.Ct. 681, 34 L.Ed. 128, 12 Ky. L. Rptr. 123 (1890). In exercising their police power in this area, the States had long enacted measures, such as price controls and licensing requirements, that had the effect of restraining trade....

The Sherman Act was enacted pursuant to Congress' power to regulate interstate commerce, and in passing the Act, Congress wanted to exercise that power "to the utmost extent." *United States v. South-Eastern Underwriters Assn.*, 322 U.S. 533, 558, 64 S.Ct. 1162, 88 L.Ed. 1440 (1944). But in 1890, the understanding of the commerce power was far more limited than it is today. See, *e.g.*, *Kidd v. Pearson*, 128 U.S. 1, 17-18, 9 S.Ct. 6, 32 L.Ed. 346 (1888). As a result, the Act did not pose a threat to traditional state regulatory activity.

By 1943, when *Parker* was decided, however, the situation had changed dramatically. This Court had held that the commerce power permitted Congress to regulate even local activity if it "exerts a substantial economic effect on interstate commerce." *Wickard v. Filburn*, 317 U.S. 111, 125, 63 S.Ct. 82, 87 L.Ed. 122 (1942). This meant that Congress could regulate many of the matters that had once been thought to fall exclusively within the jurisdiction of the States. The new interpretation of the commerce power brought about an expansion of the reach of the Sherman Act. See *Hospital Building Co. v. Trustees of Rex Hospital*, 425 U.S. 738, 743, n. 2, 96 S.Ct. 1848, 48 L.Ed. 2d 338 (1976) ("[D]ecisions by this Court have permitted the reach of the Sherman Act to expand along with expanding notions of congressional power"). And the expanded reach of the Sherman Act raised an important question. The Sherman Act does not expressly exempt States from its scope. Does that mean that the Act applies to the States and that it potentially outlaws many traditional state regulatory measures? The Court confronted that question in *Parker*.

In *Parker*, a raisin producer challenged the California Agricultural Prorate Act, an agricultural price support program. The California Act authorized the creation of an Agricultural Prorate Advisory Commission (Commission) to establish marketing plans for certain agricultural commodities within the State. 317 U.S., at 346-347, 63 S.Ct. 307, 87 L.Ed. 315. Raisins were among the regulated commodities, and so the Commission established a marketing program that governed many aspects of raisin sales, including the quality and quantity of raisins sold, the timing of sales, and the price at which raisins were sold. *Id.*, at 347-348, 63 S.Ct. 307, 87 L.Ed. 315. The *Parker* Court assumed that this program would have violated "the Sherman Act if it were organized and made effective solely by virtue of a contract, combination or conspiracy of private persons," and the Court also assumed that Congress could have prohibited a State from creating a program like California's if it had chosen to do so. *Id.*, at 350, 63 S.Ct. 307, 87 L.Ed. 315. Nevertheless, the Court concluded that the California program did not violate the Sherman Act because the Act did not circumscribe state regulatory power. *Id.*, at 351, 63 S.Ct. 307, 87 L.Ed. 315.

The Court's holding in *Parker* was not based on either the language of the Sherman Act or anything in the legislative history affirmatively showing that the Act was not meant to apply to the States. Instead, the Court reasoned that "[i]n a dual system of government in which, under the Constitution, the states are sovereign, save only as Congress may constitutionally subtract from their authority, an unexpressed purpose to nullify a state's control over its officers and agents is not lightly to be attributed to Congress." *Ibid.* For the Congress that enacted the Sherman Act in 1890, it would have been a truly radical and almost certainly futile step to attempt to prevent the States from exercising their traditional regulatory authority, and the *Parker* Court refused to assume that the Act was meant to have such an effect.

When the basis for the *Parker* state-action doctrine is understood, the Court's error in this case is plain. In 1890, the regulation of the practice of medicine and dentistry was regarded as falling squarely within the States' sovereign police power. By that time, many States had established medical and dental boards, often staffed by doctors or dentists,...and had given those boards the authority to confer and revoke licenses....This was quintessential police power legislation, and although state laws were often challenged during that era under the doctrine of substantive due process, the licensing of medical professionals easily survived such assaults. Just one year before the enactment of the Sherman Act, in *Dent v. West Virginia*, 129 U.S. 114, 128, 9 S.Ct. 231, 32 L.Ed. 623 (1889), this Court rejected such a challenge to a state law requiring all physicians to obtain a certificate from the state board of health attesting to their qualifications. And in *Hawker v. New York*, 170 U.S. 189, 192, 18 S.Ct. 573, 42 L.Ed. 1002 (1898), the Court reiterated that a law specifying the qualifications to practice medicine was clearly a proper exercise of the police power. Thus, the North Carolina statutes establishing and specifying the powers of the State Board of Dental Examiners represent precisely the kind of state regulation that the *Parker* exemption was meant to immunize.

II

As noted above, the only question in this case is whether the Board is really a state agency, and the answer to that question is clearly yes.

- The North Carolina Legislature determined that the practice of dentistry "affect[s] the public health, safety and welfare" of North Carolina's citizens and that therefore the profession should be "subject to regulation and control in the public interest" in order to ensure "that only qualified persons be permitted to practice dentistry in the State." N. C. Gen. Stat. Ann. §90-22(a) (2013).
- To further that end, the legislature created the Board "as the agency of the State for the regulation of the practice of dentistry in th[e] State." §90-22(b).

- The legislature specified the membership of the Board. §90-22(c). It defined the "practice of dentistry," §90-29(b), and it set out standards for licensing practitioners, §90-30. The legislature also set out standards under which the Board can initiate disciplinary proceedings against licensees who engage in certain improper acts. §90-41(a).
- The legislature empowered the Board to "maintain an action in the name of the State of North Carolina to perpetually enjoin any person from...unlawfully practicing dentistry." §90-40.1(a). It authorized the Board to conduct investigations and to hire legal counsel, and the legislature made any "notice or statement of charges against any licensee" a public record under state law. §§ 90- 41(d)-(g).
- The legislature empowered the Board "to enact rules and regulations governing the practice of dentistry within the State," consistent with relevant statutes. §90-48. It has required that any such rules be included in the Board's annual report, which the Board must file with the North Carolina secretary of state, the state attorney general, and the legislature's Joint Regulatory Reform Committee. §93B-2. And if the Board fails to file the required report, state law demands that it be automatically suspended until it does so. *Ibid.*

As this regulatory regime demonstrates, North Carolina's Board is unmistakably a state agency created by the state legislature to serve a prescribed regulatory purpose and to do so using the State's power in cooperation with other arms of state government.

The Board is not a private or "nonsovereign" entity that the State of North Carolina has attempted to immunize from federal antitrust scrutiny. Parker made it clear that a State may not "'give immunity to those who violate the Sherman Act by authorizing them to violate it, or by declaring that their action is lawful.'" *Ante*, at 505, 135

S.Ct. 1101, 191 L.Ed. 2d, at 48 (quoting *Parker*, 317 U.S., at 351, 63 S.Ct. 307, 87 L.Ed. 315). When the *Parker* Court disapproved of any such attempt, it cited *Northern Securities Co. v. United States*, 193 U.S. 197, 24 S.Ct. 436, 48 L.Ed. 679 (1904), to show what it had in mind. In that case, the Court held that a State's act of chartering a corporation did not shield the corporation's monopolizing activities from federal antitrust law. *Id.*, at 344-345, 63 S.Ct. 307, 87 L.Ed. 315. Nothing similar is involved here. North Carolina did not authorize a private entity to enter into an anticompetitive arrangement; rather, North Carolina *created a state agency* and gave that agency the power to regulate a particular subject affecting public health and safety.

Nothing in *Parker* supports the type of inquiry that the Court now prescribes. The Court crafts a test under which state agencies that are "controlled by active market participants," *ante*, at 510, 135 S.Ct. 1101, 191 L.Ed. 2d, at 52, must demonstrate active state supervision in order to be immune from federal antitrust law. The Court thus treats these state agencies like private entities. But in *Parker*, the Court did not examine the structure of the California program to determine if it had been captured by private interests. If the Court had done so, the case would certainly have come out differently, because California conditioned its regulatory measures on the participation and approval of market actors in the relevant industry.

Establishing a prorate marketing plan under California's law first required the petition of at least 10 producers of the particular commodity. *Parker*, 317 U.S., at 346, 63 S.Ct. 307, 87 L.Ed. 315. If the Commission then agreed that a marketing plan was warranted, the Commission would "select a program committee *from among nominees chosen by the qualified producers*." *Ibid.* (emphasis added). That committee would then formulate the proration marketing program, which the Commission could modify or approve. But even after Commission approval, the program became law (and then, automatically) only if it gained the approval of 65 percent of the relevant producers, representing at least 51 percent of the acreage of the regulated crop. *Id.*, at 347, 63 S.Ct. 307, 87 L.Ed. 315. This scheme gave decisive power to market participants. But despite these aspects of the California program, *Parker* held that California was acting as a "sovereign" when it "adopt[ed] and enforc[ed] the prorate program." *Id.*, at 352, 63 S.Ct. 307, 87 L.Ed. 315. This reasoning is irreconcilable with the Court's today.

III

The Court goes astray because it forgets the origin of the *Parker* doctrine and is misdirected by subsequent cases that extended that doctrine (in certain circumstances) to private entities. The Court requires the North Carolina Board to satisfy the two-part test set out in *California Retail Liquor Dealers Assn. v. Midcal Aluminum, Inc.*, 445 U.S. 97, 100 S.Ct. 937, 63 L.Ed. 2d 233 (1980), but the party claiming Parker immunity in that case was not a state agency but a private trade association. Such an entity is entitled to Parker immunity, *Midcal* held, only if the anticompetitive conduct at issue was both "'clearly articulated'" and "'actively supervised, by the State itself." 445 U.S., at 105, 100 S.Ct. 937, 63 L.Ed. 2d 233. Those requirements are needed where a State authorizes private parties to engage in anticompetitive conduct. They serve to identify those situations in which conduct *by private parties* can be regarded as the conduct of a State. But when the conduct in question is the conduct of a state agency, no such inquiry is required.

This case falls into the latter category, and therefore *Midcal* is inapposite. The North Carolina Board is not a private trade association. It is a state agency, created and empowered by the State to regulate an industry affecting public health. It would not exist if the State had not created it. And for purposes of *Parker*, its membership is irrelevant; what matters is that it is part of the government of the sovereign State of North Carolina.

Our decision in *Hallie v. Eau Claire*, 471 U.S. 34, 105 S.Ct. 1713, 85 L.Ed. 2d 24 (1985), which involved Sherman Act claims against a municipality, not a state agency, is similarly inapplicable. In Hallie, the plaintiff argued that the two-pronged *Midcal* test should be applied, but the Court disagreed. The Court acknowledged that municipalities "are not themselves sovereign." 471 U.S., at 38, 105 S.Ct. 1713, 85 L.Ed. 2d

24. But recognizing that a municipality is “an arm of the State,” *id.*, at 45, 105 S.Ct. 1713, 85 L.Ed. 2d 24, the Court held that a municipality should be required to satisfy only the first prong of the *Midcal* test (requiring a clearly articulated state policy), 471 U.S., at 46, 105 S.Ct. 1713, 85 L.Ed. 2d 24. That municipalities are not sovereign was critical to our analysis in Hallie, and thus that decision has no application in a case, like this one, involving a state agency.

Here, however, the Court not only disregards the North Carolina Board’s status as a full- fledged state agency; it treats the Board less favorably than a municipality. This is puzzling. States are sovereign, *Northern Ins. Co. of N.Y. v. Chatham County*, 547 U.S. 189, 193, 126 S.Ct. 1689, 164 L.Ed. 2d 367 (2006), and California’s sovereignty provided the foundation for the decision in *Parker*, *supra*, at 352, 63 S.Ct. 307, 87 L.Ed. 315. Municipalities are not sovereign. *Jinks v. Richland County*, 538 U.S. 456, 466, 123 S.Ct. 1667, 155 L.Ed. 2d 631 (2003). And for this reason, federal law often treats municipalities differently from States. Compare *Will v. Michigan Dept. of State Police*, 491 U. S. 58, 71, 109 S. Ct. 2304, 105 L. Ed. 2d 45 (1989) (“[N]either a State nor its officials acting in their official capacities are ‘persons’ under [42 U. S. C.] §1983”), with *Monell v. New York City Dept. of Social Servs.*, 436 U. S. 658, 694, 8 S. Ct. 2018, 56 L. Ed. 2d 611 (1978) (municipalities liable under §1983 where “execution of a government’s policy or custom...inflicts the injury”).

The Court recognizes that municipalities, although not sovereign, nevertheless benefit from a more lenient standard for state-action immunity than private entities. Yet under the Court’s approach, the Board, a full-fledged state agency, is treated like a private actor and must demonstrate that the State actively supervises its actions.

The Court’s analysis seems to be predicated on an assessment of the varying degrees to which a municipality and a state agency like the North Carolina Board are likely to be captured by private interests. But until today, *Parker* immunity was never conditioned on the proper use of state regulatory authority. On the contrary, in *Columbia v. Omni Outdoor Advertising, Inc.*, 499 U.S. 365, 111 S.Ct.

1344, 113 L.Ed. 2d 382 (1991), we refused to recognize an exception to *Parker* for cases in which it was shown that the defendants had engaged in a conspiracy or corruption or had acted in a way that was not in the public interest. 499 U.S., at 374, 111 S.Ct. 1344, 113 L.Ed. 2d 382. The Sherman Act, we said, is not an anticorruption or good-government statute. *Id.*, at 398, 111 S. Ct. 1344, 113 L.Ed. 2d 382. We were unwilling in *Omni* to rewrite *Parker* in order to reach the allegedly abusive behavior of city officials. 499 at 374-379, 111 S.Ct. 1344, 113 L.Ed. 2d 382. But that is essentially what the Court has done here.

IV

Not only is the Court's decision inconsistent with the underlying theory of *Parker*; it will create practical problems and is likely to have far-reaching effects on the States' regulation of professions. As previously noted, state medical and dental boards have been staffed by practitioners since they were first created, and there are obvious advantages to this approach. It is reasonable for States to decide that the individuals best able to regulate technical professions are practitioners with expertise in those very professions. Staffing the State Board of Dental Examiners with certified public accountants would certainly lessen the risk of actions that place the well-being of dentists over those of the public, but this would also compromise the State's interest in sensibly regulating a technical profession in which lay people have little expertise.

As a result of today's decision, States may find it necessary to change the composition of medical, dental, and other boards, but it is not clear what sort of changes are needed to satisfy the test that the Court now adopts. The Court faults the structure of the North Carolina Board because "active market participants" constitute "a controlling number of [the] decisionmakers," *ante*, at 511, 135 S.Ct. 1101, 191 L.Ed. 2d, at 53, but this test raises many questions.

What is a "controlling number"? Is it a majority? And if so, why does the Court eschew that term? Or does the Court mean to leave open the possibility that something less than a majority might suffice in particular circumstances? Suppose that active market participants constitute a voting bloc that is generally able to get its way? How about an obstructionist minority or an agency chair empowered to set the agenda or veto regulations?

Who is an "active market participant"? If Board members withdraw from practice during a short term of service but typically return to practice when their terms end, does that mean that they are not active market participants during their period of service?

What is the scope of the market in which a member may not participate while serving on the board? Must the market be relevant to the particular regulation being challenged or merely to the jurisdiction of the entire agency? Would the result in the present case be different if a majority of the Board members, though practicing dentists, did not provide teeth whitening services? What if they were orthodontists, periodontists, and the like? And how much participation makes a person "active" in the market?

The answers to these questions are not obvious, but the States must predict the answers in order to make informed choices about how to constitute their agencies.

I suppose that all this will be worked out by the lower courts and the Federal Trade Commission (FTC), but the Court's approach raises a more fundamental question, and that is why the Court's inquiry should stop with an examination of the structure of a state licensing board. When the Court asks whether market participants control the North Carolina Board, the Court in essence is asking whether this regulatory body has been captured by the entities that it is supposed to regulate. Regulatory capture can occur in many ways....So why ask only whether the members of a board are active market participants? The answer may be that determining when regulatory capture has occurred is no simple task. That answer provides a reason for relieving courts from the obligation to make such determinations at all. It does not explain why it is appropriate for the Court to adopt the rather crude test for capture that constitutes the holding of today's decision.

V

The Court has created a new standard for distinguishing between private and state actors for purposes of federal antitrust immunity. This new standard is not true to the *Parker* doctrine; it diminishes our traditional respect for federalism and state sovereignty; and it will be difficult to apply. I therefore respectfully dissent.

Hypotheticals

1. San Diego County has 110 gas stations. Five of them from different brands agree to increase high octane gas by 5 cents. No other gas station changes its price. Antitrust violation?

2. Costco has reduced the price for Cuisinart blenders at its warehouse locations. Cuisinart protests the low price below their competitors because it "implies we are an inferior product when we are far superior." Cuisinart threatens to stop selling its blenders to Costco unless the price is at least the recommended retail price that does not defame it. Antitrust violation?

3. A trade association of gun manufacturers is concerned about the safety of their products. Most of its members, at its suggestion, agree to include an efficient "safety device" that is attached to each handgun sold. Antitrust violation?

4. A trade association of barbers is concerned that the Cosmetology Board is letting in unqualified barbers who are using dangerous hair dyes and shaving some customers unknowingly, so they look like military cadets. They advocate for stricter education standards and a limitation on supply to the Board. Antitrust violation?

5. Five competing trash haulers agree that they will all bid on contracts with the City of Chula Vista but that due to its location, only the three southernmost haulers will bid on the Imperial Beach contract. Antitrust violation?

6. A raisin manufacturer (drying grapes) agrees with a glove manufacturer that raisin prices should go up 10%. Antitrust violation?

7. A dry cleaner in Cleveland agrees with a dry cleaner in San Diego that only Otella #2 products should be used as a cleaning agent. Antitrust violation?

8. How do the antitrust concepts of "relevant product or service market" and "relevant geographic market" relate to the last two scenarios?

FTC GUIDANCE

In October 2015, the Staff of the FTC's Bureau of Competition issued the following to provide guidance on two questions:

1. When does a regulatory board require active supervision in order to invoke the state action defense?

2. What factors are relevant to determining whether the active supervision requirement is satisfied?

As noted below, this document sets out the views of the Staff of the Bureau of Competition. The FTC is not bound by this Staff guidance and reserves the right to rescind it at a later date. In addition, FTC Staff reserves the right to reconsider the views expressed herein, and to modify, rescind, or revoke this Staff guidance if such action would be in the public interest.

*FTC Staff Guidance on Active Supervision of State Regulatory Boards Controlled by Market Participants**

* This document sets out the views of the Staff of the Bureau of Competition. The Federal Trade Commission is not bound by this Staff guidance and reserves the right to rescind it at a later date. In addition, FTC Staff reserves the right to reconsider the views expressed herein, and to modify, rescind, or revoke this Staff guidance if such action would be in the public interest.

I. Introduction

States craft regulatory policy through a variety of actors, including state legislatures, courts, agencies, and regulatory boards. While most regulatory actions taken by state actors will not implicate antitrust concerns, some will. Notably, states have created a large number of regulatory boards with the authority to determine who may engage in an occupation (e.g., by issuing or withholding a license), and also to set the rules and regulations governing that occupation. Licensing, once limited to a few learned professions such as doctors and lawyers, is now required for over 800 occupations including (in some states) locksmiths, beekeepers, auctioneers, interior designers, fortune tellers, tour guides, and shampooers.[1]

In general, a state may avoid all conflict with the federal antitrust laws by creating regulatory boards that serve only in an advisory capacity, or by staffing a regulatory board exclusively with persons who have no financial interest in the occupation that is being regulated. However, across the United States, "licensing boards are largely dominated by active members of their respective industries…" [2] That is, doctors commonly regulate doctors, beekeepers commonly regulate beekeepers, and tour guides commonly regulate tour guides.

Earlier this year, the U.S. Supreme Court upheld the Federal Trade Commission's determination that the North Carolina State Board of Dental Examiners ("NC Board") violated the federal antitrust laws by preventing non-dentists from providing teeth whitening services in competition with the state's licensed dentists. *N.C. State Bd. of Dental Exam'rs v. FTC*, 135 S. Ct. 1101(2015). NC Board is a state agency established under North Carolina law and charged with administering and enforcing a licensing system for dentists. A majority of the members of this state agency are themselves practicing dentists, and thus they have a private incentive to limit competition from non-dentist providers of teeth whitening services. NC Board argued that, because it is a state agency, it is exempt from liability under the federal antitrust laws. That is, the NC Board sought to invoke what is commonly referred to as the "state action exemption" or the "state action defense." The Supreme Court rejected this contention and affirmed the FTC's finding of antitrust liability.

In this decision, the Supreme Court clarified the applicability of the antitrust state action defense to state regulatory boards controlled by market participants:

> "The Court holds today that a state board on which a controlling number of decisionmakers are active market participants in the occupation the board regulates must satisfy *Midcal's* [*Cal. Retail Liquor Dealers Ass'n v. Midcal Aluminum, Inc.*, 445 U.S. 97 (1980)] active supervision requirement in order to invoke state-action antitrust immunity." *N.C. Dental*, 135 S. Ct. at 1114.

In the wake of this Supreme Court decision, state officials have requested advice from the Federal Trade Commission regarding antitrust compliance for state boards responsible for regulating occupations. This outline provides FTC Staff guidance on two questions. *First*, when does a state regulatory board require active supervision in order to invoke the state action defense? *Second*, what factors are relevant to determining whether the active supervision requirement is satisfied?

Our answers to these questions come with the following caveats.

→ Vigorous competition among sellers in an open marketplace generally provides consumers with important benefits, including lower prices, higher quality services, greater access to services, and increased innovation. For this reason, a state legislature should empower a regulatory board to restrict competition only when necessary to protect against a credible risk of harm, such as health and safety risks to consumers. The Federal Trade Commission and its staff have frequently advocated that states avoid unneeded and burdensome regulation of service providers.[3]

→ Federal antitrust law does not require that a state legislature provide for active supervision of any state regulatory board. A state legislature may, and generally should, prefer that a regulatory board be subject to the requirements of the federal antitrust laws. If the state legislature determines that a regulatory board should be subject to antitrust oversight, then the state legislature need not provide for active supervision.

→ Antitrust analysis—including the applicability of the state action defense—is fact-specific and context-dependent. The purpose of this document is to identify certain overarching legal principles governing when and how a state may provide active supervision for a regulatory board. We are not suggesting a mandatory or one- size-fits- all approach to active supervision. Instead, we urge each state regulatory board to consult with the Office of the Attorney General for its state for customized advice on how best to comply with the antitrust laws.

→ This FTC Staff guidance addresses only the active supervision prong of the state action defense. In order successfully to invoke the state action defense, a state regulatory board controlled by market participants must also satisfy the clear articulation prong, as described briefly in Section II. below.

→ This document contains guidance developed by the staff of the Federal Trade Commission. Deviation from this guidance does not necessarily mean that the state action defense is inapplicable, or that a violation of the antitrust laws has occurred.

II. Overview of the Antitrust State Action Defense

"Federal antitrust law is a central safeguard for the Nation's free market structures....The antitrust laws declare a considered and decisive prohibition by the Federal Government of cartels, price fixing, and other combinations or practices that undermine the free market." *N.C. Dental*, 135 S. Ct. at 1109.

Under principles of federalism, "the States possess a significant measure of sovereignty." *N.C. Dental*, 135 S. Ct. at 1110 (quoting *Community Communications Co. v. Boulder*, 455 U.S. 40, 53 (1982)). In enacting the antitrust laws, Congress did not intend to prevent the States from limiting competition in order to promote other goals that are valued by their citizens. Thus, the Supreme Court has concluded that the federal antitrust laws do not reach anticompetitive conduct engaged in by a State that is acting in its sovereign capacity.

Parker v. Brown, 317 U.S. 341, 351 52 (1943). For example, a state legislature may "impose restrictions on occupations, confer exclusive or shared rights to dominate a market, or otherwise limit competition to achieve public objectives." *N.C. Dental*, 135 S. Ct. at 1109.

Are the actions of a state regulatory board, like the actions of a state legislature, exempt from the application of the federal antitrust laws? In *North Carolina State Board of Dental Examiners*, the Supreme Court reaffirmed that a state regulatory board is not the sovereign. Accordingly, a state regulatory board is not necessarily exempt from federal antitrust liability.

More specifically, the Court determined that "a state board on which a controlling number of decisionmakers are active market participants in the occupation the board regulates" may invoke the state action defense only when two requirements are satisfied: first, the challenged restraint must be clearly articulated and affirmatively expressed as state policy; and second, the policy must be actively supervised by a state official (or state agency) that is not a participant in the market that is being regulated. *N.C. Dental*, 135 S. Ct. at 1114.

- → The Supreme Court addressed the clear articulation requirement most recently in *FTC v. Phoebe Putney Health Sys., Inc.*, 133 S. Ct. 1003 (2013). The clear articulation requirement is satisfied "where the displacement of competition [is] the inherent, logical, or ordinary result of the exercise of authority delegated by the state legislature. In that scenario, the State must have foreseen and implicitly endorsed the anticompetitive effects as consistent with its policy goals." *Id.* at 1013.

- → The State's clear articulation of the intent to displace competition is not alone sufficient to trigger the state action exemption. The state legislature's clearly- articulated delegation of authority to a state regulatory board to displace competition may be "defined at so high a level of generality as to leave open critical questions about how and to what extent the market should be regulated." There is then a danger that this delegated discretion will be used by active market participants to pursue private interests in restraining trade, in lieu of implementing the State's policy goals. *N.C. Dental*, 135 S. Ct. at 1112.

- → The active supervision requirement "seeks to avoid this harm by requiring the State to review and approve interstitial policies made by the entity claiming [antitrust] immunity." *Id.*

Where the state action defense does not apply, the actions

of a state regulatory board controlled by active market participants may be subject to antitrust scrutiny. Antitrust issues may arise where an unsupervised board takes actions that restrict market entry or restrain rivalry. The following are some scenarios that have raised antitrust concerns:

- → A regulatory board controlled by dentists excludes non-dentists from competing with dentists in the provision of teeth whitening services. Cf *N.C. Dental*, 135 5. Ct. 1101.
- → A regulatory board controlled by accountants determines that only a small and fixed number of new licenses to practice the profession shall be issued by the state each year. Cf *Hoover v. Ronwin*, 466 U.S. 558 (1984).
- → A regulatory board controlled by attorneys adopts a regulation (or a code of ethics) that prohibits attorney advertising, or that deters attorneys from engaging in price competition. Cf. *Bates v. State Bar of Ariz.*, 433 U.S. 350 (1977); *Goldfarb v. Va. State Bar*, 421 U.S. 773 (1975).

III. Scope of FTC Staff Guidance

A. This Staff guidance addresses the applicability of the state action defense under the federal antitrust laws. Concluding that the state action defense is inapplicable does not mean that the conduct of the regulatory board necessarily violates the federal antitrust laws. A regulatory board may assert defenses ordinarily available to an antitrust defendant.

1. Reasonable restraints on competition do not violate the antitrust laws, even where the economic interests of a competitor have been injured.

EXAMPLE 1. A regulatory board may prohibit members of the occupation from engaging in fraudulent business practices without raising antitrust concerns. A regulatory board also may prohibit members of the occupation from engaging in untruthful or deceptive advertising. Cf *Cal. Dental Ass'n v. FTC*, 526 U.S. 756 (1999).

EXAMPLE 2. Suppose a market with several hundred licensed electricians. If a regulatory board suspends the license of one electrician for substandard work, such action likely does not unreasonably harm competition. Cf. *Oksanen v. Page Mem'l Hosp.*, 945 F.2d 696 (4th Cir. 1991) (en banc).

2. The ministerial (non-discretionary) acts of a regulatory board engaged in good faith implementation of an anticompetitive statutory regime do not give rise to antitrust liability. See *324 Liquor Corp. v. Duffy*, 479 U.S. 335, 344 n. 6 (1987).

EXAMPLE 3. A state statute requires that an applicant for a chauffeur's license submit to the regulatory board, among other things, a copy of the applicant's diploma and a certified check for $500. An applicant fails to submit the required materials. If for this reason the regulatory board declines to issue a chauffeur's license to the applicant, such action would not be considered an unreasonable restraint. In the circumstances described, the denial of a license is a ministerial or non-discretionary act of the regulatory board.

3. In general, the initiation and prosecution of a lawsuit by a regulatory board does not give rise to antitrust liability unless it falls within the "sham exception." *Professional Real Estate Investors v. Columbia Pictures Industries*, 508 U.S. 49 (1993); *California Motor Transport Co. v. Trucking Unlimited*, 404 U.S. 508 (1972).

EXAMPLE 4. A state statute authorizes the state's dental board to maintain an action in state court to enjoin an unlicensed person from practicing dentistry. The members of the dental board have a basis to believe that a particular individual is practicing dentistry but does not hold a valid license. If the dental board files a lawsuit against that individual, such action would not constitute a violation of the federal antitrust laws.

B. Below, FTC Staff describes when active supervision of a state regulatory board is required in order successfully to invoke the state action defense, and what factors are relevant to determining whether the active supervision requirement has been satisfied.

1. When is active state supervision of a state regulatory board required in order to invoke the state action defense?

General Standard: "[A] state board on which a controlling number of decisionmakers are active market participants in the occupation the board regulates must satisfy *Midcal's* active supervision requirement in order to invoke state-action antitrust immunity." *N.C. Dental*, 135 S. Ct. at 1114.

Active Market Participants: A member of a state regulatory board will be considered to be an active market participant in the occupation the board regulates if such person (i) is licensed by the board or (ii) provides any service that is subject to the regulatory authority of the board.

→ If a board member participates in any professional or occupational sub-specialty that is regulated by the board, then that board member is an active market participant for purposes of evaluating the active supervision requirement.

→ It is no defense to antitrust scrutiny, therefore, that the board members themselves are not directly or personally affected by the challenged restraint. For example, even if the members of the NC Dental Board were orthodontists who do not perform teeth whitening services (as a matter of law or fact or tradition), their control of the dental board would nevertheless trigger the requirement for active state supervision. This is because these orthodontists are licensed by, and their services regulated by, the NC Dental Board.

→ A person who temporarily suspends her active participation in an occupation for the purpose of serving on a state board that regulates her former (and intended future) occupation will be considered to be an active market participant.

Method of Selection: The method by which a person is selected to serve on a state regulatory board is not determinative of whether that person is an active market participant in the occupation that the board regulates. For example, a licensed dentist is deemed to be an active market participant regardless of whether the dentist (i) is appointed to the state dental board by the governor or (ii) is elected to the state dental board by the state's licensed dentists.

A Controlling Number, Not Necessarily a Majority, of Actual Decisionmakers:

→ Active market participants need not constitute a numerical majority of the members of a state regulatory board in order to trigger the requirement of active supervision. A decision that is controlled, either as a matter of law, procedure, or fact, by active participants in the regulated market (e.g., through veto power, tradition, or practice) must be actively supervised to be eligible for the state action defense.

→ Whether a particular restraint has been imposed by a "controlling number of decisionmakers [who] are active market participants" is a fact-bound inquiry that must be made on a case-by-case basis. FTC Staff will evaluate a number of factors, including:

✓ The structure of the regulatory board (including the number of board members who are/are not active market participants) and the rules governing the exercise of the board's authority.

✓ Whether the board members who are active market participants have veto power over the board's regulatory decisions.

EXAMPLE 5. The state board of electricians consists of four non-electrician members and three practicing electricians. Under state law, new regulations require the approval of five board members. Thus, no regulation may become effective without the assent of at least one electrician member of the board. In this scenario, the active market participants effectively have veto power over the board's regulatory authority. The active supervision requirement is therefore applicable.

✓ The level of participation, engagement, and authority of the non-market participant members in the business of the board—generally and with regard to the particular restraint at issue.

- ✓ Whether the participation, engagement, and authority of the non-market participant board members in the business of the board differs from that of board members who are active market participants—generally and with regard to the particular restraint at issue.
- ✓ Whether the active market participants have in fact exercised, controlled, or usurped the decisionmaking power of the board.

EXAMPLE 6. The state board of electricians consists of four non-electrician members and three practicing electricians. Under state law, new regulations require the approval of a majority of board members. When voting on proposed regulations, the non-electrician members routinely defer to the preferences of the electrician members. Minutes of board meetings show that the non-electrician members generally are not informed or knowledgeable concerning board business—and that they were not well informed concerning the particular restraint at issue. In this scenario, FTC Staff may determine that the active market participants have exercised the decisionmaking power of the board, and that the active supervision requirement is applicable.

EXAMPLE 7. The state board of electricians consists of four non-electrician members and three practicing electricians. Documents show that the electrician members frequently meet and discuss board business separately from the non-electrician members. On one such occasion, the electrician members arranged for the issuance by the board of written orders to six construction contractors, directing such individuals to cease and desist from providing certain services. The non-electrician members of the board were not aware of the issuance of these orders and did not approve the issuance of these orders. In this scenario, FTC Staff may determine that the active market participants have exercised the decisionmaking power of the board, and that the active supervision requirement is applicable.

2. What constitutes active supervision?

FTC Staff will be guided by the following principles:

→ "[T]he purpose of the active supervision inquiry ... is to determine whether the State has exercised sufficient independent judgment and control" such that the details of the regulatory scheme "have been established as a product of deliberate state intervention" and not simply by agreement among the members of the state board. "Much as in causation inquiries, the analysis asks whether the State has played a substantial role in determining the specifics of the economic policy." The State is not obliged to "[meet] some normative standard, such as efficiency, in its regulatory practices." *Ticor*, 504 U.S. at 634-35. "The question is not how well state regulation works but whether the anticompetitive scheme is the State's own." *Id.* at 635.

→ It is necessary "to ensure the States accept political accountability for anticompetitive conduct they permit and control." *N.C. Dental*, 135 S.Ct. at 1111. See also *Ticor*, 504 U.S. at 636.

→ "The Court has identified only a few constant requirements of active supervision: The supervisor must review the substance of the anticompetitive decision, not merely the procedures followed to produce it; the supervisor must have the power to veto or modify particular decisions to ensure they accord with state policy; and the 'mere potential for state supervision is not an adequate substitute for a decision by the State.' Further, the state supervisor may not itself be an active market participant." *N.C. Dental*, 135 S. Ct. at 1116-17 (citations omitted).

→ The active supervision must precede implementation of the allegedly anticompetitive restraint.

→ "[T]he inquiry regarding active supervision is flexible and context-dependent." "[T]he adequacy of supervision ... will depend on all the circumstances of a case." *N.C. Dental*, 135 S. Ct. at 1116-17. Accordingly, FTC Staff will evaluate each case in light of its own facts, and will apply the applicable case law and the principles embodied in this guidance reasonably and flexibly.

3. What factors are relevant to determining whether the active supervision requirement has been satisfied?

FTC Staff will consider the presence or absence of the following factors in determining whether the active supervision prong of the state action defense is satisfied.

→ The supervisor has obtained the information necessary for a proper evaluation of the action recommended by the regulatory board. As applicable, the supervisor has ascertained relevant facts, collected data, conducted public hearings, invited and received public comments, investigated market conditions, conducted studies, and reviewed documentary evidence.

 ✓ The information-gathering obligations of the supervisor depend in part upon the scope of inquiry previously conducted by the regulatory board. For example, if the regulatory board has conducted a suitable public hearing and collected the relevant information and data, then it may be unnecessary for the supervisor to repeat these tasks. Instead, the supervisor may utilize the materials assembled by the regulatory board.

→ The supervisor has evaluated the substantive merits of the recommended action and assessed whether the recommended action comports with the standards established by the state legislature.

→ The supervisor has issued a written decision approving, modifying, or disapproving the recommended action, and explaining the reasons and rationale for such decision.

 ✓ A written decision serves an evidentiary function, demonstrating that the supervisor has undertaken the required meaningful review of the merits of the state board's action.

✓ A written decision is also a means by which the State accepts political accountability for the restraint being authorized.

Scenario 1: Example of satisfactory active supervision of a state board regulation designating teeth whitening as a service that may be provided only by a licensed dentist, where state policy is to protect the health and welfare of citizens and to promote competition.

→ The state legislature designated an executive agency to review regulations recommended by the state regulatory board. Recommended regulations become effective only following the approval of the agency.

→ The agency provided notice of (i) the recommended regulation and (ii) an opportunity to be heard, to dentists, to non-dentist providers of teeth whitening, to the public (in a newspaper of general circulation in the affected areas), and to other interested and affected persons, including persons that have previously identified themselves to the agency as interested in, or affected by, dentist scope of practice issues.

→ The agency took the steps necessary for a proper evaluation of the recommended regulation. The agency:

✓ Obtained the recommendation of the state regulatory board and supporting materials, including the identity of any interested parties and the full evidentiary record compiled by the regulatory board.

✓ Solicited and accepted written submissions from sources other than the regulatory board.

✓ Obtained published studies addressing (i) the health and safety risks relating to teeth whitening and (ii) the training, skill, knowledge, and equipment reasonably required in order to safely and responsibly provide teeth whitening services (if not contained in submission from the regulatory board).

- ✓ Obtained information concerning the historic and current cost, price, and availability of teeth whitening services from dentists and non-dentists (if not contained in submission from the regulatory board). Such information was verified (or audited) by the Agency as appropriate.
- ✓ Held public hearing(s) that included testimony from interested persons (including dentists and non-dentists). The public hearing provided the agency with an opportunity (i) to hear from and to question providers, affected customers, and experts and (ii) to supplement the evidentiary record compiled by the state board. (As noted above, if the state regulatory board has previously conducted a suitable public hearing, then it may be unnecessary for the supervising agency to repeat this procedure.)

→ The agency assessed all of the information to determine whether the recommended regulation comports with the State's goal to protect the health and welfare of citizens and to promote competition.

→ The agency issued a written decision accepting, rejecting, or modifying the scope of practice regulation recommended by the state regulatory board, and explaining the rationale for the agency's action.

Scenario 2: Example of satisfactory active supervision of a state regulatory board administering a disciplinary process.

A common function of state regulatory boards is to administer a disciplinary process for members of a regulated occupation. For example, the state regulatory board may adjudicate whether a licensee has violated standards of ethics, competency, conduct, or performance established by the state legislature.

Suppose that, acting in its adjudicatory capacity, a regulatory board controlled by active market participants determines that a licensee has violated a lawful and valid standard of ethics, competency, conduct, or performance, and for this reason, the regulatory board proposes that the licensee's license to practice in the state be revoked or suspended. In order to invoke the state action defense, the regulatory board would need to show both clear articulation and active supervision.

→ In this context, active supervision may be provided by the administrator who oversees the regulatory board (e.g., the secretary of health), the state attorney general, or another state official who is not an active market participant. The active supervision requirement of the state action defense will be satisfied if the supervisor: (i) reviews the evidentiary record created by the regulatory board; (ii) supplements this evidentiary record if and as appropriate; (iii) undertakes a de nova review of the substantive merits of the proposed disciplinary action, assessing whether the proposed disciplinary action comports with the policies and standards established by the state legislature; and (iv) issues a written decision that approves, modifies, or disapproves the disciplinary action proposed by the regulatory board.

Note that a disciplinary action taken by a regulatory board affecting a single licensee will typically have only a de minimis effect on competition. A pattern or program of disciplinary actions by a regulatory board affecting multiple licensees may have a substantial effect on competition.

The following do <u>not</u> constitute active supervision of a state regulatory board that is controlled by active market participants:

→ The entity responsible for supervising the regulatory board is itself controlled by active market participants in the occupation that the board regulates. *See N.C. Dental,*135 S. Ct. at 1113-14.

→ A state official monitors the actions of the regulatory board and participates in deliberations, but lacks the authority to disapprove anticompetitive acts that fail to accord with state policy. *See Patrick v. Burget*, 486 U.S. 94, 101 (1988).

→ A state official (e.g., the secretary of health) serves ex officio as a member of the regulatory board with full voting rights. However, this state official is one of several members of the regulatory board and lacks the authority to disapprove anticompetitive acts that fail to accord with state policy.

→ The state attorney general or another state official provides advice to the regulatory board on an ongoing basis.

→ An independent state agency is staffed, funded, and empowered by law to evaluate, and then to veto or modify, particular recommendations of the regulatory board. However, in practice such recommendations are subject to only cursory review by the independent state agency. The independent state agency perfunctorily approves the recommendations of the regulatory board. *See Ticor*, 504 U.S. at 638.

→ An independent state agency reviews the actions of the regulatory board and approves all actions that comply with the procedural requirements of the state administrative procedure act, without undertaking a substantive review of the actions of the regulatory board. *See Patrick*, 486 U.S. at 104-05.

Endnotes:

[1] Aaron Edlin & Rebecca Haw, Cartels By Another Name: Should Licensed Occupations Face Antitrust Scrutiny, 162 U. PA. l. REV. 1093, 1096 (2014).

[2] Id. at 1095.

[3] See, e.g., Fed. Trade Comm'n Staff Policy Paper, Policy Perspectives: Competition and the Regulation of Advanced Practice Registered Nurses (Mar. 2014), https://www.ftc.gov/system/files/documents/reports/policy-perspectivescompetition-regulation-advanced-practice-nurses/140307aprnpolicypaper.pdf; Fed. Trade Comm'n & U.S. Dept. of Justice, Comment before the

South Carolina Supreme Court Concerning Proposed Guidelines for Residential and Commercial Real Estate Closings (Apr. 2008), https://www.ftc.gov/news-events/press-releases/2008/04/ftcdoi-submit-letter-supreme-court-south-carolina-proposed.

END OF FTC GUIDANCE

Note: After the North Carolina case and FTC Guidance (above), three major national consumer organizations submitted the following open letter of inquiry and request for documents to the Attorneys General of each of the fifty states regarding compliance with the North Carolina case by each state, respectively.

Open letter of inquiry and request for documents, sent to the Attorney Generals of each of the 50 states re: *North Carolina State Board of Dental Examiners v. FTC*

Dear [Mr. / Madame Attorney General]:

We write to alert you to the critical significance of the U.S. Supreme Court's recent decision in *North Carolina State Board of Dental Examiners v. FTC*, 135 S. Ct. 1101 (February 25, 2015), and solicit your response as well as relevant public documents regarding its implementation in your state. As discussed below, this case holds that much of the activity conducted by your state licensing boards is not protected by the "state-action antitrust immunity" doctrine. Critically, the Court's holding hinges on the fact that the majority of the members of the state regulatory board at issue were "engaged in the active practice of the profession it regulates." *Id.* at 1107. In other words, "active market participants cannot be allowed to regulate their own markets free from antitrust accountability." *Id.* at 1111. Accordingly, your board and commission members are theoretically vulnerable to federal felony prosecution and civil treble damages—and your indemnifying state budget may be similarly exposed. We explain this apparently startling circumstance as follows:

As you know, your state has numerous agencies that regulate trades and professions. These agencies often take the form of multimember "boards" or "commissions." They commonly regulate a large portion of the state's economy—from accountants, architects, attorneys, pharmacists, dentists, and doctors, to most of the other licensed trades—contractors, brokers, barbers, nurses, and many others.

Many of the decisions these entities make on a regular basis necessarily "restrain trade." For example, they decide who is allowed to practice a trade or profession and who is excluded, with the force of law. They revoke licenses, and specify how the licensees are to practice. These acts, if committed by a cartel—or any private grouping of competitors— would be per se antitrust violations under federal law (*e.g.*, Sherman Act, 15 U.S.C. § 1 *et seq.*) For example, licensing boards control supply by limiting entry into the profession or market. These barriers to entry are effectively "group boycotts," which, as per se offenses, constitute antitrust violations without recourse to their "reasonableness" or other related defenses. The federal remedy for any violation of the Sherman Act includes potential felony prosecution, as well as private civil treble damages relief.

Virtually all of the regulation these agencies undertake sufficiently "affects interstate commerce" to invoke the supremacy jurisdiction of federal antitrust law. Because federal courts have recognized "state-action immunity" from antitrust laws, and have permitted such restraints notwithstanding their facial violation of law, that "state action" status is critical to the lawful function of every state regulatory board.

Three seminal decisions by the U.S. Supreme Court frame this special immunity, starting with *Parker v. Brown*, 317 U.S. 341 (1943). In *Parker*, the Supreme Court created the longstanding "two-pronged test" to qualify for "state-action" immunity: The challenged action must be (1) affirmatively authorized by the state, and 2) subject to active supervision by the state. *Id.* at 351-52.

The second seminal case is *California Retail Liquor Dealers Ass'n v. Midcal Aluminum, Inc.*, 445 U.S. 97 (1980), a decision that directly examined the "active state supervision" prong. That case stands partly for the proposition that "state supervision" must be specific and bona fide. *Id.* at 105-06. In other words, state "rubber stamping" of a regulatory board's action will not suffice. *Id.*

We respectfully contend that, notwithstanding these and related precedents, your state (like many others) has chosen to ignore them, and has created "state" boards that are directly controlled by members of the very trade or profession they purport to regulate. Indeed, the vast majority of occupational licensing boards and commissions nationwide are now comprised of majorities (or even supermajorities) of licensed professionals in the very economic tribal grouping with an economic interest in restraints of trade benefiting them. In fact, your state actually requires that board and commission positions be filled by those with such a conflict.[1]

It is in this context that the U.S. Supreme Court has just decided the third in this series of basic cases: *North Carolina State Board of Dental Examiners v. FTC*, 574 U.S. __, 135 S. Ct. 1101 (2015). We attach for your reference the full three-page syllabus of this 6-3 decision, with margin markings of the most pertinent passages. This decision is neither narrow nor subject to exception or avoidance. It directly and repeatedly announces a bright- line minimum test for "state action" sovereign immunity: Those controlling the decisions that might restrain trade may not be "active market participants" in the trade regulated. For every agency so afflicted, the legal status of those making such decisions is clear – they are, in the words of the Court, "nonsovereign actors" who lack any state sovereign immunity whatever. Their decisions are no different than a decision undertaken by a cartel or private combination of competitors. You are invited to review the decision en toto and draw your own conclusions, or to refer it and this letter to the leading antitrust prosecutors and experts in your jurisdiction. Significantly, the decision renders unlawful what has become the common regulatory practice across all 50 states. The holding reviews the prior *Parker* and *Midcal* decisions as described above. It states: "Limits on state action immunity are most essential when a State seeks to delegate its regulatory power to active market participants." *North Carolina State Board of Dental Examiners*, 135 S. Ct. at 1111. Either the composition of the board receiving such delegation must be changed (*e.g.*, with the addition of a supermajority of non-conflicted "public members") or all actions of a board dominated by active market participants must be subject to a state supervision mechanism that "provide[s] 'realistic assurance' that a nonsovereign actor's anticompetitive conduct 'promotes state policy, rather than merely the party's individual interests.'" *North Carolina State Board of Dental Examiners*, 135 S. Ct. at 1116, quoting *Patrick v. Burget*, 486 U.S. 94, 100-01 (1988). This alternative requires actual "active supervision" by the state. The Court does not mince words in describing the inadequacy of theoretical or general oversight to accomplish such a cure, noting that such supervision cannot be undertaken by those who are "active market participants" in the relevant trade themselves, and going beyond that threshold as follows: "[T]he supervisor must review the substance of the anticompetitive decision, not merely the procedures followed to produce it…; the supervisor must have the power to veto or modify particular decisions to ensure they accord with state policy…and the mere potential for state supervision is not an adequate substitute for a decision by the State…." 135 S. Ct. at 1116. (citations omitted).

In these regards, neither the presence of an Office of Attorney General official, nor a general rulemaking review entity, nor general legislative or other oversight will confer such immunity. Only where the decision is made by those who are not "active market participants" in the relevant trade or activity, or where decisions and acts are specifically reviewed for anticompetitive effect by a state agency lacking that bias and with the authority to veto and modify, will sovereign status be conferred. Lacking that structure—which is currently rare to non-existent—the presence of even a majority of a quorum of "active market participants" on an applicable governing board precludes or jeopardizes its immunity.[2]

The extent of current liability under federal antitrust law for many occupational licensing boards and their members is *in extremis*. Signatory Center for Public Interest Law (CPIL) is familiar with the applicable caselaw and the impact of the North Carolina decision. Professor Fellmeth personally served as a state and federal antitrust prosecutor for nine years and is the co-author of the treatise California White Collar Crime (with

Thomas A. Papageorge, Tower Publishing, 4th edition 2013), as well as other relevant publications. CPIL has studied the activities of California's regulatory agencies for 35 years, teaching the subject, and publishing the *California Regulatory Law Reporter*. Our analysis is not borne of naiveté, nor is it the product of ideological predilections—apart from sympathy with the precepts of democratic government. See http://www.cpil.org.

The Citizen Advocacy Center (CAC) is a nonprofit organization whose mission is to increase the accountability, transparency, and effectiveness of state health care professional regulatory boards and national voluntary certification organizations by offering training, researching, and networking opportunities for public members serving on these entities. The CAC supports efforts to review unjustifiable anticompetitive restrictions they impose that harm consumers. See http://www.cacenter.org.

Consumers Union is the advocacy division of the nonprofit publisher, Consumer Reports, which for nearly 80 years has empowered consumers with the knowledge they need to make better and more informed choices. The organization's Safe Patient Project has advocated for a safer health care system for the past 12 years on several fronts, covering physician accountability, health care-acquired infections, medical errors, and medical device safety. See www.consumer.org.

Each of these organizations has a longstanding interest in securing a legitimate democracy controlled by the People; one without corruptive delegation to cartel or other pecuniary special interests. We are concerned that the law upholding these core values is enforced and that the Attorneys General of the respective states perform their assigned preeminent task to assure that compliance.

We understand that a board or commission structure has advantages over a bureau or department. For example, the multimember board structure generally activates "open meeting" procedural statutes that make their operations more transparent. In contrast, a bureau or department headed by an individual may be subject to ex parte lobbying by the plethora of economically-interested trade associations who track and advocate before regulatory agencies. That pattern of hidden influence is endemic, and is also problematical where there are not proper limitations on privately-advanced contentions and secretly negotiated deals. And there are other features of the current regime in your state that we recognize warrant at least a measure of favorable consideration.[3]

You are the chief law enforcement official of your state. You also advise state agencies. As such, your predominant obligation is not to arrange or excuse violations of law, but to prevent them and, where that fails, to enforce the law. That function may place you at odds with the political and institutional prerogatives of these agencies, but we respectfully contend that your duty is not to them as clients receiving blind fealty, but to compliance with applicable Supreme Court decisions warranting your respect.

With the above in mind, we ask the following four questions divided into (a) and (b) respectively. Under (a) we respectfully ask for your response to our questions. Under (b) we separately request documents that contain related information, as described below, pursuant to your Public Records Act.

1. (a) Which agencies governed by multi-member boards regulating professions or trades are composed in majority of "active market participants" in the regulated trade or profession? Which acts and decisions of these boards are subject to "independent state supervision" for restraint of trade impact prior to their legal efficacy? Please explain which entity accomplishes this review, its authority, and its directive to consider anticompetitive implications.

   (b) Please provide documents that identify the make-up of your regulatory agencies' multi-member governing bodies, including the statutes/rules governing how many and which ones are required to be participants in the trade or profession regulated.

2. (a) How many of the members of these boards and commissions identified in your answer to Question #1 above have you notified of their potential

criminal and civil liability if they make decisions that would constitute a violation of federal antitrust law? Does that notice include the revelation that their decisions are not entitled to "state action" or other sovereign protection?

(b) Please produce copies of your notification to such persons. If the notice is the same or similar to all such persons, a single copy will suffice, with a list of recipients.

3. (a) Please explain the indemnification policy of the state in terms of criminal or civil liability if a federal criminal or civil case arises and judgment is entered against those individuals? Is publicly financed counsel provided in such a case? Are damages to be subsumed by the state treasury? Please provide estimates or calculations of possible public exposure to federal court treble damage awards.

   (b) Please produce documents that analyze or disclose antitrust liability exposure to the state treasury from potential agency antitrust violations, if any such documents exist.

4. (a) With whom have you communicated about the implications of this holding? Have you communicated with your Supreme Court Justices or Legislators or their respective offices or agents? Have you communicated with the Federal Trade Commission or the United States Attorney General or a United States Attorney's Office or its agents?

   (b) Please produce such notifications. If the notice is the same or similar to all such persons, a single copy with suffice, with a list of recipients.

Thank you for your consideration of this request. Please mail your responses to Center for Public Interest Law, University of San Diego School of Law, 5998 Alcala Park, San Diego, CA 92110 or email to cpil@sandiego.edu.

Very sincerely,

Robert C. Fellmeth, Center for Public Interest Law Executive Director, Price Professor of Public Interest

Law, University of San Diego School of Law

David Swankin, Executive Director, Citizen Action Center

Lisa McGiffert, Director, Safe Patient Project, Consumers Union of the United States Attached: 3-page U.S. Supreme Court syllabus of North Carolina

Endnotes:

[1] Political reformers are concerned about the surrender of the legislative and other elective elements of our democracy to special interest domination from campaign contribution to job interchange and lobbying domination. Indeed, there has been a marked evolution of political organization around peers and colleagues in virtually every trade, occupation, and economic grouping, such that the Congress and state legislatures increasingly function as passive mediators among the "stakeholders" so represented, and leaving diffuse and future interests unrepresented. These latter concerns, including our legacy to those who follow us, form a central value of individuals within our democracy—a value that ideally is not subjugated.

[2] For example, more than three members of a 13-member board currently participating in the industry would allow those persons to win a vote of a quorum, thus determining that decision in violation of this holding.

[3] We recognize that most members of regulatory boards and commissions believe that they are serving the public interest, are unpaid, and intend to serve democratic values. But they are necessarily part of the tribal grouping that our occupational associations have fostered. By way of illustration: State bars controlled by attorneys rarely discipline for excessive billing or intellectual dishonesty. Few require any demonstration whatever of competence in the actual practice area of law relied upon by clients. Few require malpractice insurance, or in any way ameliorate the harm from attorney incompetence. The point is, each of the many agencies within your state is empowered to carve out momentous exceptions from federal antitrust law, and those decisions in particular require a level of independence from the implicit focus of current practitioners.

> We also recognize that there is an important role for expertise in the regulation of most trades and professions. As Justice Scalia has pointed out, we have an interest in listening to neurosurgeons in evaluating the competence of new applicants to such an important and complex function. But such contributions may be received without conferring final authority over state policy to current and conflicted practitioners of that trade.

END OF LETTER

Hypotheticals

The California State Bar and Regulatory Reform

The California State Bar Board of Trustees controls the licensing of attorneys in California and is comprised of a majority of licensed attorneys (7 of the 13 members). One of the public members of the Board, Polly Paralegal, has proposed that the Board consider expanding the scope of practice for paraprofessionals to deliver certain legal services without the supervision of attorneys. According to Polly, this would help bridge the gap in access to justice by providing people with representation in court who cannot afford attorneys.

Board staff prepared a draft rule that would add a new licensing category for independent paraprofessionals and released the rule for public comment. During public comment, 19 out of 20 commenters were attorneys, and each of them were vehemently opposed to the proposed rule, claiming that the public would be at significant risk if paralegals were permitted to do any task without an attorney's supervision. One commenter, a plumber, told the Board that he recently had a contract dispute and was not able to afford the

$250/hour rate for an attorney to help him. He told the Board that he had to represent himself in court, and ultimately was unsuccessful in his case.

Discussion Questions:

1. If the board votes to deny this proposal, does the Consumer Protection Policy Center (CPPC) have grounds to bring an antitrust lawsuit against the Bar? What would the best arguments be? What might the Board argue in response?

2. Does your answer change if two of the attorney members are district attorneys who do not earn attorney's fees from clients but are paid a salary by the government?

3. Does your answer change if the California Supreme Court adopts a new rule that states that the Bar is prohibited from establishing a new licensing category for paraprofessionals?

Antitrust/ State Action Immunity

The Accountancy Board consists of 15 members: 8 public members and 7 practicing certified public accountants (CPAs). All 7 of the practicing accountants are CPAs licensed by the Board. One of the public members is married to a practicing accountant, although his spouse is not a CPA and hence is not licensed by the Board. One of the CPA members has announced his retirement, effective in 6 months, but plans to continue serving on the Board.

The California Society of CPAs, a trade association, petitioned the Board to adopt a rule which states the following:

> All individuals who practice accounting but are not CPAs must place the following caveat on any sign, ad or stationery where the word "accountant" is present, in the same sized font: "*This Accounting Practice is a Bookkeeping Enterprise that is not CPA-Qualified and is Not Licensed by the State of California.*"

The Board granted the petition, and published notice of its intent to adopt the proposed rule. After 45 days and a public hearing, the Board approved the proposed rule on a 7 to 6 vote, with all 7 of the CPA members voting for it. Two public members were absent on the day of the vote.

The Board then submitted the proposed regulation to the DCA Director, who signed it within one hour without comment, and then sent the final rulemaking package to OAL for approval. OAL rejected the proposed rule, finding it lacking clarity, and returned the rulemaking package to the Board.

The Board then revised the language and approved it. This final vote to approve was 5 to 4 in favor. Only 9 members were present for the vote, although that is a quorum; 4 of the 5 aye votes were CPA Board members.

CPPC filed a lawsuit in Federal Court, challenging this regulation as both unconstitutional and also anticompetitive pursuant to *North Carolina State Board of Dental Examiners v. FTC*, and the case has made its way to the U.S. Supreme Court.

Discussion Questions:

1. What are CPPC's best arguments? For example, what are the constitutional/antitrust objections?
2. What are the deputy attorney general's best arguments on behalf of the Board?
3. What should the California Society of CPAs argue in its amicus curiae brief?
4. What will Justice Alito ask the parties during oral arguments? Justice Kagan?

Chapter 4
Ethical Standards

Discussion

The *North Carolina* case discussed in Chapter 3, *supra*, concerns the extreme but common situation of a regulatory body directly controlled by the economic interests at issue. There is some advantage in having expertise about the nature of a business and its prerequisites and ramifications, but there is a basic problem it amplifies. The underlying premise behind American democracy is governance by the People, reflecting the diffuse and future interests that representation ideally embodies. The problem of conflicts of interest extends well beyond the extreme delegation of authority to financially interested persons.

Our democracy has serious ethical problems undermining the faithful representation of the general public by regulatory agencies and other parts of a government allegedly controlled by the People. The problems here include forms of influence that provide disproportionate influence for those with an immediate profit stake in applied policies. Two leading Constitutional law SCOTUS holdings provide much of the disruption of designed fidelity to future interests: The *Noerr-Pennington* case creating the Doctrine of the same name, and the more recent decision of *Citizens United*, giving corporations substantial political power. The *Noerr- Pennington* doctrine grants to corporations and other commercial interests a First Amendment based right to collude in petitioning government. That is, notwithstanding antitrust principles limiting collusion between competitors, especially horizontal competitors, they are afforded virtually blank check authority to communicate, plan and advocate for their financial interests as a group. That license includes all lobbying, which thusly now focuses on associations of direct competitors who hire persuasive lobbyists.

Those lobbyists commonly include former legislators and legislative staff (whose private employment may be solicited while still in public employment). In addition, current law prohibits former legislators from lobbying for three years after leaving office. However, the efficacy of such former officials in their influence over current public officials (in the legislature or agencies) is only marginally limited by the three years of direct lobbying prohibition.

The *Noerr-Pennington* doctrine allows horizontal competitors, usually organized into "trade associations," to restrain trade with impunity if they can persuade a legislative body to make such a restraint a qualifying "state action." In other words, instead of risking a felony prosecution for conspiracies that restrain trade, they can formulate such restraints among themselves and then involve the state in some manner—making it immune from antitrust liability and perhaps even protected and advanced by the powers of the state in its implementation.

Regrettably, this compromise of the most basic American principle of public control of our own government has now been exacerbated by the U.S. Supreme Court's *Citizens United* holding of 2010. That case terminally undermines democracy by equating corporations and related economic interests with the rights of "persons"—actual individuals constituting the People. This case compromises alleged controls on the financial influence of public officials (*e.g.*, through campaign contributions). Of course, a corporation is a separate and statutorily created "person" with a sacrosanct obligation of its officers, directors and lobbyists, to protect and advance the "economic interests" of the corporation's stockholders. That is a stated and pre- eminent fiduciary duty applicable to each of them. Rather, this difference is marked between these entities and individuals who vote and whose fate is at risk in governmental laws and rules, particularly future interests vis-à-vis immediate profit outcomes for corporate entities.

Beyond this pervasive imbalance, there are some laws that limit direct economic determination of official decisionmaking. Relevant statutes include the subject matter discussed below, in addition to a number of laws that have some relevance.

1. Criminal "extortion." California Penal Code sections 519 prohibits the influence of an official governmental act by "extortionate" means, *e.g.*, the threat of exposing a secret. Solicitation or attempts are enforced by the Attorney General and district attorneys in California and most states, and are also subject to federal prosecution.
2. Criminal bribery. Instead of a threat, an official act may be induced by a reward. These statutes are common at the state level and also apply federally. The key element to a criminal case conviction is the proof of a clear "quid pro quo" element. That is, the money or other reward is made on the condition and with the expectation of its influence as to a governmental decision.
3. As noted, both extortion and bribery have federal counterparts subject to prosecution by U.S. Attorneys or the Department of Justice in D.C., using mail fraud, RICO or Hobbs or Corrupt Practices Act offenses. Most of these offenses are best based on tapes or videos of the offending transaction (as with the federal ABSCAM sting case).
4. Conflicts of Interest. Governmental officials, including agency officials are prohibited from a decision (*e.g.*, a vote by a Board member) where there is a "conflict of interest." *I.e.*, where the

official has personal assets or income that will be impacted by the decision. Of course, there are some regulatory decisions that can financially influence many thousands of persons and where the official is one of a large number of those enjoying a personal benefit. That circumstance is not necessarily a limiting conflict. California has a generic statute, section 1090 of the Government Code, that requires recusal from any decision where a conflict of interest will apply.

In addition to these traditional white-collar political crime elements is a larger environment of political contributions that are allowed, and without significant limitation where accomplished through a Political Action Committee effectively exempt from limitations or effective disclosure.

There is a general visibility statute (at the state level in California)—the Political Reform Act of 1974. It essentially requires agency officials to report income, gifts and loans. Further, lobbyists must be registered and must report on sources of income and measures they were respectively paid to influence. Most of these disclosures are included in Reports to the Fair Political Practices Commission, where public access is available. Importantly, the lobbyist reporting requirements apply not only to legislative lobbying, but also to agency lobbying. However, the definition of "lobbyist" requires minimum time and expense devoted to that task and does not involve reporting of contacts between those who are regulated and public officials allegedly regulating them in the normal course.

These public reporting elements have limited efficacy in removing conflicts of interest. First, lobbying communications with agency officials (as with legislators) is generally not disclosed. These are termed "*ex parte*" contacts. In the judicial branch such communications are barred as unethical.

The problem of such influence was highlighted recently with regard to the California Public Utilities Commission (CPUC). In theory, this agency is more public in its engagement with lobbyists than others—requiring at least notice in the scheduling records of commissioners where there is a visit by a lobbyist. However, a series of private emails between regulated utility Pacific Gas & Electric and several commissioners included the request to choose a particular administrative law judge favored by the utility as to an important imminent regulatory proceeding. The request was granted after communications on the subject that were not subject to effective public disclosure.

The concept here is that allowing one interested party to have confidential communications with a court may inhibit response from others that may more fully inform the decision to be made. One issue of interest and proposed by CPPC is that all such communications between lobbyists and public officials should be disclosed, not only as to who is being heard, but given modern communications, recorded in full in a cloud that is generally accessible. Such a feature would allow others who are able to dispute or correct representations made to such public officials. It might also discourage the current practice of communicating to a public official the "deferred bribe" of a lucrative employment or contract opportunity once they leave government employment. That problem is underlined for committee and agency staff and for legislators who are now subject to a maximum term of twelve years for legislative service. If the capacity exists for such visibility, and its cost is not extreme, why is it not part of the process?

FPPC RULES FOR GIFTS, HONORARIA, TRAVEL PAYMENTS, AND LOANS[3]

Pursuant to California's Fair Political Practices Commission (FPPC), public officials and employees are subject to certain restrictions related to receiving gifts, honoraria, travel payments, and loans, as follows:

- **$10 Lobbyist Gift Limit:** Elected state officials, including members of the legislature, and legislative employees may not accept a gift or gifts totaling more than $10 in a calendar month from any individual who is registered as a lobbyist under state law. The $10 limit also applies to gifts received by officials and employees of state agencies if their agency is listed on the registration statement of the lobbyist's employer or firm.
- **$590 Gift Limit (Effective January 1, 2023–December 31, 2024)**: State and local officials and employees are prohibited from receiving a gift or gifts totaling more than $590 in a calendar year from certain sources. For elected state officials and many others, the prohibition is applicable to gifts from any source, although there are exceptions (for example, gifts from family members). For state and local officials and employees who file Statements of Economic Interests (Form 700s) under an agency's conflict of interest code, the gift limit is applicable only to individuals and entities that would have to be disclosed on Form 700. This gift limit is adjusted for inflation every odd- numbered year. (Note: Judges are not subject to the Act's gift prohibitions but are covered by the Code of Civil Procedure.)
- **Honoraria:** An honorarium is a payment received for making a speech, publishing an article or attending any public or private conference, convention, meeting, social event, meal or similar

[3] For the recent history of the Political Reform Act, including minor changes, see https://www.fppc.ca.gov/about- fppc/about-the-political-reform-act.html.

gathering. State and local elected officers and candidates for those offices and all officials holding positions listed in California Government Code Section 87200 are prohibited from receiving honoraria payments. Likewise, an employee designated under a state or local government agency's conflict of interest code is prohibited from receiving honoraria payments from any source of gifts or income the employee is required to report on his or her Statement of Economic Interests (Form 700). Some limited exceptions apply, such as income earned from a bona fide business or profession.

- **Exceptions for Travel:** Certain payments for travel are excluded from the gift limits and honoraria prohibition. Refer to the appropriate gift fact sheet to determine if your travel payment is subject to the gift limit.
- **Loan Restrictions:** Public officials who are required to file Statements of Economic Interests (Form 700s) or who are exempt employees may not receive any personal loan aggregating more than $250 from an official, employee, or consultant of, or from anyone who contracts with, their governmental agencies. In addition, elected officials may not receive any personal loan aggregating more than $500 from a single lender unless certain terms of the loan are specified in writing. Under certain circumstances, a personal loan that is not being repaid or is being repaid below certain amounts may become a gift to the official who received it.

BEHESTED PAYMENTS

Under California's transparency laws, an elected official who fundraises or otherwise solicits payments from one individual or organization to be given to another individual or organization may be required to report the payment. Generally, a payment is considered "behested" and subject to reporting if it is made:

- At the request, suggestion, or solicitation of, or made in cooperation, consultation, coordination or concert with the public official; and
- For a legislative, governmental or charitable purpose.

Behested payments subject to reporting do not include gifts made principally for personal purposes, or contributions made for election-related activity to the elected official. While state law limits the amount of gifts and campaign contributions an official may receive, there are no limits on behested payments. However, a reportable behested payment that also results in any personal benefit to the official may be considered a gift to the official even when the payment is not made principally for personal purposes. To the extent a behested payment results in a personal benefit, the payment may require additional reporting as a gift and be subject to the gift limit. State law requires the reporting of behested payments if they total $5,000 or more per calendar year from a single source.

Officials must report the behested payments within 30 days of the date on which the payment meets or exceeds $5,000 from a single source. The FPPC provides information on behested payments reported by members of the California Senate and Assembly, and statewide elected officials, at www.fppc.ca.gov/transparency/behested-payments.html.

Walking the Line: Holding Agency Counsel to Professional Standards

The following commentary, authored by Prof. Robert Fellmeth, Price Professor of Public Interest Law at the University of San Diego School of Law, was originally published in California Regulatory Law Reporter Vol. 15, No. 4 (Fall 1995). A condensed version of this article was also published in the December 20, 1995, issue of the Los Angeles Daily Journal.

> The phrase client control—as in "what kind of client control do you have to settle this?"—is familiar to litigators. Although the expression sounds patronizing, there are times when a client insists on doing what is stupid, wrong, or unlawful. At these times, counsel's ability to influence the client becomes important. When a client does not listen, counsel must often choose whether to help pilot the wayward ship to lessen anticipated damage, or row ashore and leave the vessel to its perilous fate.
>
> Sometimes, lack of client control requires counsel to leave the boat forthwith, e.g., plans to commit criminal acts, demands that spurious lawsuits be filed, positions taken, courts misled, or the legal process otherwise abused. California's Rules of Professional Conduct command the withdrawal of counsel where a client is litigating without probable cause, or where continued employment will result in a violation of the rules or the State Bar Act.[1]
>
> In turn, the State Bar Act's "duties of an attorney" include "to counsel or maintain such actions, proceedings, or

defenses only as appear to him or her legal or just (except in defense of accused criminals)."[2] And another enumerated duty is "to employ, for the purpose of maintaining the causes confided to him or her such means only as are consistent with truth, and never to seek to mislead the judge...by an artifice or false statement of fact or law."[3]

Beyond mandatory withdrawal, counsel may withdraw where a client seeks to pursue an unlawful course of action, insists upon making a claim or argument that is "not warranted," or even acts contrary to the advice of counsel (even if not prohibited by the rules or the Act).[4]

Arguably, an attorney advising an agency has a heightened obligation. First, agency counsel has duties flowing from Rule of Professional Conduct 3-600 governing representation of an "organization." The organization itself—not factions of it—is the client. Where the organization seeks to violate the law, the rule spells out duties to seek reconsideration, to appeal the matter to higher authority within the entity, and finally to resign "in accordance with rule 3-700."

There are other reasons why an agency's counsel may have special obligations. Groups do not necessarily exercise more prudent judgment than do individuals. Far from moderating excesses, group dynamics can often stimulate excesses—whether a gang, nation, political party, trade association, or other assemblage. Our species is particularly dangerous in groups.

The danger of abuse by an agency exceeds other human groupings because it wields state police powers. Most agencies have the authority to determine who may practice, or continue to practice, the trade or profession which may be the life goal of an individual.

Adding further to the obligation is the nature of the agency-advising counsel. They generally are not private attorneys who depend upon the attraction and retention of clients, but are public employees paid a salary, usually from an office of county counsel or city attorney for major local jurisdictions. At the state level, the 37 agencies within the Department of Consumer Affairs are advised by the Department's hired attorneys, and these agencies (and most others) are also advised by attorneys from the Attorney's General's Office.

The Attorney General's Office is certainly the repository of the highest obligation to comply with the standards of the Rules of Professional Conduct and the State Bar Act. Deputy attorneys general do not solely represent public agencies; they advise them on behalf of the People of the State, as officers of the State.

However, in the past twenty years, the Attorney General's Office has publicly withdrawn as an agency's counsel in only four known situations, most of which involved a political or policy-related objection of the Attorney General personally.

Critics of state and local agencies are often bewildered by the failure of counsel to "just say no" to agencies insisting on violations of law. Critics contend that violative behavior, while not prevalent, is also not rare.

Since 1987, the Office of Administrative Law has reviewed 104 complaints of alleged "underground rulemaking," allegations that a state agency unlawfully adopted a "rule" without legally required due process, including notice, an opportunity for public comment, hearing, review for necessity, clarity, authority, etc., or even publication in the California Code of Regulations. It has determined that 87 were unlawfully created.[5] Where was counsel?

Certainly a substantial number of agency decisions are close questions. But where the agency is moving against clear legislative intent and/or common decency, what should counsel do? How often has agency counsel advised against the commission of an unlawful or improper act? How often has counsel resigned from further representation of an agency under Rule 3-700 as a result of a failure to follow proper advice?

In 1986, the Center for Public Interest Law was approached by 32 Vietnamese physicians who had emigrated to California and had been denied licenses by the Medical Board, although they had passed all examinations and completed all postgraduate training requirements. An investigation disclosed that the agency had met unlawfully in private, and decided to suspend the licensing of Vietnamese physicians without explaining why and without justification. Two years of devastating career interruption, deceit from agency officials, and bureaucratic stonewalling ensued before licenses were finally issued.[6] Where was agency counsel during the process?

For years, the Board of Accountancy has been permitting a committee of private practitioners to decide disciplinary cases against colleagues and competitors. A challenge to this practice, which is obviously unlawful,[7] yielded defensiveness from the Board and indifference from its counsel. Why have counsel from both the Department of Consumer Affairs and the Attorney General's Office been advising the agency consistent with its ambitions, but contrary to basic legal principles?

Some state boards decided that the Bagley-Keene Open Meeting Act should have a loophole allowing committees to meet privately so long as they consist of "less than a quorum" of the board. In fact, the Act very clearly states and intends that a board committee of more than two members must meet in public. However, the Attorney General wrote informal opinion letters supporting the boards' position at the urging of agency clients, managed to get part of one such letter into a court's dicta (in an inapplicable case interpreting a different statute), and then cited that dicta as a holding in subsequent litigation.[8] Here, deputy attorneys general self-created a basis to undermine one of California's "sunshine" statutes—until an appellate court called them on it and noted that it would "decline...to join this circle of error."[9]

In these cases, and in others, there has been a failure to comply with the Rules of Professional Conduct and a failure of accountability. Few if any attorneys have ever been fined, sanctioned, demoted, or even publicly criticized for advising an agency to go ahead with an unlawful or unfair act. Needless to say, none has ever been sanctioned for failing to resign under the obligation of Rule 3-700(B).

One dynamic that may be at the heart of the failure to understand the proper role of public counsel to an agency is the "hired gun," "adversarial process" training received by attorneys in law school and replicated to excess in civil litigation. Schooled in the relativism of the Socratic method (there is no perfect answer; all have flaws), attorneys are taught that law is a game of one flawed argument juxtaposed against another flawed argument, and that both sides advocate to a neutral third party—who alone has the responsibility to find the correct answer.

Add to this mentality a desire to win the approval of the group one is advising, and you have a recipe for the classic "enabler"—decried by critics as the current norm in public agency representation. The "enabler" does not look with neutrality at the statutes which may be implicated in an agency action, does not attempt to ascertain the legislative intent at issue, is rarely tuned to concepts of fairness for outsiders. Instead, he or she views the agency client as seeking an end the agency determines; counsel's role is to use legal skills to help the agency achieve that end. Such a goal involves reading statutes contrary to legislative intent, finding loopholes, making supportive arguments—in essence, serving the agency by helping it do whatever it wants to do. Where advice is not followed, counsel nevertheless remains loyal, attempts to mitigate harm, and publicly defends the agency's position, using every argument and artifice available.

Many attorneys who advise agencies have a problem walking the line between a properly subsidiary role to serve a client and informing the agency when its plans breach larger obligations the agency must follow. Counsel must attempt to consider the agency's plans apart from the agency, its territory, and its ambitions, and look at what it is doing in light of legitimate competing policies and laws.

One way to do this is to make the argument from the opposite side. If, looking at the situation from the viewpoint of another legitimate interest, the direction undertaken is unlawful or simply abusive of higher values, the agency should be so advised. If the actions are unlawful and the advice is ignored, counsel must withdraw. This can be done politely, deferentially, or regretfully, but—regardless of its historical rarity—counsel is obligated to withdraw. If the action is lawful and not subject to mandatory withdrawal, but abusive of other higher values, counsel should consider withdrawal under the permissive provision of the rules.

Once a decision has been made to withdraw, there is a duty to mitigate harm that may occur from counsel's departure. Turning over files to alternate counsel, meeting approaching deadlines, and maintaining client confidences may be involved. Even here there may be limitations on assistance when the agency is pursuing an unlawful path. And it is proper to notify substitute counsel of the reason for withdrawal, enabling him or her to make a similar conscientious decision.

The Rules of Professional Conduct and the State Bar Act do not define lawyers as a profession of hired guns. The adversary process serves the higher end of truth-seeking; it is not the end itself. And the adversary process is—in particular—not an absolute shelter for public counsel who represent interests beyond the agency client.

Members of the State Bar are understandably defensive about the negative public image of attorneys. We do not understand how we are so condemned when all we are doing is professionally serving our clients. Critics argue, with some persuasive force, that we will be thought of more positively when we internalize a more sophisticated hierarchy of values, one placing compliance with the law, civility, and human kindness on a footing a step above the adversary game we have exaggerated into a self-caricature. Certainly the attorneys in a position to begin such a renaissance are those advising agencies: Their clients are capable of much damage if operating outside the law's bona fide intent. These attorneys are in a position to take a stand without serious individual sacrifice, and they have clear obligations even as counsel beyond their facial client—to the taxpayers and the body politic who create their position, pay them, and trust them to represent more than the territorial proclivities of an agency.

ENDNOTES

[1] Rule of Professional Conduct 3-700(B).

[2] CAL. Bus. & PROF. CODE § 6068(c).

[3] *Id.* at § 6068(d).

[4] Rule of Professional Conduct 3-700(C).

[5] These figures come from a survey of OAL Regulatory Determinations published in the *California Regulatory Notice Register* between 1987 and December 1995.

[6] See SB 1358 (Royce) (Chapter 1382, Statutes of 1987), resolving Le Bup Thi Dao v. Board of Medical Quality Assurance, No. 876321 (San Francisco Superior Court).

[7] See *Bayside Timber Company, Inc. v. Board of Supervisors of San Mateo County*, 20 Cal. App. 3d 1 (1971), quoting *Carter v. Carter Coal Co.*, 298 U.S. 238 (1935) ("[t]his is legislative delegation in its most obnoxious form; for it is not even delegation to an official or an official body, presumptively disinterested, but to private persons whose interests may be and often are adverse to the interests of others in the same business…").

[8] See *Funeral Security Plans v. State Board of Funeral Directors and Embalmers*, 28 Cal. App. 4th 1470 (1994) (depublished Jan. 5, 1995). See also 15:1 CAL. REG. L. REP. (Winter 1995) at 56; 13:4 CAL. REG. L. REP. (Fall 1993) at 49; 13:2&3 CAL. REG. L. REP. (Spring/Summer 1993) at 70.

[9] *Freedom Newspapers, Inc. v. Orange County Employees Retirement System Board of Directors*, 9 Cal. App. 4th 134, 147 (1992), *rev'd on other grounds*, 6 Cal. 4th 821 (1993). For a complete history of the intellectually dishonest legerdemain involved, see Robert C. Fellmeth and Julianne B. D'Angelo, *The Attorney General's "Circle of Error" Casts a Shadow Over California's Sunshine Laws*, 13:1 CAL. REG. L. REP. (Winter 1993) at 1.

END OF ARTICLE

Hypotheticals

State Legislation

CPPC has proposed AB 101, a bill to bring California into compliance with the U.S. Supreme Court's decision in *North Carolina State Board of Dental Examiners v. FTC*. The measure is authored by Assemblymember John Mountain, a member of the Business and Professions Committee that oversees the regulatory agencies within the Department of Consumer Affairs (DCA). The bill would require DCA to create a panel of experts to examine the rules and decisions of DCA boards for anticompetitive effect—including boards controlled by "active market participants" in the profession regulated by that board. The panel would *sua sponte* examine entry conditions (licensure requirements) and any action that is the subject of a colorable objection.

The California Nurses Association (CNA) opposes the measure, and does the following things:

1. CNA offers a trade association position to the chief consultant of the Business and Professions Committee at double his current salary.
2. CNA offers a lobbyist position to Assemblymember Mountain at very high pay, and notes that he would be covering Business and Professions Committee bills. Mountain is termed out from the Assembly in 16 months.
3. CNA creates a PAC to support the possible candidacy of Mountain to a state Senate position, and informs him of its purpose.
4. A group of nurses visits Mountain's district office, contending that the entire association would oppose his reelection unless he withdraws his bill.
5. CNA invites Mountain to address its statewide conference as its keynote speaker. It offers expenses and an honorarium of $5,000, or one-half of the amount normally paid to keynote speakers.
6. CNA offers a scholarship for college to Mountain's oldest child—who wishes to become a nurse.
7. In his private domain, Mountain is an avocado farmer. As the committee hearing approaches, CNA notes that it is now considering a recommendation to put avocados and guacamole into school lunches in order to "celebrate this native California crop and provide organic nutrition lacking excessive sugar."

8. CNA hires an attorney who threatens suit to invalidate any such statute due to its violation of basic occupational due process rights.

9. Do these tactics (a) violate the law, or (b) raise ethical questions? Why?

Legal Counsel to State Agency

The California State Athletic Commission (AtCom), consisting of seven commissioners, was established because of concern over (a) boxer safety and (b) the possible fixing of fights (corruption stimulated by gambling). AtCom licenses boxers, promoters, managers and others.

Boxing "promoters" are in charge of setting up and paying for everything involved in a boxing match and making sure all legal requirements are met. Only Commission licensed promoters can stage a match in California.

On March 1, 2019, AtCom posted its agenda for its March 11 Commission meeting. One of the items for the Commissioners' consideration is whether to grant a license to boxing promoter Ben King. In the days leading up to the meeting, Ben King held three separate individual meetings with Commissioners Carvelli, Lehman, and Frierson at his Sacramento hotel room. He also joined Commissioners Shen, Williams, and Sauter together at a bar nearby, where all four joined in drinking and discussing AtCom.

Deputy AG Rick Russon is the AtCom assigned attorney from the AG's Office. He knows the following:

1. Ben has three criminal convictions which he did not disclose on his license application to the Commission.

2. Commissioner Carvelli owns 10% of the stock of the corporation that owns the Olympic Auditorium, a popular boxing venue in Los Angeles. DAG Russon also becomes aware that Ben King told Carvelli in his private meeting that he wants to stage his fights at this venue.

3. He suspects that Ben may have offered Carvelli a 20% bonus beyond typical rates for the rental of the auditorium.

4. DAG Russon then learns that Commissioner Lehman has a TV show on channel 7 at 10:00 pm. In his individual meeting with Lehman, King told her that he wanted to stage a fight with big-named fighters at the Olympic Auditorium and arrange for it to be televised on channel 7 at 5:00 p.m. on the same channel for an advantageous lead in for the later show.

5. Finally, DAG Russon becomes aware that the one commissioner King did not talk to, Commissioner Ayala, has a nephew who is a young boxer and whose manager is employed by Ben King. That manager told Ayala's nephew that if he is able to secure a California promoter's license and stage a fight in California, it will be to his advantage.

Ben King has been throwing parties for all seven Commissioners, including celebrities and food at a cost of $2,000 per Commissioner per event.

You are the Assistant Attorney General supervising DAGs covering DCA agencies. DAG Russon approaches you and informs you that every single one of the Commissioners has informed him off the record that they intend to vote for Ben King's licensure. You are also aware that currently, two promoters dominate the California market and that the addition of a third could have competitive benefits for boxers and consumers.

What do you tell DAG Russon to do here, covering: Section 1090 conflicts, Bagley Keene violations, ex parte communications, extortion, bribery, illegal lobbying? Which of these is respectively implicated in these five disclosures? What should DAG be instructed to do? Be prepared to support your answer with specific citations.

Quiz

1. Under the Political Reform Act how much money may a Senator or Assemblymember earn as income in addition to the salary they earn as elected officials?

    a. Up to $50,000 in extra income
    b. Up to $100,000 in extra income
    c. No more than 25% of the salary they earn as elected officials
    d. There is no limit

2. Apart from the California Government Code's broad definition of a "conflict of interest," section 1090 applies to public officials to prohibit them from making a public governmental vote or decision (a "contract") in which he or she has a "financial interest." The available remedies for such violations include:

    a. Criminal if the act is "willful"
    b. FPPC civil penalties
    c. The voiding of the contract
    d. All of the above

3. To which of the following individuals does the Political Reform Act of 1974 apply? (more than one may be correct)

   a. Full-time, paid elected officials
   b. Part time voluntary officials
   c. Advisory board members
   d. Chief administrative officers

4. Which of the following describes a recognized exception to the Political Reform Act, in which officials are allowed to take action even if they have a conflict of interest?

   a. The permissible influence doctrine
   b. The rule of quorum
   c. The rule of necessity
   d. The qualified immunity doctrine

5. What is the FPPC's term of art for private donations made to a politician's charity or cause of choice?

   a. Directed philanthropy
   b. Directed donations
   c. Pet charities
   d. Behested payments

6. What is the limit elected state officials and legislative employees can accept as a gift from a lobbyist?

   a. $100 per month
   b. $100 per year
   c. $120 per year
   d. $10 per month

7. Pursuant to the Political Reform Act, as amended by AB 864 (Mullin), effective January 1, 2020, what constitutes a "top contributor" such that independent expenditure committees would have to disclose that contributor on campaign ads?

   a. Any donor who contributed more than $500 to the committee
   b. Any donor who contributed more than $5,00 to the committee
   c. Any donor who contributed more than $50,000 to the committee
   d. The three donors who contributed the largest amounts to the committee

8. In September 2018, the Ninth Circuit upheld which California policy pertaining to government transparency?

   a. Campaign contribution limits
   b. Lobbyist gift limits
   c. Nonprofit donor disclosure requirements
   d. Political Reform Act

9. *True or False*: A Deputy AG assigned to a board serves as its counsel and owes a "fiduciary duty of the highest order" to his client. Hence, although this attorney is free to offer advice as to what is lawful and what is advisable, he or she must honor the confidentiality of all communications with the board and its staff and follow its instructions as to court filings and legal goals.

Chapter 5
Open Meetings

BAGLEY-KEENE OPEN MEETING ACT

The impetus behind the Bagley-Keene Open Meeting Act (Cal. Gov't Code Section 11120 et seq.) is the need for accountability to the broad public. One aspect of that accountability is knowledge of the workings of our government. In California, the Bagley-Keene Act applies to the state executive branch—all state agencies. The similar but distinct Ralph M. Brown Act applies to local governments, including county boards of supervisors, city councils and the many school and special districts throughout the state.

The Bagley-Keene Act has three basic requirements: (1) meetings of bodies capable of "taking action" as state agencies must be open to the public to attend; (2) an agenda of the topics to be discussed at the meeting (items on which "action" may be taken) must be distributed at least ten days before the session (*e.g.*, posted on the agency web site and mailed to the agency's mailing list); and (3) the meeting must allow "public comment" on items on the agenda and other matters within the agency's jurisdiction (subject to reasonable time limitations).

Such open meeting laws apply to multi-member bodies that commonly govern state agencies, such as commissions and boards. A department or other entity governed by a single appointee is not subject to these laws since decisions are made separate from "meetings." Of course, many decisions are made after "meetings" with that director and lobbyists for special interests often impact those decisions, but this Act applies to bodies of more than two persons who must meet to make final decisions—broadly defined (*i.e.*, "action taken" is the applicable term of art).

Two members of a board or commission communicating is not a "meeting," but three or more may be so considered and trigger the requirements of the statute. Evasion of the public involvement through sequential emails between three or more members in discussing a decision to be made is not consistent with the statute's intent.

Meetings may occur in person or via telephone, or more recently given the COVID-19 pandemic, by video conferencing platforms. Board or commission members so participating may be expected to make the situs of their phone or computer access mechanism accessible by citizens interested in attending.

There are some exceptions to the above measures for public access. First, some matters may be discussed and decided in "closed sessions," without public participation or attendance. (See Gov't Code Section 11126.) Analogous to notions of "executive sessions," the rationale for such sessions may include the following: (1) personnel matters (such as the firing or evaluation of the Executive Director who administers the agency under the board's guidance); (2) examination questions and answers for licensure or otherwise; (3) pending litigation (to preserve the confidentiality of attorney-client relations); (4) deliberations in agency discipline matters (evidentiary hearings and oral arguments are all publicly conducted, but the actual quasi-judicial deliberations of the board members deciding the case is normally not public (see Chapter 8, *infra*); and (5) situations where an individual licensee applicant is being considered by a board committee (that individualized process may be conducted confidentially).

Such closed sessions occur as part of agenda items during public meetings, with the public excluded while the allowable matters are discussed privately. However, the board must announce any decisions made as a result of such a closed session immediately after its conclusion.

There are two other exceptions to the application of the Bagley-Keene Open Meeting Act. First, emergency meetings may be called without the full ten-day notice, and without full compliance with the public participation requirements of the law, if a majority of the board members finds there to be an emergency situation involving a work stoppage, health or safety emergency, or cripping disaster. (See Gov't Code Section 11125.5.) While the finding of such emergencies has historically been rare, the COVID-19 pandemic of 2020 and beyond triggered its occasional application.

Finally, "special meetings" preserve the requirements of the Bagley-Keene Act regarding public attendance and participation but allow an acceleration of a meeting in less than the ten-day notice period otherwise required. A special meeting may only be called for specified purposes when compliance with the ten-day notice requirement would impose a substantial hardship on the board, such as to discuss pending litigation with short timelines, or proposed legislation that may require immediate discussion and position, or the consideration of the purchase or sale of real property. (See Gov't Code Section 11125.4 for the complete list.)

Regents of University of California v. Superior Court

20 Cal. 4th 509 (1999)

Opinion by: MOSK

***

I

The Regents of the University of California are a corporation with full powers of organization and government over the university, subject only to specified control by the Legislature. (Cal. Const., art. IX, § 9, subd. (a).) The corporation is in the form of a board composed of 25 members. (*Ibid.*) It numbers seven members ex officio, including the Governor, and eighteen members appointed by the Governor and approved by the Senate (*ibid.*)—who may, in their discretion, appoint a faculty member or a student member or both (*id.*, art. IX, § 9, subd. (c)).

On July 20, 1995, having given prior notice, the Regents held an open and public meeting in order to consider two items listed on their agenda. At that time, the board comprised 26 members, including Edward P. Gomez, a student who had been appointed by the other members. Of the 26 members, 25 were present. One of the items was SP-1, entitled "ADOPTION OF RESOLUTION: Policy Ensuring Equal Treatment—Admissions," which, among other things, would prohibit the university from "us[ing] race, religion, sex, color, ethnicity, or national origin as criteria for admission to the [u]niversity or to any program of study," effective January 1, 1997. The other of the items was SP-2, entitled "ADOPTION OF RESOLUTION: Policy Ensuring Equal Treatment—Business Practices and Employment (or Employment and Contracting)," which, among other things, would similarly prohibit the university from "us[ing] race, religion, sex, color, ethnicity, or national origin as criteria in its employment and contracting practices," effective January 1, 1996. The meeting spanned 12 1/2 hours. Following deliberations, the Regents approved both SP-1 and SP-2, the former on a vote of 14 to 10 with 1 abstention, the latter on a vote of 15 to 10....

On February 16, 1996, almost seven months later, Tim Molloy and the Daily Nexus (hereafter collectively Molloy) filed a complaint in the Superior Court of the City and County of San Francisco against the Regents, including, specifically, Governor Pete Wilson in his capacity as a regent (hereafter collectively the Regents); Molloy identified himself as a taxpayer and a staff reporter and campus editor of the Daily Nexus, and the Daily Nexus identified itself as a student-run newspaper serving the students, faculty, and staff of the University of California, Santa Barbara.

Molloy asserted a first cause of action against the Regents, based on a violation of the Bagley-Keene Open Meeting Act—specifically, its notice and open-and-public-meeting requirements. He alleged, in substance, that, prior to the noticed and open and public meeting of July 20, 1995, the Regents made a collective commitment or promise to approve SP-1 and SP-2, at a "meeting" of at least a quorum of the board's members conducted in secret through a series of one-to-one telephone and other communications, each initiated by the Governor. For a right of action, he impliedly relied on what is now section 11130(a). To the same end, he also expressly relied on section 11130.3(a). In anticipation of an affirmative defense based on that provision's 30-day statute of limitations, he undertook to invoke against the Regents the doctrine that a defendant who has fraudulently concealed a cause of action may be equitably estopped from raising such a defense, alleging, in pertinent part, to the following effect: On August 3, 1995, he placed a telephone call to the Governor's press office; he asked an unidentified person whether the Governor had telephone or other communications with other regents regarding SP-1 and SP-2 prior to July 20, 1995; the unidentified person responded with a denial; over the following months, he submitted 28 requests to the Governor under the California Public Records Act, which is set out at section 6250 et seq., seeking disclosure of public records relating to telephone communications by the Governor with other regents; in response, the Governor refused disclosure; on January 17, 1996, through the Governor's several responses refusing disclosure, he was given reason to believe that the Governor had contacted at least 10 other regents concerning the proposed resolutions.

Molloy asserted a second cause of action, against the Governor, based on a violation of the California Public Records Act. He alleged his 28 requests to the Governor seeking disclosure of public records relating to telephone communications by the Governor with other regents, and the Governor's refusal of such requests. For a right of action, he relied on section 6258: "Any person may institute proceedings for injunctive or declarative relief or writ of mandate in any court of competent jurisdiction to enforce his or her right to inspect or to receive a copy of any public record or class of public records" under this act.

As for the Bagley-Keene Open Meeting Act cause of action, Molloy sought relief including: (1) a declaration that the Regents violated the act by making a collective commitment or promise to approve SP-1 and SP-2, prior to the noticed and open and public meeting of July 20, 1995, at the alleged secret serial "meeting" of at least a quorum of the board's members, including the Governor;

(2) a declaration that the Regents' approval of the resolutions at the noticed and open and public meeting of July 20 was null and void; and (3) an injunction prohibiting the Regents from implementing either of the resolutions on the ground that each was null and void.

As for the California Public Records Act cause of action, Molloy sought relief including: (1) a declaration that the Governor violated the act by refusing his 28 requests seeking disclosure of public records relating to telephone communications by the Governor with other regents; and (2) an injunction requiring the Governor to disclose such public records.

The Regents demurred to the complaint, the board as an entity and the Governor as one of its members each doing so in separate but complementary submissions. They objected that the Bagley- Keene Open Meeting Act cause of action did not state sufficient facts. In pertinent part, they argued to the effect that, under the facts alleged, Molloy did not have any right of action pursuant to section 11130.3(a) because he commenced his action almost six months after the provision's thirty-day statute of limitations had run; that that statute of limitations precluded the doctrine of fraudulent concealment; and that, even if the statute did not do so, the doctrine would nevertheless not be available in this case. They made no mention, however, as to whether he had any right of action pursuant to section 11130(a). They similarly objected that the California Public Records Act cause of action did not state sufficient facts. In pertinent part, they argued to the effect that, under the facts alleged, any public record relating to telephone communications by the Governor with other regents was exempt from disclosure under the deliberative-process, legislative, official-information, and Governor's correspondence privileges.

The superior court issued an order overruling the demurrers....

***

In advance of any peremptory writ of mandate, Division Three of the Court of Appeal for the First Appellate District, to which this matter too was assigned, caused issuance of an alternative writ. Subsequently, in an opinion not certified for publication, it rendered judgment discharging the alternative writ and denying the petition insofar as it sought a peremptory writ. At the threshold, it impliedly concluded that the superior court's order denying the Regents' summary judgment motion, and its resolution of the underlying statutory-construction issues, were subject to independent review. On the merits, it upheld the superior court's order. It concluded that the Regents were not entitled to judgment as a matter of law on Molloy's Bagley-Keene Open Meeting Act cause of action. It determined, in substance, that, under the undisputed facts, he had a right of action pursuant to section 11130(a). It believed that that right of action extends to past actions and violations as well as present and future ones. But it also determined, in substance, that, under the undisputed facts, he did not have any right of action pursuant to section 11130.3(a). It assumed for purpose of analysis only that that provision's 30-day statute of limitations did not preclude the doctrine of fraudulent concealment. But, unlike the superior court, it believed that the doctrine was not available to toll the statute through the filing of the complaint almost six months later. Because of its conclusion on Molloy's Bagley-Keene Open Meeting Act cause of action, it did not reach his California Public Records Act cause of action.

The Regents petitioned us for review in a joint submission by the board and the Governor. We granted their application. We now reverse.

II

Before we address the questions arising under the Bagley-Keene Open Meeting Act relating to the rights of action granted by section 11130(a) and section 11130.3(a), we must review the provisions of the act that bear on the answers.

A

In 1967, the Legislature enacted the Bagley-Keene Open Meeting Act, as it was subsequently entitled, in order to govern the conduct of state bodies and to impose on such bodies various obligations, including that they must generally give prior notice of their meetings and must generally cause such meetings to be open and public....

In section 11120, the act has declared since its enactment as follows: "It is the public policy of this state that public agencies exist to aid in the conduct of the people's business and the proceedings of public agencies be conducted openly so that the public may remain informed. [¶]...[I]t is the intent of the law that actions of state agencies be taken openly and that their deliberation be conducted openly." (Stats. 1967, ch. 1656, § 122, p. 4026.) In 1981, it was amended to declare in addition: "The people of this state do not yield their sovereignty to the agencies which serve them. The people, in delegating authority, do not give their public servants the right to decide what is good for the people to know and what is not good for them to know. The people insist on remaining informed so that they may retain control over the instruments they have created." (Stats. 1981, ch. 968, § 4, p. 3683.)

In section 11122, the act, as originally enacted, provided: "'[A]ction taken' means a collective decision made by the members of a state agency, a collective commitment or promise by the members of the state agency to make a positive or negative decision or an actual vote by the members of a state agency when sitting as a body or entity upon a motion, proposal, resolution, order or similar action." (Stats. 1967, ch. 1656, § 122, p. 4026.) In 1981, it was amended into its present form to replace "agency" (*ibid.*) with "body" (Stats. 1981, ch. 968, § 7.3, p. 3685).

Since its enactment, the act has generally required state bodies to give prior notice of their meetings, pursuant to section 11125 (Stats. 1967, ch. 1656, § 122, p. 4026), and to cause such meetings to be open and public, pursuant to section 11123 (Stats. 1967, ch. 1656, § 122, p. 4026).

In section 11130, the act, as originally enacted, provided: "Any interested person may commence an action either by mandamus or injunction for the purpose of stopping or preventing violations or threatened violations of" the act "by members of" a "state agency." (Stats. 1967, ch. 1656, § 122, p. 4028.) In 1969, it was amended: "Any interested person may commence an action by mandamus, injunction, or declaratory relief for the purpose of stopping or preventing violations or threatened violations of" the act "or to determine the applicability of" the act "to actions or threatened future action by members of" a "state agency." (Stats. 1969, ch. 494, § 1, p. 1106.) In 1981, it was further amended to replace "agency" (*ibid.*) with "body" (Stats. 1981, ch. 968, § 20, p. 3693). In 1997, without substantial change in any pertinent part, it was amended into its present form under its present designation as section 11130(a). (Stats. 1997, ch. 949, § 13.)

Section 11130.3 was not part of the act as originally enacted. In 1985, it was added (Stats. 1985, ch. 936, § 1, p. 2963 et seq.), and has never been amended. It provides: "(a) Any interested person may commence an action by mandamus, injunction, or declaratory relief for the purpose of obtaining a judicial determination that an action taken by a state body in violation of" the act's notice or open-and-public-meeting requirement is "null and void. Any action seeking such a judicial determination shall be commenced within 30 days from the date the action was taken. Nothing in this section shall be construed to prevent a state body from curing or correcting an action challenged pursuant to this section.

"(b) An action shall not be determined to be null and void if any of the following conditions exist:

"(1) The action taken was in connection with the sale or issuance of notes, bonds, or other evidences of indebtedness or any contract, instrument, or agreement related thereto.

"(2) The action taken gave rise to a contractual obligation upon which a party has, in good faith, detrimentally relied.

"(3) The action taken was in substantial compliance with [the act's notice and open-and-public- meeting requirements].

"(4) The action taken was in connection with the collection of any tax."

Similarly, section 11130.7 was not part of the act as originally enacted. In 1980, it was added to provide: "Each member of a state agency who attends a meeting of such agency in violation of any provision of" the act, "with knowledge of the fact that the meeting is in violation thereof, is guilty of a misdemeanor." (Stats. 1980, ch. 1284, § 16, p. 4341.) In 1981, it was amended to replace "agency" (*ibid.*) with "body" (Stats. 1981, ch. 968, § 22, p. 3693). In 1997, it was amended into its present form: "Each member of a state body who attends a meeting of that body in violation of any provision of" the act, "and where the member intends to deprive the public of information to which the member knows or has reason to know the public is entitled under" the act, "is guilty of a misdemeanor." (Stats. 1997, ch. 949, § 14.)

B

The first question before us is whether the right of action granted by section 11130(a) under the Bagley-Keene Open Meeting Act extends only to present and future actions and violations and not past ones.

Focusing on section 11130(a) itself, we are of the opinion that the answer is affirmative: the provision's right of action does indeed extend only to present and future actions and violations and not past ones.

***

Plainly, section 11130(a)'s right of action points toward the *future*: "[A]ny interested person may commence an action...for the purpose of...*preventing...threatened* violations of" the act "by members of" a "state body," or "to determine" the act's "applicability...to...*threatened future* action" by such persons. (Italics added.) In this regard, it covers violations and actions *that are yet to occur*.

Almost as plainly, section 11130(a)'s right of action also points toward the *present*: "[A]ny interested person may commence an action...for the purpose of *stopping*...violations" of the act "by members of" a "state body," or "to determine" the act's "applicability...to actions" by such persons (Italics added.). In this regard, it covers violations and actions *that are occurring, including both discrete instances and continuing patterns or practices.*

By contrast, section 11130(a)'s right of action does not point toward the *past*, plainly or otherwise.

The language of section 11130(a) argues against the past. Insofar as it deals with "preventing threatened violations" of the act and "determining" its "applicability to threatened future action," its focus is explicitly on the future. Insofar as it deals with "stopping violations" of the act and "determining" its "applicability to actions," its focus is implicitly on the present. In the phrase "stopping violations," it shows its present orientation by usage. One speaks of "stopping" present "violations," but not past ones. In the phrase "determining applicability to actions," it shows its present orientation by context. Without express adjectival modification, the noun "actions" may indeed be subject to implied modification. Its textual surroundings are the present and the future, without any reference or allusion, express or implied, to the past. Had the Legislature meant to include the past, it would have made itself plain, likely through the phrase "actions taken," which, in the singular, appears, time and again, throughout the act. (See § 11122, 11125.2, 11125.5, subds. (c) & (d), 11125.6, subd. (d), 11126, subds. (a)(2) & (f)(8), 11126.3, subd. (f), 11130.3.) It did not do so. To be sure, it might have used "actions" without modification to refer to the past as well as the present. But any evidence that it actually did is no more than conjecture and speculation.

***

Looking beyond section 11130(a) itself to its legislative history, we find confirmation for our conclusion that the provision's right of action extends only to present and future actions and violations and not past ones.

Recall that, in section 11130, the act, as originally enacted in 1967, provided: "Any interested person may commence an action either by mandamus or injunction for the purpose of stopping or preventing violations or threatened violations of" the act "by members of" a "state agency." (Stats. 1967, ch. 1656, § 122, p. 4028.)

***

In the years following 1969, section 11130 was amended twice, once in 1981 (Stats. 1981, ch. 968, § 20, p. 3693) and again in 1997 into its present form under its present designation as section 11130(a) (Stats. 1997, ch. 949, § 13). Neither time was it modified to refer to past actions or violations, or indeed to the past itself in any way. That it was not given a past orientation cannot reasonably be attributed to a belief on the part of the Legislature that it already possessed one.

***

Section 11130(a)'s legislative history, which is set out above, confirms our conclusion that the provision's right of action extends only to present and future actions and violations and not past ones. The only reference to the past existed in what was not enacted. No such reference exists in what was.

In sum, section 11130(a) grants a right of action: (1) to stop or prevent a present or future violation of the act—but not to reach back to a past one; and (2) to determine whether the act is applicable to a present or future action—but *not* a past one.

C

The second question before us is whether the right of action granted by section 11130.3(a) under the Bagley-Keene Open Meeting Act is limited by the 30-day statute of limitations contained therein.

Focusing on section 11130.3(a) itself, we are of the opinion that the answer is affirmative: the provision's right of action is indeed limited by the 30-day statute of limitations contained therein.

Section 11130.3 authorizes the nullification and voidance of an action taken by a state body in violation of the act's notice or open-and-public-meeting requirement, but only if: (1) an interested person commences an action seeking nullification and voidance within 30 days from the date the action in question was taken; (2) the action was not in substantial compliance with the requirements, and did not involve either the sale or issuance of an evidence of indebtedness or related agreement, or a contractual obligation on which a party has detrimentally relied in good faith, or the collection of a tax; and (3) the violation was not cured or corrected.

It follows, therefore, that, in enacting section 11130.3, the Legislature had as its purpose to authorize the nullification and voidance of an action taken by a state body in violation of the act's notice or open-and-public-meeting requirement, but only under strict conditions. Its purpose evidently arose as it struck a balance between two, at least potentially conflicting, objectives—to permit the nullification and voidance of certain actions, but not to imperil the finality of even such actions unduly. It accordingly chose to craft a powerful weapon, but to restrict its range....

Section 11130.3(a)'s 30-day statute of limitations does not allow any extension of time expressly. It is as it appears to be: "Any action seeking...a judicial determination" that "an action taken by a state body in violation of" the act's notice or open-and-public-meeting requirement is "null and void" "shall be commenced *within 30 days from the date the action was taken.*" (Italics added.)

Neither does section 11130.3(a)'s 30-day statute of limitations allow any extension of time by implication.

Had it fixed the inception of its limitations period not as of the date of the taking by the state body of the action to be challenged, but instead by reference, without any such date, to the accrual of the underlying cause of action or to the discovery thereof, section 11130.3(a)'s 30-day statute of limitations might be deemed to allow some extension of time by implication.

The so-called "accrual rule" is the general one for defining the beginning of a limitations period for a cause of action (Code Civ. Proc., § 312; see generally, 3 Witkin, Cal. Procedure (4th ed. 1996) Actions, § 459, pp. 580-581), setting the opening as the time "when, under the substantive law, the wrongful act is done and the...liability arises" (3 Witkin, Cal. Procedure, *supra*, Actions, § 459, p. 580, italics omitted). The so-called "discovery rule" is the "most important exception" thereto, postponing the opening for certain causes of action until discovery thereof. (*Id.*, § 463, p. 583.) If tolerantly applied, the accrual rule can effectively extend the beginning of a limitations period. (See, e.g., *Garver v. Brace* (1996) 47 Cal. App. 4th 995, 999-1001 [55 Cal. Rptr. 2d 220].) Even if strictly applied, the discovery rule can do the same, inasmuch as its very purpose is to trigger such an extension. (See generally, 3 Witkin, Cal. Procedure, *supra*, Actions, § 463-466, pp. 583-590.)

But section 11130.3(a)'s 30-day statute of limitation simply does not fix the inception of its limitations period by reference, without any date, to discovery or even accrual. It does so, rather, as of the date of the taking of the action in question. This fact is significant. Indeed, it is controlling. Section 11130.3 concerns itself exclusively with actions that have been taken in violation of the act's notice or open-and-public-meeting requirement. Which means actions occurring outside of the light of day. Which in turn means actions implicating fraud in effect if not fraud in intent. Because section 11130.3 so concerns itself, it would have been expected to allow some kind of extension of time by some kind of means. An example presents itself in subdivision (d) of section 338 of the Code of Civil Procedure, which fixes the inception of its three-year limitations period for an action for fraud by reference, without any date, to discovery thereof. That section 11130.3(a) does not allow any type of extension of time by any type of means in express terms practically bars the conclusion that it does so by implication....

Looking beyond section 11130.3(a) itself to its legislative history, we find confirmation for our conclusion that the provision's right of action is indeed limited by the 30-day statute of limitations contained therein.

In 1984, at the request of Member of the Assembly Lloyd G. Connelly, the Attorney General issued an opinion in which he concluded, as pertinent here, that, in order not to imperil the finality of actions taken by state bodies, the Legislature, in originally enacting the act, had not intended that any violation of any of its requirements would result in the nullification and voidance of any such action. (*"Specific Agenda" Requirements of the Bagley-Keene Open Meeting Act*, 67 Ops.Cal.Atty.Gen. 84, 88-93 (1984).)

***

Section 11130.3's legislative history, which is set out above, confirms our conclusion that the provision's right of action is indeed limited by the 30-day statute of limitations contained therein. That the provision does not allow any extension of time expressly shows itself on the surface. That it does not do so by implication appears beneath. Its legislative history defined strict conditions for the nullification and voidance of an action taken by a state body in violation of the act's notice or open-and-public-meeting requirement. Moreover, in its definition, it moved from strict conditions to even stricter ones. Among such strict conditions was its limitations period. It reduced it by half from 60 days to only 30 days. Its reduction was explicit. It precludes any expansion by implication—as by allowing some extension of time. Without a doubt, the provision's limitations period is indeed short. In fact, there is, apparently, none shorter. (See 3 Witkin, Cal. Procedure, *supra*, Actions, § 441, p. 558.) But, as is evident, it was surely the result of deliberate choice—a deliberate choice made in face of the fact that, as stated, the provision concerns itself exclusively with actions that have been taken in violation of the act's notice or open-and-public-meeting requirement, outside of the full light of day, implicating fraud in effect if not in intent. Had the Legislature meant to allow some extension of time of the limitations period at the same time at which it was shortening the limitations period itself, it would likely have made itself clear in the premises. It did not. What it did not speak we should not claim to hear.

In sum, section 11130.3(a)'s right of action is indeed limited by the 30-day statute of limitations contained therein.

III

We now turn to the decision of the Court of Appeal denying the Regents' petition for writ of mandate insofar as it sought a peremptory writ against the superior court in challenge to its order denying their summary judgment motion.

At the threshold, the Court of Appeal impliedly concluded that the superior court's ruling on the summary judgment motion, and its resolution of the underlying statutory-construction issues, were subject to independent review. It was right. "Rulings on such motions"—including, as here, denials—"are examined de novo." (*Buss v. Superior Court* (1997) 16 Cal. 4th 35, 60 [65 Cal. Rptr. 2d 366, 939 P.2d 766].) The same is true of the resolution of such issues, inasmuch as they are pure questions of law. (See *20th Century Ins. Co. v. Garamendi* (1994) 8 Cal. 4th 216, 271 [32 Cal. Rptr. 2d 807, 878 P.2d 566].)

A

We first consider whether the Court of Appeal correctly determined that, under the undisputed facts, Molloy did not have any right of action pursuant to section 11130.3(a) for his Bagley-Keene Open Meeting Act cause of action.

It is accepted by all that the Regents are indeed subject to the act. That is as it must be. Section 92030 of the Education Code so declares in its terms. Subdivision (g) of section 9 of article IX of the California Constitution itself states that the Regents must generally cause their meetings to be open and public, impliedly as for the former and expressly as for the latter, "with...notice requirements as may be provided by statute," including the act.

We are of the view that the Court of Appeal's determination was in fact correct. Section 11130.3(a) grants an interested person a right of action to seek the nullification and voidance of an action taken by a state body in violation of the act's notice or open-and-public-meeting requirement only if he commences an action "within 30 days from the date the action was taken." Molloy did not commence his action seeking the nullification and voiding of the Regents' approval of SP-1 and SP- 2 at the noticed and open and public meeting of July 20, 1995, within 30 days, but waited almost 7 months, until February 16, 1996.

Against our conclusion, Molloy argues that the Regents should be equitably estopped from raising section 11130.3(a)'s 30-day statute of limitations as an affirmative defense because, assertedly, they fraudulently concealed his cause of action.

As we have already explained, section 11130.3(a)'s 30-day statute of limitations does not allow any extension of time *at least as a general matter.*

Molloy argues to the contrary. He claims that section 11130.3(a)'s 30-day statute of limitations does in fact allow an extension of time. We disagree. Our analysis has demonstrated that the provision itself is without express or implied warrant in this regard, and that its legislative history stands in confirmation.

As we shall presently explain, section 11130.3(a)'s 30-day statute of limitations does not allow any extension of time *even through operation of the doctrine of fraudulent concealment.*

"Statute of limitations" is the "collective term... commonly applied to a great number of acts," or parts of acts, that "prescribe the periods beyond which" actions "may not be brought." (3 Witkin, Cal. Procedure, *supra*, Actions, § 405, p. 509.) The typical one has as its purpose the "'protection of the defendant from stale claims of a dilatory plaintiff.'" (*Bernson v. Browning-Ferris Industries* (1994) 7 Cal. 4th 926, 936 [30 Cal. Rptr. 2d 440, 873 P.2d 613], quoting 3 Witkin, Cal. Procedure (3d ed. 1985) Actions, § 529, p. 558, which is continued in 3 Witkin, Cal. Procedure, *supra*, Actions, § 691, p. 882; accord, e.g., *Kane v. Cook* (1857) 8 Cal. 449, 458; see, e.g., *Pashley v. Pacific Elec. Ry. Co.* (1944) 25 Cal. 2d 226, 228 [153 P.2d 325]–229.)

The doctrine of fraudulent concealment, which is judicially created (see, e.g., *Bernson v. Browning- Ferris Industries, supra*, 7 Cal. 4th at p. 931; *Kimball v. Pacific*

Gas & Elec. Co. (1934) 220 Cal. 203, 210–213 [30 P.2d 39] (*per curiam*); *Kane v. Cook, supra,* 8 Cal. at pp. 458-461), limits the typical statute of limitations. "[T]he defendant's fraud in concealing a cause of action against him tolls the applicable statute of limitations" (*Sanchez v. South Hoover Hospital* (1976) 18 Cal. 3d 93, 99 [132 Cal. Rptr. 657, 553 P.2d 1129]; accord, e.g., *Bernson v. Browning-Ferris Industries, supra,* 7 Cal. 4th at p. 931; *Kimball v. Pacific Gas & Elec. Co., supra,* 220 Cal. at p. 210; *Kane v. Cook, supra,* 8 Cal. at pp. 458-461; see, e.g., *Pashley v. Pacific Elec. Ry. Co., supra,* 25 Cal. 2d at pp. 229-230, 231-232.) In articulating the doctrine, the courts have had as their purpose to disarm a defendant who, by his own deception, has caused a claim to become stale and a plaintiff dilatory. (E.g., *Bernson v. Browning-Ferris Industries, supra,* 7 Cal. 4th at p. 931; *Sanchez v. South Hoover Hospital, supra,* 18 Cal. 3d at p. 100; see, e.g., *Pashley v. Pacific Elec. Ry. Co., supra,* 25 Cal. 2d at pp. 229-230, 231-232; *Kane v. Cook, supra,* 8 Cal. at p. 458.) The doctrine arose in courts of equity and not in courts of law. (See, e.g., *Kimball v. Pacific Gas & Elec. Co., supra,* 220 Cal. at pp. 210- 212; *Kane v. Cook, supra,* 8 Cal. at p. 458; see also *Bernson v. Browning-Ferris Industries, supra,* 7 Cal. 4th at p. 931 [noting that the doctrine is an "equitable principle"].) Its genesis, however, did not prove to be its confines. It was early extended to be available "in all cases" (*Kane v. Cook, supra,* 8 Cal. at p. 461; accord, e.g., *Kimball v. Pacific Gas & Elec. Co., supra,* 220 Cal. at p. 211), that is to say, in actions at law as well as suits in equity (*Kane v. Cook, supra,* 8 Cal. at pp. 458-461). It enters into a statute of limitations, if at all, from without, by being "read into" it judicially. (*Kimball v. Pacific Gas & Elec. Co., supra,* 220 Cal. at p. 212.)

To our mind, section 11130.3(a)'s 30-day statute of limitations precludes the doctrine of fraudulent concealment. The typical statute of limitations admits of the application of the doctrine of fraudulent concealment. The purposes of each are consistent the one with the other. That of the typical statute is to protect a defendant from a stale claim of a dilatory plaintiff. That of the doctrine is to disarm a defendant who, by his own deception, has caused a claim to become stale and a plaintiff dilatory. Not so the doctrine of fraudulent concealment and section 11130.3(a)'s 30-day statute of limitations, which is not a typical one. The purposes of each are inconsistent the one with the other. That of the doctrine, as stated, is to disarm a defendant who, by his own deception, has caused a claim to become stale and a plaintiff dilatory. In contrast, that of section 11130.3(a) is to authorize the nullification and voidance of an action taken by a state body in violation of the act's notice or open-and-public- meeting requirement, but only under strict conditions—which, in their absence, entails the protection of even the most deceptive defendant from the freshest claim of the most diligent plaintiff.

It is true that section 11130.3(a)'s 30-day statute of limitations would not preclude the doctrine of fraudulent concealment if the statute contained the doctrine in terms or at least by implication. But it does not do so. The statute is altogether devoid of reference or even allusion to the doctrine. In pertinent part, it states no more, and no less, than that an interested person seeking the nullification and voidance of an action taken by a state body in violation of the act's notice or open-and-public- meeting requirement "shall commence[]" an action "within 30 days from the date the action was taken."

It is also true that section 11130.3(a)'s 30-day statute of limitations would not preclude the doctrine of fraudulent concealment if the doctrine could be "read into" the statute judicially. (*Kimball v. Pacific Gas & Elec. Co.*, *supra*, 220 Cal. at p. 212.) But it cannot be. The purpose that the Legislature had in enacting section 11130.3 was to authorize the nullification and voidance of an action taken by a state body in violation of the act's notice or open-and-public-meeting requirement, but only under strict conditions. One of those strict conditions—the result of its deliberate choice—is that an interested person must commence an action within 30 days of the date the action in question was taken. For us judicially to read the doctrine of fraudulent concealment into section 11130.3(a)'s 30- day statute of limitations would upset the legislative balance.

When, as here, that balance is not constitutionally offensive, we may not do so. (See *Scheas v. Robertson*

(1951) 38 Cal. 2d 119, 125-126 [238 P.2d 982]; *Muller v. Muller* (1960) 179 Cal. App. 2d 815, 819 [4 Cal. Rptr. 419].)

Again Molloy argues to the contrary, that section 11130.3(a)'s 30-day statute of limitations does not in fact preclude the doctrine of fraudulent concealment.

Broadly, Molloy cites language in various decisions stating or implying that the doctrine is available "in all cases." (*Kane v. Cook, supra,* 8 Cal. at p. 461.) Originally, such language meant only that the doctrine could be invoked in actions at law as well as suits in equity. (*Id.* at pp. 458-461.) In current usage, it means only that it can be invoked generally. It did not, and does not, mean that it must be available here. Molloy asserts that never before has any decision held the doctrine unavailable. But never before has any decision addressed the question in this context. To arrive at an unprecedented conclusion is not to arrive at an erroneous one.

More narrowly, Molloy focuses on the general ends of the act, which, as stated in section 11120, are to cause "actions" of state bodies to be "taken openly," and to cause their "deliberation" to be "conducted openly," in order to keep "[t]he people...informed so that they may retain control over the instruments they have created." He claims that the preclusion of the doctrine of fraudulent concealment is inconsistent on the ground that it restricts the nullification and voidance of an action taken by a state body in violation of the act's notice or open-and-public-meeting requirement. But in focusing on the act's general ends, he ignores its specific means, which, as pertinent, authorize the nullification and voidance of such an action only under strict conditions, including that an interested person must commence an action within 30 days of the date the action in question was taken. The issue whether general ends prevail over specific means in case of conflict need not be resolved here. That is because there is no conflict. The act's general ends were stated in the act as originally enacted before it was amended to authorize the nullification and voidance of any actions whatsoever. Hence, they can hardly be deemed in conflict with the specific means authorizing such nullification and voidance, albeit only under strict conditions, including a limitations period of 30 days….

B

We next consider whether the Court of Appeal correctly determined that, under the undisputed facts, Molloy did indeed have a right of action pursuant to section 11130(a) for his Bagley-Keene Open Meeting Act cause of action.

Here, we are of the view that the Court of Appeal's determination was incorrect. Molloy did not have any right of action pursuant to section 11130(a), at least not to obtain the relief that he seeks. That is because that provision grants an interested person a right of action that extends only to present and future actions and violations and not past ones. Specifically, it grants a right of action: (1) to stop or prevent a present or future violation of the act—but *not* to reach back to a past one; and (2) to determine whether the act is applicable to a present or future action—but *not* a past one. Hence, it did not grant Molloy any right of action to nullify and void the Regents' *past* approval of SP-1 and SP-2 at the noticed and open and public meeting of July 20, 1995, or to prohibit the implementation of the resolutions as null and void. Neither did it grant him any right of action to determine whether the act was applicable to any *past* collective commitment or promise by the Regents to approve the proposed resolutions, prior to the noticed and open and public meeting of July 20, 1995, at the alleged secret serial "meeting" of at least a quorum of the board's members, including the Governor. And, on its very face, it did not grant him any right of action to determine whether the act was *violated* by their making of any such collective commitment or promise.

Molloy argues to the contrary, that he did indeed have a right of action pursuant to section 11130(a) to obtain the relief that he seeks. He says that that provision grants an interested person a right of action that extends to past actions and violations as well as present and future ones. But, as we have explained, the provision itself shows, and its legislative history confirms, that that is not so. He then says that we should deem the provision to grant such a person such a right of action, lest we tolerate the absence of a remedy against an action taken by a state body in violation of the act's notice or open-and-public-meeting requirement. So to deem means, in actuality, to amend—which belongs to the Legislature alone. In any event, a remedy does, in fact, exist, in the form of prevention by means of the threat of criminal liability under section 11130.7 against individual members of the state body. He complains that, without the right of action for which he contends, such persons "would be cloaked with immunity" of the most absolute sort. That is altogether false. Section 11130.7 stands in direct and complete contradiction....

C

In view of the foregoing, it follows that the Court of Appeal erred by upholding the superior court's denial of the Regents' summary judgment motion on Molloy's Bagley-Keene Open Meeting Act cause of action. For Molloy did not have any right of action pursuant to either section 11130(a) or section 11130.3(a). Hence, there was no triable issue of material fact and they were entitled to judgment as a matter of law.

Because of its error on Molloy's Bagley-Keene Open Meeting Act cause of action, the Court of Appeal did not reach his California Public Records Act cause of action. Because of its error on the former, the superior court too had not reached the latter. The superior court should be allowed an opportunity to address the issue in the first instance. Molloy so argues. The Regents have no objection.

IV

For the reasons stated above, we conclude that we must reverse the judgment of the Court of Appeal denying the Regents' petition for writ of mandate insofar as it sought a peremptory writ, and must remand the cause to that court with directions to remand it in turn to the superior court with directions to conduct proceedings not inconsistent with the views expressed herein....

It is so ordered.

George, C. J., Kennard, J., Baxter, J., Werdegar, J., Chin, J., and Brown, J., concurred.

Concur by: BROWN

Concurring.—I agree with the reasoning and result of the majority opinion which correctly resolves the statute of limitations questions. I write separately to address another significant question not directly presented by the parties here. Tim Molloy's action rests on allegations that the Governor, an ex officio member of the Board of Regents of the University of California (Regents), conducted premeeting telephone conferences with a quorum of the Regents and secured their agreement to vote for the resolutions presented at that meeting. The underlying issue in this case is whether substantive discussions of official matters—whether conducted by telephone, letter, electronic mail, or face-to- face—among the members of a state government body subject to the Bagley-Keene Open Meeting Act (Gov. Code, § 11120 et seq.; hereafter all statutory references are to the Government Code) violate the statute's injunction that "[a]ll meetings of a state body shall be open and public " (§ 11123.) The Bagley-Keene Open Meeting Act (the Act) does not, however, define "meeting."

In a handful of opinions, the Courts of Appeal have held that, at least as used in the Ralph M. Brown Act (§ 54950 et seq. [the open meeting law governing local agencies] (hereafter the Brown Act)), the term "meeting" "comprehends informal sessions at which a legislative body commits itself collectively to a particular future decision concerning the public business." (*Stockton Newspapers, Inc. v. Redevelopment Agency* (1985) 171 Cal. App. 3d 95, 102 [214 Cal. Rptr. 561] (*Stockton*).) The seminal case is Justice Friedman's opinion in *Sacramento Newspaper Guild v. Sacramento County Bd. of Suprs.* (1968) 263 Cal. App. 2d 41, 47-51 [69 Cal. Rptr. 480] (*Guild*), a Brown Act decision that is the grandfather of California's modern open meeting jurisprudence. There, newspaper journalists sued to enjoin the county board of supervisors from attending, *en masse* and in the midst of a strike by public employees, informal luncheons at the Elks Club where county counsel and the officers of the public employees labor union also appeared (and from which plaintiffs were barred). "[The Brown Act open meeting provision] is unequivocal in its central thrust upon official sessions for the transaction of official business, but somewhat ambiguous as it encounters peripheral gatherings or conversations among board members where public business is a topic," the court wrote. (*Guild*, *supra*, 263 Cal. App. 2d at p. 47.) Affirming injunctive relief against the lunches, the court held that the statute's openness requirement was "a deliberate and palpable expression of the act's intended impact," and comprehends both "deliberation and action as dual components of the collective decision-making process...[which]...cannot be split off and confined to one component only, but rather comprehends both and either." (*Ibid.*) The ban on "secret" deliberations extends to committee meetings, the court ruled, since by "the specific inclusion of committees and their meetings, the Brown Act demonstrates its general application to collective investigatory and consideration activity stopping short of official action." (*Id.* at p. 49, fn. omitted.)

In a passage that has become a shibboleth in the case law, the Guild court wrote that "[i]n this area of regulation, as well as others, a statute may push beyond debatable limits in order to block evasive techniques. An informal conference or caucus permits crystallization of secret decisions to a point just short of ceremonial acceptance. There is rarely any purpose to a nonpublic premeeting conference except to conduct some part of the decisional process behind closed doors. Only by embracing the collective inquiry and discussion stage, as well as the ultimate step of official action, can an open meeting regulation frustrate these evasive devices construed in the light of the Brown Act's objective, the term 'meeting' extends to informal sessions or conferences of the board members designed for the discussion of public business. The Elks Club luncheon, attended by the Sacramento County Board of Supervisors, was such a meeting." (*Guild*, *supra*, 263 Cal. App. 2d at pp. 50-51, fn. omitted; see also *Stockton*, *supra*, 171 Cal. App. 3d at pp. 100-102 [serial telephone conversations among board members constituted a "meeting" and violated Brown Act]; *Rowen v. Santa Clara Unified School Dist.* (1981) 121 Cal. App. 3d 231 [175 Cal. Rptr. 292] [closed session with prospective contractor was "meeting" despite absence of commitment]; *Frazer v. Dixon Unified School Dist.* (1993) 18 Cal. App. 4th 781, 791-794 [22 Cal. Rptr. 2d

641] [quorum of school board present to discuss district business was engaged in "collective acquisition and exchange of facts" and was thus a "meeting"]; *Roberts v. City of Palmdale* (1993) 5 Cal. 4th 363, 376 [20 Cal. Rptr. 2d 330, 853 P.2d 496] ["concerted plan to engage in collective deliberation" serially would violate the open meeting requirement] (dictum); see also *216 Sutter Bay Associates v. County of Sutter* (1997) 58 Cal. App. 4th 860, 876-878 [68 Cal. Rptr. 2d 492] [meetings between incumbent and newly elected supervisors were not "meeting[s]" within Brown Act since Act did not apply to supervisors-elect].)

***

Whether the Legislature intended such a broad definition of meeting is unclear. The Brown Act defines a meeting to include "any congregation of a majority of the members of a legislative body at the same time and place to hear, discuss, or deliberate upon any item that is within the subject matter jurisdiction of the legislative body or the local agency to which it pertains." (§ 54952.2, subd. (a).) It prohibits the use of "direct communication, personal intermediaries, or technological devices" employed by a majority of members "to develop a collective concurrence as to action to be taken on an item." (§ 54952.2, subd. (b).) The Brown Act defines "action taken" as "a collective decision made by a majority of the members of a legislative body, a collective commitment or promise by a majority of the members of a legislative body to make a positive or a negative decision, or an actual vote by a majority of the members of a legislative body when sitting as a body or entity, upon a motion, proposal, resolution, order or ordinance." (§ 54952.6.)

The provisions of the Bagley-Keene Open Meeting Act are more ambiguous. The Act declares the legislative intent that the deliberations of state agencies be "conducted openly" (§ 11120), specifies notice and agenda requirements, and authorizes a judicial action to determine whether an action taken in violation of these provisions is null and void. (§ 11120, 11123, 11125, 11130.3.) The definition of "action taken" (§ 11122) is identical to the Brown Act, but "meeting" is not defined and a provision prohibiting use of direct communication, personal intermediaries or technological devices to develop a collective concurrence is not included in the Act. Nevertheless, the Legislature arguably intended these provisions to be congruent with Brown Act requirements and plaintiffs here assumed they are.

However, it is not clear the Legislature's commitment to openness requires so deep an intrusion into the deliberative process of the executive branch. Indeed, substantial impairment of the essential function of a coequal branch of government would be prohibited. Under the deliberative process privilege, senior officials of all three branches of government enjoy a qualified, limited privilege not to disclose or to be examined concerning not only the mental processes by which a given decision was reached, but the substance of conversations, discussions, debates, deliberations and like materials reflecting advice, opinions, and recommendations by which government policy is processed and formulated. The case law origins of what Wright, Miller and Marcus call "the governmental" or "deliberative process" privilege (8 Wright et al., Federal Practice & Procedure (1994) § 2019, pp. 296-312; 26A Wright et al., Federal Practice & Procedure (1992) § 5680, pp. 125-157) have been codified in the federal Freedom of Information Act (FOIA) (5 U.S.C. § 552 et seq.), section 5 of which exempts from disclosure "intra and inter-agency memoranda" not ordinarily civilly discoverable. In *Times Mirror Co. v. Superior Court* (1991) 53 Cal. 3d 1325, 1338 [283 Cal. Rptr. 893, 813 P.2d 240] (*Times Mirror*), this court held that the "legislative history and judicial construction of the FOIA...'serve to illuminate the interpretation of its California counterpart,'" the Public Records Act (§ 6250 et seq.).

***

The public has a right to know what decisions government officials make and to have officials articulate fully the basis on which they act. To the extent officials seek to evade public scrutiny altogether, to avoid public discussion, to forge a majority in advance of public hearings on an issue, or to hide improper influences such as personal or pecuniary interest, public opprobrium is appropriate. The only question is whether the indirect public right to information about government activities justifies rules of engagement so stringent that the executive decisionmaking function is unreasonably impaired. There is a point beyond which open meeting requirements may effectively paralyze informed and efficient decisionmaking.

Judicial construction of the state's open meeting statutes suggesting that "serial" discussions among board members are "meetings" (and thus subject to statutory sanction) runs directly counter to a substantial and long-standing body of state and federal case law supporting the qualified privilege of confidentiality for discussions among government policy makers short of agreement and official action. Case law upholding a common law privilege of confidentiality for premeeting, prevote discussions that do not extend to a collective commitment are founded on important, even vital, common sense notions of effective government. They recognize the indispensable value of candid, unrestrained, *nonpublic* debate and discussion, where final collective agreement and action on official matters occurs publicly and in compliance with statutory "sunshine" provisions.

Whatever the Legislature's intent, the public need for access to information must be balanced against the public's right to the efficient administration of public bodies. Most sunshine laws explicitly recognize that "the administrative process cannot be conducted entirely in the public eye." (*FCC v. ITT World Communications, Inc.* (1984) 466 U.S. 463, 469 [104 S. Ct. 1936, 1940, 80 L.Ed. 2d 480] [discussing the Sunshine Act (5 U.S.C. § 552b(b))].) "'[I]nformal background discussions [that] clarify issues and expose varying views' are a necessary part of an agency's work. [Citation.] The Act's procedural requirements effectively would prevent such discussions and thereby impair normal agency operations without achieving significant public benefit." (466 U.S. at pp. 469-470 [104 S. Ct. at p. 1940], fns. omitted.)

"Inherent in an executive position is the duty to make rational decisions and to take responsibility for the consequences. Important decisions should not be made casually, but informal information may be as important as formal procedure in reaching the correct result, whether the decision needs to be rational, representative, or efficient." (*Hispanic Educ. Com. v. Houston Ind. Sch. Dist.* (S.D.Tex. 1994) 886 F. Supp. 606, 610.) "[I]t is the duty of public officials to persuade each other in an attempt to resolve issues, and it makes little sense to suggest that they may listen to a group of nonmembers on important matters but not to their colleagues, who may be more expert on the subject than any other persons." (*Moberg v. Independent Sch. Dist. No. 281* (Minn. 1983) 336 N.W.2d 510, 517.) Yet, that is the acknowledged effect of defining meeting so broadly as to preclude members of multimember bodies from engaging in any collective inquiry related to an issue within their jurisdiction.

Such a militant view of public access comes at a high price. The normal kind of give-and-take between agency members that is the essence of collegial decisionmaking is deemed illegal. Investigating, factfinding, or brainstorming among any combination of members that could constitute a quorum—even when those contacts occur seriatim—is considered a violation of the open meeting laws. In short, collegial bodies are prohibited from behaving collegially and their members may be publicly pilloried for conducting themselves in a manner that—in any other contex—would be considered supremely rational.

It thus seems evident that the demand for openness in the conduct of government decisionmaking may sometimes be at odds with the perceived value of confidentiality to effective policy deliberations, and that fine lines must sometimes be drawn by the courts in order to promote the signal values of both. It may well be that the course of judicial construction of the Bagley-Keene Open Meeting Act and the Brown Act has failed to keep that line true by glossing the open meeting statutes in ways that intrude too deeply into areas where confidential deliberations have their greatest value. A case can be made, in short, that neither of California's open meeting acts was meant to trump the established privilege from disclosure for opinions, recommendations, advice and like materials that form part of the predecisional policymaking process among senior government officials.

Arguably, the only way to reconcile these contending values would be to take a more objective view of open meeting requirements, i.e., by concluding that the requirements of these acts are met if the members of an agency or board act at a properly noticed public meeting and their votes are publicly recorded. Almost unanimously, the cases and commentaries on the open meeting acts distinguish informal, functional "meetings," composed of a quorum of a board, from gatherings, whether face- to-face or constructively, of less than a quorum. That distinction is helpful because it attempts to distinguish between predecisional discussions among less than a quorum of board members and the informal, "functional meeting" at which secret decisions are crystallized "to a point just short of ceremonial acceptance." (*Guild*, *supra*, 263 Cal. App. 2d at p. 50.) Unfortunately, the distinction is so fact-bound that any allegation, no matter how speculative or inferential, creates the potential for contentious and intrusive litigation for its resolution, a contingency that may be worse than "push[ing] beyond debatable limits in order to block evasive techniques." (*Ibid.*) In short, if government policy makers must subject themselves to lawsuits and onerous discovery as the only means of establishing their compliance with the open meeting statutes, then openness in government is achieved only at the expense of effective decisionmaking. The real impact of an expansive construction of these laws is to put a premium on ignorance.

***

Neither the Legislature nor the judiciary has been required to open every level of its deliberations to the public. Traditionally, the public has had access to governmental information through politically accountable decisionmaking. Thus, appellate courts continue to consult with their colleagues in confidential conferences; legislators may speak freely in the caucus without being required to disclose their comments. The executive branch should enjoy a similar flexibility. In this case, the Regents did hold a public meeting—one that lasted more than 12 hours. The public had a full opportunity to voice its opinions and the Regents' votes, and the basis for them, were part of the public record. Media coverage was extensive. It is difficult to see why more openness would be needed to permit the people to "retain control over the instruments they have created." (§ 11120.)

Baxter, J., concurred.

ONLINE MEETINGS

The following are excerpts from The Government of Tomorrow: Online Meetings, by the Little Hoover Commission (Report #261 June 2021) (available at https://lhc.ca.gov/report/government- tomorrow- online-meetings):

Introduction

In March of 2020, as the pandemic took hold and state government transitioned to remote work, Governor Newsom issued Executive Order N-29-20, waiving specified provisions of California's open meetings law, the Bagley-Keene Open Meeting Act. The Governor's order allowed state boards and commissions to meet entirely via remote technology, with no physical location accessible to the public. Although the Governor's order was issued as a public health measure, over the ensuing year it transitioned into an experiment in a new age of government.

The experiment was successful. As public bodies across the state met remotely, public accessibility improved while costs went down. It is time now to make the experiment a permanent feature of California government. Our statutes should catch up to our technology and experience.

This can be achieved through two simple but critical reforms – give the public remote access to every meeting, and make it easier for the members of boards to participate remotely.

First, to ensure maximum accessibility for the public, require that every meeting be accessible both through a physical location and a remote option, such as a telephone conference call or an Internet service. Californians can walk in or log on – their choice.

Second, to capture the full benefits of online meetings – such as lower travel costs and a greater diversity of potential board members – make it easier for members of

Bagley-Keene agencies to participate remotely. Current law requires that every location from which a board member joins a meeting – including a home office or a spare bedroom – must be accessible to all members of the public. That makes no sense. Members of the public have every right to watch public agencies do the public's business; they don't have a right to invade someone's home.

Combining these two key changes will increase public access, strengthen government accountability, save taxpayer money, allow for a broader representation on state boards and commissions, and bring the law into line with the modern world. California government should be an open book, but there's no reason it can't be read online.

Background

The Bagley-Keene Act is a cornerstone of California's open-government laws....With very limited exceptions, it requires that state boards and commissions meet publicly, with lengthy advance notice of the meeting and the agenda. The public must be allowed to attend and to comment on the proceedings. The law allows for remote, "teleconference" participation by members of the board or commission, but requires public disclosure and public accessibility for each of the remote locations....

These requirements posed an obvious public health issue during the pandemic, and thus the Governor, by Executive Order, waived key provisions of Bagley-Keene....In essence, state bodies were allowed to meet entirely by teleconference, with no specified physical location for the meeting, and no requirement for a physical location accessible to the public. Crucially, the Governor waived the requirement for public disclosure of the remote locations from which board members and commissioners were participating. So long as members of the public could "observe and address the meeting" by remote technology, the public agency had satisfied the requirement for meeting openly.

The Governor's order cleared the way for state boards and commissions to meet via remote technologies – such as Zoom, Microsoft Teams or some other similar service, or even by simple conference call – with members participating from their homes or private offices. Our Commission met in exactly this manner, as did most other agencies covered by Bagley-Keene.

To measure the experience of state agencies under these provisions, we surveyed 124 state boards or commissions covered by Bagley-Keene, and received a response from 46, or slightly more than a third of those surveyed....Almost all of the agencies who responded said they had held entirely remote meetings during the pandemic, and about a third said they had actually met more frequently due to their ability to meet remotely. (The other two-thirds said there had been no change in meeting frequency; no agency reported less frequent meetings.) As outlined below in more detail, most agencies reported a variety of positive outcomes from the remote meetings: greater public participation, more frequent attendance by board and commission members, and reduced costs to the state. Of those agencies that have witnesses testify, nearly half reported that it was easier to secure witnesses. Our own experience at the Little Hoover Commission echoed all of these findings.

However, as the pandemic subsides, state agencies face an uncertain future regarding their ability to meet remotely. On June 11, Governor Newsom issued a new Executive Order essentially keeping in place the pandemic Bagley-Keene requirements, but only until Sept. 30....After that, the pre- pandemic requirements of Bagley-Keene would resume.

We are supporters of Bagley-Keene; California government is stronger for its openness. But we also believe that some provisions of the law must be updated to reflect new technologies, and the practical experience of using those new technologies during the past year. Given the fast- approaching expiration of the Governor's order, we believe policymakers must act quickly to create an updated Bagley-Keene framework that increases public access while capturing the efficiency and cost-saving advantages of new technologies. Below, we outline two key reforms that we believe would accomplish these goals.

Greater Public Accessibility

Meetings are more accessible when members of the public don't have to leave their homes or offices to listen and watch....This obvious truth is critical to reform. A physical meeting location – such as a hearing room in the state Capitol or conference room in a state office building – can be accessed only by people who can come to Sacramento, take time off from work or family responsibilities, and physically attend the meeting. A meeting which the public can attend online, by contrast, can be accessed by people throughout California (and indeed around the world), often from the comfort and ease of their own homes. Especially in a state as vast as California, it is a high hurdle indeed to require that members of the public travel to Sacramento just to watch their government at work.

The empirical data from the pandemic shows that, at least in the view of the agencies that hold such meetings, they are more accessible. More than 95 percent of agencies responding to our survey said they believe that remote meetings have increased attendance, and most said there had been "a lot more public attendance."

This increased public accessibility has particular advantages for equity and inclusion. Online access does not benefit those who can attend physical meetings – often the well-heeled, retired people, special interests with a presence in Sacramento, and the like – but it clearly benefits those who traditionally face obstacles in interacting with state government, such as low-income people, rural Californians, and people with physical disabilities. Current law acknowledges the importance of such issues by requiring meeting locations that are accessible to the disabled;...for many disabled people, the Internet is surely more accessible than the state Capitol.

Online access is by no means perfect, of course. As noted in our Commission's recent Issue Brief, California's Digital Divide, as many as 2.3 million Californians lack access to broadband. Overall, the state's access to broadband is ranked 13th in the nation, with strong access to low-cost plans but slow speeds....Researchers have consistently found that poor people, people of color, and rural residents have less access to the Internet. Governor

Newsom's recent announcement of a $7 billion plan to expand broadband access is an important step toward addressing this problem, and progress in this regard will only increase the accessibility of online meetings….

But even with current rates of Internet access, a requirement that members of the public have a remote option to observe the meeting and comment upon the proceedings is a clear step forward in increased public accessibility.

Recommendation 1: Take the meeting to the public, not the other way around

We recommend that the Legislature and the Governor amend Bagley-Keene to require that boards and commissions provide public access to their meetings both in a physical location and a teleconferencing option. (For reasons we discuss below, the physical location we envision need not necessarily include board and commission members, but rather might simply be a location at which members of the public may listen to and watch audio and video of the meeting.)

Such a requirement will not be onerous for state agencies—the past year has proven that agencies can easily and cheaply provide remote public access, even when they had no warning of the need to do so and had to transition on the fly amid state budget cuts, salary reductions, and dramatically changed working conditions. After the past 12 months, no reasonable person can claim that remote meetings are simply too difficult to organize. As has been the case during the past year, agencies should be required to accommodate individuals with disabilities, publicly notice the technological means by which members of the public may attend the meeting and make public comment, and abide by other existing requirements for public notice. Current law requiring rollcall votes during teleconference meetings should also be retained.

We are aware that some public-access advocates and some state agencies have expressed concerns about technology failures – should the ability to meet be held hostage to the reliability of the Internet? The law clearly needs to make some provision for such a situation, but existing requirements face some of the same issues.

Current law, for example, allows for greater flexibility for remote participation by members of purely advisory bodies, but also requires that if the method of remote access fails, the meeting must adjourn....An Attorney General's opinion in 2016 found that the Brown Act's requirement for online agenda-posting is not necessarily violated if an agenda is inaccessible for a portion of the required period due to technical difficulties....The same opinion also found that in such a case an agency may hold its meeting if it "has otherwise substantially complied with the Brown Act's agenda-posting requirements." Existing law, in other words, already contemplates and addresses the potential for technological failure. Similar language could be incorporated into a reform statute, either allowing agencies to continue meetings without the teleconference option if a sufficient number of members were physically present, or simply requiring agencies to adjourn the meeting, much as they would do now if a power outage or fire caused their meeting room to be unavailable.

The broader point is that in a world in which so much is increasingly reliant on the Internet—business, politics, journalism, healthcare, education, etc.—a fear of technological failure cannot forestall needed reforms. California cannot create the government of tomorrow if it fears technology.

At a time when our society is rightfully focused on issues of equity and inclusion, requiring that state agencies allow the public to access meetings electronically is a simple, cheap and manageable reform that will make California government more transparent.

Benefits of Remote Participation

During the pandemic state boards and commissions have held meetings in which their own members participate via remote technology. Such meetings offer substantial benefits to the public, including reduced travel costs, a broadening of potential board members and commissioners who are able to serve, and the ability to meet more often and in a timely way. Our Commission has experienced these benefits directly, and our survey of other Bagley-Keene agencies confirms that we are not alone.

REDUCED COSTS

When board or commission members must travel to Sacramento (or any other given location in the state) to attend meetings in person, the agency bears significant costs, such as airfare, mileage, hotel accommodations and per diem. For our own Commission, pre-pandemic travel costs were the third largest component of our budget, behind only staff salaries and office space. Our ability to meet via remote technology has eliminated almost all such costs. Our survey of Bagley-Keene agencies found that more than 90 percent of responding agencies similarly reported reduced costs due to remote meetings. In the context of the state budget, the savings are not large—about half the responding agencies estimated the savings at between $10,000 and $50,000 a year—but there is no reason that taxpayers should foot any unnecessary bill.

When asked to specify what costs have been reduced or increased, the vast majority of respondents identified decreased travel and facility rental costs. Some respondents cited increased technology costs such as Zoom licenses or cameras, but these were usually more than offset by savings. Only three of the 43 agencies that responded to this question identified a net increase in costs.

BETTER ATTENDANCE BY COMMISSION MEMBERS

Californians who agree to serve on state boards and commissions often give freely of their time—many are not compensated at all. Their service is often deeply committed, but given the travel times discussed above, sometimes board members must miss meetings. That is far less likely to happen if participation in a meeting requires only that members log on. About half of agencies responding to our survey indicated that remote meetings have increased attendance by members.

BROADER POTENTIAL POOL OF PUBLIC SERVANTS

The need for travel also restricts the potential pool of people able to serve on state boards and commissions. Typically, members of a board or commission must spend an entire day, and perhaps more, in traveling to Sacramento, attending a meeting, and returning home. Given such requirements, it may be difficult for some people to accept appointment to a state body. Many people may not be able to take so much time away from work. The parents of young children, perhaps especially women, may find it impossible to be away from home. People from distant parts of the state—especially rural areas with limited airline service—may find such travel particularly time- consuming. As a result, service on state boards and commissions can be tilted toward the affluent or the retired. This should not be. California deserves the most inclusive and diverse state government possible, a goal that is furthered by reducing the burdens of service.

MORE FREQUENT AND TIMELY MEETINGS

Remote participation allows for more frequent and timely meetings. Our own Commission's experience again illustrates this fact. The Commission traditionally met 10 times a year, but during the pandemic we have roughly doubled our meeting frequency. By meeting more often, we are better able to set agendas that reflect ongoing events, creating a more timely focus for our work. About a third of agencies responding to our survey reported that they are meeting more often due to their ability to meet remotely.

BETTER WITNESSES

For agencies that call witnesses to testify, remote access has been a boon. Our survey found that roughly half of the agencies that have witnesses said it has been easier to secure high-quality speakers.

In short, remote participation by the members of boards and commissions saves taxpayer money and creates a state government that is more effective, inclusive and flexible.

However, the traditional requirements of BagleyKeene—those that were in place before the pandemic and that remain in statute today—make it extremely difficult for board and commission members to participate remotely. Prior to the pandemic, the law required public disclosure and public accessibility to every location from which a board or commission member participated. Effectively, this prohibits members from participating from their homes or even their private offices. Understandably, they are reluctant to publicly disclose their home addresses, and even more so to allow access to any member of the public who might show up. Indeed, the Department of Justice's guide to Bagley-Keene notes the difficulty of a member participating from home, and then adds, "For these reasons, we recommend that a properly equipped and accessible public building be utilized for teleconference meetings."...

Thus, if the state reverts to the traditional Bagley-Keene statute upon the expiration of the Governor's order, members of boards and commissions will effectively be unable to participate from their homes – precisely the kind of participation that has produced benefits during the past year. Our survey of state agencies confirmed that agencies will not hold remote meetings under the standards of the pre-pandemic Bagley-Keene law, with more than 85 percent saying they would not do so.

Recommendation 2: Remove barriers to remote participation.

To capture the benefits of remote meetings, including remote participation by members of state boards and commissions, we recommend that the Legislature and the Governor amend Bagley-Keene to allow for the remote participation of board and commission members without required public disclosure and public accessibility to those locations. If policymakers wish to do so, the law could limit the disclosure and accessibility exemption to the board member's private residence.

Some public-access advocates argue that much is lost when members of the public cannot sit in the same room with board or commission members during a meeting. They argue that the public's ability to witness the physical interaction of board members is a substantial benefit, and that people who wish to travel to Sacramento and attend an in-person meeting must be able to do so. Anything less is a blow to transparent government. We respect those concerns, but we reach different conclusions. First, we do not believe that physical presence in a room is critical to public access. What is critical is that members of the public have the ability to know what board members and commissioners say and do—every word at every public meeting, every vote, every action. Allowing agencies to take advantage of modern technology doesn't diminish that access. Second, even if the public's inability to be physically present amounts to some minor reduction in access, this must be counter-balanced against the improvements, discussed above, that remote participation can create—lower costs, greater inclusion, and greater flexibility. It's critical to note that these advantages benefit the public. Californians deserve an open and transparent government, but they also deserve one that takes advantage of technological change to advance goals like efficiency and inclusion.

Other objections seem to us even less convincing, for example that members of the public will not be able to see if someone else is in the room with a participating board member, or even that someone might impersonate a member of a board or commission. As for the first issue, at an in-person meeting held under current law, a lobbyist or advocate could meet with a board or commission member privately immediately before a meeting, or even during a break, or could text a member during a meeting. It is unlikely that the influence of such private interests will be markedly increased by someone sitting behind a laptop silently making gestures during a remote meeting (assuming that a board member wanted to allow such a person into their home). As for impersonation, we find this highly unlikely, but if policymakers are deeply concerned about the potential for such shenanigans, they can make it a crime to impersonate a board or commission member during remote participation at a meeting.

We recommend that the statute be permissive with regard to the disclosure and access of remote locations. If agencies wish to disclose such locations and allow public access, they should be able to do so. For example, a board member might access a meeting from a conference room with suitable public facilities, and there is no reason in such a case to prohibit public disclosure and access.

We also recognize that some agencies may wish to hold meetings in various locations around the state, and that the physical presence of board and commission members at such meetings could bring a variety of benefits. Our own

Commission is an example. We have held public hearings across the state, both to learn from diverse geographic settings, and to emphasize our role as a statewide body. Obviously we do not wish to preclude such meetings, and nothing in our proposed reforms would do so. Boards and commissions should certainly be able to meet in a physical location whenever they believe it is advantageous to their mission.

Finally, we recommend that all board and commission members be allowed to participate remotely. We anticipate that at times, nearly all members might attend in person – perhaps for a meeting focused on a particular regional issue and held at a relevant location around the state, for example. In other cases, one or two members might attend physically at a public location. At other times, all members might participate remotely. In the latter case, agencies would still have to provide at least one physical location for the meeting, which would simply be a place where members of the public could go to listen to the meeting, and from which they could make public comment. Alternatively, policymakers could choose to require that at least one member of the board or commission be present at the physical site.

Reform Process

To be most effective, the changes we have recommended must be made quickly. As noted above, the Governor's recent executive order waives the relevant provisions of Bagley-Keene only until Sept. 30.

Seeking to address these issues, the Department of Finance has prepared a trailer bill that would require state agencies to hold teleconference meetings, and allow members of the board or commission to participate remotely from undisclosed locations….In fact the bill would prohibit state agencies from disclosing remote locations, a difference from our recommendations.

Earlier this year Assemblymember Quirk, who is a member of our Commission, introduced Assembly Bill 885, which would allow for remote participation by members of boards and commissions from undisclosed locations, although it would, similar to our recommendations, require the continued existence of at least one physical location from which members of the public could watch and listen to the meeting….This bill, which did not move out of the Assembly, would have required that board and commission members participating remotely have both audio and visual connections, a specific not addressed in our recommendations. AB 885 would also not have required that every public meeting of a Bagley-Keene agency be available for remote access by the public, another difference from our recommendations.

Regardless of the precise vehicle that is used, we believe the Legislature and the Governor should act quickly to ensure that state agencies can build upon the momentum of the past year and continue to meet remotely even after the rescission of the Governor's executive order.

Conclusion

The year of the pandemic has proven that state government can take advantage of modern technology to hold meetings that are more accessible, more affordable, and more efficient. Remote access to all public meetings unquestionably increases the public's ability to monitor state government. The practical ability of board and commission members to participate remotely from their homes or private offices allows for this important segment of state government to increase efficiency, inclusion and flexibility.

***

Hypotheticals

Board of Registered Nurses

Governor Newsom has informed the Board of Registered Nurses (BRN) that the COVID-19 situation has created a shortfall in nurses, particularly at nursing homes and facilities where the elderly reside and where more intensive monitoring and testing are necessary. The Governor has a proposal to allow nursing students who have more than one year in a nursing school to engage in that work—which normally requires a license. The Board decides to hold a special meeting and to adopt a policy that will allow such persons to practice so long as it pertains to COVID-19 issues, and outlines the role of registered nurses in the supervision of these new practitioners. A meeting is scheduled to be held in five days and it is to be virtual. Several persons request permission to address the Board about issues related to that proposal. Others ask for permission to testify via Zoom as to COVID-19 more generally and related options that might be more effective. The Board's Executive Director, a practicing nurse, refuses to allow any such testimony. She declared that the discussion would be entirely in closed session, and there would be no distractions from the public, or any other testimony on this or any other issue.

Discussion Questions:

1. What issues are raised by this decision?
2. What are the implications regarding the Bagley-Keene "emergency" exception?
3. Should it apply?
4. What if supply is not currently deficient, but the need is based on a projection likely to require it in 5 to 6 weeks?
5. Can a meeting of the Board categorically exclude public testimony?

State Bar of California

Five members of the State Bar Board of Trustees have been communicating about the problem of court proceedings via Zoom. All five are practicing attorneys and their concern is that some attorneys more familiar with Zoom will have an unfair advantage over those unfamiliar with it, particularly older counsel.

They want the Bar to conduct Zoom proficiency classes as part of the Bar's operations. One member of the group notes that he has taught this subject and suggests that each of the five describe who and when such teaching shall be available, how much should be expended and the basic syllabus. He will then synthesize the comments of all five and it will be transmitted to the other members of the Board for their comments, and to a recognized expert. That proposal will then be presented for final vote at the next meeting.

Discussion Question:

1. What are the Bagley-Keene issues and problems triggered by such a process?

Chapter 6
Public Records Act

INTRODUCTION

The California Public Records Act (California Government Code Section 7920 et seq.)[4] applies to both state and local agencies. Any person may request ANY agency "record," which is broadly defined. The burden to prevent the disclosure of a record is on the AGENCY to plead and prove that a record falls within one or more of the exceptions enumerated in the act. There is no "standing" requirement to request a record, i.e., no requirement that requested records be relevant to anything nor that they be discoverable in a civil action.

Commonly asserted exemptions to the Public Records Act include:

> [1] Inter-agency / intra-agency records. (Cal. Gov't Code Section 7927.500);
>
> [2] Records that are NOT ordinarily kept in the normal course of business (i.e., drafts) that contain OPINIONS of agency officials (the purpose of this exemption is to encourage candid expression of opinion and preserve the confidentiality of agency deliberations about a particular policy issue before the final internal decision is made. Limitations: (1) If OPINION can be redacted from a responsive record and FACTUAL matter can be produced, the agency must comply, and (2) Public interest in withholding these records must "clearly outweigh" public interest in disclosure);
>
> [3] Records related to "pending litigation" (Cal. Gov't Code Section7927.200) to which the agency is a party, or to "claims made" against the agency (this allows agency officials to discuss litigation with their attorney and preserve attorney-client privilege);
>
> [4] "Personnel, medical, or similar files, the disclosure of which would constitute an unwarranted invasion of personal privacy" (Cal. Gov't Code Section 7927.700) (these records can relate to agency employees or applicants for licensure);
>
> [5] Records filed with and/or prepared by agencies that regulate the issuance of securities or financial institutions (including banks,

---

[4] On January 1, 2023, pursuant to AB 473 (Chau) (Chapter 614, Statutes of 2021) "CPRA Recodification Act of 2021," the California Public Records Act was recodified and reorganized [prior statute Government Code § 6250, et seq.]. "Nothing in the CPRA Recodification Act of 2021 is intended to substantively change the law relating to inspection of public records." Gov't Code § 7920.100. *See* Appendix for Disposition Table.

savings & loans, credit unions, insurance companies) (Cal. Gov't Code Section 7929.000);

[6] "Investigatory files" (Cal. Gov't Code Section 7923.600) (these include records of a pending investigation, and have been interpreted to also include complaints (even if uninvestigated) against agency licensees);

[7] "Test questions, scoring keys, and other examination information" (Cal. Gov't Code Section 7929.605); and

[8] "Real estate appraisals" made for or by the agency relative to the acquisition of property (Cal. Gov't Code Section7928.705).

North County Parents Organization v. Department of Education

23 Cal. App. 4th 144 (1994)

The issue in this case is whether the California Department of Education (Department) is entitled to charge its full cost of providing copies of public documents which are requested in accordance with the California Public Records Act. (Gov. Code, § 6250 et seq.)

North County Parents Organization for Children With Special Needs (appellant) is a nonprofit tax- exempt corporation which provides advisory services to parents of children with disabilities. Appellant assists such parents in enforcing their rights to special educational services provided by state and federal laws. Parents seeking review of local school district action respecting such services may take advantage of an appellate hearing process. The decisions resulting from this process are public records maintained by the Department.

Appellant requested copies of all decisions rendered in the last two years. Department charged $.25 per page for furnishing the copies, rendering a total bill of $126.50. This charge not only covered the cost of duplication of the documents, but also reimbursed Department for staff time involved in searching the records, reviewing records for information exempt from disclosure under law, and deleting such exempt information. Department refused to reduce this charge, and also refused to waive the charge upon the ground that "there is no legal authority to waive such charges." Appellant paid the charge and then brought this action seeking miscellaneous relief.

The trial court ruled for the Department, finding that section 6257 permits the Department to charge "the full direct costs of duplication," and that the Department's charge of $.25 per copy "was not in contravention of section 6257." The court made a second ruling pertaining to the potential of waiver of fees. It ruled that the Department had discretion to waive fees pursuant to section 6253.1, but that it was not required to waive fees and did not err in this case by refusing to consider waiver. Appellant contends both rulings are in error.

We agree with appellant. Section 6257 provides that one who requests copies of public documents must pay the statutory fee for same, if there is one. The parties agree there is none prescribed in this case. Lacking a statutory fee the cost chargeable is a "fee[] covering direct costs of duplication." There seems to be little dispute as to what "duplicate" means. It means just what we thought it did, before looking it up: to make a copy. (See Black's Law Dict. (4th ed. 1968) p. 593 ["to ... reproduce exactly"]; Webster's Third New Internat. Dict. (1981) p. 702 ["to be or make a duplicate, copy or transcript ..."].) Since words of a statute are to be interpreted "according to the usual, ordinary import of the language employed in framing them" (*In re Alpine* (1928) 203 Cal. 731, 737 [265 P. 947, 58 A.L.R. 1500]), we conclude that the cost chargeable by the Department for furnishing these copies is the cost of copying them.

There is no disagreement with the proposition that the Department was put to a great amount of trouble responding to appellant's request, much of which had nothing to do with copying. Records were searched, documents were read for any material to be excised, such material was removed, files were refiled, etc.

We sometimes presume too much of the Legislature, but this is assuredly not the case when we presume that the statute writers, themselves bureaucrats of a sort, knew the ancillary costs of everything government does. They specified, however, that the sole charge should be that for duplication. In order to clarify this limitation the Legislature added that the fee should be the "direct cost" of duplication. Obviously to be excluded from this definition would be "indirect" costs of duplication, which presumably would cover the types of costs the Department would like to fold into the charge.

The parties to this appeal argue earnestly about the policy considerations which should go into this momentous decision (whether to charge $.10 or $.25 per copy). We do not reach these arguments. Clearly the Legislature could have provided a different charge for copying. It simply did not, and the reason it did not is of no moment to the Court of Appeal, a body which simply interprets statutes and does not ordinarily seek their rationale.

However, if our quick conclusion needs any bolstering it is easy to find in the statutory history of this fee-setting provision. The original wording, adopted in 1968 (Stats. 1968, ch. 1473, § 39), was that "a reasonable fee" could be charged. In 1975 an amendment limited the "reasonable fee" to not more than $.10 per page. (Stats. 1975, ch. 1246, § 8.) An amendment in 1976 deleted "reasonable fee" and inserted instead "the actual cost of providing the copy." (Stats. 1976, ch. 822, § 1.) Finally, the present version of the statute was adopted in 1981 limiting the fee to the "direct costs of duplication." (§ 6257.) Thus it can be seen that the trend has been to limit, rather than to broaden, the base upon which the fee may be calculated. A "reasonable fee" or the "actual cost of providing the copy" could be interpreted to include the cost of all the various tasks associated with locating and pulling the file, excising material, etc. When these phrases are replaced by the more restrictive phrase "direct costs of duplication," only one conclusion seems possible. The direct cost of duplication is the cost of running the copy machine, and conceivably also the expense of the person operating it. "Direct cost" does not include the ancillary tasks necessarily associated with the retrieval, inspection and handling of the file from which the copy is extracted.

We apprehend that the court's second ruling was also in error. It may be thought that the error was either inadvertent or insignificant. However, being called upon herein to right wrongs which might seem inconsequential to most, we complete our task by identifying this one. As stipulated by the parties, the Department refused to waive fees because it determined there was no legal authority to do so. The trial court, to the contrary, concluded that the Department did have the power to waive fees, citing section 6253.1. This section gives an agency power to "adopt requirements for itself which allow greater access to records than prescribed by the minimum standards set forth in this chapter." The trial court apparently concluded that this provision permits an agency to waive or reduce its fees. We agree. A reduction in copy fee permits "greater access" to records.

The trial court then, however, found no obligation to reduce the fee and hence no actionable wrong by the Department. Our difficulty with this ruling is that it ignores the fact that the Department declined to exercise discretion, contending it had none. Had the Department been aware that it was vested with discretion to reduce the fee, it might have done so. We believe, therefore, that the case should be returned to the Department with instructions to consider (but not necessarily to grant) the request for fee waiver.

Section 6258 provides: "Any person may institute proceedings for injunctive or declarative relief or writ of mandate ... to enforce his or her right to inspect or to receive a copy of any public record."

This lawsuit clearly comes within this provision, and hence appellant's requests for writs, orders and declarations are proper. We decline, however, to grant such specific relief. As indicated by the general counsel, the Department will surely follow the law once it is advised of it. Appellant is entitled to a declaration of its right to obtain copies at a cost of only the expense of copying, and it is also entitled to our advice that the Department could waive this fee if it chose to do so. By this opinion we have granted these declarations. Appellant is also entitled to a refund of some portion of the fee it has already paid, and also to costs both at trial and appellate level. The statute (§ 6259, subd. (d)) contains authority for an award of attorney fees to appellant. All these matters are best determined by the trial court assuming (which we would expect is a false assumption) that the parties cannot now resolve their dispute by stipulation.

DISPOSITION

We reverse the judgment of the trial court and remand the case for further proceedings in accord with this opinion.

Work, Acting P. J., concurred.

National Lawyers Guild v. City of Hayward

9 Cal. 5th 488 (2020)

KRUGER, J.—This case concerns the costs provisions of the California Public Records Act (Gov. Code, § 6250 et seq.). As a general rule, a person who requests a copy of a government record under the act must pay only the costs of duplicating the record, and not other ancillary costs, such as the costs of redacting material that is statutorily exempt from public disclosure. (*Id.*, § 6253, subd. (b); *id.*, § 6253.9, subd. (a)(2); see *County of Santa Clara v. Superior Court* (2009) 170 Cal.App.4th 1301, 1336 [89 Cal. Rptr. 3d 374] (*County of Santa Clara*).) But a special costs provision specific to electronic records, Government Code section 6253.9, subdivision (b)(2), says that in addition to paying for duplication costs, requesters must pay for the costs of producing copies of electronic records if producing the copies "would require data compilation, extraction, or programming." Here, the City of Hayward seeks to charge a records requester for approximately 40 hours its employees spent editing out exempt material from digital police body camera footage. The City claims that these costs are chargeable as costs of data extraction under section 6253.9, subdivision (b)(2). We conclude the term "data extraction" does not cover the process of redacting exempt material from otherwise disclosable electronic records. The usual rule therefore applies, and the City must bear its own redaction costs.

I.

A.

The California Public Records Act (PRA) establishes a right of public access to government records. "Modeled after the federal Freedom of Information Act (5 U.S.C. § 552 et seq.), the PRA was enacted for the purpose of increasing freedom of information by giving members of the public access to records in the possession of state and local agencies." (*Los Angeles County Bd. of Supervisors v. Superior Court* (2016) 2 Cal.5th 282, 290 [212 Cal. Rptr. 3d 107, 386 P.3d 773].) In enacting the statute in 1968, the Legislature declared this right of access to be "a fundamental and necessary right of every person in this state" (Gov. Code, § 6250)—a declaration ratified by voters who amended the California Constitution in 2004 to secure a "right of access to information concerning the conduct of the people's business" (Cal. Const., art. I, § 3, subd. (b)(1), added by Prop. 59, Gen. Elec. (Nov. 2, 2004)). (See *Los Angeles County Bd. of Supervisors*, at p. 290.)

The Legislature that enacted the PRA recognized that increased access to government information can have both intangible and tangible costs, and it crafted the PRA accordingly. First, and most important, the Legislature recognized that increased public access to government records can come at the expense of personal privacy and other important confidentiality interests. To mitigate these sorts of intangible costs, the Legislature crafted "numerous exceptions to the [PRA's] requirement of public disclosure." (*International Federation of Professional & Technical Engineers, Local 21, AFL-CIO v. Superior Court* (2007) 42 Cal.4th 319, 329 [64 Cal. Rptr. 3d 693, 165 P.3d 488], citing Gov. Code, § 6254.) The PRA's exemptions permit public agencies to withhold a variety of records—or reasonably segregable portions of records—to protect confidential information. (Gov. Code, §§ 6253, subd. (a), 6254.) Many of these exemptions "are designed to protect individual privacy" (*International Federation*, at p. 329)—for example, the exemption for "[p]ersonnel, medical, or similar files, the disclosure of which would constitute an unwarranted invasion of personal privacy" (Gov. Code, § 6254, subd. (c)). But the exemptions are designed to protect other interests as well, including, for example, the interest in law enforcement's ability to effectively perform its duties. (See *id.*, § 6254, subd. (f) [exempting "[r]ecords of complaints to, or investigations conducted by, or records of intelligence information or security procedures of … any state or local police agency"].)

At the same time, the Legislature also recognized that increased public access to government information has costs of the more tangible, dollars-and-cents variety. Before providing access to requested records, public agencies need to locate and collect records, determine which records are responsive, determine whether any portions of responsive records are exempt from disclosure, convert the records into a reviewable format, and, if requested, create a copy of the record. To complete these tasks generally requires personnel time as well as the use of office equipment and supplies—all of which comes with a price tag. The PRA acknowledges as much and allocates certain costs to the requester, while others must be borne by the agency responding to the requests.

Precisely which costs may be allocated to the requester depends on the format of the requested record. Since 2000, the PRA has distinguished between nonelectronic records (sometimes referred to as "paper records," though the record may be in another nonelectronic medium, such as audiotape) and electronic records. Paper records are governed by a general costs provision, enacted in its earliest form by the original statute in 1968. (Gov. Code, former § 6257, added by Stats. 1968, ch. 1473, § 39, pp. 2947–2948.) Under that provision, today codified in Government Code section 6253, subdivision (b), a person requesting copies of a government record must pay "fees covering direct costs of duplication, or a statutory fee if applicable." The reference to "direct costs of duplication" has long been understood to cover "the 'cost of running the copy machine, and conceivably also the expense of the person operating it' while excluding any charge for 'the ancillary tasks necessarily associated with the retrieval, inspection and handling of the file from which the copy is extracted.'" (*County of Santa Clara*, *supra*, 170 Cal.App.4th at p. 1336, quoting *North County Parents Organization v. Department of Education* (1994) 23 Cal.App.4th 144, 148 [28 Cal. Rptr. 2d 359] (*North County*).) Nonchargeable ancillary costs include "staff time involved in searching the records, reviewing records for information exempt from disclosure under law, and deleting such exempt information." (*North County*, at p. 146.)....At least with respect to nonelectronic records, then, requesters are required to pay "direct" duplication costs, but they are not required to pay the government agencies' costs of redacting the record.

Before the statute was amended in 2000, there were no special rules for records kept in electronic format. Agencies had wide discretion to produce electronic records "in a form determined by the agency"—that is, in any form the agency saw fit. (Gov. Code, former § 6253, subd. (b), added by Stats. 1998, ch. 620, § 5, p. 4120.) Exercising this discretion, many agencies chose to print out their electronic records and produce them in paper format. This approach allowed the agencies to recover the direct costs of duplicating the paper copies, even though producing duplicates of the records in an electronic format would have been significantly cheaper. (See Sen. Com. on Judiciary, Analysis of Assem. Bill No. 2799 (1999–2000 Reg. Sess.) as amended June 22, 2000, p. 3.)

To account for differences in the costs of producing electronic versus paper records, the 2000 amendment introduced specific rules for the production of records held in electronic format. (Stats. 2000, ch. 982, § 2, p. 7142; see Sen. Com. on Judiciary, Analysis of Assem. Bill No. 2799, *supra*, as amended June 22, 2000, pp. 3–4.) In newly added Government Code section 6253.9 (section 6253.9), the Legislature cabined agencies' discretion by requiring them to make nonexempt electronic records available in "any electronic format in which [the agency] holds the information." (§ 6253.9, subd. (a)(1), added by Stats. 2000, ch. 982, § 2, p. 7142.) The amendment also created cost shifting rules specific to the production of copies of electronic records. (Stats. 2000, ch. 982, § 2, p. 7142.)

After the 2000 amendments, the ordinary rule is the same for electronic records as paper records: Requesters must pay direct duplication costs (although the statute now specifies that in the case of electronic records, the "cost of duplication shall be limited to the direct cost of producing a copy of a record in an electronic format"). (§ 6253.9, subd. (a)(2).) But the statute provides an exception specific to electronic records: Notwithstanding the usual limitations on chargeable costs, "the requester shall bear the cost of producing a copy of the record, including the cost to construct a record, and the cost of programming and computer services necessary to produce a copy of the record" if one of two conditions applies. (*Id.*, subd. (b).) First, the requester must pay these additional costs if "the public agency would be required to produce a copy of an electronic record and the record is one that is produced only at otherwise regularly scheduled intervals." (*Id.*, subd. (b)(1).) Second, the requester must pay the costs if "[t]he request would require data compilation, extraction, or programming to produce the record." (*Id.*, subd. (b)(2).) This case concerns the latter condition.

B.

In December 2014, demonstrations erupted in Berkeley, protesting grand jury decisions not to indict the police officers involved in the deaths of Eric Garner and Michael Brown, both unarmed African-American men. The Hayward Police Department provided mutual aid to the City of Berkeley in policing the demonstrations. After the demonstrations were over, plaintiff National Lawyers Guild, San Francisco Bay Area Chapter (NLG), submitted a public records request to the Department, seeking 11 categories of records relating to the Department's actions in policing the demonstrations. The requested records included relevant communications made during the demonstrations, operations and command center logs, and various reports, as well as records identifying supervisory and command officers who had approved certain police tactics used at the demonstrations and records relating to the use of those tactics. Soon after, NLG submitted a followup request for related records.

The Department's records administrator and custodian of records, Adam Perez, was responsible for identifying records responsive to the requests. For both requests, Perez first identified responsive text-based electronic records, such as written reports, logs, operational plans, and e-mails. He reviewed these documents for potential exemptions under the PRA and redacted them accordingly. He then converted the documents to portable document format (PDF), and they were emailed to NLG. NLG was never charged the costs to produce the copies of these text-based electronic records.

Perez next identified other types of electronic records potentially responsive to NLG's requests. Several

Hayward officers policing the demonstrations were equipped with body-worn cameras. Though NLG had not explicitly requested videos from these cameras, Perez believed certain videos might be responsive. In the City of Hayward, police officers upload digital video from their body- worn cameras to an online digital evidence management system known as Evidence.com, which stores videos and other digital evidence on the Internet. From Evidence.com, videos can be downloaded in MP4 format to DVDs for production, storage, or other uses. On average the City collects more than 1,000 hours of body-worn camera video per month.

Because Perez did not have access to Evidence.com, he asked the City's information technology manager of public safety, Nathaniel Roush, to search Evidence.com for videos responsive to NLG's requests. Perez provided Roush with 15 search criteria, and Roush searched Evidence.com using these criteria, identifying 141 videos totaling approximately 90 hours. Roush quickly reviewed the videos, downloaded them to DVDs, and confirmed they had successfully downloaded. This whole process—searching, reviewing, downloading, and confirming the download—took Roush 4.9 hours. Roush did not edit or redact the videos. Roush then gave the DVDs to Perez.

Perez reviewed the videos to determine whether they contained material exempt from disclosure under the PRA. After a cursory review, he concluded they contained exempt material, including personal medical information and law enforcement tactical security measures....(See Gov. Code, § 6254, subds. (c), (f).) After researching the best means for removing exempt audio and visual material from the videos, Perez downloaded the free video-editing software Windows Movie Maker. Perez quickly realized that editing 90 hours of video would be unduly burdensome, so, through the City Attorney's Office (City Attorney), the Department asked NLG to narrow its request. NLG complied, requesting six specific hours of video from the demonstrations. Perez worked with Roush to identify the six hours of video on Evidence.com and to download the videos to DVDs. The City did not charge NLG for any of Perez's or Roush's staff time completing these tasks.

With the narrower set of videos in hand, Perez began the editing process. First, he identified the exact visual and audio segments that were exempt. Next, he used Windows Movie Maker to remove all exempt audio and visual material from the video files. Before he could remove the exempt audio segments, he had to separate the audio and visual material by taking out all of the audio material from each MP4, saving that audio material as an MP3, and reuploading the MP3 audio file into Windows Movie Maker. Last, he saved the edited videos as new MP4 files and downloaded them to a thumb drive storage device. This editing process took Perez 35.3 hours.

The City Attorney then informed NLG that the videos were available for pickup. But the City Attorney warned NLG that before anyone could pick up the videos NLG would need to pay the City's costs to produce the videos. The City invoiced NLG $2,938.58...—$1 for the "DVD" (actually a thumb drive) containing the edited video copies and the remainder for 40.2 hours of staff time spent preparing the videos for production, consisting of 4.9 hours of Roush's time and 35.3 hours of Perez's time, as detailed above. NLG paid the invoiced amount under protest and received the videos.

Soon after, NLG requested additional footage from the demonstrations. The City's staff followed substantially the same procedure outlined above to identify and edit the videos....The City invoiced NLG $308.89 for the $1 "DVD" and the staff time to produce the videos. NLG again paid the amount under protest, and the City produced the videos to NLG.

After requesting the second set of videos, but before receiving them, NLG filed a petition for declaratory and injunctive relief and writ of mandate against the City and relevant City officials (collectively, Hayward). NLG sought a refund of the money it had paid to receive the first set of videos and a writ of mandate or injunction requiring immediate production of the second set of videos without costs beyond those necessary to copy the videos. Later, after paying for and receiving the second set of videos, NLG moved for a peremptory writ of mandate, arguing that Hayward's charges were excessive and seeking a refund of the money it had paid beyond the direct costs of duplicating the videos. Hayward argued in response that the invoiced costs were justified under the PRA because the City's staff had performed data extraction and compilation, as allowed under section 6253.9, subdivision (b)(2) (section 6253.9(b)(2))....

The trial court disagreed with Hayward, holding that "the phrase 'data compilation, extraction, or programming to produce the record'" does not include "making a redacted version of an existing public record." Instead, this exception "applies only when a []PRA request requires a public agency to produce a record that does not exist without compiling data, extracting data or information from [an] existing record, or programing a computer or other electronic devise [sic] to retrieve the data." The trial court thus found that Hayward's charges were unjustified and granted the petition for writ of mandate, directing Hayward to refund to NLG the charges for the City's staff time.

The Court of Appeal reversed, agreeing with Hayward that section 6253.9(b)(2) entitled Hayward to recover its costs for redacting the videos as an "extraction" of data necessary to produce the record. (*National Lawyers Guild*, *supra*, 27 Cal.App.5th at p. 941.) Finding the meaning of the term "extraction" to be ambiguous, the Court of Appeal relied on the legislative history of section 6253.9(b)(2). The court explained that before subdivision (b)(2) was added to the bill enacting section 6253.9, several groups had opposed the bill on grounds that it failed to address the costs of redacting electronic records; after subdivision (b)(2) was added, most of the opposition was withdrawn. The court concluded from this that "lawmakers were ... aware the cost of redacting exempt information from electronic records would in many cases exceed the cost of redacting such information from paper records," and therefore chose to make redaction costs recoverable under section 6253.9(b)(2). (*National Lawyers Guild*, at p. 951.) The court thus held that Hayward could recover its costs to construct a copy of the police body camera video recordings for disclosure purposes, including the "costs to acquire and utilize special computer programming (e.g., the Windows Movie Maker software) to extract exempt material from otherwise disclosable electronic public records." (*Ibid.*) We granted review.

II.

A.

The issue before us is one of statutory interpretation, so we begin by looking to the statutory language. If the language is clear in context, our work is at an end. If it is not clear, we may consider other aids, including the statute's legislative history. (*Sierra Club v. Superior Court* (2013) 57 Cal.4th 157, 165–166 [158 Cal. Rptr. 3d 639, 302 P.3d 1026] (*Sierra Club*).)

The PRA provides that public agencies may recover the costs associated with producing a copy of an electronic record, "including the cost to construct a record, and the cost of programming and computer services necessary to produce a copy of the record" (§ 6253.9, subd. (b)) when "[t]he request would require data compilation, extraction, or programming to produce the record" (§ 6253.9(b)(2)). The question here is what the Legislature meant by the term "extraction." The PRA does not define the term. Hayward argues "extraction" ordinarily is used to mean "taking something out," a usage broad enough to cover the act of redacting information from an electronic record before that record is released to the requester. By contrast, NLG argues the term "extraction" refers, in context, to a process of retrieving responsive information from a government repository in order to produce the responsive information in a newly constructed record. On this narrower understanding, extraction costs would include, for example, exporting responsive data from a large government database into a spreadsheet in order to produce the spreadsheet, but they would not include time spent redacting personally identifiable or other confidential information from the spreadsheet once constructed.

As the Court of Appeal in this case observed, both views find some support in common dictionary definitions of "extraction." The verb "extract" is commonly defined to mean "to draw forth" or "to pull out (as something embedded or otherwise firmly fixed) forcibly or with great effort." (Webster's 3d New Internat. Dict. (2002) p.

806 (Webster's Third).) This dictionary definition is capacious enough to encompass Hayward's broad interpretation as well as NLG's narrower one. (*National Lawyers Guild, supra*, 27 Cal.App.5th at pp. 947–948.)...

But general-purpose dictionary definitions are not always the most reliable guide to statutory meaning; sometimes context suggests that the Legislature may have been using a term in a more technical or specialized way. (See, e.g., Nelson v. Dean (1946) 27 Cal.2d 873, 879 [168 P.2d 16].) Section 6253.9, subdivision (b) (section 6253.9(b)) is, broadly speaking, a technical provision; it allocates the costs of "programming and computer services" and of similar processes required to produce copies of electronic records. (*Ibid.*) The term "extraction" itself appears as the middle item in a list of such technical processes, sandwiched between "data compilation" and "programming." (§ 6253.9(b)(2).) Given the evident technical focus of section 6253.9(b), it makes sense to consider the more technical usage of the term.

In the field of computing, the term "data extraction" does encompass a process of taking data out, but it is generally used to refer to a process of retrieving required or necessary data for a particular use, rather than omitting or deleting unwanted data. One computing dictionary, for example, defines the term "extract" as meaning "to remove required data or information from a database." (Collin, Dict. of Computing (4th ed. 2002) p. 139, italics added; cf. *id.* at p. 310 [defining "retrieve" as "to extract information from a file or storage device"].) Other technical sources define extraction similarly to mean retrieving data for further processing, analysis, or storage, as opposed to simply removing unwanted data. (See, e.g., Neamtu et al., Frontiers in Data Science (Dehmer & Emmert- Streib edits., 2018), ch. 7, p. 217 [defining "data extraction" as "[t]he act or process of retrieving data out of (usually unstructured or poorly structured) data sources for further data processing or data storage"].) This more technical meaning is familiar in modern parlance, as numerous judicial opinions attest. (E.g., *People v. Delgado* (2018) 27 Cal.App.5th 1092, 1105 [238 Cal. Rptr. 3d 697] [using "data extraction" to refer to retrieving information from criminal defendant's cell phone]; *Vasquez v. California School of Culinary Arts,*

Inc. (2014) 230 Cal.App.4th 35, 43 [178 Cal. Rptr. 3d 10] ["Under federal law, a nonparty cannot avoid complying with a subpoena seeking electronically stored information on the ground that it must create new code to format and extract that information from its existing systems."].)

NLG's view aligns with this more technical usage of the term "extraction," as well as with the particular context in which the term appears in section 6253.9(b)(2). Understood in this more technical way, the term "extraction" conveys an idea unique to the production of electronic records. It generally refers to a particular technical process—a process of retrieving data from government data stores—when this process is "require[d]" (§ 6253.9(b)(2)) or "necessary to produce" a record suitable for public release (§ 6253.9(b)).

The process to which Hayward refers, by contrast, is not unique to the field of electronic records; redacting exempt material is a process common to the production of virtually every kind of public record, whether in paper or electronic format. The PRA has long had a term for this process: "deletion." (Gov. Code, § 6253, subd. (a) [requiring public agencies to allow inspection of "[a]ny reasonably segregable portion of a record ... after deletion of the portions that are exempted by law"].) The Legislature's decision to use "extraction" instead of "deletion" when it enacted section 6253.9(b)(2) suggests an intent to convey a different idea. (See *Rashidi v. Moser* (2014) 60 Cal.4th 718, 725 [181 Cal. Rptr. 3d 59, 339 P.3d 344] (*Rashidi*) ["'Ordinarily, where the Legislature uses a different word or phrase in one part of a statute than it does in other sections or in a similar statute concerning a related subject, it must be presumed that the Legislature intended a different meaning.'"].)...

As a practical matter, reading section 6253.9(b)(2) to cover the costs of redacting electronic records would create peculiar distinctions between paper records and electronic ones. It would mean, for example, that an agency could charge for the time spent redacting an electronic version of a document even though it could not charge for time spent redacting a hard copy of the very same document. (See Gov. Code, § 6253, subd. (b); *North County*, *supra*, 23 Cal.App.4th at p. 148.) Given that section 6253.9 was enacted in large part to provide a less expensive alternative to paper production, an interpretation that would allow agencies routinely to charge requesters more for the electronic version seems unlikely.

Responding to this concern at oral argument, counsel for Hayward emphasized that one general definition of "extraction" refers not just to "taking something out," but to "taking out" with "special effort." Counsel suggested we could therefore construe section 6253.9(b)(2) to mean that redaction costs may be shifted to the requester if, but only if, a court finds that special effort was required to redact the record given technology reasonably available at the time. So, for example, a court could conclude that section 6253.9(b)(2) covers the cost of redacting the videos here (because of the significant staff time and effort required to operate the editing program), but that the statute would not cover redacting records in PDF, a task that is much simpler and requires less specialized technology and expertise. Moreover, courts could conclude that redactions that count as "extraction" today may not count as "extraction" tomorrow: Although the video redaction at issue here might have required special effort in 2015, advances in technology may one day make video redaction more routine and thus not chargeable as data extraction costs.

We doubt the Legislature intended us to read quite so much into the bare term "extraction." A different provision of the PRA, section 6255, does permit courts to consider context-specific burdens associated with particular requests in deciding whether and how an agency must respond. (See § 6255, subd. (a) ["The agency shall justify withholding any record by demonstrating … that on the facts of the particular case the public interest served by not disclosing the record clearly outweighs the public interest served by disclosure of the record."].) But section 6253.9(b)(2) does not resemble section 6255. Nothing in section 6253.9(b)(2) suggests it was intended to require a similar inquiry solely for purposes of cost shifting, with redaction costs deemed recoverable or not depending on a court's case-specific evaluation of how hard it was for agency officials to perform the redactions under current technological conditions.

Whatever problems its own interpretation may have, Hayward argues that NLG's interpretation is unsupportable insofar as it would limit "extraction" to responses requiring the retrieval of data for purposes of constructing a record for public release. In Hayward's view, this should be a null set, because, as a general rule, the PRA (like the federal Freedom of Information Act, on which the PRA was based) does not require agencies to "create new records to satisfy a request." (*Sander v. Superior Court* (2018) 26 Cal.App.5th 651, 665 [237 Cal. Rptr. 3d 276] (*Sander*).)

Hayward's argument misunderstands the rule described in *Sander*. The PRA does sometimes require agencies to construct records for public release. Section 6253.9(b) provides, after all, that a "requester shall bear the cost of producing a copy of the record, including the cost to *construct a record*." (Italics added.) This language would serve no purpose if agencies were not, in appropriate circumstances, in fact required to construct records.

The rule to which Hayward refers is not a general prohibition on constructing records, as such, but rather a prohibition on requiring agencies to generate new substantive content to respond to a PRA request. The rule means that, for example, agencies need not draft summary or explanatory material, perform calculations on data, or create inventories of data in response to a records request. (See, e.g., *Haynie v. Superior Court* (2001) 26 Cal.4th 1061, 1075 [112 Cal. Rptr. 2d 80, 31 P.3d 760] ["Preparing an inventory of potentially responsive records is not mandated by the []PRA."]; see also, e.g., *NLRB v. Sears, Roebuck & Co.* (1975) 421 U.S. 132, 161–162 [44 L. Ed. 2d 29, 95 S. Ct. 1504] ["The [Freedom of Information] Act does not compel agencies to write opinions in cases in which they would not otherwise be required to do so. It only requires disclosure of certain documents which the law requires the agency to prepare or which the agency has decided for its own reasons to create."]; *Students Against Genocide v. Dept. of State* (D.C. Cir. 2001) 257 F.3d 828, 837 [rejecting argument that agencies must "produce new photographs at a different resolution in order to mask the capabilities of the reconnaissance systems that took them"].) But the rule does not mean that an agency may disregard a request for government information simply because the information must first be retrieved and then exported into a separate record before the information can be released.

Sander, *supra*, 26 Cal.App.5th 651, itself explained the distinction. Plaintiffs there requested records reflecting California Bar Examination applicants' personally identifying characteristics, like race, law school, grade point average, bar exam score, and year of law school graduation. (*Id.* at p. 655.) To protect applicant privacy, the requester-plaintiffs proposed four different protocols the agency could use to "de-identify or 'anonymize'" the data requested. (*Id.* at p. 658.) Each of these protocols "'require[d] the State Bar to recode its original data into new values'" (*id.* at p. 667 [quoting trial court]), including through "recoding and binning"... data (*Sander*, at p. 659), "[data] suppression (removing information from data that might be identifying), adding 'random noise,' scrambling data or generalizing fields of information, or swapping values for generalized values" (*id.* at p. 660). In rejecting these proposals as outside the scope of the PRA, the court held the PRA does not require "reprogramming computerized data to create new records"—that is, it does not require agencies to "undertake programming that would assign new or different values to existing data, replace groups of data with median figures or variables, and collapse and band data into newly defined categories." (*Sander*, at p. 669.) By contrast, the court recognized, the PRA does require agencies to gather and segregate disclosable electronic data and to "perform data compilation, extraction or computer programming if 'necessary to produce a copy of the record.'" (*Sander*, at p. 669, quoting § 6253.9(b).) But "segregating and extracting data is a far cry from requiring public agencies to undertake the extensive 'manipulation or restructuring of the substantive content of a record'" the requester in that case had proposed. (*Sander*, at p. 669.) Put differently, the PRA does not relieve agencies of the obligation to retrieve data to construct disclosable records; it instead protects them from any obligation to generate new substantive content for purposes of public release. NLG's interpretation is perfectly consistent with that requirement.

In short, NLG's interpretation is more than supportable; it is the interpretation that more readily comports with the statutory text. Under that interpretation, section 6253.9(b)(2) permits the shifting of costs uniquely associated with the production of electronic record copies—including, as relevant here, the need to retrieve responsive data in order to produce a record that can be released to the public—but not the costs of redacting exempt information from the record. This interpretation fits with the typical usage of the term "data extraction," as well as with the usage of the term in related statutory provisions. Even so, the statute does not wholly foreclose Hayward's argument for shifting redaction costs, so we may consider other indicia of the Legislature's intent to determine the meaning of the statute. (See *Sierra Club*, *supra*, 57 Cal.4th at p. 166.)

B.

We turn, then, to the legislative history. As explained above, before the Legislature enacted section 6253.9, agencies had discretion to produce electronic records in any format they wished. (Gov. Code, § 6253, subd. (b), added by Stats. 1998, ch. 620, § 5, p. 4120.) Many agencies exercised this discretion to convert electronic records, which were often inexpensive to produce, into paper records, for which the agencies could recover often greater "direct costs of duplication" under Government Code section 6253, subdivision (b). (See Sen. Com. on Judiciary, Analysis of Assem. Bill No. 2799, *supra*, as amended June 22, 2000, p. 3.) The central purpose of the bill that enacted section 6253.9 was to "ensure quicker, more useful access to public records" by cabining this discretion. (Assem. Com. on Governmental Organization, Analysis of Assem. Bill No. 2799 (1999–2000 Reg. Sess.) as introduced Feb. 28, 2000, p. 2.) To fulfill this purpose, the bill required electronic records to be produced in electronic format. As a general rule, agencies would recover only the costs of duplication, just as they do when they produce paper records. But the bill was amended in June 2000 to add the special costs provision we are concerned with here: If data compilation, extraction, or programming was required to produce the record, the agency was entitled to recover the costs to perform those tasks. (See Assem. Bill No. 2799 (1999–2000 Reg. Sess.)

as amended June 22, 2000, pp. 5, 7; § 6253.9, subds. (a)(2), (b)(2).)

Nothing in the legislative history explains precisely what the Legislature meant by its use of "extraction" in the special costs provision, but this omission is itself telling. The overarching motivation for section 6253.9 was to improve access to electronic records by capitalizing on the relatively less expensive mechanisms for duplicating electronic records, as opposed to paper ones. As NLG reads the statute, section 6253.9(b)(2) was designed to create a narrow allowance for greater cost shifting based on the kinds of expenses that are unique to information kept in electronic format. Under Hayward's interpretation, by contrast, section 6253.9(b)(2) was designed to generally increase cost shifting for electronic records relative to paper records by making redaction costs recoverable for the former but not the latter. Given the overarching motivation for the provision, if the Legislature had intended to create such a disparity, we might expect the history to contain some affirmative indication of that intent. But it does not.

To the extent we can discern anything instructive from the legislative history, the lessons are generally consistent with NLG's view that the Legislature was primarily concerned with the costs of retrieving information from government stores, as opposed to time spent redacting exempt information. For example, in discussing Government Code section 6253, subdivision (c)(4)—the provision extending time limits for responding to records requests where data extraction is required—the Senate Judiciary Committee bill analysis noted that "sometimes the information or data requested is not in a central location nor easily accessible to the agency itself, and thus would take time to produce or copy." (Sen. Com. on Judiciary, Analysis of Assem. Bill No. 2799, *supra*, as amended June 22, 2000, p. 9.) It is fair to conclude that when the Legislature used the term "extraction" in section 6253.9(b)(2), it was similarly concerned with the process of retrieving requested data that was not easily accessible in order to produce it, as opposed to redacting exempt material.

Hayward points to other portions of the legislative record in an effort to show the Legislature intended "extraction" to cover redaction costs. Hayward argues, and the Court of Appeal agreed, that this intent can be fairly discerned by considering the views of certain outside groups that had objected to an earlier version of the bill that did not contain subdivision (b)(2). Before subdivision (b)(2) was added to section 6253.9 in June 2000, these groups opposed the bill because, among other things, it failed to account for costs associated with redacting exempt information from electronic records; after the amendment was added, many of these groups withdrew their opposition. From this, Hayward infers that subdivision (b)(2) was intended to assuage opponents' concerns by allowing agencies to shift the costs of electronic redactions to requesters.

Nothing in the record supports this inference. The opposition letters, of course, reflect only the opinions of their writers—all interested outside parties—and not those of the Legislature. (See *Hassan v. Mercy American River Hospital* (2003) 31 Cal.4th 709, 723 [3 Cal. Rptr. 3d 623, 74 P.3d 726] ["letters state the views of the writers, not the intent of the Legislature," absent "support for [the proposed] interpretation from any source within the Legislature itself"]; *Altaville Drug Store, Inc. v. Employment Development Department* (1988) 44 Cal.3d 231, 238, fn. 6 [242 Cal. Rptr. 732, 746 P.2d 871]; cf. *People v. Dennis* (1998) 17 Cal.4th 468, 501, fn. 7 [71 Cal. Rptr. 2d 680, 950 P.2d 1035] [declining to take judicial notice of letters in support of a bill in part because they "simply state[d] the views of two groups specially interested in supporting the bill's passage"].) Hayward does point to a pre-amendment "Question and Answers" sheet by the bill's author acknowledging the letter writers' concerns. But nothing in that document, or any other document in the available legislative history, indicates the Legislature shared—much less acted on—the writers' concerns about the costs of electronic redaction.

Nor is it fair to infer from the timing that subdivision (b)(2) must have been added to section 6253.9 to respond to redaction cost concerns, as opposed to any of the other concerns raised by opponents of the bill. Those other concerns included worries about the cost of producing responsive data stored in massive databases. (See Violet Varona-Lukens, California Association of Clerks and Election Officials, letter to Assemblywoman Carole Migden, May 11, 2000, p. 2 [raising concern that bill failed to address costs of providing requested information that, "due to the size or complexity of the database from which the information is extracted," would be "extremely burdensome to provide … 'on demand'"]; see also Assem. 3d reading analysis of Assem. Bill No. 2799 (1999–2000 Reg. Sess.) as amended May 23, 2000, p. 3 [acknowledging concern of some commentators that, before June 2000 amendments, bill did not address costs of "separating disclosable electronic records from nondisclosable electronic records" "retain[ed] [in] massive databases"].) It is entirely possible that the bill's opponents succeeded in persuading the Legislature to address this concern about the costs of retrieving responsive information from large electronic repositories, but failed in their efforts to secure an amendment that would have shifted redaction costs as well.

It is true, as Hayward notes, that many of the groups that had previously opposed the bill withdrew their opposition after subdivision (b)(2) was added to section 6253.9. But the withdrawal letters do not reflect an understanding that the new provision would cover redaction costs. Neither did the author nor the bill's sponsor ever mention that the amendments would allow agencies to charge for redaction costs. By contrast, at least one bill analysis suggests the bill as amended would not cover redaction costs. That analysis noted the amended bill's "fiscal effect" would include "[p]otential costs … for workload in redacting nondisclosable electronic records from disclosable electronic records," without mentioning the possibility that public agencies might recover some of those costs by charging requesters for time spent redacting exempt material. (Assem. Conc. Sen. Amends. to Assem. Bill No. 2799 (1999–2000 Reg. Sess.) as amended July 6, 2000, p. 2.)

In sum, the legislative history offers little support for Hayward's proposed interpretation of section 6253.9(b)(2)'s extraction costs provision as covering the costs of redacting electronic records. But it does clearly reflect other concerns, including the difficulties associated with retrieving responsive data from massive, potentially intractable databases. The language of section 6253.9(b)(2)—which permits charging requesters for the cost of "extract[ing]" data to produce or construct electronic records—is consistent with that narrower focus.

Neither the text of section 6253.9 nor its history permits us to comprehensively catalog what types of processes will or will not qualify as "extraction" within the meaning of the statute, but they do provide some guideposts. As the legislative history makes clear, the term is designed to cover retrieving responsive data from an unproducible government database—for example, pulling demographic data for all state agency employees from a human resources database and producing the relevant data in a spreadsheet. But the term "extraction" does not cover every process that might be colloquially described as "taking information out." It does not, for example, cover time spent searching for responsive records in an e-mail inbox or a computer's documents folder. Just as agencies cannot recover the costs of searching through a filing cabinet for paper records, they cannot recover comparable costs for electronic records. Nor, for similar reasons, does "extraction" cover the cost of redacting exempt data from otherwise producible electronic records. That is the conclusion that best accords with the statutory text and the history of its enactment.

C.

To the extent any doubt remains, California's constitutional directive to "broadly construe[]" a statute "if it furthers the people's right of access" confirms our conclusion that redaction costs are not chargeable as costs of data extraction. (Cal. Const., art. I, § 3, subd. (b)(2).) All else being equal, interpreting the term "extraction" in section 6253.9(b)(2) to cover redaction costs would make it more difficult for the public to access information kept in electronic format. Redaction costs are often nontrivial. Take this case, where NLG was charged more than $3,000 for six hours of responsive video. For many requesters, such costs may be prohibitive. Article I, section 3 of the state Constitution favors an interpretation that avoids erecting such substantial financial barriers to access.

Hayward counters that shifting costs to the requester would actually improve public access to electronic records. Hayward theorizes that allowing agencies to recoup redaction costs reduces the overall burden on the agency, which in turn allows the agency to (1) produce records more quickly; (2) redact records with greater fidelity to any claimed exemptions; and (3) rely less frequently on the catchall exemption in section 6255, subdivision (a), the exemption permitting agencies to withhold records where the public interest in nondisclosure "clearly outweighs" the interest in disclosure. (See *California Public Records Research, Inc. v. County of Stanislaus* (2016) 246 Cal.App.4th 1432, 1451 [201 Cal. Rptr. 3d 745] [suggesting time and convenience concerns, in addition to cost concerns, affect public's ability to access records].)

While we do not doubt that greater funding for PRA compliance would yield many of the access benefits Hayward describes, we are not convinced that shifting redaction costs to requesters is the right way to secure those benefits under the statute. Redaction costs could well prove prohibitively expensive for some requesters, barring them from accessing records altogether. Even if higher costs to the agency mean slower disclosure rates or greater inconvenience to the requester, these burdens on access are insignificant if the alternative is no access at all.

To the extent Hayward is concerned about being made to respond to overly burdensome requests without adequate funding, the PRA does provide various solutions to ease those burdens. For example, Government Code section 6253, subdivision (a) requires agencies to disclose nonexempt portions of records only if they are "reasonably segregable" from portions exempted by law. Section 6255, subdivision (a) allows agencies to withhold records if "the public interest served by not disclosing the record clearly outweighs the public interest served by disclosure of the record," which may encompass requests that place undue burdens on an agency. (See *American Civil Liberties Union Foundation v. Deukmejian* (1982) 32 Cal.3d 440, 453 [186 Cal. Rptr. 235, 651 P.2d 822] ["Section 6255 speaks broadly of the 'public interest,' a phrase which encompasses public concern with the cost and efficiency of government."].) And Government Code section 6253.1, subdivision (a)(3) allows agencies to suggest ways requesters can reduce practical barriers to agency compliance with any request—a technique Hayward appears to have used in this very case.

But no similar provisions protect requesters from costs that unduly burden their right of access to government information. Consideration of that right favors a rule that avoids shifting routine redaction costs as a condition of gaining the access the PRA promises....

Hayward argues that requests for body camera footage present unique concerns for government agencies with limited resources. We do not doubt the point. Video footage has a unique potential to invade personal privacy, as well as to jeopardize other important public interests that the PRA's exemptions were designed to protect. Redacting exempt footage can be time-consuming and costly. But section 6253.9(b)(2) is not a provision directed to body camera footage alone; it covers every type of electronic record, from garden-variety e-mails to large government databases. Whether the unique burdens associated with producing body camera footage warrant special funding mechanisms is a question only the Legislature can decide. We hold only that section 6253.9(b)(2), as presently written, does not provide a basis for charging requesters for the costs of redacting government records kept in an electronic format, including digital video footage.

III.

Applying this understanding here, we conclude the trial court was correct to disallow the City's charges for time its staff spent responding to NLG's requests.

The City charged for Nathaniel Roush's time spent searching Evidence.com for responsive videos, reviewing videos, downloading them to DVDs, and confirming their download. Roush never edited the videos; more specifically, he did not extract responsive data from any video. Hayward does not argue Roush performed data extraction with respect to the videos. We agree with this implicit concession. Roush's tasks of searching Evidence.com for video records and downloading them were akin to searching a filing cabinet for responsive paper records. Such actions are not extraction under the PRA.

The City also charged for Adam Perez's time spent editing the videos. But to the extent Perez merely deleted exempt data from the videos (i.e., redacted them), he did not "extract[]" data in order to produce new videos within the meaning of section 6253.9(b)(2). This is not to say the process was entirely straightforward. As Hayward notes, to delete the exempt data, Perez separated the audio and visual material, spliced out the exempt data from each set of material, and then saved the redacted video as a new MP4. But in video-editing terms, what Perez did was not substantively different from using an electronic tool to draw black boxes over exempt material contained in a document in electronic format. As noted, the paradigmatic example of when section 6253.9(b)(2) applies is when the government agency is required to pull certain data from a large database in order to construct a record that can be disclosed to the requester. In some cases, certainly, the process to extract responsive data might also, simultaneously, separate out data that is exempt from disclosure.

But this is not such a case. What Perez did was simply perform redactions of an otherwise producible record, albeit through technologically more advanced means.

Hayward raises one final argument to justify at least some of its charged costs: It argues that Roush performed "data compilation," as the term is used in section 6253.9(b)(2), when he searched for, located, and collected the responsive videos from Evidence.com. Neither the trial court nor the Court of Appeal addressed this argument, and we decline to address it in the first instance. We thus leave this argument, and any related forfeiture issues, for consideration on remand.

IV.

We reverse the judgment of the Court of Appeal and remand for further proceedings consistent with this opinion.

Cantil-Sakauye, C. J., Chin, J., Corrigan, J., Liu, J., Cuéllar, J., and Groban, J., concurred.

Concur by: Cuéllar, J.

CUÉLLAR, J., Concurring.—The majority opinion concludes that when City of Hayward employees spent hours editing out portions of digital body camera footage that were exempt from disclosure, those hours didn't fall within the ambit of data "extraction" encompassed by Government Code section 6253.9, subdivision (b)(2)….I agree but write separately to stress what I take to be the limited scope of our holding, and to anticipate the somewhat distinct variations on a theme this case portends.

The California Public Records Act (PRA; § 6250 et seq.) was enacted to further "access to information concerning the conduct of the people's business," which the Legislature characterized as "a fundamental and necessary right of every person in this state." (§ 6250.) Allowing government agencies to charge potentially steep sums for mere redactions that must be routinely performed by municipal employees for PRA requests—fees that could very well stand as a practical obstacle to the public's right of access—would hinder that purpose. Nothing in the statute's text or context demonstrates a legislatively enacted expectation that requesters of government records pay for what Hayward employees did here: edit the responsive videos to redact audio and visual material exempt from disclosure under the PRA.

But because such electronic data can be stored in nearly infinite ways, jurisdictions such as Hayward can respond to public records requests using technologies that continue to evolve. Imagine a not-so- distant future when government entities deploy more thoroughly automated, artificially intelligent systems for responding to PRA requests. Such systems would likely weave into a nearly seamless quilt—either because of the software's design and functionality, or because of how the relevant data were classified—the search of government databases for responsive records, their extraction from the databases, and the editing of portions of the data exempt from disclosure. Such technology could readily help agencies be more accurate, efficient, and thorough in responding to public records requests—and allow members of the public to receive quicker access to government records.

(See Gomez, *MuckRock request data shows big difference in backlogs between states* (Mar. 21, 2019) Muckrock <https://www.muckrock.com/news/archives/2019/mar/21/feature-state-data/> [as of May 26, 2020] [average response times for state public records requests filed through one organization range from 11 days in Vermont to 148 days in Oregon].)...

This technology will also merit nuanced application of statutory provisions such as the one at issue here. A "paradigmatic example of when section 6253.9(b)(2) applies" and requires payment to the relevant government agency, the majority opinion explains, is when the agency "pull[s] certain data from a large database in order to construct a record that can be disclosed to the requester." (Maj. opn., *ante*, at p. 509.) What our opinion does not address is how the statute ought to be interpreted if that function becomes part and parcel of tasks not encompassed by "extraction"—such as editing exempt material from responsive records. Consider, for example, software that surveys records replete with metadata about matters such as physical location and time, isolates responsive records, and retrieves only those portions of the records that are relevant and not subject to an exemption under the PRA—without ever having to delete information from an existing file. (See maj. opn., *ante*, at p. 500 [government agencies may not charge requesters for the deletion of material exempt from disclosure under the PRA].)

Someone eventually needs to pay for the development, refinement, and maintenance of such technologies—even in a world where people and firms extensively use open source software and loss leading products. Although certain now-familiar business models pivot on presenting the monetary costs of these systems to users as low enough to appear negligible or even nonexistent, such products may impose a host of subtle or unexpected costs in other forms. As we've observed, products that "attract[] users with 'free' and low-priced services" may in fact lock in dependence on expensive support services, or enable private companies "to mine, exploit, and market their users' data to third parties." (Day & Stemler, *Infracompetitive Privacy* (2019) 105 Iowa L.Rev. 61, 63, fn. omitted; see also Newman, *The Myth of Free* (2018)

86 Geo. Wash. L.Rev. 513, 563 [product users "systematically underestimate the amount of information costs they are willing to incur in exchange" for products that are advertised as "free"].) That software offered by such business models may be suitable for public agencies in some situations doesn't remotely mean it would make sense in every instance. (See, e.g., Paquette et al., *Identifying the Security Risks Associated with Governmental Use of Cloud Computing* (2010) 27 Gov. Inf. Q. 245, 251 ["prevent[ing] unauthorized access to both data and code" and the "[p]reservation of information and documents" are among the risks associated with the government's use of cloud services and third party software]; Schooner & Greenspahn, *Too Dependent on Contractors? Minimum Standards for Responsible Governance* (2008) 6 J. Cont. Mgmt. 9, 14 [among the challenges of privatizing government responsibilities is the dependence of agencies on contractors for service and support].) Click-wrapped gift horses are best looked in the mouth.

Government agencies willing to do so may often find that what's most consistent with their public mission is not to opt for the system with the cheapest sticker price. They may instead take best account of the full range of interests and concerns by selecting products that require subscriptions or otherwise involve greater up-front expenses but allow for greater certainty about long-term costs or otherwise evince fidelity to the civic values at stake. (Cf. Re & Solow-Niederman, *Developing Artificially Intelligent Justice* (2019) 22 Stan. Tech. L.Rev. 242, 285 [advocating for the use of technologies that are "more democratically legitimate" and advance goals other than profit maximization].) And because that technology may perform some tasks that overlap with those that constitute "compilation, extraction, or programming" of data as used in section 6253.9, subdivision (b)(2)—by culling data from a larger database, for example, to construct a disclosable record—government agencies may find it not only prudent, but well within their statutory power, to share some of the costs of their infrastructure with requesters of government records.

I don't construe the majority opinion's interpretation of the statutory scheme to foreclose that approach. Our interpretation and application of terms such as "extraction" should avoid, to the extent possible, making pivotal distinctions based on subtle technical details of the digital architecture used by government agencies. We should instead seek to advance the interplay of legislative purpose underlying the statutory scheme. (See *Weatherford v. City of San Rafael* (2017) 2 Cal.5th 1241, 1246–1247 [218 Cal. Rptr. 3d 394, 395 P.3d 274].) Our decision today is in that vein: It prudently recognizes that, in this particular context, Hayward may not shift its costs to records requesters for the time its employees spent redacting exempt material from digital body camera footage. Yet it continues to give leeway for government agencies to depend less on having employees cobble together edited reels of material, and more on making thoughtful choices about how best to navigate the full range of considerations relevant to making public records retrieval in the digital age as responsive and effective as possible.

Stevenson v. City of Sacramento

55 Cal. App. 5th 545 (2020)

BLEASE, Acting P. J.—Under Code of Civil Procedure section 529,...a court generally must require a party who has obtained a preliminary injunction to post an undertaking in an amount determined by the court. Courts set this amount based on their estimate of the harmful effect the injunction is likely to have on the restrained party and, in the event they later conclude the injunction was wrongly issued, they may require some or all of this amount to be distributed to the restrained party to compensate it for the harm it suffered. These requirements provide a measure of protection to parties who are mistakenly enjoined.

The question here is whether parties enjoined under the California Public Records Act (the PRA; Gov. Code, § 6250 et seq.) are entitled to section 529's protections. Appellants Richard Stevenson and Katy Grimes contend they are not for two general reasons. First, they allege section 529's undertaking requirement conflicts with the PRA's own requirements. Second, they assert that requiring a party to post an undertaking before obtaining an injunction is an unlawful prior restraint under the First Amendment. Because we find neither argument persuasive, we affirm the trial court's order requiring appellants to post an undertaking as a condition to obtaining their requested injunction.

BACKGROUND

Government Code section 34090 authorizes the heads of city departments, "with the approval of the legislative body by resolution and the written consent of the city attorney," to destroy most city records that are at least two years old unless the law requires otherwise. Based on this authority, the city council for respondent City of Sacramento (Sacramento or the City) adopted a resolution in 2007 approving the destruction of records as allowed under Government Code section 34090 and authorizing its city clerk to adopt a new records retention policy.

Acting pursuant to this resolution, Sacramento's city clerk adopted in 2010 a new records retention schedule allowing the destruction of all correspondence, including e-mails, older than two years old, subject to certain exceptions. But because Sacramento lacked the technological ability to automatically delete older e-mails at the time, it delayed implementing this policy for several years.

In 2014, Sacramento finally attained the technological ability to automatically delete older e-mails under its 2010 policy. Before moving forward to delete these emails, the City informed various media and citizen groups around December of 2014 that it would begin automatically deleting e- mails under its 2010 policy on July 1, 2015.

In late June of 2015, less than a week before Sacramento planned to begin deleting its older e-mails, appellants each submitted requests to the City for records set for destruction. Both submitted their requests under the PRA—an act that "provide[s] the public with a right of access to government information." (*Sierra Club v. Superior Court* (2013) 57 Cal.4th 157, 164 [158 Cal. Rptr.

3d 639, 302 P.3d 1026]; see Gov. Code, § 6253.) Stevenson requested "[a]ll emails currently scheduled to be deleted from City records July 1, 2015," and Grimes requested, among other things, all e-mail records "by the City of Sacramento and its employees, elected and appointed officials and anyone acting on the City's behalf from January 1, 2008 until the present date." At the time, Sacramento was retaining about 81 million email records. Stevenson's request concerned about 53 million of these records, and Grimes's request concerned about 64 million. Sacramento staff estimated it would take well over 20,000 hours to comply with appellants' requests.

Sacramento informed appellants that their requests were excessive but offered to postpone its planned deletion date by a week to allow appellants an opportunity to narrow the scope of the records they sought. Appellants, in response, agreed to narrow the scope of their requests. But at the same time, they sued Sacramento for "refus[ing] to provide Petitioner's [*sic*] access to the records they request" in violation of the PRA and the California Constitution.

On the same date they filed suit, appellants also asked the trial court to issue a temporary restraining order barring Sacramento from deleting records potentially responsive to their requests. Without considering the merits of the request, the court issued a temporary restraining order for the sole purpose of maintaining the status quo. The court also scheduled a followup hearing to consider whether a preliminary injunction should issue, and directed appellants to submit, in advance of that hearing, new PRA requests to address the City's objections that the initial requests were too broad. The following day, appellants submitted new requests covering 30 categories of records. Sacramento identified about 15 million potentially responsive e-mails.

A month later, the court granted appellants' request for a preliminary injunction and directed Sacramento to preserve the 15 million potentially responsive e-mails. But the court, over appellants' objection, conditioned the grant of the injunction on appellants posting an undertaking per section 529—a statute providing that courts, on granting an injunction, must require the moving party to post an undertaking. (§ 529, subd. (a).) The court initially set the undertaking in the amount of $80,000 based on Sacramento's representations that it would need to expend over $80,000 a year to retain all its e-mails indefinitely. But the court afterward reduced the undertaking amount to $2,349.50, following supplemental briefing in which Sacramento said it in fact anticipated expending as little as $2,349.50 to comply with the injunction.

Appellants timely appealed, alleging the trial court wrongly required them to post an undertaking in connection with the injunction....

DISCUSSION

I

Appellants first contend that section 529's undertaking requirement conflicts with the PRA's own requirements and is thus inapplicable in PRA cases. In support, they rely on two principles of statutory construction—namely, the principles that (1) a specific statute controls over a general statute in the event of conflict, and (2) a more recent statute controls over an older statute when the two conflict. But because we find no conflict between section 529 and the PRA, we find neither principle applicable.

A

Sections 525 through 533 provide the primary statutory authority for injunctions pending trial. (Weil & Brown, Cal. Practice Guide: Civil Procedure Before Trial (The Rutter Group 2019) ¶ 9:501, p. 9(II)-2.) Under section 529, a court, on granting an injunction, "must require an undertaking on the part of the applicant to the effect that the applicant will pay to the party enjoined any damages, not exceeding an amount to be specified, the party may sustain by reason of the injunction, if the court finally decides that the applicant was not entitled to the injunction." (§ 529, subd. (a).) This rule serves to afford compensation to parties who are ultimately found to have been wrongly enjoined. (*City of South San Francisco v. Cypress Lawn Cemetery Assn.* (1992) 11 Cal.App.4th 916, 922 [14 Cal. Rptr. 2d 323].)

Compliance with section 529's requirements is typically a necessary condition to obtain a valid preliminary injunction. (See *Biasca v. Superior Court* (1924) 194 Cal. 366, 367 [228 P. 861] [an undertaking under § 529 is "definitely" required in connection with a preliminary injunction]; *Paiva v. Nichols* (2008) 168 Cal.App.4th 1007, 1024 [85 Cal. Rptr. 3d 838] (Paiva) [absent an exception, "the filing of an undertaking in connection with the issuance of a preliminary injunction is required by statute"]; *Griffin v. Lima* (1954) 124 Cal.App.2d 697, 699–700 [269 P.2d 191] [§ 529's undertaking requirement is "expressly required" and "mandatory"].)

But several statutes expressly exempt certain parties from section 529's requirements. Some of these statutes supply general exemptions that apply in all cases involving injunctions. Section 529, subdivision (b)(3), for example, exempts public entities from its requirements. Other statutes offer narrower exemptions for specific statutory schemes. For example, a student injured by an educational travel organization's false advertising may seek injunctive relief without needing to post an undertaking. (Bus. & Prof. Code, § 17556, subd. (a); see also *id.*, § 17555.) Similarly, an Indian tribe seeking to enjoin certain gaming activities need not post an undertaking "in connection with any action to seek the preliminary or permanent injunction." (§ 1811, subd. (a).) Similar exceptions also exist for a variety of other statutory schemes. (See, e.g., Civ. Code, § 1812.602; Pub. Resources Code, § 30803, subd. (a).)

The PRA, however, is not one of those statutory schemes that specifically bars application of section 529. Although it expressly allows parties to obtain an injunction (Gov. Code, § 6258), it says nothing at all on the topic of undertakings.

B

With that background in mind, we now turn to appellants' offered reasons for finding section 529's undertaking requirement impermissibly conflicts with the PRA's own requirements.

First, they contend the PRA and section 529 conflict because both discuss injunctions, but only section 529 discusses the need for an undertaking. (See § 529; Gov. Code, § 6258.)...This variance, they claim, is enough to invoke the rule of statutory construction "'that a specific provision prevails over a general one relating to the same subject.' [Citation.]" (*Pacific Lumber Co. v. State Water Resources Control Bd.* (2006) 37 Cal.4th 921, 942 [38 Cal. Rptr. 3d 220, 126 P.3d 1040] (*Pacific Lumber*).) But that rule "only applies when an *irreconcilable* conflict exists between the general and specific provisions." (*Id.* at pp. 942–943, italics added.) And we find no such conflict here. Section 529, as appellants accept, provides a general rule: in the event the court grants an injunction, it must require the party that obtained the injunction to post an undertaking. (See *Paiva*, *supra*, 168 Cal.App.4th at p. 1024; *Griffin v. Lima*, *supra*, 124 Cal.App.2d at p. 700.) But the PRA offers no conflicting specific rule. It in fact says nothing at all on the topic of undertakings. We thus decline to find the requisite irreconcilable conflict.

Consideration of how courts have treated similar statutory schemes strengthens this conclusion. Various statutory schemes specifically allow for injunctive relief, yet many, like the PRA, are silent about the need for an undertaking. That is true, for example, of the Safe Drinking Water and Toxic Enforcement Act of 1986, more commonly known as Proposition 65. Proposition 65 expressly authorizes courts to enjoin those who violate or threaten to violate its provisions but says nothing about whether an undertaking is required. (Health & Saf. Code, § 25249.7.) Courts nonetheless have found section 529's undertaking requirement applicable in Proposition 65 cases. (*Mangini v. J.G. Durand International* (1994) 31 Cal.App.4th 214, 218–219 [37 Cal. Rptr. 2d 153] (*Mangini*).)... And reasonably so. In both Proposition 65 and the PRA, the Legislature certainly could have included a specific exemption from section 529's requirements had it wanted. Indeed, the Legislature has done so for various other laws that specifically do away with any undertaking requirement. (See, e.g., Code Civ. Proc., § 1811, subd. (a); Bus. & Prof. Code, § 17556, subd. (a).) But for whatever reason, the Legislature did not provide a similar exception in the PRA. And its declining to do so is telling, as we """"must assume that the Legislature knew how to create an exception if it wished to do so...." [Citation.]'

[Citation.]" (*DiCampli–Mintz v. County of Santa Clara* (2012) 55 Cal.4th 983, 992 [150 Cal. Rptr. 3d 111, 289 P.3d 884].)

Second, appellants assert that the PRA describes the specific costs that PRA applicants can be expected to pay, and those costs are expressly limited to copying costs and, in frivolous cases, court costs and attorney fees. In support, appellants point to Government Code section 6253, subdivision (b)—which allows public agencies to charge those seeking records "fees covering direct costs of duplication" or "a statutory fee if applicable"—and Government Code section 6259, subdivision (d)—which requires courts to award "court costs and reasonable attorney's fees to the public agency" when the "requester's case is clearly frivolous." But that the Legislature found PRA applicants should be required to pay certain specific costs does not mean the Legislature, by implication, believed PRA applicants should be exempt from other generally applicable requirements. Or to put it differently, that the Legislature expressly granted public agencies certain protections in PRA cases (e.g., the right to be reimbursed for the cost of duplication) does not mean the Legislature implicitly took away other protections provided by law (e.g., § 529's undertaking requirement). (See *Pacific Lumber*, *supra*, 37 Cal.4th at pp. 942–943 [requiring "irreconcilable conflict" to invoke the rule that a specific provision prevails over a general one].) Had the Legislature in fact intended to remove from PRA cases any undertaking requirement—a fundamental feature of injunction procedure—we would expect the Legislature to have spoken far more clearly. (See *DiCampli-Mintz v. County of Santa Clara*, *supra*, 55 Cal.4th at p. 992.)

Third, appellants suggest that accepting the trial court's ruling will leave indigent litigants unable to pursue PRA cases—conflicting with the PRA's purpose to allow the public broad access to public records. California law, however, already allows courts to except indigent parties from section 529's undertaking requirements. The Bond and Undertaking Law (§ 995.010 et seq.) generally governs all bond and undertaking requirements, including those in section 529. (§ 995.020, subd. (a); see *Smith v. Adventist Health System/West* (2010) 182 Cal.App.4th

729, 740 [106 Cal. Rptr. 3d 318].) And this law expressly grants courts discretion to "waive a provision for a bond in an action or proceeding ... if the court determines that the principal is unable to give the bond because the principal is indigent and is unable to obtain sufficient sureties, whether personal or admitted surety insurers." (§ 995.240.) Appellants, however, never acknowledge these protections for indigent plaintiffs in their briefing....

Fourth, appellants contend that "[a]ny restriction to the public's right to access records"—including any undertaking requirement—"must be expressly and unambiguously stated by the Legislature within the PRA; if not, the restriction is invalid." But this position proves too much. Although, as appellants note, the California Constitution requires courts to narrowly construe statutes limiting the right of access to public records (Cal. Const., art. I, § 3, subd. (b)(2)), that requirement does not nullify unambiguous statutory requirements. For that reason, for example, a plaintiff seeking relief under the PRA must still pay various court filing fees absent a waiver—even though these fees incidentally burden the plaintiff's right to access public records. (See, e.g., Gov. Code, §§ 70611, 70617; see also *id.*, § 68630 et seq.) So too, we find, must a PRA plaintiff, absent a waiver, comply with section 529 when applicable.

Fifth, appellants assert the trial court wrongly imported section 529's requirements into the PRA, even though the PRA is silent on the issue. But this argument suggests the default rule is that section 529 does not apply unless another statutory scheme, like the PRA, specifically incorporates it. The law, however, is otherwise. Application of section 529 is the default rule, not the other way around. (See *Paiva*, *supra*, 168 Cal.App.4th at p. 1024 [absent an exception, "the filing of an undertaking in connection with the issuance of a preliminary injunction is required by statute"].)...

Finally, we address briefly the arguments of certain amici curiae who, like appellants, contend section 529 conflicts with the PRA. Their first argument relies on Government Code section 6259, subdivision (d), which, again, requires courts to award "court costs and reasonable attorney's fees to the public agency" when the "requester's case is clearly frivolous." In their view, Government Code section 6259's specific requirements override Code of Civil Procedure section 529's general requirement based on the rule of statutory construction that a specific provision prevails over a general one relating to the same subject. (See *Pacific Lumber*, *supra*, 37 Cal.4th at p. 942.) But again, this rule "only applies when an irreconcilable conflict exists between the general and specific provisions." (*Id.* at pp. 942–943.) And we find no conflict at all between the two mentioned statutes, let alone an irreconcilable one. That public agencies are entitled to court costs and attorney fees in frivolous PRA cases, per Government Code section 6259, does not somehow conflict with the right of public agencies to demand an undertaking under section 529.

Second, appellants' amici curiae contend it would be "absurd" to find that public agencies "never have to post a bond," per section 529, subdivision (b)(3), but private individuals seeking injunctions against public agencies under the PRA "always have to post a bond." But we do not find it absurd that the Legislature opted to exempt public agencies from section 529's requirements but not private individuals. In any event, amici curiae's premise that individuals "always have to post a bond" when seeking injunctions under the PRA is incorrect. Again, courts have discretion to exempt indigent individuals from bonding requirements. (§ 995.240.)...

II

Appellants next contend that requiring a party seeking records under the PRA to post a bond "is an unlawful prior restraint" under the First Amendment. We disagree.

A "prior restraint," for First Amendment purposes, is a governmental action """"*forbidding* certain communications when issued in advance of the time that such communications are to occur." [Citation.] Temporary restraining orders and permanent injunctions—i.e., court orders that actually forbid speech activities—are classic examples of prior restraints.' [Citation.]" (*DVD Copy Control Assn., Inc. v. Bunner* (2003) 31 Cal.4th 864, 886 [4 Cal. Rptr. 3d 69, 75 P.3d 1].)

But the trial court here did not forbid appellants from engaging in any communications. It simply asked them to post an undertaking per section 529. And requirements of this sort, which are not concerned with speech at all, are not prior restraints within the meaning of the First Amendment simply because they may incidentally affect expression. (See *Thomas v. Chicago Park Dist.* (2002) 534 U.S. 316, 322–323 [151 L. Ed. 2d 783, 122 S. Ct. 775] [content-neutral permit scheme regulating speech in a public forum was not a prior restraint on speech]; *DVD Copy Control Assn., Inc. v. Bunner, supra,* 31 Cal.4th at p. 886 ["only content-based injunctions are subject to prior restraint analysis"].)

DISPOSITION

The court's order is affirmed. Respondent Sacramento is entitled to recover its costs on appeal. (Cal. Rules of Court, rule 8.278(a)(1) & (2).)

Murray, J., and Butz, J.,...concurred.

AFFIRMATIVE DISCLOSURES

Public information about agency decisions and consumer welfare includes more than the PRA itself. Commenting on the broader issue of appropriate disclosures by crucial regulatory agencies is the following testimony from CPPC's Administrative Director. Her 2001 testimony remains relevant to the underlying issues.

DEPARTMENT OF CONSUMER AFFAIRS:
Hearing on Proposed Standards for Consumer Complaint Disclosure
November 5, 2001 • State Capitol

Testimony of Julianne D'Angelo Fellmeth
Administrative Director, Center for Public Interest Law

Introduction

My name is Julie D'Angelo Fellmeth, and I am the Administrative Director of the Center for Public Interest Law (CPIL) at the University of San Diego School of Law.

For 21 years, CPIL has studied the state's regulation of business, trades, and professions. We have attended literally thousands of the meetings of your agencies, and we publish the California Regulatory Law Reporter, a journal that chronicles the activities and decisions of 25 different California regulatory agencies, including many Department of Consumer Affairs (DCA) boards.

For 21 years, we have focused heavily on the enforcement programs of California occupational licensing agencies.

As the State Bar Discipline Monitor appointed by former Attorney General John Van de Kamp in 1987, we played a key role in overhauling the attorney discipline system of the State Bar.

As the self-appointed Medical Board Discipline Monitor, we have drafted and sponsored two major bills—one in 1990 and one in 1993—that have significantly improved that board's physician discipline system and placed it largely under the oversight of the Attorney General's Office.

We are currently participating in a similar discipline monitor experiment at the Contractors State License Board, and I am the co-author (with CSLB Enforcement Monitor Tom Papageorge) of the Initial Report of the Contractors State License Board Enforcement Program Monitor.

We have tried to improve and strengthen the enforcement programs of your agencies. In an ideal world, your enforcement programs would be adequately funded, professionally staffed, quick and efficient, decisive, fair, and thoroughly capable of promptly removing dangerous or dishonest practitioners from the marketplace, and we would not need a public disclosure policy because the bad apples would be removed.

But we do not live in an ideal world.

We live in a world where many of your agencies are still controlled by members of the very trades and professions they regulate. Licensees largely control their own regulation, and enforcement is clearly not always their highest priority.

We live in a world where it takes a minimum of five decisionmaking steps—fragmented out among at least three executive branch agencies plus the courts—to take the license of a dangerous or dishonest licensee (see attached flowchart of the enforcement process). That's at least two more steps than are afforded criminal defendants before they are deprived of their liberty.

We live in a world where it can take anywhere from four to eight years to remove the license of a dangerous or dishonest licensee, and—during that time period in 99% of the cases—that dangerous or dishonest licensee retains a full and unrestricted license to injure people.

We live in a world where trades and professions finance their own regulation and enforcement programs. Enforcement is expensive. The agency has to pay enforcement staff, investigators, prosecutors, the administrative law judge, and—the most expensive component of all—the court reporter at the hearing. The lower the licensing fee, the less enforcement an agency can do. And many trade associations are extremely active in this building, ensuring that their licensing fees are as low as possible. Licensing fees are influenced not by the needs of the public but by the wishes and demands of the organized trades and professions through legislative lobbying.

And we live in a world where each agency no matter how big or how small—is expected to run its own enforcement program, funded by its own licensee base, staffed by its own staff. That staff may not include any trained investigators, and usually does not include anyone trained in the law. A few large agencies are capable of running a fairly competent enforcement program; the small agencies with small licensee populations are rarely capable of doing so. One good enforcement case against a litigious licensee will bankrupt a small board.

This is not an ideal world when it comes to public protection—which is supposed to be the highest priority of DCA and its agencies.

Thus, because the enforcement process—structured and financed as it is—is generally not capable of acting quickly and decisively and aggressively to protect consumers and prevent harm, we have to enable consumers to protect themselves.

And we do that by giving them information so they can make informed choices about the various kinds of businesspeople they want to deal with.

That's why an agency's public disclosure policy is so important—it helps consumers help themselves, because they are rarely helped by enforcement.

<u>DCA's Current Complaint Disclosure Policy</u>

The Department has a complaint disclosure policy—it was drafted in 1979 and it is not remarkably different from the one you now propose. The problem with your 1979 policy is that you have no authority to impose it on any of your boards, so all of your boards have done whatever they want—meaning you now have a mishmosh of different public disclosure policies largely dictated by board members listening to trade associations of their licensees.

In most cases, what your boards do is to disclose a complaint only after it has been fully investigated, approved for disciplinary action by agency staff, forwarded to the Attorney General's Office, and the accusation (written notice of charges) has been filed. This process is very lengthy. Where the licensee refuses to cooperate with an investigation, the investigative phase alone can take a year or more, and in too many instances we have seen the Attorney General's Office take 6–8 months just to file the accusation. That's almost two years—and during that entire time, if a consumer calls the agency and inquires about that licensee, the agency will respond: "His license is clear." That is extremely misleading where one or two or five or ten investigations are winding their way toward or are in the Attorney General's Office.

The other problem is that most of your agencies disclose only their own disciplinary actions—which are few and far between for many agencies. Many fail to collect and/or disclose other information about licensee misconduct that is relevant to consumer choice, such as civil judgments or settlements or arbitration awards, criminal convictions, other-state disciplinary actions, and business bankruptcies—<u>all of which is public information</u>.

When an agency has that kind of information and refuses to disclose it to an inquiring consumer, the agency appears to be protecting the licensee. Obviously, that is not what your agencies are supposed to do, and that perception certainly does not encourage consumers to trust your agencies.

CPIL's Suggestions

How would CPIL change your complaint disclosure policy? Here are eight bullet points in response to some of the questions posed in your background paper:

1. We believe public disclosure can and should be generally consistent across all of your agencies.

   A lot of people will testify today that "my profession is special," "don't lump me in with all those others," "nurses are different from doctors," or "doctors are different from contractors."

   That may be true in some respects, but we don't believe that's the case when it comes to public disclosure. We believe that it is possible to fashion rules of public disclosure that can and should be followed consistently by all DCA occupational licensing agencies.

2. **We believe that agencies should affirmatively collect and disclose all public information about their licensees to consumers**—that includes civil judgments, settlements, arbitration awards, criminal convictions, business bankruptcies, disciplinary actions by other states, and other types of <u>public information</u> about licensee misconduct or business problems.

Obviously, some of these kinds of actions may not be relevant to a licensee's business practices—so you can adopt regulations to draw lines around those and not disclose them.

For example, I don't really care if a licensee has been involved in a messy divorce or a dispute with his or her neighbor about a boundary problem or a barking dog. Those things are not relevant to the competence or professional performance of my doctor, architect, or hairdresser, so you don't need to disclose those.

However, the California Public Records Act expresses a strong public policy favoring the disclosure of public records. And under Business and Professions Code section 101.6, the role of your agencies is to protect the public from licensees who are incompetent, negligent, or impaired. If your agencies—for whatever reason—are not able to fashion disciplinary programs that quickly and decisively excise problem practitioners from the marketplace, then the very least they can do is actively and aggressively collect and disclose public information to consumers about what other social actors have done to them. Your agencies should want that information anyway—so that they can make more informed licensing and enforcement decisions. And once they get it, they should disclose it to inquiring consumers.

3. **With regard to disciplinary activity performed by your agencies, we strongly support disclosure of the filing of an accusation (written statement of charges) and everything that follows. That is state law, and that should not be changed.**

   With regard to the disclosure of pending complaints and investigations prior to the filing of an accusation, we believe SB 135 (Figueroa) probably draws a fair line.

   Under that bill (recently passed by the legislature and signed by the Governor, and applicable to the Contractors State License Board), some complaints and some investigations—not all of them—will be disclosed prior to the filing of the accusation: serious complaints (not minor ones, but only those justifying the revocation or suspension of a license) that have been investigated sufficiently to determine a "probable violation." And the disclosure will be accompanied by a disclaimer informing consumers that the complaint is still in the allegation and investigation stage.

   The State Bar also has precedent in this area. Under Business and Professions Code § 6086.1, the Bar's general rule is the same as that of your agencies: Don't disclose a complaint or investigation until formal charges have been filed. However, the Bar's statute provides the Bar's Chief Trial Counsel and the Bar President with the discretion to confirm the fact that a formal investigation is pending "when warranted for protection of the public" and "after notice to'' the State Bar member who is under investigation.

And Bar policy requires consideration of a number of factors when determining whether to disclose such an investigation, such as whether there is a continuing pattern of ongoing misconduct, any record of prior discipline, the severity of probable disciplinary sanctions, the expected completion date of the investigation, and the member's cooperation with the Bar. So this statute permits the Bar to warn the public of an ongoing investigation in an egregious case prior to the filing of formal charges.

Please understand: We are not contemplating that you or your agencies will hold press conferences to affirmatively publicize every meritorious complaint you get. We are simply saying you should respond truthfully to a consumer who has the initiative to inquire, and whose protection is the paramount priority of your agencies.

Regarding the disclosure of both "naked" complaints and resolved complaints, CPIL has some concerns. CPIL generally does not support the disclosure of raw complaints that identify the complainant and that have not yet been investigated. You are government, and you need to be concerned about the due process rights of your licensees—which are not absolute, I hasten to add. However, there is much room for mischief here. We know of too many instances where businesses file frivolous or sham complaints against their competition in order to gain a competitive edge. Disclosure of frivolous complaints that have not been investigated would be unfair. So we have concerns about the disclosure—by government—of raw uninvestigated complaints.

By the same token—and this is a closer question—we have concerns about the disclosure of resolved complaints. We think that a licensee who has made a mistake ought to be able to negotiate a settlement with a consumer in good faith, and should not be penalized for resolving a complaint. However, if there is a pattern of numerous resolved complaints indicating that the licensee is using the licensing board as his quality control mechanism— in other words, if the licensee is clearly acting in bad faith and simply resolving numerous complaints filed by "squeaky wheels" who have the resources and initiative to file a complaint—that might warrant disclosure. That might be kind of a difficult line to draw, but I'd be happy to help you try.

4. However, we do support the notion that **the websites of your agencies should provide, in appropriate cases, links to the websites of the Better Business Bureau** and other similar private organizations that collect and disseminate information on businesses and their practices and complaints—just as an additional source of information. Those private businesses are not limited by due process concerns, and we think it is not inappropriate that government advise consumers of these alternate sources of information—with appropriate disclaimers.

5. **We also support much greater use of the interim suspension remedy that your agencies have**—when your agencies come upon an egregious case or a pattern of substandard or dishonest conduct that is harming the public, they should move quickly

and decisively to suspend that license pending conclusion of the disciplinary process, and then <u>disclose that action</u>. Your recent annual report reveals that very few of your agencies make meaningful use of that remedy.

6. **Regardless of the details of any policy that you or any of your boards adopt, <u>we believe consumers should be told what they are NOT being told</u>.**

   Example: The Medical Board discloses civil malpractice judgments against doctors, but not malpractice settlements. It discloses felony convictions against doctors, but not misdemeanor convictions. Nowhere does the website tell consumers that it does not disclose that information—lulling consumers into believing that there are no settlements or misdemeanor convictions, which may be erroneous.

   Another example: The Contractors State License Board's website does not disclose criminal convictions. Yet it does not tell consumers that it does not disclose criminal convictions, leading consumers to believe there are none. That is misleading. Your agencies' websites should clearly state what is being disclosed and what is not being disclosed, so as not to mislead consumers. Some of that undisclosed information is actually public information, and consumers may be able to get it elsewhere if they so desire.

7. The mere fact that your agencies have websites is a sign of the times. Fifteen years ago, when I first started out, we barely had computers much less the Internet. So, to the extent that your agencies have websites and disclose any information about their licensees, that's an improvement over the past decade. However, many of your agencies' websites could be vastly improved—**not only should they disclose more information, they should**

disclose information in a manner that is understandable to the general public.

Many of your agencies' websites suffer from problems that make them decidedly consumer- unfriendly. They are filled with terms of art and legal jargon that may have meaning to insiders at the agency but have no meaning to anyone else. Some of them fail to include a glossary defining those terms. Some of them use legal terms incorrectly or in a misleading fashion. Others fail to include important information that could give the consumer some context or perspective when considering negative information. This is an area where the Department should be able to impose its will on its agencies. The Department should convene a focus group to review the websites of its agencies and clean them up for these types of problems.

8. **Finally, I want to address the privacy rights of licensees**, because I am not insensitive to them. A lot of people are going to complain to you today that your disclosure (or your boards' disclosure) of certain information would violate their personal privacy rights. Some will refer to these as constitutional privacy rights, and they will cite Article I, section 1 of the California Constitution.

Let's be clear: What you are proposing to disclose, and what we are agreeing should be disclosed, is not personal information. I don't want a licensee's home address or social security number or credit report.

We propose that you disclose **accurate** and **complete** and **truthful** information that is relevant to the professional performance of a licensee. If a licensee is the subject of five completed investigations that are sitting on a Deputy Attorney General's desk awaiting the filing of an accusation, I don't want to be told that "his record is clean"—which is what almost all of your boards are going to tell me.

> If a licensee has two civil settlements and a judgment related to her business practices (all of which is public information), I don't want to be told that "her record is clean"—which is what almost all of your boards are going to tell me. If my doctor has two misdemeanor DUI convictions, I don't want to be told "no problem" by the Medical Board—but that is exactly what it will tell me under its current policy.
>
> I am asking for **accurate** and **complete** and **truthful** information that is relevant to the professional performance of a licensee and that will help me make an informed choice when choosing a licensed professional. No constitutional provision prevents you or your agencies from giving me that information, and no court decision that I am aware of supports the notion that government consumer protection agencies may secrete factual information regarding the professional performance of a licensee in a regulated industry.
>
> In fact, many courts would go in the other direction, under the "highly regulated industry'' doctrine. By definition, your licensees are regulated. They are regulated for a reason— because government has found that, in the absence of regulation, their incompetence may harm the public. Under the "highly regulated industry" doctrine, licensees are deemed to have consented to some public intrusion—not into their personal lives or personal information—but certainly into their conduct of their licensed businesses.

The California Public Records Act says that "access to information concerning the conduct of the people's business is a fundamental and necessary right of every person in this state" (emphasis added).

The Bagley-Keene Open Meeting Act says that "the people of this state do not yield their sovereignty to the agencies which serve them. The people, in delegating authority, do not give their public servants the right to decide what is good for the people to know and what is not good for them to know. The people insist on remaining informed so that they may retain control over the instruments they have created" (emphasis added).

Give people information—factual information about a licensee's professional performance and history—and let them make the choice. That's what the marketplace is all about.

Thank you for convening this hearing and for having the courage to raise this issue—which is long overdue for reexamination. We support your approach and look forward to working with you to implement it.

***

Quiz

1. How many days does an agency have to respond to a Public Records Act request?

   a. 30 days
   b. 60 days
   c. 10 days
   d. 90 days

2. The California Public Records Act applies to which of the following entities?

   a. State agencies
   b. Legislature
   c. Courts
   d. All of the Above

3. The California Public Records Act is modeled after which Federal law?

   a. Freedom of Information Act
   b. McCarran Ferguson Act
   c. Noerr Pennington Doctrine
   d. United States Constitution

4. What must an individual requesting a public record from an agency include in a Public Records Act request?

   a. The reason for the request
   b. The statutory authority supporting the request
   c. Both of these
   d. None of these

5. A government employee's private emails and texts may be searched pursuant to a CPRA request.

   a. True
   b. False

6. Which of the following are NOT exempt under the CPRA?

   a. Intra-agency memos
   b. Court filings
   c. Personnel files
   d. Investigatory files

7. A balancing test may be utilized to determine whether which of the following exemptions applies?

   a. Intra-agency memos
   b. Investigatory files
   c. Both of these
   d. None of these

8. An agency may charge the requestor for which of the following items in connection with a Public Records Act Request?

   a. Staff time in gathering responsive documents.
   b. Costs of duplication
   c. Processing fees
   d. All of the above

9. Who bears the burden of proving whether an exemption to the Public Records Act applies?

   a. Agency
   b. Requestor
   c. Both
   d. Neither

Chapter 7
APA Rulemaking

INTRODUCTION

Agencies may exercise quasi-legislative powers through "rulemaking," the adoption of rules and regulations that function as effective public obligations as designated. The process most agencies must follow in order to engage in rulemaking is set forth in the Administrative Procedure Act (APA) (California Government Code Section 11340 *et seq.*). Unlike the state or federal legislature, a state agency's powers must not only comport with applicable constitutional standards for law making, but must also be authorized. That is, this power is purely derivative—it can be exercised only by an agency given that authority by a constitutional or statutory provision, and it is necessarily circumscribed by that applicable intent.

Interestingly, any person may petition any agency to commence rulemaking within its scope of authority (Cal. Gov't Code Section 11340.6).

Once the agency has decided to consider or propose a new or altered rule, it must give notice—with required elements, usually including publication in the *California Regulatory Notice Register* and the provision of a 45-day public comment period. The notice must include the date, time, and place of a public hearing (if any). If the agency has not scheduled a public hearing, any interested person can compel one by simply requesting it in writing no later than 15 days prior to the close of the comment period. The initial notice must also include the statutory or other authority for the action; an informative digest (explanation of impact of the proposal); and disclosure that an initial statement of reasons and the text of the exact changes are available on the agency's website or upon request (the actual text of the proposed changes need not be included in the notice itself).

The notice must also include disclosures regarding many potential impacts added to the rulemaking process over the years, including impacts on small business, housing, jobs, *et al.*

Finally, it must provide the name and contact information for the identified contact person for the agency. Following the 45-day public comment period, an agency may withdraw notice of changes (published in the Notice Register); adopt changes exactly as proposed, and move on to prepare the final rulemaking file; or adopt changes with minor modifications (which requires the publication of the modified language for an additional public comment period; grammatical or non-substantive changes may trigger an additional 15-day period for public comment while a major change may require a new full 45-day period).

The adoption of rules by agencies may be subject to review and possible approval or rejection by other sources of authority. That function may lie within a supervening review agency. An example in California is the Department of Consumer affairs (DCA), which oversees many agencies operating under its aegis. Also, as to those agencies and others, generic review authority rests with the Office of Administrative Law (OAL) (see the flowchart below).

The DCA Director may veto regulatory changes adopted by DCA boards (but the board may override the Director's veto by a unanimous vote). More extensive review is provided by OAL, which reviews the rulemaking file of all proposed rules adopted by an agency prior to its effective entry. OAL reviews the rulemaking file to ensure proper notice and hearing procedures, and to ensure that the agency provided an adequate response to any public comments received (including objections and comments made during the public hearing, if one was held). Finally, as the flow chart illustrates, OAL reviews all rulemaking files submitted by agencies subject to the APA under six criteria: authority, clarity, consistency, reference, necessity, and nonduplication (Cal. Gov't Code Sections 11349 and 11349.1). If OAL disapproves the proposed rulemaking action, the agency may appeal to the Governor's Office. The Governor exercises a one-way decision—he/she may overrule OAL and accomplish rule adoption but does not have the power to veto an OAL decision of approval. The Governor appoints the OAL Director, who serves at his/her pleasure, so examples of Gubernatorial overruling of OAL are extremely rare.

Of course, OAL's approval is subject to judicial review via a petition for writ of mandate or other civil action to invalidate a rule.

Under the APA, an agency may determine various aspects of its internal operations (e.g., details of its internal investigative steps) without public rulemaking. This internal confinement is particularly compelled where such disclosure would facilitate detection avoidance by violators. On the other hand, an agency may not engage in what is termed "underground rulemaking"—where they effectively change or specify a required operational element without adhering to the APA steps set forth in the flowchart below (usually by terming the action a "policy" or "letter," or something other than a rule or regulation.

Any person may directly petition OAL for a regulatory determination and request its opinion as to whether an agency has engaged in underground rulemaking as noted above. Such an opinion does not directly cancel the non-rule policy under challenge, but it has substantial weight, similar to an opinion by the Attorney General (described as more than ordinarily persuasive). OAL designations of policies as lacking required rulemaking compliance are commonly obtained, perhaps partly because one of the steps accomplished through rulemaking avoidance is the denial of OAL review.

CPPC Critique of the APA Rulemaking Process

Although the APA rulemaking process was created to (and intended to) cut red tape and regularize rulemaking, it requires agencies to make a large number of assessments, evaluations, and declarations as to the impact of proposals under consideration. These have proliferated to the point where they are, interestingly, highly duplicative, generally not applicable, and would not, themselves, withstand OAL review.

The six criteria reviewed by OAL ironically violate themselves. *I.e.*, any rule that is unnecessary is properly rejected, as is any rule that is found to be duplicative. One might argue that a duplicative rule is also unnecessary, making the duplicative objection itself unnecessary.

Although OAL generalist lawyers are generally able to judge authority and perhaps clarity, they may not be able to judge necessity and will simply buy whatever the agency is selling. The agency is supposed to be the subject matter expert—why/how should an OAL generalist be expected to second-guess it based on a record proferred by the specialist agency? The Department of Finance also engages in its own review of some rules and that process is similarly flawed. Both are also subject to concealed special interest lobbying influence—either directly or through the Governor's or legislators' offices (see Chapter 4 above).

An ideal process combines independence (from special interests with an economic stake) with expertise on the subject and on its consequences. And ideally, it is done in one high-quality process, not sequential deficient steps lacking independence or expertise (or both).

STEPS OF THE APA RULEMAKING PROCESS

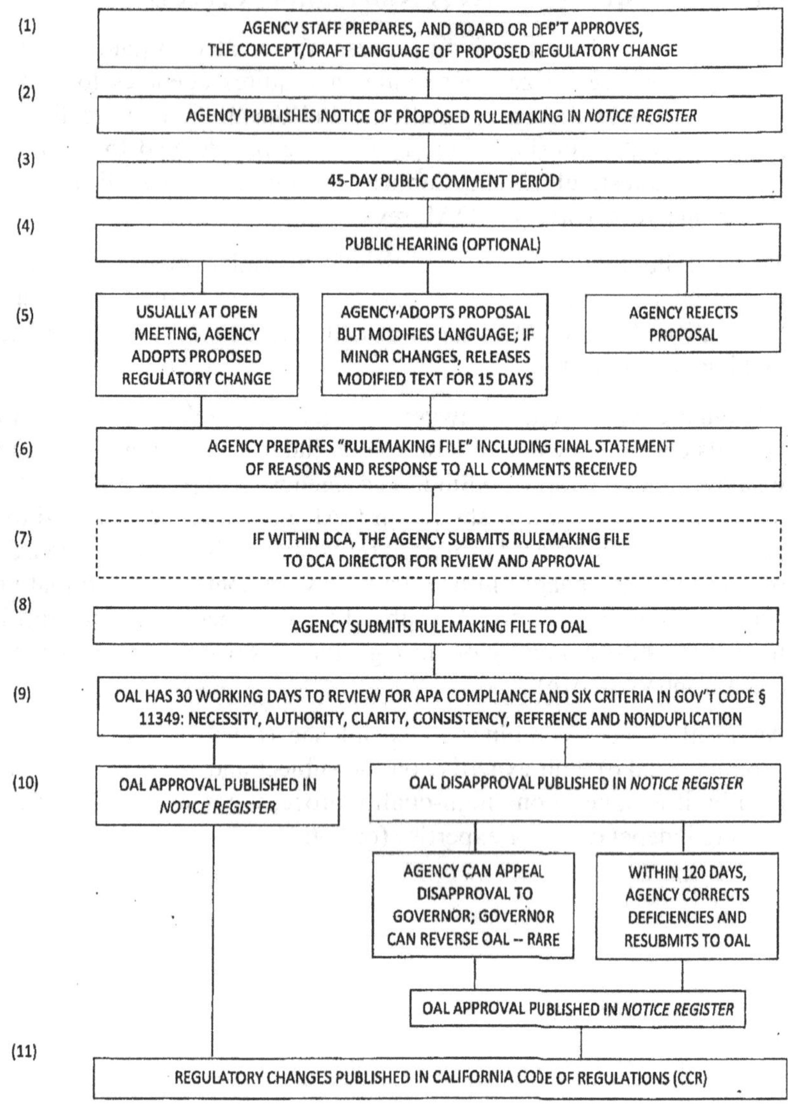

Emergency Rulemaking

Emergency rulemaking is described by OAL as follows:[5]

> **Emergency Adoption of Rules**
>
> A state agency may adopt emergency regulations in response to a situation that calls for immediate action to avoid serious harm to the public peace, health, safety, or general welfare, or if a statute deems a situation to be an emergency under the APA. Because emergency regulations are intended to avoid serious harm and require immediate action, the emergency rulemaking process is substantially abbreviated compared to the regular rulemaking process. OAL reviews emergency regulations for compliance with the APA's emergency rulemaking requirements.
>
> The emergency rulemaking process generally includes a brief public notice period, a brief public comment period, review by OAL and an OAL decision. In addition, some agencies have requirements related to emergency rulemakings that are unique to that particular agency.
>
> ***
>
> **What constitutes an emergency?**
>
> An "emergency" means a situation that calls for immediate action to avoid serious harm to the public peace, health, safety, or general welfare. (Government Code section 11342.545.) In order for an emergency regulation to be approved, an emergency situation must be shown to exist. Unless a situation is expressly deemed in statute to meet the emergency standard, an agency must make a finding of emergency by describing specific facts supported by substantial evidence that demonstrate its existence. In addition, if the emergency existed and was known by the agency in sufficient time to have been addressed through nonemergency regulations, the finding of emergency shall include facts explaining the failure to so address the situation. A finding of emergency based only upon expediency, convenience, best interest, general

---

[5] See https://oal.ca.gov/emergency_regulations/ and https://oal.ca.gov/emergency_regulations/Emergency_Regulation_Process/.

public need, or speculation, is not adequate to demonstrate the existence of an emergency.

***

How may the public comment on a proposed emergency rulemaking action?

Emergency rulemakings have a five calendar day comment period that begins when OAL posts the notice of the pending emergency action on the OAL web site. OAL may approve an emergency rulemaking without public comment if "the emergency situation clearly poses such an immediate, serious harm that delaying action to allow public comment would be inconsistent with the public interest." (Government Code section 11349.6(b).)

Comments on a proposed emergency rulemaking action must be submitted directly to OAL within five calendar days from when OAL posts the proposed emergency regulation on the OAL web site, with a copy of the comment also submitted to the rulemaking agency's contact person. OAL will confirm that the agency has received the comment before considering it. The comment must state that it is about an emergency rulemaking action currently under OAL review and include the topic of the emergency....

The rulemaking agency is not required to respond to comments submitted in connection with an emergency rulemaking action. If the agency chooses to respond, however, it must submit its response to OAL within eight calendar days after the date of submission of the proposed emergency rulemaking action to OAL...unless specific exceptions apply.

What must the rulemaking agency submit to OAL for review in an emergency rulemaking action?

The agency proposing an emergency regulation must include the following in the file submitted to OAL (Title 1, CCR, section 50):

- Proposed Emergency Regulation Text and STD. Form 400 (7 copies).
- Finding of Emergency (1 copy)

- Agency statement of specific facts demonstrating existence of emergency and by substantial evidence need for immediate action (unless deemed an emergency by statute). (Government Code Section 11346.1(b)(2).)
- Information required by Government Code Section 11346.5(a), including:
- Authority and Reference citations
    - o Informative Digest
    - o Specific Agency Statutory Requirements
    - o Local Mandate Determination
    - o Fiscal Impact Estimate and Form 399
- Identification of each technical, theoretical, and empirical study, report, or similar document, if any, upon which the agency relies.
- Facts explaining the failure to address the situation through nonemergency regulations (only necessary if the emergency existed and was known by the agency in sufficient time to have been addressed through nonemergency regulations). (Government Code section 11346.1(b)(2).)

What is OAL's review process for the proposed emergency rulemaking?

OAL has 10 calendar days within which to review and make a decision on the proposed emergency rulemaking file. If OAL approves the emergency rulemaking, OAL will file the approved regulation with the Secretary of State. If OAL disapproves the regulation, it must write a decision explaining the reasons for disapproval.

OAL reviews the file for the following (Government Code section 11349.6(b)):

- Does the agency's finding of emergency demonstrate that the situation addressed by the regulations is an emergency?

- Do the proposed emergency regulations comply with the six substantive standards of Government Code section 11349.1?
- Did the agency comply with the procedural requirements of Government Code section 11346.1?

What is the effective period of an approved emergency regulation?

An emergency regulation usually becomes effective when filed with the Secretary of State. An emergency regulation generally remains in effect for 180 days unless OAL approves a readoption of the emergency regulation during that time period. If an agency requests a readoption of an emergency, it should be submitted to OAL at least 10 calendar days prior to the expiration of the emergency effective period to avoid the possibility that the regulation lapses by operation of law during OAL's 10-day review. If approved by OAL, the emergency readoption extends the emergency regulation for an additional 90 days; however, no more than two readoptions are permitted.

Can an emergency regulation become permanent?

Yes. An emergency regulation can become permanent if the agency adopts the emergency regulation through the regular rulemaking process within the time period the emergency regulation is in effect. This is commonly referred to as filing a "certificate of compliance." When the agency submits a timely certificate of compliance to OAL, the emergency regulation stays in effect during OAL's review. OAL reviews the certificate of compliance action to ensure it satisfies all APA requirements for a regular rulemaking. (Government Code section 11346.1(e).) OAL has 30 working days to review a certificate of compliance.

If a certificate of compliance is submitted, the maximum time period for OAL review is 30 working days, although OAL may act earlier. A proposed rulemaking submitted with a certificate of compliance usually becomes effective on filing by OAL with the Secretary of State.

Americana Termite Co. v. Structural Pest Control Bd.

199 Cal. App. 3d 228 (1988)

Opinion by: ASHBY

***

Appellants Americana Termite Company, Inc., a California corporation, Gary Woolery, individually and doing business as Americana Termite Company, Inc., Paul Allen Ellis and Michael Andrew Gerritse appeal from a superior court judgment denying a writ of mandate upholding the suspension of their licenses as pest control operators by respondents Structural Pest Control Board, Department of Consumer Affairs of the State of California (Board), and Mary Lynn Ferreira. We affirm.

Facts

In 1982 Dennis Patzer, deputy registrar in charge of Board enforcement programs, had the responsibility for the Board's active enforcement program (AEP). The program was originally designed to uncover fraud in the pest control business. In 1982, focus shifted to consumer protectionism by seeking administrative action against negligent and incompetent inspectors and termite companies. Patzer submitted to the Board a yearly prepared proposal indicating the general scope of the program but not delineating the specific companies to be investigated. After obtaining Board approval for the general description of the program, Patzer would select companies with the largest number of complaints within a specific geographical area. A Board investigator contacted various homes in the geographical area to request the homeowner participate in the program. Investigators would inspect each home to determine if there were infestations or conditions likely to lead to infestations. Thereafter, the homeowner called the companies designated by Patzer and requested termite inspections. After the companies inspected the homes, they filed the required reports with the Board. The inspection reports were then analyzed to determine if the reports uncovered the problems previously identified by the Board investigators. The filed reports were evaluated on a point system.

In the underlying matter, in November-December 1982, three homes were selected in the Long Beach area. One hundred points were assigned to each home. If a filed report scored less than seventy, or if it missed any one of the most serious violations, or three of the next most serious violations it would be referred to the division of investigations to seek discipline.

Accusations were filed against appellants when they filed inadequate reports on the three homes....In a writ of mandate proceeding, the superior court upheld the administrative decision to discipline each appellant due to inspection and reporting violations.

Appellants do not contest the factual findings below. In this appeal they question the legal validity of the AEP.

Structural Pest Control Act

Appellants contend that the AEP deprived them of statutory rights under the Structural Pest Control Act. Appellants' contention lacks merit.

Business and Professions Code section 8500 et seq., the Structural Pest Control Act, authorizes the Board to regulate, administrate, license, and discipline structural pest control operators. The Board is authorized to investigate, hold hearings, and impose discipline not only on the filing of a complaint by a consumer, but also "upon its own motion." (Bus. & Prof. Code, § 8620.) If a complaint is filed by a consumer, Business and Professions Code section 8622 delineates the procedures which are to be followed. Citizen complaint procedures include giving notice to the company that a complaint has been filed and providing the company 30 days in which to cure any defect. Contrary to appellants' assertion, the Board need not follow the procedures as outlined in Business and Professions Code section 8622 when it files a complaint on its own motion pursuant to Business and Professions Code section 8620....Thus, appellants were not entitled to notice, or an opportunity to cure the defect, or the other procedures outlined in Business and Professions Code section 8622 and were not denied rights under the act....

Equal Protection

Appellants contend that the AEP violated their equal protection rights. Appellants' contention lacks merit.

"[The] Constitution, federal and state, [requires] that persons similarly situated with respect to the legitimate purpose of the law receive like treatment." (*Educational & Recreational Services, Inc. v. Pasadena Unified Sch. Dist.* (1977) 65 Cal.App.3d 775, 785 [135 Cal.Rptr. 594], fn. omitted.) In cases involving occupational licensing, "'[the] conventional "rational relationship" test is traditionally applied '" (*Bib'le v. Committee of Bar Examiners* (1980) 26 Cal.3d 548, 555 [162

Cal.Rptr. 426, 606 P.2d 733], quoting *D'Amico v. Board of Medical Examiners* (1974) 11 Cal.3d 1, 17 [112 Cal.Rptr. 786, 520 P.2d 10].) According to this test, if the classifications rationally relate to a legitimate state interest, the equal protection clause is not violated even if the classifications made by its laws are imperfect, not mathematically precise, or result in some inequality. (Cf. *Agricultural Labor Relations Bd. v. Superior Court* (1976) 16 Cal.3d 392, 410 [128 Cal.Rptr. 183, 546 P.2d

687].)

There is no question that protecting the public from negligent or incompetent pest control operators is a legitimate state interest. Further, in selecting the companies with the most complaints to investigate, the Board has chosen a method which is rationally related to that purpose. Neither the grading system nor the selection process (i.e., utilizing the number of complaints as the triggering mechanism without reference to a company's size or volume of business) makes the selection process irrational. Contrary to appellants' suggestion, there is no showing that appellants "were purposefully and intentionally selected for discrimination," or that it was inappropriate to treat appellants differently from others against whom disciplinary action was pending, or that the program operated at the "whim" of Patzer. The program was an organized system for evaluating the professional competency of pest control investigators and bringing forth charges when warranted.

Administrative Procedure Act

Appellants contend that the AEP was a “regulation” and thus the Board erred in not following the procedural requirements of the Administrative Procedure Act. Appellants’ contention lacks merit.

Under the Administrative Procedure Act, Government Code section 11342 et seq., an administrative agency must follow certain procedures, including giving notice to interested parties, when the agency formulates a “regulation.” Government Code section 11342, subdivision (b), set forth below...defines a “‘Regulation’” as “every rule...or standard of general application. or standard adopted by any state agency to implement, interpret, or make specific the law enforced or administered by it “ Specifically excluded from the definition of a regulation are those rules which relate “only to the internal management of the state agency.”

Contrary to appellants’ argument, for which they cite no authority, the AEP was not a regulation and therefore the Board did not have to comply with the procedural requirements of the Administrative Procedure Act. The AEP did not determine if a licensee violated the Structural Pest Control Act, but was merely an internal enforcement and selection mechanism. The termite inspection industry was aware of the existence of the AEP due to the open legislative hearings. The AEP investigative procedures were subject to disclosure under the California Public Records Act. (Cf. *Cook v. Craig* (1976) 55 Cal.App.3d 773, 784 [127 Cal.Rptr. 712].) Therefore the process was not “surreptitious” as suggested by appellants. Inasmuch as the process did not violate appellants’ equal protection rights, and the administrative hearings which followed provided appellants with due process protections, the AEP was a proper exercise of the Board’s powers.

The judgment is affirmed.

Grier v. Kizer

219 Cal. App. 3d 422 (1990)

Opinion by: KLEIN

Factual & Procedural Background

Grier was a provider under the Medi-Cal program. In August or September of 1982, the Department audited claims for payment filed by Grier during the period between December 1980 and March 1982. The total amount paid to Grier for the period was $ 932,642.

Fan Yee (Yee), an operations research specialist for the Department, developed a random sampling plan to audit physician claims. As to Grier, Yee selected a sample size of 200 pages from a 9,711- page record of all claims for services rendered to Medi-Cal beneficiaries by Grier during the period in question and submitted for payment.

After the selected samples were audited, the audit results were extrapolated, which process disclosed an estimated overpayment to Grier of $654,592, with a 95 percent confidence at a projection of plus or minus $16,344.

Grier filed an audit appeal with the Department. A hearing was held before the Department's administrative law judge (ALJ) on December 4, 1985. Grier, his expert, Dr. Michael Intriligator, and Yee testified. Grier testified as to the wide variety of patients seen in his practice. In his testimony, Intriligator attacked Yee's methodology, opining that in view of the heterogeneity of Grier's practice, a stratified sampling method would have yielded a more accurate result than simple random sampling....

***

On September 29, 1986, Grier filed a petition for writ of mandate, alleging, inter alia, the sampling methods utilized by the Department were arbitrary and capricious, there was no evidence to support the findings of the ALJ, and the ALJ employed by the Department was biased. Grier subsequently filed an amended petition, alleging the sampling methods adopted by the Department were in violation of the APA and thus void and unenforceable.

***

During this time frame, the Union of American Physicians and Dentists requested the OAL to determine whether the Department's policy of using a statistical sampling and extrapolation method for determining overpayment when auditing physicians' claims constituted a regulation as defined in section 11342, subdivision (b).

After considering the Department's arguments, the OAL filed an opinion concluding: the challenged audit method was a regulation, none of the recognized exceptions to the APA rules was applicable, and because the method had not been duly adopted as a regulation and filed with the Secretary of State in accordance with the APA, it was invalid and unenforceable. (1987 OAL Determination No. 10 [Docket No. 86-016] Aug. 6, 1987.)

***

The trial court ruled "the statistical methods utilized by [the Department] in this case are invalid and unenforceable for failure to comply with the requirements of the Administrative Procedure Act, Gov. Code Sections 11342 et seq., [sic] and as a separate and independent basis for judgment, having also determined that there is not substantial evidence to support the findings of fact of the Director...that the statistical methods utilized by the Department in this case were valid or adequate[.]"

The trial court granted Grier's petition to set aside the Department's decision and ordered the Department to refrain from making any claim against Grier based upon the sampling and extrapolation methods utilized herein.

***

Contentions

The Department contends: (1) Grier's challenge to its authority to use statistical sampling audit techniques is untimely and therefore Grier has waived any right to challenge same; (2) Grier's challenge to its authority to utilize such method is without merit; (3) the subject sampling methodology is appropriate and valid; and (4) its application of the audit methodology was proper.

Discussion

1. *Grier's challenge to the Department's authority to use the subject audit method is properly before this court.*

The Department contends Grier's challenge to its authority to use statistical sampling techniques is untimely because Grier did not make the argument at the administrative level but instead, first raised the issue in his petition for writ of mandate. The trial court properly rejected this argument.

Futility is an exception to the exhaustion of administrative remedies doctrine. (*McKee v. Bell-Carter Olive Co.* (1986) 186 Cal.App.3d 1230, 1245 [231 Cal.Rptr. 304].) Here, the Department consistently has maintained it has the authority to utilize the audit method in issue, even after the OAL's 1987 determination which found the sampling method to be an invalid regulation. In view of the Department's unyielding position that it has statutory authority to audit providers by way of sampling and extrapolation, an administrative challenge by Grier based on the Department's failure to promulgate the regulation pursuant to the APA certainly would have been futile.

2. *OAL review of administrative regulations mandated by APA.*

The APA was enacted to establish basic minimum procedural requirements for the adoption, amendment or repeal of administrative regulations promulgated by the state's many administrative agencies. (Stats. 1947, ch. 1425, §§ 1, 11, pp. 2985, 2988; former Gov. Code § 11420, see now § 11346.) Its provisions are applicable to the exercise of any quasi-legislative power conferred by statute. (§ 11346.) The APA requires an agency, inter alia, to give notice of the proposed adoption, amendment or repeal of a regulation (§ 11346.4), to issue a statement of the specific purpose of the proposed action (§ 11346.7), and to afford interested persons the opportunity to present comments on the proposed action (§ 11346.8). Unless the agency promulgates a regulation in substantial compliance with the APA, the regulation is without legal effect. (*Armistead v. State Personnel Board* (1978) 22 Cal.3d 198, 204 [149 Cal.Rptr. 1, 583 P.2d 744].)

In 1979, the Legislature established the OAL and charged it with the orderly review of administrative regulations. In so doing, the Legislature cited an unprecedented growth in the number of administrative regulations being adopted by state agencies as well as the lack of a central office with the power and duty to review regulations to ensure they are written in a comprehensible manner, are authorized by statute and are consistent with other law. (§§ 11340, 11340.1, 11340.2)....

The APA defines a regulation as "every rule, regulation, order, or standard [of] general application...adopted by any state agency to implement, interpret, or make specific the law enforced or administered by it, or to govern its procedure, except one which relates only to the internal management of the state agency." (§ 11342, subd. (b).)....

Section 11347.5 thereof states: "(a) No state agency shall issue, utilize, enforce, or attempt to enforce any...rule, which is a regulation as defined in subdivision (b) of Section 11342, unless the...rule has been adopted as a regulation and filed with the Secretary of State pursuant to this chapter. [para.] (b) If the [OAL] is notified of, or on its own, learns of the issuance, enforcement of, or use of,...[a] rule which has not been adopted as a regulation and filed with the Secretary of State pursuant to this chapter, the [OAL] may issue a determination as to whether the...rule, is a regulation as defined in subdivision (b) of Section 11342."

OAL determinations as to whether a rule is a regulation are filed with the Secretary of State and published in the California Regulatory Notice Register. (§ 11347.5, subd. (c)).

Any interested person may obtain judicial review of a given determination by the OAL by filing a written petition with the court within 30 days of the date the determination is published requesting the determination of the OAL be modified or set aside. (§ 11347.5, subd. (d).) Also, if the OAL disapproves a proposed regulation submitted for its review, the adopting agency has recourse to the Governor, who may overrule an OAL decision disapproving a proposed regulation. (§ 11349.5.)

a. Application of the APA to the Department.

The California Medi-Cal Act explicitly makes the Department's rule making subject to the provisions of the APA. (Welf. & Inst. Code, §§ 14000 et seq., 14000.4, 14124.5.)

Welfare and Institutions Code section 10725 provides in relevant part: "The director [of the Department] may adopt regulations, orders, or standards of general application to implement, interpret, or make specific the law enforced by the department, and such regulations, orders, and standards shall be adopted, amended, or repealed by the director only in accordance with the provisions of [the APA]."

Similarly, Welfare and Institutions Code section 14124.5, found within the Medi-Cal Act, states in pertinent part: "(a) The director may, in accordance with the provisions of Section 10725, adopt, amend or repeal, in accordance with [the APA], such reasonable rules and regulations as may be necessary or proper to carry out the purposes and intent of this chapter and to enable it to exercise the powers and perform the duties conferred upon it by this chapter, not inconsistent with any of the provisions of any statute of this state."...

Despite the clear directive of the above mentioned statutes, the Department argues that other sections of the Medi-Cal Act provide sufficient authorization for its use of the challenged audit method without the formality of regulation promulgation and OAL review.

The Department invokes, inter alia, Welfare and Institutions Code section 14170, which states in relevant part: "Amounts paid for services provided to Medi-Cal beneficiaries shall be audited by the department i*n the manner and form prescribed by the department.*" (Italics added.) The Department also cites Welfare and Institutions Code section 14133, as authorizing "(c) Postservice postpayment audit, which is review for medical necessity and program coverage after service was rendered and the claim paid. The department may take appropriate steps to recover payments made if subsequent investigation uncovers evidence that the claim should not have been paid."

It is a fundamental rule of statutory construction that every statute should be construed with reference to the whole system of law of which it is a part so that all may be harmonized and have effect. (*Brown v. Superior Court* (1984) 37 Cal.3d 477, 484 [208 Cal.Rptr. 724, 691 P.2d 272].) Accordingly, while the above-cited sections and others authorize the Department to audit providers, these sections must be read in conjunction with the balance of the Medi-Cal scheme, specifically, Welfare and Institutions Code sections 10725 and 14124.5, which require the Department to comply with the APA in adopting regulations.

The issue to be determined by this court is whether the challenged audit method constitutes the subject of a regulation within the meaning of section 11342, subdivision (b), of the APA, or amounts only to an exempt internal management rule. If the method were properly the subject of a formal regulation, the Department's failure to comply with the APA would render the method invalid and unenforceable. (§ 11347.5.)

3. Standard of appellate review.

The trial court ruled the Department's use of the subject statistical method was invalid for failure to comply with the requirements of the APA.

Review of that decision is a question of law for this court's independent determination, namely, whether the Department's use of an audit method based on probability sampling and statistical extrapolation constitutes a regulation within the meaning of section 11342, subdivision (b). (See *California Teachers Assn. v. San Diego Community College Dist.* (1981) 28 Cal.3d 692, 699 [170 Cal.Rptr. 817, 621 P.2d 856]; *Shoban v. Board of Trustees* (1969) 276 Cal.App.2d 534, 541 [81 Cal.Rptr. 112].)

***

Because section 11347.5, subdivision (b), charges the OAL with interpreting whether an agency rule is a regulation as defined in section 11342, subdivision (b), we accord its determination due consideration.

4. The Department's audit method should have been promulgated as a regulation pursuant to the APA.

As indicated, the OAL filed an opinion concluding the challenged audit method amounted to a regulation within the meaning of the definition set forth in section 11342, subdivision (b)....

The OAL's analysis set forth a two-part test: "First, is the informal rule either a rule or standard of general application or a modification or supplement to such a rule? [para.] Second, does the informal rule either implement, interpret, or make specific the law enforced or administered by the agency or govern the agency's procedure?" (1987 OAL Determination No. 10, *supra.*)

The OAL concluded this particular audit method was a standard of general application "applied in every Medi-Cal case reviewed by [Department] audit teams and...used to determine the amount of overpayment." Further, the method implemented Welfare and Institutions Code sections 14170 and 14133, which authorize the Department to audit providers and to take appropriate steps to recover overpayments. The Department thus had the rulemaking authority to adopt regulations concerning the use of probability sampling and statistical extrapolation, and was required to comply with the APA before utilizing such audit method. (1987 OAL Determination No. 10, *supra.*)

We accord due consideration to the OAL's determination and also examine case law which has construed the APA's definition of regulation. The case law, which is sparse, discloses generally that the definition of regulation is broad, as contrasted with the scope of the internal management exception, which is narrow.

a. The Department's method is not entitled to deference as an administrative interpretation.

The Department urges that while the OAL's construction of the APA is entitled to deference, the probability sampling and extrapolation method should be given weight as the Department's administrative interpretation of the Medi-Cal Act.

In rejecting a similar contention, the Supreme Court in *Armistead* observed that a major aim of the APA was to provide a procedure whereby people to be affected by proposed regulatory action may be heard on the merits of proposed rules. (*Armistead v. State Personnel Board, supra*, 22 Cal.3d at p. 204.) "Yet we are here requested to give weight to [a rule] in a controversy that pits the [agency] against an individual member of exactly that class the APA sought to protect before rules like this are made effective. That, we think, would permit an agency to flout the APA by penalizing those who were entitled to notice and opportunity to be heard but received neither." (*Ibid.*)

The Department's argument is clearly answered by the *Armistead* rationale and therefore the audit method in issue merits no weight as an agency interpretation. (*Armistead, supra*, 22 Cal.3d at p. 205.) "To hold otherwise might help perpetuate the problem" of """"house rules of the agency"""" which are promulgated without public notice, opportunity to be heard, filing with the Secretary of State, and publication in the California Code of Regulations. (*Ibid.*)

b. Internal management exception inapplicable.

As set forth above, the APA defines regulation as "every rule, regulation, order, or *standard [of] general application*...adopted by any state agency to implement, interpret, or make specific the law enforced or administered by it, or to govern its procedure, *except one which relates only to the internal management of the state agency*." (§ 11342, subd. (b), italics added.)

Armistead v. State Personnel Board, supra, 22 Cal.3d at pages 200-201, determined that an agency rule relating to an employee's withdrawal of his resignation did not fall within the internal management exception. The Supreme Court reasoned the rule was "designed for use by personnel officers and their colleagues in the various state agencies throughout the state. It interprets and implements [a board rule]. It concerns termination of employment, a matter of import to all state civil service employees. It is not a rule governing the board's internal affairs. [Citation.] 'Respondents have confused the internal rules which may govern the department's procedure...and *the rules necessary to properly consider the interests of all...under the...statutes*') [Fn. omitted.]" (*Id.*, at pp. 203-204, italics added.)

***

Relying on Armistead, and consistent therewith, *Stoneham v. Rushen* (1982) 137 Cal.App.3d 729, 736 [188 Cal.Rptr. 130], held the Department of Corrections' adoption of a numerical classification system to determine an inmate's proper level of security and place of confinement "extend[ed] well beyond matters relating solely to the management of the internal affairs of the agency itself[,]" and embodied "a rule of general application significantly affecting the male prison population" in its custody.

By way of examples, the above mentioned cases disclose that the scope of the internal management exception is narrow indeed. This is underscored by *Armistead's* holding that an agency's personnel policy was a regulation because it affected employee interests. Accordingly, even internal administrative matters do not per se fall within the internal management exception.

Nonetheless, the Department argues the provider is not required to do anything differently when the Department uses probability sampling to prove an overpayment than it would be required to do in a full scale audit. However, the Department's use of probability sampling might cause a provider to leave the Medi-Cal program to avoid the potential for large recoupments based on probability sampling. Further, whether a regulation requires affirmative conduct by an affected party is not dispositive. In *Stoneham v. Rushen, supra*, 137 Cal.App.3d at page 736, the adoption of a standardized scoring system to determine an inmate's classification invoked the APA because it was "a rule of general application significantly affecting the male prison population," although it does not appear the new system imposed an additional burden on the inmates.

In a case decided before *Armistead*, *City of San Joaquin v. State Bd. of Equalization* (1970) 9 Cal.App.3d 365, 374-375 [88 Cal.Rptr. 12], a statistical accounting technique was held not to be a regulation within the meaning of the APA.

Briefly, in that case, revenues from sales taxes imposed on over-the-counter sales were allocated to each taxing jurisdiction in direct proportion to the reported sales attributable to such jurisdiction. But, as to sales taxes derived from construction contracts, the taxes were returned to the cities and the county in the same ratio as such cities and county received revenues from over-the-counter sales for the same quarterly periods. Thus, each taxing jurisdiction received its prorated share of revenues from construction contracts under a formula which was geared to the revenues it received from over- the-counter sales. (*City of San Joaquin v. State Bd. of Equalization, supra*, 9 Cal.App.3d at p. 375.)

The *San Joaquin* court held the challenged pooling procedure was "not a regulation, order or standard of general application" but "merely a statistical accounting technique to enable the Board to allocate, as expediently and economically as possible, to each [participating city], its fair share of sales taxes collected by the Board on that city's behalf." (*City of San Joaquin, supra*, 9 Cal.App.3d at p. 375.)

In view of the Supreme Court's subsequent recognition in *Armistead* of the distinction between purely internal rules which merely govern an agency's procedure and rules which have external impact so as to invoke the APA (*Armistead, supra*, 22 Cal.3d at pp. 203-204), *San Joaquin's* holding that statistical accounting techniques are exempt from the APA appears to have lost its precedential value. After *Armistead*, it would appear an accounting procedure resulting in a possibly disproportionate allocation of tax revenues would be the appropriate subject of a regulation adopted pursuant to the APA, allowing interested parties to be heard on the merits of the proposed rule.

Further, because the Legislature adopted the APA to give interested persons the opportunity to provide input on proposed regulatory action (*Armistead, supra*, 22 Cal.3d at p. 204), we are of the view that any doubt as to the applicability of the APA's requirements should be resolved in favor of the APA.

We are also aware of *Americana Termite Co. v. Structural Pest Control Bd.* (1988) 199 Cal.App.3d 228 [244 Cal.Rptr. 693], decided after Armistead, which held an agency enforcement program was not a "regulation" subject to the APA.

There, pursuant to the enforcement program, the agency inspected the homes of participating homeowners. Thereafter, the homeowner contacted the companies designated by the agency and requested termite inspections. The agency then analyzed the companies' inspection reports to determine if the reports uncovered the problems previously identified by the agency's investigators. (*Americana Termite Co.*, *supra*, 199 Cal.App.3d at pp. 230-231.) Without citation to authority, the *Americana* court concluded the enforcement program was not a regulation but merely "an internal enforcement and selection mechanism." (*Id.*, at p. 233.)

Thus, the *Americana* court apparently concluded "internal management" and "enforcement" are synonymous. Its reasoning is not fully developed. The fact that a rule pertains to enforcement does not establish that it relates only to internal management. In the instant case, while the challenged audit method facilitated enforcement, it also was a standard of general application adopted to implement the Department's statutory auditing authority.

Having made an independent determination as to what constitutes a regulation for purposes of the APA, we conclude the internal management exception is inapplicable. We therefore concur in the OAL's conclusion that the challenged audit method was an improper regulation not promulgated pursuant to the APA; it was a standard of general application which, in implementing the Department's statutory auditing authority, affected Medi-Cal providers statewide.

c. *The Department's other arguments are unavailing.*

The Department further submits there was no need to promulgate a regulation because the only legally tenable interpretation of its statutory auditing authority is that statistical sampling and extrapolation procedures must be utilized. The argument is without merit. While sampling and extrapolation may be more feasible or cost-effective, it does not follow that such method is the sole tenable interpretation of Welfare and Institutions Code sections 14133 and 14170. A line by line audit is an alternative tenable interpretation of the statutes.

The Department also urges that by refraining from the adoption of a formal regulation, it advanced the APA's goal of reducing the number of administrative regulations. (§ 11340.1.) The argument is unpersuasive. It is for the OAL to determine whether a regulation is necessary and nonduplicative; a regulation found to be unnecessary or duplicative will be disapproved. (§ 11349.1, subds. (a)(1) and (a)(6).)

5. *The Department acquiesced in the OAL's determination that the subject audit method constitutes a regulation.*

Lastly, we note the Department acquiesced in the OAL's adverse 1987 determination. Following that determination, it formally promulgated a regulation under the APA, providing for statistical extrapolation of Medi-Cal provider reviews. (Cal. Code Regs., tit. 22, § 51458.2, operative May 13, 1988.) The regulation requires "probability sampling to extrapolate the recoverable amount when the extrapolated recovery amount exceeds the cost to the Department of doing the audit." (Cal. Code Regs., tit. 22, § 51458.2, subd. (a).) The regulation further provides: "Probability sampling will be done in conformance with generally accepted statistical standards and procedures described in any textbook on statistical sampling methods." (Cal. Code Regs., tit. 22, § 51458.2, subd. (b).)...

While the Department contends the formal regulation was a mere codification of its audit procedures, its failure to object to the OAL's adverse 1987 determination, compounded by its subsequent compliance with the APA, in effect constitutes an acquiescence in the OAL's determination.

Conclusion

***

Because the challenged audit method was a standard of general application implementing the Department's statutory auditing authority, the OAL properly determined the method was an improper "underground" regulation which should have been adopted pursuant to the APA.

The Department's failure to comply with the APA renders the method invalid and unenforceable. Therefore, we do not reach the statistical validity of the method, whether it was correctly employed, or any other contentions....

We affirm the judgment barring the Department from making any claim against Grier based on the sampling and extrapolation method it utilized in the audit. Grier to recover costs on appeal.

Safeco Ins. Co. v. Garamendi

27 Cal. App. 4th 400

Opinion by: BOREN, J.

This appeal involves the nature and finality of the former Insurance Commissioner's so-called "amended decision" of June 15, 1990. It presents the question of the extent to which the present commissioner is bound by certain agency determinations which resulted from hearings held by his predecessor to devise a plan for the implementation of Proposition 103....We find that the amended decision did not address specific issues as to specific insurers, but did develop general principles to be applied in future cases and set forth a plan for the implementation of Insurance Code sections 1861.01 and 1861.05 and related portions of Proposition 103. Accordingly, the amended decision was not an adjudicatory decision. Rather, it constituted quasi-legislative rulemaking of generic procedures to be followed and thus did not bind the new commissioner, who was free to rescind his predecessor's regulations and establish new and different regulations.

PROCEDURAL AND FACTUAL HISTORY

This case arises out of unfocused early efforts to implement Proposition 103. As enacted, Proposition 103 provided that rates on policies written between November 8, 1988, and November 8, 1989, would be "rolled back" to 20 percent below their 1987 levels. The initiative contemplated that all rates modified after November 7, 1989, would be subject to the "prior approval" of the Insurance Commissioner. The initiative provided for an automatic rollback, giving the Department of Insurance (DOI) a full year before it would have to hold rate hearings. However, the Supreme Court in *Calfarm Ins. Co. v. Deukmejian* (1989) 48 Cal.3d 805 [258 Cal.Rptr. 161, 771 P.2d 1247] (hereinafter, *Calfarm*), upholding all but two severable portions of the insurance reform initiative, essentially revised the automatic rollback procedure such that each company would be permitted to file for exemption from the rollback requirement until the commissioner determined that the rate as applied to each company would not be confiscatory....Following *Calfarm*, hundreds of insurers filed thousands of applications for exemption from Proposition 103's requirement that each insurer roll back its levels 20 percent below the November 8, 1987, levels.

In response to the deluge of applications for exemptions, in August of 1989, former Insurance Commissioner Roxani Gillespie commenced a series of company-by-company adjudicatory hearings to determine the rollback liability of several insurers under the *Calfarm* confiscation standard. By October of 1989, it became apparent that there were a number of generic issues common to virtually all insurers' rates and that these issues could be resolved in a similar manner for all insurers. The former Insurance Commissioner then suspended individual hearings and gave notice of the bifurcation of proceedings and the consolidation of proceedings and hearings regarding common, generic insurance rate issues.

The proceedings concluded approximately eight months later, and the former commissioner signed on June 15, 1990, a so-called "amended decision" which reflected the commissioner's policies on generic issues involved in both rollback and prior-approval applications, subject to the right of each insurer to request variances from those policies. The amended decision, which by its terms was "effective June 15, 1990," addressed inter alia the following issues: (1) the reasonable industry-wide rate of return (11.2 percent) to be used to determine the insurers' rates for the rollback year, absent a showing by an insurer that its individual circumstances warranted a variance from that rate of return; (2) the determination of the amount of capital to which that rate of return would be applied, again absent an insurer's showing that it was entitled to a variance; (3) the disallowance of certain expenses incurred by insurers during the rollback year; and (4) the provisions for a company-specific adjudicatory hearing to determine whether insurers are entitled to any requested variances.

The amended decision was in the format of a lengthy narrative to which a detailed outline of definitions and procedures entitled "Exhibit A" was appended. The narrative portion described the various provisions of Proposition 103, the Supreme Court's opinion in *Calfarm*, and the commissioner's procedures for setting rollback rates, prior-approval rates and variances. The detailed "Exhibit A," captioned "California Department of Insurance Plan for the Implementation of Insurance Code Sections 1861.01 and 1861.05 and Related Portions of Proposition 103," was an outline with headings and subheadings which were substantively consistent with the descriptive narrative which preceded it.

Following the amended decision, Commissioner Gillespie scheduled the resumption of company- specific rollback exemption hearings for numerous companies. Several insurers, including Safeco and Allstate, filed actions challenging the amended decision. Safeco sought a writ of mandate "[o]rdering the Commissioner to set aside the findings, determinations, and rulings contained in her Amended Decision." Allstate sought a writ of mandate "requiring the Commissioner to vacate and annul the Amended Decision." None of the insurers specifically challenged the portions of the amended decision regarding the right to seek variances from the generic determinations. Nor did any of the insurers seek to prohibit the commissioner or the DOI from rendering any decisions or promulgating any future rules or regulations regarding insurance rates. However, each petition and complaint filed by the insurers sought to invalidate various portions of the June 15, 1990, amended decision, and each contained at least one broadside attack against the amended decision in its entirety or against the portion of it addressing rollbacks.

On July 31, 1990, the superior court ruled on related cases brought by several insurers, including Safeco and Allstate. The court denied the motions to enjoin the commissioner from holding company-specific hearings under the guidelines in the June 15, 1990, amended decision and dismissed the insurers' petitions for a writ of mandamus or mandate or for injunctive relief. The court ruled that the June 15, 1990, amended decision was not a final order and that the insurers had not exhausted their administrative remedies. The court observed that not one application seeking exemption from the rollback requirement had been decided and no orders had yet been issued that any particular insurer was required to roll back its rates and make a refund. The court reasoned that since the rate adjustment process entailed company-specific hearings following the consolidated generic hearings, as contemplated by *Calfarm* and as then ordered by the commissioner who had established bifurcated hearings, until a company-specific hearing is concluded "[T]here is no final rate rollback adjudication as to any insurer." The court emphasized, "It is possible that a particular rollback applicant may establish at the company's specific hearing that its application for variance should be granted. If the application is not granted, judicial review will available of both the Commissioner's methodology and its application to the insurer."...

Following the superior court's decision, a company-specific hearing applying the amended decision commenced as to Safeco and California State Automobile Association (CSAA). The claims of these two insurers were reviewed at a joint hearing before an administrative law judge (ALJ) who issued a proposed decision for review by the commissioner. Before Commissioner Gillespie rendered a decision on the Safeco and CSAA company-specific hearing, she was replaced by the newly elected (see Ins. Code, § 12900) Commissioner John Garamendi. The new commissioner rejected the ALJ's proposed decision after the company-specific joint hearing and remanded the matter for a further hearing. Commissioner Garamendi indicated that new regulations were forthcoming and that Safeco and CSAA should have their rollback liability ultimately determined under the new regulations which would also govern the liability of other insurers who came thereafter. No final decision has yet issued in any company-specific hearing held under the June 15, 1990, amended decision.

As Commissioner Garamendi's regulatory program took shape, insurers became increasingly attached to the former commissioner's previously reviled amended decision. Although the insurers continued to press the present appeal from their unsuccessful challenge to the amended decision, the insurers also defended the amended decision. On March 19, 1991, the insurers filed a complaint for declaratory and injunctive relief and a petition for a writ of mandate challenging the right of the commissioner to ignore and redecide various ratemaking determinations in the amended decision. On April 8, 1991, the superior court denied the insurers' request to enjoin the commissioner from proceeding with new rate component determinations hearings and denied the attempt to require adherence to the former commissioner's amended decision....

After extensive rulemaking hearings, Commissioner Garamendi subsequently adopted and implemented regulations regarding a reasonable industry-wide rate of return for rollback purposes (10 percent) and other generic issues common to all insurers' rates. The regulations promulgated new and different guidelines than those in the amended decision regarding several key ratemaking determinations.

The insurers view the regulations as politically motivated and unwarranted changes from the now largely satisfactory guidelines in the amended decision. On the other hand, the new commissioner portrays the amended decision as the product of hearings infected with wholesale irregularities, including the denial of discovery, denial of the right to cross-examination, unwarranted and capricious limitations on issues and evidence deemed important by consumer interveners, and purported ex parte communications and alleged conflicts of interest by the hearing officer. However, the commissioner's motivation in rescinding the guidelines in the amended decision and in enacting superseding generic issue determinations by way of regulations is irrelevant to this appeal.

The commissioner thereafter directed the ALJ to determine the rollback liability of Safeco and CSAA based on the new regulations, which had been adopted to replace the determinations contained in the June 15, 1990, amended decision. The financial rollback obligations of Safeco and CSAA would be less onerous under the generic determinations in the amended decision than under subsequent regulations by the commissioner. (Among other things, the new regulations specified that 10 percent, rather than 11.2 percent, constituted a reasonable industry-wide rate of return.) Pursuant to the guidelines in the amended decision, the ALJ determined (in a company-specific "proposed decision" before Commissioner Garamendi replaced Commissioner Gillespie) that the rollback obligations initially were $41 million for Safeco and $92 million for CSAA. After allowable variances, the ultimate rollback obligations would have been $17.5 million for Safeco and nothing for CSAA. However, pursuant to calculations based on the subsequent regulations, Commissioner Garamendi advised the insurers that the rollback obligations would be $88.7 million for Safeco and $126.2 million for CSAA, although new company-specific hearings under Commissioner Garamendi's regulations have apparently not been pursued by Safeco and CSAA. The insurers' present attachment to the previously attacked amended decision is thus understandable.

Meanwhile, seemingly stuck at first in an administrative morass, Commissioner Garamendi's regulations regarding generic issues common to all insurers' rates are now in an apparent state of flux. The generic issue regulations formulated after extensive rulemaking hearings were submitted by the commissioner to the Office of Administrative Law (hereinafter, the OAL), were twice rejected by the OAL (see Gov. Code, § 11343.1), but, after appeals by the commissioner to the Governor (see Gov. Code, § 11349.5), were twice approved on order of the Governor.

Nonetheless, we are most recently advised that once again the OAL has rejected the commissioner's comprehensive generic regulations. According to the OAL's notice disapproving of the commissioner's regulations, the regulations lack the statutorily required consistency and clarity (see Gov. Code, § 11349.1, subd. (a)(3) & (4)) in that they "go too far in restricting an insurer from showing at a rate hearing that a rate is not 'excessive' or 'inadequate'" and that the "definitions of 'excessive' and 'inadequate' (primary standards established by Proposition 103 for approval of a rate) cannot easily be understood." The OAL's notice also suggested to the commissioner that he may seek judicial review of the OAL's decision. (See Gov. Code, § 11350.3.)...The insurers maintain that the OAL's actions illustrate that the commissioner has no coherent regulatory program. Moreover, the insurers suggest that upholding the trial court's decision would produce anomalous results and impede the effective resolution of numerous pending rollback cases.

However, the commissioner notes that, despite the apparently uncertain status of his regulations in the OAL, the superior court's ruling which permitted him to rescind the amended decision and to enact generic issue regulations also permitted a coherent regulatory program which has resulted, albeit not in this case, in voluntary rollbacks of $300 million and a final administrative decision on another $100 million in rollbacks. Thus, the commissioner urges that predictable and actual effects of the trial court's denial of the insurers' request for an injunction and the public interest in the consequences of the denial are relevant in reviewing the order denying the insurers' request for equitable relief....

DISCUSSION

I. *NATURE AND EFFECT OF THE SO-CALLED "AMENDED DECISION" OF JUNE 15, 1990*

The insurers urge that the amended decision was a final decision which was adjudicatory in nature. The insurers would thus like to see Commissioner Garamendi essentially a prisoner of his predecessor's determinations on June 15, 1990, even if he deems those determinations unwise or erroneous. According to the reasoning of the insurers: (1) the amended decision of June 15, 1990, was final for the purposes of judicial review with the DOI retaining no jurisdiction (see *Heap v. City of Los Angeles* (1936) 6 Cal.2d 405, 407-408 [57 P.2d 1323]); (2) the amended decision was final for the purposes of collateral review with the DOI not entitled to modify the decision and with no inherent jurisdiction to correct any errors or to alter policy determinations in continuing administrative proceedings (see *Long Beach Unified Sch. Dist. v. State of California* (1990) 225 Cal.App.3d 155, 169 [275 Cal.Rptr. 449]); and (3) the commissioner must determine rollback liability based on the amended decision regardless of whether equitable principles preclude the insurers from binding the commissioner to the amended decision which the insurers themselves chose to challenge. The necessary underlying premise for the entire position taken by the insurers is that the June 15, 1990, amended decision was adjudicatory and final, rather than quasi-legislative ratemaking and thus always open to correction or modification as warranted by experience, a change in conditions, or a change in policy.

Contrary to the contention of the insurers, we find that the amended decision was not adjudicatory. When an agency formulates generic rules of general applicability and develops principles to be applied in future cases, the agency acts in its quasi-legislative and nonadjudicatory capacity. (*Strumsky v. San Diego County Employees Retirement Assn.* (1974) 11 Cal.3d 28, 34-35, fn. 2 [112 Cal.Rptr. 805, 520 P.2d 29].) "'[A] legislative action is the formulation of a rule to be applied to all future cases, while an adjudicatory act involves the actual application of such a rule to a specific set of existing facts.'" (*Dominey v. Department of Personnel Administration* (1988) 205 Cal.App.3d 729, 736 [252 Cal.Rptr. 620].) It is the function performed, not the label attached, which governs whether an agency is engaged in quasi-legislative rulemaking. (*Pitts v. Perluss* (1962) 58 Cal.2d 824, 834 [27 Cal.Rptr. 19, 377 P.2d 83].) Even where an agency develops an evidentiary record on technical facts, the fundamentally legislative character of the proceeding is not altered. (See *Stauffer Chemical Co. v. Air Resources Board* (1982) 128 Cal.App.3d 789, 794 [180 Cal.Rptr. 550].) Indeed, the very requirement that the agency make findings based on a huge record of technical facts may itself constitute a basis for classifying the agency's actions as quasi-legislative. (See, e.g., *Rivera v. Division of Industrial Welfare* (1968) 265 Cal.App.2d 576, 586 [71 Cal.Rptr. 739].)

Moreover, an agency's ratemaking function is uniformly recognized as quasi-legislative. (See, e.g., *New Orleans Pub. Serv. v. New Orleans* (1989) 491 U.S. 350, 371 [105 L.Ed.2d 298, 318, 109 S.Ct. 2506]; *California Hotel & Motel Assn. v. Industrial Welfare Com.* (1979) 25 Cal.3d 200, 211 [157 Cal.Rptr. 840, 599 P.2d 31]; *Wood v. Public Utilities Commission* (1971) 4 Cal.3d 288, 292 [93 Cal.Rptr. 455, 481 P.2d 823].) As the court explained in *Rivera v. Division of Industrial Welfare, supra,* 265 Cal.App.2d 576, an agency acts in its quasi-legislative capacity when it sets rates by acting "to receive and consider economic and social data, as well as opinion and argument, covering large numbers of people and wide sectors of the economy; to select a series of positions aimed at the statutory objectives but shaped by discretion and policy; finally, to express its selection in rules regulating the future conduct of relatively broad classes of persons. Thus its function was quasi- legislative rather than adjudicative." (*Id.* at p. 586.)

Whether an agency acts in its quasi-legislative or in its adjudicative mode is significant regarding the finality of its actions. An adjudicatory action within the scope of the Administrative Procedure Act (Gov. Code, § 11500-11529) (hereinafter, APA) is final and judicially reviewable 30 days after delivery or mailing of the decision, unless an earlier effective date for the decision is set by the agency, and the agency then loses power to reconsider its decision. (Gov. Code, § 11521, subd. (a), 11523.) On the other hand, it is well established that an agency's quasi-legislative action is like an act by a legislative body which can reconsider and change its action at any time. (See *Hollywood Circle, Inc. v. Dept. of Alcoholic Beverage Control* (1961) 55 Cal.2d 728, 732 [13 Cal.Rptr. 104, 361 P.2d 712]; *Olive Proration etc. Com. v. Agri. etc. Com.* (1941) 17 Cal.2d 204, 208-209 [109 P.2d 918]; *California Optometric Assn. v. Lackner* (1976) 60 Cal.App.3d 500, 505 [131 Cal.Rptr. 744].) An administrative agency concerned with furtherance of the public interest is not bound to rigid adherence to precedent. "'The [agency's] view of what is best in the public interest may change from time to time. Commissioners themselves change, underlying philosophies differ, and experience often dictates changes.'" (*New Castle County Airport Commission v. C.A.B.* (D.C. Cir. 1966) 371 F.2d 733, 735, fn. 4.) Indeed, government could not properly function if administrators were bound in perpetuity to initial determinations, and the lessons of experience and the input of varied personnel could not influence and enrich government policy.

In the present case, the former commissioner's amended decision of June 15, 1990, was captioned on the first page as if it were an adjudicatory opinion and the document was labeled a "decision." However, merely labeling the document a decision is not determinative of its adjudicatory rather than quasi-legislative nature. (See *Perdue v. Crocker National Bank* (1985) 38 Cal.3d 913, 935-936, fn. 25 [216 Cal.Rptr. 345, 702 P.2d 503]; *Dominey v. Department of Personnel Administration, supra*, 205 Cal.App.3d at pp. 736-738; *Independent Broker-Deal T. Ass'n v. Securities & E. Com'n* (D.C. Cir. 1971) 442 F.2d 132, 140-141.)

Nor is the caption of the amended decision conclusive of its nature, though it may be indicative. Here, the caption of the amended decision is typed as if it were a judicial opinion, but it does not refer to any specific parties and only describes generic issues of general applicability. The caption refers to rate increase matters and issues related to the control, review and approval of insurance rates pursuant to pertinent statutory provisions, indicative of its quasi-legislative nature.

The text of the amended decision and an analysis of its substance and function further reveal its general applicability and quasi-legislative nature. The document contains a description of the provisions of Proposition 103, the effect of the *Calfarm* opinion, and a narrative discourse on general insurance industry characteristics. The document specifically discusses the desirability of developing generic rules, disclaims any findings as to any specific insurer, and selects approaches from competing methodologies regarding ratemaking.

The general rulemaking, quasi-legislative nature of the decision is also consistent with the notice announcing the generic hearings which resulted in the amended decision. The notice announcing the generic hearings revealed, in pertinent part, that the hearing would "result in the adoption of methods for controlling, reviewing and approving insurance rates" and would "determine whether exceptions should be made to the general methodologies for on-going rate review, prior approval or Rollbacks, and if so, what the methodologies for such exceptions should be."

Conclusively revealing the quasi-legislative rulemaking nature of the amended decision is the lengthy exhibit A appended to the decision. The exhibit consists in outline format of numerous definitions, formulas and procedural rules for calculating rates which were written precisely in the form of regulations. In fact, such regulations were promptly enacted.

We acknowledge, as the insurers point out, that pursuant to Proposition 103, Insurance Code section 1861.05, subdivision (a) "govern[s] rate regulation during the first year of the initiative's operation" (*Calfarm*, *supra*, 48 Cal.3d at p. 823), and that hearings under section 1861.05 must be conducted pursuant to the adjudicatory hearing provisions of the APA (Ins. Code, § 1861.08). Nonetheless, the Supreme Court in *Calfarm* emphasized the commissioner's broad implied powers which go beyond the adjudicatory provisions of the APA. The commissioner's "powers are not limited to those expressly conferred by statute; 'rather, "[i]t is well settled in this state that [administrative] officials may exercise such additional powers as are necessary for the due and efficient administration of powers expressly granted by statute, or as may fairly be implied from the statute granting the powers.'"...(*Calfarm*, *supra*, 48 Cal.3d at p. 824, citations omitted.) Accordingly, Insurance Code section 1861.08 merely requires a hearing in conformity with APA adjudicatory procedures on each company's contested rate application. The procedural requirements of Proposition 103 apply to the adjudicatory hearings contemplated by the initiative, but do not apply to what *Calfarm* described as the commissioner's implied "broad discretion to adopt rules and regulations as necessary to promote the public welfare" and to "tak[e] whatever steps are necessary to reduce the job to a manageable size."

(*Ibid.*) "No provision [in Proposition 103] bars the commissioner from consolidating cases or issuing regulations of general applicability." (*Ibid.*)

The insurers also assert the adjudicatory nature of the amended decision because the hearings which led to the amended decision included the right of cross-examination, discovery and subpoena, which are normally associated with adjudicatory hearings. However, courts have long acknowledged that an agency's decision to ascertain facts in a court-like hearing does not alter the nature of a quasi- legislative proceeding. (*City of Santa Cruz v. Local Agency Formation Com.* (1978) 76 Cal.App.3d 381, 388 [142 Cal.Rptr. 873].) "'The Legislature and administrators exercising quasi-legislative powers commonly resort to the hearing procedure to uncover, at least in part, the facts necessary to arrive at a sound and fair legislative decision....Hence, the presence of certain characteristics common to the judicial process does not change the basically quasi-legislative nature of the subject proceedings.'" (Ibid.) Moreover, the agency's determination "to hold hearings, take evidence and make findings creates characteristics shared by adjudicatory proceedings but does not stamp the function with an adjudicative character." (*Rivera v. Division of Industrial Welfare, supra*, 265 Cal.App.2d at p. 587, fn. omitted.)...

Accordingly, the former commissioner's amended decision of June 15, 1990, was not adjudicatory but was quasi-legislative in nature and thus was lawfully reconsidered, rescinded and superseded by new and different regulations regarding generic ratesetting issues of general applicability....

II. *MOOTNESS*

Safeco filed an action to enjoin enforcement of the June 15, 1990, amended decision and to order "the Commissioner to set aside the findings, determinations, and rulings contained in her Amended Decision" Likewise, Allstate sought injunctive relief and a writ to require "the Commissioner to vacate and annul the Amended Decision." By validly rescinding the amended decision and superseding it with new and different regulations, the new commissioner has effectively accorded the insurers the relief they requested.

Safeco protests that "while [the insurers] originally filed their actions to challenge certain aspects of the Amended Decision, the current appeal is not for the purpose of attacking the Amended Decision, but rather to establish the current legal significance of the Amended Decision."

Nonetheless, the current legal significance of the amended decision is its quasi-legislative and regulatory nature, which leads to the conclusion that the amended decision was validly rescinded by the new commissioner and thus that Safeco administratively obtained the relief requested in the present case. We therefore find the appeal by Safeco moot based on the well-settled principle that the termination of an administrative action renders a challenge to that action moot. (*Dawson v. Town of Los Altos Hills* (1976) 16 Cal.3d 676, 687 [129 Cal.Rptr. 97, 547 P.2d 1377]; *Paul v. Milk Depots, Inc.* (1964) 62 Cal.2d 129, 132-133 [41 Cal.Rptr. 468, 396 P.2d 924].)

DISPOSITION

The appeal is dismissed as moot. Appellant insurers are to bear all costs on appeal.

Turner, P. J., and Grignon, J., concurred.

***

Hypotheticals

Veterinary Medical Board

The Veterinary Medical Board discussed a problem involving dog groomers (who are not veterinarians) who are cleaning the teeth and injuring the gums of Pekinese known to have sensitive mouths. As the discussion proceeded, the Executive Officer (EO) spoke up: "I know this is a problem, but it does not require us to adopt a rule to deal with it. All we need to do is to simply send those who are engaged in that activity a letter stating current law and noting that it is unauthorized practice." One of the Board members interjected: "I think you need to send that out as a general informative bulletin, stating that those who clean the teeth of dogs must have a veterinarian present to supervise that delicate and important task."

Would the letter proposed by the EO violate the APA? Would the "general informative bulletin" do so? Would it help if there were an existing court decision holding that teeth cleaning is the practice of veterinary medicine and that decision were simply reproduced and published by the EO?

Dental Board of California

On October 15, 2020, the Dental Board of California posted notice of a public meeting on October 25, 2020. The agenda contained a single item: "Adoption of investigation policy for online provision of orthodontic treatment." The Board posted a staff memo in the meeting materials accompanying the draft policy, explaining that it is designed to implement AB 1519, which the governor recently signed. That bill amends section 1680 of the Business and Professions Code, to require dentists and orthodontists licensed in California to review X-rays of a patient's teeth in person before providing orthodontic treatment. The proposed policy sets forth in detail the Board's internal strategy for investigating online companies to ensure compliance with the new statute.

After hearing public comments, and one hour of deliberation in public, the Board voted to adopt the policy as proposed, effective in 30 days from the date of the meeting. After the meeting, SmileDirect Club, an online orthodontic treatment company, filed a petition for regulatory determination with the OAL. What should OAL rule?

Quiz

1. Which of the following best describes the statutory requirements for initiating a petition for rulemaking pursuant to California Government Code Section 11340.6?

    a. An individual petitioning for rulemaking must establish standing before a Board may consider the petition.
    b. Any interested person may initiate a petition for rulemaking absent a statutory restriction.
    c. An individual petitioning for rulemaking need not state the reason for the request.
    d. All petitions for rulemaking must first be approved by the Governor.

2. How many days notice must an agency provide before submitting emergency regulations to OAL?

    a. 5 calendar days
    b. 10 calendar days
    c. 45 calendar days
    d. 15 working days

3. The statutory provision governing the adoption, amendment, and repeal of emergency regulations is ___________.

4. How many days is the initial effective period of an emergency regulation?

   a. 45 days
   b. 90 days
   c. 180 days
   d. There is no limit.

5. How do agencies determine when a proposed regulation is a "major regulation" triggering review by the Department of Finance?

   a. The economic impact of the regulation exceeds $50 million.
   b. The DCA Director deems the regulation to be "major."
   c. A vote of the board.
   d. None of the above.

6. How long must a board release a proposed regulation for public comment?

   a. 30 days
   b. 15 days
   c. 45 days
   d. 90 days

7. To whom can the agency appeal if the OAL disapproves its proposed rulemaking?

   a. The Legislature
   b. The Governor
   c. The California Supreme Court
   d. The U.S. Supreme Court

8. Which of these is NOT required to be posted with the notice of proposed rulemaking?

   a. Final statement of reasons
   b. Applicable section of the California Code of Regulations
   c. Hearing date
   d. Public comment deadline

9. Which of these is NOT one of the six criteria OAL must consider when reviewing proposed regulations?

   a. Comprehensibility
   b. Clarity
   c. Necessity
   d. Authority

10. What is the name of the required "plain language" document that describes proposed rulemaking?

   a. Initial statement of reasons
   b. Modified text
   c. Final statement of reasons
   d. Plain text

11. For the most part, the scope of an agency's authority to adopt regulations is derived from:

   a. Article 1 Section 1 of the California Constitution
   b. The Legislature
   c. The California Code of Regulations
   d. None of the above

12. If OAL rejects an agency's proposed rulemaking, how long does the agency have to resubmit the regulatory package to address OAL's concerns?

   a. 30 days
   b. 45 days
   c. 90 days
   d. 120 days

13. In *Grier v Kizer*, the agency argued that what principle exempted its claims auditing procedure from the APA?

   a. Modification rule
   b. Standard of general application
   c. Express statutory exemption
   d. Internal management rule

14. OAL's determination of underground rulemaking is governed by which statutory provision?

15. If an agency's standard or procedure is one of ____________, it is subject to the rulemaking procedures under the California APA.

   a. Express exemption
   b. General application
   c. Internal management
   d. None of the above

Chapter 8
Agency Quasi-Judicial Enforcement

INTRODUCTION

As discussed in the previous chapter, executive branch agencies exercise quasi-legislative powers through rulemaking. They also conduct adjudications as part of their enforcement of applicable standards. The imposition of due process is required in particular whenever an agency removes or threatens a "vested right." Once licensure has been granted, the right to practice as specified becomes such a right, and it may be removed or seriously restricted only where warranted after a quasi-judicial proceeding. To this end, the Administrative Procedure Act (APA) specifies not only rulemaking powers, but also the procedures for enforcing agency requirements; those procedures may be undertaken confidentially in some circumstances, but formal hearings and decisions are normally subject to a public process. However, certain agencies operate quasi-judicial enforcement—and d under other agency specific statutory requirements outside of the APA.

Accusations may be subject to an Interim Suspension Order (ISO) pending further litigation. Such an order may be entered by an ALJ or by a superior court judge. If a licensee has been charged with a crime in a pending matter, the Attorney General (AG) can request license suspension or restriction as a condition of bail (see Cal. Pen. Code Section 23).

APA ADJUDICATION PROCESS – Formal Hearing

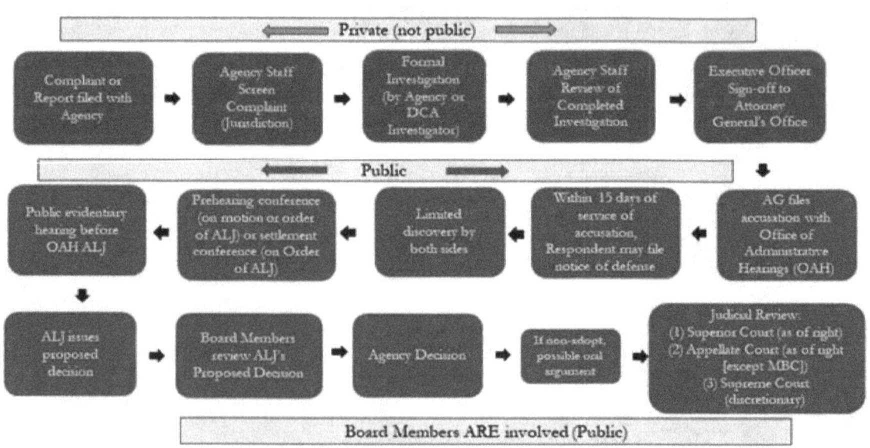

As the above figure indicates, the adjudication process under the APA generally begins with a complaint or report filed with the agency. In addition to complaints filed by individuals, various agencies have other sources of information to trigger discipline. These include mandatory reporting provisions, insurance company filings, hospital actions, and court proceedings involving a licensee (which may include malpractice judgments or settlements and criminal convictions).

The matter is then screened by assigned agency staff. If it states a colorable claim, it will be investigated by assigned agency staff (or by Department of Consumer Affairs (DCA) investigators). After completion, the agency's Executive Officer reviews it, and if approved, it goes to the Office of the Attorney General. In addition to a deputy AG being assigned to such a case, each agency also has an assigned deputy AG adviser. Those reviewing this process consistently advise that such deputy AG's enter into and direct the initial investigation. Termed "vertical enforcement," this process allows investigations to proceed in a way most likely to elicit the evidence effectively relevant to the judicial process to follow. The deputy AG then may file an "accusation" with the Office of Administrative Hearings (OAH), consisting of a group of trained Administrative Law Judges (ALJs) who perform the direct and initial adjudication. This is a very different entity than the Office of Administrative Law (OAL), discussed in Chapter 7, which reviews quasi-legislative rules.

Within 15 days of accusation service, the accused Respondent may file a notice of defense. Discovery may then occur between the parties. However, because a hearing is imminent, it is not typical to engage in or allow the kind of extensive discovery typical of civil court proceedings. Documents may be exchanged, but depositions of witnesses are normally not countenanced—unless a witness's testimony is germane and cannot be produced at the hearing to follow shortly. There then may be a prehearing conference, or a settlement conference, on the motion of parties or upon the order of the assigned ALJ. If the case is not settled, it will proceed to a public hearing. The executive officer serves as the named prosecutor for the agency, with the assigned deputy AG serving as agency counsel. The hearing often involves expert testimony, with licensees usually retaining their own counsel and with liberally allowed cross-examination. The AG bears the burden of proof. That burden is harsher than "preponderance of the evidence" in civil proceedings but is less than "beyond a reasonable doubt" applicable to criminal cases. The intermediate standard here applied is "clear and convincing evidence."

Minor violations may trigger citations, fines, letters of warning, or other mild sanctions that may be accepted by Respondents or may not trigger required hearings or other due processes.

As the chart above indicates, the ALJ prepares a written proposed decision. It must contain findings of fact, conclusions of law, and recommended discipline. Those recommendations may be based on pre-existing agency "disciplinary guidelines" specifying sanctions for enumerated offenses. The members of the agency's Board or Commission review the decision and may decide to adopt or reject it, or may schedule additional arguments before the Board, which is publicly presented. A final decision involving discipline is then subject to conventional judicial review based on the traditional "substantial evidence" test. The initial review is by a superior court (as of right), then to the state court of appeal (as of right, except for the Medical Board of California, as discussed below), and finally to the California Supreme Court by discretionary writ.

The case may also impose a "cost recovery" imposition on the Respondent to pay investigative and enforcement costs (including the AG office's attorney's fees up to the date of the hearing) (see Cal. Bus. and Prof. Code Section 125.3).

ADMINISTRATIVE PROCEDURE ACT REFORM

The following article was originally published in California Regulatory Law Reporter, Vol. 10, No. 1 (Winter 1990). Since its publication, some facets of regulations and names of agencies have changed, but most of the following analysis remains applicable.

> The way we regulate California's licensed professionals and tradespersons makes little sense. We license people—whether they are accountants, morticians, doctors, or lawyers— because we believe that such licensees who are dishonest or incompetent will cause irreparable harm. We tell people they cannot become an accountant, mortician, doctor, or lawyer unless they pass through an "entry barrier" and assure us in advance of their likely honesty and competence. We impose this "prior restraint," generally disfavored in the American model, because of the consequences of dishonesty or incompetence to the public.
>
> It is ironic that in the two areas where the potential for irreparable harm from dishonesty or incompetence is most easily acknowledged—the medical and legal professions—the initial licensing barriers to entry imposed by the state do not address it effectively. As to honesty, the screening process is of little use—very few practitioners are eliminated on this basis. Dishonesty is best dealt with by license revocation and the deterrent

punch of criminal prosecution. It is not easily predictable, and its absence cannot be reliably assured by a written examination or a criminal record check at the age of 25. As to competence, the state grants a very basic license enabling a lawyer or physician to practice in any aspect of the profession. A person may be able to pass a general bar examination in torts, contracts, and civil procedure, but know virtually nothing about bankruptcy, immigration, tax, divorce, or other area of specific practice. If a consumer goes to an attorney for a bankruptcy, tax, or other specific matter, the fact that the practitioner has passed a general bar exam at the age of 25 may be a sign of general intelligence or understanding of legal vocabulary, but it does not relate directly to competence or knowledge in the area of actual practice, upon which the consumer relies.

The same lack of nexus holds true for physician licensing. As far as the California Medical Board is concerned, a licensed physician may perform as a neurosurgeon, radiologist, proctologist, anesthesiologist, or dermatologist. Neither doctors nor lawyers are licensed or tested in their specialty.

This initial failure is baffling since each area of law or medicine is separate and distinct; persons cannot competently practice in more than one or two areas, and the skills and information required for each are quite different. Yet, as far as the state is concerned, one may practice in any or all areas. After this abdication, doctors and lawyers are not at any point retested or required to demonstrate their competence in their actual area of practice for the thirty to fifty years they practice. In addition, neither the legal nor medical regulatory systems require malpractice insurance, or otherwise provide for the assured recovery of damages from incompetence that may be suffered by consumers. In other words, although the rationale for intrusive "prior restraint" licensing of lawyers, physicians, and other professions is the prevention of irreparable harm flowing from incompetence, the applicable regulatory systems do not seriously address it.

The failure to assure honesty or competence at point of entry arguably imposes a special burden to provide that assurance through *post-licensure* discipline. Where dishonesty or incompetence occurs *post facto*, the *raison d'etre* of regulation is manifest, and decisive, quick public protection, including license revocation or restriction, is compelled.

Where there is cause to believe that licensed physicians or other professionals are dishonest or incompetent, the discipline systems work under standard procedures dictated by an Administrative Procedure Act (APA) common in most states, including California.[1] These acts are designed to afford due process by specifying procedures for administrative adjudicative hearings and for their judicial review. Unfortunately, this process has evolved into a series of confused hearings and review where unqualified people make inconsistent decisions, which are then purportedly reconciled by review in yet another series of dilatory steps. While this seven- to eleven-year minuet is danced, interim remedies to suspend, restrict, or review licenses to protect the public are non-existent or ineffectual. The obligation to assure honesty and competence implicit in a decision to license is betrayed by an impotent and irrational Rube Goldberg procedure. Let's review how it works.

Our Adjudicative System

(1) The Disciplinary Hearing. First, there is an evidentiary hearing on the agency level. The presiding officer is usually a professional administrative law judge (ALJ), either from the independent Office of Administrative Hearings within state government or one employed directly by the agency performing the administrative enforcement itself. Sometimes (but rarely) an agency head or board will decide to hear a case and judge it directly itself. When the agency does this, it will use an ALJ to make legal rulings, but the agency head or licensing board (or a committee thereof) makes the decision (findings of fact, conclusions of law, and punishment).

Where the agency itself hears the case, the panel of "judges" is usually a board, commission, or committee of appointed officials who direct the agency. Although the ALJ who rules on objections and evidence is generally a professional with a legal background, the findings of fact and the actual discipline, i.e., the adjudicatory order, will be entered by the commission, board, committee, or agency director, not by the ALJ.

(2) Agency Review. Most often, however, an ALJ working alone presides over the disciplinary hearing. The extreme part-time format of most state commissions and boards compels the use of ALJs to handle the initial hearing. However, under the APA as it exists in most states, the board, commission, or agency may then review this decision; indeed, the ALJ's opinion is merely a "proposed" decision to the agency. The agency may adopt the proposed decision, reject it, or modify it. To alter the decision, the agency may have to afford an opportunity for oral argument, but the part-time commission or board may alter it as it sees fit. In its review of the ALJ's proposed decision, the agency, board, commission, or director does not hear the evidence directly. It revises a decision based on a review of the record, written briefs, and several minutes of oral argument.

(3) Judicial Review: Superior Court. Perhaps because of a lack of confidence in the agency's adjudication, the APAs in virtually every state allow for judicial review by a superior court of agency final decisions. Any one of a large number of possible superior courts may review the hearing transcript (and may take additional evidence in unusual or extraordinary cases) and re-evaluate the entire matter on an "independent judgment" basis. That is, where a "vested right" is at issue-almost always the case in discipline matters—the court looks at the record and is required to "substitute its judgment" in interpreting and applying the facts. The court may uphold the agency decision, reject it, or remand the case to the agency for further proceedings.

(4) Judicial Review: Court of Appeal/Supreme Court. In California, the matter may then be appealed to one of six district courts of appeal. There, it will be reviewed under a "substantial evidence" test, *i.e.*, the decision of the superior court will be upheld if it is supported by substantial evidence (and includes no critical legal errors). It then may be reviewed by petition to the California Supreme Court.

This process has serious problems. First, it takes anywhere from seven to eleven years. There is little opportunity for interim suspension of an accused licensee during this entire period.[2]

These individual proceedings have their own respective deficiencies:

(1) *The Discipline Hearing.* If the hearing is conducted by an ALJ, it is usually one from a centralized Office of Administrative Hearings. These judges lack the prestige, independence, or trappings of the judiciary. They often lack expertise in the subject matter at hand. While the ALJ has knowledge of administrative law and administrative law precedents, he/she may be assigned in fragmented fashion to liquor license cases, occupational health and safety cases, water rights cases, complex discipline cases, et al., across a panoply of subject areas. ALJs from such centralized offices do not know of each others' decisions (which are generally not reported formally), and lack consistency and predictability in their decisions.

Where the administrative law judge is, however, not from a centralized ALJ office, but is a creature of the agency, we encounter the problem of the agency/prosecutor hiring, promoting, and supervising the judge. That is, the accuser and the judge are the same entity. How fair can a hearing be if the judge feels some responsibility for the decision to prosecute and is part of the prosecution team, especially when the judge also functions—as here—as the jury?

The initial hearing is the one forum where live testimony is most likely and observing the demeanor of witnesses is critical. It is where the "on-the-scene" fact finding function of the adjudicator takes place. It is here where the quality hearing should be held. Is it possible to have a defined group of persons in a given agency who have requisite judicial independence, judicial and legal skills, knowledge of precedents, and required expertise? The answer is yes, as we discuss below. But that is not what we have.

(2) *Agency Review.* Although the licensing agency *(i.e.*, the board, commission, or director) does not hear the

evidence or make the initial recommendation, it reviews a proposed opinion and is authorized to make the final decision. The review process by this part-time group of practitioners (with perhaps some public members) generally involves a partial review of the record by some members of the board (sometimes a task assigned to one member for a given case), written briefs, and oral argument often lasting five to ten minutes.[3]

In most states, the governing boards which regulate trades and professions generally consist of people who are currently practicing the very trade or profession being regulated. The bias resulting from this derivation may cut unjustly in either of two directions. The member of the profession may be so offended by the behavior of one of his/her peers that the punishment imposed may be excessive. More likely, the natural rationalizing process leads us to filter facts in sympathy with those with whom we identify. This bias will lead the colleague of the person accused into a more sympathetic frame of mind about his/her wrongdoing and its appropriate sanction.

Perhaps more important than bias is the question of the competence of these decisionmakers. As noted above, members of these boards and commissions at the state level are volunteer part-timers. They meet once a month or, in some cases, once every three months. They are not professional adjudicators; as noted above, they are usually members of the profession or trade regulated by that board. In their review function, they do not directly see the witnesses or the evidence. They make their decisions with little knowledge of agency precedent, and little knowledge of court decisions reviewing similar judgments. They themselves are not schooled in the rules of evidence. In our court system, and for a good reason, criminal sentences and civil penalties are decided not by a jury, but by a court, applying rules of law and attempting to impose a consistency which is the hallmark of an equitable judicial system, *i.e.*, people who commit similar transgressions are treated similarly.

Amazingly, the power of this commission or board to review and overturn, in a radical fashion, the ALJ who was on-the-scene and who has at least some legal training, is without the traditional limitations of an appeal; the agency has complete discretion to rewrite the ALJ's decision.[4]

One reported justification for allowing the agency board or commission this discretion rests with its purported substantive "expertise". However, this "expertise" is not necessarily on point. Most discipline cases do not involve esoteric questions of professional practice. Persons disciplined have often committed offenses such as child molestation, drug dealing, and violent acts against their patients or clients. Subtle knowledge about the optimum surgical procedure is not required to pass judgment as to the factual issues normally in dispute. However, in the occasional case where a technical matter is in dispute, the expertise of the board or commission rendering final review is very unlikely to be "on point." The fact that a physician who practices neurosurgery is on a regulatory board does not assure competent expertise on a technical question involving violation by a psychiatrist, internist, or even an orthopedic surgeon. In summary, the final administrative decision is made by a group of persons with a vested interest in the profession, and perhaps in the practices being disputed; very little knowledge of court precedent reviewing related decisions; very little knowledge of legal proceedings, including rules of evidence; and who did not observe the witnesses directly.

(3) Superior Court Review. The agency's "final decision" is then subject to a writ of mandate procedure, usually involving "independent judgment" review by one of over 1,000 superior court judges. Here we have a reconsideration by someone schooled in the law, precedent, and the rules of evidence. However, the superior court judge lacks expertise in the subject matter and familiarity with the policies of the agency. Rather than delegating review to an identified body of adjudicators who may have both substantive and legal expertise and who handle all cases emanating from a major agency, the system scatters review to any one of hundreds of superior court judges whose calendars are full of probate, criminal, and other non-administrative matters.[5]

Although it is possible for the superior court judge to hear additional (or repetitive) evidence, this is usually not the case. Rather, the superior court judge exercises his/her "independent judgment" in reviewing the transcript of the proceedings before the administrative law judge and the entire "administrative record." This means that the superior court judge is being asked to substitute his/her judgment for the judgment of the administrative law judge and, as with the agency review, without seeing the demeanor of the witnesses or directly confronting the evidence. That such a course is dangerous and antithetical to basic principles of judicial resolution should be obvious.

(4) *Court of Appeal.* Once again, perhaps because the previous series of procedures is not considered trustworthy, the respondent has the opportunity to appeal the matter yet again to any one of six different courts of appeal. Any number of three-judge panels sitting on a rotating basis in any one of these courts of appeal will receive the case and review it under a "substantial evidence" test. Because different panels in different courts of appeal sometimes disagree on the application of standards and rules of law, it is often necessary for the Supreme Court to grant a petition for review in order to reconcile them.

A Reform Proposal

The end result? The adjudicator in this five-step system—which consumes between seven and eleven years-lacks expertise, independence, or both. However, it is possible to design a system with a quality hearing and a quality review—in two steps, consuming less than eighteen months, conducted by persons who are both expert and independent. It is also possible to create a system which offers both *on point* legal and substantive expertise from a group of independent, competent adjudicators who render consistent decisions, who know each others' decisions, and who are capable of issuing interim orders while the litigation is proceeding to protect the public (*e.g.*, to suspend a license or to impose supervision or other restrictions). We have proposed such a system concerning the discipline of attorneys, who are generally not within the APA rubric. California attorneys have accepted that system, and it is now successfully operating through SB 1498 (Presley) (Chapter I 159, Statutes of

1988). We have proposed a somewhat similar system to revise the APA-governed discipline of physicians in California, through SB 2375 (Presley). Using physician discipline as an example, our model works as follows:

First, one of three designated expert ALJs appointed to a Medical Quality Panel (MQP) within the centralized Office of Administrative Hearings would preside over the disciplinary hearing. The MQP ALJs would hear all medical discipline cases. Hence, they would become expert in the subject matter, familiar with each others' decisions, and able to render a consistent and predictable outcome. Each would be knowledgeable in administrative law issues and familiar with court precedents. They would also have at least one year of education in basic medical courses—a working knowledge of pharmacological and medical terminology. Replicating this example in other fields, similar specialized panels or (where only a small number of cases is likely) an assigned judge with some expertise in an agency's specific subject matter could be created within a centralized Office of Administrative Hearings.[6]

Next, our proposal calls for the ALJs to have available to them panels of expert witnesses. These persons may be called by the ALJ himself/herself to answer questions, clarify matters, or comment on the testimony of other expert witnesses. The contribution of these expert witnesses would be "on the record" and fully subject to cross-examination by all parties.

The advantage of such an expert panel and its use by the ALJ should be obvious. Where esoteric questions are at issue, both sides usually call expert witnesses to testify. But it is sometimes difficult for a trier of fact to achieve complete understanding simply from the testimony of vigorously contending expert witnesses hired by both sides. The notion that two partisan presentations—each excluding a substantial truth which hurts their conclusion—leads directly to the revelation of optimum truth is a theory belied by human experience. However, where the adjudicator has not only knowledge of the rules of evidence, but of the basic terminology and subject matter in dispute, *and* where he/she is able to call an impartial expert witness to answer questions, a more informed decision is likely.

Our reform then provides for a "substantial evidence" judicial review by a single assigned panel of appellate court judges. The state Judicial Council (*i.e.*, the Supreme Court) would direct these cases consistently to the same group of judges. Hence, rather than having to reconcile decisions among various courts of appeal, the Supreme Court would have to intervene only if there were error in the first instance. Further, the assignment to a single panel would enhance consistency and predictability, and would lead to greater expertise by the reviewing court.

Our recent reforms enacted under SB 1498 (Presley) in California for the State Bar have created a twelve- to eighteen- month system. We removed the initial evidentiary hearing from the hands of 450 volunteer practicing attorneys and put it in the hands of full-time, independent State Bar Court Judges appointed directly by the California Supreme Court. The administrative appeal is now referred to a full- time three-judge panel also appointed by the Supreme Court. The system now produces a high-quality hearing and a high-quality review, consistency, predictability, and adjudication by people with both independence and expertise. It is a system which should be the model for APA state reform in general.

The ABA Model Under Discussion: Heading the Wrong Way

The American Bar Association's Administrative Law Section and others have been considering a number of proposals for model APA reform.[7] On at least one point, the ABA's still-pending recommendation for a model APA includes some counterproductive features. It is the position of some scholars, especially those with federal administrative law background, that ALJs should be within the control of the agency conducting the decisionmaking process, that they should make recommended decisions, and that these decisions should be reviewed by the commission or board with absolute discretion to alter—*i.e.*, the current failed model. The reason for this position taken by those in the ABA section is puzzling.

The ABA's tentative position is based on the following theory: agencies "make policy" in two ways-through rulemaking (the adoption of generic standards applicable to all licensees), and through adjudication (the formulation and application of rules on an individual, case--by-case basis). The distinction between rulemaking and adjudication is a difficult one. In fact, adjudications are often a vehicle for policy change. A very broad statute or rule which is adjudicated may establish a rule of law. Hence, to the extent that the agency controls rulemaking and performs that quasi-legislative function, it must also control the adjudicators—by controlling its ALJs and by reviewing their decisions to implement its policies.

Such a picture is interesting, but is much divorced from the reality of state administrative law. It suffers from the following defects:

(1) The first problem is a conceptual one. Would those proposing such a system agree that criminal cases should be appealed for final resolution to the judiciary committees of the state legislature (or of the U.S. Congress where federal prosecutions are involved)? Certainly, criminal prosecutions often involve interpretations of the reach and nature of the criminal statutes enacted by these legislative bodies. However, few scholars would ever seriously recommend such an alteration. This is because there is, in fact, some qualitative difference between quasi-legislative and quasi- adjudicative functions in government. It is simply *not* the job of legislators to adjudicate. They are not good at it and they are not constituted to do it. Many of the same reasons leading us to that conclusion also apply in the administrative law arena to agency commission and board members, except that the reasons here are even more pronounced, as discussed below.

(2) It is unclear why the proponents feel so strongly that the agency must be in control of these adjudications, where under the current system of judicial review, the entire matter is then transferred to a superior court judge who will exercise his/her independent judgment as an

adjudicator. The agency does not have the last word anyhow.

(3) The picture presented by the "agency-in-control-of-adjudications" theorists is marred by a factual flaw. The proponents assume that large numbers of adjudications involve serious policy questions. This is not the case at the state level. Certainly there are such adjudications, and these may properly lead to changes in legislation or rulemaking where the adjudicative results contravene legislative or regulatory intent—as is normally the case. But the vast majority of adjudications are just that: adjudications. They attempt to determine whether a standard or rule or statute, which is reasonably well defined, was violated by the respondent (accused licensee). The function of these adjudications is not to establish policy so much as it is to determine (a) what happened, and (b) the appropriate punishment. These judgments require skilled factfinding, knowledge of the rules of evidence, some expert knowledge where appropriate, and consistency and predictability in judgment.

These are critical decisions involving public protection and the livelihood of a licensee whose future is at stake. They are sobering decisions commanding serious and effective procedures. The people making them should know what they are doing. They should know how to make them, and they should have the independence to justify the confidence of the public and the accused. 'If one were to sit in on the many adjudications occurring at the state level, one would see that the issues raised and skills required are not suited to legislators, but to adjudicators in a traditional sense.

(4) The ABA also overlooks the nature of the decisionmakers on the state level. Those in the ABA Administrative Law Section who advocate agency control of adjudication are well familiar with the federal system—where the agencies, boards, or commissions are run by professional full-time persons subject to congressional oversight and high visibility.[8] At the state level, these conditions are generally not present. Instead, state agency decisionmakers are usually current members of the trade or profession being regulated. They operate

out of the visibility of media attention or public scrutiny, and they are volunteers without legal or judicial experience.

Although they may have a vested profit stake interest in the profession, they may or may not have any expertise in the subject matter of a particular adjudication. We may want (with hesitation) to vest these people with some quasi-legislative power. Part-time amateur legislatures are part of the American tradition. But when it comes to the adjudication of someone's right to practice, their possible incarceration, or the imposition of a civil or criminal fine, we turn to professional adjudicators for good reason.

There are others who object to the reforms we have proposed. Chiefly, they consist of those from the industries and trades which may be affected. These "special interests" argue for maximum "due process," the weakening of discipline and the interim remedy powers of any entity, and control of adjudications by practitioners who are politically active in the state, preferably operating at the local level in "peer review."

These persons seek a kind of "medieval guild" where the members of the profession or trade determine who is in it and how they are to be treated. These proponents have largely determined the system currently in effect. Decisions are made by persons who are colleagues or competitors of the accused—in either case, an unacceptable bias in a serious adjudication. We have a process where there is no expertise/independence combined, and where expertise—to the extent it does exist—is rarely relevant to the issues in a given adjudication. We have a system which lasts anywhere from seven to eleven years (where resisted by a respondent). We have no entity with the experience, expertise, self- confidence, or authority to issue interim suspension orders or other license restrictions to protect the public as litigation proceeds.

The end result of the current system is a fraud on the public. It is a system of purported public protection pursuant to state APAs which are actually a cartel recipe for inaction. The output of state agency discipline systems, even those regulating professions where irreparable harm is a very real danger (*e.g.*, medicine), is pathetic. In 1987 (the last year for which such figures are available), the national average of state disciplinary actions per 1,000 doctors in the United States was 2.78. California is an example of the failure of the APA process. In California during 1987–88 (the last year for which this statistic is available), 715 physicians suffered malpractice judgments or agreed to malpractice settlements in excess of $30,000. These are not merely accusations or cases filed: they are substantial judgments and/or settlements—many of them in the millions of dollars. The level is a record number, up 50% from two years before. Also in 1987–88, the hospital privileges of 249 physicians were revoked for incompetence. During that same time period, the number of physicians publicly disciplined by the Medical Board for incompetence—either by public reprimand, suspension, or revocation—amounted to 12.

Litigation of the average discipline case takes over seven years from the act giving rise to discipline to final resolution. And during this interim, the number of physicians subject to interim suspension over the last three years? Trivial. In California, that number is three-approximately one per year.

The number of complaints flowing into the physician discipline system continues to increase. After initial filtering, those with facial merit and within the jurisdiction of the Medical Board amounted to 4,800 in 1989. The number anticipated for this year [1990]? Over 6,000. One does not have to be a sophisticated mathematician or actually review the failure of the system in microcosm, as those of us at the Center have done on many occasions, to see the complete failure of the current system of detection, investigation, and APA adjudication. Nor does the minor tinkering proposed by the ABA Administrative Law Section address the issue squarely, or with the appropriate diagnosis or prescription.

The creation of a system which works is not that difficult, absent the political power of the cartels manipulating the current celebration of impotence. It is not an arrangement over which reasonable persons should be differing. The reforms needed should be supported by scholars, responsible professionals, and the public in order to fulfill the promise and purpose of the regulation of our trades and professions: the protection of the public and the discipline, restriction, or excision of those who, because of their dishonesty or incompetence, threaten irreparable harm to the consuming public.

ENDNOTES

[1] Government Code § 11500 *et seq.* Some professions, including attorneys, have generally created their own administrative procedures separate from the generic administrative procedure acts of the various states, but most of these *sui generis* systems have defects similar to those described in this commentary.

[2] In APA-governed administrative proceedings, interim suspension is normally obtained by a separate motion for temporary restraining order (TRO) or preliminary injunction to one of a large number of superior court judges rotating through the law and motion departments of the superior courts of our counties. These judges have heavy caseloads, know little about the trade or profession, and receive few cases involving interim suspension of an occupational license in general. They are extremely hesitant to interim suspend or to otherwise limit practice for public protection, and years of lack of success have led to abandonment of the attempt. For example, the California Medical Board obtains approximately one interim suspension order each year against a practicing physician.

[3] During argument, board or commission members frequently ask questions inappropriate for a legal argument—including factual questions which are often answered on a hearsay basis by counsel who are not under oath.

[4] A normal appeal consists of written briefs and oral argument to a reviewing court, which decides whether there are "errors of law" or whether there is "substantial evidence" to support findings. However, the agency review of an ALJ's decision is without limitations. The ALJ's decision is only "proposed" to the agency, and it may change it even if there is substantial evidence in support of the ALJ's findings and no errors of law. A change may require opportunity (albeit brief) for written and oral argument, but the agency's director, board, or commission may and often does alter these decisions without directly hearing the evidence.

[5] As noted in note 2, *supra*, this large group of undifferentiated superior court adjudicators is also relied upon for interim suspension decisions.

[6] This option is superior to the assignment of these cases

to ALJs with-in the control of the agency itself. There is no reason why an independent Office of Administrative Hearings cannot assign panels or individual judges to hear all of the cases in a particular subject area for consistency and expertise purposes. The outcome for such an arrangement combines both independence and expertise.

[7] *See, e.g.*, Asimow, *Updating California Administrative Law. California Regulatory Law Reporter* Vol. 9, No. 3 (Summer 1989) at 1.

[8] Note that federal agency adjudications also involve more policy-laden issues. A stark example is the Federal Trade Commission, where cease and desist orders (adjudications) and trade regulation rules interplay in defining a very broad statute prohibiting "unfair" business practices (section 5 of the Federal Trade Commission Act). In general, state adjudications take place in a substantially more defined legal setting, where the rule or policy is not seriously in dispute or altered by the process.

End of Article

Excerpts From Final Report of the Former State Bar Discipline Monitor

by Robert C. Fellmeth

EDITOR'S NOTE: In 1986, the California legislature passed SB 1543 (Presley), establishing the post of State Bar Discipline Monitor in Business and Professions Code section 6086.9. The Monitor was delegated the investigative powers of the Attorney General; charged with analyzing the State Bar's system of receiving, investigating, prosecuting, and adjudicating complaints against licensed attorneys; and directed to make recommendations for legislative and administrative changes to improve the Bar's discipline system.

In January 1987, Professor Robert C. Fellmeth, Director of the Center for Public Interest Law, was appointed to the position. During his tenure as Bar Monitor, Professor Fellmeth published an Initial Report in June 1987 and eight subsequent progress reports; helped to draft SB 1498 (Presley) (Chapter 1159, Statutes of 1988), which made substantial structural changes to the Bar's discipline system; and oversaw the Bar's implementation of hundreds of changes mandated by statute, suggested by the Monitor, or initiated by the Bar itself. Pursuant to Business and Professions Code section 6140.8, the

Monitor published his Final Report on September 20, 1991. The following is an excerpt from that 143-page report, which necessarily excludes detailed descriptions and statistical tables and exhibits.

In 2022, Professor Fellmeth provided to the State Bar, at its request, a critique of its discipline system. That critique included a number of the same criticisms and reform proposals extant in the 1991 report excerpted below.

***

III. THE DISCIPLINE SETTING: RECOMMENDATIONS CONCERNING COMPETENCE AND HONESTY ASSURANCE

The above description of the State Bar's evolution from 1987 to the present focuses on the reforms accepted and implemented by the Bar, and presents indices showing their impact. That discussion is not intended to be a testimonial; however, candor compels that the remarkable changes accomplished be catalogued and acknowledged. Having noted overall progress, an important caveat is in order. One of the factors accentuating Bar improvement is the degree of inadequacy of the Bar's discipline system in January 1987. Hence, progress to a much better system—which has occurred—does not mean that the Bar has created a perfect or model system. The State Bar has not yet created a final system which is ideal.

The final test of a properly functioning discipline system is its empirical impact on the profession. Certainly, the enhanced discipline of the most visibly errant attorneys is important. More are being removed from the profession more quickly than ever before. But the fact remains that the legal profession remains disturbingly deficient in the two areas most critical to regulatory purpose: the personal dishonesty and incompetence of large numbers of licensees—large numbers.

The State Bar has failed to accomplish one of the two reasons justifying a regulatory system involving "prior restraint" licensing: It has not acted in any reasonable way to *assure competence*. It does not license in the actual area of attorney practice. It does not limit any attorney from practicing immigration law, patent law, bankruptcy law, family law, antitrust law, and criminal defense, or all of them, as counsel sees fit. It administers a single general knowledge and skills examination once at the beginning of an attorney's career. It requires minimal standards of the schools whose degrees make persons eligible for this single examination. It requires no evidence of actual competence, does not limit scope of practice, and does not require retesting—not once or in any area—over the entire thirty- to fifty-year career of a licensee. Ironically, the major purpose of prior restraint licensing is to prevent irreparable harm to consumers which flows from incompetent practice. And consumers do indeed rely on the license of the state in entrusting their affairs to counsel. Except for a new continuing legal education program, which does not assure competence by itself, the State Bar has abjectly failed to address this issue in an effective manner.

In addition to its failure to meaningfully address incompetence by way of licensure barriers to entry or by post-entry requirements, the Bar has not seriously disciplined incompetence, nor has it removed the incompetent from the profession except in the extreme cases of disability or client abandonment. Moreover, it has failed to require malpractice insurance of its licensees, and has limited its own Client Security Fund to reimbursing clients victimized by the dishonest acts of attorneys, precluding recovery from it for even gross incompetence. As discussed below, the measures undertaken by the Bar over the past four years to address the incompetence problem have been well- intentioned, but are grossly inadequate to accomplish a substantial result.

The failure of the Bar to establish overall standards of personal honesty is similarly stark. The prevalence of dishonesty among attorneys in their everyday behavior—particularly in civil practice billing, promises to clients, representations to the court, even in their points and authorities routinely submitted—is rightfully a source of profound embarrassment to many in the profession.

The requirement that attorney fee agreements be in writing, an ethics hotline, some fee arbitration reforms, the introduction of public members to some local bar panels, a substantial increase in informal discipline (particularly letters of warning), and the advent of pattern detection are all positive steps toward encouraging honesty. They are perhaps more significant than efforts in the area of competence. But the problem remains, as discussed below. We are less certain here of viable solutions. However, it may well rest in the education of law students and of attorneys, the revision of the Rules of Professional Conduct, the further reform of billing practices, and in the basic revision of the extreme "adversary"—all is fair—ethic, particularly in civil proceedings. This last problem has created a kind of amoral atmosphere which permeates and poisons much of the profession—without reliably producing the "truth from conflict" which is its raison d'etre.

We have some doubt that these kinds of reforms can be accomplished given the regrettable structure of Bar governance; that is, a system where the state agency regulating the profession in the interests of the larger body politic consists largely of members of the profession selected by the profession. Political reality makes it difficult for the Bar's governors or its electorate (here, attorneys electing the Board of Governors) to burden themselves substantially for the benefit of a larger population or purpose. That some such changes have happened in discipline, and in the institution of some continuing education requirements, is heartening. But taking a few loosely specified classes (which often assume over time the characteristics of professional tax-deductible tourism opportunities), and raising dues by over $100 per year to strengthen a discipline system (which will rarely apply to the more ethical and conscientious members of the profession sitting as its governors) does not exhaust the burdens required of the profession to truly as- sure competence and honesty. The State Bar of California is a long way from assuring acceptable attorneys for the public, particularly in terms of everyday personal honesty (short of financial theft) and competence. Here, the system remains only marginally effective. Here, it is not yet a model. Many of the measures needed to address these problems do not rest within the jurisdiction of the discipline system itself—but they burden that system, and undermine its purpose.

A. Competence

Pursuant to SB 905 (Davis), beginning in 1992 attorneys must complete 36 units of minimum continuing legal education (MCLE) every three years. The requirement is welcome and is justified for at least three reasons: first, the number of sole practitioners or small offices staffed by young or inexperienced attorneys is large and growing larger. Second, as noted above the Bar's discipline system attacks the incompetence problem *post facto* and at the extremes, focusing its resources on the obvious high-priority need to address dishonest conduct rather than incompetence. Third, the Bar's Client Security Fund only recompenses for dishonest attorney conduct, not for incompetence—even gross incompetence. The possibility of civil recompense is limited by the Bar's failure to require legal malpractice insurance. A disproportionately high percentage of small law offices lack such insurance and account for a disproportionately high source of complaints to the Bar's discipline system.

As noted above, the Bar has done little to assure competence in the past. It administers a generalized Bar exam. It does not require demonstration of competence in the specific area of practice engaged in by a licensee. A licensee may practice criminal law, bankruptcy law, antitrust law, tax law, probate law, and immigration law simultaneously without check by the Bar. Until 1992 no continuing education is required whatever, despite the uniquely fast changing world of law. There are no retesting requirements.

The Bar has been studying these problems, both on its own and pursuant to statutory command. A consortium on competence including private practitioners, law professors, legal secretaries, and consultants has issued a report studded with recommendations to enhance the competence of attorneys; many of the consortium's recommendations focus on areas highly relevant to the current discipline workload. A Standing Committee on Competence was formed in 1990.

We do not comment here on the individual proposals of the consortium retesting requirements, or other options. The suggestions made vary from those likely to have marginal impact on discipline to those promising a measurable ameliorating impact. Taken as a whole we believe the training, pre-admission practice, continuing legal education, peer review panels, two-year residency malpractice insurance, and other recommendations included in the pending proposals are likely to assist the discipline system in the most cost- effective manner, by preventing much of the behavior now complained about. Not only does such prevention lighten the load on discipline; it affects the many cases where abuses occur but are not reported to the Bar.

B. Honesty

The Bar must begin to search for ways to deter attorney deceit, particularly in the practice of civil law. The level of attorney dishonesty in representations to the court, in promises to clients, in dealings with adverse counsel, and perhaps especially in points and authorities and legal briefs, is embarrassing to anyone with a measure of intellectual pride. Regrettably, the large city practice, where an attorney's previous abuses do not become widely known so that his or her statements are then discounted based on reputation, means that misleading behavior is not deterred by the courts adequately, and can even be rewarded by the system.

Part of the problem has to do with the lack of certain sanctions for deceit. And part of it has to do with an adversary system which has gone awry. In the criminal case context the adversary system is more likely to work well since one of the two adversaries—the prosecutor—isn't really an adversary, but a public official whose primary obligation is the truth and the fair application of justice. On the civil side, the ethic has been distorted to justify deceit on a grand and institutionalized scale. It has reached the stage where any trier of act is going to have difficulty in ferreting out the truth from two persons each bound and determined to mislead as much as possible.

What is needed are some bounds, some clear and defined limits. The Bar should consider examining with special care and with a fresh eye some of the underlying ground rules of civil representation. It is possible to develop new rules of behavior supervening adversary representation, and restoring a measure of honor to a profession which is in a current state of well-deserved dishonor.

C. Malpractice Insurance

Mandatory malpractice insurance is one issue relevant to competence where the Bar should consider action. The consequences of the Bar's failure to require such insurance are serious and embarrassing, especially in light of the avoidance of competence-related cases by the discipline system and the exclusion of negligence as a basis for recovery from the Client Security Fund.

Over 25% of practicing attorneys currently practice "naked," or without coverage. This percentage has been increasing over the past decade. Moreover, the group avoiding coverage is disproportionately subject to discipline, and is without question disproportionately committing malpractice. Sole practitioners and marginal attorneys are overrepresented in both groups. Their clients are disproportionately middle class and poor.

We have interviewed legal malpractice specialists and are convinced that the problem causes clear and present harm to those whom the Bar's statutory charter requires it to protect. Malpractice attorneys generally will not file an action without insurance coverage on the defendant. Marginal practitioners without coverage can and do cause irreparable harm to consumers. Since the Bar fails to license by actual practice specialty, discipline the incompetent, provide financial redress for incompetence, or require any retesting following initial Bar exam passage, the least it can do is to require malpractice insurance so that existing private remedies will allow consumers to collect on their meritorious judgments.

One argument against such a requirement is the concern that some practitioners may not be able to obtain insurance. We believe that there has been an increase in the number of carriers providing coverage, somewhat ameliorating this problem. However, the insurance industry has at times historically allocated territories or otherwise left certain markets in a highly concentrated format.

The Bar attempted to impose such a requirement several years ago and was presented with regrettable political opposition. We are not certain whether the same interests would oppose such a system under present circumstances but we don't believe they should be allowed to prevent a needed requirement for the protection of the public.

The Bar is now involved in overseeing and developing a "State Bar approved professional liability insurance program." One goal is to assure a stable provider of such services should existing carriers suddenly leave the California market, as has been the case in the past. This effort does not address the underlying problem facing victims of legal malpractice.

We would recommend that the Bar create an insurance pool analogous to the California Automobile Assigned Risk Plan (CAARP) for auto insurance. Where an applicant is refused insurance by two carriers, or certifies that no carrier is offering insurance in his or her geographic or subject area, the pooled program would provide it as an alternative. Rates would be actuarially responsible. With such an alternative, the Bar could sponsor appropriate legislation to require malpractice coverage at a minimum level.

IV. CONCLUSION

We have acknowledged the significant empirical improvement in the Bar's disciplinary performance, and noted some areas in which the Bar's system excels. Moving beyond the statistics, however, we offer the unsettling experience of listening to the hotline operation of the State Bar's toll-free complaint number. For two days (July 11 and 12, 1991), the Bar Monitor personally listened to the intake system, primarily to survey the efficacy of the complaint analysts. That is, we were able to listen to conversations between callers and Bar intake personnel without either knowing of the monitoring. Compensating for a number of factors—including the large number of attorneys currently practicing, the contentious nature of legal disputes, possible unrealistic expectations of litigants, and the fact that the caller is simply presenting one side of what may be a much more complicated factual situation—the experience was nevertheless deeply troubling. It is one highly recommended for the "defenders of the profession" who deny serious and endemic abuses practiced upon the public by the legal profession. The sheer force of call after call after call after call is momentous. The vast majority of the callers did not project anger, hatred, or irrational expectations. In both tone and content, the callers, in general, conveyed befuddlement, disappointment, simple curiosity. They want to know why the attorney they called took a $5,000 retainer and has done nothing, has not called them, has not sent them any documents, and won't return their phone calls. They want to know if an attorney can agree to handle a matter for $20,000 and get a trust deed on their home to secure the amount, and then without discussion or warning bill for $40,000. They want to know if there is anything they can do when an attorney has promised to file a case, but has let the statute of limitations pass and has now told them they did not have that good a case anyway—after the matter has been involuntarily dismissed and without prior discussion. The tone of most of these many, many calls is not "I'm outraged, off with his head." It is "Hey, is this normal? And what do I do now?"

The first call: "My daughter went to a local nightclub and one of the employees injured her. It may have been an accident, but she has some serious bills. I went to Attorney Jones who has an office in the neighborhood and he told me I had no case, so I forgot about it. Yesterday I found out that this attorney is part owner of the night club. Isn't he supposed to tell me that before he tells me I have no case?"

Next call: "I had a family law problem and saw Attorney Johnson. She said it would cost $5,000. I paid. Some clerk--type person filled out some forms and now they've billed me for another $9,000. I only talked to the attorney twice and we never went to court and she never told me it would cost more than $5,000. This bill has some very strange entries on it. Can attorneys just bill you like that? She seems to thinks she's on my checking account with me, with one problem—she doesn't know my balance."

Next call: "I gave Attorney Smith $1,000 to file bankruptcy for me. It was really the last money I had. I want to pay my creditors, but I need more time, and this attorney said this was what I had to do, so I gave him the money. But I haven't heard anything from him since." "How long has it been?" "Eight months, and I've called over fifteen times, but he never will take my calls. He hasn't filed anything and now I'm getting my furniture repossessed. They took my car yesterday. What should I do? Can you recommend another attorney? Can I do something myself? What should I do?"

The number of calls of this type to the Bar is simply overwhelming. They represent a large proportion of about 75,000 calls to the Bar each year—two for every three attorneys in the state annually; one coming in every 80 seconds every business day. Switching from line to line for ten to twelve hours and listening to calm recitation after calm recitation of these alleged practices, whether all meritorious or not, elicits in any listener a sense of profound sadness.

The State Bar must understand that the disrepute of what should be a proud profession is not the product of media bias, and is not curable through public relations campaigns—such as the Bar periodically suggests. We believe that it is the cumulative impact of thousands upon thousands of these experiences, endured and then shared by word of mouth. This kind of problem is addressable only by a profound change in the way attorneys are educated, trained (the two are perhaps somewhat different), selected, monitored, and disciplined.

The State Bar, despite its acknowledged progress and new sensitivity, has yet to face up to the magnitude of its problem.

End of Excerpt

Another major regulatory agency with crucial adjudication authority is the Medical Board, responsible for ensuring competent physicians. The following testimony from CPPC outlines the current status of that process. It is a part of the sunset process that systematically reviews an agency's performance. As outlined above, a failure to win continuation results in the removal of those currently governing the agency.

March 3, 2021

Honorable Richard D. Roth, Chair and Members,
Senate Business, Professions, and Economic Development Committee
State Capitol, Room 2053
Sacramento, CA 95814

Honorable Evan Low, Chair, and Members
Assembly Business and Professions Committee
Legislative Office Building, Room 379
Sacramento, CA 95814

Re: Joint Sunset Oversight Hearing, Medical Board of California

Dear Senator Roth, Assemblymember Low, and Members of the Committees:

The Center for Public Interest Law (CPIL) respectfully submits the following testimony relevant to the Committees' sunset review of the Medical Board of California (MBC). As public comments and remarks from members of the Senate Rules Committee recently made clear at its February 3, 2021 hearing on the confirmation of three licensee members of MBC, **public trust in the Board's ability to protect patients is extremely low**. To that end, CPIL proposes retention of the Board but makes the following major recommendations (which are explained more fully below):

1) **Establish a Public Member Majority on the Board:** Add two public members to the composition of the Board—one from each house of the Legislature—to ensure public protection remains the highest priority of the Board.
2) **Appoint an Enforcement Monitor:** As the Board itself recognizes in its Sunset Report, investigation and case processing times are simply unacceptable for public protection. The Committees need not look further than the Board's February 21, 2021 accusation of Santa Clara County's former chief pediatrician for children in foster care, Patrick Steven Clyne, **filed 20 years after allegations surfaced that he had sexually abused foster youth living in his home**, to be convinced that a thorough investigation of the Board's enforcement process is imperative.
3) **Create an Ombuds Office:** An independent Ombudsperson to facilitate the complaint process and improve dialogue with patient advocates would improve public trust and improve internal efficiencies at the Board.
4) **Increase Licensing Fees:** A robust enforcement program is impossible with starved resources. This is a must.

Center for Public Interest Law
5998 Alcalá Park, San Diego, CA 92110-2492
P: (619) 260-4806 | F: (619) 260-4753 | www.cpil.org

About the Center for Public Interest Law

CPIL is a nonprofit, nonpartisan academic and advocacy organization based at the University of San Diego School of Law. For over 40 years, CPIL has studied occupational licensing and monitored California agencies that regulate business, professions, and trades, including the Medical Board and other Department of Consumer Affairs (DCA) health care boards. CPIL has focused heavily on MBC since 1989 when it published *Physician Discipline in California: A Code Blue Emergency* ("*Code Blue*"), a 100-page report based on three years of research which revealed the minimal output, fragmented structure, and questionable priorities of the Medical Board's enforcement program. Based on that report, the Legislature passed at least five MBC enforcement program reform bills between 1990 and 2000.[1] After continuing reports of problems at MBC's enforcement program were published in 2002, the Legislature passed SB 1950 (Figueroa) in 2002, which required the DCA Director to appoint a "Medical Board Enforcement Monitor." After a competitive bidding process, the Director appointed CPIL's then Administrative Director, Julianne D'Angelo Fellmeth, to that position in October 2003. Over a two-year period, she directed an in-depth investigation and review of MBC's enforcement and diversion programs, culminating in two reports containing 65 concrete recommendations for reform.[2] At least five pieces of reform legislation (SB 231 in 2005; SB 1438 in 2006; AB 1127 in 2011; SB 304 in 2013; AB 1886 in 2014) have been enacted in response to these reports, mirroring many of the recommendations.

Increase Public Member Representation on the Board

CPIL wholeheartedly supports the suggestion that Senate President pro Tempore Toni Atkins made at the conclusion of the February 3, 2021 Rules Committee hearing that **two public members should be added to the Board** to give the public—and not physicians—the majority of the Board. This is a recommendation for which we have been advocating for decades—particularly following the U. S. Supreme Court's decision in *North Carolina State Board of Dental Examiners v. Federal Trade Commission*, 574 U.S.494 (2015). This holding included the bold general rule that where a regulatory board is controlled by active market participants in the occupation the board regulates, it lacks state sovereignty and thus is subject to federal antitrust liability unless the state can show that it is actively supervising these boards. Currently, California exercises no such supervision according to the standards set forth by the Court. In fact, CPIL sponsored legislation to provide that review for all such vulnerable state agencies in SB 1195(Hill) in 2016, but it was defeated after vigorous trade association lobbying. Thus, as it stands, boards with a majority of licensee members, like MBC, are at significant risk of exposure to an antitrust lawsuit and the treble damages that would result. Changing the Board's composition to a public member majority is not only the right thing to do for public protection, but it will decrease the Board's risk of exposure to lawsuits.

---

[1] SB 2375 (Presley) (Chapter 1597, Statutes of 1990); SB 916 (Presley) (Chapter 1267, Statutes of 1993); SB 609 (Rosenthal) (Chapter 708, Statutes of 1995); AB 103 (Figueroa) (Chapter 359, Statutes of 1997); SB 16 (Figueroa) (Chapter 614, Statutes of 2000).

[2] Julianne D'Angelo Fellmeth and Thomas A. Papageorge, *Initial Report of the Medical Board Enforcement Monitor* (November 1, 2004) (hereinafter "*Initial Report*"); Julianne D'Angelo Fellmeth and Thomas A. Papageorge, *Final Report of the Medical Board Enforcement Monitor* (November 1, 2005).

For the same reasons, the current public member vacancies on the Board are troubling. At this writing, there are three public member vacancies on the Board—two to be appointed by the Governor and one by the Speaker of the Assembly. The public is woefully underrepresented on MBC, and its current supermajority of physician members increases the potential for anticompetitive decisionmaking.

Appoint an Enforcement Monitor to Assess the Existing Program and Recommend Improvements for Public Protection

As mentioned above, in 2002, after continuing reports of problems at MBC's enforcement program, the Legislature passed SB 1950 (Figueroa), which required the DCA Director to appoint a "Medical Board Enforcement Monitor," a position ultimately filled by CPIL's then Administrative Director, Julie Fellmeth. Notably, a May 2002 committee analysis of the bill described the circumstances which ultimately resulted in the appointment of the Enforcement Monitor, "[It is] apparent . . . that public confidence in the Board's enforcement program and the transparency of its public disclosure policies is thin and, if possible, getting thinner; on the verge of evolving into a 'crisis.' For physicians and patients it makes sense to have a vigorous, trusted regulatory program in place that prevents as many patients as possible from being damaged in the first place." These same concerns exist today.

Just last week, the San Jose Mercury News reported[3] that MBC filed an accusation seeking to revoke Santa Clara County's former chief pediatrician's medical license for children in foster care, Dr. Patrick Clyne. Shockingly, the report details **20 years of reports of abuse before the Board filed the accusation,** specifically, that Clyne had been accused of sexual abuse for decades by Santa Clara County social workers, parents, guardians, therapists, a juvenile probation officer, and staff at two residential group homes based on the accounts of 13 children; had been the subject of a civil lawsuit filed on behalf of a former foster youth who alleged that Clyne had sexually abused him when he was eight years old and living in Clyne's home; was removed from his position as chief pediatrician for the foster care system by Santa Clara County in 2011 after the Santa Clara County District Attorney's Office found substantial evidence that Dr. Clyne committed multiple crimes of moral turpitude, specifically sexual assaults; was barred by the California Department of Social Services in 2013 from ever becoming a foster parent again, and prohibited him from working with any children or adults in state-licensed facilities. In a testament to this incredibly broken system, a license search for Clyne on the Board's BreEZe database lists his license as "Renewed and Current," although it does show that an accusation has been filed. None of the above troubling past would be known to the parents of any of his patients. **This means he will continue to practice—where he serves low-income clients in a rural, immigrant community south of Santa Cruz—likely for years before his case is resolved.**

While it is unclear at this point (to the public anyway) why it took the Board so long to file an accusation against Dr. Clyne, what is clear is that this case alone exemplifies the dire need to quickly identify and remedy the breakdowns in the system that allowed—and continues to allow—Dr. Clyne to prey on the most vulnerable of our society.

---

[3] *See* Karen De Sá, *After decades of sex abuse claims, state moves to stop former Santa Clara chief pediatrician from practicing medicine*, San Jose Mercury News, February 23, 2021.

Regardless of whether the Committees determine that an Enforcement Monitor is warranted at this time, the following pressing issues with respect to the Board's enforcement program must be expeditiously addressed during this Sunset Review process:

- ***Inefficient Investigations and Lack of Collaboration with Prosecutors***: As the Board mentioned in its Sunset Report, and as some members of these Committees may recall, the Board's Vertical Enforcement program[4] was repealed at MBC's request in 2019. A central recommendation of the Enforcement Monitor's Initial Report in 2004, Vertical Enforcement (also known as "VE" or Vertical Prosecution), required MBC and the Health Quality Enforcement (HQE) unit of the Attorney General's Office to utilize VE in investigating and prosecuting MBC disciplinary matters, and—in order to fully and efficiently implement VE—transfer MBC's investigators into HQE where the prosecutors who specialize in physician discipline matters are located. The Enforcement Monitor cited a number of benefits that would likely result from the use of VE and the transfer, including (1) improved efficiency and effectiveness arising from better communication and coordination of efforts—including more efficient recognition of cases deserving interim suspension order (ISO) treatment due to the early involvement of the prosecutor, (2) reduced case cycle times—including decreased time to procure needed medical records due to the earlier involvement of the prosecutor, (3) the earlier closure of investigations where the Board will not be able to sustain its burden of proof, (4) improved commitment to cases by both investigator and prosecutor, (5) improved morale, recruitment and retention of investigators, (6) improved training for investigators and prosecutors, and (7) the potential for improved perception of the fairness of the process (in that the investigators would no longer be subject to actual or perceived pressures or undue influence by the physician-dominated Medical Board).[5]

  While the Legislature did accept the recommendation to institute VE at the Board, it did not transfer the investigators to the AG's office. Thus, the program was never implemented as intended, and the structural and geographical separation of investigators from prosecutors created a host of problems throughout the program's tenure. To complicate matters, the Legislature—effective July 1, 2014—transferred MBC's investigators not to the Attorney General's Office as suggested by the Monitor, but to the Department of Consumer Affairs, thus introducing a third party into the already fraught relationship between MBC and HQE. This transfer caused investigator attrition and investigative case cycle times to skyrocket immediately. Ultimately, these problems led to the sunset of the program and the return to the "hand-off" model of investigation, in which investigators at the Department of Consumer Affairs' Health Quality Investigations Unit (HQIU) investigate the complaints on their own, and then "hand-off" the investigations to the Attorney General's Office.[6] We are only now

---

[4] Gov't Code § 12529.6 (enacted in 2006).

[5] *Initial Report* at Chapter VII, pages 138–40. Note that complex white collar crime cases, including civil unfair competition matters in the offices of the district attorney throughout California, are routinely investigated by investigators supervised by deputy district attorneys. These are not simple cases that can be investigated and then "handed off" to a prosecutor previously uninvolved in the matter. Issues including the elements of the offense, what evidence is needed to prove those elements, and how such evidence can be obtained and organized for effective and admissible presentation require early attorney involvement.

[6] For a complete history of the implementation and eventual sunset of VE, *see* the following issues of the *California Regulatory Law Reporter*, available at https://digital.sandiego.edu/crlr/: Volume 23, Issue 1 (Fall 2017) at 37–40; Volume 23, Issue 2 (Spring 2018) at 46–47; Volume 24, Issue 2 (Spring 2019) at 44–45.

seeing the impact of this sunset, and the numbers are not good. The investigation times and overall case processing times are at unacceptable levels. The Board itself recognized that it did not realize the cost savings or reduction in investigation times that it anticipated after the program's sunset.

At the Board's February 2021 meeting, it held a lengthy discussion with a representative from the Attorney General's office representing HQE. The Board members expressed concern as to the increasing number of days it was taking the AG's office to file a case. The AG's office reported that a contributing factor is the sunset of VE. Alarmingly, the AG's office reported that HQE returned 77 cases to the Board for further investigation in FY 19/20—**11 times the number returned in FY 16/17** before VE was sunset. Not only that, but the Board's Sunset Report reveals that investigation cycle times increased by two months since the sunset of VE. Delayed investigations—including investigations of egregious matters—delay the filing of accusations against physicians, which filing makes the matter public so patients can protect themselves from potentially dangerous doctors. Obviously, this is a multi-pronged problem that has severe public safety impacts.

In light of the significant public protection implications of the current state of the Enforcement Program, the Board's recommendation for "improved communication" with HQIU set forth in New Issue #3 of its Sunset Report is dangerously insufficient.

CPIL again reiterates its recommendation that the **investigators should move to the Attorney General's Office as originally proposed** so that all of the team members (prosecutors and investigators) can work together as expeditiously as possible to maintain consumer protection. At a minimum, the Legislature should consider reverting to the system in which the investigators are employed by the Board, and the Attorney General assigns a Deputy in District Office (DIDO) to work in each MBC field office to provide legal assistance and guidance to investigators.[7]

- *Inadequate Compliance with Mandated Reporting:* The Board's Sunset Report recognizes some troubling instances. It does not believe it is receiving critically important mandated reports set forth in sections 800, *et seq* of the Business and Professions Code. For example, MBC reported it only received one report from a coroner in FY 19/20 pursuant to section 802.5, which requires coroners to report to the Board if the cause of death may be the result of a physician's gross negligence.[8] It also rightly suspects that entities are not submitting reports pursuant to section 805.01, which requires peer review bodies to report certain actions being taken against a licensee after an investigation if the conduct relates to incompetence or gross or repeated deviation from the standard of care involving death or serious bodily injury, the use of controlled substances, repeated acts of excessive prescribing, or sexual misconduct. These are the most serious forms of misconduct, and yet the Board has never received more than 18 reports in a single year according to its Annual Reports; in fact, in four out of the six years since the statute was enacted, the Board received less than ten reports pursuant to 805.01. And even with respect to the reports MBC does receive, there is no mechanism in place that

[7] *See Initial Report*, Chapter VII.

[8] *See* MBC Sunset Review Report at p. 99.

will allow the Board to proactively audit and ensure that it is actually receiving these statutorily-mandated reports.[9]

The Enforcement Monitor found the reporting of adverse peer review events pursuant to section 805 to be the single highest source of information for the Board with respect to the detection of unethical and dangerous physicians. Yet it has no mechanism in place to ensure adequate reporting, nor does it appear to be utilizing this powerful tool to its full potential.[10] Indeed, in a recent Public Records Act request to the Board, CPIL requested all documents evidencing discipline issued for failure to file reports pursuant to sections 805 *et seq.*, and received only a list of four physicians and two hospitals for the entirety of the requested five year period.

In addition, the Clyne case raises questions as to whether enhanced reporting and communication needs to take place between county officials and the Board when such rampant complaints about a physician's sexual misconduct are being raised.

- *Subversion of Business and Professions Code § 2220.7 by physicians and their lawyers*: In the past 15 years, CPIL has spearheaded an effort to ban the insertion of so-called "regulatory gag clauses" into civil settlement agreements by licensees of state regulatory boards. These clauses generally prohibit a regulated defendant in a malpractice/ negligence action who agrees to pay a monetary settlement from requiring the plaintiff to agree to: (1) not complain to the defendant's licensing board, (2) withdraw any previously-filed complaint to the licensing board, and/or (3) refuse to cooperate in any investigation initiated by the licensing board. Essentially, these clauses allow an unscrupulous licensee to conceal from that licensee's own regulator information about misconduct committed by the licensee.

  In 2006, the Medical Board included a provision in an omnibus licensing bill that prohibits doctors from including a regulatory gag clause in a civil settlement agreement; Governor Schwarzenegger signed that bill, that language is now in Business and Professions Code section 2220.7.[11] In 2012, then-Assemblymember Jerry Hill successfully carried AB 2570 (Hill), which expands section 2220.7's prohibition to all licensees of all DCA boards and bureaus (*see* Business and Professions Code section 143.5). [12]

---

[9] *See, e.g., id.* at p. 100 ("Board relies on outreach" to assure it receives reports from clerks of courts pursuant to section 803, 803.5, 803.6 involving licensee felony convictions or judgments in which licensee is responsible for death or personal injuries); p. 101 (Board reports that new forms were created and placed on its website with respect to required reporting by health care facilities if any written allegation of sexual abuse or sexual misconduct is made against a licensee pursuant to section 805.8, but does not disclose whether it has *received* any such reports since the law's effective date on 1/1/2020, or how it intends to track them); p. 101 ("Adverse events appear to be reported as required" pursuant to section 2216.3, which requires accredited Outpatient Surgery Settings to report adverse events to the Board within five days of the incident, but Board does not report how it can verify this information; similarly, the Board states that licensees must report deaths that occur outside the hospital setting to the Board, but does not indicate whether or not it receives these reports).

[10] *See Initial Report* at 111–112.

[11] Our first two efforts—AB 320 (Correa) (2004) and AB 446 (Negrete McLeod) (2005)—were vetoed by Governor Schwarzenegger.

[12] This legislation continues longstanding legal precedent and policy established by the Legislature in Business and Professions Code section 6090.5 (a 35-year-old statute prohibiting lawyers who are defendants in legal malpractice

CPIL is aware that—despite sections 143.5 and 2220.7 and the considerable caselaw that preceded them—defendants in civil malpractice/ negligence actions are inserting vague confidentiality clauses in civil settlement agreements. **These clauses can be interpreted by plaintiffs as regulatory gag clauses masquerading as confidentiality agreements, causing them to hesitate to report misconduct to regulatory boards.** Even worse, the vague confidentiality clauses are often accompanied by oral assertions and threats asserting that plaintiffs cannot report the misconduct to the regulatory boards, but which cannot be proven and/or are made in the context of mediation and are thus privileged.

CPIL knows of only one case in which the Medical Board has enforced section 2220.7; in 2009, it imposed a public letter of reprimand on a physician for including a vague confidentiality clause in a civil settlement agreement (details available upon request). The clause read as follows: "To preserve the confidentiality of the terms and conditions of this settlement, including the settlement amount, **the Parties agree that neither they nor their attorney nor representative shall reveal to anyone, other than may be mutually agreed to in writing, any of the terms of this Settlement Agreement,** the allegations giving rise to this litigation, and the name, likeness, or address of the Released Defendants. The parties further agree that neither they nor their attorneys will disclose in any manner the facts relative to any released defendants' involvement in this case. The above provision is meant to include publication, fictionalization, recitation or other disclosure of any of the facts of this case relative to any released defendant." (emphasis added). MBC learned about the settlement because it was over $30,000, and it was reported to the Board under section 801.01 of the Business and Professions Code.

Additionally, another case challenging the validity and legality of an almost identical confidentiality clause is pending in the First District Court of Appeal (again, details available upon request). In that case, counsel for the physician not only included the vague confidentiality clause which they now insist bars the plaintiff from complaining to the Medical Board but is also insisted on structuring the agreed-upon $100,000 settlement amount as follows: **Defendant physician will pay $70,000.01 from her own funds, leaving her malpractice insurance company to pay $29,999.99 from her insurance policy—thus evading not only section 2220.7 but also section 801.01.** If this gambit succeeds, MBC will never learn of this $100,000 settlement—nor will this physician's patients ever become aware

---

actions from including gag clauses in civil settlement agreements) and reinforced by multiple courts striking down gag clauses as void as against public policy. *See, e.g., Cariveau v. Halverty*, 83 Cal. App. 4th 126 (2000) ("[T]he inclusion of a restrictive confidentiality clause in the Forbearance Agreement is not only directly connected to [defendant's] misconduct, but is an instance of misconduct in itself. …To countenance this agreement would encourage future … violators to hide their misdeeds in a secret agreement free from the light of regulatory scrutiny."); *Picton v. Anderson Union High School*, 50 Cal. App. 4th 726 (1996) (applicable to teachers); *Mary R. v. Division of Medical Quality of the Board of Medical Quality Assurance*, 149 Cal. App. 3d 308 (1983) ("[T]he stipulated order of confidentiality is contrary to public policy, contrary to the ideal that full and impartial justice shall be secured in every matter and designed to secrete the evidence in the case form the very public agency charged with the responsibility of policing the medical profession. … Such a stipulation is against public policy, similar to an agreement to conceal judicial proceedings and to obstruct justice.").

of these and other settlements given the disclosure requirements set forth in sections 803.1 and 2027.[13]

The Medical Board and the Legislature should explore this issue in order to ensure that MBC is receiving information about physician misconduct that it is entitled and mandated to receive. As the Medical Board Enforcement Program Monitor said in her Initial Report, "regulatory gag clauses cause many serious problems—both for the Medical Board that is being deprived of information about its own licensees by its own licensees and for unsuspecting patients who continue to be exposed to unscrupulous and/or incompetent physicians because MBC cannot take appropriate disciplinary action against them…."[14]

A vague confidentiality clause such as the one quoted above is no more than a regulatory gag clause masquerading as a confidentiality clause and should also be banned and/or clarified to expressly say that the clause does not preclude the plaintiff/consumer from contacting the defendant's regulatory agency.

- *Physician Health and Wellness Program:* CPIL welcomes the Board's suggestion in New Issue #6 that it should be more proactive in identifying potential areas of patient harm before that harm actually occurs. However, we caution these Committees, and the Board itself, that any newly-established Physician Health and Wellness Program must be carefully monitored in order to avoid the dire patient safety consequences of the Board's former diversion program.[15] We are especially concerned by the Board's use of the term "confidential" when describing this program (*see* Sunset Report at p. 216). The secret nature of the diversion program was devastating to patients, and patients and the Board must continue to be apprised of participants in any Board-sponsored program in order to adhere to the Board's statutory obligation to protect the public as its paramount priority.

<u>An Independent Ombuds Office Would Improve Public Trust and Operational Efficiencies</u>

MBC's Sunset Review Report identifies consumer complaints as the "heart" of the Board's enforcement program. This makes the dismal scores from customer satisfaction surveys about the complaint process—not to mention the heart-wrenching stories from patient advocates about their experience with the Board and the complaint process—an area of grave concern as to the public's trust in the Board and its ability to protect the public.

---

[13] We are aware that the practice of settling civil cases just below the $30,000 level is common. Regrettably, so is the more clearly unlawful practice of reporting $29,999 and then rewarding the plaintiff beyond this amount, as has been documented to us. This practice is now joined with the vague but seemingly comprehensive confidentiality provisions which are reasonably interpreted (especially by non-attorneys or those unfamiliar with applicable law) as prohibiting patient-initiated reporting of licensee wrongdoing to the Medical Board. These two practices must be policed by the Board, with explicit prohibitions and serious sanctions where pursued. Not only must the Board police these practices; it should notify the State Bar where any attorney is involved in them.

[14] *Initial Report* at 113.

[15] *Id.* at Chapter XV; *Final Report* Chapter XV (finding significant patient safety concerns and recommending safeguards for continued operation); *See also* Elaine M. Howle, State Auditor, *Medical Board of California's Physician Diversion Program: While Making Recent Improvements, Inconsistent Monitoring of Participants and Inadequate Oversight of Its Service Providers Continue to Hamper Its Ability to Protect the Public* (June 7, 2007), available at http://bsa.ca.gov/pdfs/reports/2006-116R.pdf. (report leading to ultimate abolishment of the program).

The Board reports that over the past four years, those consumers who have completed the Board's survey **consistently rank the handling of their complaints as either "poor" or "very poor."** And of the complainants who were unable to get the assistance they desired from MBC, zero were provided alternatives. Results like these erode public trust in the Board, whose paramount priority is to protect consumers.

After studying the problem, CPIL recommends an independent ombudsperson (or ombuds office) to better manage consumer complaints. Scandinavian for "representative," ombuds offices work in a variety of contexts across the globe, including government agencies, colleges and universities, corporations, hospitals and other medical facilities, and news organizations. The two primary duties are typically (1) to work with individuals and groups to explore and assist them in determining options to help resolve conflicts, problematic issues, or concerns, and (2) to bring systemic concerns to the organization for resolution. Ombuds offices have proliferated in U.S. federal agencies over the past 50 years but are still rare in California government (two examples are in the Medi-Cal Managed Care and Mental Health Office and the Department of Aging).

A 2016 report on the value of the Ombudsman in Federal Agencies[16] emphasized the neutral role as promoting public trust, characterizing ombudsmen as a powerful way to ensure government is accessible and responsive to the needs and concerns of both external and internal stakeholders. Ombudspersons "humanize government" and help people navigate with and within an agency. They also triage problems and prevent escalation, exploring less adversarial means of resolution and avoiding the formal complaint processes when appropriate. Perhaps the most valuable service an ombuds provides is helping to identify themes and systemic issues that support the improvement of an organization's mission.

Despite the Board's efforts to host patient advocate meetings and update consumer informational brochures, there remains a significant disconnect between individuals who have deeply suffered due to doctors' actions regulated by the Board. It is clear that improved communication alone will not bridge this growing divide; a systemic solution is desperately needed.

Additionally, as observers of MBC Board meetings for the past four decades, it is apparent to us that there has been an increasing and unfortunate breakdown in the relationship between the Attorney General's office and the Board in recent years. This not only impacts the day-to-day operations of the Board, but it has grave consequences for consumer protection in terms of case processing times, during which unethical or incompetent physicians continue to practice. An independent ombuds office could also play a role as a neutral party in facilitating and streamlining disputes as they arise in relationships such as these going forward.

Increase Licensing Fees

It has been 15 years since any kind of fee increase has occurred. The Board has more than justified its need for additional funds—funds which are critical to enhancing the enforcement program so that it may achieve the Board's paramount priority of public protection. CPIL also supports the Board's additional requests for enforcement enhancements, specifically as to conditions for tolling

[16] Administrative Conference of the United States, *The Ombudsman in Federal Agencies--FINAL REPORT* (2016), available at https://www.acus.gov/report/ombudsman-federal-agencies-final-report-2016.

the statute of limitations, increased inspection powers, and established timeframes for pharmacies to turn over records to the Board.

CPIL appreciates your consideration of this testimony and these recommendations.

Sincerely,

Bridget Fogarty Gramme
Administrative Director and Supervising Attorney
Center for Public Interest Law
University of San Diego School of Law

cc Kristina Lawson, President, Medical Board of California
William Prasifka, Executive Director, Medical Board of California
Kimberly Kirchmeyer, Director, Department of Consumer Affairs
Hon. Toni Atkins, Senate President pro Tempore
Hon. Anthony Rendon, Speaker of the Assembly

End of Letter

An important case involving the avoidance of reporting requirements to the Medical Board of California was recently litigated. Any civil case with a settlement over a certain amount precludes the blockage of disclosure to the Board. Attorneys engaged in malpractice settlements often seek to avoid such disclosure in order to maximize monies to the aggrieved patient. CPPC's (then CPIL) amicus brief filed in that case is presented below.

Helen Pappas v. Carolyn Chang, M.D.

Case Nos. A159792 and A160293 (Cal. Ct. App., 1st Dist.)

Brief of Amicus Curiae Center for Public Interest Law in Support of Helena Pappas

INTRODUCTION

Based on its four decades of experience advocating for public policy in California that protects patients from unsafe physicians, the Center for Public Interest Law (CPIL) submits this amicus curiae brief to provide the Court with some additional perspective as to the critically important public policy and patient protection implications that this matter presents.

Article I, Section 1 of California's Constitution enumerates safety as an "inalienable right" held by the people of California. When it comes to the safety of California's patients, the state's chief mechanism in protecting them from incompetent and unethical physicians and surgeons is the Medical Board of California (MBC or the Board). Pursuant to the Medical Practice Act,[7] MBC issues licenses to practice medicine in California, and has the authority to limit and/or revoke these licenses if necessary to prevent further patient harm.

But the Board can only take action against its licensees if it is alerted to conduct that violates the Medical Practice Act, thus prompting an investigation. Thus it relies heavily on patient complaints and mandated reports from other entities, such as insurers, hospitals, and courts, about its licensees.

In its oversight role over the Board, the Legislature has addressed, and passed laws to mitigate, unscrupulous tactics by physicians and their lawyers to prevent the Board from ever receiving information about a physician's conduct and allowing them to continue practicing without any scrutiny by the Board.

The facts presented by this case demonstrate precisely such tactics, and the policies put in place to prevent them. In its efforts to adjudicate this matter based on the contract negotiations alone, the trial court appears to have overlooked the Respondent's blatant attempts to avoid disclosure of the underlying incident to the Board in violation of two critical statutes: section 2220.7 of the Business and Professions Code, which prohibits "regulatory gag clauses," and section 801.01, which requires malpractice insurers to report malpractice settlements in excess of $30,000 to MBC.[8]

As set forth in detail below, upholding the trial court's order would set a dangerous precedent by condoning physician attempts to circumvent regulation. It would also significantly hamper the Board's ability to identify and investigate physicians who may be imposing significant harm on their patients, and undermine the Legislature's express intent to stop these practices.

Accordingly, CPIL respectfully submits that the trial court's order should be reversed and remanded.

ARGUMENT

Where, as here, the terms of an agreement run counter to public policy – especially where that public policy is articulated in legislation – that term is unenforceable. *See Cariveau v. Halferty* (2000) 83 Cal.App.4th 126, 131–32, citing Rest.2d Contracts, § 178. Specifically, the term is unenforceable on the grounds of public policy if the interest in its enforcement is "clearly outweighed" in the circumstances by a public policy against the enforcement of such terms. *Ibid.*

In this case, the evidence admitted at trial makes clear that Respondent, in negotiating the terms of the "more comprehensive settlement agreement," had every intention of prohibiting Ms. Pappas from proactively reporting any information to MBC about 1) Respondent's underlying conduct pertaining to Appellant's medical treatment, and 2) the terms of the settlement agreement itself as to the distribution of payments between the Respondent's personal funds and her insurer. Each of these prohibitions violates distinct but equally important statutes, adopted to ensure that the Medical Board has the information it needs to protect California's patients.

Such terms must be deemed void as against public policy; indeed, they will become standard practice if upheld here. The trial court erred in dismissing Appellant's arguments in this regard.

A. Respondent's Proposed Confidentiality Agreement Was Effectively a Gag Clause and Violates Express Public Policy in Bus. & Prof. Code, § 2220.7

Settlement terms which prohibit consumers from disclosing wrongful conduct about a licensee to their licensing board, known as "regulatory gag clauses," present many serious problems — both for the agency that is being deprived of information about its own licensees, and for the unsuspecting consumer who continues to be exposed to unscrupulous and/or incompetent state licensees because their regulators cannot take appropriate disciplinary action against them. Indeed they are the very antithesis of the purpose of regulatory agencies.

Based on our experience monitoring the regulated professions, we supported AB 2260 (Negrete McCloud) (Chapter 565, Statutes of 2006), which added section 2220.7 to the Business and Professions Code to prohibit physicians and surgeons from utilizing these clauses, and later in in 2012 with the enactment of AB 2570 (Hill), a prohibition applicable to all boards within the Department of Consumer Affairs, now codified as section 143.5 of the Business and Professions Code. All of this legislation was driven by three public policy concerns regarding the use of these types of confidentiality clauses.

First, regulated licensees should not be able to unilaterally deprive regulators of information about their own misconduct committed in the course and scope of the regulated business.

Second, concealment from the regulator should not be "on the table" during civil settlement negotiations. The civil tort system and the administrative process have very different purposes and standards. An outcome in one system (civil) should not necessarily dictate the outcome in the other (regulatory). Agencies should not be deprived of the discretion to investigate complaints.

Finally, an injured patient or consumer should not be put in the position of having to decide between two competing incentives: "I should take the money and run" vs. "I'd really like to help prevent what happened to me from happening to others." This is precisely the "Catch 22" scenario in which the Appellant found herself in this case, and her unwillingness to agree has since deprived her of the agreed-upon settlement funds.

With this background in mind, and particularly keeping in mind that the Board's discipline system is entirely reliant on the receipt of complaints which prompt the Board to initiate investigations and the disciplinary process, it is clear that Respondent's counsel's proposed terms for the confidentiality agreement were expressly designed to prevent Appellant from proactively alerting the Board about Respondent's conduct pertaining to her case.

The terms of the confidentiality agreement, as proposed by Respondent's counsel on July 6, 2018 would have required Appellant to agree that she would not disclose the "Agreement, the terms of the Agreement, or the amount of the settlement, to *any third parties unless she is legally required to do so*." (JA 8) (emphasis added). When Ms. Pappas, through her counsel, challenged the breadth of the proposed confidentiality clause because it would prohibit her from communicating with the Board, Respondent's counsel's carefully worded response on July 18 speaks volumes. Her proposed revision, "This provision does not prohibit Releasor from disclosures to the California Medical Board or any other government agency *if such information is requested by the Board* or another government authority," is carefully limited to disclosures only if the Board requests information from her. (JA 16) (emphasis added) Any ambiguity about the intent to preclude Appellant from proactively approaching MBC about this incident is cleared up by the final line of the email. "I am concerned that she might make a complaint to the Board. She is not legally required to do that." (*Ibid.*)

Business and Professions Code § 2220.7 provides, in pertinent part:

> (a) A physician and surgeon shall not include or permit to be included any of the following provisions in an agreement to settle a civil dispute arising from his or her practice, whether the agreement is made before or after filing the action:
>
> > (1) A provision that prohibits another party to the dispute from contacting or cooperating with the board.
> >
> > (2) A provision that prohibits another party to the dispute **from filing a complaint with the board**.
> >
> > (3) A provision that requires another party to the dispute to withdraw a complaint he or she has filed with the board.
>
> (b) A provision described in subdivision (a) **is void as against public policy**. (emphasis added) created by

AB 2260 (Negrete McCloud) (Chapter 565, Statutes of 2006).

In finding that that the proposed confidentiality clause did not violate section 2220.7, the trial court erred by failing to consider the critical distinction between Appellant's ability to *proactively report* the underlying facts of the lawsuit to the Board on the one hand, and any obligation she may have to respond to the Board if asked for information on the other– a distinction which would prevent the Board from ever learning about Respondent's conduct in the first place. The court rejected Ms. Pappas's argument that her counsel's email exchange with defense counsel on 7/18/18 demonstrated evidence that the agreement was designed to preclude her from making a complaint with the Board (see JA 16), and concluded that the agreements did not violate § 2220.7 because both the 6/29/18 Settlement Agreement and the 7/6/18 proposed Confidential Release Agreement permitted disclosures "required by law." "The two agreements do not preclude a complaint to the Medical Board, but as worded provide for confidentiality of the *case and the terms and amount of the settlement agreement* unless disclosure is required by law." (Statement of Decision at p. 9, lines 7-9) (emphasis in original)

But this conclusion entirely misses the fact that, as Respondent's counsel rightly pointed out, Appellant is not "legally required" to file a complaint with the Board. (JA 16). The issue here is not the right of a victim to refuse to answer a subpoena from the Medical Board, it is to essentially inhibit the Board from knowing about the issue in the first place. Indeed, the terms of the Settlement Agreement expressly provided for mutual confidentiality as to the "underlying case," without any exception for reports to the Board, and the proposed release permitted disclosures only "*if such information is requested by the Board*" (*ibid.*, emphasis added). This effectively "gags" Appellant from going to the Board on her own and filing a complaint about her physician's conduct. It is silencing a victim from reporting her physician's potential misconduct to the public regulator of that physician, and therefore violates the letter and intent of applicable law.

The trial court's error in overlooking Respondent's intentions in this regard, as evidenced by the July 18 email (JA 16), validates this unscrupulous behavior. If allowed to stand it will reverse a decade of successful and publicly beneficial reforms, and will have implications beyond the medical profession alone.[9] As noted above, these provisions were enacted after it came to light that it had been common practice for licensed professionals to use the leverage of a money settlement to deprive the regulatory agency of notice that a potentially negligent (or other harmful) act has occurred. Moreover, allowing such malfeasance as a precedent assures that any attentive attorney will incorporate such "gag" provisions as a matter of course.

Critically, the trial court did not conduct any sort of balancing test in considering the public policy issues at stake. See *Cariveau, supra*, 83 Cal.App.4th at 134-137 (weighing the public policy of encouraging investors to report wrongdoing against the general interest in resolving disputes without litigation, and finding confidentiality clause in a settlement agreement that restricted reporting to the securities regulator to be void as against public policy after applying balancing test set forth in Restatement of Contracts § 178). "To permit [defendant's] violations of rules and shield them from administrative review in an agreement to silence wrongdoing would undermine the public's confidence in the integrity of securities oversight. This type of secret settlement should not be left in some dark oubliette, leaving investors unprotected. To countenance this agreement would encourage future NASD violators to hide their misdeeds in a secret agreement free from the light of regulatory scrutiny." *Id.* at p. 137.

These precise policy implications are at play in this case, yet the Statement of Decision is devoid of any such analysis. The confidentiality clause, as proposed, violates the spirit and the letter of section 2220.7 of the Business and Professions Code and should be found to be void as against public policy.

B. The Proposed Release Appears to Have Been Designed to Avoid Malpractice Settlement Disclosure to the Board

Just as it too quickly dismissed Ms. Pappas's argument with respect to the proposed language of the confidentiality clause, the trial court also erred in overlooking the proposed agreement's clear design to avoid statutory reporting obligations regarding civil settlements of malpractice claims.

Section 801.01 of the Business and Professions Code begins with express legislative findings that emphasize the underlying public policy rationale for the provision: "The Legislature finds and declares that the filing of reports with the applicable state agencies required under this section is essential for the protection of the public. It is the intent of the Legislature that the reporting requirements set forth in this section be interpreted broadly in order to expand reporting obligations." It goes on to require, in pertinent part, professional liability insurers to send a "complete report to the Medical Board of California" regarding a licensee's "settlement over $30,000 . . . of a claim or action for damages for. . . personal injury caused by the licensee's alleged negligence, error, or omission in practice." Bus. & Prof. Code § 2220.7, subd. (a)(1), (b)(1). Subdivision (b)(2) requires the licensee or her counsel to make the report "*if the licensee does not possess professional liability insurance*." (emphasis added)

Respondent's proposed Release dated July 6, 2018 at ¶ 5 purports to divide the settlement into two payments: a check for $29,999.99 to be paid by Respondent's professional liability carrier, and $70,000.01 to be paid by Respondent personally. (JA 11) In considering Ms. Pappas's argument that this proposed division of payment was designed to avoid reporting to MBC and should be void as against public policy, the trial court again failed to conduct any sort of balancing test or consider the public policy implications behind section 801.01. *Cariveau, supra*, 83 Cal.App.4th at 134-137. Without citing to the record, the court merely concludes that the "7/6/18 Release . . . clearly states that the amount of the settlement is $100,000.00 and obligates the insurer to report the settlement to the Medical Board." (Statement of Decision at p. 8 lines 21-23) But the proposed Release makes no such aggregate calculation of the settlement nor does it contain any such requirement that the settlement be reported.

Instead it appears to be cleverly worded to avoid such disclosure. Subdivision (b)(1) requires an insurer to report settlements over $30,000 to the Board, but under the terms of the agreement, it will only be paying $29,999.99. One could certainly argue that the insurer, therefore would not be technically required to report to the Board. And subdivision (b)(2) only requires the licensee or her counsel to report to the board *if she does not have liability insurance*. But in this case, she does have insurance, so she could argue she is not obligated to report either.

The court found Respondent to be credible in her testimony that "she paid the additional

$70,000.01 because she wanted to be done with the case and conclude the litigation with a former patient" (Statement of Decision at lines 23-26), but acknowledges that "[f]urther testimony as to why there were two settlement checks was limited due to the mediation and attorney/client privileges." (Id. at p. 4, n. 2) Particularly given the 7/18/18 email indicating Respondent's counsel's fear that Ms. Pappas would report her client's conduct to MBC, it is difficult to imagine any logical reason why the agreement would be structured so that the professional liability company would pay one cent less than the amount which triggers reports to the Board.

Just as with the regulatory gag clause discussed above, to permit this type of contractual provision to stand, without any commentary or consideration as to the public policy implications of permitting such provisions, will merely encourage future physicians accused of misconduct and their attorneys from continuing to structure secret agreements so as to hide their misdeeds from MBC's scrutiny. The court erred when it so cavalierly dismissed these policy arguments.

CONCLUSION

The medical profession involves extraordinary reliance of patients and dire potential consequences from incompetent practice. Certainly, making a mistake that gives rise to damages may not warrant licensure revocation or even serious discipline. But it needs to be known by those whose duty it is to assure competent practice. Accordingly, the law prohibits the inclusion of any provision in any settlement agreement that stymies not only compliance with the law and proper inquiries made, but also the *right of the victim to report the applicable events to the agency*. The law also requires outside entities, such as professional liability insurers to report certain settlements to the Board to facilitate its oversight over physicians. We respectfully ask this Honorable Court to reject the proposed settlement provisions at issue in this case clearly and decisively. Its survival will result in their likely universal inclusion in all settlement agreements because of the incentives discussed above, and will undermine the public policy objectives mandated by the Legislature.

***

Endnotes:

[1] Cal. Gov't Code, § 12529 et seq.

[2] *Id.* at §§ 11371 et seq.

[3] Since 1993, CPIL has sponsored, drafted, and/or supported at least two dozen other pieces of successful legislation to strengthen the Medical Board's physician discipline system; additionally, it has helped to block or amend numerous pieces of legislation sponsored by the medical profession that would have served to protect the medical profession rather than patients.

CPIL has also participated actively in the Legislature's periodic "sunset reviews" of the Medical Board's performance in 1997, 2002, 2005, 2013, and 2017, and is now actively involved in the Board's current sunset review.

[4] See Julianne D'Angelo Fellmeth and Thomas A. Papageorge, *Initial Report of the Medical Board Enforcement Monitor* (November 1, 2004); Julianne D'Angelo Fellmeth and Thomas A. Papageorge, *Final Report of the Medical Board Enforcement Monitor* (November 1, 2005).

[5] See AB 2260 (Negrete McCloud) (Chapter 565, Statutes of 2006).

[6] See SB 1438 (Figueroa) (Chapter 223, Statutes of 2006).

[7] Business and Professions Code sections 2000, *et seq.*

[8] Both of these statutes were adopted one year after CPIL's Administrative Director published her final report as the Medical Board's legislatively-appointed Enforcement Monitor, and were among the 65 recommendations she made to improve the Board's enforcement program to better protect the public. See Julianne D'Angelo Fellmeth and Thomas A. Papageorge, Final Report of the Medical Board Enforcement Monitor (November 1, 2005) at p. 204 (Recommendation #17;) and 206 (Recommendation #49).

[9] See Bus. & Prof. Code, § 143.5 (applying the regulatory gag clause provision in § 2220.7 to all boards in the Department of Consumer Affairs).

End of Amicus Brief

VARIATIONS AMONG AGENCIES IN THE ENFORCEMENT PROCESS AND THE CPPC CRITIQUE

	BRN (APA)	CSLB (APA)	MBC (APA)
Investigation	DCA's Division of Investigation (generalists)	in-house non-sworn investigators (specialists)	DCA's Health Quality Investigative Unit (sworn specialists)
Prosecution	AG Licensing Section (generalists; no VE)	AG Licensing Section (generalists, no VE)	AG Health Quality Enforcement Section (specialists; as of 1/1/19 no VE)
Hearing	OAH – general ALJ panel	OAH – general ALJ panel	OAH – Medical Quality Hearing Panel (Gov't Code § 11371) (specialists)
Review of ALJ Decisions/ Stipulated Settlements	board members (entire board)	Registrar (EO)	board members (2 panels) – must give "great weight" to ALJ's findings of fact
Judicial Review	1. Superior Court (as of right) 2. Ct of Appeal (as of right) 3. California Supreme Court (discretionary)	1. Superior Court (as of right) 2. Ct of Appeal (as of right) 3. California Supreme Court (discretionary)	1. Superior Court (as of right) 2. Ct of Appeal (pet'n for extraordinary writ - *Leone)* 3. California Supreme Court (discretionary)

	Dep't of Insurance (APA)	State Bar (not APA)	PUC (not APA)
Investigation	in-house investigators (specialists)	in-house investigators (specialists)	in-house investigators (specialists)
Prosecution	in-house attorneys (specialists) (also has intervenor compensation mechanism to encourage consumer group participation)	in-house prosecutors (Office of Chief Trial Counsel) (specialists who use VE)	in-house attorneys (specialists); Office of Ratepayer Advocates; Intervenor compensation mechanism to encourage consumer participation
Hearing	in-house DOI ALJs (specialists)	Hearing Panel of the State Bar Court (specialists)	in-house ALJs (specialists); assigned commissioner under Pub. Util. Code § 1701.1(b)
Review of ALJ Decisions/ Stipulated Settlements	Insurance Commissioner (elected)	3-judge Review Department of the State Bar Court (specialists)	5-member Commission (appt'd by Governor to 6-year terms) (specialists)
Judicial Review	1. Superior Court (as of right) 2. Ct of Appeal (as of right) 3. California Supreme Court (discretionary)	California Supreme Court (discretionary) (*In Re Rose)*	Court of Appeal and/or Supreme Court

As the matrix above indicates, there are differences among state agencies in their respective enforcement processes. The discussion above captures the process in most agencies and is the generic norm, as represented by the first entry—the Board of Registered Nursing (BRN). However, five agencies have variations—some substantial—from these standard steps. The first of these five, as the matrix above indicates, is the Contractors State License Board (CSLB). This Board confers substantial powers to its Executive Officer, termed the "Registrar," who exercises the review and approval powers for ALJ decisions without reference to Board member consideration or vote. The CSLB investigation is conducted not by general DCA investigators as is the norm, but by in-house CSLB investigators with a measure of specialized expertise. The ALJ hearing the case, however, comes from the general list of ALJs within the Office of Administrative Hearings (OAH).

The second varying agency is the Medical Board of California (MBC). As proposed by CPPC, this system enjoys a specialized unit of deputy AGs in a "Health Quality Enforcement Section" to encapsulate the often- useful subject matter expertise involved in medical profession discipline. In addition, and also reflecting the advantage of expertise, the ALJs of OAH are here grouped into a "Medical Quality Hearing Panel." So, the ALJs conducting these hearings have expertise in medical issues. After the hearing and the issuance of a proposed decision by one of those ALJs, one of two groupings ("panels") of the Medical Board review of the proposed ALJ decision. Further, the Board members are statutorily required to give "great weight" to the ALJ's findings of fact. This measure of weight reflects the fact that the ALJ hears the witnesses and is in a position to judge credibility more effectively than a panel seeing only a transcript and hearing oral argument. Finally, the normal appellate process of appeal to superior court, and then to a court of appeal and then discretionary appeal to the California Supreme Court is somewhat streamlined. There is an appeal right to superior court, but further appeals to a court of appeal or to the Supreme Court are both discretionary. That is, a full process of appeal will require a minimum finding of justification for that review by either of these two appellate bodies.

These changes in the Medical Board process reflect long-standing reform proposals by CPPC based on the following critique: The standard process discussed above lacks subject matter expertise over subject matter suited to familiarity with applicable nomenclature and history. And the ALJ hearing live witnesses warrants a measure of credibility over a body of officials with uncertain knowledge and a lack of percipient absorption of actual witnesses and evidence. Finally, the existence of the proceeding and appeal steps in the standard model also involves time spans of three to seven years for a final case resolution. Indeed, a case adjudicating capital punishment, in the normal course, has a trial, a court of appeal review and a discretionary petition to the state supreme court. In contrast, licensee enforcement for most agencies involves a hearing before an ALJ, a hearing before a Board, an appeal to superior court, then to a court of appeal, followed by discretionary review by the State Supreme Court—a five-step rather than the three-step travail of a homicide case. And that three- to seven-year period does not generally involve interim remedies. The major such remedy might be an interim suspension—understandably subject to respondent protecting due process. In addition to advocating for a reasonable process of fewer steps, CPPC has advocated for more easily imposed interim remedies short of complete practice suspension, but with conditions assuring specific consumer protection *pendente lite*. For example, if sexual transgressions are alleged, a physician may be required to have a nurse present during patient contact, or if embezzlement is alleged, a designated accountant could handle cash and finances. Such interim remedies might afford public protection without precluding or seriously inhibiting continued practice.

State agencies outside of the Medical Board have generally escaped all of these reforms. And the Medical Board itself has recently escaped one of the most crucial agency enforcement reforms, what is termed "vertical prosecution." This term refers to the practice of assigning specialized attorneys to direct investigations from the outset. The specifically-qualified Health Quality Enforcement Section of deputy AGs was so assigned for obvious reasons, *e.g.*, with specialized expertise these attorneys are not only relatively knowledgeable about medical aspects of a case, but know what must be proven at trial (hearing) and know how to gather such evidence so it will be admissible. However, the supervision of agency investigators by attorneys from another agency caused a territorial conflict that was resolved by eliminating such a "vertical" case structure and ceding all investigatory processes to non-attorney personnel under the direction of the agency.

The remaining three agencies in the above matrix have features separate from the usual pattern, including the Department of Insurance, the State Bar, and the Public Utilities Commission.

The Department of Insurance's first variation from the common model is that it is not governed by a multi- member governing board or commission, but rather by a single, statewide elected "Insurance Commissioner." Second, the entire operation is "in house"—without involvement of OAH or the Office of AG. It has in-house investigators specializing in insurance matters, and an in-house group of Insurance Department counsel. Even the Administrative Law Judges are not from OAH but are part of the Department of Insurance as well. The final review is by the Commissioner operating individually, followed by the normal right of appeal to superior court, a court of appeal and with discretionary review by the State Supreme Court. One additional feature of the Department is unique—any contribution made to its proceedings (usually quasi-legislative in nature) can yield attorneys' fees to any intervenor who contributes to the result of the proceeding in a way bereft of normal billing. I.e., an intervenor who raises issues and provides evidence and argument beyond the direct pecuniary stake of a client, may be rewarded with a fee that includes billable hours constructively expended times a usual fee amount, and often with a "multiplier" enhancing it more where deemed warranted.

The State Bar of California is not subject to the Administrative Procedure Act in its basic operations and has its own process. From 1987–1992, CPPC served as an outside "Discipline Monitor" of the State Bar's enforcement system, authorized by legislation, appointed by then Attorney General John Van De Kamp, and reporting to the then California Supreme Court Chief Justice Malcolm Lucas. The State Bar is controlled by a Board of Trustees, a majority of whom are practicing attorneys. As with the Department of Insurance, it does not use the state Office of Attorney General but has its own Office of Chief Trial Counsel to direct investigations and bring cases. CPPC's Bar Monitor work did lead to a major change in its enforcement adjudications, which had been presided over by State Bar officials—meeting in 18-member groupings to consider discipline cases; however, legislation enacted from the Discipline Monitor recommendations created a unique, independent State Bar Court consisting of hearing judges and a Review Department of three judges. These judges are independent of the State Bar and have their own budget and sources of authority. Their decisions are final and only subject to discretionary review by the California Supreme Court. Prior to the creation of this new system, the Supreme Court felt obligated to review every single discipline case, demarking a major share of its workload. The new system is relatively efficient and independent, but additional reforms are commended, as detailed in Chapter 9, below. These include adequate resources for the enforcement of basic standards. The license fees funding this agency were at $410 per attorney in 1992 and have remained close to that level while inflation would require over $800 in standard annual fees to maintain resources.

The final variant from the generic model described above is the Public Utilities Commission (PUC), which regulates monopoly utilities and some aspects of transportation and water regulation. The PUC is governed by a five-member Commission appointed by the Governor, and each serving six-year terms. As with the above two agencies, the PUC does not use the Office of Attorney General or the OAH. Rather, it has its own in-house investigators, attorneys, and administrative law judges. The ALJ selected for a particular case is joined by an assigned Commissioner for their respective proceedings. Its final decisions can be appealed to a court of appeal, and to the Supreme Court. Interestingly, the agency also has a special Office of Ratepayer Advocates (ORA) who advocate in hearings and otherwise on behalf of consumers. And as with the Department of Insurance discussed above, it will pay "intervenor compensation" attorney fees, and with a possible "multiplier" beyond billed hours. While such intervention on behalf of consumers and intervenor reward payments are uncommon at the Department of Insurance, they have a long history at the PUC. In fact, two major consumer organizations—TURN (Toward Utility Rate Normalization) based in Northern California, and UCAN (Utility Consumer Action Network), based in San Diego and initiated by CPPC in the 1990s—are the most active outside intervenors (consumers) in PUC proceedings. PUC proceedings may be rate setting, investigative, or rulemaking proceedings.

As to the overall efficacy of agency quasi-judicial enforcement, critics have cited the following problems and suggested reforms:

1. As discussed in Chapter 3, governing agency boards or commissions should not be under the control of those who practice in the licensed profession. This common flaw removes "state action" defense from any act of an agency in violation of federal antitrust law. It is not exempt "state action." And disciplinary actions to effectively boycott persons from competitive practice, as well as supply reduction that lessens competition, can be per se violations of the federal Sherman Act—implicating both treble damages and possible felony liability. While expertise in the subject matter of the regulation can be helpful, that may be provided by expert witnesses, or by an advisory board or by an opportunity for outside opinions and comments.

2. Length of time, expense, and excessive number of proceedings, especially Board review of adjudicative hearing results with no clear limit on any basis for rejection. Further, the members deciding often are part of the profession involved and may have income related biases. Finally, none of them were present when witnesses testified—an important part of the fact-finding part of any adjudication provided by expert witnesses, or by an advisory board or by an opportunity for outside opinions and comments.

3. The three- to seven-year length of time for proceedings that are appealed is excessive and lacks the full range of interim remedies appropriate for such a travail. Although interim suspension is sometimes imposed, it is possible to directly require practice elements that prevent further incidence of accused violations while the case proceeds (as discussed above). Indeed, most states require only proof by a "preponderance" of the evidence to impose discipline. Some other states, including California, require a higher "clear and convincing" standard of proof. Although lower than the criminal "proof beyond a reasonable doubt" requirement, its requirement above "preponderance" may be justified by a proceeding that can end the vested right to continue to practice one's profession. While the lower standard is common in a public decision to deny a license or permission to practice in a regulated field, the "clear and convincing" higher burden is justified where the state is removing an existing vested right. But that arguably justifiable burden of proof should not apply to interim remedies that protect the public

but do not foreclose continued practice. For example, in the well-known abuses of attorney Girardi allegedly embezzling or improperly managing case proceeds (and other alleged abuses) over a 30-year period of 105 complaints and Bar investigations, it would have made sense to appoint an independent accountant to manage the handling of monies in his practice. That would not have stopped or even fatally curtailed his legal representations over the many years of abuse but would have precluded the most serious ethical transgressions alleged. Similarly, physicians who are alleged to engage in sexual misconduct with patients could be required to always have a nurse or other third-party present in doctor/patient interactions. These and many other interim remedies pending adjudication outcome should be allowed and affirmatively sought under a "preponderance" test since they do not preclude effective practice. Regrettably, virtually no regulatory agency engages in such interim remedies short of total suspension as the case proceeds—which understandably requires clear and convincing proof.

4. It would be helpful if the attorneys and Administrative Law Judges had a measure of expertise in the regulated operations at issue. And ALJs should be allowed to call expert witnesses themselves, subject to questions and cross examination. Such expert contribution not from a party who will pre-select a favored expert can provide better understanding of the specialized and relevant evidence and give the ALJ additional on-point information.

5. Attorneys with expertise in the substantive areas of law they are adjudicating, particularly in areas requiring specialized knowledge. The Deputy AGs who handle Medical Board enforcement are all part of the specialized unit of attorneys focusing on medical care issues. The State Bar does have one member of the Office of Chief Trial Counsel who handles attorney discipline cases specializing in immigration law. But there are many other areas of law where specialized knowledge would enhance that process, including wills and estates, bankruptcy, family law, and other areas involving specialized practice. In fact, attorneys are given a license permitting practice in any one of more than 24 separate substantive areas involving very disparate courts, procedures, and evidentiary requirements. State Bar prosecutors should include experts in each major area of practice. And part of their duties should include not just the more informed imposition of public protection standards, but also the consideration of preventive measures in education and testing and licensing that would serve the public. Finally, licensees should be required to carry malpractice insurance at levels allowing for reasonable recovery for victimized consumers. In particular, the State Bar's failure to do so has caused obvious difficulties for consumers seeking recovery for malpractice.

6. It is not necessary for agency discipline of licensees to have five adjudicative steps: ALJ hearing and decision, board final decision after oral argument, full appeal at the superior court level, right of appeal to the court of appeal, and discretionary review by the state supreme court. Ideally, the ALJ decision would be final, with a single step appeal to either the superior court, or in some circumstances to the court of appeal—i.e., two steps plus discretionary review. The State Bar Court creates such a reasonable number of such steps, but almost all agencies operate in a world where the number of steps is more than is required to impose capital punishment in the criminal sphere. And as noted above, some of those steps lack balance and adequate evidentiary consideration.

7. One recurring problem, perhaps related to domination of agency decisions by vested interests, is the consistent reduction in monies and adequate resources for effective enforcement. The Medical Board, State Bar, and many other agencies are financed through "special funding" outside the general fund process. Usually, that consists of license renewal fees or other related revenue. However, there is rarely an adjustment for inflation, hence, funding is strangled over time into ineffective totals. The Bar license renewal was $410 in 1992 and is only marginally higher now. This produces just over 50% of that historical level in terms of its inflation adjusted amount. The same is true of the Medical Board. Those enforcement attorneys and investigators need to receive substantial increases to simply maintain enforcement. Instead, like a victim of a neck-choking python, they are cut and cut and cut. Insufficient pay to encourage retention of effective personnel and inadequate numbers betray this basic mission of regulation. Although any economist will testify that a renewal fee increase is passed onto consumers and is actually borne by them, because it comes from payment by licensees, they are in a strong position to oppose any increase—even one which maintains spending power. And their control of the relevant agency board underlines that flaw.

8. One common enforcement problem is the "repeat offender" who triggers multiple but separate investigations. They are often not considered as a group. In an extreme example involving the State Bar, attorney Girardi triggered well over 100 separate investigations over 30 years, and CPPC has reviewed over 40 attorneys triggering more than 15 complaints and inquiries each. Similarly, a number of physicians, particularly those with sexual offenses, have practices for many years while evidence of abuse is sporadically received. In cases of repeated complaints or investigations, particularly where over five such triggers in a five-year period, the agency properly assigns a single attorney investigator to review the entire practice of the licensee, including affirmative inquiry into patients or clients involving areas of suspected abuse.

9. The power of the agencies and Attorney General to assess costs from the Respondent is of dubious merit. It does not merely apply to bad faith or disingenuous defenses but may be assessed if an accusation of five alleged offenses results in a finding of culpability for one. Why should such costs be assessed? That practice might inhibit *bona fide* tests of disciplinary tactics and might apply not merely to physicians and attorneys, but to drywallers and other contractors, or barbers or to the brunt of licensees who do not have income or savings to risk.

10. Each agency should have a reporter publishing every decision rendered by an ALJ and any court appellate proceedings. That compilation should be a part of Board and licensee education. In addition, each agency should have disciplinary guidelines to promote consistency in punishment. These guidelines must be adopted through rulemaking discussed in the preceding chapter. In addition, an agency might specifically label a decision as precedential to stimulate general consistency. (See Gov't Code Sections 11425.50(e) and 11425.60.)

Hypotheticals

APA Adjudication

In the early morning hours of August 17, 2011, Dee, a registered nurse with more than 20 years of experience, was at work at San Diego Memorial Hospital. One of her patients was Frank, a 55–year–old man with Down syndrome (the patient). The patient began to suffer from respiratory distress around 4:00 a.m., and Dee paged the medical resident doctor on call, Dr. Night, for assistance.

Dee had examined the patient herself over the course of her shift but did not discuss her findings with Dr. Night. When Dr. Night arrived in the room, he concluded that the patient was too unstable to be transported to the ICU and needed his airway secured first. Dr. Night called in his supervisor, who concurred that the patient was unstable and needed to be intubated.

Dr. Night then informed everyone in the room that the patient was to be intubated and instructed Dee to intubate the patient. Dee told Dr. Night that she could not intubate the patient on the floor and that the patient was first to be taken to the ICU. Dr. Night repeated his intention to intubate the patient immediately, but Dee proceeded to unplug the bed from its electrical outlet and maneuver the bed out of the room. All personnel in the room, including Dr. Night, followed the patient as Dee transported him to the ICU, which was on another floor of the hospital; the trip to the ICU took approximately five minutes. The patient was transported without any device for monitoring his cardiac status or vital signs; he received oxygen from a portable tank during the transport.

The patient and entourage arrived at the ICU at approximately 6:50 a.m.; morphine sulfate was administered, and Dr. Night successfully intubated the patient at that time. At 7:20 a.m., a code blue was initiated; cardiopulmonary resuscitation began at 7:23 and the patient died at 7:30. There was no evidence the delay in intubating the patient caused or contributed to his death.

Dr. Night entered a "code blue note" on the patient's record at 7:45 a.m., recording the incident substantially as described above. At 9:00 a.m., Dee wrote an "occurrence report" of the incident, which included the statement that she "countermanded the order of Dr. Night." She wrote that when Dr. Night ordered her to intubate the patient in the room, Dee said the equipment and staff were not adequate, and the patient should be moved to the ICU. Dee further observed that the patient was "awake, but lethargic," was "breathing spontaneously with palpable pulses," was "viable at the time" and would have had to be transported to the ICU after intubation "at much risk due to the obvious complications"; an "unnecessary intubation and code blue on the lower floor, especially at change of shift" would compromise all the patients on the floor.

A few days after the incident, the hospital terminated Dee's employment, listing "gross negligence—failure to follow direction from treating physician" as the reason for the termination. The hospital's discharge memorandum stated Dee had refused the physician's order and transported the patient to the ICU. Dee is currently employed at Snail Medical Center.

In April 2014, the Board of Registered Nursing filed an accusation in connection with the August 17, 2011, incident, alleging unprofessional conduct and gross negligence, and incompetence and seeking the revocation or suspension of Dee's license. A hearing was held before an administrative law judge in January 2015. The ALJ heard testimony from Dr. Night, Dr. Day, and other nurses working on the floor with Dee on the night of the incident. Dee presented testimony from an expert witness who opined that it is always preferable to intubate a patient in the ICU. It is appropriate for a nurse to question a doctor's order under the circumstances such as those which occurred in this case. The Board's expert opined that, while Dee may have believed she was acting in the best interest of the patient, she was wrong; while it is permissible for a registered nurse to disobey an order that is inaccurate or unsafe, the documentation reviewed did not indicate this was such a case.

After hearing all the evidence, the ALJ concluded there was clear and convincing evidence of gross negligence and incompetence within the meaning of the applicable statute and regulations and recommended revocation of Dee's license but staying that revocation and placing her on probation for three years.

The Board adopted the ALJ's proposed decision in January 2016. Dee then filed a writ of administrative mandamus, petitioning the Court to require the Board of Registered Nursing to set aside its decision. The trial court upheld the Board's decision, and Dee appealed.

Discussion Questions:

1. BRN's regulations, stated in Section 1443.5, Title 16 of the CCR, provide that the standards of competent performance also require the nurse to act "as the client's advocate, as circumstances require, by initiating action to improve health care or to change decisions or activities which are against the interests or wishes of the client...." How should Dee's attorneys use this provision to argue that the Board's decision should be overturned?

2. What should the attorneys for the Board argue?

3. What was the standard of review for the Superior Court? What about the appellate Court?

4. How should the Court rule? Should the Board's decision be upheld? Why or why not?

Board of Pharmacy

Jack Straightshooter is a licensee of the Board of Pharmacy. The Board initiated an investigation of Jack in 2014 after receiving complaints that he was not correctly tracking his opioid prescriptions as required by the Board's regulations.

After hearing from several witnesses who confirmed the allegations from the complaints received, the Board filed an accusation against Jack under the Administrative Procedure Act in 2017. Included in the accusation was notice that the Board would seek an order directing Jack to pay all of the costs assumed by the Board in its investigation and prosecution if any part of the accusation were sustained under the APA (which included 11 counts involving different aspects of alleged improper prescriptions or recordkeeping). Additionally, the notice advises Jack that these costs of prosecution include attorneys' fees to the Office of Attorney General representing the Board that is incurred "right up to the date of the hearing." If he agreed to the remedy sought immediately and did not incur state investigative costs or AG costs of hearing preparation—which are considerable—he would not owe any such funds.

Jack requested a hearing before an Administrative Law Judge, asserted his defenses, and challenged the constitutionality of the regulation authorizing the Board to charge him for the costs of investigation and prosecution. At the hearing, Jack argued that there is no legal aid or other public sources of legal representation available to him and that his own costs would amount to over

$100,000 for the one year plus travail of a completed investigation leading to hearing and then a final decision. The addition of prosecution costs and attorney fees for those persons accusing him, and which would be assessed if even one or a small number of accusations were confirmed, would bankrupt him.

After the hearing, the ALJ issued a proposed decision recommending revocation of Jack's license but staying the revocation and placing him on probation for three years, subject to certain conditions, including paying $75,000 for the Board's costs of prehearing investigation and prosecution. The Board voted not to adopt the ALJ decision, and after considering the administrative record, issued a decision finding the allegations of misconduct to be true, revoked Jack's license, but stayed it pending five years' probation, subject to certain conditions including a 60-day suspension, and also paying $75,000 for the Board's costs of prehearing investigation and prosecution.

Jack filed a petition for administrative mandate in Superior Court, alleging that the Board's findings were contrary to the weight of the evidence and challenging the cost assessment as unconstitutional. The trial court denied the petition, and Jack appealed. The appellate court found that substantial evidence supported the Superior Court's decision upholding the Board's finding of misconduct but held that the Board's order requiring Jack to pay for the Board's prehearing investigation and prosecution costs violated his right to due process of law. The Board appealed, and the Supreme Court of California granted review.

Discussion Questions:

1. What are the best arguments that can be made by the state to support the constitutionality of this statutory assessment?

2. Are there other examples of this kind of "fee shift" to a defendant where a meritorious action is brought? For example, a private civil rights case against the government or an antitrust case against a large corporation?

3. What might Jack argue distinguishes this situation from those private civil litigation examples?

4. Is there a criminal counterpart? Is there any statute that allows the state to assess its costs in indicting or convicting a defendant? What would the objections be? To what extent do those considerations and factors apply to the state's termination of a license to practice one's profession?

5. How should the Supreme Court rule with respect to Jack's due process argument?

Chapter 9
Excessive Regulation

INTRODUCTION

As Chapter 1 discusses, there are bases for regulation, including measures to restore or enhance an effective marketplace with informed consumer choice dictating competitive choice and the prevention of unnecessary external costs. Ideally, regulation has a rationale for each of its measures, including the consideration of more efficient alternatives. However, the actual impetus for regulation tends to emanate from profit stake interests of the trade or industry regulated, particularly where those self-interested actors control that government involvement.

Where unnecessary, regulation may involve supply diminution that increases prices. To be sure, an assurance of competence may justify some entry barrier measures—but what is the relevant need, and how does that relate to the specific measures limiting supply? Beyond that initial regulatory control are a phalanx of rules defining the "how" of practice. Those measures may also increase costs and diminish effective supply. Indeed, regulation may arrange and increase market restraints and their state source immunizes them from alternatives or competitive check.

Do the benefits of applicable regulation justify their costs? Are there alternatives to assure effective services benefiting consumers other than regulation or other than the specific measures imposed? Any study of regulation properly considers the market flaw addressed, its scope and the efficacy of its mitigation. Regulation properly connects to a justification. And each choice is ideally examined in light of less restrictive or costly alternatives. Chapter 1 discusses the alternatives of market restoration, public (required) disclosure, criminal prohibition, strict rule of liability, and financial incentives/disincentives as alternatives.

A primary rationale for prior restraint licensure is the reduction of irreparable harm threatened by unregulated enterprise and the inadequacy of other alternatives. The elements common to justification here tend to involve (a) irreparable harm from competency failure; (b) a lack of consumer knowledge; (c) a single major transaction/event that exacerbates risk; and (d) ability of the state to judge/assure competence.

As Chapter 1 discusses, the argument for competence assurance declines where damages from normal practice are unusual or easily detected, especially where repeat business is required to operate successfully. For example, the argument for landscape architects, where the purchasers tend to have their own expertise in detecting incompetence; or barbers, where repeat business and consumer capacity to evaluate practice makes prior restraint regulation suspect.

And where there is a rationale for prior restraint regulation, does the system created to accomplish that need without extraneous cost create excessive ancillary regulation? For example, boxing may warrant regulation due to physical safety issues, but does that justify the licensure of wrestlers? Of ticket takers? Recent proposals have suggested the prior restraint licensure of interior designers, aerobics instructors, dog groomers, et al. Some states, including California, now require what are called "sunrise" criteria to justify the creation of prior restraints or other regulations in a new area of commerce where it has not been applied historically. CPPC sponsored the California Sunrise statute and has prevented numerous proposals, almost always by practitioners, to create supply-limited qualifications.

At the same time, many states have partially followed the lead of Colorado to enact what are termed "sunset" provisions requiring the repeated justification for an existing regulatory system, usually at five- year intervals. If the regulation is excessive or unnecessary, it is to be terminated (sunsetted) unless affirmatively renewed by the state legislature. Many states, such as California, do not sunset the entire regulatory system but rather the board or director running it. That position or those positions will all be terminated, and an alternative system of governance created if the sunset is not affirmatively removed prior to its invocation date. Usually, this process involves a report from the agency detailing areas of controversy or change (see Chapter 11).

The discussion below highlights excessive or detailed but misplaced regulations with three examples. First is the excessive regulation of trucking. While vehicle safety is certainly an area of potential irreparable harm and state legitimate interest, historical federal and some state regulations have focused on dispensation to allow price fixing or to curtail effective competition otherwise. Second is an example of a student study of an agency of dubious formation merit—the California Board of Fabric Care (laundry and dry cleaning). Finally, a detailed study of attorney regulation in California (also generally applicable in other states as well) does not demonstrate a system focused on the legitimate need for competence to prevent irreparable harm but limits entry without a clear connection to such competence and otherwise regulates for purposes of anticompetitive advantage for practitioners, not for public benefit.

Public Utilities Administrative Law Judge Proposes Cartel Price Proposals and Minimum Floors for Trucking

> The Interstate Commerce Commission (ICC) regulates interstate surface transport, including common carriage

trucking. The California Public Utilities Commission (PUC) regulates similar operations within the state of California. During the 1960's and 1970's, independent economists and consumerists devastatingly documented abuses in the regulation of surface transportation. Chief among the complaints was the cartel-like regulatory system which had been created to protect truckers from competition. Truckers operating in interstate commerce often were given very narrow licenses to haul goods. They were perhaps licensed to carry particular commodities from particular points to particular points. The ICC set up minimum rate floors, and allowed "rate bureaus" to form. These bodies are not governmental bureaus at all, but are collections of private truckers, who meet in groups and collusively propose prices. Without the permission of the Interstate Commerce Act and the Interstate Commerce Commission, such behavior is a serious antitrust violation.

The end result of the horizontal price fixing, minimum pricing and narrow licensing grant system was a nightmare of inefficiency and cross subsidy. Theoretically, the ICC reviewed rates for reasonableness, but it did so in a passive way. Rates were reviewed when they were protested. Those capable of protesting were those specifically organized around a profit stake in transport carriage. This included major carriers and the very large shippers (whose goods are carried). Most of the litigation before the ICC was not that the rates were too high because of the collusive price fixing by the rate bureaus, but that they were too low and unfairly competed with the rate someone else was charging who was able to protest.

Three decades of abuse eventually led to hearings and a series of deregulation measures, including the Surface Transportation Act of 1980. Trucking became increasingly subject to competition. Rate bureaus were abolished as horizontal price fixing entities.

The question then confronting many states was what position they should take as competition began to increase in trucking. Could the state, for legitimate purposes, restrict competition for operations within its borders notwithstanding a more competitive federal policy? The answer appeared to be "yes." States have been grappling with either following or not following the federal precedent. California has been holding hearings on the question since 1982. Unsurprisingly, the very same kinds of interests which have historically dominated ICC proceedings have been omnipresent at the state proceedings. The intermittent PUC hearings included testimony during 1985 before Administrative Law Judge Turkish. In late 1985, the ALJ issued a proposed report to the Commission, which is now considering final adoption in the form proposed.

The proceedings leading to this report consisted, in 1985, of testimony of 29 witnesses, all but a very few of whom represent interests with a direct profit stake in the policy question before the PUC. Carriers, the affected labor unions and the more organized shippers all stand to gain in various ways from the continuation of rate bureau price fixing. Those carriers not subject to direct rate bureau price fixing know that the process artificially inflates rates charged by other carriers. Those in the rate bureaus, and the rate bureaus themselves, profit from the opportunity to engage in horizontal voluntary price fixing. Many larger shippers (those whose goods are carried) gain because the very specific nature of the tariffs allows them to protest the low rates of competing small shippers giving them lower rates. The smaller shippers cannot afford counsel in San Francisco (before the PUC) and are at a competitive disadvantage. The labor unions benefit because artificially high prices may be used to support higher wage demands.

Except for two witnesses, James C. Miller, IV, and Gloria J. Hurdle, representing the view of virtually any independent economist who has ever studied the subject matter of this proposed report, the other witnesses (i.e., except one other staff witness and a traffic safety official from the state of California) were directly financed by one of the groups with a profit stake such as is identified above. The proposals and the record in support of those proposals advanced by these groups, including the alleged "expert testimony" proferred, consisted almost entirely of the kind of policy contention common to legislative debate. The tenor of the record is reminiscent of the end-of-legislative-session pork barrel remonstrations of those seeking special privilege and exemption.

Missing from this record, except for the witnesses noted above, is representation of the interests of consumers, small shippers who are not organized, taxpayers or the economic infrastructure relying upon efficient and inexpensive motor carriage. The proposed report itself reflects, in vector-like fashion, the demands and requests of those constituent groups represented in the proceedings.

Having considered the requests of the various contending groups, ALJ Turkish finds that the trucking industry is subject to "destructive rate competition" without rate bureaus. He finds that rate bureaus help guarantee service to small, little-traveled communities, assure adequate expenditure of monies for highway safety, guarantee that adequate wages are paid and that truckers do not go out of business because competitors unfairly charge a lesser amount. He finds that rate bureaus save the administrative costs of many individual carriers having to file individual tariffs with the Commission, and that rate bureaus facilitate a stable rate structure and reliable supply of common carriage services to the benefit of all. At the same time, the proposed report concludes that rate bureaus do not result in higher rates at all because truckers are free to take independent action outside the rate bureau if they so desire. Hence, a rate bureau also does not significantly impede the proper competitive forces setting rates.

The proposed report concluded with an extraordinary series of recommendations. This report would continue the rate bureaus and allow private horizontal price fixing as condemned in current federal policy. And it would go even further. The lowest rate which may be lawfully published and filed by a common carrier or assessed by a contract carrier shall be the lowest rate in existence when the transition tariffs are canceled. Current levels are then established as a minimum. They are then to escalate without the need for further proceedings according to a "truck freight cost index." This index, inevitably based on factors applying with great variability to individual carriers, will raise that floor *seriatim*. Those who wish to lower rates, even to meet competition, may do so only if there is a new filing with cost justification. The report also proposes that cost justifications in all contexts must include compensatory rates not in terms of actual compensatory levels, but assuming "prevailing rates" for all labor costs as the Commission determines them. (Thus precluding any shipper or consumer benefit flowing from decreased labor costs for relevant individual carriers.) The report includes in the regulatory scheme both haulers and subhaulers of general commodity freight. The ALJ, with an apparent straight face, issued as a finding of fact that "the regulatory system adopted here will contribute to greater rate and service competition among motor carriers."

Flaws in the PUC's Proposed Report

Rate Cutting Down to Competitive Levels is the Sine Qua Non of the American Free Enterprise System.

There is a premise implicit in much of the proposed report that it is the duty of the Public Utilities Commission to paternalistically protect entrepreneurs subject to its regulation from "going out of business." Hence, the report finds that "destructive rate cutting is one of the major causes of the decline of the trucking industry."

How does one define "decline?" Natural selection is an axiom of a healthy marketplace system. Those who are inefficient *should* go out of business. The Public Utilities Commission has no mandate to protect inefficient carriers at consumer cost. The Commission is well aware that it is its duty to protect the public from commercial abuses, not vice versa. The Commission must be concerned that commercial shippers and the public have available an adequate and reliable trucking system. Such a system, however, hardly depends upon horizontal price fixing and minimum rate floors, nor guaranteed commercial survival. There is no natural scarcity to the supply of trucking. Americans are no less likely to suffer serious immediate shortages in a competitive trucking system than they have in the purchase of the thousands of products and services competitively priced— from shoes to bread.

It is ironic that economists almost universally agree that there is hardly an industry in America more amenable to competition than is trucking. The units of production are relatively small and discrete. This is not a natural monopoly in any sense, but rather an industry where the units of production are by definition mobile, capable of moving to the place of greatest demand and divisible to be allocated where and as that demand exists.

The Trucking Industry is Among Those Least Likely to Suffer Public Harm from Predatory Pricing, and there are Other Remedies for Predation.

What is the traditional harm which flows from predatory pricing? Entities engage in predatory practices (utilizing their deep pocket to go below costs) for a reason. The reason is to drive others out of business. And you drive others out of business to obtain sufficient market power to jack prices up for a profit premium. The traditional predatory pricer is not interested in going below cost to drive others out of business unless the effort will yield some return. That return depends upon a barrier to entry into that business. For once the smaller entrepreneurs are driven out, one is unable to raise prices to capture the reward unless one can price very high. One can price very high only if new entrants are impeded from taking advantage of those high prices by undercutting-at still profitable levels—and stealing the business. Competition drives prices toward cost. With trucking, assuming that the PUC does not create an artificial system of entry barriers, such enrichment is highly problematical. Why should deep pocket X spend money and time driving smaller Y and Z out of a market when, after they are out, and the reward for all this effort might be forthcoming, X will inevitably be foreclosed by new entrants A and B.

This is not an industry amenable to traditional predatory pricing concern.

There is a remedy to rectify and to pre-vent any predation which might occur. A sophisticated body of law exists in both federal and state jurisdictions making such predatory practices unlawful. At the federal level, the Robinson-Patman Act (Section 2 of the Clayton Act as amended) and at the state level, the Unfair Practices Act (Business and Professions Code Sections 17000 *et seq.*) make going below cost with the intent to reduce or eliminate competition unlawful. The remedies are not weak. Both federal and state authorities prosecute these violations. Violation is a criminal offense. The public prosecutors on the state level may bring an additional action under Section 17200 of the Business and Professions Code, the Little FTC Act. This section allows for civil penalties, restitution and attorneys' fees. Furthermore, these civil penalties go to the county treasury, or to the state treasury if the Attorney General brings the action. The recompense of these civil penalties, in addition to attorney fee recovery, make these actions particularly attractive to public authorities. As if that isn't enough, the victim can file suit as well in either jurisdiction. The remedy? Treble damages and attorneys' fees.

The Wrong Sought to be Addressed does not Match the Remedy Chosen.

It would be possible for a PUC, if it were legitimately concerned about demonstrable harm from "destructive rate competition," to provide an imaginative solution to the problem short of the proposed report. The overwhelming impact of a proposal which allows 1,200 carriers to get together in five or more rate cartels to privately price fix, buttressed by Commission enforced minimum rate floors, lacks a nexus to the rationale here justifying it. To an outsider considering these issues, the "rate cutting" danger does not appear to be a very substantive excuse for the overwhelming impact of the system proposed.

If the auto dealerships of California were to approach the Commission with the same proposal *de novo* (assuming PUC jurisdiction over car dealerships), they would get short shrift. Or, if one wishes to consider industries with a "ripple effect" because they're relied upon by other enterprises, ask the same question with regard to health, food, fuel or other areas. Gasoline is certainly an underlying industry fueling our economic system. If the gas stations of California approach the Commission with the same proposal (assuming jurisdiction), what would the response be? What should the response be? The stations have safety concerns. The stations have environmental impacts. The stations have the same ripple effect trucking does, and operators often are driven out of business. Moreover, because stations are limited by land use regulation, there may be entry barriers creating a real danger of predatory practice.

D. A Rate Bureau Cannot be Justified as Competitive Because it is "Voluntary."

The proposed report argues throughout that rate bureaus are necessary to guarantee high enough prices to minimize the external harm of carriers "going out of business." The report also argues incorrectly, and in conflicting fashion, that higher prices will not be the result because competitive pressure remains. In a misunderstanding of the notion of horizontal price fixing, the report argues that the fact that the rate bureaus are "voluntary" minimizes their anticompetitive impact. An arrangement where 1,200 carriers get together, by themselves, subject only to minimal review by the PUC upon protest, is hardly a minor compromise of free enterprise rules. But for the protection to be afforded by "state action," the offense would be a massive horizontal price fixing conspiracy, prosecutable even under the current federal administration standards, as a felony criminal offense. Its harsh treatment as such is grounded in 100 years of economic experience.

The system advanced by the proposed report not only allows such an impact, it facilitates it. The Commission itself serves as the important "detection mechanism" through which the conspirators communicate.

An important element in any price fixing conspiracy based on voluntary adherence is a detection mechanism to ferret out any who might price lower. It is relatively easy to enforce a voluntary price fix if everyone knows when and if a participant undercuts the agreement. If a participant knows others will know if he undercuts the price fix, he is unlikely to do so. The result will be a like reduction by his competitors, after which he will be where he was in the first place. After attempting to undercut several times, followed by its detection and equivalent reductions by competitors, the participants eventually learn that the only course which pays for all of them is to escalate up together. No member gains otherwise. And they may be expected to do so. The fact that the proposed report not only establishes the detection mechanism but makes it extremely difficult to undercut it due to PUC standards and intervention, further underlines the problem.

The proposed report notes that the rates are effective unless they are reviewed, and that hearings are consistently held. In fact, as our review of the Interstate Commerce Commission indicated, almost all protests leading to regulatory intervention concern rates which are rates for new commodities *et al.* which allegedly are at "too low" a level, according to competing carriers or shippers who wish to maintain higher prices. This was illustrated for the popular press in the amusing Yak Fat Case of the late sixties, where a small trucker, in order to make his point, invented a mythical commodity called "Yak Fat." He filed a high tariff for it and then was met by the automatic protest of other carriers and shippers organized in Washington that this rate was not "compensatory" and should be higher. The PUC (or ICC) process for protest, suspension and hearing is hardly going to be of use where the system relies upon passive review by the PUC of those who are already aggressively organized around a profit stake in those rates. Very large shippers and other carriers will be active. Those whose interest the PUC must protect will not be.

There is No External Costs Amelioration or External Benefit Advantage to Horizontal Price Fixing Which Cannot be Addressed by More Effective Means and Without the Costs Implicit in Overwhelming Competition Diminution.

The proposed report argues that there is a public benefit to a "healthy" trucking system. Allegedly, rate bureaus enhance that health without competitive drawback because they increase the flow of information about prices. This argument rests on the notion that there is a market flaw without rate bureaus from such lack of information. The proposed report quotes approvingly from the testimony of Paul MacAlheny, appearing for the Cal West Rate Bureau, to the effect that small carriers "due to their lack of experience operating a business ... or plain lack of knowledge for determining what their costs are, will operate below their costs, thinking they are being competitive and they will eventually go bankrupt. Collective rate making is more apt to assure the economic viability of carriers to the transportation network."

While collective rate making is certainly apt to assure the "economic viability" of inefficient carriers, it is more than a little insult to America's small entrepreneurs that they need the assistance of rate bureaus to prevent them from setting prices below costs of operation. The notion that any American entrepreneur will set a price out of ignorance at a level which will drive him into bankruptcy illustrates the lengths to which proponents of horizontal price fixing must go to justify their scheme. One can picture this businessman seeing his account dissipate month after month as his costs exceed his revenue. Although competitively able to price higher because of his own efficient operation, he neglects to do so out of "ignorance." Month after month his bank account level decreases until he finally reaches bankruptcy. At no time does it dawn on him that he requires more revenue and that there is a relationship between revenue and rates.

One does not have to be an expert witness to know that the most fundamental task properly resting with any small businessman is the independent setting of prices for his operation. You can bet that trucker knows his costs, and every one of them. You can bet he knows exactly what his rates are and exactly the kind of revenue they will produce as time goes by. Indeed, you can bet that is what he thinks about as much as the operations of the business itself. If he is able to raise rates, he will do so. Competition and his own efficiency will determine that. He will win his business by competitive rates, superior service and compliance with the law to minimize fines or penalties.

There is no question that society has a stake in a healthy transportation system. The proposed report's analysis is correct that common carriers hold themselves out to all alike in a nondiscriminatory manner. And it is also true that common carriers assume certain liability for the goods placed in their care during transport. But these characteristics are not unlike the common law rules governing much of American enterprise. One can point to virtually any industry and note dynamic policies of nondiscrimination, the "implied covenant of good faith and fair dealing," the notion of "fair competition" (see Section 17200 of the Business and Professions Code), strict product liability, *res ipsa loquitor* doctrines, etc. None of these policies requires a horizontal price fixing system for their continued viability.

You do not have to allow horizontal price fixing and set minimum rate floors with all the attendant social costs thereto in order to rightfully demand common carriage duty compliance. It is possible to identify a requirement or rule which benefits society at large and which is demanded of all those who participate in an industry, without exchanging for that obligation a horizontal price fix or other *quid pro quo*.

Farmers are circumscribed in pesticide use. Several hundred major equipment requirements apply to manufacturers of automobiles. Government makes harsh demands on the operations of insurance firms, banks, savings and loans (many of which have obligations similar to the common carriage concepts applicable to trucking). California regulates some forty trades and over fifty thousand pages of administrative regulations apply to the rights and obligations of accountants, attorneys, physicians, engineers, contractors and thirty others, from barbers to psychologists. One could put on the stand an expert to testify to the uniqueness of any of these professions or industries. E.g., the honorable and special responsibility of members of the Bar to represent the oppressed-even to the point of being required by the court to represent indigent defendants at their own cost (see *Yarbrough v. Superior Court of Napa County*, 39 Cal. 3d 197 (1985)). One could persuasively argue that for any of these professions or industries, an important part of America's economy depends upon its help. And one can argue that the fulfillment of these "extra" societal responsibilities is absolutely essential to the benefit which society demands from it. It does not follow, however, that we yield as a gratuitous price for that benefit, horizontal price fixing.

F. Neither Trucking Highway Safety Nor Service Improvement is a Legitimate Justification for Horizontal Price Fixing.

The proposed report argues that vigorous competition drives some entrepreneurs close to the line of bankruptcy. The implicit message is that while close to bankruptcy, they may cut costs on equipment to the detriment of safety and may drive long and dangerous hours. There is, in fact, no evidence anywhere indicating that there is a predictable correlation between safety and degree of competition. That aspect of trucking subject to competitive pricing (e.g., the transportation of agricultural commodities) in interstate commerce for many years has never had a markedly worse safety record as compared to carriers subject to rate bureau cartel pricing. Indeed, published studies of trucking safety in the late 1960s, in the midst of minimum pricing floors and overwhelming cartel practices under ICC jurisdiction, revealed prevalent violation of rules limiting the number of hours drivers could drive, and of various equipment violations within the regulated sector.

One of the reasons for this lack of connection is the absence of relationship between horizontal price fixing and monies devoted to safety enhancement. Instead of setting a minimum rate floor and allowing voluntary price fixing, simply imagine the PUC somehow taxing all shippers and consumers and handing over to each trucker a check every six months equal to the difference between competitive rates and the rates allowed in this system as proposed. How much of that money will be spent on safety? Is there any requirement that this money be spent on safety? What are the forces which drive entrepreneurs to spend money for safety-related purposes? Is it because they have a natural predilection, where they have a little extra money, to spend it on safety?

There is a far more effective way to address safety concerns. That is to regulate safety. One does that by requiring certain equipment standards as a prerequisite to licensure, and by enforcing length of time rules. If the PUC is concerned about compliance, it might wish to require a small bond of all truckers to guarantee the payment of fines or damages where there are violations.

The proper solution to safety violations may be standards, bonding, strict liability, insurance requirements and enforcement, in any number of combinations.

Nor does the proposed report stimulate superior service. What guarantees outstanding service is the right to raise prices slightly where the costs of service are somewhat greater and the uncertainty of knowing that unless operations are kept efficient, prices low and service satisfactory, another entrepreneur will be chosen and the result will be loss of business. Ironically, it is not the security and insulation of guaranteed comfortable minimum rates which assures adequate service historically, it is insecurity and the need to please every possible customer in order to survive and prosper which does so. One might imagine the kind of service one might receive if our hamburgers were being sold by DMV, to cite an extreme example.

Some carriers, in competition with interstate carriers, will attempt to use the extra profit available because of the state proposed system to compete in areas where federal policy wisely is pro- competition. The misallocations from the system as proposed are somewhat predictable. The result will be declining sensitivity to rural service and low volume traffic because of the inflexibility of the rate structure, a movement of high volume traffic into exempt interstate carriers wherever possible, discrimination against current shippers as new shippers may be able to establish new rates without reference to the "me too" limitations of the proposed report, an inability to carry commerce at a profit where it has not been carried within the past year and the new prices are lower than current rates. This is a very partial list of the kinds of immediate dislocations which the report's system will create. These dislocations, as well as the decline in service, higher inefficiency and, over time, substantially higher rates, will be a momentous price for shippers and consumers. This momentous price will be paid by those diffuse interests it is the PUC's solemn trust to protect.

G. The Proposed Report does not Provide "Independent State Supervision" as Required by Law.

The proposed report rightfully describes the current law as requiring a two-pronged test to meet "state action" exemption from federal antitrust exposure. If this report were to be adopted as policy, California would be countenancing, and insulating from prosecution, the most heinous of all Sherman Act violations. Hence, the requirements allowing exemption may be construed strictly.

The first requirement is statutory authorization for the restraint. The second requirement is independent state supervision. It is unclear whether the statutory authorization in Public Utilities Code section 496 is specific enough so that a federal court will find that it manifests a legislative intent for minimum rate floors *et al.* However, in the area of independent state supervision, the report may be more seriously flawed. The United States Supreme Court has held that it is not "independent state supervision" for the state to simply defer to private bodies the critical decisionmaking which restrains trade. (See *California Retail Liquor Dealers Assn. v. Midcal Aluminum, Inc.*, 445 U.S. 97 (1980).) In *Midcal*, the Alcoholic Beverage Commission had allowed the manufacturers of liquor to set resale prices. It had routinely rubber-stamped their implementation. The court held that such a rubber-stamp procedure does not constitute the kind of *independent* state supervision necessary to compensate for an absent marketplace. Arguably, a system where 1,200 entrepreneurs are invited to get together in groups and fix prices, subject to review only if the prices exceed some index and if there is a complaint about them, would appear rather close to the rubber-stamp procedure condemned in *Midcal* and other cases. The fact that the proposed report involves horizontal price fixing, a much more serious violation than the vertical price fixing condemned in *Midcal*, should be cause for concern by PUC counsel.

If the marketplace is to be eschewed in favor of horizontal price fixing, whether voluntary or not, the resulting rates bear the same general dangers to the population as do the unfettered rates set by a monopolist. For reasons we have enumerated briefly above, the voluntary cartel, with a successful detection mechanism, may accomplish monopoly power pricing in the same way a power utility might. There is no independent state supervision unless the same kind of rate of return analysis is made to the profit levels of those entrepreneurs, where establishing prices by cartel private agreement.

Conclusion

In general, benefits from a horizontal price-fixing-assured profit level philosophy are ephemeral. Even the one concern most appropriate for consideration by the PUC, external costs which might flow from safety degeneration, are addressable by other means. The proof of benefits from the proposed report is essentially mere assertion.

If one eliminates those economists who serve as expert witnesses for the carriers, labor unions or large shippers, one finds an extraordinary unanimity of view from economists of a wide variety of ideology and orientation about this issue, to wit: the system of license restrictions, minimum rate floors and voluntary horizontal price fixing results in massive inefficiency, dislocations and shipper and consumer costs. The ascribed benefits to horizontal price fixing through rate bureaus (safety enhancement, administrative cost savings, service improvement) are illusory or are, in fact, impeded.

It is an axiom of the American economic system that the free market is the presumptive mechanism for distribution of goods and services. There may be good reason to compromise that principle, particularly in order to prevent abuse by natural monopolists or to confer an external benefit or minimize an external cost flowing from an unfettered marketplace. But before such intervention occurs, particularly intervention as extraordinary as massive voluntary horizontal price fixing with rate floors, one should have a very clear understanding of the external benefit or cost being addressed. And there should be overwhelming evidence of the relationship between the remedies selected and the results desired. Not only should the evidentiary standards be harsh, but the remedy should be the least restrictive alternative to maximum competition in achieving that result. The proposed report of the ALJ would sacrifice the heart of the free enterprise system as it benefits an important segment of commerce in order to achieve public benefits which are self-servingly described, lacking in demonstrable support and contrary to the elementary rules of the marketplace.

The proposed report begins by postulating that "a healthy motor carrier industry...is required by the prescription we have discussed." In fact, a healthy motor carrier system requires competition, particularly price competition. The reasoning of the proposed report to justify an extraordinary system of what is otherwise, and should be, prison term yielding felonies, is openly to benefit those who the PUC is created to regulate for the public interest. The proposed report revealingly notes in the synopsis "that the ad hoc proposal (a carrier proposal), with some modifications, best meets the concerns of all interested parties and offers a balance among the conflicting interests of the effected groups…." The effected groups, in this case, are those groups the PUC is mandated to limit and obligate in the interests of those who were *not* a party to the proceedings.

The protection of the consumer has been here turned upside down, into a corrupting system of favor dispensation. He who is organized and capable of burdening the PUC and private interests with administrative costs will obtain some advantage. Most PUC reviews will be interminable squabbles between interests contending that the proposed rates are too low and should be raised. Such has been the federal experience. To be sure, restricting price reductions, even to meet competition, to carriers who have carried *that* traffic within the past year, and setting floors at PUC-determined "prevailing wage rates" will limit the number of such disputes. Pricing low will become rather difficult.

The message is clear—everybody stays alive—nobody cuts into anyone else's territory. We all make out. It is an old siren song. The PUC should not be seduced by it. To embrace it, if the reader will pardon the harsh but appropriate hyperbole, is to commit regulatory adultery.

End of Excerpt

THE STATE BOARD OF FABRIC CARE: IT DOESN'T CARE FOR YOU

By John S. Moot

> *Is there anything in this business, or calling, constituting a substantial menace to the public peace, health or welfare to which such restriction has a reasonable relation?...We are unable to find it. Looking at the dry cleaning and/ or pressing business in the light of the record and briefs and applying such common knowledge of the subject as we are permitted to use, we are confirmed in our view that it is an ordinary simple occupation which, conducted in the normal way, involves no special danger to the public peace, health or welfare....We hold the Act to be unconstitutional...in that it attempts to exclude from an ordinary harmless occupation, upon insufficient grounds, those who are entitled...to engage in it, and thereby creates a monopoly in the group to which such privilege is extended.*
>
> —The North Carolina Supreme Court, when declaring that state's Dry Cleaner's Commission unconstitutional and invalid.

In a new political era in which the President strongly opposes the regulation of private businesses, and legislation on California State Government Organization and Economy (the Little Hoover Commission) conducted a study of the State Board of Dry Cleaners (presently the State Board of Fabric Care). The Commission concluded:

This board and licensing program should be abolished. The program offers no significant public protection and as such constitutes an unwarranted interference with [the free marketplace].[6] [note: footnote numbers are changed from original]

Following the Commission's report, two pieces of legislation were introduced, both designed to repeal the enabling act which created the Board. S.B. 338 (Miller, 1967) and S.B. 588 (Knox, 1968) both passed their

---

6 A report of findings and recommendations of the Commission on California State Government and Economy. *An Examination of the Department of Professional and Vocational Standards*, State of California (September 1967), p. 25.

respective policy committees and were approved by the Senate. However, after a flurry of last-minute, fervent lobbying by the California Dry Cleaners Association (the industry's trade association) and its full-time lobbyist, the bills were voted down on the Assembly floor. Yet, the battle over the dry cleaning board was far from over. In 1971, Governor Reagan introduced a government reorganization plan to abolish the State Board of Dry Cleaners and transfer its funds and duties to the State Fire Marshal.[7] This time the dry cleaners' trade association was more prepared and they quickly dispatched their professional lobbyists to the capitol steps. The reorganization plan was voted down by the Assembly. Again in 1975, Governor Brown tried to eliminate the Board by zero budgeting the agency in his appropriations budget bill. California Advocates, Inc. went back to the hill, and the Board's budget was reinstated. Finally, in 1978, in a sweeping attempt to sunset a number of agencies including the Board of Fabric Care, Speaker of the House Leo T. McCarthy ordered a lengthy survey of the Board's activities. This last legislative attempt to repeal the Board of Fabric Care died along with McCarthy's two sunset bills, A.B. 3145 and A.B. 46.

Despite the many protracted and heavily-lobbied legislative battles waged in defense of the Board of Fabric Care, the consensus about the Board's uselessness has remained unchanged. In 1979, the Department of Consumer Affairs, the state agency which oversees the Board of Fabric Care, recommended its abolition. The Department's report concluded that the Board did not materially affect the health, safety, or welfare of the consumer.[8] Apparently, the only thing that had changed in the 12 years since the Little Hoover Commission's 1967 report was, by 1979, no one could find a legislator willing to take on the industry's lobby.

To fully understand why the industry desires to be regulated and thus strongly opposes all attempts to terminate the Board, it is necessary to explore the Board's origins and its symbiotic relationship with the dry

---

[7] Reorganization Plan No. 2 of 1971.

[8] Department of Consumer Affairs Licensing Boards and Regulatory Programs, *Overview Budget Reduction* (Sacramento, 1979), p. 5.

cleaning industry. From its inception, the State Board of Dry Cleaners was the brainchild of dry cleaners. Enacted in 1945 under the state's police power to protect the public's health, safety, and welfare, the Dry Cleaners Law[9] was the product of a successful lobbying effort by a group of dry cleaners from the East Bay of San Francisco. Prior to 1945, dry cleaning was under the jurisdiction of the State Fire Marshal. It was during this period that Alameda County District Attorney Earl Warren was concerned about organized crime gaining a foothold in the industry. When Warren later became Governor of California, dry cleaners who were acquainted with the Governor decided the time was ripe. These original promoters reasoned and argued that if they were going to be regulated anyway (by the Fire Marshal), they should at least have some say in the matter. In addition, by 1945 at least three other states had experimented with dry cleaning commissions.[10] Many in the industry felt the licensing of dry cleaners would bring more respect to the industry as a whole.[11] While price-cutting and organized crime were a small undercurrent in the movement, the primary argument in favor of a board was that it would keep bad dry cleaners out of the business and confine the trade to those individuals who were competent.

The proposed dry cleaning law did, however, encounter opposition. Among the original provisions of the proposed law was a schedule of minimum prices for certain services. When Governor Warren objected to inclusion of the minimum price schedule, the minimum price provisions were replaced by a less objectionable clause which authorized the dry cleaning Board to establish minimum price schedules only when the Board deemed it necessary and only after receiving a request for the establishment of minimum price schedules from seventy-five percent (75%) of the licensed dry cleaners in

[9] Chapter 18, Division 3, Business and Professions Code Sections 9500, *et seq.*
[10] New Mexico (abolished by statute, Sections 61-201, 1978); Florida (abolished by statute, Sections 515.01, 1943); North Carolina (abolished judicially, *State v. Harris*, 6 S.E. 2d 854 (1940)).
[11] See 44 UNIVERSITY OF CHICAGO LAW REVIEW 6 (1976). Also, particular information regarding California comes from the author's interview with George Sheppard, former President of CFI. (CFI is the successor to the California Dry Cleaner's Association, the industry's trade association.)

a particular area. As one might suspect, the Alameda dry cleaners were able to get a minimum price schedule approved by the Board within a few years.[12] In 1953, however, the California Supreme Court struck down the price setting powers of the dry cleaning Board. In *State Board of Dry Cleaners v. Thrift-D-Lux Cleaners, Inc.*, the court ruled that while other sections of the 1945 Act could be justified as designed to protect the public health and safety, the minimum price schedules have no function to that end, but [instead] constitute an unnecessary and unreasonable restriction on the pursuit of private and useful business activity.[13]

In retrospect, the California Dry Cleaning Board walked away from its constitutional challenge wounded but not dead. The North Carolina Supreme Court, exercising a more rigorous review of the public health, safety, and welfare justification for its state Dry Cleaning Commission concluded the entire licensing act, Commission and all, was an unjustified delegation of the legislature's police power.[14] Florida's Supreme Court exhibited greater deference to their legislature's determination of what was in the "public interests" when in 1938 it upheld the act creating the Florida Dry Cleaning and Laundry Board.[15] The Florida Legislature, however, had second thoughts and repealed the law in 1943.[16]

While many of the California Board's formative years were spent in courtrooms defending its administrative powers,[17] by the late 1960s and 1970s the Board had managed to ally itself with some of the largest and most powerful dry cleaners in the state. The list of past presidents of the state Board is a virtual "who's who" in California dry cleaning. In fact, the list even includes the very man who challenged the original validity of the Dry Cleaners Law in the California Supreme Court. Yet, as the industry and its trade association became more active in

---

[12] *French Art Cleaners v. State Board of Dry Cleaners*, 91 Cal.App.2d 890 (1949).
[13] 40 Cal.2d 436 (1953).
[14] *State v. Harris,* 6 S.E.2d 854 (1940).
[15] *Miami Laundry Co. v. Florida Dry Cleaning & Laundry Board,* 183 So. 759 (1938).
[16] Chap. 21666, Florida Annotated Statutes, section 1.51501.
[17] *See Duskin v. State Board,* 58 Cal.2d 156 (1962).

its support of the Board, legislative skepticism was growing. In 1967 during the Senate hearings on S.B. 338 (Miller), representatives of the Dry Cleaners Association sought to justify the public need for regulation in California by referring to an article in the *Saturday Evening Post* about a Mafia don who ran his illicit operations from a New England dry cleaning store. The trade association argued for the state Board's continued existence by stating, "With the present law we can prevent this from happening [in California]." A year later while Senator Knox's bill was being debated, it was asserted that the Board was necessary to prevent dry cleaning stores from becoming fronts for "dope peddling, bookmaking and all this type of activity." This last preposterous proposition finally prompted Assemblyman Brown (presently Speaker Willie Brown) to state that (1) none of this had anything to do with the cleaning of his clothes, and (2) even if it did, such threats to the public welfare were not an administrative but rather a police problem.[18]

While some legislators were not persuaded by the association's public welfare and protection arguments, others never questioned either the sincerity or the propriety of the trade association's efforts on behalf of the Board. On February 9, 1973, the California Fabricare Institute (formerly the California Dry Cleaners Association) sent a letter to its capitol lobbyist to see if the legislature would appropriate $25,000 a year to the Board of Fabric Care[19] to study the environmental impact of dry cleaning. The request was passed on to State Senator George Deukmejian who, after limiting the appropriation to two successive years, introduced S.B. 501. In contrast to earlier bills opposed by the industry, S.B. 501 sailed through both houses and was signed into law. Upon receiving its first year's $25,000, the Board of Fabric Care promptly and incestuously awarded the full amount to the California Fabricare Institute's (CFI) parent organization, the International Fabricare Institute (IFI). The contract with IFI resulted in a report entitled

---

[18] From a report by the Department of Consumer Affairs. *Professional Licensing in California* (Sacramento, 1978), p. A-17.

[19] Not surprisingly, the Board requested a name change soon after the association changed its name.

Experimental Study on Solvent Discharge to the Environment. IFI was less fortunate the next year. Instead of ordering a follow-up study, the Board apparently allocated the next year's $25,000 to CFI to conduct a series of seminars. As of this date, the Board has neither a copy of the IFI report nor any records of its contracts concerning the expenditure of the S.B. 501 funds.[20]

LICENSE FEES: AN INESCAPABLE TRAP

While the foregoing may be regarded as an historical incident as unlikely to be repeated as the Board's early decision to set minimum prices, it is, nonetheless, illustrative of another key point. When Senator Deukmejian made his notations on the association's proposed bill asking for the $50,000, he stated "no fiscal impact." This same comment appears on all the legislative analyst's comments concerning monies for the Board. This is because the Board of Fabric Care, like many other state regulatory agencies, is financed through licensing fees. Instead of receiving its budget appropriation from the state's general fund, the Board is authorized by the Dry Cleaners Law to charge its licensees certain licensing fees. These fees provide the Board with an independent and secure source of revenue. Historically, the budgets of license fee-supported Boards, like the Board of Fabric Care, are not subject to legislative scrutiny. Legislators do not care how fee boards spend their money, and consequently rarely object to the appropriations for licensing boards.

The Board of Fabric Care charges fees for cleaning establishment licenses ($200 every two years), fees for shop licenses ($60 every two years), and fees for operator certification ($25 every two years). In addition, there is a $20 charge for taking the required examinations. Before an applicant is allowed to take an examination for any license, including that of hat renovator or fur renovator, the applicant must also have as much as 12 months experience or 360 hours of training, or as little as four months experience or 120 hours of training, depending on the license. This, of course, helps keep the dry cleaning

[20] Richard B. Spohn, Director of the Department of Consumer Affairs, has directed that the board not make any contracts with CFI without competitive bids.

schools in business ($250 annual license fee). With over 13,000 licensees, the Board of Fabric Care's major problem is concocting ways to spend all its money.[21]

While this ingenious licensing-fee method makes the Board fiscally autonomous and thus "free" to the legislature, it is far from free to the consumer. The licensing fees charged to dry cleaners are eventually passed on to the consumer in the price he or she pays for dry cleaning services. In effect, the legislature, through the Board of Fabric Care, exacts a direct but "hidden tax" from the over 7.5 million people who use the services of a dry cleaner every year.[22]

Yet, the particularly cruel feature of special-fund financing is that it fosters a regulatory attitude and system which produces an agency that is little more than a consumer relation board for the industry. A few examples clarify this point. At a recent meeting, Board members were discussing legislation which would permit the Assembly to borrow interest-free the excess monies in the Board's Special Fund. The Executive Secretary's response to this proposal was: "The industry should do something to protect their (the industry's) funds." In response, the President of the Board turned to a member of the California Fabricare Institute who was present at the meeting and said that CFI should certainly look into this. What is interesting about this exchange is that the Board clearly regards the money raised by its licensing fees as belonging to the industry—to be spent only on dry cleaning--related projects. While this is a common notion, it is nothing short of a total fallacy. As noted previously, the license fees charged by the Board are in fact a special tax on the consumer. As such, there is nothing sacred about the Board's fee generated revenue which compels the Board to spend its money only on dry cleaners. In New

---

[21] At one point in 1981, the Board was told it was going to have to lower its licensing fees because of its large special fund surplus. Instead, the Board managed to include a $217,200 appropriation in A.B. 103 (Robinson) which saved them from having to lower fees.

[22] This figure is taken from *Fieldscope Report, a Summary of California Adults Concerning Consumer Complaints.* Department of Consumer Affairs Report on *Professional Licensing in California,* Part IV (Sacramento, 1978), p. 11 in the Summary of Field Poll.

York, which is typical of the 48 other states, the legislature readily permits counties and municipalities to directly tax dry cleaning establishments. There is no requirement that the money raised be spent on dry cleaners.[23] Furthermore, the California Legislature itself abolished the special fund system briefly in 1961 and merged all revenues into the general fund (A.B. 1833, Unruh).

The notion that the funds raised by the Board belong exclusively to Board licensees combines with another even more pernicious by-product of the licensing-fee system to aggravate an already deplorable situation. Boards which generate revenue solely from licensing fees are put in the rather unique and difficult position of having to regulate and discipline those who pay for its activities. As one consumer group noted, this method of financing tends to blur the distinction between regulator and licensee:

> By funding the board, licensees obtain a customer-like status The result is a perversion of the regulatory process which transforms regulatory agencies into little more than dues- financed vocational social clubs, dedicated to promoting the general welfare *but only to the degree which the membership is willing to pay.* (emphasis added.)[24]

While past Boards of Fabric Care may have been "dues-financed social clubs"[25] such criticism is less accurate when applied to the present Board. Limited progress has been achieved.[26]

---

[23] McKinney's Consolidated Laws of New York Annotated, Tax Law, Article 29, section 1210.

[24] Quoted from a report by the National Community Consumer Education Project for Occupational Licensing: *A New Role for Consumers.* Paul H. Douglas (Washington, 1978) p. 27. The actual statement comes from San Francisco Consumer Action.

[25] A former member of the Board recalls the days when a quick meeting and some golf were not unknown.

[26] However, it should be noted that critics of the Board do not attribute the recent progress made by the Board to reform-minded industry members. Any progress made by the Board in recent years is directly and solely attributable to the addition of public members to the Board. Absent the addition of public members, the Board would be as backward as ever.

THE BOARD'S RECENT SORDID HISTORY

Yet the subtle effects of special-fund financing takes its toll even on the most conscientious and hardworking of Boards. For example, the Board of Fabric Care *has revoked only one license since 1976*. It is hard to see how consumers are protected from fraud and dishonesty in the industry when the Board fails to make even a colorable attempt to exercise its policing function over the industry. While this lack of discipline may be partly due to the angelic qualities of the majority of dry cleaners, certainly one other factor is simply the Board's reluctance to bite the hand that feeds it. For example, last year in Contra Costa County, a Spanish-speaking woman was charged $170 by Cleanco Cleaners for the cleaning and boxing of two dresses. While the Board readily admitted that the woman had been vastly overcharged, the Executive Secretary told the woman, "There is no violation [of law] because you left the items without first obtaining a price; there is nothing more this board can do to assist you."[27] But there is something the Board could have done. A year before the Contra Costa woman was so flagrantly overcharged, the staff counsel for the Department of Consumers Affairs issued an informal opinion stating that the Board did in fact have the power to require and enforce price posting. The Board simply chose not to exercise that power.

The problem is that when push comes to shove, the Board ultimately adopts the position most favorable to the industry. Two other examples stand out. Recently, a public member proposed that the Board develop a complaint disclosure policy so consumers would have a readily available means of avoiding an incompetent dry cleaner. The proposal was quickly abandoned with the consensus that a fair system *to the dry cleaner* could not be developed. Secondly, there was a big falling out when the Board put together its otherwise commendable *Consumer's Guide to Fibers, Fabrics, and Finishes*. Some public members strongly argued that a brief section on small claims court should be included in the last section of the booklet entitled, "Help for the Consumer." The booklet was printed without any mention of small

[27] "State Joins Cleaning Dispute," *Contra Costa Times,* March 22, 1981.

claims court. This was undoubtedly due to the fact that the vast majority of dry cleaners taken to small claims court are found liable to the consumer. Once again, and in revealingly dramatic fashion, the Board chose to protect those who fund them and neglect those they are required by law to protect.

If Board inaction is illustrative of how the agency fails to vigorously protect consumers, Board "action" is equally illustrative of the thesis that the Board performs an effective and essentially free consumer relations function for the industry. The Board of Fabric Care's consumer information and continuing education seminars are probably the most notable projects the Board performs. In these seminars, lectures are presented on such topics as garment mislabeling and problem trends with new fabrics difficult or impossible to clean. Not surprisingly, however, these lectures and periodic bulletins are largely (90%) prepared for and attended by dry cleaners. The theory, of course, is that the information and benefits eventually "trickle down" to the consumer.

Another example of the valuable consumer relation function the Board performs is complaint mediation. The Board receives over 1,222 complaints in any given year. The Board seeks to "resolve" these complaints by talking to the consumer and the dry cleaner involved. Sometimes the Board has the consumer send the damaged garment to the trade association's testing laboratory for analysis. Yet, if the consumer is still not satisfied after the Board's hand--holding efforts, the complaint is considered resolved. *Rarely is the consumer referred to small claims court where he can get a quick dollar settlement for his or her damaged clothes.*

The attitude adopted in complaint handling is that dry cleaners cannot be held responsible for mistakes made by the consumer. If the consumer brings in a fabric which is mislabeled or difficult to clean, and it is ruined by the dry cleaner, the Board does not feel the dry cleaner should be responsible. While this is certainly a beneficial position as far as the industry is concerned, it leaves the consumer out in the cold. As many of the state's small claims courts recognize, it is the dry cleaner, not the consumer, who is trained and in a better position to know whether or not a garment can be safely cleaned. As such, the dry cleaner should have a duty to inspect and return those clothes which cannot be safely cleaned, or bear the risk of loss once a garment is accepted for cleaning.

Because the argument over whether the Board of Fabric Care is in fact the vanguard for the consumer, or merely a beneficial sounding board for the industry, could be continued for eternity, *it is more productive to explore the question whether any regulation of the dry cleaning industry is necessary*. Historically, the state only invokes its police power to license and regulate business when serious social problems exist and there are no economic incentives within the offending business that will encourage "self-regulation." Child labor and air pollution are the classic examples. On the other hand, the licensing and regulation of occupations like dry cleaning for the alleged purpose of protecting the public welfare has recently come under scrutiny because of a re-evaluation of the need for, and effectiveness of, such programs. All of us would acknowledge the need to regulate against serious specific social abuses. However, there is an equally strong, if not more fundamental belief in a free and unfettered market place. In this country, the market forces of supply and demand are generally regarded as the most efficient and effective means of allocating resources and promoting the general public welfare.

DO ADEQUATE MARKET FORCES EXIST?

Dry cleaning by its very nature is a business particularly sensitive to the self-regulating forces of our free market. Most importantly, there is a large, plentiful supply of dry cleaning services available throughout the state. Consumers who are not satisfied with how their clothes are being cleaned can, and will, take their business elsewhere. This is a particularly strong self-regulating force in the dry cleaning business because, as any dry cleaner will tell you, repeat customers are the heart and soul of a successful operation. This dependence on repeat customers interacts with the large capital expenditures necessary to start a dry cleaning shop to provide further free market incentives to "self-regulate." It costs anywhere between sixty and ninety thousand dollars to purchase and install the modern equipment necessary to make a dry cleaning plant competitive. The prospect of losing this substantial capital investment is a strong economic incentive which, when combined with the repeat nature of the business, is capable of curtailing most of the abuses in the industry. *Certainly, this is the most logical explanation why the overwhelming majority of the states manage to survive without a regulatory agency for dry cleaners.*

Yet, even when abuses do occur in the interaction between consumer and dry cleaner, many state institutions already exist that are more capable of adequately handling possible problems than the Board of Fabric Care. The most common problem within the system is damaged clothes. The injury the consumer suffers, however, is not irreparable. Small claims court provides an effective and quick process whereby a consumer can obtain a dollar award for his damaged clothes. Also, the nature of the transaction between consumers and dry cleaner is one that occurs at arm's length. There is nothing particularly sophisticated about the dry cleaning process which renders a consumer especially vulnerable to an unscrupulous dry cleaner. Gross breaches of trust are, of course, actionable by the District Attorney under the criminal code or the unfair business and advertising section of the Business and Professions Code (section 17200 and section 17500). Routine complaints can be handled by the Better Business Bureau.

THE SINGLE REAL PROBLEM

The use of potentially toxic and volatile chemicals is the only real public health and safety problem within the dry cleaning industry. Here again, however, there are other state and local agencies more capable of addressing the problem. The use of toxic chemicals involves two separate issues. First, there is the problem of the stationary or closed system use of perchlorethylene and stoddard. These are primary cleaning agents used in dry cleaning. In high concentrations perchlorethylene is a potential (though unproven) carcinogen. In addition, high concentrations of perchlorethylene pose environmental problems when released into the atmosphere or improperly disposed of in non-class 1 chemical waste dumps. Stoddard, on the other hand, is dangerous only because it is highly flammable. At present the State Board of Fabric Care does very little regulating concerning the in- plant use of these chemicals.[28] The reason that this conspicuous lack of meaningful regulation does not pose any particular problem is that the State Air Resources Board and Cal-OSHA are in fact better equipped and more on top of the potential hazards. The State Air Resources Board oversees and sets guidelines for the local Air Pollution Control Districts. Local pollution control agencies make a thorough inspection of every dry cleaning plant for all potential environmental and pollution problems. A permit from the local Air Pollution Control District is required by law and must be renewed every year, subject to inspection every six months by the local control boards. A dry cleaner who operates without a permit can be fined and enjoined from operating. Secondly, Cal-OSHA conducts studies and sets the appropriate concentration levels for the industrial use of chemicals. Both Cal-OSHA and the dry cleaners trade associations have made extensive studies on the use of perchloroethylene. Cal-OSHA typically has offices in every community in California and can readily respond to any dangers posed by the chemical solvents used in dry cleaning. Furthermore, Cal-OSHA has strong administrative powers which can be used to enforce its guidelines and regulations. There is no need for the Board of Fabric Care to poorly and wastefully duplicate the functions of Cal-OSHA and the Air Pollution Control Districts.

A more pressing problem involves the use of chemicals in what is known as "on-site" dry cleaning. This term merely refers to the dry cleaning of draperies, rugs, and furniture in consumers' homes. On-site cleaning poses a serious and immediate problem. While the Board of Fabric Care should be strongly commended for its hard work in instigating and procuring legislation (A.B. 103) on this problem, it is, however, entirely incapable of executing an effective program. This is largely due to the fact that the Board only has jurisdiction over "on-site" drapery

[28] The Board's one regulation merely mimics the levels already set by the federal government.

cleaning and not over carpet and upholstery cleaning. This means that a substantial majority of those doing on-site dry cleaning are not even regulated by the Board.

The present program designed by the Board would expend $182,000 to license and inspect only on- site drapery cleaners. The program totally ignores the fact that the same dry cleaner in the same home could be chemically cleaning carpets and furniture without a license and without being subject to disciplinary action. Such a result is clearly absurd and would hardly protect the consumer from the real dangers posed by the on-site use of chemicals. The use of chemicals in people's homes is a health hazard whose enforcement ramifications extend well beyond the means of a small regulatory agency like the Board of Fabric Care which cannot even effectively inspect and discipline all its licensees.[29] Moreover, according to conservative estimates, 10-20% of the industry is unlicensed.

Yet, given the recent fervor over on--site cleaning, the California Legislature will undoubtedly hear cries and requests from the rival trade associations of carpet cleaners that they too should become licensed and regulated. They, of course, will demand membership on the Board of Fabric Care or maybe even suggest a whole new agency—the State Board of On-site Carpet Cleaning. One need only look at the history and evolution of the old State Board of Dry Cleaners to see what a mistake this would be.

A MERCIFUL DEATH THAT IS LONG OVERDUE

From its very birth, the State Board of Dry Cleaners was little more than a private lobby to enhance the occupational status of the industry. The original enabling legislation also had the beneficial side effect of allowing an industry-dominated state agency to set prices at the request of the industry. At that time such state-sanctioned activity was called regulation. Today, it would more appropriately be called a violation of the antitrust laws.

---

[29] The number of unlicensed dry cleaning shops in the state may be as high as 10% to 20% based on the averages of existing figures compiled by the Board. Furthermore, some plants, like the Board President's, had not been inspected for five years, at least until he mentioned the fact at a recent meeting.

Yet, despite its many setbacks in the courts, the Board survived and continued to grow and evolve. At times the distinction between the regulated and the regulator became so blurred that not even the legislature perceived the impropriety of the trade association requesting appropriations for the state Board which, in turn, merely awarded the money right back to the trade association.

Ultimately, however, the majority of the legislature was, and probably still is, perfectly willing to tolerate the Board of Fabric Care. Special-fund financing makes the Board "free" to the legislators and, as such, most are unwilling to take the inevitable political heat from a well-organized lobby should they propose the elimination of the Board. Besides, the 7.5 million people who are subject to the legislature's "hidden" tax never make it to capitol hill to complain. The loser, of course, is the consumer. While the Board may no longer be a "dues-financed social club," its system of special funding practically insures that it will not vigorously pursue still unresolved and in some cases unconsidered nuts and bolts consumer issues. The moment fee-paying licensees object to price posting, complaint disclosure, or small claims court, the Board buckles under.

Because it is neither a threat to the industry (in the sense that it might occasionally adopt a pro- consumer stance) nor a financial burden to the legislature, it is easy to understand how the State Board of Fabric Care survives despite the current "deregulatory" political winds. Yet, clearly, the Board is unnecessary. Forty-eight other states manage without one. The local Air Pollution Control Districts, Cal-OSHA, and possibly the Bureau of Home Furnishings can more than adequately take care of any present or future safety problems posed by the industry. Our free market economy combines with the inherent nature of a highly capitalized, repeat--oriented business structure to adequately self-regulate the industry. Furthermore, the vast majority of dry cleaners are conscientious and hardworking. These dry cleaners *and their customers* do not need the Board of Fabric Care. Neither does the State of California.

Cartel Control of Attorney Licensure and the Public Interest*

by Robert C. Fellmeth, Bridget Fogarty Gramme,
C. Christopher Hayes**

8 BRIT. J. AM. LEGAL STUD. 193, Fall 2019

* The word "cartel" is used purely according to its economic definition—" a grouping of producers who work together to protect their interests." See Cartels, Economics Online, www.economicsonline.co.uk/Business_economics/Cartels.html.

***

I. Introduction

An incompetent or dishonest attorney can visit irreparable harm upon his or her clients, and lessen the fairness and efficacy of the judicial system that is central to our democracy. Attorneys and physicians have a more compelling justification for a licensure requirement to practice than do barbers or astrologers (which California once seriously considered licensing). But these supply constraints have their own negative effects. They mean higher prices and diminished availability of needed services. So how do we reconcile these two legitimate and somewhat conflicting features? The question raised here is how to accomplish that balance, and just as importantly who should be doing the balancing.

It is critical to recognize that existing systems of entry in the licensed professions are controlled by those currently practicing in the professions. Although current practitioners may have advantageous knowledge about needed performance, the professions' control of their own supply gives rise to the appearance of a serious conflict of interest. Our regulatory systems raise the proverbial drawbridge for the benefit of those already in the castle. Those with an occupational self-interest decide who will be allowed to offer services in the future. This article questions whether this process reflects functioning democracy—one in which the People control the state, not the special interests.

Two facts make this a timely legal and ethical issue.

First, supply control through licensure is a restraint of trade that artificially affects prices—a per se antitrust offense when performed by horizontal competitors.

Second, the U.S. Supreme Court in *North Carolina State Board of Dental Examiners v. Federal Trade Commission*, 574 U.S. __, 135 S. Ct. 1101, 191 L. Ed. 2d 35 (2015), recently held that state regulatory boards controlled by "active market participants" in the trade or profession being regulated categorically lack sovereign status, and may not claim state action immunity for anticompetitive decisions made in the regulatory context unless an independent state body actively supervises all final decisions.

This profound legal circumstance raises particular questions as to the supply of attorneys in an era in which an increasing number of people in the U.S. report that they cannot afford a lawyer—and in which an estimated 75% of litigants in civil court are unrepresented.[1] It is time to revisit the wisdom and motivations behind deeply-engrained barriers to entering the legal profession. These barriers have been erected and maintained by attorney-dominated state bars across the country, with little-to-no supervision. Of specific and immediate concern are: 1) unprecedented student debt resulting from the skyrocketing costs of education (both undergraduate and at law schools); 2) unparalleled higher education prerequisites to licensure compared to other nations, without proof that seven years of higher education provides actual assurance of attorney competence; 3) declining bar exam pass rates nationwide, on an exam that has not been proven in content or cut score to correlate at all with competence assurance (especially given the evolution of legal practice in this technological age); and 4) un-redressed consumer harm resulting from failure to measure attorney competence at any point after the bar examination, and a profession-controlled system that generally does not provide a safety net to compensate victims who are injured by attorney error.

We ended the medieval guilds that controlled entry into occupations with good reason. Have we now resurrected them without proper checks?

This article seeks to measure and evaluate the performance of the legal profession in its own regulation, not based on our self-interested notions of public-spirited dedication to the common good, but based on what actually happens, what it costs, and how its justifications may not exist by any good faith measure.

It is possible to have both enhanced supply of attorneys and assured competence. Currently, we have neither. Here we propose ten reasonable corrections to the existing system that will bring about much-needed reform to the legal profession.

II. The Anticompetitive Underpinnings of Attorney Licensure in the United States

A. Attorney Self-Regulation and the State of the Legal Services Market

It has been well-documented for quite some time that indigent populations cannot access the legal services they need. According to a 2017 report, 86% of the civil legal problems reported by low- income Americans over the scope of one year received inadequate or no legal help.[2] And 71% of low-income households experienced at least one civil legal problem, including problems with domestic violence, veterans' benefits, disability access, housing conditions, and health care.[3] These problems are not limited to the indigent. More and more individuals across the U.S. report that they cannot afford a lawyer.[4] Indeed a recent report found that a full 76% of civil cases in state courts involve a self-represented party.[5]

The diminishing ability of a majority of people in the United States to access legal services calls for a careful reexamination, starting with the origins of our current system. We can no longer ignore that onerous barriers to enter the profession, and ethics rules preventing the delivery of legal services through less expensive means, are the direct result of regulatory capture. Indeed, all of these artificial barriers—from exorbitantly difficult bar examinations to outright prohibitions on providing less expensive and more accessible legal services despite clear market demand—have been erected under the guise of "public protection" by those who directly benefit from their exclusionary outcomes: attorneys themselves.[6]

How has this occurred? Attorneys are regulated on a state-by-state basis, in varying forms and with varying levels of oversight by the respective state supreme courts. But this state regulation necessarily involves state rules and practices that may violate federal antitrust law. By its very nature, licensing is a means of controlling supply; the profession is establishing through its admissions rules an artificial barrier to entering the legal profession. In doing so, it artificially affects prices. This is a form of price fixing, considered unreasonable "per se" under the Sherman Act.[7]

State regulators, including state bars, may nevertheless impose otherwise anticompetitive policies if they qualify for "state action immunity." The problem is, the U.S. Supreme Court has made clear that regulatory boards controlled by "active participants" in the trade or profession being regulated (*e.g.*, state bars comprised of a majority of attorneys, and all of them are) cannot qualify for this immunity unless they can show that they are being independently and actively supervised by the state.

As noted, this principle was cemented by the Supreme Court's holding in *North Carolina State Board of Dental Examiners v. Federal Trade Commission.*[8] In that holding, Justice Kennedy wrote for the majority as follows:

> Limits on state-action immunity are most essential when the State seeks to delegate its regulatory power to active market participants, for established ethical standards may blend with private anticompetitive motives in a way difficult even for market participants to discern. Dual allegiances are not always apparent to an actor. In consequence, active market participants cannot be allowed to regulate their own markets free from antitrust accountability.[9]

This is precisely what has been allowed to occur for decades with respect to the regulation of the legal profession, and the reason why the market for legal services is in desperate need of reform.

But state bars (and state supreme courts) across the country have been slow to recognize the anticompetitive implications of the landmark *North Carolina* holding on the existing regulatory structures for attorneys in every single state—structures that are obviously controlled by active market participants. Per the Supreme Court's decision, the only way to ensure that these state bars are not adopting anticompetitive policies is to ensure that their actions are "clearly articulated and affirmatively expressed as state policy," and that the state is independently and "actively" supervising them.[10] The Supreme Court, and the Federal Trade Commission in its subsequently- issued Staff Guidance on Active Supervision of State Regulatory Boards Controlled by Active Market Participants,[11] have set forth clear minimum requirements for establishing active supervision to assure that public decisions are made by an entity other than one controlled by the regulated trade or profession.

The Court has identified only a few constant requirements of active supervision:

> The supervisor must review the substance of the anticompetitive decision, not merely the procedures followed to produce it; the supervisor must have the power to veto or modify particular decisions to ensure they accord with state policy; and the "mere potential for state supervision is not an adequate substitute for a decision by the State." Further, the state supervisor may not itself be an active market participant.[12]

State supreme courts—the state entities that are charged with "supervising" attorney regulation— are ill-equipped to actively supervise decisions by market participants. They are passive bodies, accustomed to resolving disputes brought before them. They lack the mechanisms for independent supervision, or for analysis as to the potential anticompetitive impacts of the policies adopted and implemented among the state bars.[13] To the authors' knowledge, no state Supreme Court has engaged in the type of supervision set forth in the *North Carolina* decision—with independent decisionmakers who do not participate in the market reviewing the substance of potentially anticompetitive decisions with veto power.[14]

Furthermore, such courts tend to embody confidence in their own profession and its membership, particularly where those persons are respected leaders, and may have been appointed to their state regulatory posts by the court itself. For example, as discussed *infra*, the California Supreme Court is currently, to its credit, investigating the bar exam cut score, and other entry restraint practices that lead the majority of examination takers in California to flunk. But it is delegating the information gathering and consideration of alternatives to State Bar entities controlled by practicing attorneys. State supreme courts may qualify as independent supervisors for antitrust purposes. But they must be "active." It should go without saying that they must not delegate their supervisory role straight back to the very entities with an ulterior economic interest in the outcome.[15]

In the four years since the Supreme Court issued the *North Carolina* decision, state supreme courts have done little to supervise or curb protectionist behavior by state bars across the country. For example, in 2018, the Washington State Bar Association refused to add Limited License Legal Technicians (LLLT) and Limited Practice Officers (LPOs) to its Board of Governors, even despite the Washington Supreme Court's order that they do so.[16] In 2018, the Florida Bar sought an injunction against TIKD, an app which connects consumers to lawyers to represent them in traffic court, for the unauthorized practice of law.[17] The New Jersey Supreme Court declined to review a bar ethics opinion prohibiting lawyers from participating in fixed fee legal services platforms such as Avvo Advisor—an action which ultimately prompted Avvo to cease this service nationwide.[18] State supreme courts' practice of delegating competition-related decisions to their attorney-controlled state bars is prevalent across the nation. Their impact is acutely felt by those who cannot afford legal services as a result of the radical supply diminution and absence of alternative legal services from these cartel restrictions.

B. The Role of the ABA as Cartel Overseer

Headquartered in Chicago, the American Bar Association ("ABA") is a horizontal trade group of attorneys.[19] It boasts 400,000 members across the country, and its law school accreditation process affects every member of the public who seeks out a lawyer. Nineteen states and four territories require a degree from an ABA-accredited law school in order to take their bar exams.[20] If a law school does not conform to the standards of the ABA and pay the fees associated with accreditation,[21] its graduates cannot sit for the bar in other states that require it.[22] Indeed, any law school administrator is likely to admit that a major concern is the ABA accreditation visit that involves inspections, interviews and critiques of law school governance and policies. Even though the ABA is not a government entity,[23] part of its function is so closely intertwined with attorney regulation that it effectively functions as one—albeit one run by lawyers and lacking democratic legitimacy. Its actions all but carry the force of law.[24] Although its officers and agents are well-intentioned and engage in many salutary projects, it stands as a substantial impediment to attorney licensure in the public interest.[25]

As this article will explore, many of the factors contributing to what can best be described as a "failed market" for legal services have at their origin policies that were developed, and in some cases enforced, by the ABA. From stringent standards for law school accreditation (including a minimum number of costly tenured faculty and a unique-to-the-U.S. bachelor's degree requirement for all entering law students), to its model rules of professional conduct (prohibiting multijurisdictional practice, corporate ownership of law firms, and "fee sharing" with non-lawyers), the ABA has played a significant role in erecting the barriers to entering the legal profession and the high costs of legal services.[26] On the other hand, if willing, it has the potential to implement sweeping positive changes to the profession.

III. Existing Barriers to Entering the Legal Profession

A. *Law School Qualification: The Undergraduate Travail*

Undergraduate College Education Costs

Undergraduate college education costs nationally continue to rise rapidly above inflation. In 1988, public college tuition cost an average of $3,360 per year.[27] That figure was $10,230 per year in 2018-19.[28] Over the same period, tuition and fees at private non-profit colleges climbed from $17,010 to $35,830 per year.[29] For all four years at private non-profit schools, the total has risen from $68,040 to $143,320 for tuition alone.[30]

Room and board has also increased. When including room and board with tuition those numbers jump from $9,480 per year in 1988 to $21,370 per year in 2018–19 for public schools and from $24,800 per year in 1988 to $48,510 in 2018-19 for private non-profits.[31] Including only basic tuition and room and board, the total cost of a four year undergraduate education is now $85,480 for in-state public college students, $149,720 for out-of-state public college students, and $194,040 for private school students.[32] And these figures exclude other often-substantial costs that have also suffered major increases beyond inflation over the last thirty years, including transportation, communications, clothing, books, and food—all beyond what a college would provide.

College education today puts an unprecedented burden on families. Students and their parents are borrowing and sacrificing pensions to pay for education. In contrast to the dramatic rise of college costs, median family income in constant dollars nationally went up marginally from $51,973 in 1987 to $57,617 in 2016—the most recent Census Department figure. Basic college costs have increased from 20.4% of median income in 1971 to 51.8% today.[33]

Certainly there are benefits to a liberal arts education, including many of the courses discussed *infra*, but the evolving economy offers work in diverse, changing, and specialized fields increasingly unconnected to this lengthy and expensive precursor. The issue raised is not whether we must eliminate non-career-oriented courses altogether, but whether such courses need to include up to 40 three-unit subjects over four years, as opposed to a somewhat smaller number.

Four Years of Undergraduate Expense and Coursework as a Prerequisite to Law School

Throughout the United States, law school entry is essentially barred to anyone without a full undergraduate degree.[34] The crushing debt load on today's students, and the questionable relevance of many curricular choices, properly raises the following question: can four years of undergraduate education be conscionably justified as a mandatory prerequisite to law school? Virtually the entire world requires five years of total higher education to practice law. The United States generally requires seven. Is this burdensome prerequisite justified?

The United Kingdom teaches law as an undergraduate course of study lasting three years, followed by a one-year full-time practical skills training course, followed in turn by a one-year pupillage or apprenticeship in the case of barristers,[35] or two years of a practice-based training contract in the case of solicitors.[36] From the moment most law students begin university study, the education focuses on the practice of law. The doctrinal study in the first three years serves as a basis for future practical training.[37] For both solicitors and barristers, that practical training takes the form of a one- year course, designed to bridge the gap between the academics of the first few years and the apprenticeship to follow.[38] Thereafter, pupillage is a requirement before any student becomes a barrister,[39] as is two years of practice-based training for solicitors.[40]

In contrast to this British model, the pattern of most other nations,[41] or even the specialized undergraduate education undertaken (or necessitated) for graduate degrees in engineering or medicine (*e.g.*, pre-med), American law schools do not require any particular type of prerequisite learning beyond a bachelor's degree.[42] As a result, some law students begin learning legal doctrine four years after their English counterparts.[43] By that point, middle or lower-class American law students have borrowed six figures to pay for four years of required university study in what is often unrelated subject matter.[44]

To be sure, there is value in a general liberal arts education and in courses separate and apart from a future occupation. But as time and expenses increase, more careful thought as to the connection between the required number of courses and an articulable end purpose is warranted. At some point, relevance becomes relevant. For example, a review of the undergraduate courses for recent applicants to the University of San Diego School of Law[45] includes one typical student with the following courses: Peace Theories, Intermediate Arabic, Physical

Education, African Music, Human Sexual Behavior, Visual Design and Dress, Intermediate Poetry Writing, Motivation, Trigonometry, Living in Multi-Cultural Society, Human Osteology, Introduction to Archeology, Strategies in Stress Management, and Artist's Perspective: Drawing. Another student in this law school application pool took the following college classes: Keyboard Skills, Harmony, Jazz Combo, History of Rock Music, Instrumental Improvisation, Poetic Imagination, Comic and Tragic Vision, Wild Times, Prison Gangs, French Cinema, Juvenile Gangs, and Realism and Romance.

While many courses listed on some applicants' transcripts do suggest law school relevance, such as courses in economics, sociology, history, and even direct law content choices in constitutional or criminal law subjects, they tend not to be the majority or even a substantial percentage of courses undertaken by law school applicants.

In light of the dubious relevance of many undergraduate courses to the practice of law, we must consider the costs to students' families, the ever-growing burden of student debt,[46] and the supply reduction impact for those who would benefit from affordable legal services. Over the last two decades, burgeoning creativity of course ideas—ranging from a course on Beyoncé to two units for "bowling"—raise concerns over these factors in our regulation of entry into the legal profession.

B. *Increasing Law School Costs And Debt*

Increasing Costs of Law School

Adding to the sobering financial situation facing many of today's entering law students is an even more extreme upward trend—the cost of law school itself. Often starting out with debt from four years of mandatory undergraduate education, students without independent sources of funding must borrow three more years' worth of tuition and housing, in addition to other expenses. Law school is thus a substantial financial barrier to entry into remunerative attorney employment in the U.S.

The total cost of a legal education now approaches or exceeds the median cost of a home in the United States.[47]

In terms of tuition alone, Columbia leads the pack at $69,916 per year.[48] The average private non-profit law school tuition nationally is $47,754 in 2018 dollars.[49] For public law schools the average tuition is $27,160. Tuition by itself is now at an expected sum of approximately $80,000 to $144,000 for the typical three-year term of law school attendance. This sum does not include housing, transportation, food, books, or bar exam review courses—or the opportunity costs of three years' foregone employment.

This tuition increase is not a product of inflation. A recent study concludes: "[L]aw school tuition increases exceed the inflation rate between 1985 and 2018. In 1985, the average private school tuition was $7,526 (1985 dollars), which would have cost a student $17,520 in 2018. Instead, average tuition was $47,754 (2018 dollars)."[50] Accordingly, private law school was 2.73 times as expensive in 2018 as it was in 1985 after adjusting for inflation.

> In 1985, the average public [law] school tuition was $2,006 (1985 dollars) for residents, which would have cost a student $4,670 in 2018 dollars. Instead, average tuition is $27,160 (2018 dollars) for residents. In other words, public [law] school [tuition for in-state students] was 5.82 times as expensive in 2018 as it was in 1985 after adjusting for inflation.[51]

In addition to law school tuition, students must find a way to pay for three years of living expenses. A survey of the 203 ABA-accredited law schools nationally from 2011-12 to 2018–19 found only 43 with small decreases in living expenses, whereas 153 had increases—104 of which exceeded the 11.4% cost of living (CPI) increase for this period.[52]

On average, a law student can expect to spend $20,000 to $24,000 per year on living expenses, with California school living expenses often between $30,000 and $37,000.[53] Assuming a conservative $20,000 figure, this adds $60,000 over three years to the total law school tuition figures discussed above, for a total of $140,000 for tuition and living expenses at a public law school, and $200,000 for a private non-profit law school. These figures are on top of the sums already paid for undergraduate tuition and housing of $50,000 to $188,000 for those previous four years.

In short, the seven-year cost of public education for attorney licensure, including only tuition and housing, is now an expected $190,000 at public schools for in-state students[54] and $388,000 at private non-profit— with these unprecedented numbers likely to continue to increase well above inflation.[55]

The Setting: Actual Law School Tuition and Market Dysfunction

Assuming a competitive market, how do prices of this type increase at levels largely disparate from cost factors? The adage "competition drives prices toward costs," with higher demand rewarding those who offer a comparable product at a lower price, does not seem to apply to this service market. Costs have increased somewhat for faculty salaries, but at no level close to tuition increases.[56] Nor are other cost increases apparent that explain them. One major factor in this competitive failure is what may be termed the "Cuisinart effect." *Cuisinart*[57] was a vertical price fixing case in which an appliance manufacturer cut off retailers who lowered prices below the suggested retail price of its products. The reason for insisting on higher prices than others rested on Cuisinart's public relations approach—that its products were "clearly superior" to others, and that its superiority was understandably reflected in its higher price. If its price were to be lowered to those of competitors, the public implication would be that others were of equal or higher quality. The same concern demarks the public persona of many trade names, from Mondavi Cabernet to Cadillac.

This perception, that comparative quality is manifested in price, is a core part of law school tuition increases. It is common for the administration and faculty of law schools to measure their tuition levels based on those of their competitors, with subjective quality of the school a major factor. Hence, when law school faculties consider increasing tuition by two-to-three times inflation levels, the discussion is invariably as follows: "We would note that our three rival law schools, not up to our caliber, have increased their tuition 3–5% and will be at a higher level than are we. We risk a public impression that we are of inferior quality if we fail to match or exceed their tuition levels." And the pattern of such effective "price leadership" increases suggests that this same conversation is hardly unusual.

The "Cuisinart effect" in its original application involved a vertical price fixing case, but its anticompetitive impact in the horizontal context has a much more deleterious impact. It allows these prices to be raised well above theoretically competitive levels through a pattern of price leadership and replication. Any one competitor who raises tuition then causes other law schools to move up in price by a similar degree. The normal drive of competition seeking to win customers through efficiencies or reducing costs— and hence prices—is not a predominant factor.[58] Recent trends in applications and admissions illustrate the market anomaly for law school education. Law school applications fell dramatically from 2010 to 2016—perhaps partly reflecting tuition increases, as well as other factors.[59]

With demand reduced, the typical competitive response would be to lower prices to generate additional business (applicants). This would be particularly true for any high fixed-cost enterprise, such as law schools.[60] But that did not and does not occur. One source summarizes the trend: "Compared to the peak in JD enrollment in 2010 (147,525 students), overall JD enrollment was down 24.3% in 2018."[61] But even this extraordinary demand reduction did not yield the normal market response in the form of enhanced price competition. Instead, law schools continue to eschew transparent price competition in favor of a burgeoning, but secretive means of competing, as reflected in the actual tuition charged to each student.[62]

A law school advertising $50,000 in annual tuition does not necessarily charge $50,000 per student. According to a 2017 study analyzing ABA grant and scholarship data, the median private law school discounted tuition by 28.3%, with an average scholarship of $20,129.[63] Few are aware that such discounts (and affordable law school opportunity, for many) are primarily driven by two numbers: Law School Admission Test (LSAT) scores and college grade point average (GPA).[64] While certainly important indicators, the disproportionate weight of these particular factors is driven by the pervasive influence of, and law school preoccupation with, the *U.S. News & World Report* law school rankings.[65] Indeed, law school admissions offices meticulously calculate exact medians for a prospective entering class and offer tuition subsidies to those with the highest scores.[66]

The over-emphasis on two numbers distorts student evaluation and inhibits a more balanced judgment. But those two numbers make up 90% of the *U.S. News* rating of law school "selectivity."[67] Students lacking financial resources that might otherwise allow them to enroll in an LSAT prep course or pay for tutoring in college suffer financial barriers to law school entry and a legal career. Instead, they borrow to pay the "sticker price" tuition—often hundreds of thousands of dollars, on top of what they may have already had to borrow to go to college. In doing so, these individuals end up subsidizing tuition discounts for those with higher college GPAs and LSAT scores.[68]

Public Subsidy and Loans: Overall Student Debt

Law school graduates carry record debt into their bar examination crucible. Of the 181 law schools tracked by *U.S. News*, the percentage of 2018 students carrying substantial debt varied from 34% to 100%.[69] The amount of the debt of graduating students by school varied from $68,743 at University of North Dakota to $212,576 at Southwestern Law School.[70]

These education loans are rarely dischargeable—even in bankruptcy. Available and secured federal and non-federal loans for law students (and indeed all students) have declined markedly since 2010.[71] Total student loans grew to $125.6 billion in 2010, but have since declined to $105.5 billion in 2017-18, while tuition and living costs climbed substantially over the same period.[72]

C. *LAW SCHOOL AND THE EDUCATION OF ATTORNEY PRACTITIONERS*

Existing Law School Curriculum

As discussed above, undergraduate education does not necessarily have the same connection to law school as does the typical academic record of those seeking engineering, science or medical advanced degrees. Then, once a student is admitted, the law school curriculum itself lacks correlation to the actual practice of law.

Most law schools present a core of required courses that consume the first year and sometimes part of the second year. Traditionally, required courses include contracts, torts, property, civil procedure, constitutional law, legal ethics, and several other courses varying by school. But there are several deficiencies in most curricula. First, the courses tend to focus on the judicial branch, with most of them revolving around a "casebook" text. The adjustment of curricula to changes in society, including our political and legal systems, is glacial.[73] For example, a large portion of current law practice involves, in some way, the legislature and executive branch agencies. The former enacts the laws, and the latter implement the laws through important rulemaking and enforcement procedures. Attorneys must often interpret these laws in order to advise their clients on compliance, or litigate alleged violations. But few law schools include substantial curriculum offerings in those and other areas of burgeoning practice.

Second, the courses typically do not lead students into actual areas of practice in terms of functional knowledge. The era of Abraham Lincoln, where an attorney practices "law" and will draft a will, defend a client in criminal court, and then litigate a divorce, is no longer practical. We present 24 areas of law commonly practiced in the United States, as follows: (1) immigration law; (2) criminal law; (3) property law; (4) probate, trust and estate planning law; (5) general corporate, securities and commercial law; (6) family law; (7) environmental law; (8) civil rights law; (9) administrative and regulatory law; (10) antitrust and economic crime law; (11) personal injury and consumer law (including product liability, property damage, and class action law); (12) labor/employment law and worker compensation; (13) real estate and construction law; (14) insurance law; (15) admiralty law; (16) bankruptcy law; (17) elder law; (18) education law; (19) health care law; (20) medical malpractice; (21) legal malpractice; (22) military law; (23) patent and trademark law (IP); and (24) tax law.

It is possible for some attorneys to practice in two, or perhaps three, of these 24 areas. But each involves substantial differences. An attorney who practices as a criminal defense attorney (or prosecutor) follows very different precedents and procedures from one handling divorces in family court. An attorney in bankruptcy court will have little in common in terms of the "what" or the "how" of practice with one practicing in juvenile dependency court. Many of these areas involve entirely disparate courts, with their own complex rules and procedures: juvenile dependency or delinquency court, bankruptcy court, probate court, Offices of Administrative Hearings adjudicating regulatory cases, immigration courts, military JAG proceedings and others—have marked differences. Each requires substantial specialized knowledge and experience to practice competently.

The generality of law school coursework is based on a collegial ethic that the Socratic Method (the practice of challenging students in class with repeated and pointed questions) leads to a superior mind—one able to identify inconsistencies. It facilitates the ability to pierce shallow rhetoric and sophistry. It allows students to "think like a lawyer." These fundamentals are undoubtedly valuable. But they begin only in the fifth year of American legal education—after four years of potentially unrelated (but still mandatory) undergraduate coursework. The assumption that the Socratic Method alone constitutes an effective means of educating 21st century attorneys seems dubious. Skyrocketing education costs, increasing practice specialization, technology, and the need for attorneys who are ready to begin practicing upon licensure should prompt a reevaluation of the way our country teaches law. How should we balance doctrinal coursework and practical skills training?

Moreover, even after four years of potentially irrelevant college coursework, three years of substantive law classes, and life-altering debt, aspiring attorneys are not even finished with doctrinal work. For the vast majority of bar applicants, existing law school coursework is insufficient to prepare graduates to take and pass the required state bar examinations. As described *infra*, the esoteric and impractical nature of the exams has spawned a national cottage industry of "Bar Preparation" providers, which charge ever-increasing sums of thousands to teach—*after* law school has concluded—the 10 to 15 subject areas most states cover, including the standard Multistate Bar Examination (MBE) given as a part of the bar exam in all states.[74] This cottage industry (perhaps understandably) does not advocate for bar exam reform that might lessen demand for its services.

The Practical Skills Training Movement

In the spring of 2012, the State Bar of California created the Task Force for Admissions Regulation Reform ("TFARR"), to examine whether the State Bar should develop a regulatory requirement for a pre-admission practical skills training program. In finding that the Bar should adopt a new set of regulations to focus on competency and professionalism, TFARR's Phase I report observed that "the rapidly changing landscape of the legal profession, where, due to the economic climate and client demands for trained and sophisticated practitioners fresh out of law school, fewer and fewer opportunities are available for new lawyers to gain structured competency training early in their careers."[75] The Task Force identified three specific and interrelated sources of concern that prompted the need for its action, with crushing student debt burden as the common thread: 1) recent law graduates with no prospects are forced into solo practice to pay off loans before they may be competent to practice, at great risk to the clients they serve; 2) with fewer young attorneys in a financial position to perform pro bono or public service work, low-income access to the judicial system suffers; and 3) law school debt puts becoming an attorney beyond reach for those lacking pre-existing family wealth.[76]

Ultimately, TFARR recommended three new requirements to practice law in California: (1) fifteen units of practical coursework before bar admission;[77] (2) fifty hours of legal services to pro bono clients or clients of modest means (before or after admission); and (3) ten hours of Mandatory Continuing Legal Education focused on practical skills.[78] Phase II of the Task Force issued a second report with recommended implementation strategies for each of these three recommendations the following year.[79]

These recommendations superficially addressed some problem areas. But they left untouched a system that foists deeply indebted, brand-new market entrants with no experience onto the most vulnerable segments in our society—and only for brief stints, so they could avoid meaningful commitments to client service. Indeed, the new recommendations would make it even more difficult to become a lawyer, without addressing the root causes of harm to consumers as a result of the supply reduction imposed by the current regulatory framework.[80]

D. *STATE BAR EXAMINATIONS AS ENTRY BARRIERS*

Today, all 50 states require that applicants pass some version of a bar examination to qualify for attorney licensure.[81] This examination is a significant barrier to entering the legal profession, and at the same time is produced and administered by what the U.S. Supreme Court deems "active market participants" in the trade or profession involved—lawyers.[82] Nearly every state in the union delegates the regulation of lawyers to lawyers themselves, who then, in turn, often defer in matters of entry policy to the nationwide trade association they control—the American Bar Association—as discussed above.

The conflict of interest in our system of attorney regulation is apparent. When a profession is allowed to regulate itself—to gauge the appropriate incoming supply and the amount of competition it will encounter (i.e., the number of new attorneys admitted with each bar exam administration)—it runs afoul of both the Sherman Act and also fundamental principles of our democracy.[83] The state is supposed to make decisions in the interests of the people—all of the people—not only professionals with a vested interest in high entry barriers.

General Format of Existing Bar Examinations

Generally, bar exams are administered by each state twice a year for two days, and include the MBE, a 200-question multiple choice test developed by the National Committee of Bar Examiners (NCBE),[84] and an essay portion of the exam. The Uniform Bar Examination ("UBE"), now adopted by 33 states, is coordinated by NCBE and is composed of the Multistate Essay Examination, two Multistate Performance Test tasks, and the MBE.[85] It is uniformly administered, graded, and scored by user jurisdictions and results in a portable score that can be transferred to other UBE jurisdictions.[86] Other states, like California, develop their own essay portion of the exam.[87]

Even though the MBE and UBE are nationally-administered tests, each state sets its own "cut score" that will ultimately determine who passes the exam, and what the level of new attorney supply will be in that state.[88] And these cut scores vary wildly from state to state, from 144 and 145, respectively, in California and Delaware, to 129 in Wisconsin, with a national average around 135.[89] Not surprisingly, these variations yield varying pass rates among the states.

California's Ongoing Travail

California's pass rate, which has been consistently declining and hit a record low in July 2018 at 40.7% overall,[90] has driven California law schools in recent years to petition the Supreme Court, and the State Bar, to revisit its high cut score and take a closer look at the content of the exam itself.[91] Indeed, California's current cut score was set in 1986.[92] The Court ordered the Bar to study this issue, and the Bar underwent a series of studies in 2017 and 2018 on a compressed timeline at the Court's direction.[93] Over significant opposition from the Committee of Bar Examiners, which advocated for no change to the cut score, the Board of Trustees of the State Bar of California, after considering the results of the studies, and holding two public hearings, voted to present the Court with three options with respect to the cut score: 1) maintain the status quo at 144 overall; 2) lower it to 141; 3) lower it to 139.94 The Court ultimately declined to lower the cut score, instead ordering the Bar to conduct further study.[95]

While these studies were ongoing in 2017, the California legislature added section 6064.8 to the Business and Professions Code, directing the Bar to "oversee an evaluation of the bar examination to determine if it properly tests for minimally needed competence for entry-level attorneys" and mandating that it "shall make a determination, supported by findings, whether to adjust the examination or the passing score based on the evaluation" at least every seven years or more frequently if so directed by the California Supreme Court. The Supreme Court likewise added California Rule of Court 9.6, effective January 1, 2018, which also requires a regular evaluation of the bar examination's validity. The California State Bar announced that it was commencing a California-specific Attorney Practice Analysis in December 2018 to "ensure that the California Bar Exam is relevant and tests what is needed by entry-level California attorneys."[96]

Also in December 2018, the Bar released the results of its fourth study on the California Bar Examination, *Performance Changes on the California Bar Exam, Part Two*. Based on data from 11 ABA-accredited California law schools who volunteered to participate, the study was designed to examine the correlation between California's steadily declining pass rate and law school attendee credentials (both prior to and during law school).[97] The study concluded, unsurprisingly, that law school GPA was the single best indicator of predicting success on the California Bar Exam.[98] Interestingly, however, the study found that the slight decline in undergraduate GPA and LSAT scores for law school applicants admitted in the most recent five years could only be attributed to some (between 20–50%) of the decline in bar exam pass rates; with the remaining portion of the decline "unexplained."[99]

As these studies—which are likely to take years—continue, the Bar is continuing to administer the same exam, with the same cut score, with no imminent plans to make further changes.

Questions Pertaining to Bar Exam Efficiency

As noted at the outset above, the core purpose of public regulation of attorneys (and many other trades and professions) is to assure practitioner competence and honesty. This assurance is paramount for members of the public, who rely on the state to keep incompetent and dishonest people—who may impose irreparable harm on unsuspecting clients—from practicing law.[100]

Consider the following questions in evaluating whether a single examination (in the present format of bar examinations across the country) is properly achieving that stated purpose:

1. While a bar examination may have some relevance to competence, to what extent does it actually measure the knowledge, skills, and abilities that new lawyers entering the profession actually need to competently practice? This is a central tenet in justifying occupational licensure, and requirements to regularly validate the content of licensing exams via psychometric evaluation have been in place for all other occupations—from physicians to architects— (at least in California) for decades.[101] The State Bar of California is now undergoing this process, beginning with its California-specific "Attorney Practice Analysis," discussed above, and the NCBE is also now undergoing a three year study of the examinations it administers.[102] Only when these studies have been completed can one properly evaluate whether the content of the exams are actually measuring for these skills.[103]

2. In determining their respective bar examination "cut scores," are state bars appropriately ensuring that they are only excluding from admission those who are not "minimally competent" to practice law? While this is the psychometrically appropriate standard by which to measure and set the cut score for a licensing exam, state bars across the country have not typically adhered to this "do no harm" standard of entry into our profession.[104] Can any other standard be justified under the antitrust laws?

3. What are the implications of a system of undergraduate and then law school education now extant, in which graduates must pay thousands of additional dollars and three months of intense study to pass a purported general competence examination? In addition, should law students be forced to choose between courses on subjects that will be tested on the bar and courses covering the subject matter in areas where they intend to practice?[105]

4. All practice areas are not equal in their potential to impose irreparable consumer harm. A criminal prosecutor is usually supervised by expert guides; a

corporate contract attorney often has models and supervision, and sophisticated clients who are able to determine for themselves whether their attorney is performing competently. So which specialties deserve attention for competence assurance? Arguably, these would include areas where: (1) the client is not in a position to gauge competence; (2) the attorney is not subject to assured training and review before or during legal practice; and/or (3) counsel may engage in a single case or task that, standing alone, portends irreparable harm. What test for assurance of competence is provided for immigration law, juvenile law, family law, or landlord/tenant law—topics not tested on bar examinations, yet practice areas with enormous potential for consumer harm?

5. Do any states have any mechanism to ensure continuing competence in any given practice area over the entire 50-year career of an attorney? Do any require a minimum body of continuing legal education in the area of actual practice? Do any ever provide tests relevant to competence in such areas of practice relied upon by consumers?

6. Are supplemental tests designed for state certified "specializations" designed to protect consumers or do they serve as marketing tools enabling these specialists to charge higher prices to willing (and well-heeled) clients?[106] Does it matter that each of them is a label awarded by a group of practitioners currently practicing in that respective area of law?[107]

The answers to these questions at this time are not favorable to the public interest.

IV. The State of the Market for Legal Services Nationwide

A. The Current Supply Of Attorneys In The United States: Categories And Trends

Analyses of attorney employment divide the market into three basic parts: (a) the "legal services market" offering legal services to the public directly, (b) "in-house" attorneys working directly for corporations or other entities, and (c) government lawyers.[108]

The first market, offering services to the public, primarily work in law offices (95.1%); only 1% work for non-profit legal aid entities.[109] The second category, that of "in-house" lawyers, has increased 203% from 1997-2017—almost seven times more than those providing direct legal services to the public.[110] These are lawyers working for "industries other than legal services or government," (e.g., counsel for corporations or trade associations or other commercial entities). The third major sector consists of government attorneys, up 49% over the same 20-year period. The largest proportion work for local governmental entities (county counsel, district attorneys, city attorneys, et al.) the next largest grouping for the state (legislative staff, agency counsel, attorney general, et al., and the smallest for the federal government.[111]

Of the 1.3 million practicing attorneys in the U.S. in 2018,[112] however, there is a noticeably declining number who are actually representing individuals in areas such as personal injury, family law, or housing matters (also known as the "PeopleLaw" sector), as opposed to attorneys representing corporate or other entities (the "Organizational Client" sector).[113] Indeed, for the most recently- reported year of 2012, U.S. Census Bureau Economic Census data indicate that the amount of money individual consumers spent on legal services declined substantially—$7 billion—over just a five year period.[114] By contrast, the Organizational Client sector *increased* its spending by over $26 billion.[115] Put another way, individuals in the U.S. spent an average of $187 per capita on legal expenses, while government entities spent approximately $100,000 annually, and Fortune 500 companies spent $160 million.[116]

Meanwhile, the price of legal services has been increasing markedly. From 1987 to 2016, the cost of legal services rose nearly twice as fast as the overall Consumer Price Index-Urban.[117] Legal services are not alone in this phenomenon. Prices for other "human-intensive" services, such as medical expenses and college tuition, have likewise been increasing at a much higher rate than worker income.[118] While consumers are continuing to pay the higher prices for medical services and tuition, however, they are largely choosing to forego legal services, regardless of the need.[119]

In economic terms, the decline of the PeopleLaw sector of the legal services market can be attributed to higher relative cost, shrinking demand, and an emerging market of "substitutions" for traditional attorney services in the form of "legal tech" services.[120] At the same time, in the Organizational Client sector, profits have increased much faster than the nation's GDP or the Consumer Price Index.[121]

As of 2017, 12.3% of Americans lived below the federal poverty line.[122] Legal aid addresses only a small percentage of their legal needs and remains a very small public subsidy account. But the current supply shortfall, combined with a lack of price bargaining, reaches well beyond impoverished Americans. It is not merely children in family or dependency court, or the victimized elderly, or immigrants whose children are taken from them, who lack legal services. The problem reaches into the middle and upper-middle classes. At this point it undoubtedly includes not only most of the population, but the vast majority.

One manifestation of the attorney services collapse is the growth of unrepresented parties in court. This is one setting where most citizens would want some attorney representation. One study by the National Center for State Courts looked at 925,344 cases—a sample drawn from a variety of ten urban counties nationally and representing 5% of the total court cases during the one year surveyed. It found that 76% of those cases involved at least one party who was "self-represented"—appearing without counsel. The range of costs in most of these cases was $40,000 to $120,000. The median value of a judgment obtained was $2,441.[123] Were affordable counsel to be available and competently functioning, how many of those court cases would be resolved between counsel quickly and at lower cost?

What is the relationship between the current and increasing inability for most individuals in the U.S. to pay for and obtain legal representation and recent underlying trends? The data suggest three interacting dynamics: (a) a shift to high-profit organizational (predominantly corporate) representation, (b) the trend towards high-remuneration "partnership status" as the ambition and focus of attorneys, and (c) a failure to lower prices to generate demand—the normal market response where unmet demand remains. Underlying these factors is a setting of supply restriction—barriers to entry that are imposed by the current system of high and increasing tuition costs and time covering seven years of higher education, followed by a bar examination obstacle of unclear relevance to on- point competence.

B. Legal Tech And Prospective Supply Of Needed Legal Services

One new grouping of legal services has not been included in the surveys discussed above. They are commonly referred to as alternative legal services providers ("ALSPs").[124] These involve a mix of attorneys and business executives, increasingly using the Internet and often new technology termed artificial intelligence ("AI") to deliver legal services to consumers (likely those who may be unwilling or unable to pay for a private attorney).[125] Their potential market is vast, for it includes the millions of people—now the majority of the nation—who are not being served by traditional attorneys. This grouping includes entities such as Axiom, Intergreon, Elevate, Quislex, and UnitedLex.[126] They are private corporations, often financed by venture capital and private equity funding. They have evolved to provide specialized help to corporate counsel or others where such specialization can be used. On the "PeopleLaw" side, several have arisen to provide help to the largest area of unmet demand, the need for routine legal services to draft a will or review a contract or even start a small corporation.[127] These and other new legal assistance ventures use attorneys and the Internet. Some jurisdictions, such as the British Columbia model, even engage in online mediation to minimize the need for expensive court proceedings.[128]

These efforts and many more potential ventures of this type are impeded by two ABA Model Rules of Professional Conduct adopted by virtually every state: Rule 5.4, prohibiting non-lawyer ownership of a law firm,[129] and Rule 5.5, prohibiting "unauthorized practice of law," i.e., attorney functions performed by a non-attorney.[130] The rationale for these restrictions involves the preservation of "lawyer independence" and the prevention of "fee splitting" or financial arrangements providing funds to someone with a fiduciary duty to make the optimum referral—not influenced by a fee received from the beneficiary.[131]

There are some legitimate concerns related to these rules, but circumstances have made them largely disingenuous. In fact, private non-attorney ownership and control inhabits every corporation or other for-profit entity hiring an attorney as one of its officers or employees. If someone believes such persons are truly exercising "legal advice" separate from the profit-making purpose of the corporation, they are unfamiliar with the realities of law practice. Indeed, in the starkest example, the Big Four accounting firms employ attorneys providing legal services to all sorts of clients— individuals and entities. They are private corporations with investors and are not attorney-owned or controlled. They are in theory "under the supervision" of the client's other attorneys. Such other attorneys have the private interest of their client as a preeminent concern. And that reality is separate and apart from principles of legal ethics, which dictate attorneys' various duties to their clients.[132]

Three aspects of this new dimension for legal services warrant consideration. First, AI and the Internet are increasingly used for consumer benefit in many contexts, and across many professions, from automatic car braking to the reading of complex MRIs (possible for examinations 10,000 miles away). Second, given the extreme supply constriction from barriers to entry and the depletion of services for individuals discussed above, there is substantial unmet need likely reachable through modern technology.[133] Third, the costs of these services may be a fraction of the individualized attorney services option.

While it would make sense for those regulating the legal industry in the U.S. to recognize these overwhelming market signals and embrace new and innovative methods of increased access to legal services, the pattern thus far is to seek their limitation or elimination.[134] However, in 2018, the Board of Trustees of the State Bar of California formed the Task Force on Access Through Innovation of

Legal Services, comprised of a mix of attorney and non-attorney members (a majority of whom are not attorneys), and charged with identifying possible regulatory changes to enhance the delivery of, and access to, legal services through the use of technology, including AI and online legal service delivery models.[135] It remains to be seen whether an attorney-dominated Board of Trustees will consider any recommended changes in this space.

Emerging developments in the legal technology space also raise issues with respect to attorney continuing competence and law school curriculum. With technology's increasing ability to replicate work that attorneys have traditionally performed (document review, contract drafting, legal research, etc.), regulators and law schools alike must reconsider the knowledge skills and abilities that lawyers as humans can uniquely deliver. Are existing continuing legal education models ensuring that attorneys are keeping up with this technology, and offering their clients the most efficient and accurate method of services?[136] Are attorneys incentivized to do so given the existing billable hour business model? Are law schools training law students about this emerging marketplace? Are "essential skills" such as empathy, technology, problem-solving, writing, time management, and client communication incorporated into law school core curricula?[137]

V. Ten Steps to a Lawful System of Attorney Entry and Regulation in the Public Interest

The data support increasing the supply of attorneys by multiple measures: the need for indigent representation, the lack of attorneys providing services to individual (as opposed to corporate) clients, and the high price of legal services—which now often places quality (or any) legal representation out of the reach of even the middle class. The dilemma becomes "how do we increase the supply of attorneys to address increasingly unmet legal needs without compromising competence?"

It is beyond time for us to recognize that the existing cartel-controlled legal profession in the United States is ill-equipped to address this dilemma. It does not stimulate supply, competitive pricing, or any kind of competence assurance (or other consumer protections) in actual areas of attorney practice. A review of the problems and available cures commend the following ten major reforms in legal practice regulation.

A. *Reform The Entire Socratic Tradition For Legal Education*

As a rational issue examined tabula rasa, how would we arrange the years of college education to qualify persons for attorney licensure and consumer reliance in relevant areas of law? If we were fashioning one from scratch, would we require four years of often substantially unrelated courses with the delay and costs noted above, followed by three years of largely cerebral generality, often lacking connection to the future practice of those students?

Today, law schools do not accept applicants without bachelor's degrees, and the American Bar Association will not accredit schools that do.[138] A rational prescription to stimulate both supply and competence, and which relevant evidence commends, would include three reform elements:

Employ a Five-Year Total Higher Education Path for Bar Licensure

The first two years would include liberal arts or other courses of interest to students. But of these likely 16 to 20 courses, three to five would have some colorable relationship to law: political science, economics, legal history, et al. Such college students could be admitted to law school following their second year.

Restructure Law School Curriculum

Law school would occupy the final three years, with the first year including Socratic Method teaching of fundamental subject areas (contracts, torts, civil procedure, constitutional law, property, legal ethics, evidence). Moreover, existing law school courses reflect an arcane mindset that elevates judicial precedents to the exclusion of other areas of legal practice. In particular, the legislative and executive branches are largely ignored, despite their obvious relevance to legal practice. Courses on legislation and on administrative law[139] are thus properly part of these first two years, as are courses involving newly emerging "essential skills," and elective courses related to areas of specialized interest: criminal, juvenile, environmental, or civil rights law. Of the typical eight to nine courses taken during the third year of law school, three could be follow-up courses in one of those separate areas of common practice explored in the second year, and the rest of the third year should consist of practical experience in an area of actual prospective practice. Hence, for the final year—and particularly the final semester—law schools would offer clinics, internships, externships and perhaps one semester of advanced placement in a particular area of practice.

Require "Concentrations" Pertaining To Desired Practice Area

The law school would formulate "majors" or areas of "concentration," consisting of collections of properly-sequenced courses and practical skills training relevant to an area of law.[140] Students who concentrate their studies develop a specific, heightened proficiency that is relevant to their future career. In addition, concentrations would be reflected on students' transcripts so that future employers may consider them in hiring. These features would facilitate student progress into a legal career, and ensure competence and readiness to practice in a specific practice area. Law schools should hire practicing attorneys in the relevant practice areas to serve as adjuncts, and provide contemporary skills-based training for law students.

B. HOLD LAW SCHOOLS ACCOUNTABLE FOR TUITION PRICING

The antitrust division of the U.S. Department of Justice should create a monitoring enforcement team to detect any and all indicia of price fixing in higher education, including law schools. This includes patterns of "price leadership," and other coordination by law schools, whether though the American Association of Law Schools, the American Bar Association, or any other mechanism.

Furthermore, law schools and other institutions of higher learning should be open and transparent to their prospective students about differential pricing options and data, including number and amounts of tuition "discounts" based on pre-admission statistics such as GPA or LSAT scores. These strategies, and the extent of their influence, must be disclosed to accomplish pricing information and tuition competition. Prospective students should know how much they are paying relative to other admitted students and the variables dictating those differences. Actual tuition, including net tuition amounts after "individual scholarship" reductions by the law school (not involving actual gifts or outside funded accounts) should be comparatively reported and published.

C. Establish Robust Loan Forgiveness And Legal Education Subsidy Programs

One way to ameliorate high education costs, while simultaneously addressing the widespread unmet legal needs in our country, is to provide loan forgiveness (also known as "loan repayment assistance programs") to attorneys who may be working to address those legal needs but earning a lower salary than they would if they chose to represent corporate clients.

Other professions have established systems for such assistance. Nationally, the Public Service Loan Forgiveness Program has been in effect since 2007, although its future is in doubt.[141]

More relevant, particularly for California, is the example provided by and for the medical profession: the California State Loan Repayment Program (SLRP).[142] It provides assistance to a broad array of health professionals, including doctors, dentists, nurses, social workers, therapists and pharmacists. The beneficiary must commit to practice in medically underserved areas for a minimum of two years and a maximum of four years, with $50,000 available the first year, $20,000 the second and third years and $10,000 the fourth year.[143]

Specifically, in 2002, the California Legislature established the Physician Corps Loan Repayment Program within the Medical Board of California.[144] In 2004, it was renamed the Steven M. Thompson Physician Corps Loan Repayment Program, and its administration was subsequently transferred to a foundation.[145] The Program is currently funded by an earmarked, mandatory surcharge on physician and osteopath licensing fees, an annual allocation of $1 million from the Managed Care Administrative Fines and Penalties Fund,146 donations, grants, voluntary contributions, and interest earned on surplus money investments.[147] The Program provides $105,000 in loan forgiveness for three years of service in designated "Medically Underserved Areas."[148] Although this and related programs do not create health care services for even a substantial part of the indigent, since 2013 this one program involving medical profession creation and contribution, has received 1,228 applications to 2018. The program has awarded more than $47 million and monitored the progress of 538 physicians providing direct patient care in 47 of California's 58 counties. Consistent with the intent of the program, 80 percent of the total recipients are certified in a primary care specialty.[149]

In contrast, attorney loan forgiveness has a very different record. Nationally, over 100 law schools do offer Loan Repayment Assistance Programs (LRAP) for graduates who pursue public interest work.[150] However, the number of recipients and the amounts involved are small and, although laudable, serve mostly as a symbolic commitment.[151] Aware of the problem of law school debt, some advocates in California attempted to create a credible system of repayment for those representing impoverished clients or doing public interest work for qualified 501(c)(3) charities. In 2001, Assemblymember Robert Hertzberg authored a bill to establish a "Public Interest Attorney Loan Repayment Program."[152] While the law has been on the books for over 18 years,[153] it has never been funded.

Subsidies for law school education should be enhanced from both public and charitable sources. Using the STLRP program as a model, the bars of every state should identify specific geographic and practice areas with the lowest rates of access to legal services and establish substantial loan forgiveness programs for attorneys who work to meet those needs. These programs should be funded with a mandatory surcharge on annual attorney licensing fees. They should also work with their respective state Attorneys General to earmark a percentage of civil penalties assessed to stabilize this fund, similar to the Managed Care Administrative Fines and Penalties Fund.

D. *Rethink The Bar Examination*

Each state should undertake, as California and the NCBE are now (and as other professions have done for decades), a regular psychometric evaluation of its licensing exam to ensure that the cut scores are properly evaluating minimum competence to practice law as it is currently being practiced.[154] Ideally, after completing law school, 80–90% of applicants should be passing the bar exam.

Specifically, the bar examination should test basic legal vocabulary and concepts, including the concept of judicial "precedents," and overarching legal principles pertinent to all practice areas: professional responsibility, contract law, torts, civil procedure, constitutional law, basic rules of evidence, and remedies. The additional competence assurance required for certain actual areas of practice requiring particular knowledge and where negligence will portend serious harm, should have additional qualification respectively, and regularly evaluated to ensure continuing competence.

Public protection, the purported justification for this arbitrary and notoriously difficult-to-pass examination, will be better achieved without an extreme barrier entry into the legal profession.

E. *Require Law Schools To Achieve Minimum Bar Pass Rates*

Once states have undertaken the appropriate analyses to ensure that the content and cut score of their respective bar exams are valid, they should then take measures to ensure that law schools within their jurisdictions are achieving a minimum pass rate.[155] For example, schools with less than 65% of their graduates passing the Bar within two years would be placed on probation, and ultimately be barred from access to the bar examination in their state, and required to return all tuition collected from the students who failed to meet that minimum and reasonable standard.

Such a standard is designed to ensure that schools not be tempted to admit students who do not have the skills necessary to pass the bar exam. The purpose of a law school is not to generate tuition, academic positions, law review articles, or conference gatherings. It is to prepare students for practice as ethical, competent attorneys serving the public. If their operation instead takes many thousands of dollars from youth and their families, incurs momentous debt, and yields little or no remunerative opportunity, that institution is not meeting the *raison d'etre* for its existence. On the other hand, it does not make sense to impose such a standard until we can be sure that the exam itself, and the cut score, is designed to exclude only those who are not minimally competent to practice law.

F. Identify Specific Areas Of Law Where Specialized Competence Is Required

Rather than require a rigorous bar examination spanning multiple specialized practice areas as a requisite condition for all bar applicants, states should instead offer a basic examination (as described above), and then design a certification mechanism for attorneys who choose to practice in areas which pose the greatest risk of irreparable harm to the public. Indeed, some areas of law, such as immigration, juvenile dependency, criminal defense, landlord/tenant, and family law, are fields which may have devastating results on a client with just one case (i.e. deportation), and in which clients generally lack the ability to judge attorney competence for themselves (unlike corporate clients with general counsel who may more easily determine whether their attorneys are best serving their interests).

The bars of each state should consider which practice areas have the potential to impose the greatest harm to consumers, and then require attorneys who choose to practice in one of these areas to demonstrate minimal competence in their chosen field. This could include a state-issued "certification," which attorneys may achieve by passing a psychometrically-sound, practice area-specific examination, and/or working under the direct supervision of a current practitioner for a specified number of hours as an apprentice.[156] Attorneys would then be required to renew these certifications at regular intervals (such as every seven to ten years) to demonstrate continued competence, including knowledge of contemporary legal precedents.[157] These measures need not be expensive, onerous, or time consuming, and elective law school courses covering these fields could be designed to prepare applicants for the desired certification.[158]

G. Reform Continuing Legal Education To Require Continuing Competence In The Substantive Areas Of Actual Practice

Many state bars require that attorneys complete a certain number of hours of "continuing legal education" ("CLE") over a specified number of years as a condition of license renewal. However, many do not require that these courses coincide with an attorney's area of actual practice, nor do they typically require any kind of assessment demonstrating retention of the information.

Such CLE requirements should be amended to require that at least half of the CLE hours be taken in the attorney's designated area of actual legal practice. Additionally, state bars should administer a psychometrically-sound, basic test in an attorney's chosen practice area at least every ten years as a condition of license renewal. If the attorney cannot initially pass the exam, he or she may be placed on probation for 60 days to retake the test. If unable to pass such a test in that specialty area after repeated attempts, the attorney should move to another area of practice where client reliance will not have the same consequences or where relevant competence is demonstrated.

H. Revise Existing Ethics Rules To Permit New And Innovative Methods For Delivering Legal Services

The use of modern technology is growing and permeating many trades and professions, including legal practice. As discussed in Section IV.B. above, the challenge facing all state bars is how to embrace emerging technologies to benefit those in need of legal services. Two variables are at issue which must be appropriately balanced: the advantage of additional services meeting demand, and the danger of abuse or malpractice with consumer harm resulting.

It is important that those regulating attorneys not over-enforce the "unauthorized practice of law" mantra in order to protect attorneys' "turf" and preserve their ability to charge higher hourly fees.[159] On the other hand, one obligation of regulators is to protect consumers from abuse by commercial interests in areas legitimately a part of, or closely related to, legal services.

Each state should appoint a commission, including (and perhaps a comprised of a majority of) non- attorneys to revisit rules governing the unauthorized practice of law, multijurisdictional practice, advertising, fee sharing, corporate practice, etc. Specifically, the commission should assess the historical purpose and impetus behind these rules, determine whether existing rules are achieving the aforementioned balance of access to legal services and public protection, and assess whether these rules are stifling the innovative delivery of legal services to a public which is in great demand of these services. Moreover, such a commission should consider not only potential reforms to business structures and technological innovations, but also consider whether new categories of licensure (akin to nurse practitioners in the medical profession) may be implemented in order to maximize access to legal services.

I. *Consider Mandatory Liability Insurance*

Another measure that would protect the public from incompetent and unethical attorneys—but has been largely opposed by attorney-dominated state bars—would be to require attorneys to carry liability insurance as a condition of licensure. Indeed, existing attorney discipline systems across the country generally do not police negligent acts that may cause harm to consumers, and consumers are generally unable to recover against attorneys who do not carry insurance.[160]

The result of a lack of coverage is effective immunity from damage or restitution assessment for the vast majority of such attorneys. Plaintiffs' malpractice attorneys will not normally pursue cases where payment of judgments obtained is unlikely or uncertain. Further, states do not generally assure payment of malpractice judgments. In the case of California, the State Bar has a Client Security Fund, but it deliberately includes only dishonesty or damages arising from disciplinary proceeding proof, and excludes negligence or malpractice judgments.[161]

While many countries require attorneys to carry liability insurance to protect clients from precisely these harms, only two states in the U.S., Idaho and Oregon, maintain the same requirement.[162] In 2018, California convened a malpractice insurance working group to study this issue pursuant to a statutory mandate.[163] On March 15, 2019, however, the working group submitted a report to the Board of Trustees of the State Bar reflecting a sharply divided group, and finding that more data is required prior to making a recommendation regarding whether mandatory malpractice insurance is necessary.[164]

J. Reformulate State Bar Governance Structures to Comply with Antitrust Laws

Antitrust policy and compliance is a major issue for all state regulatory agencies; licensure decisions directly control the supply of legal services, with per se federal Sherman Act unlawful implications.[165] Thus, decisionmaking by state bar entities controlled by attorneys—i.e. "active participants" in the legal market—cannot enjoy immunity from the antitrust laws by claiming they are a state agency.[166] To protect themselves from potential antitrust liability—and more importantly to ensure the adoption of policies that prioritize consumer (and not attorney) protection—state bar governance structures must be reformed in at least the following ways.

Eradicate Conflict of Interest Inherent in "Unified Bars"

Several bars across the country maintain a "unified" or "integrated" governance structure. Under this structure, a state bar serves as a trade association and also as a regulatory agency—in a single entity. This model gives rise to the appearance of impropriety. It poses an inherent conflict of interest between acting in the best interests of the legal profession and acting in the best interests of the public. This is a profound ethical problem. Recently, it has started to be addressed.

By way of example, in 2018, after 25 years of study and consideration of this proposition, the State Bar of California was statutorily required to "deunify," spinning off its 16 practice area-specific sections and other aspects that constitute direct trade association activities into a separate trade association, the California Lawyers Association.[167] The California Bar has been implementing this deunification in recent years, aiming to streamline what has expanded into a panoply of "sub- entities" operating under the umbrella of the Bar, and boasting 250 volunteers, even after the split of the sections.[168]

States that maintain an integrated structure should follow California's lead.

Comply with *North Carolina State Board of Dental Examiners v. FTC*

Ideally, governing boards charged with making decisions impacting the regulation of the legal profession should not be controlled by practicing attorneys who stand to benefit from the policies they adopt. Instead, boards should be comprised of a "public member" majority—who may consult attorneys for their expertise in the field, but whose ultimate allegiance is to public protection alone.[169]

If this option is not exercised, and the states opt to maintain an attorney-member majority, the only way to ensure that the boards are not acting anticompetitively and to guarantee state action immunity from federal antitrust laws is to establish a supervisory entity that reviews the board's decisions for anticompetitive effect. That review must explicitly not be symbolic or perfunctory, but must include analysis of anticompetitive impacts and have the clear authority to amend or reject all or any part of any decision being made.

For example, state supreme courts could appoint a body of experts, ideally including economists with antitrust expertise, educators, and others, to evaluate complaints, gather relevant evidence and advise the justices accordingly as to the potential anticompetitive impact of policies adopted by an attorney-controlled board.[170]

VI. Conclusion

The purpose of state licensure is to assure access to competent practitioners, especially when incompetence threatens irreparable harm. It is not to serve as a means for professions being regulated to artificially restrict supply so as to drive prices out of reach of the lower and middle classes.

As the 21st century ushers in a new era of technology and innovation, we find ourselves at a crossroads. Both the legal profession and the several states must choose whether they will continue to allow special interests to capture professional regulatory bodies and infect them with abject self- interest. Or, will they truly act in the best interests of the public?

As it stands, the fox guards the henhouse. There is little question that lawyers govern the legal profession for lawyers. The American Bar Association decides what law schools can and cannot do from sea to shining sea. This lawyer monolith all but decides how to become a lawyer, on behalf of lawyers, for the people of the United States.

And the cartel has acted exactly as one would expect—in line with its own interests. It has made it exorbitantly expensive to become a lawyer. A legal education takes seven years—four of which are unrelated to law. A law student must mortgage his or her future, at a total cost ranging from $190,000 and $380,000. And perhaps most disturbingly of all, the legal training that students do receive (in their final three years of those seven) often leaves them woefully unprepared. A student's textbook legal education is tangentially relevant at best to the one or two of 24 heavily specialized practice areas of modern law in which that student will eventually practice. Even the doctrinal classes are insufficient—students are almost universally funneled into expensive "bar preparation" classes to get them through licensing exams.

Those licensing exams have virtually nothing to do with the practice of law. They consist almost entirely of memorized subject matter that bears little resemblance to what lawyers do on a daily basis, scored by an arbitrary "cut score" to guarantee a high percentage of failures—in California, 60%.

Meanwhile, the state bars:

(a) Do not rank negligent acts as a normal basis for discipline (outside of extreme incapacity);

(b) Do not require malpractice insurance—allowing attorneys to effectively escape sanctions or the obligation to pay for harm caused to their clients;

(c) Ensure that their "client security fund[s]" compensate injured clients for only theft, not malpractice (even where a judgment exists);

(d) Do not require continuing legal education to be in the areas in which attorneys practice;

(e) Most significantly, never test any attorney in any area of actual practice relied upon by consumers—ever, even in areas of law where clients are unable to gauge competence and a single case can mean ruination; and

(f) Confront and attempt to dismantle artificial intelligence and other technological solutions to legal problems, as an affront warranting elimination—even in situations when these solutions could be cheaper and more effective to clients than live lawyers.

The societal costs of lawyers regulating lawyers are dire. Legal services are so expensive that three quarters of legal cases involve an unrepresented party. The poor have token access to legal representation at best, and the situation is not much better for the middle class. At a certain point, it starts to look like the sticker price of legal education is rather the point of this endeavor—to drive up the cost of becoming a lawyer and to reduce competition for existing practitioners. The point of regulation should be to help the people who hire lawyers, not the lawyers themselves.

Critically, no area of state regulation more consistently overlooks the specter of federal antitrust liability than does the legal profession itself. The Supreme Court of the United States unambiguously held in 2015 that any state body controlled by "active participants" in the profession being regulated is not a sovereign entity for antitrust purposes. And yet the legal profession continues to use state machinery to regulate itself without active state supervision. Licensing without state action is supply control—price fixing, a per se Sherman Act violation. This poses an obvious problem, which should be a great motivator for change. State action immunity would be available if a state body without a conflict of interest actively supervised the attorney-run regulatory process. But so far, that has not happened.

The question remains. Will states seize upon the momentum of the 2015 *North Carolina State Board of Dental Examiners v. FTC* opinion and regulate in the interests of the people? Or will they continue to forsake their responsibility and allow special interests to grasp the reins?

Endnotes

** For educational use only.

Robert C. Fellmeth (A.B. Stanford U., J.D. Harvard U.) is a consumer advocate and former state and federal antitrust prosecutor. He holds the Price Chair in Public Interest Law at the University of San Diego School of Law and directs the Center for Public Interest Law and the Children's Advocacy Institute there, with offices in Sacramento and Washington, D.C. Bridget Fogarty Gramme (B.A. University of San Diego, J.D. University of San Diego) was the Administrative Director of the Center for Public Interest Law and adjunct professor at the University of San Diego School of Law. Prior to joining the Center, she was a civil litigator for ten years, primarily focused on antitrust and consumer protection matters. C. Christopher Hayes (A.B. Stanford, J.D. University of San Diego) is a practicing attorney in San Diego, California. Hayes was Volume 52 Articles Editor of San Diego Law Review and Magister of the Wigmore Inn of the Phi Delta Phi Legal Honor Society. The authors would like to thank Jena Scarborough and Taylor Brewer for their invaluable research assistance in drafting this article.

1. William D. Henderson, *Legal Market Landscape Report Commissioned by the State Bar of California*, at 20 (July 2018).

2. Legal Services Corporation, *The Justice Gap: Measuring the Unmet Civil Legal Needs of Low- Income Americans* at 6 (June 2017). Prepared by NORC at the University of Chicago for Legal Services Corporation, Washington, DC.

3. *Id.*

4. Henderson, *Legal Market Landscape Report*, *supra* note 1, at 19–21.

5. *See* Paula Hannaford-Agor JD, Scott Graves & Shelley Spacek Miller, *The Landscape of Civil Litigation in State Courts*, at iv (National Center for State Courts 2015).

6. Henderson, *Legal Market Landscape Report*, *supra* note 1, at 21.

7. *U.S. v. Socony-Vacuum Oil*, 310 U.S. 150 (1940). Regulatory schemes also implicate a separate "per se" antitrust offense in the form of a horizontal "group boycott"—an exclusion of competitors by a group of professionals already in the field. *See Klor's, Inc. v. Broadway-Hale Stores, Inc.*, 359 U.S. 207 (1959).

8. *N.C. State Bd. of Dental Exam'rs v. FTC*, 574 U.S ___, 135 S. Ct. 1101, 191 L. Ed. 2d 35 (2015).

9. *Id.* at 1111. *See also Id.* (quoting *Goldfarb v. Virginia State Bar*, 421 U.S. 773, 791, 95 S. Ct. 2004, 44 L. Ed. 2d 572 (1975)) ("The fact that the State Bar is a state agency for some limited purposes does not create an antitrust shield that allows it to foster anticompetitive practices for the benefit of its members.").

10. *N.C. State Bd. of Dental Exam'rs*, 135 S. Ct. at 1110 (citation omitted).

11. https://www.ftc.gov/system/files/attachments/competition-policy-guidance/active_supervision_of_state_boards.pdf

12. *N.C. State Bd. of Dental Exam'rs*, 135 S. Ct. at 1116-17 (citations omitted); *See also* FTC guidance, *supra* note 11, at 9.

13. Some have even questioned whether state Supreme Court justices themselves are "active market participants" since they are attorneys capable of returning to private practice and may stand to benefit from the protectionist policies adopted by the state bars. *See* Tom

Gordon, State Bar of California Governance in the Public Interest Task Force, Responsive Law (Apr. 22, 2016), https://www.responsivelaw.org/uploads/1/0/8/6/108638213/responsive_law_comments_to_ca_governance_task_force.pdf

14. The *North Carolina* holding calls into question earlier Supreme Court precedent pertaining to anticompetitive conduct by State Bars. For example, *Bates v. Arizona*, 433 U.S. 350 (1977), held that the Arizona State Bar qualified for state action immunity from the antitrust laws, finding that the Arizona Supreme Court itself had adopted the rules in question and the Bar was merely enforcing those rules. *Id.* at 361. But this decision long preceded North Carolina's poignant discussion of precisely how a state must actively supervise "active participants" in a profession who are engaged in anticompetitive practices using the state regulatory apparatus. Nor did the *Bates* court consider the extent to which the Arizona Supreme Court had delegated its regulatory power to active market participants. *Hoover v. Ronwin*, 466 U.S. 558 (1984), which contained a similar holding pertaining to the Arizona Supreme Court, similarly lacks the active supervision analysis.

15. *See* http://www.cpil.org/download/4.4.17.letter.Supreme.Court.follow.up.pdf.

16. *See, e.g., Washington State Bar Association Bylaws VI. 2. c.; In the matter of the approval of amendments to WSBA Bylaws regarding members of the Board of Governors*, Supreme Court of Washington, Case No. 25700-B-483 (January 4, 2018).

17. *TIKD Servs. LLC v. Fla. Bar*, No. 17-24103-CIV, 2018 WL 4521198 (S.D. Fla. Sept. 20, 2018).

18. ACPE Joint Opinion 732, CAA Joint Opinion 44, UPL Joint Opinion 54, http://www.judiciary.state.nj.us/notices/2017/n170621f.pdf.

19. American Bar Association, About the American Bar Association, https://www.americanbar. org/. Although much of this article focuses on the self-interested practices of the ABA and state bar organizations, a caveat is appropriate. The attorneys who are a part of these organizations engage in laudatory and admirable work that is in the public interest. They include,

for example, just within the ABA, the Center for Professional Responsibility, the Commission on Homelessness and Poverty, the Center on Children and the Child Litigation Rights Committee, among others. The critique herein is not intended to impugn a large part of the work of the ABA or state bars. Far from it. But the incidence of self-interested regulatory practice remains a serious problem that functions apart from conscious intent, and separate from the admirable work of many of its leaders and members.

20. *See* Judith Gundersen and Claire Guback, *Comprehensive Guide to Bar Admission Requirements 2019* at 10 (ABA 2019), http://www.ncbex.org/assets/BarAdmissionGuide/ NCBE-CompGuide- 2019.pdf.

21. American Bar Association, *Schedule of Law School Fees* (Mar. 18, 2019 11:00 AM), https://www.americanbar.org/groups/legal_education/accreditation/schedule-of-law-school-fees/. Annual fees range from $18,175 for schools with enrollment of fewer than 400 full-time JD students to $29,480 for schools with enrollment of 1,201 or more full-time JD students. *Id. See also* Letter from Hon. Solomon Oliver, Jr., Chairperson, & Barry Currier, Managing Director of the ABA Section of Legal Education and Admissions to the Bar, to ABA Law School Deans, http://www.americanbar.org/content/dam/aba/administrative/legal_education_and_admissions_to_the_bar/governancedocuments/2014_memo_re_law_school_fees.authcheckdam.pdf (explaining a three-percent increase in annual fees and an increase in the fee to apply for provisional ABA approval from $30,000 to $80,000).

22. *Id.*

23. *See supra* note 20 ("The American Bar Association is one of the world's largest voluntary professional organizations, with nearly 400,000 members and more than 3,500 entities.").

24. Law schools are free to choose not to pursue ABA accreditation, but their graduates will be unable to practice in nearly a third of the states in the union. See ABA Standards and Rules of Procedure for Approval of Law Schools 2018–2019, https://www.americanbar.org/content/dam/aba/publications/misc/legal_education/Stan

dards/2018-2019ABAStandardsforApprovalofLaw Schools/2018-2019-aba-standards-rules-approval-law-schools-final.pdf;
See also ABA-Accredited Law School, The Princeton Review, https://www.princetonreview.com/law-school-advice/law-school-accreditation ("Since passing the bar is a requirement for the practice of law almost everywhere, a degree from a school without ABA- accreditation is usually a ticket to nowhere.").

25. Notably, the antitrust division of the U.S Department of Justice has, on occasion, brought actions against the ABA. *See, e.g. U.S. v. American Bar Ass'n*, 135 F. Supp. 2d 28 (D.D.C. 2001) (challenging certain anticompetitive practices the ABA used in its law school accreditation process).

26. The full time tenured faculty requirement for law schools noted above is a typical example of an ABA-facilitated restraint of trade as it prevents law schools from hiring more adjunct faculty. *See* https://www.americanbar.org/groups/legal_education/resources/standards/. Bringing adjuncts into law schools to teach practical skills has several advantages. These are practicing professionals with experience their tenured peers often lack. And a long-term rise in the number of adjuncts could allow for the hiring of fewer tenured faculty, thereby allowing for tuition reductions. However, the ABA's accreditation guidelines for law schools mandate a minimum size for full-time faculty. See also Deborah L. Cohen, *To Teach or Not to Teach: Adjunct Work Can Come with a Hefty Price*, ABA Journal (Aug. 1, 2012), http://www.abajournal.com/magazine/article/to_teach_or_not_to_teach_adjunct_work_can_come_with_a_hefty_price/; *See also* Debra Cassens Weiss, *Adjunct Law Prof: A Low-Paying Job, If You Can Get It*, A.B.A. J. (Sep. 30, 2010), http://www.abajournal.com/news/article/adjunct_law_prof_a_low-paying_job_if_you_can_get_it/.

27. See https://trends.collegeboard.org/college-pricing/figures-tables/tuition-fees-room-and-board- over-time.

28. *Id.*

29. *Id.*

30. *Id.* Note these figures use 2018 dollars to adjust for inflation.

31. CollegeBoard, *Trends in College Pricing 2018*, at 9 (2018), https://trends.collegeboard.org/sites/default/files/2018-trends-in-college-pricing.pdf.

32. Attendance at a public college for a non-resident of that state may be compelled based on limited facilities in a student's home state—particularly in the many states of small population. It may also be compelled due to family, spousal, military or employment changes or needs. Some states will allow a shift into resident tuition status prior to the completion of four or more years of college there. Such students may incur tuition/room and board charges in the $70,000 to $90,000 range while attending over four years.

33. https://college-education.procon.org/view.resource.php?resourceID=005532; note that these figures are gathered by gender and these are the median percentages as to males. The percentages as to females, with somewhat lower median income, are measurably higher.

34. As part of its accreditation process, the ABA requires four years of undergraduate education as a prerequisite to law school entry. See ABA Standards and Rules of Procedure for Approval of Law Schools 2018-2019, *supra* note 24, at Standard 502(a). Note that the ABA does permit "three plus three" programs, where students enroll in three years of undergraduate study followed by three subsequent years of study at a law school to earn both a bachelor's degree and a JD. *Id.* at Standard 502(b); *See, e.g.*, 3 + 3 Law Program with Albany Law School, University at Albany, State University of New York, http://www.albany.edu/advisement/albany_law_3+3.shtml Prospective Students, Tulane University Law School, http://www.law.tulane.edu/tlsadmissions/index.aspx?id=208. While certainly a step in the right direction to reduce student debt, these programs are rare and do not substantially address the mix of current problems, including the excessively irrelevant and costly undergraduate years.

35. www.barstandardsboard.org.uk/qualifying-as-a-

barrister/becoming-a-barrister/,www.barcouncil.org.uk /becoming-a-barrister/how-to-become-a-barrister/. The three stages of training are known as the academic stage, the vocational stage, and the pupillage.

36. See https://www.lawsociety.org.uk/law-careers/ becoming-a-solicitor/;https://www.barcouncil.org.uk/ careers/general-information-and-faqs/faqs/.

37. https://www.barstandardsboard.org.uk/qualifying -as-a-barrister/becoming-a-barrister/.

38. *Id.*

39. *Id.*

40. *See* https://www.lawsociety.org.uk/law-careers/ becoming-a-solicitor/.

41. *See, e.g.*, University of Sydney's description of four-year bachelor of laws program, https://sydney.edu.au/law/study-law/our-law-degrees/ bachelor-of-laws.html; Trinity College of Dublin (four year law program), https://www.tcd.ie/ law/programmes/undergraduate/llb#Structure; University of Cambridge, UK (three year program), https://ba.law.cam.ac.uk/ studying-law-at- cambridge/.

42. *See* Law School Admissions Council, Statement on Prelaw Preparation, it should be noted that the current British requirement for three years of study for a 'qualifying LLB' will shortly no longer apply and will be replaced by a requirement to pass the Solicitors' Qualifying Examination (SQE). *See* https://www.lawsociety.org.uk/law-careers/becoming-a-solicitor/sqe-overview/ ("The ABA does not recommend any undergraduate majors or group of courses to prepare for a legal education. Students are admitted to law school from almost every academic discipline.").

43. *See Id.*; The Bar Council, *supra* note 35; The Law Society, *supra* note 36 at 6.

44. See American Bar Association, Preparing for Law School, http://www.americanbar.org/groups/ legal_education/resources/pre_law.html.

45. Co-author Fellmeth has served on the University of San Diego School of Law Admissions Committee since 1993. These examples are from the transcripts of reasonably typical student applicants.

46. Education loans are rarely dischargeable, even in bankruptcy, and can have a pervasive effect on the credit rating of delinquent borrowers, including employment, apartment rentals, and other needed borrowing.

47. As of December 2018, the median home price in the United States was $240,000. Home Prices in the 100 Largest Metro Areas, Kiplinger (March 10, 2019, 10:00 AM), https://www.kiplinger.com/tool/real-estate/T010-S003-home-prices-in-100-top-u-s- metroareas/index.php.

48. https://data.lawschooltransparency.com/costs/tuition/?scope=schools.

49. https://data.lawschooltransparency.com/costs/tuition/?scope=national.

50. *Id.*

51. *See Id.* Tuition for out-of-state attendees is substantially higher—approximately $35,000.

52. https://data.lawschooltransparency.com/costs/living-expenses/.

53. *Id.*

54. As discussed *supra*, in the context of undergraduate costs, out-of-state students attending a public law school will pay somewhere between these two figures, likely in the $250,000 to $300,000 range.

55. These totals assume maintenance of low-cost room and board for undergraduate education and assume no further increases above inflation for tuition or law school living expenses. Both of these assumptions are unlikely. As noted above, these numbers do not include many other costs, including books, loan interest, clothes, or transportation.

56. *See* Scott Jaschik, *What You Teach is What You Earn*, *Inside Higher Ed*, https://www.insidehighered.com/news/2016/03/28/study-finds-continued-large-gaps-faculty-salaries-based-discipline.

57. *See In re Grand Jury Investigation of Cuisinarts, Inc.*, 516 F. Supp. 1008, 1010-11 (D. Conn.) (recounting the proceedings in the criminal case, which resulted in a nolo contendere plea and a $250,000 fine). The DOJ also brought a companion civil case that was resolved by consent decree. *See United States v. Cuisinarts, Inc.*, Civ. No. H80-559, 1981-1 Trade Cas. (CCH) ¶ 63,979 (D.

Conn. Mar. 27, 1981).

58. David Segal, *Law School Economics: Ka-Ching!*, N.Y. TIMES, July 16, 2011, https://www.nytimes.com /2011/07/17/business/law-school-economics-job-market-weakenstuition- rises.html.

59. Applicants per year fell from 100,000 in 2002 to 82,900 in 2009-10 to 56,500 in 2015-16. See https://data.lawschooltransparency.com/enrollment/demand-for-law-school/.

60. Law schools have a high percentage of fixed costs that do not vary with added students (*e.g.*, real estate, staff and faculty with tenure who are not easily reduced in size notwithstanding fewer students). Indeed, when a law school's attendance drops 20% to 30%—as has occurred in many campuses after 2010—a natural response in an assumed competitive market would be to lower prices as necessary to fill the empty seats, each one of which involves little additional marginal cost. A tuition of just $5,000 would add significant net income to such an enterprise. Note that such reductions and bargains are part of the fabric of other high fixed cost service industries, e.g., hotels and airlines among many others—all of which compete vigorously with discounts and bargains for customers to occupy otherwise empty rooms or seats. *See also* Segal, *supra* note 58.

61. https://data.lawschooltransparency.com /enrollment/ all/. Although interestingly, law school enrollment increased slightly for the first time in nearly a decade in 2017-2018 in a phenomenon some experts deem the "Trump bump," this increase does not make up for the near decade of decline. *See* Staci Zaretsky, *Law School Enrollment Is Up for the First Time in Nearly a Decade*, Above the Law, Dec. 14, 2018, https:// abovethelaw.com/2018/12/law-school- enrollment-is-up-for-the-first- time-in-nearly-a-decade/; Ilana Kowarski, *Law School Applicant Increased This Year*, U.S. NEWS & WORLD REPORT, Jan. 29, 2018, https:// www.usnews.com/education/best-graduate-schools/top-law- schools/articles/2018-01-29/law-school-applications -increased-during-president-trumps-first-year.

62. Law schools are convinced that price is not the factor that influences choice, and, in fact, its reduction is

viewed as a competitive problem consistent with the *Cuisinart* scheme described *supra*. They would rather suffer serious customer shortfall than admit to lower price as a basis for consumer selection. *See also* Segal, *supra* note 58.

63. Tyler Roberts, *How Much Law Schools Are Discounting Tuition*, 21 PRELAW, at 13 (Winter 2018); Tyler Roberts, *Which Schools Are Discounting Tuition the Most?*, 27 NAT'L JURIST, at 13 (Winter 2018).

64. *Id.*

65. The degree of influence of these rankings is extreme. Many law schools have staff and faculty focusing substantial time and resources to the ratings of this publication and believe that it is a major factor in school selection by students. The direct ranking vis-à-vis rival law schools has a major effect. Note that many elements of the U.S. News ranking have merit in judging quality. For example, it measures class size per faculty member, faculty publications and citations, ratings of faculty by peers, bar passage rates, and timely employment of graduates. But it also excludes aspects important to legal education—from assuring competent attorneys in areas of actual practice, to a curriculum that is directed to that purpose.

66. Co-author Fellmeth has been on his Law School Admissions Committee since the 1990s and contends that there are many factors properly relevant apart from the GPA raw number. They commonly include obstacles: A student achieving a 3.3 GPA while having to work full time and/or take care of a child or ill grandparent might be more impressive than a 3.5 from a full time student at a school with a relatively liberal grading pattern. Another student may have suffered a major injury or disease and managed to overcome it, manifesting courage and tenacity. Or a student may have had a weak freshman year, a first year away from home, and then recover to sequentially increase the GPA every year thereafter to a 4.0 senior year performance. In addition, difficult courses may warrant more consideration, but the overall GPA is not so adjusted in the U.S. News rankings. Similar excluded variables compromise the accuracy of the LSAT test score. Take an immigrant from Bosnia whose family was forced to flee to Russia when she was 8, and then at

age 16 immigrated to the United States, who achieved an LSAT score in the 60th percentile—in her third and newest language. Should she be dismissed in favor of a student from a wealthy family in the 70th percentile, who attended private schools and had access to tutors?

67. *See* Methodology: 2019 Best Law Schools Rankings, https://www.usnews.com/ education/best-graduate-schools/articles/law-schools-methodology; *See also* Malcolm Gladwell, *The Order of Things*, THE NEW YORKER, https://www.newyorker.com/magazine /2011/ 02/14/the-order-of-things.

68. This is not to say that equitable factors enjoy no consideration. For those with LSAT and GPA scores on "the bubble" (not as high as desired but close) there will be more particularized consideration. But the ranking based on the two numbers must be overcome with a burden not easily met. In contrast, unless there is a criminal or ethical issue, a high score will usually qualify an applicant for admission ipso facto, and usually with a generous tuition discount. See also Roberts, *supra* note 63 (How Much Law Schools are Discounting Tuition) at 13.

69. See www.usnews.com/best-graduate-schools/ top-law-schools/grad-debt-rankings/page+4.

70. *Id.*

71. *See* https://trends.collegeboard.org/student-aid/figures-tables/total-federal-and-nonfederal-loans-over-time.

72. *Id.*; *See also* https://data.lawschool transparency.com/costs/living-expenses/; https://data.law schooltransparency.com/costs/tuition/?scope=national.

73. Law school administration and faculty are understandably influenced by their own experience. We all have a tendency to project our own model onto those we wish to teach. But practical legal experience is not common among tenured law faculty. Not many have conducted a trial, argued appellate cases or had to deal with a caseload of clients. Their concerns are with important ethical and philosophical issues, which do facilitate legal and citizen intelligence. But we are not educating large numbers of future appellate justices or law professors. Even for these latter functions, professors also specialize in only one or several subject areas

themselves. The vast majority of graduates will be practitioners faced with client problems such as an unruly child, a fraudulent business partner, or a grandfather who wants to emigrate from South Korea. The skills to enable competent services in this latter domain of real world problems warrant high priority in law school education.

74. A typical charge ranges from $1,000 to $4,200, with several months of study—including lectures, written material and practice examination. *See* https://abovethelaw.com/2013/05/which-bar-exam-prep-course-is-the-best-2/.

75. *See Phase I Final Report* at 14 (June 2013), http://www.calbar.ca.gov/Portals/0/documents/bog/bot_ExecDir/ADA%20Version_STATE_BAR_TASK_FORCE_REPORT%28FINAL_AS_APPROVED_6_11_13%29_062413.pdf.

76. *Id.* at 1, 5.

77. Around the same time, the ABA adopted a new experiential learning requirement, requiring six hours of study for ABA-accredited law schools, as articulated in Standards 303 and 304. https://www.americanbar.org/content/dam/aba/publications/misc/legal_education/Standards/2018-2019ABAStandardsforApprovalofLawSchools/2018-2019-aba-standards-chapter3.pdf.

78. *See Phase I Final Report*, *supra* note 75 at 1.

79. *Phase II Report*, (Sept. 2014), available at http://www.calbar.ca.gov/portals/0/documents/bog/bot_ExecDir/2014_TFARRPhaseIIFinalReport_092514.pdf; http://www.calbar.ca.gov/Portals/0/documents/bog/bot_ExecDir/2014_AttachmentA_ImplementingRulesfor15units.pdf; http://www.calbar.ca.gov/Portals/0/documents/bog/bot_ExecDir/2014_AttachmentB_ImplementingRulesfor50hoursprobono.pdf; http://www.calbar.ca.gov/Portals/0/documents/bog/bot_ExecDir/2014_AttachmentC_ImplementingRulesfor10hourscompetencytra.

80. TFARR's final recommendations were released just as the Bar was facing a period of political and internal turmoil as the Board of Trustees voted to terminate the Bar's Executive Director, Joseph Dunn, just two months

later. With long and protracted litigation pending, as well as new executive leadership and increased scrutiny from the legislature, these recommendations largely fell by the wayside for several years. Ultimately, the pro bono recommendation was opposed by the legal services sector, who did not have the resources to supervise the influx of attorneys under this recommended regime. And Governor Jerry Brown vetoed a 2016 bill, SB 1257 (Block), which would have imposed the 50 hour pro bono requirement, stating that a state mandate for pro bono service cannot be justified, as "[l]aw students in California are now contending with skyrocketing costs ... and many struggle to find employment once they are admitted to the Bar." He further stated that, "it would be unfair to burden students with the [pro bono] requirements ... [and] [i]nstead, we should focus on lowering the cost of legal education and devising alternative and less expensive ways to qualify for the Bar Exam. By doing so, we could actually expand the opportunity to serve the public interest." The 15 hours of practical coursework recommendation was never implemented either. The bar did, however, adopt the recommendation for ten hours of MCLE for new attorneys. See 23:1 CAL. REG. L. REP. 172 (2017).

81. Four states (California, Vermont, Virginia, and Washington) permit individuals who have worked a designated period of time as an apprentice to a licensed attorney to skip law school all together and sit for the bar exam using their experience as a substitute for the law school experience. *See, e.g.*, Rules of State Bar of California, Rule 4.26; Rules of Admission to Bar of Vermont, Rule 7; Washington Courts Admission and Practice Rules, APR 6; Va. Code Ann. § 54.1-3926 (West). Very few applicants, however, are able to, or do, avail themselves of this unusual route. Additionally, Wisconsin admits students with diplomas from in-state law schools (University of Wisconsin and Marquette University) without taking the Wisconsin bar examination. *See* Wisconsin Supreme Court Rule 40.03 (Diploma Privilege).

82. *See N.C. State Bd. of Dental Exam'rs*, 135 S. Ct. at 1114.

83. *See supra*, Section II.

84. The MBE covers seven core subjects: civil procedure, constitutional law, contracts, criminal law, evidence, real property and torts. http://www.ncbex.org/exams/mbe/preparing/.

85. http://www.ncbex.org/exams/ube/.

86. *Id.*

87. http://www.calbar.ca.gov/Admissions/Examinations/California-Bar-Examination.

88. See National Committee of Bar Examiners, *Comprehensive Guide to Bar Admission Requirements 2018* at 33-34, http://www.ncbex.org/pubs/bar-admissions-guide/2018/ mobile/index.html#p=44.

89. *Id.*

90. www.calbar.ca.gov/About-Us/News-Events/News-Releases/state-bar-releases-july-2018- bar-exam-results.

91. *See State Bar of California Bar Exam Evaluations Results*, March 15, 2018, http://www.calbar.ca.gov/Portals/0/2018BarExamReport.pdf.

92. *Id.* at 8.

93. For a detailed history of the controversy spurred by the July 2016 bar exam results, and the studies conducted during this period, See 23:1 CAL. REG. L. REP. 158-161 (2017). Note that co-author Gramme served as the Assembly Judiciary Committee's appointee subject matter expert on the Standard Setting and Content Validation studies in 2017.

94. *See State Bar of California Bar Exam Evaluation Results*, *supra* note 91, at 3.

95. 23:1 CAL. REG. L. REP., *supra* note 93, at 158-161; 23:2 CAL. REG. L. REP. 254-58 (2018).

96. See www.calbar.ca.gov/About-Us/News-Events/News-Releases/state-bar-launches-california-attorney-practice-analysis-to-continue-bar-exam-study. To the authors' knowledge, California is the only state that imposes this level of psychometric analysis and validity with respect to its bar exam.

97. Roger Bolus, PhD., Performance Changes on the California Bar Examination: Part 2 (Research Solutions Group, State Bar Dec. 20, 2018), http://

www.calbar.ca.gov/Portals/0/documents/admissions/Examinations/Bar-Exam-Report-Final.pdf.

98. *Id.* at ii.

99. *Id.* at viii. This finding was significant in that much of the public comment in support of maintaining California's high cut score has attributed declining pass rates to law schools' willingness to accept lesser qualified applicants in the face of widespread declines in law school enrollment since 2011.

100. *See, e.g.*, Cal. Bus. & Prof. Code § 6001.1 ("Protection of the public, which includes support for greater access to, and inclusion in, the legal system, shall be the highest priority for the State Bar of California and the board of trustees in exercising their licensing, regulatory, and disciplinary functions. *Whenever the protection of the public is inconsistent with other interests sought to be promoted, the protection of the public shall be paramount.*") (emphasis added).

101. *See* Cal. Bus. & Prof. Code § 139; Center for Public Interest Law's Amicus Brief to Supreme Court of California dated October 2, 2017, discussing and attaching the California Department of Consumer Affairs' Licensure Examination Validation Policy, http://www.cpil.org/download/S244281_LB_CPIL.pdf.

102. The National Committee of Bar Examiners also established a "Testing Taskforce" in 2018, that will similarly conduct a three year comprehensive study of the bar exam. *See* https://www.testingtaskforce.org/about/.

103. *See* Michael T. Kane, *So Much Remains the Same: Conception and Status of Validation in Setting Standards (2001)*, published in Setting Performance Standards: Concepts, Methods, and Perspectives 53–88 (Gregory J. Cizek & Robert J. Sternberg eds., 2001).

104. See *Standards for Educational and Psychological Testing* (AERA, APA, & NCME, 2014); R.K. Hambleton & M.J. Pitoniak, *Setting Performance Standards, in Educational Management* 433-70 (R.L. Brennan ed., 2005).

105. *See* February 1, 2017 letter from deans of 20 out of California's 21 ABA-accredited law schools to the California Supreme Court at 3 ("California's high cut scores generate pressure for California law schools to

design their educational programs with even more focus on the bar exam itself than is required in other states. This may, in the margins, drive schools and students to additional emphasis on memorization, multiple-choice exam skills and overt test preparation rather than the full range of skills necessary for effective lawyering."), http://www.calbar.ca.gov/Portals/0/2018BarExamReport.pdf at 142–146.

106. Many states offer "certification" programs for practitioners in various legal specialties. Such specialization, with required examinations, work experience, etc. can contribute to market knowledge about a given practice area. However, that "label" is separate and apart from licensure, and is not required to practice in that area of law. Equally troubling is that the criteria for certification are overwhelmingly controlled by individuals who have already obtained these specializations—giving them a profit stake interest in raising the barriers for new market entrants. *See N.C. State Bd. of Dental Exam'rs*, 135 S. Ct. at 1114.While it may be useful to advertise skills to sophisticated clients, it does not protect average consumers who are most likely to be irreparably harmed by attorney misconduct.

107. By way of illustration, the following are specialties certified as such by the California State Bar or its recently devolved associations: 1. Admiralty and Maritime Law, 2. Appellate Law, 3. Bankruptcy Law, 4. Criminal Law, 5. Estate Planning, Trust and Probate Law, 6. Family Law, 7. Franchise and Distribution Law, 8. Immigration and Nationality Law, 9. Legal Malpractice Law,10. Taxation Law. In addition, the Bar "accredits" private attorney associations to certify attorneys in 11 additional areas of specialization, including: 1. Business Bankruptcy Law, 2. Consumer Bankruptcy Law, 3. Creditors' Rights Law (American Board of Certification) 4. Civil Trial Advocacy, 5. Criminal Trial Advocacy, 6. Family Law Trial Advocacy, 7. Social Security Disability Law (National Board of Trial Advocacy), 8. Elder Law (National Elder Law Foundation), 9. Legal Malpractice, 10. Medical Malpractice (American Board of Professional Liability Attorneys), 11. Juvenile Law (Child Welfare) (National Association of Counsel for Children).

108. *See, e.g.*, Henderson, *supra* note 1 at 1-9. As discussed below, there is also a small but increasing fourth category, "Alternative Legal Service Providers (ALSPs)" and legal technicians— using internet and artificial intelligence tools to provide law related assistance.

109. U.S. Census Bureau 2012 Economic Census; Henderson, *supra* note 1 at 2.

110. *Id.* at 4-5.

111. *Id.*

112. According to ABA statistics, there are 1,338,678 resident attorneys in the United States in 2018. See https://www.americanbar.org/content/dam/aba/administrative/market_research/Total_National_Lawyer_Population_1878-2018.authcheckdam.pdf.

113. Henderson, *supra* note 1 at 12–16. *See also* John P. Heinz & Edward O. Laumann, *Chicago Lawyers: The Social Structure of the Bar* (rev. ed. 1994) ("Chicago Lawyers I"); John P. Heinz et al., Urban Lawyers: *The New Social Structure of the Bar* at 6–7 (2005) ("Chicago Lawyers II").

114. U.S. Census Bureau 2012 Economic Census; Henderson, *supra* note 1, at 13.

115. *Id.*

116. *Id.* at 14.

117. *Id.* at 17-18. Note that Consumer Price Index-Urban is the inflation measure used in relevant studies by the Bureau of Labor Statistics.

118. *Id.*

119. *Id.*; Bureau of Labor Statistics Consumer Expenditure and Income data, https://www.bls.gov/opub/hom/cex/home.htm.

120. Henderson, *supra* note 1, at 19. Note that this market is currently being hampered by existing ethics rules nationwide pertaining to the "unauthorized practice of law," multijurisdictional practice, corporate ownership, fee sharing, and advertising. *Id.*

121. *Id.*

122. *See* Income and Poverty in the United States: 2017, United States Census Bureau, https://

www.census.gov/library/publications/2018/demo/p60-263.html.

123. The time period of the study was July 1, 2012 to June 30, 2013, *See* Paula Hannaford-Agar JD, Scott Graves, and Shelley Spacey Miller, *The Landscape of Civil Litigation in State Courts* (National Center for State Courts, 2015); *See* related information, http://www.courtstatistics.org/; *See also* Henderson, *supra* note 1, at 19.

124. Thomas Reuters, Alternate Legal Service Providers 2019 (Jan. 2019), https://legal.thomsonreuters.com/content/dam/ewp-m/documents/legal/en/pdf/reports/alsp-report-final.pdf?cid=9008178&sfdccampaignid=7011B000002OF6AQAW&chl=pr.

125. *Id.*

126. *Id.*; *See also* Henderson, *supra* note 1, at 10-12.

127. *Id.*

128. *Id.* at 20. Additionally, the UK and Australia permit and regulate ALSPs. *Id.* at 26–27.

129. American Bar Association Model Rules of Professional Conduct, Rule 5.4 (professional independence of a lawyer), https://www.americanbar.org/groups/professional_responsibility/publications/model_rules_of_professional_conduct/rule_5_4_professional_independence_of_a_lawyer/.

130. American Bar Association Rules of Professional Conduct, Rule 5.5 (unauthorized practice of law), https://www.americanbar.org/groups/professional_responsibility/publications/model_rules_of_professional_conduct/rule_5_5_unauthorized_practice_of_law_multijurisdictional_practice_of_law/.

131. *See* Comments on American Bar Association Rules of Professional Conduct, Rule 5.4, https://www.americanbar.org/groups/professional_responsibility/publications/model_rules_of_professional_conduct/rule_5_4_professional_independence_of_a_lawyer/comment_on_rule_5_4/.

132. *See, e.g.*, Rules 1.1-1.18 of the ABA Model Rules of Professional Conduct. Also note that even as to government attorneys, the notion that counsel operates

with independent integrity is not an empirically verifiable proposition. *See* Fellmeth, Walking the Line, 15 CRLR 4 (Fall 1995) (reviewing judgments for violation of state Open Meeting, Public Records, and Administrative Procedure Acts and finding that even without the profit motive issue, government counsel have a cultural allegiance to the client to advance his or her or its interests provisions) *See* http://www.sandiego.edu/cpil/documents/Walking %20the%20Line.pdf.

133. *See* Victoria Hudgins, Survey: 69 percent of people would use online legal services over attorneys, Law.com (Dec. 2018) (citing a Harris Poll where 82 percent of U.S. adults surveyed said they wanted alternatives to traditional lawyers when dealing with small legal matters, such as making a will and document review), https://www.law.com/legaltechnews/2018/12/12/survey-69-percent-of-people-would-use-online-legal-services-over-attorneys/.

134. Daniel Conte, *Avvo Shuts Down its Legal Services Product in Wake of Ethics Opinions Warning Attorneys Not to Participate* (Aug. 14, 2018), https://www.hinshawlaw.com/newsroom- updates-avvo-shuts-down-its-legal-services-product-in-wake-of-ethics-opinions-warning- attorneys-not-to-participate.html; *See* New York State Bar Association, Opinion 1132 (Aug. 8, 2017), http://www.nysba.org/EthicsOpinion1132/; See also Tom Gordon, *ABA To Consider Proposed "Best Practices" for Online Document Preparers*, (Jan. 23, 2019), https://www.responsivelaw.org/blog/ny-bars-proposed-regulation-of-online-document-preparers-to-go-before-aba. *See also* Xiumei Dong, *Survey Finds Legal Industry in Last Place in AI, Machine Learning Adoption*, Law.com, (Nov. 19, 2018), https://www.law.com/therecorder/2018/11/19/survey-finds-legal-industry-in-last-place-in-ai-machine-learning-adoption/.

135. Co-author Gramme is serving as an attorney member of this task force, as well as the Association of Professional Responsibility Lawyers' Future of Lawyering Committee studying similar issues with respect to the ABA model rules.

136. *See* comment 8 to ABA Model Rule of Professional Conduct 1.1 ("To maintain the requisite

knowledge and skill, a lawyer should keep abreast of changes in the law and its practice, including the benefits and risks associated with relevant technology, engage in continuing study and education and comply with all continuing legal education requirements to which the lawyer is subject.").

137. *See* Catherine Sanders Reach, *Essential Tech Skills for the New Lawyer*, ABA for Law Students (November, 2017), https://abaforlawstudents.com/2017/11/02/essential-tech-skills-for-the-new- lawyer/.

138. American Bar Association, ABA Standards and Rules of Procedure for Approval of Law Schools 2018–19, at 32, https://www.americanbar.org/content/dam/aba/publications/misc/legal_education/ Standards/2018-2019ABAStandardsforApprovalofLawSchools/2018-2019-aba-standards-rules-approval-law-schools-final.pdf

139. State regulatory agencies are particularly ignored, with few law schools teaching anything about a subject that determines the regulation of all trades and professions (including attorneys), the environment, education, and health. These agencies function primarily at the state level and knowledge of what they do and the procedural rules determining their transparency, accountability, and legality should be a part of the curriculum of all schools.

140. An example is the University of San Diego, offering concentrations in: (1) Business and Corporate law, (2) Children's Rights, (3) Civil Litigation, (4) Criminal Litigation, (5) Employer and Labor Law, (6) Environmental and Energy Law, (7) Health Law, (8) Intellectual Property, (9) International Law, and (10) Public Interest Law. http://www.sandiego.edu/law/academics/jd-program/concentrations/. Each area has one or several required courses and a number of allowable electives. Completion of the requirements for such an area of concentration is part of the student's official transcript.

141. The program allows people working for qualified organizations to repay some of their federal student loans based on a portion of their monthly income. After making 120 monthly payments, the remaining federal student loans are forgiven, with no cancellation-of-debt income tax consequences. Private loans are not eligible for PSLF.

At this writing the program is still in effect, although there are competing bills pending in Congress to limit it (Promoting Real Opportunity, Success, and Prosperity through Education Reform Act (the “PROSPER Act”), 115th Congress (2017-2018), H.R. 4505, Rep. Foxx, https://www.congress.gov/bill/115th-congress/house-bill/4508/text#toc-H0DD0FF2E45414041A8FACE65 B4BD4B73) and to expand it (Aim Higher Act, 116th Congress (2018-2019), H.R. 6543, Rep. Scott, https://www.congress.gov/bill/115th-congress/house-bill/6543.

142. *See* https://oshpd.ca.gov/loans-scholarships-grants/loan-repayment/slrp/.

143. https://oshpd.ca.gov/loans-scholarships-grants/loan-repayment/slrp/#provider eligibility.

144. AB 982 (Firebaugh) (Chapter 1131, Statutes of 2002).

145. The Health Professions Education Foundation (HPEF) is a non-profit 501(c)(3) public benefit corporation housed within the Office of Statewide Health Planning and Development (OSHPD). Pursuant to Health & Safety Code sections 128330-128370, HPEF is required to submit an annual report to the California State Legislature documenting the performance of the Steven M. Thompson Physician Corps Loan Repayment Program (STLRP).

146. This fund is administered by the Department of Managed Health Care in California and consists of administrative fines and penalties assessed in the process of licensing and regulating Health Care Service Plans. *See* Cal. Health & Safety Code § 1341.45(a).

147. *See* Steven M. Thompson Physician Corps Loan Repayment Program Annual Report to the Legislature, at 3-4 (June 2017), https://oshpd.ca.gov/ml/v1/resources/document?rs:path=/Loan- Repayments-Scholarships-Grants/Documents/HPEF/Publications-Reports/HPEF-STLRP-Annual- Report-to-Legislature-2017.pdf. The total amount spent from all sources on this program from July 2015–November 2016 was $6 million. *Id.* at 4.

148. STLRP guidelines are in California Health and Safety Code Section 128550–128558 and the California

Code of Regulations are in Title 22, sections 97931.01-97931.06.

149. *See* Steven M. Thompson Physician Corps Loan Repayment Program Annual Report to the Legislature, *supra* note 147.

150. *See* ABA description at https://www.americanbar.org/groups/legal_education/resources/student_loan_repayment_and_forg iveness/; *see also* https://www.psjd.org/getResourceFile.cfm?ID=112 for a discussion of the confluence of LRAPs with other potential assistance.

151. Based on the authors' survey of individual law school programs, amounts obtained in these programs vary under complicated formulae but are generally at or below $7,000 per year. These amounts here are generally less than one fifth the amount paid to physicians. Some LRAP programs may provide benefits for a longer period (many for up to five years and some for up to 10) where public interest law practice continues and with total income below $60,000 per year (with benefit reductions common where income is above $40,000). The average amounts provided are relatively small, particularly in relation to the over $140,000 in average accrued law school debt for graduates, and in relation to the benefits afforded by the professions. The percentage of a law school's graduates receiving assistance is typically less than 2%. They depend on law school created "funds" fed from charitable contributions and other limited sources.

152. AB 935 (Hertzberg) (Chapter 881, Statutes of 2001).

153. *See* Cal. Ed. Code § 69740, et seq.

154. *See supra* Section III.D.

155. At this writing, the ABA has been engaged in a three-year debate as to whether to amend Standard 316 of its Standards and Rules of Procedure for Approval of Law Schools to require 75 percent of a school's bar exam takers to pass within two years of graduation, rather than the five years currently allowed. See Lyle Moran, ABA Legal Ed Council Delays Decision on Stricter Bar Passage Standards, ABA Journal, February 22, 2019, http://www.abajournal.com/web/article/aba-legal-

education-council-delays-decision-on-stricter-bar-passage-standards.

156. Note that these proposed certifications are different than the existing "specialization" models, which currently serve as marketing tools, enabling attorneys to charge higher prices to sophisticated clients for the privilege of being represented by a legal specialist. *See supra* Section III.D. Instead, these certifications would be issued by the bar, subject to relevant antitrust laws, and psychometrically validated, in order to ensure public protection.

157. Indeed, to maintain certification for Cardiopulmonary Resuscitation ("CPR"), one must take a refresher course every two years. Why do we not require the same for licensed professionals?

158. Flexible standards for practice in the event that a longstanding practitioner fails the re- certification exam could be available; for example, a 90-day probationary period could be imposed to allow time for a retake. This flexibility can be important for the clients of practitioners who might be harmed by the interrupted practice of their attorney. If competence cannot be demonstrated at the end of 90 days, the specialized practice in that area would cease.

159. The North Carolina State Board of Dental Examiners was seeking to sanction and halt the practice of teeth whitening as the unauthorized practice of dentistry and to confine such brightening to practicing dentists. *See N.C. State Bd. of Dental Exam'rs*, 135 S. Ct. at 1111; discussion in Section II.A, *supra*.

160. *See* Leslie C. Levin, *Lawyers Going Bare and Clients Going Blind*, 68 Fla. L. Rev. 1281 (2016), http://scholarship.law.ufl.edu/flr/vol68/iss5/2; Testimony of Robert C. Fellmeth to the State Bar of California's Malpractice Insurance Working Group, July 9, 2018, http://www.sandiego.edu/cpil/documents/20180709_RCF%20Testimony_Final.pdf; Illinois Attorney Registration & Disciplinary Commission Annual Report of 2016, https://www.iardc.org/AnnualReport2016.pdf at 16 (finding 41% of sole practitioners in Illinois reported they did not carry malpractice insurance).

161. See Cal. Bus. & Prof. Code § 6140.5; *See also* Testimony of Robert Fellmeth, *supra* note 160.

162. See https://www.americanbar.org/content/dam/aba/administrative/professional_responsibility/chart_implementation_of_mcrld.authcheckdam.pdf.

163. *See* Cal. Bus. & Prof. Code § 6069.5; http://www.calbar.ca.gov/Portals/0/documents/702-Malpractice-Insurance-Working-Group.pdf.

164. *See* http://board.calbar.ca.gov/docs/agendaItem/Public/agendaitem1000023886.pdf.

165. *See* detailed discussion in Section II, *supra.*

166. *N.C. State Bd. of Dental Exam'rs*, 135 S. Ct. at 1116.

167. *See* SB 36 (Jackson) (Chapter 422, Statutes of 2017).

168. *See* Memo to the Board of Trustees from Richard Schauffler, Analyst of the Office of Research and Institutional Accountability, July 19, 2018 at 5, http://board.calbar.ca.gov/docs/agendaItem/Public/agendaitem1000022371.pdf.

169. The landmark 2017 California legislation deunifying the State Bar of California also revised the composition of the State Bar Board of Trustees—eliminating six positions which were elected by California attorneys, and providing for more even distribution of attorneys (7) and non-attorneys (6). *See* SB 36 (Jackson), *supra* note 168. Although moving away from the extreme cartel structure of the past 80 years, the new governing body remains under the control of "active market participants." *N.C. State Bd. of Dental Exam'rs*, 135 S. Ct. 1101.

170. There is little doubt that those involved in public regulation, including attorneys, generally believe that they serve the public interest, usually receiving little or no compensation. They subjectively believe that their mission is to serve the public interest. But the accumulation of persons into trade associations creates empathy lines that are rarely discussed openly. To illustrate, how often does a state bar discipline attorneys for over-billing? How often is the issue of knowing deceit in points and authorities, et al. subject to sanction or professional approbation? Or even discussed? How often

do state bars study the impact of supply limitations vis-à-vis hourly prices?

End of Article

Hypotheticals

The Antitrust head of the State Attorney General's Office contacts you with this question:

1. As you review the regulation of trades and professions, where is regulation excessively anticompetitive or unnecessary?

2. What areas of commerce might the market perform more efficiently without unnecessary barriers to entry of other regulatory costs? Barbers? Auctioneers? Stockbrokers?

Chapter 10
Inadequate Regulation

INTRODUCTION

As Chapter 1 outlines, regulation has multiple purposes. One is to ensure effective competition in a manner that may lessen the need for aspects of regulatory control. Where regulatory systems operate to shield those regulated from competitive discipline, the very purpose of state involvement is undermined. The areas of current inaction or erroneous action are many. We have a patent system with purposes that ideally do not include pricing at 50 times the cost of medicines important to health and survival. But America's pharmaceutical prices are the highest globally, with drug companies enjoying monopoly power pricing over essential treatment.

We have an oil industry centered on an international horizontal price fix on the price of oil that extends worldwide. The time taken for state bars or medical boards to stop damaging practices in the normal course of regulatory discipline portends unnecessary and severe irreparable harm. And the range of inadequacy extends from allowing dangerous practitioners to obtain licensure to not requiring basic disclosures that allow consumer choice to be an effective market check.

The U.S. Supreme Court decision in *AT&T v. Concepcion*, 563 U.S. 333 (2011), exacerbates such non- feasance, seriously impairing the viability of class action remedies by groups of consumers who have been victimized. This 5–4 decision upheld AT&T Mobility's right to compel the plaintiffs and all members of the large group of consumers, which comprised the class, to proceed in individual arbitrations if they wish to pursue a claim. All any merchant needs do is include in "terms and conditions," rarely reviewed by consumers, that all grievances are subject to compulsory and individual arbitration as a sole remedy. After 2011, such provisions became commonplace in each and every business/consumer transaction.

Some of the results of inadequate or misplaced regulation include the continuing horizontal price fix of licensed real estate broker commissions at 6% of the sale price of a property. Those resale prices have spiked many times more than inflation, with $60,000 median homes now approaching $600,000. Inflation may have halved the value of money, but the static application of the 6% price fix multiplies revenue for brokers to more than five times the previous levels. The regulation of those licensees is not only inadequate, but it facilitates a widespread and general felony horizontal price fix. Nor are real estate broker regulators alone in non-feasance. Title insurance, purportedly subject to state regulation, has price and kickback defects.

Regrettably, there are many examples of serious market abuse and felony offenses that regulation shields from market-based criminal remedies. The abuses of private for-profit schools in corruptly luring hundreds of thousands of our youth into an expensive curriculum at increasingly high tuition rates have created both serious burdens on federal and state education subsidies and also decades of debilitating debt. Cases against ITT Tech, Corinthian, and many other schools have illuminated egregious and massive abuses without the important benefits of higher education for a large number of our students. To be sure, public prosecutors have started to sanction many of the offenders, but the "school rating" systems and other forms of quasi- regulation are largely illusory.

Some of the most noteworthy examples of regulation failure include physicians committing sexual misconduct and, hospitals failing to report physician problems.

We present one example of such failure in examining the regulation of finances, mortgages, commercial representations, et al., that magnified from 2000 to 2008—leading to a massive economic breakdown and tragedy, one that could have created a national crisis on the 1929 depression scale. It represents the confluence of inadequate regulation or regulation that erroneously allowed massive abuse. It concerns a widespread practice evolving after 2000 to use what is termed "bait and switch" tactics in financing home purchases throughout the nation. Mortgagors offered low interest or even no interest for a period of time to attract consumers to purchase real property at a time of price increases. After three to five years of "bait," the mortgages "switched" to a high-interest assessment, usually pegged at something just over the extant "prime rate." This game resulted in the purchase of not just hundreds or thousands but millions of homes, with payment obligations increasing to untenable levels soon after the "switch" to an often unanticipated high-interest rate. The consequences in terms of loss of homes and personal bankruptcies were startling and massive.

This recent area of regulatory/market failure and harm is an important example to study and involves both state and federal regulatory failure.

Excerpt from California White Collar Crime and Business Litigation, by Thomas A. Papageorge and Professor Robert C. Fellmeth (Tower Publishing, 2019):

***

D. Predatory Real Property Lending, Securitization and National Financial Crisis

§6.27 1. Background

"Predatory lending" in the real estate context refers to a range of abusive lending practices: (a) deception and fraud in appraisals or loan terms, (b) "bait and switch" arrangements that begin with below-prime rates (or collection of interest through additions to principal)—followed by later imposition of markedly higher interest rates, (c) loans made on properties beyond their market value and without regard to the payment ability of borrowers, and (d) repeated refinancings imposed upon consumers threatened with foreclosure, with additional fees and subsequent foreclosure notwithstanding those assessments. (For a similar discussion of "predatory lending" see *American Financial Services Association v. City of Oakland* (2005) 34 Cal.4th 1239, 1244 [104 P.3d 813].)

The subprime variable interest rate pattern in home mortgages became endemic after 2000. The mortgages then became securitized instruments traded among and between major financial institutions previously limited in speculative transactions, with their accounting implications concealed from investors and regulators. The resulting bubble had many of the characteristics of the traditional white collar crime Ponzi scheme—with late-arriving purchasers holding empty or toxic assets. The scale of the bubble and the 2008 collapse nationally in terms of pension and stock market diminution, unemployment and economic dislocation, was unprecedented since the Great Depression of 1929. Ten public policy/statutory subject areas, each related to white collar crime prevention, facilitated the expansion and collapse:

(1) **Usury Application to Real Property Financing**. The non- application of California's 10 percent and 12 percent constitutional usury limitations added speculative value to the relevant mortgage backed securities (see discussion of California usury exemptions at §6.26, *supra*). That non-application allows an initial temporary level below the "prime rate" guiding funds acquisition for the lender. Or, in the alternative, interest

rates may be at or above prime, but payments may be lowered temporarily to cover only part of the interest, with the remainder adding onto principal and future obligation. Where the initial interest rate is low, the lender may rely on a later substantial increase (the "switch") to levels that may be unaffordable for the consumer but allow an extraordinary profit for the lender above the acquisition cost of money loaned. This premium future value, lacking a usury ceiling, provides one inducement to market real property under arrangements of no-interest or low interest temporary "arms"—with uncertain or unclear increase at some future date. Such prospective profit also drove purchases and refinancing of homes without required money down (and for loan amounts totaling more than the actual market value of the property). That prospective future value also drove the transformation of mortgages into securities traded to third parties who to some extent were able to determine the "switch" free from defenses that may be available by the borrower vis-a-vis the initial lender (see discussion of "holder in due" course status for securitization below).

(2) **Predatory Real Property Lending and Bank Regulation**. In 1994, the Congress addressed predatory real estate loans by enacting the Home Ownership and Equity Protection Act (HOEPA, Pub. Law 103- 325, see esp. 15 U.S.C. § 1639 et seq.). It limited some predatory practices, but only applied to loans with upfront fees exceeding 8% of the loan amount, and was easily loopholed with smaller up-front charges and the later "switch" profit potential, as noted above. In 2000, the Federal Deposit Insurance Corporation, the Federal Reserve and the Office of Thrift Supervision considered rules to restrict predatory loans. However, the Federal Reserve Rules only prohibited a small number of egregious practices. More expansive safeguards took the form of non-binding "guidelines." Nor were existing standards enforced—from 2003–07 the Federal Reserve took only three enforcement actions nationwide. From 2004–06 the Office of the Comptroller of the Currency—with authority over 1,800 banks—also took three enforcement actions. Meanwhile, during this period, subprime loans grew to 20% of annual home mortgage lending. Some states outside of California (e.g.,

Massachusetts, New York, New Jersey, New Mexico) enacted anti- predatory lending laws that substantially reduced their incidence. (See Wei Lie and Keith Ernst, *The Best Value in the Subprime Market: State Predatory Lending Reforms*, Center for Responsible Lending (February 23, 2006).)

In 2001, California enacted some restrictions on predatory loan issuance (Fin. Code, §§ 4970– 4979.8, see discussion in §6.338 below). In 2003, the Office of the Comptroller of the Currency (OCC) invoked a clause from the 1863 National Bank Act to issue formal opinions preempting, and effectively voiding, the brunt of state predatory lending laws. In 2004, it issued rules preempting all state regulation of national banks. While federal banks did not originate the largest proportion of predatory home loans, some of them suffering serious shortfalls (e.g., Wachovia) were major originators. More critically, these OCC-controlled banks became major holders of securities backed by the loans of others (see discussion below). The preemption move of the OCC did not directly affect California because its "predatory lending" statute, enacted in 2001, already excluded from its coverage "persons chartered by Congress to engage in secondary mortgage market transactions." (Fin. Code, § 4979.8, see § 6.27 et seq., *infra*).

(3) **Securitization of Mortgages and Security Buyer Immunity as "Holder in Due Course."** The instrument for speculative expansion of sub-prime mortgage depended upon "holder in due course" status to collect on mortgage debts backed by real property; i.e., the initial mortgage lender making the sale to the consumer could treat the mortgage instrument as if it were currency—entitled to full faith and credit regardless of how the giver or seller obtained the instrument. Unless fraud or other violation of law appears on the face of the instrument, the mortgage may be bought free from any defenses the homeowner obligor may have against the initial lender. Contrary to this concept is the "assignee liability" principle, which holds those receiving such instruments responsible for unlawful acts in their creation. Consumer interests favoring such liability argue that it provides an incentive on such recipients to inquire into the business practices of initial lenders—persons in a better

position to monitor prudent loan practices than the general public. The 1994 House Ownership and Equity Protection Act discussed above provided for holder-in-due-course status for all mortgage instruments, except those categorized as "very high cost"—where the definition did not include typical subprime loans. Hence, initial lenders (often loan brokerage firms) would sell mortgages to other financial institutions, and they would be packaged in large numbers as "mortgage backed" securities by large commercial or investment banks. The mortgage value (based on the obligation of a consumer to pay under its stated terms) was secure regardless of misrepresentation or fraud by the original lender. Consumer advocates argued that such protected status limited buyer or assignee incentive to verify sales practices and precluded consumer redress except against the original lender. Importantly, any such defenses as to the original lender would not impede (or be raisable) against a foreclosure action by the current holder of the mortgage security.

(4) **Investment Bank Deregulation and Speculation Expansion**. The Financial Services Modernization Act of 1999 (Pub. Law 106-102, 15 U.S.C. § 6801 et seq.) repealed the Glass- Steagall Act of 1933. The latter was enacted to curb depression era abuses and limit bank speculation. The repeal further blurred lines between banks, insurers, and securities trading firms ("investment" banks). Those lines had been drawn after the speculative bubble of 1929 depleted banks of assets necessary to pay depositors. The limitation on bank securities trading or speculative activity in general was based on the public need for protection of consumer deposited assets— buttressed by the Federal Deposit Insurance Corporation's backing for its security from public funds. The role of banks as (1) a steady source of loans to business without undue disruption from stock market cycles, and (2) provider of steady consumer credit, are additional cited reasons for bank conservative investment. Similarly, insurers have long been subject to limitations on speculation, with industry regulation focused on stable assets to meet contingent policy claims. But almost all insurance regulation occurs at the state level, allowing substantial insurer speculation. Federal regulation of investment banks had been subject to post-

1975 rules requiring a debt-to-net capital ratio of less than 12 to 1 in order to trade in securities. And brokers were required to set- aside capital based on the risk level of investments undertaken. Hence, highly leveraged speculation had some limit. However, in 2004 the SEC deregulated net ratio and set-aside requirements, allowing borrowing for highly leveraged securities trading.

(5) **Fannie Mae and Freddie Mac Purchase of Mortgage Backed Securities**. The Federal National Mortgage Association ("Fannie Mae") and the Federal Home Loan Mortgage Corporation ("Freddie Mac") are private, shareholder owned entities created by Congress to stimulate real property lending and home ownership. They do not originate loans, but purchase them, and began to convert them into mortgage backed securities (MBSs) in the 1970s. By selling those securities to investors it increases the monies it can then devote to buying new mortgages and stimulates liquidity for home purchase. Further, when it sells those securities, it backs collection of payment on the underlying mortgages— removing risk and stimulating more financing at lower interest rates. Hence, Fannie Mae and Freddie Mac were in a position to impose standards on mortgages that they would so guarantee (as prudence would dictate). And it traditionally required a 20% down payment so non-payment would yield a foreclosure covering the entire loan. In 1992, the Congress enacted the Federal Housing Enterprises Financial Safety and Soundness Act (12 U.S.C. 4501 et seq.) to create the Office of Federal Housing Enterprise Oversight to monitor Fannie and Freddie. Although Fannie softened standards for loan acceptance in 1999, most subprime loans did not meet them, and few were sold to them directly. But Fannie and Freddie engaged in buying mortgage backed securities marketed by Wall Street, purchasing close to a third of these securities offered from 2004–06. Doing so made them vulnerable to asset diminution should the value of those securities decline. Federal law and accounting practices did not require them to report such losses on their balance sheets. Efforts by House Republicans to impose tougher restrictions on their risky loan repurchase practices were defeated in 2005 (and thereafter) by the Bush White House and Democrats, with Fannie and

Freddie expending $176 million on Congressional lobbying during the 1998–2008 decade prior to their financial demise.

During 2008, both entities became effectively insolvent and late that year entered into a federally compelled conservatorship—taxpayer backed protection compelled by their ownership or guarantee status over $5 trillion in real property mortgages nationally. As of 2009, $200 billion in federal monies have been transferred to Fannie and Freddie, with more likely to follow (see Housing and Economic Recovery Act of 2008; see §6.28 below).

(6) **"Off the Books" Accounting**. After the energy/high technology firm collapses of 2001, measures were undertaken to address the problem of off-balance sheet liabilities. Enron, for example, had over $13 billion in debt hidden from its publicly disclosed audits prior to its market collapse. The resulting Sarbanes-Oxley Act of 2002 (Pub. Law 107-204, 15 U.S.C. § 78 et seq.) was intended to impose some reforms on accounting fraud and abuses that facilitated concealed speculation and fraudulent stock manipulation. But it allowed a major role in carving exceptions and standards to the privately controlled Financial Accounting Standards Board (FASB), which in turn allowed "Qualified Special Purpose Entities" and "Special Investment Vehicles" to evade balance sheet inclusion and public disclosure for mortgage backed securities. Accordingly, liability and risk might be concealed from the public and regulators until an unavoidably visible collapse exposed them. (See discussion of FASB Statement 140 evasion and history of (2), (3) and (4) above in R. Weissman and J. Donahue, *Sold Out*, Essential Information/Consumer Education Foundation (March 2009) at 22–35.)

The "off the books" status of these assets are joined by reliance on accountants for neutral information in public audits and financial statements. Such reliance is underlined by caselaw limiting recourse by investors against accounting firms whose reports mislead them (see *Bily v. Arthur Young & Co.* (1992) 3 Cal.4th 370 [11 Cal.Rptr.2d 51]). Consumer advocates contend that such misleading filings may be partly the product of conflicts of interest between publicly perceived profess- ionals advising the public, and those who pay them (see discussion in (9) below). Accountants rely heavily for compensation on the entities they are auditing. Although Sarbanes- Oxley reforms following the Enron collapse of 2000 implemented some measures to increase the independence of financial statement audits, including limits on non-audit compensation, they did not address the underlying conflict—a firm is being paid directly by the entity it is purportedly evaluating for the benefit of investors who provide it with no direct compensation and have uncertain or no standing to recover for reliance on misleading information.

(7) **Financial Derivative Trading Deregulation**. The Commodi- ties Future Trading Commission (CFTC) has jurisdiction over futures, options and other derivatives connected to commodities. At the behest of Clinton Treasury Secretary Robert Rubin and Fed Chair Alan Greenspan, CFTC regulation was prevented from including financial derivative trading within its regulatory ambit. Derivatives represent a bet on the value of some underlying financial asset, such as a stock, bond, or mortgage contract. They can be highly leveraged, meaning that under a deregulated regime, they can be purchased with borrowed funds, replicating the "stock purchased on margin" pattern of 1929 and facilitating expansion of a speculative bubble. Unlike the trading on the value of commodities, such as oranges or pork bellies, the financial derivative trading was permitted without required public disclosure or public supervision. "Credit default swaps" (CDSs) were created as a particular hedge instrument, a kind of insurance policy against default by an obligated debtor. With increasing defaults, the sellers of these CDSs were now required to reimburse the buyers for losses—commonly at levels many times the sale price of the security.

In 2000, the Congress enacted the Commodities Future Moderniza- tion Act, rejecting the attempts of previous CFTC Chair Brooksley Born to implement safeguards, and allowing Enron to market energy securities in a deregulated setting. Mortgage backed securities enjoyed similar deregulated status. After 2000, the global market value of CDSs world- wide (their "notional value") reached $60 trillion in 2007, surpassing the gross domestic product of the world. The value of the entire global derivative market reached $683 trillion by mid-2008, more than 20 times the value of the U.S. stock market.

(8) **Restriction of Private Lawsuit Remedy for Securities Fraud**. In 1995, Congress enacted the Private Securities Litigation Reform Act (Pub. Law 104-67, 15 U.S.C. § 78 et seq.), partly to curb the growing securities fraud litigation of private plaintiff counsel. The Congress rejected amendments that would have exempted CDSs and other financial derivative trading from the statute's protections against such suits.

(9) **Ratings and Referral Incentives**. The real property loans and securities are both guided by professional entities supposedly guiding prudent consumer choice. Hence, individual home buyers/owners rely on real estate brokers and loan brokers to steer them to optimum providers of mortgage funds. However, those making referrals to lenders (and to escrow firms and title insurers) deal only episodically with consumers relying on them, and more substantially with the beneficiaries of their referrals. That pattern stimulates concealed payments or commissions for such referrals, not based on advantageous terms for consumers who believe the referral is made in their interests, but on payment from the commercial actors getting the referral. This pattern of "dishonest services" as a species of mail fraud under federal law, or "commercial bribery" under California law. (See Pen. Code, § 641.3; Bus. & Prof. Code, § 17045 (secret rebates in general); Bus. & Prof. Code, §10177.4 (real estate brokers); Ins. Code, § 12404 (title insurance agents); Fin. Code, §§ 102, 752 (lenders).) Enforcement of these provisions is difficult and has not been common. Such secreted referral compensation may lead consumers into predatory loan terms above otherwise available alternatives, including those with lower fees, or less onerous "switch" liability into higher and unaffordable interest levels.

Related to possible predatory loan guidance is the role of ratings entities in recommending securitized mortgage instruments. The three major securities "rating firms"—Moody's Investor's Service, Standard & Poor's and Fitch

Ratings Ltd.—are relied upon by investors to measure the risk of investments, including mortgage backed securities. All three of these agencies, with longstanding relationships with the banks and other traders marketing these securities, gave mortgage backed securities their highest ratings. Such ratings are widely relied upon by investors as reflecting an independent evaluation of risk. A reduction in rating generally requires additional security or capital set-aside to reassure investors. Although evidence of falling home prices and concomitant risk became apparent during 2006, it was not until June of 2007 that the credit agencies downgraded these securities. The delay here was similar to the delay during the "dot.com" bubble collapse of the late 1990s, and the collapse of firms such as Worldcom, Tyco, and Enron in 2003. As a result of the extraordinary failure to warn in 2006, the Congress enacted The Fair Credit Reporting Agencies Reform Act of 2006 (15 U.S.C. § 78 et seq.), which purportedly gave the SEC oversight over these private entities. However, the law requires the approval of these agencies so long as they adhere to their own standards—however flawed they may be in measuring risk. As with the commercial bribery problem for individual consumers choosing among lenders, the lenders here as well are major financiers of the rating entities. Banks paid high fees to the rating entities to advise them on "how to achieve the highest rating." Those rating entities have extremely high profit margins.

Hypotheticals

You are the chief of staff of the California Business & Professions Committee. The Chair asks you about the current problems with Artificial Intelligence (AI).

1. What regulation is needed and appropriate?

    a. Regulation to identify the work product of AI work product?

    b. Regulation to prevent child abuse, particularly sex trafficking?

    c. Where else?

Chapter 11
The California Legislative Process[30]

INTRODUCTION: CALIFORNIA LEGISLATION AND ITS SIGNIFICANCE FOR THIS COURSE

All agencies are guided by either constitutional provisions or legislative enactments that create and guide them. Most are legislatively created. And the lawful functions they perform are necessarily derivative— depend wholly on the legislative intent in their creation. Part of that authority is the creation of resources for agency functioning. Most of this derives from what is termed "special funding." That is, the agency charges licensing, renewal, and other fees that largely fund their respective operations. That funding depends on legislative authority, making the legislature critical in allowing such assessments—albeit the increase in such revenue typically involves payment by licensees. Hence, to the extent such licensee groups control the agency (or influence the legislature, which needs to adjust maximum fees in existing legislation), amounts may be influenced counter to public protection. To increase ethical standards or discipline, consumer advocates must contend with the trade association of licensed practitioners who commonly oppose fee increases.

Importantly, the budget activities of the legislature focus on the state's "general fund" of income, sales, and property taxes, et al., not on special fund spending. For this latter category, specific spending is decided by agencies from a "special fund" sum not related to the general fund spending where legislative discretion is paramount. Hence, the special funding of agencies tends to reduce legislative interest in their monitoring vis-à-vis those accounts where the legislature has substantial discretion to control who gets how much. For this reason, CPPC was among the first to advocate for what is called a "sunset process." This is a practice that started in Colorado in 1976. It provides that periodically (e.g., at five-year intervals), an agency will "sunset" or cease to exist (its enabling statute effectively revoked) unless affirmatively renewed by a date certain. This burden then requires the agency to justify its existence and current practices, or it will automatically terminate. Currently, 47 have some form of sunset review in place. California replicated the basics of the Colorado statute in the early 1980s, except instead of terminating the entire regulatory statute, it terminated the governing entity or persons—requiring new leadership. Although less severe than the total excision of a

---

[30] Vocabulary and discussion by Thomas Papageorge, for the predecessor course Public Interest Law & Practice, taught historically by Professor Papageorge with Professor Fellmeth.

regulatory system, it is of obvious importance to those controlling any state agency whose jobs are at risk. This process is crucial in elevating legislative attention to agencies that would otherwise lack oversight. CPPC (historically known as the Center for Public Interest Law or CPIL) triggered these statutes and coalesces consumer participation in complaints and reform proposals around this legislative process, commonly requiring "special reports" from the agency prior to the crucial hearings on the affirmative renewal of the agency leadership. These reports are designed to present basic performance data and to respond to consumer and other complaints about agency operations.

OVERVIEW OF THE LEGISLATIVE PROCESS

The legislative process is the mechanism by which bills are considered and laws enacted by the California State Legislature. In California, the state legislature is made up of two houses: the Senate and the Assembly. There are 40 Senators and 80 Assembly Members. The Legislature maintains a legislative calendar governing the introduction and processing of legislative measures during its two-year regular session. The text, status, and other information about past and current bills may be obtained at https://leginfo.legislature.ca.gov/.

- **Bill idea**. All legislation begins as an idea or concept originating from a variety of possible sources, including citizens, government officials, interest groups, and industry associations. The person or group that proposes the legislative idea is called the sponsor. The process begins when a Senator or Assembly Member decides to author a bill.

- **Bill author**. A legislator sends the idea for the bill to the Office of the Legislative Counsel, where it is drafted into bill form. The draft of the bill is returned to the legislator for introduction. If the author is a Senator, the bill is introduced in the Senate. If the author is an Assembly Member, the bill is introduced in the Assembly.

- **First reading/introduction**. A bill is introduced or read the first time when the bill number, the name of the author, and the descriptive title of the bill are read on the floor of the house. The bill is then sent to the Office of State Publishing. No bill except the Budget Bill may be acted upon until 30 days have passed from the date of its introduction.

- **Committee hearings**. After introduction, a bill goes to the rules committee of the relevant house, where it is assigned to the appropriate policy committee for its first hearing. Bills are assigned to policy committees according to subject area. For example, a Senate bill dealing with occupational licensure agencies would typically be assigned to the Senate Business and Professions Committee for policy review. (Bills that require the expenditure of funds must also be heard in the fiscal committees, Senate Appropriations and Assembly Appropriations.) Each committee is made up of a specified number of Senators or Assembly Members.

During the committee hearing, the author presents the bill to the committee, and testimony may be heard in support of or opposition to the bill. Sponsors and other witnesses in support testify and then witnesses in opposition appear and speak. Live witness testimony often plays an important role in the committee's evaluation. The committee then votes on whether to pass the bill out of committee or that it be passed as amended. Bills may be amended several times. It takes a majority vote of the committee membership for a bill to be passed and sent to the next committee or to the floor. Each house maintains a schedule of legislative committee hearings. Prior to a bill's hearing, a **bill analysis** is prepared that explains the intended effect of the bill on current law, together with background information. Typically, the analysis also lists organizations that support or oppose the bill. Thus, this document is typically a key source of information about the bill's meaning, and about its supporters and opponents.

- **Second and third reading**. Bills passed by committees are read a second time on the floor in the house of origin and then assigned to third reading. Bill analyses are also prepared prior to third reading. When a bill is read the third time it is explained by the author, discussed by the Members, and voted on by a roll call vote. Bills that require an appropriation, or that take effect immediately, ordinarily require 27 votes in the Senate and 54 votes in the Assembly to be passed. Other bills generally require 21 votes in the Senate and 41 votes in the Assembly. If a bill is defeated, the Member may seek reconsideration and another vote.

- **Process repeated in second house**. Once the house of origin has approved the bill, it proceeds to the other house where the procedure described above is repeated.

- **Deadlines for legislative process**. Each step of the state legislative process has a deadline mandated by each house's rules. For example, the bill introduction deadline is typically in late February, and deadlines for clearing the policy committees and fiscal committees are similarly specified. **Waivers** of these deadlines can be approved by the respective Rules Committees and are often critical to the passage of controversial or difficult bills.

- **Resolution of differences**. If a bill is amended in the second house, it must go back to the house of origin for concurrence, meaning agreement on those amendments. If the house of origin does not concur in those amendments, the bill is referred to a two-house conference committee to resolve the differences. Three members of the committee are from the Senate and three are from the Assembly. If a compromise is reached, the bill is returned to both houses for a vote. Bills not passed in the first year of a legislative session may become "two-year bills" and may be reconsidered, on an expedited basis, at the beginning of the second year of the session.

- **Governor's role**. If both houses approve a bill, it goes to the Governor. The Governor has three choices: sign the bill into law, allow it to become law without his or her signature (a process different in California than some other states), or veto it. Governors typically issue a "**veto message**," a brief statement of the reasons for the Governor's disapproval of the bill (this is typically a political statement, but it can be important in subsequent efforts to promote a similar bill). A governor's veto can be overridden by a two-thirds vote in both houses. Most enacted bills go into effect on the first day of January of the next year. **Urgency bills**, and certain other measures, take effect immediately after they are enacted into law.

- **Bill becomes law**. Each bill that is passed by the Legislature and approved by the Governor is assigned a chapter number by the Secretary of State (e.g., "Stats.2010, c.123"). These chaptered bills are statutes, and ordinarily become part of the California Codes.

- **Constitutional amendments**. The California Constitution sets forth the fundamental laws by which the State of California is governed. All amendments to the California Constitution come about as a result of constitutional amendments approved by the voters at a statewide election, most commonly by the initiative process (below).

OVERVIEW OF THE INITIATIVE PROCESS

An initiative is a proposal to change statutory law or the California Constitution, submitted directly by members of the public rather than by the Legislature, and requiring voter approval at a statewide election. To qualify for a statewide ballot, a statutory initiative must receive signatures equal to 5 percent—and a constitutional amendment initiative must receive signatures equal to 8 percent—of the votes for all candidates for Governor at the last gubernatorial election. Information about initiatives may be obtained at www.ss.ca.gov.

- **Introduction**. In 1911, California became the 10th state to adopt the initiative process. Governor George Hiram Johnson began his term by promising to give citizens a tool they could use to adopt laws and constitutional amendments without the support of the Governor or the

Legislature. The new Legislature put a package of Constitutional amendments together, which included the ability to recall elected officials, the right to repeal laws by referendum, and the ability to enact state laws by initiative. The Initiative is the power of the people of California to propose statutes and amendments to the California Constitution (Cal. Const., art. II, Sec. 8 (a)). Generally, any matter that is a proper subject of legislation can become an initiative measure. However, no initiative measure addressing more than one subject area may be submitted to the voters, nor will it have any effect (Cal. Const., art. II, Sec. 8 (d) and 12).

- **Drafting the text of the law**. The first step in the process of qualifying an initiative measure is to write the text of the proposed law. Proponents must present the idea for the law to the Legislative Counsel and 25 or more electors must sign the request draft of the proposed law. The Legislative Counsel will draft the proposed law (Government Code Section 10243), or the proponents may choose to write the text themselves.

- **Request for title and summary**. The proponents must submit a draft of the proposed initiative measure to the Attorney General with a written request that a title and summary of the chief purpose and points of the proposed initiative measure be prepared (Section 9002). The proponent(s) must pay a fee of $2,000, which is refunded if the initiative measure qualifies.

- **Role of the Attorney General**. The Attorney General prepares a title and summary, which will be the official summary of the initiative measure. The Attorney General provides a copy of the title and summary to the Secretary of State within 15 days after the receipt of the final version of a proposed initiative measure. If the Attorney General determines that the initiative measure requires a fiscal analysis, the Department of Finance and the Joint Legislative Budget Committee are required to prepare an analysis. Fiscal analysis includes either the estimate of the amount of any increase or decrease in revenues or costs to state or local governments, or any opinion as to the result, if the proposed initiative measure is adopted. When the official title and summary is complete, the Attorney General sends it to the proponents, the Senate and the Assembly, and the Secretary of State. The Legislature may conduct public hearings on the proposed initiative measure but cannot amend it.

The **official summary date** is the date the title summary is sent to the proponents by the Attorney General and the date the Secretary of State uses to calculate calendar deadlines.

- **Circulation of initiative**. Based on the official summary date, the Secretary of State prepares a calendar of filing deadlines. Proponents are allowed a maximum of 150 days to circulate petitions and collect signatures (Sec. 336). The initiative measure must qualify at least 131 days before the next statewide election at which it is to be submitted to the voters (Sec. 9013; Cal. Const., art. II, Sec. 8 (c)).

  In order to qualify for the ballot, the initiative measure must be **signed by a specified number of registered voters** depending on the type of initiative measure submitted. An initiative statute must be signed by registered voters. The number of signatures must be equal to at least 5% of the total votes cast for Governor at the last gubernatorial election. An initiative constitutional amendment must also be signed by registered voters. The number of signatures must be equal to at least 8% of the total votes cast for Governor at the last gubernatorial election.

  The format for the **initiative petition** is specified by law. A petition may have several sections. Each section of the petition must contain the Attorney General's title and summary and the full text of the initiative measure. The petition must have room for the signature of each petition signer as well as his or her printed name, residence address, and city or unincorporated community name.

  Each section must have attached thereto a declaration signed and dated by the circulator of the petition. The petition may be circulated by a variety of individuals carrying separate, identical parts of the petition called "sections." Each petition circulator who obtains signatures must complete the attached declaration to the petition. The declaration must be signed under the penalty of perjury. Only persons who are registered, qualified voters at the time of signing are entitled to sign the petition. A person can only sign a petition that is being circulated in his or her county of registration.

  The Elections Code imposes certain **criminal penalties for abuses** related to the circulation of initiative petitions. It prohibits circulators from misrepresenting the purpose or contents of the petition to potential petition signers. It also prohibits offering or giving payment or anything of value to another in exchange for signing an initiative petition. Any person who is paid by the proponents to obtain signatures on any initiative is subject to severe penalties for refusing to surrender the petition to the proponents for filing (Sec. 18640).

- **Filing of initiative**. Once the requisite number of signatures has been collected, they need to be filed with the appropriate county election officials. Once filed, petitions may not be amended except by order of a court of competent jurisdiction.

Within eight working days after filing the petition, the county elections officials begin the process of **verification** by determining the total number of signatures on the petition sections submitted in that county, and report the total to the Secretary of State. If the Secretary of State determines that the raw count of petitions submitted throughout the state lack 100 percent of the signatures required, the Secretary of State must immediately notify the county election officials of the failure of the initiative measure and no further action is taken on that measure. (Sec. 9030)

If the raw count equals 100 percent or more of the total number of signatures needed to qualify the initiative measure, the Secretary of State notifies the county election officials. The county election officials verify the validity of the signatures filed with their office using a **random sampling technique of verification**.

If the total number of valid signatures is less than 95 percent of the number of signatures required to qualify the initiative measure, the initiative measure will fail to qualify for the ballot. If the number of valid signatures is greater than 110 percent of the required number, the initiative measure is considered qualified without further verification.

If the result of the random sample process indicates that the number of valid signatures represents between 95 percent and 110 percent of the required number of signatures to qualify the initiative measure for the ballot, the Secretary of State directs the county election officials to verify every signature on the petition.

- **Vote and initiative measure effective date**. A properly verified initiative measure is placed on the relevant election's ballot and is typically approved by a simple majority vote of the electorate.

  An initiative measure approved by a majority vote takes effect the day after the election unless the initiative measure provides otherwise (Cal. Const., art. II, Sec. 10 (a)). If the provisions of two or more measures approved at the same election conflict, the measure receiving the highest affirmative votes prevails (Cal. Const., art. II, Sec. 10 (b)). The Legislature may amend or repeal an initiative statute; however, any proposed legislative action becomes effective only when approved by the voters unless the initiative statute permits amendment or repeal without voter approval (Cal. Const., art. II, Sec. 10 (c)).

Tracking Legislation

Bill format and bill information of importance:

- **Bill Number**
- **Author** (and co-authors)
- **Date introduced and amended** (CAUTION-Keep bill VERSIONS straight; always check for bill amendments and changes, and always refer to the bill "as amended XXX date" to be sure you are referencing the same version)
- Statutory sections added or amended
- **Legislative Counsel digest** (what bill does and how it impacts current law)
- **Substantive bill content**. The content of the bill is indicated, and changes are indicated with strikeouts and italics to show deletions and additions respectively (CAUTION- Each amended version typically only includes strikeouts and italics indicating THAT version's changes to prior versions; be sure to track the bill back through its amended versions to be sure you are properly following these changes.)
- **Committee and house analyses**. These include the name and contact number of the "committee consultant," who is the permanent staff person assisting the committee members by reviewing bills and preparing a written analysis distributed to the committee members and the public. Bill analyses are often of great importance as a source of insights into the bill and its prospects, usually providing questions or issues for the committee to consider (and for proponents or opponents to be sure to address).

Critical Analysis of California Legislative Process

- **Imbalance of lobbying influence and presence**. More than 1200 registered lobbyists, mostly for powerful private interests. There are generally very few representatives of the public as a whole, consumers, children and the elderly, and other under-represented or underfunded groups. The influence of money (campaign contributions and other funding) is undeniable in the state legislative process, and public interest law often seeks to redress this.
- **Lack of institutional memory and expertise**. After Proposition 140 term limits, both legislators and, increasingly, high-quality permanent staff turnover so rapidly that institutional memory, process skills, and knowledge of how to get things done all suffer.

"Frequent changes in the membership and leadership of legislative committees, especially in the Assembly, diminish their expertise in many important policy areas. Many committees lack the experience to weed out bad bills and to ensure that agencies are acting efficiently and in accordance with legislative intent." (Public Policy Institute of California, Rpt. #94, Nov. 2004). This also exacerbates the general problems associated with the differences between long-term and short-term interests (political careers, rather than sound long- term policies, often drive such lawmaking).

- **"Revolving door"** of legislative staff and lobbyists.
- **Inadequate media coverage and public understanding of the legislative process**.
- **Super-majorities rules**. Budget rules inserted into the State Constitution by special interest initiatives have resulted in "super-majority" requirement of **two-thirds vote** to pass the **annual state budget** (and other super-majority requirements elsewhere). This permits a small and/or unrepresentative or extreme minority to hold the state budget process "hostage" and impose its will on the majority. (In the Senate, 14 out of 40 votes can derail the state budget process—and small caucus majorities, say nine votes out of a caucus of 16, can dictate such outcomes.) Only three states have this procedurally extreme rule.
- **Abuse of time limits and last-minute brokering**. Abuse of this process often takes the form of waiting until the eleventh hour (literally) and then using poorly disclosed last-minute tactics, such as "gut and amend" bills, to frustrate fair deliberations and open public scrutiny.
- **The "suspense file" use and abuse**. Small dollar amounts of projected expense can result in bills being directed to "suspense files" for later consideration by fiscal committees. This can permit abuse of the process, last-minute manipulation, and permanent derailment of important bills. Crucially, most bills are subject to suspense file assignment to one of the two appropriations committees (either Assembly or Senate) and the criteria for such assignment is based on cost estimates of $150,000 or more from the Department of Finance or other sources that are often disparate from actual costs—and commonly do not consider savings. Importantly, unless a bill is affirmatively removed from this "suspense" category, it simply dies without the accountability of any recorded vote. The politics of removal

from this "file" for public vote can reflect the influence of money in the process.

- **Single-subject rule often ignored**. Technical requirement of "germaneness" is frequently abused or ignored, allowing complex bills with riders and attachments serving unrelated purposes. This undermines proper consideration of these issues.

DISCUSSION OF ADDITIONAL PUBLIC INTEREST ISSUES IN LEGISLATIVE INVOLVEMENT

A number of dynamics stimulate legislative passivity over agency performance. As noted above, these include the separation of their funding from the general fund accounts that are the legislative focus. Further, the California legislature has been subject to "term limits" that were intended to stop the historical practice of a single person serving as Assembly Speaker or Senate President Pro Tempore for many decades. Instead, there is now a twelve-year limit on legislative service, including both Assembly and Senate terms. The passage of Proposition 140 in 1990 had effects beyond these limits, including a ceiling placed on legislative appropriations for its own operations, including oversight. Hence, many legislative entities gathering evidence and informing the legislature of agency (and other governmental) performance were terminated or devolved into the control of other parts of government. The California state auditor became a part of the Little Hoover Commission, and research assets from the legislature itself became limited.

The impacts of these changes have included the enhanced lobbying power of special interests who make job offers to legislators (who now must seek non-legislative employment within twelve years, or in many cases eight to ten years). Such special interest/legislator financial interaction also extends strongly to legislative staff, both of the legislators leaving, and committee staff appointed by chairs changing identity with retirement limits.

The rise in special interest influence is reflected in the practice and vocabulary of Sacramento operations. At one time, the legislator introducing a measure was labeled the "sponsor" of the bill. Now, that legislator is deemed the "Author" of the bill. The "sponsor" of legislation is now openly and directly the special (usually private) interest writing it (and submitting it to Legislative Counsel) and organizing its advocacy, including the addition of "co-sponsors" and "supporters" from interest groups.

In addition to the revolving door problem alluded to above, is the strong imbalance of lobbying and information provision to legislators. The California system does involve a Fair Political Practices Commission (FPPC) and requires disclosures by lobbyists, including those lobbying both the legislature and agencies. These reports detail the proposals being addressed by each lobbyist, as well as the monies expended for that purpose. However, a great deal of lobbying occurs apart from the professional lobbyists so reporting. Attorneys commonly engage in agency lobbying for special interest clients without the required lobbyist registration. And, in fact, involvement in litigation involving an agency issue or even party involvement is not "lobbying" for FPPC reporting purposes.

Importantly, contacts between lobbyists and agency officials or legislators (aside from actual public hearings) are secret. What is contended factually or promised politically is effectively confidential and lacking in the checks and opportunity for rebuttal that demark our judicial system.

In terms of balance, some $600 to $800 million are expended each year by special interests with profit incentives. Leading spenders include the Petroleum Association, SEIU (union of service employees), Chevron, physician groups, pharmaceutical industry, among many others.

The ethics discussion of Chapter 4 discusses some of the agency influence issues now extant. These sources of influence concerning the Governor and senior legislators rebound to agencies. Agency officials are commonly appointed by the Governor or senior legislators, and that involvement, including allowable and common confidential contacts between an agency official and his or her appointer, can have an obvious impact on decisions made.

Beyond lobbying imbalance favoring special interests are campaign contributions to those appointing those officials noted above. Over $200 million is now contributed to political committees in California per election. Further, the *Citizens' United* holding that profit stake interests have essentially the same 1st Amendment rights to "associate" into lobbying trade and other commercial groups as do citizens who constitute the "People" allegedly controlling state government. The dichotomy between persons seeking immediate profit enhancement and asset protection from the populace concerned about diffuse and future interests is arguably not trivial.

The legislative orientation toward special interests is further exacerbated by the decline in media coverage of Sacramento decisions.

In addition to influence imbalance are legislative rules that exacerbate disparate influence. It is important to understand basic vocabulary in the legislative process. The "single subject rule" is intended to prevent the historical practice of placing special benefit provisions in bills covering separate subject matter with strong popular support. Of greater concern are common practices undermining legislative accountability. Among those are the following issues: (1) the "Suspense file" game, discussed above, that purports to prioritize legislation and public cost but allows measures to be routinely killed without any vote or related accountability. (2) The practice of taking a bill that has progressed substantially through the legislature and altering it through what is termed "gut and amend" to include entirely different and unrelated provisions and avoiding full hearing or other examination. (3) Use of "omnibus bills" or "budget trailer bills" to avoid hearings that might reveal negative consequences. (4) Bills generally require a majority of their assigned committees to move on. But absence of a vote by a particular legislator has the effect of a negative vote. Termed "taking a walk", it allows such a vote of rejection to escape full disclosure.

As discussed in Chapter 4, many ethics issues join efficacy performance in the budget process. The timeline for the state budget, including agencies, is as follows:

- January 10: Governor releases the Proposed Budget for following fiscal year (July 1 through June 30), including all general fund agency and special fund agency budgets. The 2022–23 total state budget was $286.4 billion.
- February 10: Legislative Analyst's Office (LAO) releases its Analysis of Governor's Budget.
- Feb-April: Legislative hearings by subject-matter budget committees
- May: "May Revise" of Governor's Proposed Budget released.
- May-June: Legislature fashions Budget Bill (which may not amend substantive law) and "budget trailer bills" (which can amend existing law and are tied to the budget bill).
- June 15: Constitutional deadline for legislature to pass budget bill; must be passed by a majority vote (used to be a 2/3 vote requirement; that was changed in 2010 with Prop 25). But tax changes and new fees still require 2/3 vote.
- July 1: Governor must sign (and may veto some parts of) budget bill for new fiscal year.

Approximately $60 billion of the total $286 billion is special funding, including agencies.

The Common Pattern for Special Funding for agencies is to include in legislation a Maximum Ceiling for Licensing Fees. The agency then has the discretion to charge an amount under that limit for its financing. Of course, inflation requires attention to adjusting that maximum over time, a common problem in adequate agency financing of operations. In general, industry opposition to any increase in the statutory limit commonly precludes its increase.

MAJOR FACTORS INFLUENCING AGENCY BUDGETS

A general fund deficit has impacts on special funded agencies. In fact, historically, agency budgets have been raided by the state to resolve general fund deficit problems. Borrowing from agency reserve funds has been common where general fund deficits arise. It might also cause "travel freezes" to be imposed on agencies. This problem is related to the fact that a state cannot engage in "deficit spending" as the United State has irresponsibly done federally. It cannot issue "bonds" or any instrument, promising interest and requiring repayment at some point.

In addition, Proposition 13 has had a major and continuing impact on state and local public funding. A major source of state funding (apart from general fund sales, income and corporate taxes) are property taxes. These particularly fund cities, counties, and special districts. Proposition 13 was enacted in 1978 to limit these taxes. However, the system in place raises extreme ethical issues. The enacted system limits taxation to 1% of the assessed valuation of the home or other real property involved. And most important, it limits that calculated assessment to no more than 2% per annum over the purchase price. Since real property values have gone up much more than 2% per year from 1978, seniors buying then or in the 80s or 90s now are paying much less than the next generation now purchasing homes or commercial property. This gives an enormous fiscal advantage to commercial longstanding owners over new possible competition. And it means that current buyers will commonly pay six to ten times the property tax for properties recently purchased vis-à-vis those who purchased more than 20 years ago. This disparity includes a marked advantage for established businesses and seniors paying a fraction of the home property taxes their children and grandchildren will bear living in identically valued property.

Another factor influencing public spending budgets and rarely examined closely is the issue of "tax expenditures", including state tax credits, deductions and exemptions, now at around $80 billion per year foregone. These expenditures are not part of the traditional budget. Moreover, they are rarely revisited or even monitored closely. They remain unchanged absent a 2/3 vote to change or eliminate them.

Finally, a future issue will be public employee pensions, which are generous and amount to a commitment of $500 billion that is unfunded.

Review of agency budgets beyond the sunset process is rare. Those agencies within the Department of Consumer Affairs (DCA) are subject to some administrative (executive branch) budgetary review. The DCA has particular power over bureaus or departments within its domain and where it has a direct supervisorial role. Even as to boards and commissions with separate governance, there is some review over each agency's budget, at least in theory. In addition, the independent Little Hoover Commission may sometimes initiate studies with budget aspects, and the Bureau of State Audits operating under the State Auditor has expertise and some potential role in budgetary review. A legislator can request a Bureau of State Audits review of any agency or account. The Senate Office of Research that survived the term and Legislature spending limits examines agency related issues, but not budgetary aspects normally. In contrast, the Legislative Analyst's Office can examine agency budgets but focuses not on special fund agencies but on general fund issues.

THE LEGISLATIVE OPEN RECORDS ACT

The executive branch, including all agencies, is subject to the Open Meetings and the Public Records Act. But the Legislature and courts have different open government rules and standards. The equivalent of the Public Records Act applicable to all executive branch agencies is the Legislative Open Records Act. While it provides for public inspection of documents produced or used by the legislature, it has a much broader list of exceptions and limitations. The Act, codified at Cal. Gov. Code Section 9070 et seq., includes the following major exceptions:

- Preliminary drafts, notes, or legislative memoranda.
- Records pertaining to pending litigation to which the Legislature is a party, until the litigation or claim has been finally adjudicated or otherwise settled.
- Personnel, medical, or similar files, the disclosure of which would constitute an unwarranted invasion of personal privacy.
- Records pertaining to the names and phone numbers of senders and recipients of telephone and telegraph communications, provided that records of the total charges for any such communication shall be open for inspection.
- Records in the custody of or maintained by the Legislative Counsel, except those records in the public database maintained by the Legislative Counsel that are described in Section 10248. Legislative records shall not be transferred to the custody of the Legislative Counsel to evade the disclosure provisions of this chapter.
- Records in the custody of or maintained by the majority and minority caucuses and majority and minority consultants of each house of the Legislature.
- Correspondence of and to individual Members of the Legislature and their staff, except as provided in Section 9080.

- Records the disclosure of which is exempted or prohibited pursuant to provisions of federal or state law, including, but not limited to, provisions of the Evidence Code relating to privilege.
- Communications from private citizens to the Legislature, except as provided in Section 9080.
- Records of complaints to or investigations conducted by, or records of security procedures of, the Legislature.

The current version of California's Legislative Open Records Act can be accessed for free at https://leginfo.legislature.ca.gov/faces/home.xhtml.

Hypothetical

Sunshine Statutes

On August 15, the Senate appointed Phyllis Pupil to serve as a public member on the California State Board

of Optometry. Her husband, Dr. Peter Pupil, is a retired optometrist whose term as President of the California Optometrists Association (COA) expired on July 31.

Dr. Peter Pupil's platform during his presidency at the COA was to improve the standards for optometrists in California and ensure that only those with the highest qualifications serve as California optometrists. In his parting speech Dr. Pupil advocated for a more difficult licensing exam to reflect these higher standards.

At her first Board meeting, which was held virtually, Phyllis attended from her home in Pasadena. Throughout the meeting, her husband was visible on the screen sitting in the chair just behind her.

On the agenda for the Board meeting was the following item: "Discussion and possible action regarding elimination of the optometric clinical licensing exam."

In advance of the meeting, staff prepared a memo citing a report revealing that applicants of color fail the optometric clinical licensing exam at disproportionately higher rates than white applicants. Because of this staff recommended that the Board eliminate the exam in this format and rethink the clinical portion of the licensing exam.

When the item came up for discussion, 50 optometrists, including the new president of COA spoke during public comment arguing against the elimination of the clinical exam, citing the board's obligation to protect the public. One public comment from a representative from the Consumer

Protection Policy Center (CPPC) at USD argued in support of the proposal to eliminate the clinical exam.

On Zoom, several members of the Board could be seen texting on their phones during the presentation and public comments.

After public comment was over, Phyllis made the following comment: "I think it is clear from the overwhelming opposition we've heard today that not only must we maintain the clinical exam, but we should increase the cut score on the exam by 100 points to make sure that we are only licensing optometrists of the highest quality." She made a motion to this effect and the motion passed unanimously.

The next day the Los Angeles Times published an article quoting several text messages from optometrists to one of the Board members threatening to move their practice to Arizona if the Board votes to eliminate the licensing exam, which apparently one of the board members leaked to the Times on the condition of anonymity.

Discussion Questions:

1. You are an attorney for CPPC and wish to challenge the vote at the board meeting. How would you utilize each of the sunshine statutes to support your position?
2. You are the Deputy Attorney General for the California State Board of Optometry. What should you advise the Board to do?

Chapter 12
Judicial Review

Discussion

The most common mechanism for review of regulatory decisions within the judiciary is the filing of a writ of mandamus. These filings are by "petitioners" against "respondents." It is an action "in equity" with court decisions made without jury participation. That facet makes this review less costly and more expeditious.

There are two common mandamus actions relevant to regulatory action appeal. The first is authorized by the California Code of Civil Procedure Section 1085, termed "ordinary mandamus." It lies wherever there has been an "abuse of discretion" by a public official. This cause of action may lie where the official acts in a manner that violates the federal or state constitution. And alleged violations of federal civil rights law (42 U.S.C. Section 1983) may create such a mandamus-eligible case. But violation of any federal or state law may constitute such an abuse. Further, an official may fail to act where legally obligated to do so— which also can be a basis for ordinary mandamus. It is not uncommon for third parties to join such actions as alleged "real parties in interest" since public official actions or refusals to act often directly involve the interests of such third parties. This writ can be initially filed in any court (superior, appellate, or supreme court), although it is likely that where factual evidence is implicated, the matter may be remanded down to the superior court for writ decision.

The second major avenue of mandamus relief is California Code of Civil Procedure Section 1094.5, or petition for writ of administrative mandamus. It applies where there is a proceeding below in the executive branch (such as licensee discipline) appropriate for court review. A decision by a regulating agency that involves the taking of evidence, a record and findings of fact and conclusions of law commonly qualify for this mode of review. Here, the court can order a revised outcome or remand the matter back for revision that complies with applicable law. The review includes a determination whether the findings of fact are supported by the evidence and whether the decision is supported by those factual findings and whether the penalty imposed is within the agency's discretion and is not an abuse of that discretion. This review is normally filed in superior court.

The standard of review for mandamus actions under Section 1094.5 will involve "independent judgment" if a vested right (*e.g.*, a license to practice) may be revoked. The California Supreme Court has held that a reviewing court must undertake "heightened review" of findings that require "clear and convincing" evidence. *I.e.*, could a reasonable fact finder make the finding with confidence that it was "highly probable" the fact was true. In contrast, the reviewing court will use the more deferential "substantial evidence" test where no vested right is at stake (*e.g.*, a license has been not revoked but initially denied).

The initial court review under Section 1094.5 may take the form of a "paper review," where the court examines the transcript of the hearing, the documentary evidence, and the decision below. A party may present live evidence where a witness was unable to testify in the agency proceedings or for extraordinary reasons.

In terms of Section 1085 ordinary mandamus, the writ will invalidate an agency action (or require action) only if the alternative is "arbitrary and capricious." The agency's action will be upheld if there is any reasonable basis to support it, reflecting judicial deference to executive branch decision making.

Apart from the two writ alternatives, judicial review may also proceed through a "petition for declaratory relief" (see Cal. Civ. Proc. Code Section 1060). This action is also court determined and is often an additional cause of action in a mandamus petition.

There are some important overall prerequisites to filing for judicial review of an agency action. First, the petitioner must exhaust any administrative remedies available (*e.g.*, a motion for reconsideration). However, if others have made such efforts or if it is apparently "futile," it may be excused. Second, the action must be filed prior to the application of the statute of limitations. Often, a writ must be filed within thirty days after the last day on which the agency could order reconsideration of its decision, although precise timelines can vary by agency statute. Apart from this limitation, there may be a statutory three- or four-year period from a violation applicable as a statute of limitation in a relevant case. However, many matters subject to possible statute of limitations bar may be what are termed "continuing violations." If the agency decision that was challenged continues its operation, its challenge may well be allowed until that period expires after the practice has ceased.

As in any judicial proceedings, cost and delay make the availability of attorney fees crucial in obtaining practical access to court action. Many statutes provide for attorney fees for a prevailing party. And federally, any prevailing party filing under 42 U.S.C. Section 1983, the civil rights statute, is eligible for such fees. But mandamus by itself does not provide so, nor are such remunerative laws necessarily involved in a challenge to agency action. However, apart from statutory fees, California and several other states have an alternative basis for attorney compensation. Under California Code of Civil Procedure Section 1021.5, a court may award to a "successful party" in litigation fees where the action resulted in the "enforcement of an important right affecting the public interest." That public interest benefit need not be pecuniary and need not involve any state statute authorizing such fees. Called the "private attorney general" basis for fees, it vindicates such successful actions where the benefit redounds well beyond the parties to the suit. Further, the statute allows a "multiplier" to the market fees rates times hours common in attorney billings. The fee award under this section can be and often is, at two to three times the normal fee times hours billed.

For more information, see The Rutter Group, *California Practice Guide—Administrative Law*, Ch. 13 (Bringing the Action for Judicial Review).

Hypotheticals

Medical Board of California

In 2017, the Medical Board of California (MBC) charged Dr. Lucy Lion with professional misconduct. After a hearing, the Administrative Law Judge recommended that her license be revoked, and the Board unanimously voted to adopt this recommendation and revoke her license to practice medicine in California.

Dr. Lion sought judicial review of the Board's decision by petitioning the superior court. The superior court upheld the license revocation.

Business and Professions Code Section 2337 provides that the Court of Appeal shall review the superior court's decision, not by direct appeal, but "pursuant to a petition for an extraordinary writ," meaning that the appellate court's review is discretionary, and Dr. Lion is not automatically entitled to an appeal.

Despite this provision, however, Dr. Lion did not file an extraordinary writ. Instead, she filed a notice of appeal. Citing Section 2337, MBC moved to dismiss the appeal. The appellate court denied the Board's motion to dismiss and found Section 2337 to be unconstitutional because "the Legislature does not have the power to destroy the right of an appeal that is constitutionally granted."

Article VI, section 11 of the California Constitution states in relevant part that, "The Supreme Court has appellate jurisdiction when judgment of death has been pronounced. With that exception, courts of appeal have appellate jurisdiction when superior courts have original jurisdiction…."

The Supreme Court granted MBC's petition for review to determine whether the Legislature has the authority to specify the mode of appellate review of physician discipline, as it did in enacting Section 2237, without infringing on the constitutionally granted "appellate jurisdiction" of the Court of Appeal.

Discussion Questions:

1. Which form of mandamus did Dr. Lion use to challenge MBC's revocation of her license? (cite to a code section)
2. What are Dr. Lion's best arguments that Section 2337 is unconstitutional?
3. What should MBC's attorneys argue?
4. What should the court rule?

California State Athletic Commission

The California State Athletic Commission (Atcom) regulates professional boxing, licensing boxers, trainers, managers, and promoters. Jack Masher is a professional boxer whom Atcom licensed from the mid-1990s until 2009, when the Commission revoked his license.

Masher has held several welterweight world titles. He was scheduled to fight for that title again in January 2009. Masher's trainer was Carl Careful, a licensed trainer for 18 years, who had served as Masher's trainer for 11 years. Before the January fight, Careful was wrapping Masher's hands with gauze pads in the presence of three Atcom inspectors and Masher's opponent's trainer, who intervened during the wrapping to object and ask that it be examined. The pads were removed from both hands and found to be impermissibly "hard." And, in fact, Masher noted at the time that one of them did feel "kind of hard." The inspectors confiscated the pads and sent them to a lab for a forensic analysis.

Shortly thereafter, Atcom notified Masher that his boxing license was temporarily suspended pending a final determination of the case and informed Masher that he was being investigated for a potential violation of Rule 323, which limits the use of gauze and tape on an athlete's hands and requires that both contestants be represented while the gauze and tape are applied. The letter informed Masher that the forensics lab results concluded that the confiscated hand wraps contained a "plaster element," which would improperly give his fist greater power when connecting with an opponent.

Atcom held a disciplinary hearing itself in February 2009, with all seven commissioners present, and an ALJ made judicial rulings (a variation on normal adjudications). Masher contended that he did not request any adulteration nor know anything about it and that he relied upon the expertise of the Commission- licensed trainer to properly equip him for the fight.

After the hearing, Atcom voted 7–0 to revoke Masher's professional boxing license. In a follow-up written decision, the Commission found that Masher had violated Rule 323 and rejected Masher's argument that he did not know that his trainer had inserted the illegal pads, noting "the Commission's laws and rules, enacted to protect public health and safety, do not require either knowledge or intent for a violation to occur."

Masher hires you to represent him in getting his license reinstated. After reviewing the record, you decide your best option is to argue that Rule 323, as written, does not provide for strict or vicarious liability, and therefore, Atcom erred as a matter of law when it revoked Masher's license.

Discussion Questions:

1. What procedural vehicle should you use to challenge the Commission's decision?
2. How long do you have to file it?
3. What do you think the Commission will argue to justify its strict liability application?
4. What evidence would you ideally want to produce to more significantly challenge this revocation?

Index